Semantic Information Theory

Semantic Information Theory

Guest Editors

Meixia Tao
Kai Niu
Youlong Wu

MDPI

Basel • Beijing • Wuhan • Barcelona • Belgrade • Novi Sad • Cluj • Manchester

Guest Editors
Meixia Tao
Department of Electronic Engineering
Shanghai Jiao Tong University
Shanghai
China

Kai Niu
The Key Laboratory of Universal Wireless Communications
Beijing University of Posts and Telecommunications
Beijing
China

Youlong Wu
School of Information Science and Technology
Shanghai Tech University
Shanghai
China

Editorial Office
MDPI AG
Grosspeteranlage 5
4052 Basel, Switzerland

This is a reprint of the Special Issue, published open access by the journal *Entropy* (ISSN 1099-4300), freely accessible at: https://www.mdpi.com/journal/entropy/special_issues/Z5DLC3A359.

For citation purposes, cite each article independently as indicated on the article page online and as indicated below:

Lastname, A.A.; Lastname, B.B. Article Title. *Journal Name* **Year**, *Volume Number*, Page Range.

ISBN 978-3-7258-5807-1 (Hbk)
ISBN 978-3-7258-5808-8 (PDF)
https://doi.org/10.3390/books978-3-7258-5808-8

Contents

About the Editors

Meixia Tao

Meixia Tao is a Professor with the School of Information and Electronic Engineering at Shanghai Jiao Tong University, China. She received a B.S. degree in electronic engineering from Fudan University, Shanghai, China, in 1999 and a Ph.D. degree in electrical and electronic engineering from the Hong Kong University of Science and Technology in 2003. Her current research interests include wireless edge learning, semantic communications, integrated communication–computing–sensing, AI-based channel modeling, and beamforming. She has published over 330 research papers in peer-reviewed journals and conferences. Dr. Tao is a Fellow of the IEEE. She has received the 2019 IEEE Marconi Prize Paper Award, the 2013 IEEE Heinrich Hertz Award for Best Communications Letters, the IEEE/CIC International Conference on Communications in China (ICCC) 2015 Best Paper Award, and the International Conference on Wireless Communications and Signal Processing (WCSP) 2022 and 2012 Best Paper Awards. She has also received the 2009 IEEE ComSoc Asia-Pacific Outstanding Young Researcher Award.

Kai Niu

Kai Niu received a B.S. degree in information engineering and a Ph.D. degree in signal and information processing from the Beijing University of Posts and Telecommunications (BUPT), Beijing, China in 1998 and 2003, respectively. He is currently a Professor with the School of Artificial Intelligence, BUPT. His research interests include channel coding theory and applications, semantic communication, and broadband wireless communication. He has published more than 200 academic papers, and his proposed high-performance compilation code algorithm for polar code has become the mainstream scheme for standard 5G, and he won the first prize of the Natural Science of Science and Technology Award from the Chinese Institute of Electronics.

Youlong Wu

Youlong Wu is an associate professor at the School of Information Science and Technology, ShanghaiTech University. His research interests include information theory and its applications, e.g., coded caching/computing, task-oriented communications, and machine learning. Youlong Wu obtained his B.S. degree in electrical engineering from Wuhan University, Wuhan, China, in 2007. He received his M.S. degree in electrical engineering from Shanghai Jiaotong University, Shanghai, China, in 2011. In 2014, he received a Ph.D. degree at Telecom Paris Tech, Paris, France. In December 2014, he worked as a postdoctoral researcher at the Institute for Communication Engineering, Technical University Munich (TUM), Munich, Germany. In 2017, he joined the School of Information Science and Technology at Shanghai Tech University. He obtained a TUM Fellowship in 2014 and was selected for the Shanghai Pujiang Talent Program in 2018. He is an Alexander von Humboldt research fellow.

Preface

Information theory has laid the foundation for modern communication systems by quantifying information and establishing fundamental limits for reliable data transmission over noisy channels. However, it primarily focuses on the syntactic aspects of data transmission without considering the semantic meaning. Semantic communication, in contrast, concentrates on the semantic or effectiveness levels and aims to extract and convey the information needed to allow the receiver to accomplish a goal with the desired effectiveness. This paradigm shift is envisioned to enhance efficiency and timeliness in a variety of emerging applications, such as autonomous driving, remote robotics, the meta-universe, drone inspection, and more. Due to its exceptional advantages in communication efficiency and its compatibility with emerging AI applications, semantic communication has garnered significant attention.

Despite the notable progress achieved in semantic communications as empowered by AI, a unified theoretical foundation and operational analytical tools for semantic communications remain elusive. The relationship between traditional information theory and semantic communications is not yet fully established.

This Reprint is firmly grounded in bridging the established principles of information theory with the emerging field of semantic communications. Its aim is to contribute a unified theoretical foundation while showcasing practical advancements. This collection comprises two comprehensive review articles, which provide holistic perspectives on the theory and its applications in areas like the Internet of Vehicles, alongside ten original research articles. These are organized into two complementary themes: advancing semantic rate–distortion theory and designing efficient semantic communication systems. By collecting these works, we hope to provide a foundational resource that not only deepens theoretical understandings but also offers rigorous methodologies for designing future intelligent communication networks.

This Reprint is addressed to academic researchers, industrial R&D engineers, and graduate students in information theory, signal processing, machine learning, and next-generation wireless communication. We believe the insights contained herein will inspire further innovation in the pursuit of truly goal-oriented and semantic-aware communication technologies.

Meixia Tao, Kai Niu, and Youlong Wu
Guest Editors

entropy

MDPI

Editorial

Semantic Information Theory and Applications

Meixia Tao [1], Kai Niu [2] and Youlong Wu [3,*]

[1] Department of Electronic Engineering, Shanghai Jiao Tong University, Shanghai 200240, China; mxtao@sjtu.edu.cn
[2] The Key Laboratory of Universal Wireless Communications, Beijing University of Posts and Telecommunications, Beijing 100876, China; niukai@bupt.edu.cn
[3] School of Information Science and Technology, ShanghaiTech University, Shanghai 200240, China
* Correspondence: wuyl1@shanghaitech.edu.cn

Traditional information theory provides a rigorous foundation for information compression and reliable symbol transmission. However, in emerging applications such as autonomous driving, remote healthcare, and industrial Internet of Things (IoT), the key communication challenge has been shifted from accurate delivery of raw data to the efficient transmission of task-relevant information [1–4]. For instance, autonomous vehicles require timely awareness of driving-critical events rather than full sensor streams, while remote healthcare relies on essential medical features rather than complete high-resolution images. These task-driven communication scenarios are inherently bandwidth-constrained and latency-sensitive, calling for integrating downstream task objectives into information processing and transmission to improve the communication efficiency.

Semantic communication has emerged as a new paradigm that operates at the semantic or effectiveness level, aiming to extract and convey only the information necessary for a receiver to accomplish a specific goal [5–10]. The rapid advancement of artificial intelligence (AI) has significantly accelerated research in this field. By leveraging AI techniques, transmitters can efficiently extract, compress, and encode task-relevant information, thereby reducing communication overhead and enabling more intelligent, goal-oriented transmission. Consequently, semantic communication has attracted increasing attention as a key enabler of next-generation intelligent networks.

Despite the notable progress made in semantic communications, a unified theoretical foundation and operational analytical tools remain elusive. The relationship between traditional information theory and semantic communication is not yet fully established, particularly regarding the extent to which information-theoretic principles can address the unique challenges posed by semantic communication. This Special Issue aims to bridge this gap by promoting the convergence of information theory and semantic communication, thereby fostering deeper theoretical insights and practical advancements. After going through a rigorous review process, twelve articles are selected in this Special Issue, including two review articles and ten research articles. The review articles provide holistic perspectives on the semantic information theory and semantic communications, respectively. The novel contributions in the research articles can be broadly categorized into two directions: semantic rate–distortion theory, which investigates source compression under task-specific semantic distortion measures, and efficient semantic communication system design, which focuses on optimizing transmission efficiency while preserving semantic relevance.

The review article [11] takes a complementary perspective, advocating for a generalization of Shannon's framework rather than a parallel theory. It introduces a "G theory" that replaces the traditional distortion constraint with a semantic constraint, employing

 https://doi.org/10.3390/e27111092

truth functions to quantify semantic distortion, information, and loss. The paper illustrates the broad applicability of this theory across domains ranging from machine learning to statistical physics and further proposes refining Friston's minimum free energy principle into the maximum information efficiency principle. The review article [12] presents a systematic review of the state-of-the-art semantic communications in the Internet of Vehicles (IoV). It covers key technologies, including semantic information extraction, system architectures, and resource allocation, and demonstrates their effectiveness in traffic perception, intelligent driving, and traffic management. The survey emphasizes the vast potential applications of semantic communications within IoV.

The six papers dedicated to semantic rate distortion theory [13–18] collectively push the boundaries of theoretical analysis by introducing new analytical frameworks and algorithms. Specifically, paper [13] proposes a new semantic arithmetic coding (SAC) method for semantic lossless compression. By leveraging the concept of synonymity and constructing synonymous mappings, the SAC method achieves higher compression efficiency for meaning-contained source sequences, approximating the semantic entropy limits. Paper [14] proposes a framework to quantify the rate-distortion tradeoff for semantic communication under various task-specific semantic distance measures. The authors derive closed-form expressions for the semantic rate-distortion functions for classification and signal generation tasks, providing theoretical results verified by extensive experiments. Paper [15] integrates the perceptual dimension into the rate-distortion paradigm. This work clarifies the role of perceptual constraints common and private randomness and projects an increase in expected traffic in intelligent communication networks when perceptual quality is considered. The paper demonstrates how a modest increase in rate can significantly enhance the perceptual quality of reconstructions. Paper [16] extends the fundamental BA algorithm to the semantic domain. It introduces the Extended Blahut–Arimoto (EBA) algorithm, which iteratively computes the semantic rate-distortion function based on synonymous mapping. The paper also proposes an optimization framework combining EBA with simulated annealing to handle scenarios with unknown synonymous mappings and analyzes the role of the semantic knowledge base size. Paper [17] characterizes the optimal transition probability distribution for reproducing an intrinsic state in a composite source model. The paper interprets this optimal solution as a "soft classifier" that generalizes the traditional "classify-then-compress" scheme. It demonstrates that this approach, which uses soft classification to guide lossy compression, outperforms existing coding schemes. Paper [18] addresses a distributed source coding problem relevant to task-oriented semantic communication. It characterizes the exact rate-distortion function for scenarios where a central decoder aims to recover a latent variable from independently encoded sources. The paper also develops a distributed Blahut–Arimoto (BA) algorithm to numerically compute the rate-distortion function.

The four papers on theoretically guided semantic communication scheme designs [19–22] demonstrate the practical application of these ideas. Specifically, paper [19] proposes a new semantic communication system for image transmission that addresses bandwidth limitations. The system uses a non-uniform quantization technique based on the differential impact of features on image recovery at the receiver. This dynamic bit allocation algorithm ensures image reconstruction quality under limited bandwidth. Paper [20] fills a key gap by providing an operational interpretation of partial information decomposition. It connects this decomposition to the capacity of the broadcast channel, rigorously interpreting the synergistic information as a cooperative gain. This provides a clear theoretical basis for the technique's applications. Paper [21] proposes a separate source–channel coding framework for semantic communications in MIMO systems, improving adaptability and model reusability compared to joint source–channel coding. The framework combines a VAE-based semantic coder, a communication-informed bottleneck attribution for feature importance, and an importance-aware resource allocation scheme. Ref. [22] proposes a task-oriented framework for multimodal digital semantic communications. It leverages a pre-trained transformer to extract semantic information and designs three semantic source-coding schemes: quantization-based coding, compression via clustering, and a vector-quantized autoencoder-based learned codebook. By combining these semantic codes with standard channel coding, the study demonstrates that the proposed approaches achieve comparable classification accuracy while significantly improving system time efficiency over learning-based baselines.

This Special Issue underscores the pivotal role of information theory in shaping the emerging paradigm of semantic communication. The collected articles demonstrate how classical tools—most notably rate–distortion theory and joint source–channel coding—can be extended to support more efficient and reliable approaches to data compression and information transmission. Information theory thus provides indispensable theoretical guidance for the advancement of semantic communication, while the rapid progress of semantic communication simultaneously expands and deepens the research frontiers of information theory itself. Looking forward, we envision semantic information theory not only as a bridge between these two domains but also as a source of practical insights and rigorous methodologies that will inform the design of next-generation communication networks.

Acknowledgments: The Guest Editors extend their sincere gratitude to all contributing authors for their excellent work, to the anonymous reviewers for their insightful and constructive feedback, and to the Editorial Team of *Entropy* for their professional support on this Special Issue. The work by M. Tao was supported by the National Natural Science Foundation of China (NSFC) under Grant 62125108. The work by K. Niu was supported by NSFC (No. 62293481). The work by Y. Wu was supported by NSFC (No. 62571329).

Conflicts of Interest: The authors declare no conflicts of interest.

References

1. Shi, Y.; Zhou, Y.; Wen, D.; Wu, Y.; Jiang, C.; Letaief, K.B. Task-Oriented Communications for 6G: Vision, Principles, and Technologies. *IEEE Wirel. Commun.* **2023**, *30*, 78–85. [CrossRef]
2. Ferrag, M.A.; Friha, O.; Kantarci, B.; Tihanyi, N.; Cordeiro, L.C.; Debbah, M.; Hamouda, D.; Al-Hawawreh, M.; Choo, K.R. Edge Learning for 6G-Enabled Internet of Things: A Comprehensive Survey of Vulnerabilities, Datasets, and Defenses. *IEEE Commun. Surv. Tutor.* **2023**, *25*, 2654–2713. [CrossRef]
3. Yang, W.; Du, H.; Liew, Z.Q.; Lim, W.Y.B.; Xiong, Z.; Niyato, D.; Chi, X.; Shen, X.S.; Miao, C. Semantic Communications for Future Internet: Fundamentals, Applications, and Challenges. *IEEE Commun. Surv. Tutor.* **2022**, *25*, 213–250. [CrossRef]
4. Tao, M.; Zhou, Y.; Shi, Y.; Lu, J.; Cui, S.; Lu, J.; Letaief, K.B. Federated Edge Learning for 6G: Foundations, Methodologies, and Applications. *Proc. IEEE* **2024**, 1–39. [CrossRef]
5. Wever, W. Recent contributions to the mathematical theory of communication. In *ETC: A Review of General Semantics*; Institute of General Semantics: New York, NY, USA, 1953; pp. 261–281.
6. Gündüz, D.; Qin, Z.; Aguerri, I.E.; Dhillon, H.S.; Yang, Z.; Yener, A.; Wong, K.K.; Chae, C.B. Beyond Transmitting Bits: Context, Semantics, and Task-Oriented Communications. *IEEE J. Sel. Areas Commun.* **2023**, *41*, 5–41. [CrossRef]
7. Wu, Y.; Shi, Y.; Ma, S.; Jiang, C.; Zhang, W.; Letaief, K.B. Toward Effective and Interpretable Semantic Communications. *IEEE Netw.* **2024**, *38*, 55–62. [CrossRef]
8. Xie, H.; Qin, Z.; Li, G.Y.; Juang, B.H. Deep Learning Enabled Semantic Communication Systems. *IEEE Trans. Signal Process.* **2021**, *69*, 2663–2675. [CrossRef]
9. Niu, K.; Zhang, P. A mathematical theory of semantic communication. *J. Commun.* **2024**, *45*, 7–59. Available online: https://www.joconline.com.cn/zh/article/doi/10.11959/j.issn.1000-436x.2024111/ (accessed on 15 October 2025).
10. Niu, K.; Zhang, P. *The Mathematical Theory of Semantic Commnication*; Springer: Singapore, 2025.
11. Lu, C. A Semantic Generalization of Shannon's Information Theory and Applications. *Entropy* **2025**, *27*, 461. [CrossRef] [PubMed]
12. Ye, S.; Wu, Q.; Fan, P.; Fan, Q. A Survey on Semantic Communications in Internet of Vehicles. *Entropy* **2025**, *27*, 445. [CrossRef] [PubMed]

13. Liang, Z.; Niu, K.; Xu, J.; Zhang, P. Semantic Arithmetic Coding Using Synonymous Mappings. *Entropy* **2025**, *27*, 429. [CrossRef] [PubMed]
14. Chai, J.; Zhu, H.; Xiao, Y.; Shi, G.; Zhang, P. On the Rate-Distortion Theory for Task-Specific Semantic Communication. *Entropy* **2025**, *27*, 775. [CrossRef] [PubMed]
15. Niu, X.; Bai, B.; Guo, N.; Zhang, W.; Han, W. Rate–Distortion–Perception Trade-Off in Information Theory, Generative Models, and Intelligent Communications. *Entropy* **2025**, *27*, 373. [CrossRef] [PubMed]
16. Han, Y.; Liu, Y.; Sun, Y.; Niu, K.; Ma, N.; Cui, S.; Zhang, P. Extended Blahut–Arimoto Algorithm for Semantic Rate-Distortion Function. *Entropy* **2025**, *27*, 651. [CrossRef] [PubMed]
17. Cao, Y.; Liu, J.; Zhang, W. Soft Classification in a Composite Source Model. *Entropy* **2025**, *27*, 620. [CrossRef] [PubMed]
18. Tang, J.; Yang, Q. Rate-Distortion Analysis of Distributed Indirect Source Coding. *Entropy* **2025**, *27*, 844. [CrossRef] [PubMed]
19. Zhang, J.; Zhang, Y.; Ji, B.; Chen, A.; Liu, A.; Xu, H. Feature-Driven Semantic Communication for Efficient Image Transmission. *Entropy* **2025**, *27*, 369. [CrossRef] [PubMed]
20. Tian, C.; Shamai (Shitz), S. Broadcast Channel Cooperative Gain: An Operational Interpretation of Partial Information Decomposition. *Entropy* **2025**, *27*, 310. [CrossRef] [PubMed]
21. Cao, Y.; Wu, Y.; Lian, L.; Tao, M. Importance-Aware Resource Allocations for MIMO Semantic Communication. *Entropy* **2025**, *27*, 605. [CrossRef] [PubMed]
22. Kutay, E.; Yener, A. Harnessing the Power of Pre-Trained Models for Efficient Semantic Communication of Text and Images. *Entropy* **2025**, *27*, 813. [CrossRef] [PubMed]

entropy

MDPI

Article

Broadcast Channel Cooperative Gain: An Operational Interpretation of Partial Information Decomposition

Chao Tian [1,*] and Shlomo Shamai (Shitz) [2]

[1] Department of Electrical and Computer Engineering, Texas A&M University, College Station, TX 77840, USA
[2] Department of Electrical Engineering, Technion Institute of Technology of Israel, Haifa 3200003, Israel; sshlomo@ee.technion.ac.il
* Correspondence: chao.tian@tamu.edu

Abstract: Partial information decomposition has recently found applications in biological signal processing and machine learning. Despite its impacts, the decomposition was introduced through an informal and heuristic route, and its exact operational meaning is unclear. In this work, we fill this gap by connecting partial information decomposition to the capacity of the broadcast channel, which has been well studied in the information theory literature. We show that the synergistic information in the decomposition can be rigorously interpreted as the cooperative gain, or a lower bound of this gain, on the corresponding broadcast channel. This interpretation can help practitioners to better explain and expand the applications of the partial information decomposition technique.

Keywords: network information theory; channel capacity

1. Introduction

Shannon's mutual information has been widely accepted as a measure to gauge the amount of information that can be revealed by one random variable regarding another random variable. Partial information decomposition (PID) is an approach to refine and further decompose this fundamental quantity to explain the effect of interactions among several random variables. Recently, this approach has found applications in biological information processing [1–7] and machine learning [8–10].

There exist different approaches to decompose the total information [11–27], but the general idea in the case with two observables is as follows: the total information revealed by X and Y regarding a third quantity T is the mutual information between (X, Y) and T, i.e., $I(X, Y; T)$ (see [28]), and it needs to be decomposed into four non-negative parts:

- The common (or redundancy) information in X and Y, regarding T;
- The unique information in X, but not in Y, regarding T;
- The unique information in Y, but not in X, regarding T;
- The synergistic information (or complementary) information in X and Y, regarding T, which only becomes useful when combined, but is useless otherwise.

This decomposition helps to explain the effect of combining X and Y, or separately using X or Y, to infer T. For example, in multi-modality machine learning, X can represent one modality such as the vision image of the event, Y another modality such as the soundtrack of the event, and T the event's label. In this case, we can use the amounts of synergistic and unique information to determine which multi-modality models will be the most effective in capturing the interactions and therefore are most likely to be accurate. In neural signal processing, the quantities can be used in a similar manner to interpret different biological signals.

One of the most influential notions of partial information decomposition was proposed by Bertschinger et al. [13], sometimes referred to as the BROJA PID (the initials of the authors; we will simply refer to it as partial information decomposition as it is the only decomposition we consider). The desirable properties of this definition were thoroughly studied in [13], but in terms of the operation meaning, only a qualitative justification in a decision-making setting was given. The intuition and motivation were that these quantities can help explain how rewards can be optimized via decision-making in such a setting, either using only X (or only Y) as the observations, or using X and Y jointly as the observations (a refinement was given in [29]). However, this qualitative justification is far from satisfying, as it does not provide the exact quantitative interpretation and requires an artificially introduced utility function, which makes its meaning quite vague. In this work, we fill this gap by connecting PID to the well-studied broadcast channel in information theory [30–32], and show that there is indeed a quantitative connection between PID and the sum-rate capacity of the broadcast channel. More precisely, the synergistic information defined in [13] can be interpreted as either the cooperative gain or a lower bound of the cooperative gain in the broadcast channel, under a fixed signaling distribution.

2. Partial Information Decomposition

2.1. A Few Examples

Before formally introducing the PID defined in [13], let us consider a few simple settings to understand intuitively how the decomposed information should behave.

1. Common information dominant: X is a uniformly distributed Bernoulli random variable and $Y = T = X$. It is clear that $I(X,Y;T) = 1$. In this case, the common information should be one, since X and Y are exactly identical. The other components should all be 0, since there is no unique information in either X or Y regarding T, and there is no synergistic information when combining X and Y.
2. Synergistic information dominant: X and Y are uniformly distributed Bernoulli random variables independent of each other, and $T = X \oplus Y$, where $\oplus$ is the XOR operation. Here, the synergistic information should be 1, and the other components should be 0. This is because X or Y alone do not reveal any information regarding T, and since they are completely independent, they do not share any common information either, but their combination reveals the full information on T.
3. Component-wise decomposition: $X = (X_1, X_2)$ and $Y = (Y_1, Y_2)$, where X_1, X_2, Y_1, Y_2 are all uniformly-distributed Bernoulli random variables, mutually independent of each other. Let $T = (X_1, Y_1, X_2 \oplus Y_2)$. Clearly, in this case, the common information is still 0, but the two kinds of unique information are both 1, and the synergistic information is also 1.

2.2. Partial Information Decomposition

We next introduce the formal definition for the PID given in [13]. Let X, Y, and T be three random variables in their respective alphabet $\mathcal{X}$, $\mathcal{Y}$, and $\mathcal{T}$, which follow the joint distribution $P_{X,Y,T}$. The total information between X, Y, and T is their mutual information, i.e., $I(T;X,Y)$; however, from here on out, we shall write it as $I_P(T;X,Y)$ to make the dependence on the distribution more explicit. As mentioned earlier, the decomposition first needs to satisfy the total information rule:

Total information:

$$I_P(T;X,Y) = I^{(C)}(T;X,Y) + I^{(U_X)}(T;X,Y) + I^{(U_Y)}(T;X,Y) + I^{(S)}(T;X,Y), \quad (1)$$

where the superscript C indicates common (or redundancy) information, U_X indicates unique information from X, U_Y indicates unique information from Y, and S indicates synergistic (or complementary) information. This condition simply states that the total information is the summation of four parts. The decomposition also needs to satisfy the individual information rule:

$$\textbf{Individual information:} \quad \begin{aligned} I_P(T;X) &= I^{(C)}(T;X,Y) + I^{(U_X)}(T;X,Y) \\ I_P(T;Y) &= I^{(C)}(T;X,Y) + I^{(U_Y)}(T;X,Y). \end{aligned} \tag{2}$$

This rule dictates that the information that can be revealed from X regarding T needs to be the summation of the unique information in X, and the common information in both X and Y. Note that the synergistic information is not included here, since it can only manifest when combining X and Y.

We now already have three linear equations for the four quantities in the decomposition, and the authors of [13] introduced the following definition of synergistic information:

$$I^{(S)}(T;X,Y) \triangleq I_P(T;X,Y) - \min_{Q \in \mathcal{Q}} I_Q(T;X,Y), \tag{3}$$

where the set of distributions $\mathcal{Q}$ is defined as

$$\mathcal{Q} = \{Q \in \Delta_{\mathcal{X}\times\mathcal{Y}\times\mathcal{T}} : Q_{T,X} = P_{T,X}, Q_{T,Y} = P_{T,Y}\}, \tag{4}$$

where $\Delta_{\mathcal{X}\times\mathcal{Y}\times\mathcal{T}}$ is the probability simplex on $\mathcal{X} \times \mathcal{Y} \times \mathcal{T}$; in other words, $\mathcal{Q}$ is the set of all joint distributions such that the pairwise marginals of $P_{T,X}$ and $P_{T,Y}$ are preserved. As a consequence, this definition, together with (1) and (2), also specifies the values of the other three quantities $I^{(C)}(T;X,Y)$, $I^{(U_X)}(T;X,Y)$, and $I^{(U_Y)}(T;X,Y)$. It can be easily verified that in the examples discussed earlier, this decomposition gives the quantities matching our expectations.

It was shown in [13] that this PID definition enjoys several desirable properties, for example, the following: (1) All the quantities $I^{(C)}(T;X,Y)$, $I^{(U_X)}(T;X,Y)$, $I^{(U_Y)}(T;X,Y)$, and $I^{(S)}(T;X,Y)$ are non-negative. (2) They satisfy certain extremal relations in the sense that the shared information $I^{(S)}(T;X,Y)$ is the minimum among all possible definition under an additional axiom that the unique information only depends on the two marginal distributions. (3) They satisfy the symmetry, self-redundancy, and monotonicity axioms stipulated in [11].

3. Broadcast Channels

The broadcast channel is a well-studied communication system in classic information theory [30], where a transmitter wishes to send two independent messages to two receivers through a channel with a single input signal that induces two separate output signals; see Figure 1a. To accomplish this goal, the transmitter must encode the messages in such a way that the individual messages can be decoded by the intended receivers. Clearly, if the first receiver is completely ignored, the transmitter can send more information to the second receiver, and vice versa. In other words, there is a tradeoff between the amounts of information that can be sent to the two receivers. One particular important quantity here is the sum of the rates that can be supported on this channel, often referred to as the sum-rate capacity.

Next, we provide a rigorous definition of the broadcast channel capacity region, where the channel is allowed to be used many times at a time, i.e., a block code where the block length approaches infinity. A *two-user broadcast channel* is specified by an input alphabet $\mathcal{T}$, two output alphabets $\mathcal{X}$ and $\mathcal{Y}$, and a conditional probability distribution $P_{X,Y|T}$ that gives the channel law for each symbol $t \in \mathcal{T}$ and $(x, y) \in \mathcal{X} \times \mathcal{Y}$. The alphabets are usually assumed to be finite, though the results usually hold under more general assumptions [33].

Definition 1. *For a blocklength $n \in \mathbb{N}$, let M_1 and M_2 be two positive integers. An (n, M_1, M_2)-code for the broadcast channel $P_{X,Y|T}$ consists of the following:*

- *Two message sets:*

$$\mathcal{M}_1 = \{1, 2, \ldots, M_1\}, \quad \mathcal{M}_2 = \{1, 2, \ldots, M_2\}.$$

- *An encoding function*

$$f : \mathcal{M}_1 \times \mathcal{M}_2 \to \mathcal{T}^n,$$

which assigns to each pair of messages (m_1, m_2) a length-n input sequence $T^n = (T_1, T_2, \ldots, T_n)$.

- *Two decoding functions:*

$$g_1 : \mathcal{X}^n \to \mathcal{M}_1, \quad g_2 : \mathcal{Y}^n \to \mathcal{M}_2,$$

where $\hat{M}_1 = g_1(X^n)$ is the estimate of message M_1 by receiver 1, and $\hat{M}_2 = g_2(Y^n)$ is the estimate of message M_2 by receiver 2.

Definition 2. *For an (n, M_1, M_2)-code, let (M_1, M_2) be chosen uniformly from $\mathcal{M}_1 \times \mathcal{M}_2$. The average probability of error is defined as*

$$P_e^{(n)} = \Pr\{(\hat{M}_1, \hat{M}_2) \neq (M_1, M_2)\}.$$

A sequence of codes (indexed by n) is said to have vanishing error probability if $P_e^{(n)} \to 0$ as $n \to \infty$.

Definition 3. *A rate pair (R_1, R_2) is said to be* achievable *for the broadcast channel $P_{X,Y|T}$ if there exists a sequence of $(n, M_1^{(n)}, M_2^{(n)})$-codes with vanishing error probability such that*

$$\liminf_{n \to \infty} \frac{1}{n} \log M_1^{(n)} \geq R_1, \quad \liminf_{n \to \infty} \frac{1}{n} \log M_2^{(n)} \geq R_2.$$

The capacity region $\mathcal{C}$ of the two-user broadcast channel is the closure of the set of all achievable rate pairs. The sum-rate capacity is $C_{sum} \triangleq \max_{(R_1,R_2) \in \mathcal{C}} R_1 + R_2$.

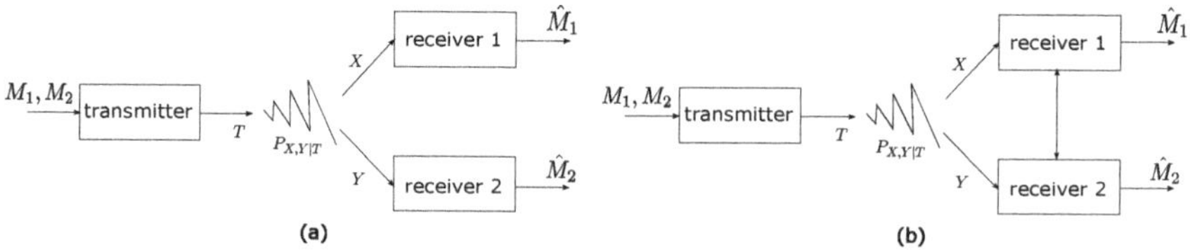

Figure 1. Standard broadcast channel vs. broadcast channel with receiver cooperation.

4. Main Result: An Operational Interpretation of PID

In this section, we provide the main result of this work, which is an operational interpretation of partial information decomposition.

4.1. PID via Sato's Outer Bound

Researchers in the information theory community have made numerous efforts to identify a computable characterization of the capacity region of general broadcast channels (see the textbook [33] for a historical summary); yet, at this time, a complete solution is still elusive. Nevertheless, significant progress has indeed been made toward this goal. Particularly, Sato [34] provided an outer bound for $\mathcal{C}$, and it can be specialized to yield an upper bound for the sum-rate capacity of the general broadcast channel as follows:

$$C_{\text{sum}} \leq C_{\text{Sato}} \triangleq \min_{Q \in \mathcal{Q}'} \max_{P_T} I_{P_T Q_{X,Y|T}}(X,Y;T), \tag{5}$$

where the set $\mathcal{Q}'$ is defined as

$$\mathcal{Q}' = \{Q \in \Delta_{\mathcal{X}\times\mathcal{Y}|\mathcal{T}} : Q_{X|T} = P_{X|T}, Q_{Y|T} = P_{Y|T}\}, \tag{6}$$

i.e., the set of conditional distributions for which the marginal conditional distributions $P_{X|T}$ and $P_{Y|T}$ are preserved. The inner maximization is over the possible marginal distribution of the random variable P_T in the alphabet $\mathcal{T}$. The form already bears a certain similarity to (4). Note that for channels on general alphabets (i.e., not necessarily optimized on a compact space), the maximization should be replaced by the supremum and the minimization by the infimum. Due to the minimax form, the meaning is not yet clear, but the max–min inequality (weak duality) implies that

$$\min_{Q \in \mathcal{Q}'} \max_{P_T} I_{P_T Q_{X,Y|T}}(X,Y;T) \geq \max_{P_T} \min_{Q \in \mathcal{Q}'} I_{P_T Q_{X,Y|T}}(X,Y;T) = \max_{P_T} \min_{Q \in \mathcal{Q}} I_{Q_{X,Y,T}}(X,Y;T), \tag{7}$$

where the equality is by the definition of $\mathcal{Q}'$, and the set $\mathcal{Q}$ is exactly the one defined in (4) with $Q_{X,T} = P_T Q_{X|T}$ and $Q_{Y,T} = P_T Q_{Y|T}$. The inner minimization of this form is exactly the same as the second term in (3). Though the max–min form does not yield a true upper bound of the sum-rate capacity, in the PID setting we consider, P_T is always fixed; therefore, the max–min and min–max forms are in fact equivalent in this setting. The equivalence in mathematical forms does not fully explain the significance of this connection, and we will need to consider Sato's bound more carefully. Let us define the following quantity for notational simplicity:

$$R_{P_T} \triangleq \min_{Q \in \mathcal{Q}'} I_{P_T Q_{X,Y|T}}(X,Y;T). \tag{8}$$

Sato's outer bound was derived using the following argument. For a channel that has a single input signal T and a single output signal Y on a channel $P_{Y|T}$, Shannon's channel coding theorem [28] states that the channel capacity is given by $\max_{P_T} I_{P_T P_{Y|T}}(Y;T)$. Moreover, for any fixed distribution P_T, the rate $I_{P_T P_{Y|T}}(Y;T)$ is achievable, where the probability distribution P_T represents the statistical signaling pattern of the underlying codes. Turning our attention back to the broadcast channel with a transition probability $P_{X,Y|T}$, if the receivers are allowed to cooperate fully and share the two output signals X and Y—i.e., they become a single virtual receiver (see Figure 1b)—then clearly the maximum rate achievable would be $\max_{P_T} I_{P_T Q_{X,Y|T}}(X,Y;T)$. However, Sato further observed that the error probability of any code should not differ on any broadcast channel $Q_{X,Y|T} \in \mathcal{Q}'$, even if the transition distribution $Q_{X,Y|T}$ is different from the true broadcast channel transition probability $P_{X,Y|T}$. This is because the channel outputs only depend on the marginal transition probabilities $P_{X|T}$ and $P_{Y|T}$, respectively, and the decoders only use their respective channel outputs to decode. Therefore, we can obtain an upper bound by choosing the worst channel configuration $Q \in \mathcal{Q}$, i.e., the outer minimization in (5).

With the interpretation of Sato's upper bound above, it becomes clear that R_{P_T} is essentially an upper bound on the sum rate of the broadcast channel where the receivers are not allowed to cooperate, when the input signaling pattern is fixed to follow P_T. On the other hand, the quantity $I_{P_T P_{X,Y|T}}(X,Y;T)$ is the rate that can be achieved by allowing the two receivers to fully cooperate, also with P_T being the input signaling pattern. In this sense, $I^{(S)}(T;X,Y)$ defined in (3) is a lower bound on the difference between the sum rate with full cooperation and that without any cooperation, with the input signaling pattern following P_T.

This connection provides an operational interpretation of PID for general distributions. Essentially, synergistic information can be viewed as a surrogate of the cooperative gain. When this lower bound is in fact also achievable, $I^{(S)}(T;X,Y)$ would be exactly equal to the cooperative gain. In the corresponding learning setting, it is the difference between what can be inferred about T by using both X and Y in a non-cooperative manner, and what can be inferred by using them jointly. This indeed matches our expectations for the synergistic information. In the next subsection, we consider a special case when Sato's bound is indeed achievable, and the lower bound mentioned above becomes exact.

In one sense, this operational interpretation is quite intuitive as explained above, but on the other hand, it is also quite surprising. For example, in broadcast channels, a more general setup allows the transmitter to also send a common message to both receivers [35,36], in addition to the two individual messages to the two respective receivers. It would appear plausible to expect this generalized setting to be more closely connected to the PID setting with the common message related to the common information, yet this turns out to be not the case here. Moreover, a dual communication problem studied in information theory is the multiple access channel (see, e.g., [28]), where two transmitters wish to communicate to the same receiver simultaneously. The readers may also wonder if an operational meaning should be extracted on this channel, instead of on the broadcast channel. However, note that in the PID setting, we are inferring T from X and Y, which is similar to the decoding process in the broadcast channel, instead of the multiple access channel. Moreover, in the multiple access channel, the joint distribution of the two transmitters' inputs is always independent when the two transmitters cannot cooperate, and this will not match the PID setting under consideration. Another seemingly related problem setting studied in the information theory literature is the common information between two random variables [37,38]; however, for the PID defined in [13], this approach also does not yield a meaningful interpretation.

4.2. Gaussian MIMO Broadcast Channel and Gaussian PID

One setting where a full capacity region characterization is indeed known is the Gaussian multiple-input multiple-output (MIMO) channel [32,39]. In the two-user Gaussian MIMO broadcast channel, the channel transition probability $P_{\vec{X}|\vec{T}}$ and $P_{\vec{Y}|\vec{T}}$ are given, with $\vec{T}$ being the transmitter input variable, and $\vec{X},\vec{Y}$ the channel outputs at the two individual receivers. The channel is usually defined as follows:

$$\vec{X} = H_X\vec{T} + \vec{n}_X \tag{9}$$
$$\vec{Y} = H_Y\vec{T} + \vec{n}_Y, \tag{10}$$

where H_X and H_y are two channel matrices, the additive noise vector $\vec{n}_X$ is independent of $\vec{T}$, and similarly, $\vec{n}_Y$ is independent of $\vec{T}$. For a fixed input signaling distribution P_T, the pairwise marginal distributions $P_{\vec{T},\vec{X}}$ and $P_{\vec{T},\vec{Y}}$ are well specified. Conversely, for any joint distribution $P_{\vec{T},\vec{X},\vec{Y}}$, where the marginals $P_{\vec{T},\vec{X}}$ and $P_{\vec{T},\vec{Y}}$ are jointly Gaussian, respectively, we can represent their relation in the form above via a Gram–Schmidt orthogonalization. Note that the joint distribution of $\vec{n}_X,\vec{n}_Y$ is not fully specified here, as the noise vectors $\vec{n}_X$ and $\vec{n}_Y$ are not necessarily jointly Gaussian, but can be dependent in a more sophisticated manner. The standard Gaussian MIMO broadcast problem usually specifies the noises zero-mean Gaussian with certain fixed covariances, and there is also a covariance constraint on the transmitter's signaling $\vec{T}$. The problem can be further simplified using certain linear transformations, as discussed below.

Let us assume $\Sigma_{\vec{n}_X}$ and $\Sigma_{\vec{n}_Y}$ are full rank for now (when $\Sigma_{\vec{n}_X}$ and $\Sigma_{\vec{n}_Y}$ are not fully rank, a limiting argument can be invoked to show the same conclusion holds), and in this case, it is clearly without loss of generality to assume that $\Sigma_{\vec{n}_i}$'s are in fact identity matrices, since otherwise, we can perform receiver-side linear transforms to make them so, i.e., through a transformation based on the eigenvalue decomposition of $\Sigma_{\vec{n}_X}$ and $\Sigma_{\vec{n}_Y}$, respectively. For the same reason, we can assume $\Sigma_{\vec{T}}$ is an identity matrix, through a linear transformation at the transmitter. These reductions to independent noise and independent channel input are often referred to as the transmitter precoding transformation and the receiver precoding transformations in the communication literature; see, e.g., [39].

For the two-user Gaussian broadcast channel, the worst channel configuration problem we discussed in the general setting is essentially the least favorable noise problem considered by Yu and Cioffi [39] with the simplification above, where the noise relation between $\vec{n}_X$ and $\vec{n}_Y$ needs to be identified for a channel that makes it the hardest to communicate. It was shown in [39] that the least favorable noise problem can be recast as an optimization problem:

$$\text{minimize: } \log \frac{|H\Sigma_{\vec{T}}H^T + \Sigma_{\vec{n}}|}{|\Sigma_{\vec{n}}|} \tag{11}$$

$$\text{subject to: } \Sigma_{\vec{n}_x} = I, \tag{12}$$

$$\Sigma_{\vec{n}_y} = I, \tag{13}$$

$$\Sigma_{\vec{n}} \succeq 0, \tag{14}$$

where $H^T = [H_X^T, H_Y^T]$, and $\vec{n} = (\vec{n}_X, \vec{n}_Y)$, when $H\Sigma_{\vec{T}}H^T$ is nonsingular. It can be shown that the problem is convex.

Yu and Cioffi also showed that in this setting, Sato's upper bound is achievable—i.e., it is exactly the sum-rate capacity. Moreover, for any input signaling $P_{\vec{T}}$ that is Gaussian-distributed, the corresponding R_{P_T} can be achieved on this broadcast channel through a more sophisticated scheme known as dirty-paper coding [40]. Therefore, when the pairwise marginals $P_{\vec{T},\vec{X}}$ and $P_{\vec{T},\vec{X}}$ are jointly Gaussian, respectively, the synergistic information $I^{(S)}(\vec{T};\vec{X},\vec{Y})$ is exactly the cooperative gain of the corresponding Gaussian broadcast channel using this specific input signaling pattern $P_{\vec{T}}$. The connection in the Gaussian setting is of particular interest, given the practical importance of the Gaussian PID, which was thoroughly explored in [41].

4.3. Revisiting the Examples

Let us now revisit the examples given earlier, and attempt to understand them in the broadcast channel setting:

1. Common information dominant: Here, the two receivers both know the transmitted signal completely, and therefore, there is no difference even if they are allowed to cooperate, and the cooperative gain is 0.
2. Synergistic information dominant: Clearly, here, T is a uniformly distributed Bernoulli random variable. When the two receivers are not allowed to cooperate, they cannot decode anything because the channel $T \to X$ is completely noisy, and similarly for the channel $T \to Y$. When the receivers are allowed to cooperate, then from X and Y, we can completely recover T—i.e., the channel becomes noiseless. Therefore, the full information in T can be decoded. The cooperative gain is then one, matching the synergistic information.

3. Component-wise decomposition: Here, T has three uniformly distributed Bernoulli random variable components, mutually independent of each other. In the channel $T \to X$, the first component is noiseless, and the second component is completely noisy. This is similarly the case for $T \to Y$. When the receivers are not allowed to cooperate, the sum rate on the channel is two. However, when the channels are allowed to cooperate, the last component in T becomes useful (noiseless), and the total communication rate becomes three. Therefore the cooperative gain is $3 - 2 = 1$, equal to the synergistic information.

5. Conclusions

We provide an operational interpretation of the PID given in [13] via a connection to the well-studied broadcast channel capacity in the information theory literature. The synergistic information is directly connected to the cooperative gain on the corresponding broadcast channel, either quantitatively exactly equal or being a lower bound. This interpretation can help us better understand why such decomposition can be used to guide model selection in machine learning and in the analysis of biological signals, and potentially design new methods to utilize it.

We note that in the information theory literature, broadcast channels with cooperative receivers have been studied carefully [42], where the two receivers are allowed to communicate on rate-limited links. It may be of interest to consider the corresponding notion of partial information decompositions, when the synergistic information can be parametrized by the degree of cooperation between the receivers. Moreover, the concept of Renyi information has found applications in many fields [43], and the decomposition of Renyi information has not been explored; it may be beneficial to study how our approach can be applied to such decompositions.

Author Contributions: Conceptualization, C.T.; Formal analysis, C.T.; Investigation, S.S.; Writing—original draft, C.T.; Writing—review & editing, C.T. and S.S. All authors have read and agreed to the published version of the manuscript.

Funding: The work of S. Shamai was supported by the German Research Foundation (DFG) via the German-Israeli Project Cooperation (DIP) under Project SH 1937/1-1 and the Ollendorff Minerva Center of the Technion.

Data Availability Statement: No new data were created or analyzed in this study. Data sharing is not applicable.

Acknowledgments: C. Tian wishes to acknowledge his discussion with Paul Liang of the Massachusetts Institute of Technology regarding the application of PID in multimodality learning. This work was partially completed while C. Tian was on a faculty development leave at the Massachusetts Institute of Technology.

Conflicts of Interest: The authors declare no conflicts of interest.

References

1. Wibral, M.; Priesemann, V.; Kay, J.W.; Lizier, J.T.; Phillips, W.A. Partial information decomposition as a unified approach to the specification of neural goal functions. *Brain Cogn.* **2017**, *112*, 25–38. [CrossRef] [PubMed]
2. Feldman, A.K.; Venkatesh, P.; Weber, D.J.; Grover, P. Information-theoretic tools to understand distributed source coding in neuroscience. *IEEE J. Sel. Areas Inf. Theory* **2024**, *5*, 509–519. [CrossRef]
3. Wibral, M.; Finn, C.; Wollstadt, P.; Lizier, J.T.; Priesemann, V. Quantifying information modification in developing neural networks via partial information decomposition. *Entropy* **2017**, *19*, 494. [CrossRef]
4. Ehrlich, D.A.; Schneider, A.C.; Priesemann, V.; Wibral, M.; Makkeh, A. A measure of the complexity of neural representations based on partial information decomposition. *Trans. Mach. Learn. Res.* **2023**, *5*, 2835–8856.

5. Timme, N.; Alford, W.; Flecker, B.; Beggs, J.M. Synergy, redundancy, and multivariate information measures: An experimentalist's perspective. *J. Comput. Neurosci.* **2014**, *36*, 119–140. [CrossRef]
6. Stramaglia, S.; Cortes, J.M.; Marinazzo, D. Synergy and redundancy in the Granger causal analysis of dynamical networks. *New J. Phys.* **2014**, *16*, 105003. [CrossRef]
7. Timme, N.M.; Ito, S.; Myroshnychenko, M.; Nigam, S.; Shimono, M.; Yeh, F.C.; Hottowy, P.; Litke, A.M.; Beggs, J.M. High-degree neurons feed cortical computations. *PLoS Comput. Biol.* **2016**, *12*, e1004858. [CrossRef]
8. Liang, P.P.; Cheng, Y.; Fan, X.; Ling, C.K.; Nie, S.; Chen, R.; Deng, Z.; Allen, N.; Auerbach, R.; Mahmood, F.; et al. Quantifying & modeling multimodal interactions: An information decomposition framework. *Adv. Neural Inf. Process. Syst.* **2024**, *36*, 27351–27393.
9. Liang, P.P.; Zadeh, A.; Morency, L.P. Foundations & trends in multimodal machine learning: Principles, challenges, and open questions. *ACM Comput. Surv.* **2024**, *56*, 1–42.
10. Liang, P.P.; Deng, Z.; Ma, M.Q.; Zou, J.Y.; Morency, L.P.; Salakhutdinov, R. Factorized contrastive learning: Going beyond multi-view redundancy. *Adv. Neural Inf. Process. Syst.* **2024**, *36*, 32971–32998.
11. Williams, P.L.; Beer, R.D. Nonnegative decomposition of multivariate information. *arXiv* **2010**, arXiv:1004.2515.
12. Schneidman, E.; Bialek, W.; Berry, M.J. Synergy, redundancy, and independence in population codes. *J. Neurosci.* **2003**, *23*, 11539–11553. [CrossRef] [PubMed]
13. Bertschinger, N.; Rauh, J.; Olbrich, E.; Jost, J.; Ay, N. Quantifying unique information. *Entropy* **2014**, *16*, 2161–2183. [CrossRef]
14. Bertschinger, N.; Rauh, J.; Olbrich, E.; Jost, J. Shared information—New insights and problems in decomposing information in complex systems. In Proceedings of the European Conference on Complex Systems 2012, Agadir, Morocco, 5–6 November 2012; pp. 251–269.
15. Griffith, V.; Koch, C. Quantifying synergistic mutual information. In *Guided Self-Organization: Inception*; Springer: Berlin/Heidelberg, Germany, 2014; pp. 159–190.
16. Harder, M.; Salge, C.; Polani, D. Bivariate measure of redundant information. *Phys. Rev. E—Stat. Nonlinear Soft Matter Phys.* **2013**, *87*, 012130. [CrossRef]
17. Olbrich, E.; Bertschinger, N.; Rauh, J. Information decomposition and synergy. *Entropy* **2015**, *17*, 3501–3517. [CrossRef]
18. Porta, A.; Bari, V.; De Maria, B.; Takahashi, A.C.; Guzzetti, S.; Colombo, R.; Catai, A.M.; Raimondi, F.; Faes, L. Quantifying net synergy/redundancy of spontaneous variability regulation via predictability and transfer entropy decomposition frameworks. *IEEE Trans. Biomed. Eng.* **2017**, *64*, 2628–2638.
19. Lizier, J.T.; Bertschinger, N.; Jost, J.; Wibral, M. Information decomposition of target effects from multi-source interactions: Perspectives on previous, current and future work. *Entropy* **2018**, *20*, 307. [CrossRef]
20. Quax, R.; Har-Shemesh, O.; Sloot, P.M. Quantifying synergistic information using intermediate stochastic variables. *Entropy* **2017**, *19*, 85. [CrossRef]
21. Barrett, A.B. Exploration of synergistic and redundant information sharing in static and dynamical Gaussian systems. *Phys. Rev. E* **2015**, *91*, 052802. [CrossRef]
22. Chatterjee, P.; Pal, N.R. Construction of synergy networks from gene expression data related to disease. *Gene* **2016**, *590*, 250–262. [CrossRef]
23. Rauh, J.; Banerjee, P.K.; Olbrich, E.; Jost, J.; Bertschinger, N. On extractable shared information. *Entropy* **2017**, *19*, 328. [CrossRef]
24. Ince, R.A. Measuring multivariate redundant information with pointwise common change in surprisal. *Entropy* **2017**, *19*, 318. [CrossRef]
25. Finn, C.; Lizier, J.T. Pointwise partial information decompositionusing the specificity and ambiguity lattices. *Entropy* **2018**, *20*, 297. [CrossRef] [PubMed]
26. James, R.G.; Emenheiser, J.; Crutchfield, J.P. Unique information via dependency constraints. *J. Phys. A Math. Theor.* **2018**, *52*, 014002. [CrossRef]
27. Varley, T.F. Generalized decomposition of multivariate information. *PLoS ONE* **2024**, *19*, e0297128. [CrossRef]
28. Cover, T.M.; Thomas, J.A. *Elements of Information Theory*; John Wiley & Sons: Hoboken, NJ, USA, 2006.
29. Kolchinsky, A. A novel approach to the partial information decomposition. *Entropy* **2022**, *24*, 403. [CrossRef]
30. Cover, T. Broadcast channels. *IEEE Trans. Inf. Theory* **1972**, *18*, 2–14. [CrossRef]
31. Cover, T. An achievable rate region for the broadcast channel. *IEEE Trans. Inf. Theory* **1975**, *21*, 399–404. [CrossRef]
32. Weingarten, H.; Steinberg, Y.; Shamai, S.S. The capacity region of the Gaussian multiple-input multiple-output broadcast channel. *IEEE Trans. Inf. Theory* **2006**, *52*, 3936–3964. [CrossRef]
33. El Gamal, A.; Kim, Y.H. *Network Information Theory*; Cambridge University Press: Cambridge, UK, 2011.
34. Sato, H. An outer bound to the capacity region of broadcast channels (Corresp.). *IEEE Trans. Inf. Theory* **1978**, *24*, 374–377. [CrossRef]
35. Geng, Y.; Nair, C. The capacity region of the two-receiver Gaussian vector broadcast channel with private and common messages. *IEEE Trans. Inf. Theory* **2014**, *60*, 2087–2104. [CrossRef]

36. Tian, C. Latent capacity region: A case study on symmetric broadcast with common messages. *IEEE Trans. Inf. Theory* **2011**, *57*, 3273–3285. [CrossRef]
37. Gacs, P.; Korner, J. Common information is far less than mutual information. *Probl. Control Inf. Theory* **1973**, *2*, 149–162.
38. Wyner, A. The common information of two dependent random variables. *IEEE Trans. Inf. Theory* **1975**, *21*, 163–179. [CrossRef]
39. Yu, W.; Cioffi, J.M. Sum capacity of Gaussian vector broadcast channels. *IEEE Trans. Inf. Theory* **2004**, *50*, 1875–1892. [CrossRef]
40. Costa, M. Writing on dirty paper (corresp.). *IEEE Trans. Inf. Theory* **1983**, *29*, 439–441. [CrossRef]
41. Venkatesh, P.; Bennett, C.; Gale, S.; Ramirez, T.; Heller, G.; Durand, S.; Olsen, S.; Mihalas, S. Gaussian partial information decomposition: Bias correction and application to high-dimensional data. *Adv. Neural Inf. Process. Syst.* **2024**, *36*, 74602–74635.
42. Dabora, R.; Servetto, S.D. Broadcast channels with cooperating decoders. *IEEE Trans. Inf. Theory* **2006**, *52*, 5438–5454. [CrossRef]
43. Liese, F.; Vajda, I. On divergences and informations in statistics and information theory. *IEEE Trans. Inf. Theory* **2006**, *52*, 4394–4412. [CrossRef]

entropy

MDPI

Article

Feature-Driven Semantic Communication for Efficient Image Transmission

Ji Zhang [1,2,3,*], Ying Zhang [1,2], Baofeng Ji [1,2], Anmin Chen [1,2], Aoxue Liu [1,2] and Hengzhou Xu [4]

[1] School of Mathematics and Statistics, Henan University of Science and Technology, Luoyang 471000, China; 230320080769@stu.haust.edu.cn (Y.Z.); baofengjihkd@163.com (B.J.); 220320080764@stu.haust.edu.cn (A.C.); 17739127399@163.com (A.L.)

[2] Intelligent System Science and Technology Innovation Center, Longmen Laboratory, Luoyang 471000, China

[3] Engineering Research Center of Intelligent Swarm Systems, Ministry of Education, Zhengzhou University, Zhengzhou 450001, China

[4] School of Computer, Henan University of Engineering, Zhengzhou 450001, China; xhz05228@126.com

* Correspondence: zhangji@haust.edu.cn

Abstract: Semantic communication is an emerging approach that enhances transmission efficiency by conveying the semantic content of information more effectively. It has garnered significant attention in recent years. However, existing semantic communication systems for image transmission typically adopt direct transmission of features or uniformly compress features before transmission. They have not yet considered the differential impact of features on image recovery at the receiver end and the issue of bandwidth limitations during actual transmission. This paper shows that non-uniform processing of features leads to better image recovery under bandwidth constraints compared to uniform processing. Based on this, we propose a semantic communication system for image transmission, which introduces non-uniform quantization techniques. In the feature transmission stage, the system performs varying levels of quantization based on the differences in feature performance at the receiver, thereby reducing the bandwidth requirement. Inspired by quantitative quantization techniques, we design a non-uniform quantization algorithm capable of dynamic bit allocation. This algorithm, under bandwidth constraints, dynamically adjusts the quantization precision of features based on their contribution to the completion of tasks at the receiver end, ensuring the quality and accuracy of the transmitted data even under limited bandwidth conditions. Experimental results show that the proposed system reduces bandwidth usage while ensuring image reconstruction quality.

Keywords: semantic communication; non-uniform quantization; image feature extraction

1. Introduction

The global deployment and application of 5G technology have brought existing wireless communication systems closer to the Shannon limit in terms of performance [1]. This makes it difficult to further increase the channel capacity, and they cannot meet the massive and high-frequency data transmission demands under limited bandwidth conditions [2]. The development of artificial intelligence technology has provided new pathways for overcoming the limitations of traditional communication, driving the development of a communication paradigm aimed at transmitting semantic information–semantic communication. Compared to traditional communication, semantic communication emphasizes the transmission of information's semantic content, thereby improving communication efficiency and task execution accuracy [3].

Current research mainly focuses on semantic communication for data types such as text, speech, and images. For example, Wang et al. [4] designed a semantic communication system for speech transcription based on the masked autoencoder; Xie et al. [5] combined visual and semantic data to design a semantic communication system for visual question answering. Hu et al. [6,7] used variational autoencoders to design a semantic communication system for image classification; Pan et al. [8] utilized semantic features from vehicle perception images to design an image segmentation semantic communication system for vehicle driving decision-making. However, these studies mainly focus on using the transmitted data to complete tasks at the receiver end, and they do not adequately address the issues related to data recovery and reconstruction, especially considering the high dimensionality and noise sensitivity of image data.

As a result, some researchers have focused on semantic communication systems for image transmission. E. Bourtsoulatze et al. [9] proposed an image transmission system based on convolutional neural networks (CNNs), which achieved better image recovery quality than traditional image transmission methods. K. Tonchev et al. [10] designed a semantic communication system based on graph convolutional networks (GCNs) to achieve the transmission and recovery of 3D video data. In addition to CNN-based communication systems, K. Yang et al. [11] used the self-attention mechanism and global modeling capability of transformers to design an image transmission system based on the Swin Transformer architecture, which showed superior image recovery performance compared to traditional communication systems and some semantic communication systems based on CNN architectures.

Although the image reconstruction results from the aforementioned semantic communication systems are satisfactory, they all aim to improve the quality of information recovery at the receiver end, with little consideration of the differential contribution of semantic information to the receiver.

This limitation has led to further consideration of how to optimize the transmission of semantic information, particularly how to apply differentiated encoding based on the contribution of different semantic information to the receiver. To address this, Lin et al. [12] proposed a semantic importance-based encoding algorithm that aggregates image channel features to obtain the importance weights of feature maps for task results, prioritizing the transmission of high-importance semantic feature maps to reduce redundant information in the transmission process. Considering the limited bandwidth issue in practical transmission, Huang et al. [13] divided the image into a base layer and an enhancement layer, prioritizing the transmission of key information at low bit rates to reduce transmission resource consumption. These approaches bear some resemblance to adaptive quantization methods in prior work. For instance, Wu et al. [14] proposed an adaptive quantization scheme based on semantic segmentation, dividing images into regions of interest (ROIs) and regions of non-interest (RONIs) with distinct encoding to optimize transmission efficiency. Gupta et al. [15] developed a method that dynamically adjusts quantization levels for neural network weights based on their statistical distribution, targeting memory reduction. Han et al. [16] introduced a technique combining pruning and quantization, adaptively assigning fixed bit-widths to weights based on magnitude for computational efficiency. Lei et al. [17] designed an ROI-based adaptive quantization for image compression, adjusting bit allocation to prioritize predefined regions critical for tasks like classification. However, these methods have notable limitations, that is, Wu et al. and Lei et al. relied on predefined ROI distinctions, restricting global optimization and adaptability to dynamic conditions; Gupta et al. and Han et al. applied uniform quantization across layers or parameters, neglecting feature-specific importance and bandwidth constraints during transmission.

In contrast, this paper proposes a feature-driven semantic communication framework that advances beyond these methods with non-uniform quantization based on feature contribution factors. Unlike Wu et al. [14] and Lei et al.'s [17] region-specific approaches or Gupta et al. [15] and Han et al.'s [16] uniform quantization, our method introduces a feature contribution factor to dynamically allocate bits across all image features according to their reconstruction importance. It optimizes global image recovery rather than predefined regions and adapts in real-time to bandwidth constraints, ensuring both efficiency and high-quality reconstruction under limited resources. The main contributions are as follows:

- We designed a feature-driven semantic communication framework that uses non-uniform quantization methods based on the contribution factor of image features, optimizing bandwidth usage while ensuring image quality.
- This paper designs a non-uniform quantization algorithm for transmitted features, which is based on fixed-point quantization technology. The algorithm dynamically adjusts the quantization precision by combining the contribution factors of features and the transmission bandwidth requirements, maximizing data transmission efficiency and image quality during the transmission process.
- The performance of the proposed system was validated under additive white Gaussian noise (AWGN), Rayleigh fading channels, and a composite channel model. This composite model combines Rician fading, multipath effects, and time-varying noise. The simulation results demonstrate the improvements in image transmission efficiency and quality of the proposed system compared to traditional uniform quantization. These improvements are particularly evident under limited bandwidth conditions across all tested channel environments.

The remainder of this paper is organized as follows: Section 2 describes the quantization techniques and the development of semantic communication. Section 3 presents the problem formulation, along with the system model and the design of the non-uniform quantization algorithm. Section 4 analyzes the existing simulation results. The conclusion is provided in Section 5, and Section 6 outlines potential directions for future work.

2. Related Works

2.1. Quantitative Methods

Quantization techniques were initially used for the digital processing of analog signals [18]. In particular, during the analog-to-digital conversion (ADC) process, continuous analog signals are discretized into a finite number of digital values, achieving a digital representation of the signal [19]. Quantization methods are divided into uniform and non-uniform quantization based on the difference in quantization intervals. Uniform quantization divides the data range into multiple equal-sized intervals for quantization, while non-uniform quantization performs quantization with unequal intervals based on the statistical properties of the data to improve quantization efficiency. In the field of image processing, quantization methods are widely applied in image compression, especially in early image compression standards such as JPEG [20], which uses uniform quantization techniques to quantize the coefficients after discrete cosine transform (DCT), adjusting the balance between compression ratio and image quality.

With the rise of deep learning and the increasing complexity of neural network models, quantization techniques have been redefined as an important method for neural network compression. Lin et al. [21] demonstrated the potential of quantization as a regularization technique by applying different bit quantization methods to multiple neural networks. Jacob et al. [22] proposed a pure integer quantization method, where both the weight and activation values were uniformly quantized to the INT8 type, further optimizing network performance. Notably, Liu et al. [23] introduced the binary neural network (BNN) quantization method, where all network weight and activation values are quantized to +1 and −1, significantly simplifying the model structure and reducing storage requirements. Inspired by this method, subsequent research has proposed various improvements and optimization methods [24].

In recent years, to improve the flexibility and applicability of quantization methods, mixed-precision quantization based on parameter differences has garnered significant attention [25]. This approach, which we refer to as a method of non-uniform quantization, allocates different bit precisions to parameters in different layers.

Chen et al. [26] designed a deep neural network model compression algorithm based on a three-value weight network, where full-precision weights were quantized into four states, enhancing the flexibility of weight quantization. Zhen et al. [27] introduced Hessian-aware quantization (HAWQ), which analyzes the curvature information of network layer outputs to establish a quantization sensitivity evaluation model, allocating the optimal bit width for each layer. Similarly, Zhang et al. [28] proposed a mixed-precision quantization method for depth-separable convolutional networks, assigning different bit widths to each layer based on the weight distribution and importance of each layer to reduce model size.

Uhlich et al. [29] proposed a method where the dynamic range and step size of the quantizer were parameterized as differentiable variables. By dynamically updating these parameters during training, they achieved the optimal bit width for mixed-precision quantization. In the ImageNet task, this method achieved less than 0.5% accuracy loss while compressing the ResNet-18 model by 4.24 times. Wu et al. [30] proposed the differentiable neural architecture search (DNAS), where a supernetwork with different bit-width candidate operations is constructed. By relaxing discrete bit-width choices to continuous probability distributions using Gumbel-Softmax, they assigned lower precision to redundant layers and retained high precision for sensitive layers, achieving model compression.

Wang et al. [31] proposed the APQ framework, which uses an evolutionary algorithm to search for mixed-precision strategies on a pre-trained "Once-For-All" network. By estimating latency and energy consumption for each layer at different bit-widths, the framework quickly computes model accuracy and resource usage, enabling pruning and mixed-precision quantization. Van et al. [32] introduced a Bayesian quantization framework that decomposes weights into multiple sets of power-of-two bit-width residuals. Using a variational inference approach, they jointly optimized bit-width and pruning gates, achieving mixed-precision quantization.

Additionally, some works have utilized reinforcement learning methods to dynamically select the appropriate quantization bit-width for each layer of neural networks. This helps maintain model inference accuracy while reducing storage and computational resource consumption. For example, Wang et al. [33] used the deep deterministic policy gradient (DDPG) to optimize per-layer bit-widths, incorporating hardware feedback (e.g., delay, energy consumption) to achieve multi-objective constraint optimization. In MobileNet-V2, this method achieved 8.03x model compression with only a 1.14% accuracy loss, considering FPGA resource constraints. Elthakeb [34] et al. proposed an LSTM-based reinforcement learning framework with an asymmetric reward function to balance accuracy and compression, prioritizing high precision for key layers and avoiding model collapse due to low precision.

Liu et al. [35] introduced a hierarchical reinforcement learning architecture (HLC and LLC controllers), jointly optimizing network architecture and per-core mixed precision. Using hardware model predictions, they reduced real deployment costs. This method, when applied to ResNet-50, reduced latency by 39% and energy consumption by 33%, compared to traditional methods. In summary, the development of non-uniform quantization techniques has greatly improved the efficiency of neural network models, enabling them to maintain high accuracy while reducing storage and computational demands.

2.2. Semantic Communication

As early as 1953, Weaver introduced the concept of semantics [36]. It focuses on transmitting semantic information rather than raw data [37,38]. Early communication theory mainly focused on the reliability of channel transmission. It paid limited attention to the semantics of the transmitted information [39]. However, with evolving communication needs [40] and advances in deep learning technology [41], semantic communication systems have gained increasing attention. Traditional communication systems focus on the accurate transmission of data. They do not consider the semantic relevance of the transmitted information. In contrast, using semantic encoding modules to extract and compress semantic features can improve communication efficiency and optimize the process [42–45]. Yet, many existing semantic communication systems face challenges in information transmission. These include high model complexity [46], large computational resource demands [47], and limited transmission efficiency.

To address these issues, some researchers have explored importance-based encoding. This approach aims to prioritize and encode information features based on their importance. It seeks to enhance transmission efficiency and reduce redundant data. These methods typically rank features and prioritize the transmission of higher-ranked ones. Zhou et al. [48] used feature importance and robustness as priority metrics. They prioritized the transmission of top-ranked features to ensure key image features are sent even under poor channel conditions. Gao et al. [49] defined semantic value to measure the importance of semantic information. They selected top-ranked semantic triples for transmission. Ma et al. [50] applied generative artificial intelligence (GenAI) to divide visual data into semantic segments. They ranked these segments by task relevance and transmitted only those with higher priority. Although these methods work in some cases, they generally face issues. These include high computational overhead, poor real-time performance, and complexity in dynamically assessing feature importance. In bandwidth-limited or resource-constrained environments, efficiently transmitting key features without adding computational burden remains a critical challenge. To address this, we propose a semantic communication framework based on feature contribution factors and non-uniform quantization. Compared to existing methods, our framework avoids complex feature ranking and predictive computation. It adjusts quantization precision according to each feature's contribution to image recovery quality. Our method can adapt to the varying impacts of features on image reconstruction.

3. Feature-Driven Semantic Communication System

In this section, we discuss our proposed method in detail. First, we provide a theoretical analysis to demonstrate that, under resource-constrained conditions, applying non-uniform quantization to features, as opposed to uniform quantization, leads to better image reconstruction quality. Next, we introduce the semantic communication system model that we have designed. Finally, we elaborate on the non-uniform quantization method for features that we developed and explore its application in image reconstruction.

3.1. Problem Formulation

In communication systems, to reduce transmission bandwidth, quantization is applied to the extracted features before transmission. This process discretizes continuous-valued features, reducing data size while maintaining essential information. In semantic communication systems for image transmission, it is commonly assumed that all features contribute equally to image reconstruction at the receiver. Under this assumption, uniform quantization is applied to all features, treating them as equally important. However, in practice, different features have varying levels of significance. Some features play a more critical role in enhancing image quality, while others contribute less. Ignoring the non-uniform impact of features and applying uniform quantization can lead to the following issues:

1. Information loss: Important features may suffer excessive quantization errors, resulting in significant degradation of image quality.
2. Inefficient resource allocation: Less important features may receive unnecessary bit allocation, leading to inefficient transmission.

To address these issues, this paper proposes a feature-aware non-uniform quantization method that adapts quantization parameters based on the varying contributions of features. We introduce the contribution factor, c_i, to measure the importance of each feature in the image reconstruction. It is defined as follows:

$$c_i = \frac{r(x_i)}{\sum_{i=1}^{n} r(x_i)}, \tag{1}$$

where c_i represents the contribution factor of feature x_i, n denotes the total number of features, and $r(x_i)$ quantifies the impact of feature x_i on image reconstruction quality. Our objective is to design an adaptive quantization algorithm that optimizes transmission efficiency while maintaining high image recovery quality. In the next section, we analyze the advantages of non-uniform quantization in reducing quantization error.

3.2. *Analysis of the Advantages of Non-Uniform Quantization in Image Recovery*

Through analysis, we demonstrate the advantages of non-uniform quantization over uniform quantization in image recovery quality under a fixed bit budget.

3.2.1. Assumptions

To facilitate the theoretical analysis, we make the following assumptions:

Assumption 1 (feature distribution): The extracted features $X = \{x_1, x_2, \ldots, x_N\}$ are assumed to have a smooth probability distribution within their dynamic ranges. While deep neural networks may produce feature distributions that are approximately Gaussian or slightly non-uniform, we assume that within each feature's dynamic range, the values can be approximated as locally uniform. This assumption can simplify the quantization error model and allow for an analytical derivation of the mean squared error (MSE).

Assumption 2 (quantization as the sole source of distortion): We assume that quantization is the sole source of distortion in the system, excluding factors such as channel noise or encoding errors.

Assumption 3 (bit budget constraint): We assume that the total available bits for quantization, denoted by R, is the sum of the bit allocations b_i for each feature x_i, as follows:

$$R = \sum_{i=1}^{N} b_i, \quad \text{where} \quad b_i \in \mathbb{Z}.$$

Additionally, the total bit budget is constrained by the maximum channel capacity $R_{\max}$, such that we have the following:

$$R \leq R_{\max}.$$

Assumption 4 (mean squared error as the quality metric): We use mean squared error (MSE) as the metric for evaluating image reconstruction quality, defined as follows:

$$MSE = \frac{1}{N} \sum_{i=1}^{N} (x_i - \hat{x}_i)^2,$$

where x_i represents the original image and $\hat{x}_i$ denotes the reconstructed image.

Assumption 5 (quantization error model): We assume that the quantization error for each feature x_i follows a uniform distribution within its respective quantization interval:

$$\varepsilon_i = x_i - \hat{x}_i \sim \text{Uniform}\left(-\frac{\Delta_i}{2}, \frac{\Delta_i}{2}\right),$$

where Δ_i is the quantization step size.

With these assumptions, we have the following theorem.

3.2.2. Theorem and Proof

Theorem 1. *Under Assumptions 1–5, the optimal bit allocation for minimizing the Mean Squared Error (MSE) in image recovery follows a non-uniform quantization scheme. The number of bits b_i assigned to each feature x_i is proportional to the logarithm of its contribution factor c_i, given by the following:*

$$b_i^* = \frac{1}{2}\log_2\left(\frac{2c_i \cdot C \cdot \ln 2}{\lambda}\right). \quad (2)$$

Furthermore, non-uniform quantization results in a lower overall MSE compared to uniform quantization:

$$MSE_{non\text{-}uniform} \leq MSE_{uniform}. \quad (3)$$

Proof. Step 1: Formulating the MSE Expression According to Assumption 5, the quantization error ε_i follows a uniform distribution in its quantization interval, leading to a quantization noise variance:

$$E[\varepsilon_i^2] = \frac{\Delta_i^2}{12}. \quad (4)$$

By Assumption 4, the total MSE is given by the following:

$$MSE = \sum_{i=1}^{N} c_i \cdot \frac{\Delta_i^2}{12}. \quad (5)$$

Substituting the quantization step size, we have the following:

$$\Delta_i = \frac{x_{i,\max} - x_{i,\min}}{2^{b_i} - 1}, \quad (6)$$

we obtain the following:

$$MSE = \sum_{i=1}^{N} c_i \cdot \frac{(x_{i,\max} - x_{i,\min})^2}{12(2^{2b_i} - 1)}. \quad (7)$$

Step 2: optimization problem formulation. The objective is to minimize the total MSE subject to the bit budget constraint given in Assumption 3:

$$\sum_{i=1}^{N} b_i = R. \quad (8)$$

Using the Lagrange multiplier method, we define the Lagrangian function as follows:

$$L = \sum_{i=1}^{N} c_i \cdot \frac{(x_{i,\max} - x_{i,\min})^2}{12(2^{2b_i} - 1)} + \lambda\left(\sum_{i=1}^{N} b_i - R\right). \quad (9)$$

Following the standard derivation using the Lagrange multiplier method, the optimal bit allocation is obtained as follows:

$$b_i^* = \frac{1}{2}\log_2\left(\frac{2c_i \cdot C \cdot \ln 2}{\lambda}\right). \tag{10}$$

Step 3: Performance Comparison Applying the arithmetic-geometric mean (AM-GM) inequality, we have the following:

$$\frac{1}{N}\sum_{i=1}^{N} a_i \geq \left(\prod_{i=1}^{N} a_i\right)^{\frac{1}{N}}, \tag{11}$$

we establish the following:

$$MSE_{\text{non-uniform}} \leq MSE_{\text{uniform}}. \tag{12}$$

This completes the proof. □

The above theoretical analysis establishes that the proposed non-uniform quantization strategy effectively reduces MSE compared to uniform quantization. Equation (16) indicates that the number of bits assigned to each feature depends on its relative importance, leading to a more efficient representation of the image data. This result ensures reduced storage and transmission bandwidth requirements while maintaining image recovery quality.

3.3. Overall Architecture

Based on the above theory, this paper designs a feature-contribution-factor-based non-uniform quantization semantic communication system, which reduces data storage and transmission bandwidth requirements while ensuring image recovery quality. The semantic communication system considered in this paper consists of two main parts, namely, the transmitter and the receiver. The system flow is shown in Figure 1.

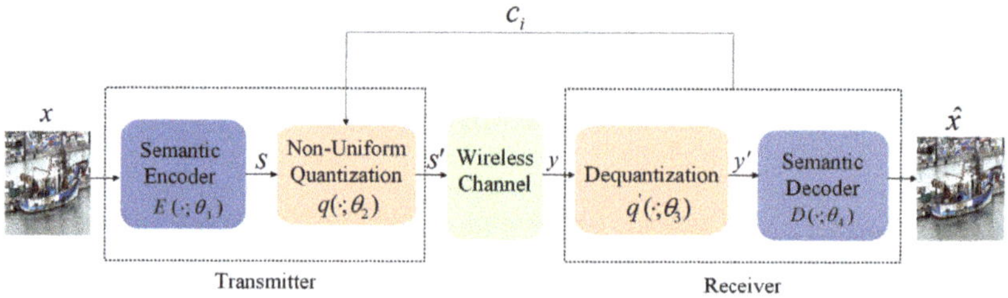

Figure 1. The overall architecture diagram of the proposed non-uniform quantization semantic communication system.

The transmitter extracts features from the input image, x, through the encoder, E, and obtains the encoded feature vector, s; the transmission process is represented as follows:

$$s = E(\cdot;\theta_1), \tag{13}$$

where θ_1 represents the parameter set of the encoder. Based on the contribution factors of the features, the representation of the feature s is non-uniformly quantized to obtain the compressed feature $s' = q(\cdot;\theta_2)$, where θ_2 is the parameter set used for non-uniform quantization. Before transmitting the compressed feature through the wireless channel, power normalization is performed to ensure that the signal satisfies the specified average power constraint. In this paper, we consider a general fading channel model, where the transmission process is represented as follows:

$$y = h \odot s' + n, \tag{14}$$

where h denotes the channel state information (CSI) vector, representing the channel characteristics, $\odot$ denotes element-wise multiplication, and n is the noise vector, with each component independently sampled from a Gaussian distribution. The noise distribution is characterized by noise power σ_n^2, and I_k is the identity matrix. The receiver performs the corresponding dequantization on the received feature vector y to obtain $y' = q'(\cdot;\theta_3)$. The decoder D is then used to reconstruct the dequantized feature into the image $\hat{x}$, which can be expressed as follows:

$$\hat{x} = D(\cdot;\theta_4), \tag{15}$$

where θ_3 represents the parameter set for dequantization, and θ_4 represents the parameter set of the decoder.

3.4. Non-Uniform Quantization Algorithm Based on Feature Contribution Factors

This section designs a non-uniform quantization algorithm based on feature contribution factors. The algorithm can assign differential quantization precision to image features based on their contribution, maintaining the integrity of key information while reducing the data size, lowering transmission cost, improving transmission efficiency, and facilitating compatibility with digital communication systems. This foundation optimizes bandwidth utilization for efficient data transmission in practical communication environments. The core idea of the algorithm is to first classify features into different categories based on their contribution factors. Then, the total bit count is allocated to each category of features, followed by the allocation of bits to the symbol, integer, and fractional parts, and calculating the quantization step sizes for each part. As depicted in Figure 2, the n features after semantic encoding are divided into m feature categories based on their contribution factors, denoted as $D_1, D_2, \ldots, D_m$. Each category contains $t_1, t_2, \ldots, t_m$ features, and their sum equals n. For each feature category D_j, the total number of bits allocated for the feature quantization representation is denoted as b_k, where k represents the feature category, and quantization is performed according to a specific bit allocation formula.

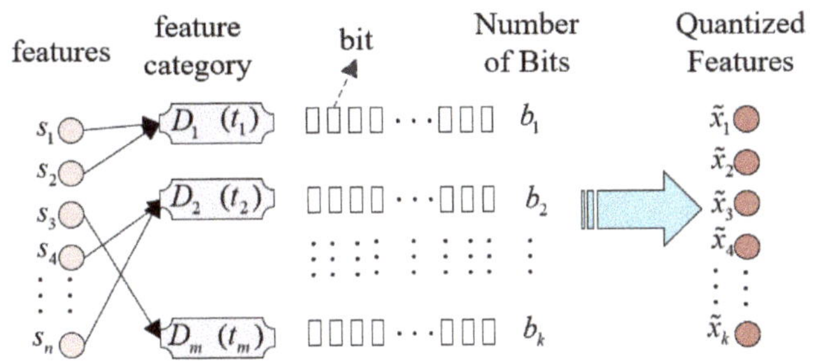

Figure 2. The overall architecture of the proposed non-uniform quantization.

First, based on the feature contribution factors, the sender classifies the features into priority categories before transmission. The larger the contribution factor, the higher the priority of the corresponding feature. These features are divided into m categories according to their priority. For each feature category D_j, the total number of bits allocated for feature quantization representation is denoted as b_k, where k represents the feature category. The bit allocation formula is defined as follows:

$$b_k = \left\lfloor \frac{\sum\limits_{i=1}^{k} c_i}{\sum\limits_{k=1}^{M} \sum\limits_{i=1}^{k} c_i} \cdot B \right\rfloor \tag{16}$$

where B is the total bit budget of the system, and c_i represents the contribution factor of feature x_i, typically determined by the task objective or reconstruction quality. In an ideal scenario, these factors exhibit certain patterns. However, in practical applications, the complexity of task objectives and reconstruction quality makes it difficult to directly obtain the contribution factors. In this paper, the gradient values are used as a measure of the feature contribution factors. Next, for each feature category, based on the allocated bit count b_k, the bits are divided into symbol bits b_k^0, integer bits b_k^1, and fractional bits b_k^2, with the constraint that $b_k^0 = 1$. The quantization step size formulas for the integer and fractional parts are as follows:

$$\Delta_k^1 = \frac{|x_k|_{\max} - |x_k|_{\min}}{2^{b_k^1 - 1}}, \quad \Delta_k^2 = \frac{|x_k|_{\max} - |x_k|_{\min}}{2^{b_k^2 - 1}} \tag{17}$$

For each feature x_k^i in the category, the corresponding quantization step size is used to quantize the feature, and the integer and fractional parts are combined to yield the final quantized feature value $\tilde{x}_k^i$. The expression is as follows:

$$\tilde{x}_k^i = \Delta_k^1 \times \left\lfloor \frac{|x_k^i| - |x_k|_{\min}}{\Delta_k'} + \frac{1}{2} \right\rfloor \cdot L(b_k'') + \Delta_k^2 \times \left\lfloor \frac{|x_k^i| - |x_k|_{\min}}{\Delta_k''} + \frac{1}{2} \right\rfloor \tag{18}$$

where $L(\cdot)$ represents the left shift operation, which is used to combine the integer and fractional parts according to their allocated bit precision. Algorithm 1 summarizes the entire workflow of the non-uniform quantization algorithm.

Algorithm 1 Contribution factor-based non-uniform quantization.

Input: Feature set X, contribution factors C, total bit budget B, number of categories m.
Output: Quantized feature set $\tilde{X}$.
Step 1: Feature classification
for each feature x_i in X **do**
  Assign contribution factor c_i based on task or reconstruction quality.
  Classify features into m categories based on c_i.
end for
Step 2: Bit allocation
for each category D_j **do**
  Allocate bits b_k to each category based on the contribution factors:

$$b_k = \left\lfloor \frac{\sum_{i=1}^{k} c_i}{\sum_{k=1}^{M} \sum_{i=1}^{k} c_i} \cdot B \right\rfloor.$$

end for
Step 3: Bit splitting
for each category D_j **do**
  Split b_k into symbol bits $b_k^0 = 1$, integer bits b_k^1, and fractional bits b_k^2,
  Calculate the quantization step sizes Δ_k^1 and Δ_k^2:

$$\Delta_k^1 = \frac{|x_k|_{\max} - |x_k|_{\min}}{2^{b_k^1 - 1}}, \quad \Delta_k^2 = \frac{|x_k|_{\max} - |x_k|_{\min}}{2^{b_k^2 - 1}}.$$

Algorithm 1 *Cont.*

end for
Step 4: Quantization
for each feature x_k^i in D_j **do**
    Quantize the feature using Δ_k^1 and Δ_k^2:

$$\tilde{x_k^i} = \Delta_k^1 \cdot \left\lfloor \frac{|x_k^i| - |x_k|_{\min}}{\Delta_k^1} + 0.5 \right\rfloor \cdot L(b_k^2) + \Delta_k^2 \cdot \left\lfloor \frac{|x_k^i| - |x_k|_{\min}}{\Delta_k^2} + 0.5 \right\rfloor.$$

end for
Step 5: Output
Return quantized feature set $\tilde{X}$.

At the receiver end, the received quantized values need to be dequantized. First, the received quantized feature values are separated into integer and fractional parts according to the given integer bits b_k^1 and fractional bits b_k^2. Then, based on the quantization step sizes for the integer and fractional parts, they are dequantized. The restored integer and fractional parts are combined to form the final dequantized feature value $\hat{x}_k^i$. The detailed dequantization algorithm is shown in Algorithm 2.

Algorithm 2 Dequantization algorithm for contribution factor-based non-uniform quantization.

Input: Quantized feature set $\tilde{X}$, feature categories $D_1, D_2, \ldots, D_m$, contribution factors C, total bit budget B, quantization step sizes Δ_k^1, Δ_k^2.
Output: Restored feature set X.
Step 1: Bit splitting and inverse bit allocation
for each feature category D_j **do**
    Split each category's total bit allocation b_k into symbol bits b_k^0, integer bits b_k^1, and fractional bits b_k^2,
    Input: Inverse quantization step sizes Δ_k^1 and Δ_k^2 from the sender.
end for
Step 2: Dequantization of each feature
for each quantized feature $\tilde{x_k^i}$ in D_j **do**
    Extract the integer part and fractional part from $\tilde{x_k^i}$ using the left shift operation $L(b_k^2)$:

$$\hat{x}_{\text{int}} = \left\lfloor \frac{\tilde{x_k^i}}{L(b_k^2)} \right\rfloor,$$

$$\hat{x}_{frac} = \tilde{x}_k^i \bmod L(b_k^2).$$

    Restore the original value for integer and fractional parts:

$$x_{\text{int}} = |x_k|_{\min} + \hat{x}_{\text{int}} \cdot \Delta_k^1,$$

$$x_{\text{frac}} = |x_k|_{\min} + \hat{x}_{frac} \cdot \Delta_k^2.$$

    Combine the integer and fractional parts:

$$x_k^i = x_{\text{int}} + x_{\text{frac}}.$$

end for
Step 3: Output
Return the restored feature set $X = \{x_1, x_2, \ldots, x_n\}$.

To preserve the gradient information during the quantization process, this paper adopts the straight-through estimator (STE). Using the STE technique, during backpropagation, an approximate gradient is used to replace the non-differentiable part of the quantization process, ensuring that the model can be properly optimized.

4. Experiments and Discussion of Results

In this section, we first introduce the experimental setup, including the dataset, comparison methods, and experimental details. Finally, the experimental results are presented and discussed.

4.1. Experiment Settings

Experimental environment: The experiments were conducted on a Windows 11 64-bit operating system. The computer was equipped with an Intel i9-12700H processor, an NVIDIA GeForce RTX4060 graphics card, and 8 GB of RAM. The project environment was based on the PyTorch framework and implemented in Python 3.9.

Datasets: The experiments were conducted using the CIFAR10 dataset, consisting of 10 categories of color images, with each category containing 6,000 images, for a total of 60,000 images. In addition, we evaluated our approach on the CIFAR100 dataset and Tiny ImageNet. CIFAR100 comprises 100 categories, with 600 images per category, totaling 60,000 images, offering greater diversity in image classes compared to CIFAR10. Tiny ImageNet consists of 200 categories, with 500 images per category, totaling 100,000 images, providing increased variation in both content and complexity while remaining computationally feasible within the scope of our experimental setup. During training, all images from the datasets were randomly cropped into 256 × 256 patches to ensure consistency across evaluations.

Evaluation metrics: To evaluate image reconstruction quality, we analyzed it from two perspectives, namely, image fidelity and perceptual quality, using the following three key metrics: PSNR, MS-SSIM, and LPIPS.

On the one hand, PSNR and MS-SSIM served as metrics for assessing image fidelity, quantifying the consistency between the reconstructed image and the original image by measuring pixel-wise differences and structural similarity. For PSNR, we used mean squared error (MSE) as the loss function to optimize the model. MSE is defined as the squared difference between the pixel values of the original and reconstructed images, and PSNR is derived by applying a logarithmic transformation to map MSE to a signal-to-noise ratio, expressed in decibels (dB). For MS-SSIM, we used the multi-scale structural similarity (MS-SSIM) index as the loss function to guide model training. In the result analysis, we report the absolute value of MS-SSIM to ensure consistent comparison and analysis with other metrics such as PSNR.

On the other hand, to evaluate the perceptual quality of the generated images, we introduced learned perceptual image patch similarity (LPIPS), a deep learning-based metric. Specifically, for both the original and generated images, we used a pre-trained VGG model to extract multi-level deep features. The perceptual difference between the images was then quantified by calculating the weighted L_2 distance in the feature space. In this study, we used LPIPS only as an evaluation metric to assess the perceptual similarity in image reconstruction quality.

Training U: We used an end-to-end approach to train the model as a whole. The training process was divided into two stages. In the first stage, we trained the model to effectively extract feature representations of the image. Here, we used its variant, Swin Transformer, as the semantic encoding module for the image. The parameter settings are the same as those proposed in [22], namely $[N_1; N_2] = [2; 4]$, $[C_1; C_2] = [128; 256]$, with a window size of 2. In the second stage, we loaded the parameters trained in the first stage and applied the method designed in this paper to process the semantic encoded image features. To reduce computational complexity, we set the feature category $m = 3$. We explored the effects of different bit allocation strategies on the reconstructed image quality when the total bit count B was fixed. We use the Adam optimizer with a learning rate of 1×10^{-4} and a batch size of 128.

4.2. Results and Analysis

Through comparative experiments, the performance of the proposed model under different channel conditions and compression ratios was validated. Figure 3 depicts a comparison of image recovery quality on the AWGN channel without considering bandwidth limitations during transmission. "Origin" represents the PSNR performance when no quantization is applied to the features. "Uniform_10" indicates the PSNR value when 10-bit quantization is applied to all features. "Hierarchical_10" represents the PSNR value when all features are divided into three feature levels, and 10-bit quantization is applied. The bit allocation for the three feature levels, based on their contribution factors, is set as follows: 5, 3, and 2. The division of the symbol bits, integer bits, and fractional bits is as follows: 5:131, 3:111, 2:110.

As shown in Figure 4, after quantizing the features, the image recovery quality at the receiver is noticeably affected compared to the case without quantization. As the available bandwidth increases (i.e., as the bit count per feature increases), the impact of quantization gradually diminishes. In both the AWGN and Rayleigh channels, at low signal-to-noise ratios (SNRs), the image recovery quality for both uniform and non-uniform quantization methods is similar. However, in the Rayleigh channel, the non-uniform quantization method slightly underperforms. At high SNR values, the image recovery quality still lags behind that of the unquantized case, but this gap diminishes, possibly due to the image recovery quality falling within an acceptable range.

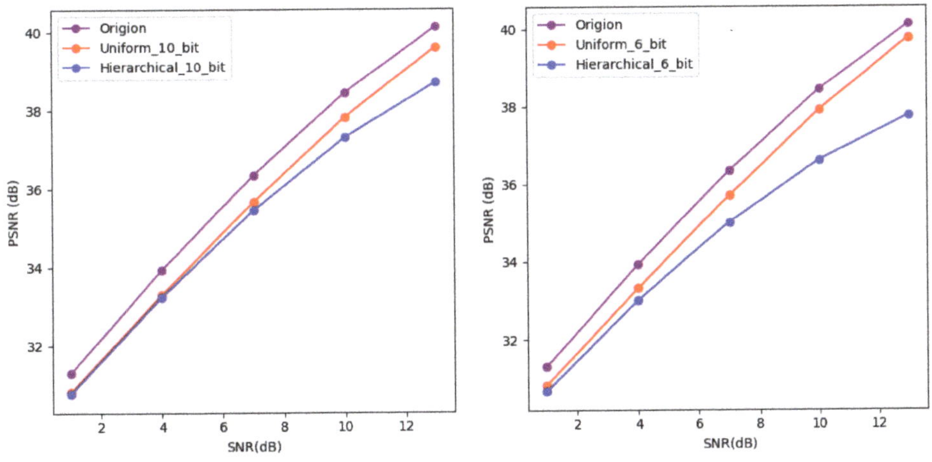

(a) (b)

Figure 3. *Cont.*

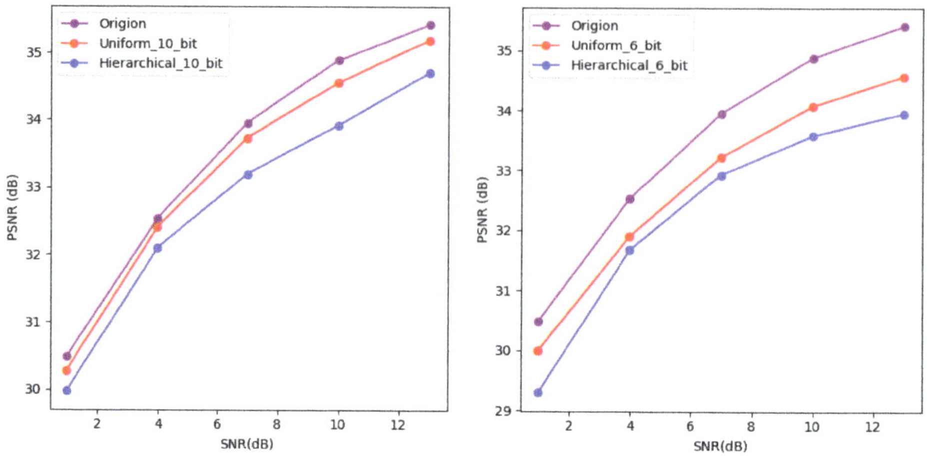

(c) (d)

Figure 3. (**a**,**b**) Describes the image reconstruction PSNR values and MS-SSIM for the CIFAR10 dataset under the AWGN channel, with features transmitted using 10-bit uniform quantization, 6-bit uniform quantization, and no feature compression. (**c**,**d**) Show the PSNR values for image reconstruction of the CIFAR10 dataset under the Rayleigh channel.

To comprehensively evaluate the performance of the proposed model, we also tested and trained our model using the MS-SSIM metric. MS-SSIM is a commonly used image quality assessment metric that performs a weighted calculation of brightness, contrast, and structural similarity across multiple scales, providing a more accurate reflection of the perceptual quality of the image. The MS-SSIM performance of the model under different conditions is illustrated in Figure 4.

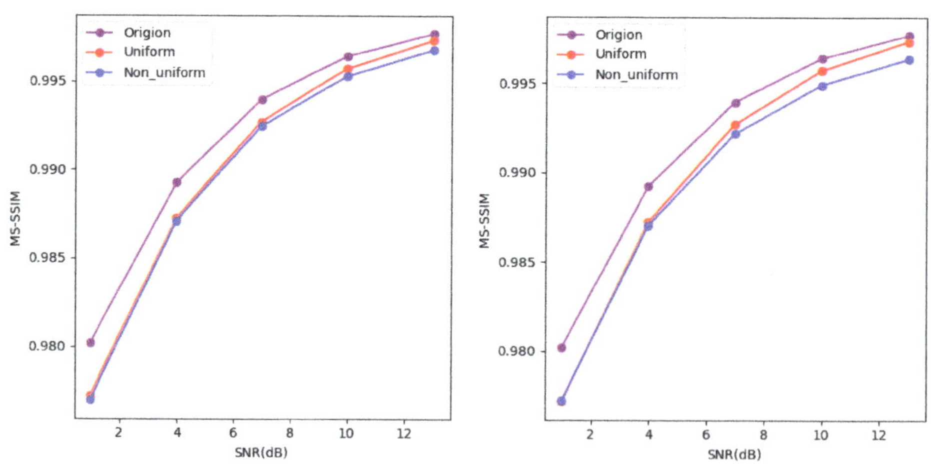

(a) (b)

Figure 4. *Cont.*

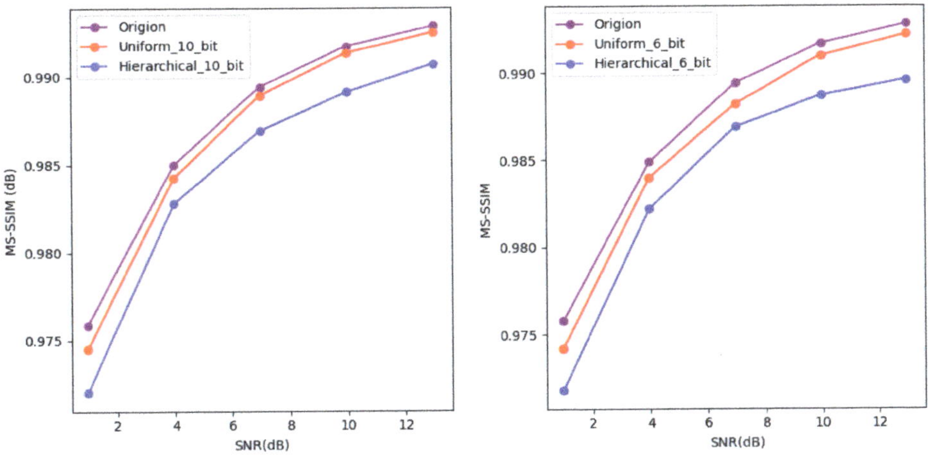

(c) (d)

Figure 4. (**a**,**b**) Describe the image reconstruction MS-SSIM values for the CIFAR10 dataset under the AWGN channel, with features transmitted using 10-bit uniform quantization, 6-bit uniform quantization, and no feature compression. (**c**,**d**) Describe the MS-SSIM values for image reconstruction of the CIFAR10 dataset under the Rayleigh channel.

As presented in Figure 4, with the increase in bandwidth, the MS-SSIM values of different quantization methods gradually increase. The model proposed in this paper performs better in the AWGN channel compared to the Rayleigh channel.

To evaluate the perceptual quality of the image reconstruction, we used the LPIPS metric, which assesses the perceptual similarity between the reconstructed and original images. The results are shown in the figures below.

Figure 5 shows the LPIPS values for image reconstruction of the CIFAR10 dataset under both AWGN and Rayleigh channels using different quantization methods. As the SNR increases, the LPIPS values decrease for all methods, indicating better perceptual quality of the reconstructed images. Both uniform and non-uniform quantization methods have higher LPIPS values compared to the unquantized method, as quantization inevitably affects image quality. However, the LPIPS values for all three methods are below the threshold for high-quality image recovery (0.05). This indicates that the proposed methods in this paper maintain the perceptual quality of the reconstructed images within an acceptable range, despite a slight decrease in quality.

Figure 6 presents the reconstruction results for the CIFAR10 dataset over an AWGN channel with 8-bit transmission. The experimental findings reveal that, under the constraint of limited transmission bits, the proposed non-uniform quantization method outperforms the uniform quantization method across the PSNR, MS-SSIM, and LPIPS metrics.

Specifically, in the PSNR metric (Figure 6a), non-uniform quantization shows significant improvement, particularly at higher SNR values. In terms of the MS-SSIM metric (Figure 6b), the non-uniform quantization method consistently maintains higher values compared to the uniform quantization method, indicating its superior ability to preserve structural details. Additionally, the LPIPS metric (Figure 6c) demonstrates that non-uniform quantization results in fewer perceptual differences from the original image, emphasizing its effectiveness in preserving perceptual quality.

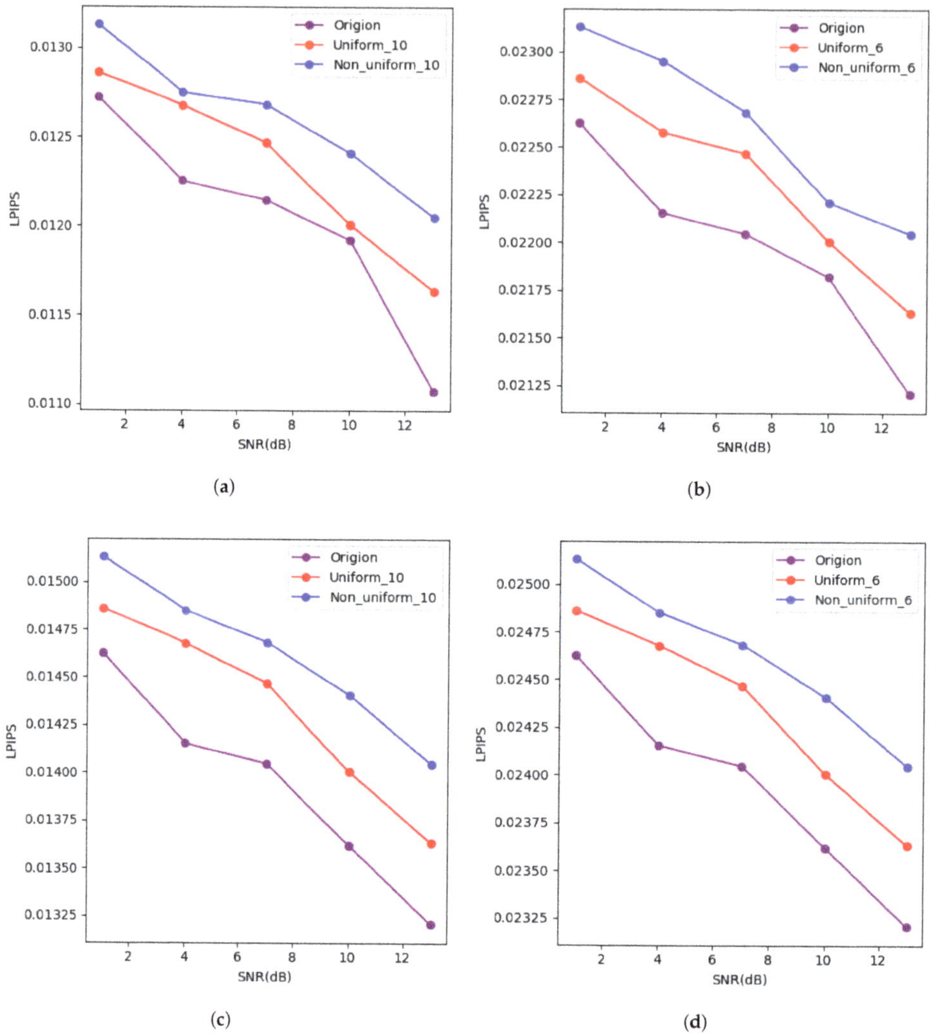

Figure 5. (**a**) Shows the LPIPS values for image reconstruction of the CIFAR10 dataset under the AWGN channel with no bandwidth limitations, comparing three methods: 10-bit uniform quantization for each feature, 10-bit non-uniform quantization, and no feature quantization. (**b**) Presents the LPIPS values for the CIFAR10 dataset under the AWGN channel with no bandwidth limitations, comparing the same three methods: 6-bit uniform quantization, 6-bit non-uniform quantization, and no feature quantization. (**c**) Describes the LPIPS values for image reconstruction of the CIFAR10 dataset under the Rayleigh channel with no bandwidth limitations, comparing 10-bit uniform quantization for each feature, 10-bit non-uniform quantization, and no feature quantization. (**d**) Shows the LPIPS values for the CIFAR10 dataset under the Rayleigh channel with no bandwidth limitations, comparing 6-bit uniform quantization, 6-bit non-uniform quantization, and no feature quantization.

To assess the robustness of our method in real wireless environments, we designed a composite channel model with multipath fading and time-varying noise. This model combines Rician fading ($K = 3$), which includes a dominant line-of-sight component, and time-varying noise modulated as a sinusoidal waveform ($\sin(t/10)$, where $t \in [0, 100]$) to simulate dynamic signal-to-noise ratio (SNR) changes. This model reflects more realistic conditions in daily wireless communication compared to simplified AWGN and Rayleigh models. We conducted a small-scale experiment using this real channel model to evaluate the performance of our method. In the experiment, the CIFAR-100 and Tiny ImageNet datasets were tested at SNRs of 4 dB and 10 dB, with SBR values of 1, 4, 7, 10, and 13, with a bit budget of 8 bits.

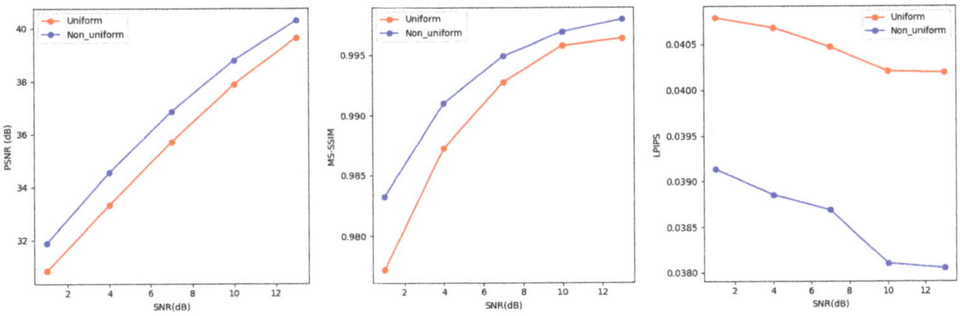

Figure 6. (**a**) Describes the relationship between PSNR and SNR under different quantization methods (Uniform and Non_uniform) in an AWGN channel with an 8-bit transmission limit. (**b**) Describes the relationship between MS-SSIM and SNR under different quantization methods (Uniform and Non_uniform) in an AWGN channel with an 8-bit transmission limit. (**c**) Shows the effect of 8-bit transmission on CIFAR10 images in an AWGN channel in terms of LPIPS.

The results (shown in Figures 7 and 8) show that at low SNR, such as SNR = 1 dB, our method achieves a minimum PSNR of 30 dB, an MS-SSIM of 0.97, and an LPIPS value below 0.2, which indicates good image reconstruction quality. At high SNR, while our method achieves an MS-SSIM of 0.98 and an LPIPS value below 0.014, the PSNR reaches only 33 dB. This PSNR value, although acceptable, is still relatively low, which may result in some loss of fine details and image quality. Therefore, there is still room for improvement in terms of preserving detailed structures and achieving higher-quality image restoration.

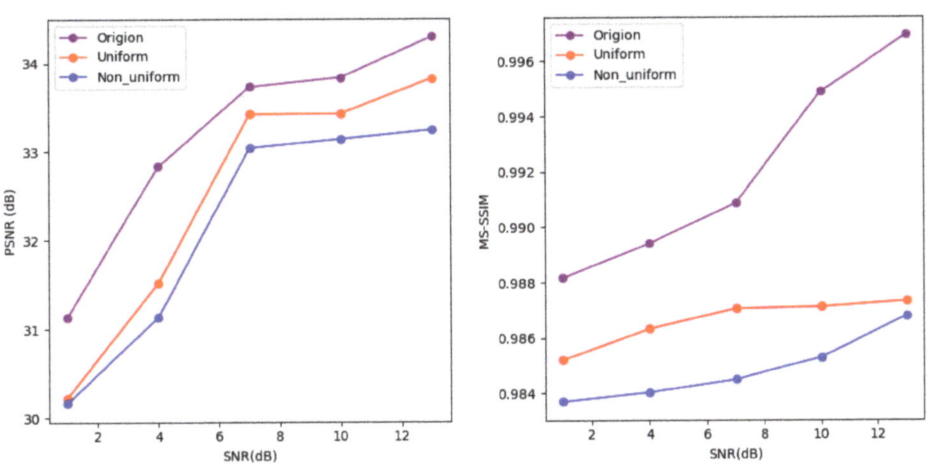

Figure 7. *Cont.*

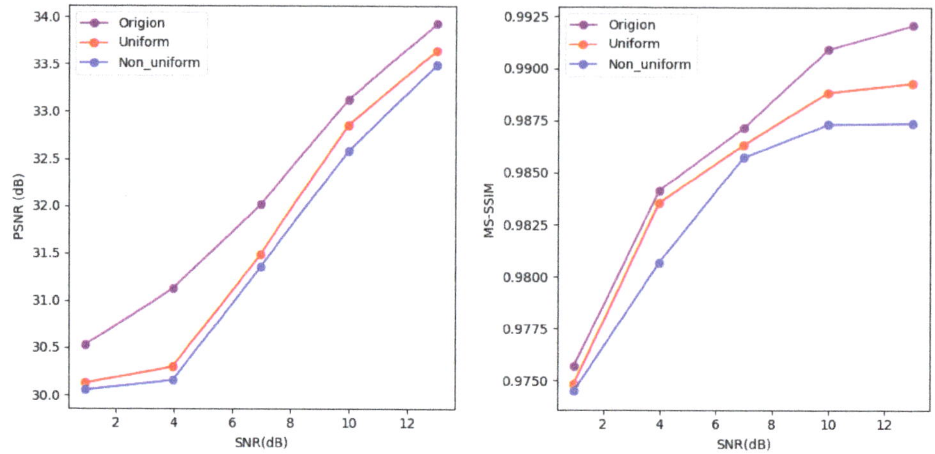

(c) (d)

Figure 7. (**a**) Describes the relationship between PSNR and SNR for the CIFAR100 dataset under the composite channel with 8-bit transmission. (**b**) Describes the relationship between MS-SSIM and SNR for the CIFAR100 dataset under the composite channel with 8-bit transmission. (**c**) Describes the relationship between PSNR and SNR for the Tiny ImageNet dataset under the composite channel with 8-bit transmission. (**d**) Describes the relationship between MS-SSIM and SNR for the Tiny ImageNet dataset under the composite channel with 8-bit transmission.

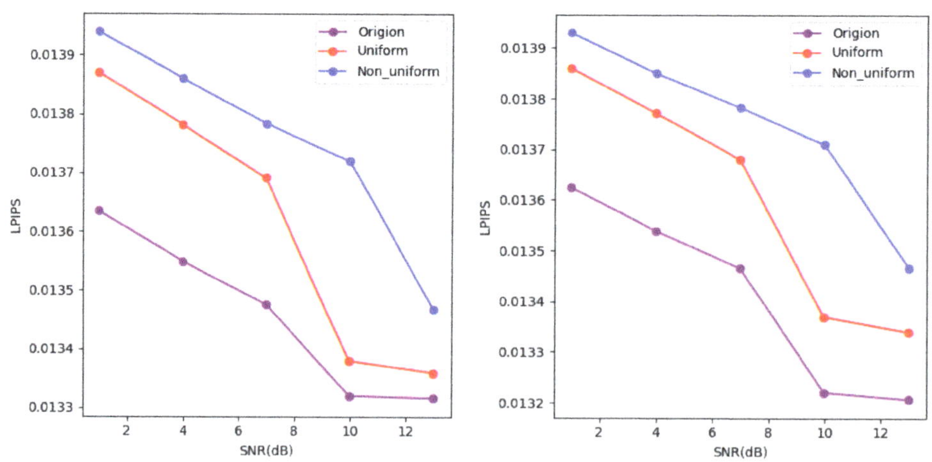

(a) (b)

Figure 8. (**a**) Describes the relationship between LPIPS for the CIFAR100 dataset under the composite channel with 8-bit transmission. (**b**) Describes the relationship between LPIPS for the Tiny ImageNet dataset under the composite channel with 8-bit transmission.

Table 1 shows the image reconstruction quality of the Tiny ImageNet dataset under AWGN, Rayleigh, and composite channels with 8-bit transmission.

Table 1. Performance across channels (SNR = 4 dB).

Channel	PSNR (dB)	LPIPS	MS-SSIM (dB)
AWGN	33.12	0.0135	0.982
Rayleigh	32.07	0.021	0.984
Composite	30.10	0.0133	0.981

The results indicate that while there is a decrease in performance in the composite channel compared to the AWGN and Rayleigh channels, the image quality remains within an acceptable range. Specifically, the PSNR value in the composite channel (30.10 dB) is lower than in both the AWGN (33.12 dB) and Rayleigh (32.07 dB) channels, reflecting a slight reduction in reconstruction quality. However, the LPIPS value for the composite channel (0.0133) is very close to that of the AWGN channel (0.0135), suggesting that the perceptual quality of the reconstructed image is still maintained at an acceptable level.

4.3. Computational Overhead Analysis

To assess the computational feasibility of our non-uniform quantization scheme, which incorporates feature classification and bit-allocation logic, we conducted a profiling analysis and compared it to uniform quantization. This evaluation was conducted on the Tiny ImageNet dataset using test images under an AWGN channel (SNR = 10 dB, 8-bit transmission), consistent with the experimental setup used in previous sections. We measured the training time per epoch (epoch = 128), inference time per image, and peak memory usage for both methods.

For training, we profiled the full pipeline, including feature extraction, gradient-based contribution factor computation, bit allocation, and quantization. For inference, we measured the end-to-end process from the input image to the reconstructed output. The results are presented in Table 2. Compared to uniform quantization, our non-uniform approach increases training time by 20% (from 30 minutes to 36 minutes per epoch). Inference time rose by 12% (from 0.175 seconds to 0.195 seconds per image). Peak memory usage increased by 7.6% (from 6.5 GB to 7.0 GB). Despite these increases, our approach remains practical for resource-limited systems, especially when considering the gains in bandwidth efficiency under fixed bit budgets.

Table 2. Computational overhead comparison (Tiny ImageNet, SNR = 10 dB).

Method	Training Time (min/epoch)	Inference Time (s/image)	Peak Memory (GB)
Uniform Quantization	30	0.175	6.5
Non-Uniform Quantization (Ours)	36	0.195	7.0

4.4. Ablation Studies on Feature Weighting

To evaluate the effectiveness of our gradient-based weighting approach for determining contribution factors, we conducted an ablation study, comparing it with two simpler heuristics, namely, the largest magnitude and the standard deviation of feature values. The experiment was performed on the Tiny ImageNet datasets, using both an AWGN ideal channel (SNR = 10 dB, 8-bit transmission) and the designed composite channel. Reconstruction quality was evaluated using PSNR and LPIPS. As shown in Table 3, our gradient-based method achieved a PSNR of 34.52 dB and an LPIPS of 0.028, outperforming the largest magnitude heuristic (PSNR = 30.25dB, LPIPS = 0.046) and the standard deviation heuristic (PSNR = 32.12 dB, LPIPS = 0.054). Similarly, under the composite channel, our method also outperformed the heuristics in both PSNR and LPIPS, as shown in Table 4. These results demonstrate that our gradient-based approach effectively captures contextual dependencies, leading to better accuracy and perceptual quality compared to the simpler heuristics in both channels.

Table 3. Ablation study results (SNR = 10 dB, Tiny ImageNet, AWGN channel).

Weighting Method	PSNR (dB)	LPIPS	MS-SSIM	Inference Time (s)
Gradient-based (Ours)	34.52	0.028	0.975	0.195
Largest magnitude	30.25	0.046	0.925	0.143
Standard deviation	32.12	0.054	0.930	0.162

Table 4. Ablation study results (SNR = 10 dB, Tiny ImageNet, composite channel).

Weighting Method	PSNR (dB)	LPIPS	MS-SSIM	Inference Time (s)
Gradient-based (Ours)	32.45	0.035	0.960	0.215
Largest magnitude	28.55	0.062	0.910	0.175
Standard deviation	30.47	0.070	0.920	0.190

5. Conclusions

In this paper, we propose a semantic communication system for image transmission, which utilizes a non-uniform quantization method and feature contribution factors to achieve efficient transmission under bandwidth constraints. The core of the system is a non-uniform quantization algorithm that dynamically allocates bit rates based on the contribution of each feature. This approach enhances both image transmission quality and compression performance. Additionally, we present an implementation of this non-uniform quantization system for image transmission, based on the Swin Transformer. To validate the feature importance measurement based on contribution factors, we conducted ablation experiments comparing our method with other approaches. Under limited bandwidth and varying signal-to-noise ratio (SNR) conditions, the experimental results demonstrate that our method outperforms both unquantized and uniform quantization approaches. The proposed quantization framework effectively balances image reconstruction quality and compression efficiency, providing reliable support for semantic communication systems.

6. Future Work

While our current framework focuses on single-user image transmission, the non-uniform quantization approach based on feature contribution factors offers promising extensions to broader scenarios. Below, we outline several directions for future research, which are based on potential extensions of our approach to multi-user systems, multimodal data, and dynamic network environments.

In multi-user scenarios, our method could be extended through a joint optimization strategy. By considering individual user requirements (such as image quality preferences) and network conditions (such as available bandwidth), we can dynamically allocate bits and bandwidth across users. This would ensure fair resource distribution while maintaining transmission efficiency, and could potentially incorporate game-theoretic or fairness-based optimization techniques.

For multimodal data, such as combined image and audio inputs, our approach can evolve by incorporating multimodal feature selection. By jointly assessing the contribution factors of features across modalities, we can optimize quantization bits to prioritize critical information (such as key visual details or audio cues). This would enable efficient cross-modal transmission, particularly suited for tasks like multimedia streaming or multimodal perception.

In dynamic network environments, real-time adaptive bit allocation could be optimized through the integration of reinforcement learning. This would enable the system to adjust quantization thresholds dynamically based on fluctuating channel conditions (e.g., signal-to-noise ratio under AWGN or Rayleigh fading), ensuring a balance between image quality and bandwidth usage. Such an approach would enhance robustness and adaptability in practical deployments.

Another important extension in future work will focus on dynamic bandwidth variations. We plan to explore how fluctuations in available bandwidth can affect the performance of our system. By incorporating real-time bandwidth adaptation, we can further optimize the system's ability to maintain image quality and transmission efficiency under conditions of varying available bandwidth, simulating more realistic scenarios encountered in mobile or dynamic environments.

These extensions will broaden the applicability of our feature-driven semantic communication framework, addressing diverse real-world challenges. Future work will further explore these directions through both theoretical modeling and experimental validation. In addition, beyond current datasets (CIFAR-10, CIFAR-100, Tiny ImageNet), we also plan to validate our method on larger, more complex datasets like ImageNet and COCO, which include high-resolution images and diverse scenes, to further test its scalability in real-world semantic communication scenarios.

Author Contributions: Conceptualization, methodology, formal analysis, and investigation: J.Z. and Y.Z.; writing—original draft preparation: A.C. and A.L.; writing—review and editing: J.Z., H.X. and B.J. All authors have read and agreed to the published version of the manuscript.

Funding: This work was supported in part by the Major Science and Technology Projects of Longmen Laboratory (grant no. 231100220400, 231100220300); the Key Scientific Research Project in Colleges and Universities of Henan Province of China (grant no. 21A510003); the Key Science and Technology Research Project of Henan Province of China (grant no. 222102210053); and the Open Found of the Engineering Research Center of Intelligent Swarm Systems, Ministry of Education (grant no. ZZU-CISS-2024003).

Institutional Review Board Statement: Not applicable

Data Availability Statement: Data are contained within the article.

Conflicts of Interest: The authors declare no conflicts of interest.

References

1. You, X.H. Shannon theory and future 6G's technique potentials. *Sci. Sin. Inf.* **2020**, *50*, 1377–1394. (In Chinese) [CrossRef]
2. Attaran, M. The impact of 5G on the evolution of intelligent automation and industry digitization. *J. Ambient Intell. Hum. Comput.* **2023**, *14*, 5977–5993. [CrossRef]
3. Zhang, Y.M.; Wang, F.Y.; Xu, W.J.; Liu, C.Y. Intelligence Semantic Communications: A New Paradigm for Networked. In Proceedings of the 2022 IEEE 32nd International Workshop on Machine Learning for Signal Processing (MLSP), Xi'an, China, 22–25 August 2022.
4. Weng, Z.; Qin, Z. Robust Semantic Communications for Speech Transmission. *arXiv* **2024**, arXiv:2403.05187.
5. Xie, H.; Qin, Z.; Li, G.Y. Task-Oriented Multi-User Semantic Communications for VQA. *IEEE Wirel. Commun. Lett.* **2022**, *11*, 553–557. [CrossRef]
6. Hu, Q.; Zhang, G.; Qin, Z.; Cai, Y.; Yu, G.; Li, G.Y. Robust Semantic Communications Against Semantic Noise. In Proceedings of the 2022 IEEE 96th Vehicular Technology Conference (VTC2022-Fall), London, UK, 26–29 September 2022.
7. Hu, Q.; Zhang, G.; Qin, Z.; Cai, Y.; Yu, G.; Li, G.Y. Robust Semantic Communications With Masked VQ-VAE Enabled Codebook. *IEEE Trans. Wirel. Commun.* **2023**, *22*, 8707–8722. [CrossRef]
8. Xu, W.; Zhang, Y.; Wang, F.; Qin, Z.; Liu, C.; Zhang, P. Semantic Communication for the Internet of Vehicles:A Multiuser Cooperative Approach. *IEEE Veh. Technol. Mag.* **2023**, *18*, 100–109. [CrossRef]
9. Tonchev, K.; Bozhilov, I.; Manolova, A. Semantic Communication System for 3D Video. In Proceedings of the 2023 Joint International Conference on Digital Arts, Media and Technology with ECTI Northern Section Conference on Electrical, Electronics, Computer and Telecommunications Engineering (ECTI DAMT and NCON), Phuket, Thailand, 22–25 March 2023.

10. Bourtsoulatze, E.; Burth Kurka, D.; Gündüz, D. Deep Joint Source-Channel Coding for Wireless Image Transmission. *IEEE Trans. Cogn. Commun. Netw.* **2019**, *5*, 567–579. [CrossRef]
11. Yang, K.; Wang, S.; Dai, J.; Tan, K.; Niu, K.; Zhang, P. WITT: A Wireless Image Transmission Transformer for Semantic Communications. In Proceedings of the ICASSP 2023—2023 IEEE International Conference on Acoustics, Speech and Signal Processing (ICASSP), Rhodes Island, Greece, 4–10 June 2023.
12. Lin, S.; Liu, F.; Guo, C.; Tong, W. Research on Semantic Coding Algorithm Based on Semantic Importance. *J. Beijing Univ. Posts Telecommun.* **2024**, *47*, 10–16.
13. Huang, D.; Tao, X.; Gao, F.; Lu, J. Deep Learning-Based Image Semantic Coding for Semantic Communications. In Proceedings of the 2021 IEEE Global Communications Conference (GLOBECOM), Madrid, Spain, 7–11 December 2021.
14. Wu, J.L.; Wu, C.; Lin, Y.F.; Yoshinaga, T.; Zhong, L.; Chen, X.F.; Ji, Y.S. Semantic segmentation-based semantic communication system for image transmission. *Digit. Commun. Netw.* **2024**, *10*, 519–527. [CrossRef]
15. Gupta, K.; Asthana, A. Reducing the Side-Effects of Oscillations in Training of Quantized YOLO Networks. In Proceedings of the IEEE/CVF Winter Conference on Applications of Computer Vision (WACV), Steamboat Springs, CO, USA, 24–26 March 2014; Volume 11, pp. 2440–2449.
16. Han, S.; Mao, H.; Dally, W.J. Deep compression: Compressing deep neural networks with pruning, trained quantization and huffman coding. *arXiv* **2016**, arXiv:1510.00149v5.
17. Lei, L.; Hong, X.; Shi, J.; Su, M.; Lin, C.; Xia, W. Quantization-Based Adaptive Deep Image Compression Using Semantic Information. *IEEE Access* **2023**, *11*, 118061–118077.
18. Tsumura, K.; Maciejowski, J. Optimal Quantization of Signals for System Identification. In Proceedings of the 2003 European Control Conference (ECC), Cambridge, UK, 1–4 September 2003.
19. Xia, X.; Sun, G.; Zhang, K.; Wu, S.; Wang, T.; Xia, L.; Liu, S. NanoSats/CubeSats ADCS Survey. In Proceedings of the 2017 29th Chinese Control And Decision Conference (CCDC), Chongqing, China, 28–30 May 2017.
20. Wallace, G.K. The JPEG still picture compression standard. *IEEE Trans. Consum. Electron.* **1992**, *38*, xviii–xxxiv.
21. Lin, J.; Tang, J.; Tang, H.; Yang, S.; Chen, W.-M.; Wang, W.-C.; Xiao, G.; Dang, X.; Gan, C.; Han, S. AWQ: Activation-aware Weight Quantization for LLM Compression and Acceleration. *arXiv* **2024**, arXiv:2306.00978.
22. Jacob, B.; Kligys, S.; Chen, B.; Zhu, M.; Tang, M.; Howard, A.; Adam, H.; Kalenichenko, D. Quantization and Training of Neural Networks for Efficient Integer-Arithmetic-Only Inference. In Proceedings of the 2018 IEEE/CVF Conference on Computer Vision and Pattern Recognition, Salt Lake City, UT, USA, 18–23 June 2018.
23. Liu, Z.; Wu, B.; Luo, W.; Yang, X.; Liu, W.; Cheng, K.-T. Bi-Real Net: Enhancing the Performance of 1-bit CNNs with Improved Representational Capability and Advanced Training Algorithm. *arXiv* **2018**, arXiv:1808.00278.
24. Srikotr, T.; Mano, K. Sub-band Vector Quantized Variational AutoEncoder for Spectral Envelope Quantization. In Proceedings of the TENCON 2019—2019 IEEE Region 10 Conference (TENCON), Kochi, India, 17–20 October 2019.
25. Sun, J.H. Mixed-precision quantization technology of convolutional neural networks. *Inf. Technol.* **2020**, *6*, 66–69.
26. Chen, Y.; Cai, X.; Liang, X.; Wang, M. Compression algorithm for weights quantized deep neural network models. *J. Xidian Univ.* **2019**, *46*, 132–138.
27. Dong, Z.; Yao, Z.; Gholami, A.; Mahoney, M.; Keutzer, K. HAWQ: Hessian AWare Quantization of Neural Networks With Mixed-Precision. In Proceedings of the 2019 IEEE/CVF International Conference on Computer Vision (ICCV), Seoul, Republic of Korea, 27 October–2 November 2019.
28. Zhang, C.; Zuo, G.; Zheng, Z.; Zhang, W.; Rao, Y.; Jiang, Z. Quantizing Separable Convolution of MobileNets with Mixed Precision. *J. Electron. Imaging* **2024**, *33*, 013013. [CrossRef]
29. Uhlich, S.; Mauch, L.; Kazuki, Y.; Fabien, C.; Javier, A.G.; Stephen, T.; Thomas, K.; Akita, N. Differentiable Quantization of Deep Neural Networks. *arXiv* **2019**, arXiv:1905.11452v1.
30. Wu, B.C.; Wang, Y.H.; Zhang, P.Z.; Tian, Y.D.; Vajda, P.; Kurt, K. Mixed Precision Quantization of ConvNets via Differentiable Neural Architecture Search. *arXiv* **2018**, arXiv:1812.00090.
31. Wang, T.Z.; Wang, K.; Cai, H.; Lin, J.; Liu, Z.J.; Han, S. APQ: Joint Search for Network Architecture, Pruning and Quantization Policy. *arXiv* **2020**, arXiv:2006.08509.
32. van Baalen, M.; Louizos, C.; Nagel, M.; Amjad, R.A.; Wang, Y.; Blankevoort, T.; Welling, M. Bayesian Bits: Unifying Quantization and Pruning. *arXiv* **2020**, arXiv:2005.07093.
33. Wang, K.; Liu, Z.J.; Lin, Y.J.; Han, S. HAQ: Hardware-Aware Automated Quantization. *arXiv* **2018**, arXiv:1811.08886.
34. Elthakeb, A.T.; Pilligundla, P.; Mireshghallah, F.; Yazdanbakhsh, A.; Esmaeilzadeh, H. ReLeQ: A Reinforcement Learning Approach for Deep Quantization. *arXiv* **2018**, arXiv:1811.01704.
35. Lou, Q.; Guo, F.; Liu, L.T.; Kim, M.J.; Lei, J. AutoQ: Automated Kernel-Wise Neural Network Quantization. *arXiv* **2019**, arXiv:1902.05960.
36. Weaver, W. Recent contributions to the mathematical theory of communication. In *ETC: A Review of General Semantics*; Institute of General Semantics: Fort Worth, TX, USA, 1953; pp. 261–281.

37. He, K.; Zhang, X.; Ren, S.; Sun, J. Deep Residual Learning for Image Recognition. In Proceedings of the 2016 IEEE Conference on Computer Vision and Pattern Recognition (CVPR), Las Vegas, NV, USA, 27–30 June 2016.
38. Yang, W.; Du, H.; Liew, Z.Q.; Lim, W.Y.B.; Xiong, Z.; Niyato, D.; Chi, X.; Shen, X.; Miao, C. Semantic Communications for Future Internet: Fundamentals, Applications, and Challenges. *IEEE Commun. Surv. Tutor.* **2023**, *25*, 213–250.
39. Rothstein, J. Review of "Science and Information Theory" by Leon Brillouin. *Science* **1956**, *124*, 492–493.
40. Sudan, M. Communication Amid Uncertainty. In Proceedings of the 2012 IEEE Information Theory Workshop, Lausanne, Switzerland, 3–7 September 2012.
41. O'Shea, T.J.; Karra, K.; Clancy, T.C. Learning to Communicate:Channel Auto-Encoders, Domain Specific Regularizers, and Attention. In Proceedings of the 2016 IEEE International Symposium on Signal Processing and Information Technology (ISSPIT), Limassol, Cyprus, 12–14 December 2016.
42. Shi, G.; Xiao, Y.; Li, Y.; Xie, X. From Semantic Communication to Semantic-Aware Networking: Model, Architecture, and Open Problems. *IEEE Commun. Mag.* **2021**, *59*, 44–50.
43. Feng, Y.; Xu, J.; Liang, C.; Yu, G.; Hu, L.; Yuan, T. Decoupling Source and Semantic Encoding: An Implementation Study. *Electronics* **2023**, *12*, 2755. [CrossRef]
44. Xie, H.; Qin, Z. A Lite Distributed Semantic Communication System for Internet of Things. *IEEE J. Sel. Areas Commun.* **2021**, *39*, 142–153.
45. Xu, X.; Xiong, H.; Wang, Y.; Che, Y.; Han, S.; Wang, B.; Zhang, P. Knowledge-Enhanced Semantic Communication System with OFDM Transmissions. *Sci. China Inf. Sci.* **2023**, *66*, 172302.
46. Zhang, W.; Zhang, H.; Ma, H.; Shao, H.; Wang, N.; Leung, V.C.M. Predictive and Adaptive Deep Coding for Wireless Image Transmission in Semantic Communication. *IEEE Trans. Wirel. Commun.* **2023**, *22*, 5486–5501.
47. Qi, Z.; Feng, Y.; Qin, Z. Adaptive Sampling and Joint Semantic-Channel Coding under Dynamic Channel Environment. *arXiv* **2025**, arXiv:2502.072362025.
48. Zhou, K.Q.; Zhang, G.Y.; Cai, Y.L.; Hu, Q.Y.; Yu, G.D. FAST Feature Arrangement for SemanticTransmission. *arXiv* **2019**, arXiv:2305.03274.
49. Gao, S.; Qin, X.Q.; Chen, L.; Han, K.F.; Zhang, P. Importance of Semantic Information Based on Semantic Value. *IEEE Trans. Commun.* **2024**, *72*, 5443–5457.
50. Ma, Y.; Xu, C.M.; Liu, Z.Y.; Zhang, S.Q.; Tafazolli, R. Importance-Aware Source-Channel Coding for Multi-ModalTask-Oriented Semantic Communication. *arXiv* **2025**, arXiv:2502.16194.

entropy

MDPI

Article

Rate–Distortion–Perception Trade-Off in Information Theory, Generative Models, and Intelligent Communications

Xueyan Niu *, Bo Bai, Nian Guo, Weixi Zhang and Wei Han

Theory Lab, 2012 Labs, Huawei Technologies Co., Ltd., No. 3 Xinxi Rd., Beijing 100085, China; baibo8@huawei.com (B.B.); guonian4@huawei.com (N.G.); zhangweixi1@huawei.com (W.Z.); harvey.hanwei@huawei.com (W.H.)

* Correspondence: niuxueyan3@huawei.com

Abstract: Traditional rate–distortion (RD) theory examines the trade-off between the average length of the compressed representation of a source and the additive distortions of its reconstruction. The rate–distortion–perception (RDP) framework, which integrates the perceptual dimension into the RD paradigm, has garnered significant attention due to recent advancements in machine learning, where perceptual fidelity is assessed by the divergence between input and reconstruction distributions. In communication systems where downstream tasks involve generative modeling, high perceptual fidelity is essential, despite distortion constraints. However, while zero distortion implies perfect realism, the converse is not true, highlighting an imbalance in the significance of distortion and perceptual constraints. This article clarifies that incorporating perceptual constraints does not decrease the necessary rate; instead, under certain conditions, additional rate is required, even with the aid of common and private randomness, which are key elements in generative models. Consequently, we project an increase in expected traffic in intelligent communication networks with the consideration of perceptual quality. Nevertheless, a modest increase in rate can enable generative models to significantly enhance the perceptual quality of reconstructions. By exploring the synergies between generative modeling and communication through the lens of information-theoretic results, this article demonstrates the benefits of intelligent communication systems and advocates for the application of the RDP framework in advancing compression and semantic communication research.

Keywords: rate–distortion–perception trade-off; perceptual fidelity; lossy compression; AI-empowered communication

1. Introduction

For decades, rate–distortion (RD) theory has served as the de facto standard for evaluating real-world applications involving compression and communication. With the advances in artificial intelligence technologies, the dimension of perceptual fidelity has been increasingly recognized as a crucial aspect. While traditional distortion measures like mean squared error (MSE) have served well in many applications, they fail to capture the perceptual quality that humans actually experience [1–3]. This disconnect has motivated the integration of perceptual measures into RD, leading to the emergence of the rate–distortion–perception (RDP) framework [4]. The information RDP function incorporates an additional perceptual constraint measured by the divergence between the input and reconstruction distributions within the context of lossy compression using machine learning. Unlike conventional distortion measures, perceptual fidelity captures the global properties of the entire coding block rather than focusing on individual sample positions, giving rise to new coding theorems. Consequently, RD plots, which have long been used to evaluate practical source coding algorithms, should be updated to incorporate this new dimension in alignment with the emerging coding theorems (see Figure 1b,c for a comparison of the RDP frontier with the RD curves). This development has also inspired a variety of innovative source coding methods that rely on generative models [5–11]. As emerging techniques are increasingly applied to lossy source coding and communication systems in general, the RDP trade-off offers a novel perspective for evaluating the performance of machine-learning-aided systems. Recent advances in AI-empowered communication have reimagined communication systems as a joint optimization of transmitter and receiver through end-to-end training for reconstruction tasks [12,13]. Therefore, in communication systems where downstream tasks demand high perceptual fidelity, such as interactive AI agents and the reconstruction of visually pleasing content, the RDP framework is particularly useful. This paper explores the critical role of perceptual constraints in information theory and their impact on practical generative modeling scenarios, which drives the development of a wide range of compression and communication algorithms that integrate various generative model architectures with end-to-end training objectives. We demonstrate how incorporating perceptual constraints into the traditional RD framework offers a comprehensive perspective for evaluating the performance of AI-empowered systems in communication and potentially increases network traffic.

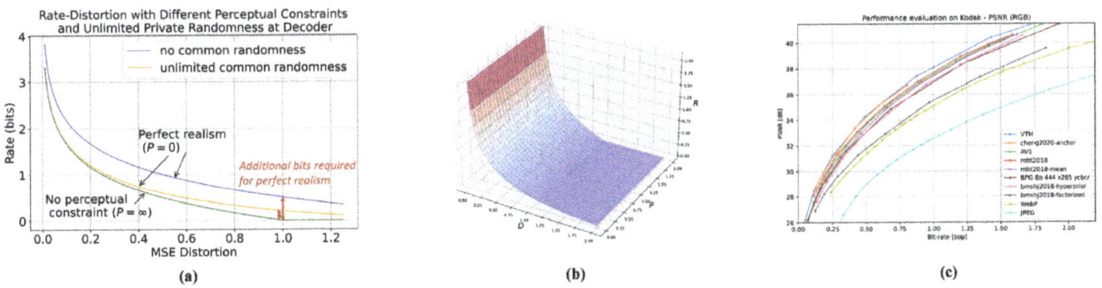

Figure 1. Rate–distortion–perception trade-off. (**a**) Rate–distortion curves with and without the realism constraint for a Gaussian source. The perceptual constraint slightly increases the bitrate required in theory, suggesting an increase in traffic in communication networks. (**b**) Information rate–distortion–perception frontier for a Gaussian source with MSE distortion and 2-Wasserstein perceptual constraint. (**c**) Rate–distortion performance evaluation of various practical image compression algorithms using the PSNR distortion metric. The evaluation is conducted with the CompressAI package [14], covering a range of methods from the standard JPEG to SoTA learning-based compression techniques such as [15].

The capacity to perceive, communicate, and learn from the environment, as well as to construct mental models that internally simulate potential outcomes, is fundamental to both human and artificial intelligence. In early neuroscience research, perception was conceptualized as a form of hypothesis testing [16], a notion that naturally aligns with the divergence measure for perceptual quality in information theory. More recently, the theory of predictive coding has posited that generative models of the world are derived from sensory input, perception being understood as the minimization of prediction errors [17,18]. Developing models capable of mimicking human-like perception and reasoning, including visual aesthetics and consistency; language perplexity and fluency, among others, is essential for the creation of useful generative models. Contemporary large language models (LLMs) and multi-modal models have demonstrated remarkable capabilities, such as memorization [19], generation of images and videos based on descriptive prompts [20], retrieval and reasoning [21]. During the training of these generative models, the loss function typically combines both distortion-oriented MSE and perception-oriented cross-entropy losses, weighted to balance distortion and perception constraints (see Equation (21)). For downstream tasks such as image synthesis, a key challenge is to balance the faithfulness to user inputs and the realism of the generated outputs [22]. Within the RDP framework, the perceptual quality of reconstruction is assessed by the similarity between the distributions of the input and the reconstruction, with the encoder and decoder potentially aided by generative models. This alignment naturally supports the objectives of generative modeling. Thus, in contemporary intelligent compression and communication systems, the quality of reconstruction should be evaluated based on both the perceptions of end users, whether human or machine, and the average distortions.

The perception axis plays a pivotal role in both source coding and communication systems in general. In information theory, the source coding problem aims to minimize the amount of information needed to transmit a message by eliminating redundancy, thereby achieving effective compression. To assess the performance, a certain level of reconstruction error is permissible. For instance, when compressing and subsequently recovering a bit string using a decoder, the Hamming distance can be used to quantify the number of errors, thereby providing a measure of distortion. Conventional RD theory, originally developed by Claude Shannon, has effectively characterized the minimal rate required to satisfy distortion constraints. For stationary sources, it is well established that deterministic encoders and decoders can achieve asymptotically optimal RD performance [23]. However, the introduction of perceptual constraints suggests that deterministic coding may no longer be optimal [24]. Randomization has been demonstrated to be essential for achieving realism constraints through stochastic coding [25–27]. The requirement for the output to conform to a specified distribution is known as the realism constraint [28–31]. The zero-distortion constraint corresponds to the well-known zero-error source coding problem [23], which also implies perfect realism. However, perfect realism, which requires the distributions of the source and reconstruction to be identical, does not necessarily imply zero distortion. Nevertheless, perceptual constraints restrict the reconstruction process, thereby increasing the required rate. For example, consider a pangram—a sentence using each letter of the English alphabet with balanced letter counts. If a decoder is required to reconstruct a sentence while adhering to a specific letter distribution, this scenario exemplifies the perfect realism condition. A "perfect pangram" is extremely rare due to the overuse of common letters and the scarcity of rare ones; for instance, the classic pangram "The quick brown fox jumps over a lazy dog" contains repeated Es and Os. This suggests that perceptual constraints are closely related to semantics and can be highly restrictive, thereby carrying significant amounts of information.

In practical communication systems, the idealized assumptions underlying the separation theorem, upon which modern communication systems are founded, are rarely met. The separation theorem posits that separate source and channel coding (SSCC) is theoretically optimal in terms of distortion, with source coding eliminating data redundancy and channel coding ensuring reliable transmission in noisy and interference-prone environments. Moreover, under certain conditions, incorporating perceptual constraints renders separation suboptimal in the absence of common randomness between the encoder and decoder [32]. Recent research has increasingly focused on AI-empowered communication systems, where communication nodes are enhanced through machine learning techniques, such as generative modeling, to improve the comprehension and generation of high-fidelity content for downstream tasks, including image and video transmission, augmented and virtual reality (AR/VR), the Internet of Things (IoT), and vehicular-to-everything (V2X) applications. These systems are trained end-to-end for downstream tasks using generative objectives that inherently incorporate perceptual measures. Inspired by these information-theoretic results, which suggest that common and private randomness at the encoder and decoder provide advantages in terms of the RDP trade-off, AI-empowered generative models can be deployed at the transmitter and receiver nodes, with these randomness sources serving as shared or private random seeds.

As the main purpose of this paper, we are devoted to highlighting efforts in the field of information theory aimed at elucidating the fundamental limits of source coding and communication with perceptual-oriented metrics. Inspired by these findings, we demonstrate the utility of common and private randomness in generative modeling architectures, such as variational auto-encoders (VAEs), generative adversarial networks (GANs), diffusion models, and transformers, through the lens of the RDP trade-off. These generative modeling architectures can be designed and deployed at communication nodes to support downstream tasks requiring high perceptual fidelity. We provide a comprehensive overview of common perceptual measures in Section 2. Subsequently, Section 3 discusses the information-theoretic results and their implications with respect to the additional rate required to meet the new perceptual constraint. Section 4 introduces several generative modeling architectures, including VAEs, GANs, diffusion models, and transformers, used in communication systems, emphasizing the importance of high perceptual fidelity in downstream machine learning tasks. Section 5 characterizes the role of generative models in AI-empowered semantic communication systems. Finally, Section 6 explores future directions in information theory and communication. Through the lens of the RDP trade-off, we demonstrate that the introduced perceptual constraint leads to an increase in expected traffic within communication networks. The key takeaways include the following:

- Perceptual constraints fundamentally alter the rate–distortion trade-off, requiring additional rate even with unlimited common randomness.
- Generative models naturally align with RDP objectives, making them powerful tools for developing perceptually optimized communication systems.
- The practical implementation of RDP-aware systems faces challenges related to computational complexity and the need for robustness across diverse channel conditions.

Notations

We use capital letters such as X to denote random variables, lowercase letters such as x to denote their corresponding instances, and calligraphic letters such as $\mathcal{X}$ to denote sets of alphabets. Let $\text{Prob}(\mathcal{X})$ denote the set of probability measures defined on $\mathcal{X}$, and let $P_X(x), P_{XY}(x,y)$, and $P_{Y|X}(y|x)$ denote the probability distribution of X, the joint distribution, and the conditional distribution of Y given $X = x$, respectively. We omit the arguments of the distributions when doing so does not cause ambiguity. The n-sequence $(X_1, X_2, \ldots, X_n)$ is denoted by X^n. Suppose that $\{X_i\}_{i=1}^{\infty}$ and $\{Y_i\}_{i=1}^{\infty}$ are memoryless sources; then, $P_{X^nY^n} = \prod_{i=1}^{n} P_{XY} = \otimes_{i=1}^{n} P_{X_iY_i}$. We use $[m]$ to denote the set $\{1, 2, \ldots, \lfloor m \rfloor\}$ for $m > 0$, and we use $\mathcal{C}$ to denote the codebook. For sequences $(x^n, y^n) \in \mathcal{X}^n \times \mathcal{Y}^n$, the empirical distribution is defined as

$$\hat{P}_{x^n,y^n}(x,y) = \frac{1}{n}\sum_{i=1}^{n} \mathbf{1}\{(x_i, y_i) = (x,y)\}. \tag{1}$$

Extensions to multiple arguments can be defined similarly. Throughout the paper, we use $\Delta(\cdot,\cdot) : \mathcal{X}^n \times \mathcal{X}^n \mapsto \mathbb{R}$ to denote an additive distortion measure, and we use the calligraphic letter $\mathcal{D}(\cdot,\cdot) : \text{Prob}(\mathcal{X}^n) \times \text{Prob}(\mathcal{X}^n) \mapsto \mathbb{R}$ to denote the measure of perceptual fidelity. We define $\overline{\mathbb{R}}_{\geq 0} := \mathbb{R}_{\geq 0} \cup \{+\infty\}$.

2. Distortion and Perceptual Measures

We set out to explore the interplay between conventional distortion measures and the recently introduced perceptual measures. Details regarding the emerging class of perceptual measures, including the total variation (TV) distance, the Kullback–Leibler (KL) divergence, and the Wasserstein distance, are provided. Additionally, we present a set of assumptions and a series of distance–divergence inequalities. These elements highlight the fundamental differences and connections between distortion and perceptual measures, thereby motivating the information-theoretic results. We demonstrate that neither the distortion measure nor any of the perceptual measures, including the TV distance, KL divergence, and Wasserstein distance, dominate each other. Instead, they synergistically contribute to the RDP trade-off.

2.1. Distortion Measures

In the conventional additive distortion setting, the distortion measure is defined as the average of a per-letter distance.

Definition 1. *Given a per-letter distortion measure $\delta : \mathcal{X} \times \mathcal{X} \mapsto [0, d_{\max}]$ with $d_{\max} < \infty$, the (average) distortion between two sequences x^n and y^n is defined as*

$$\Delta(x^n, y^n) := \frac{1}{n} \sum_{i=1}^{n} \delta(x_i, y_i).$$

Here, we assume that the distortion is upper-bounded by $d_{\max}$.

This bounded distortion enables the derivation of a bound relating the distortion measure to the perceptual measure, as shown in Equation (11), which will be introduced below.

2.2. Perceptual Measures in Information Theory

To quantify the proximity between the reconstruction distribution and another probability distribution, several perceptual measures are widely studied in information theory. These include the total variation (TV) distance, the Kullback–Leibler (KL) divergence, and the Wasserstein distance.

2.2.1. Total Variation Distance

The TV distance defined in the following is widely used in information theory. Given two distributions P_X and P_Y defined on the same σ-algebra $(\mathcal{X}, \mathcal{F})$, the TV distance is defined as

$$\mathcal{D}_{\text{TV}}(P_X, P_Y) = \sup_{S \subseteq \mathcal{X}} |P_X(S) - P_Y(S)|.$$

The TV distance is equivalent to the L_1 norm when the alphabets are finite, making it a natural choice in the Lebesgue space, i.e., when P_X and P_Y are probability mass functions,

$$\mathcal{D}_{\text{TV}}(P_X, P_Y) = \frac{1}{2}\|P_X - P_Y\|_1 = \frac{1}{2} \sum_{x \in \mathcal{X}} |P_X(x) - P_Y(x)|. \quad (2)$$

From Equation (2) and the triangle inequality for real numbers, we have the triangle inequality

$$\mathcal{D}_{\text{TV}}(P_X, P_Y) \leq \mathcal{D}_{\text{TV}}(P_X, P_Z) + \mathcal{D}_{\text{TV}}(P_Z, P_Y).$$

This implies that the TV distance does not tensorize. In fact, we have the following folklore knowledge:

$$\mathcal{D}_{\text{TV}}(P_{X_1X_2}, P_{Y_1Y_2}) \leq \mathcal{D}_{\text{TV}}(P_{X_1}, P_{Y_1}) + \mathcal{D}_{\text{TV}}(P_{X_2}, P_{Y_2}) - \mathcal{D}_{\text{TV}}(P_{X_1}, P_{Y_1}) \cdot \mathcal{D}_{\text{TV}}(P_{X_2}, P_{Y_2}). \quad (3)$$

2.2.2. KL Divergence

Another widely used divergence measure in information theory is the KL divergence. Given two distributions P_X and P_Y defined on the same σ-algebra $(\mathcal{X}, \mathcal{F})$, when $\mathcal{X}$ is finite,

$$\mathcal{D}_{\mathrm{KL}}(P_X \| P_Y) = \sum_{x \in \mathcal{X}} P_X(x) \log \frac{P_X(x)}{P_Y(x)}.$$

When P_X and P_Y are probability density functions, the KL divergence is defined as

$$\mathcal{D}_{\mathrm{KL}}(P_X \| P_Y) = \int_{x \in \mathcal{X}} P_X(x) \log \frac{P_X(x)}{P_Y(x)} \, \mathrm{d}x,$$

and, by convention, $\mathcal{D}_{\mathrm{KL}}(P_X \| P_Y) = \infty$ when P_X is not absolutely continuous with regard to P_Y. The KL divergence is not a distance metric because it is asymmetric between the two arguments and does not satisfy the triangle inequality.

2.2.3. Wasserstein Distance

The Wasserstein distance, rooted in the theory of optimal transport, is a powerful tool with broad applications in deep learning as a perceptual measure [33]. It has also garnered significant attention in information theory, particularly following the pioneering work of Marton on distance–divergence inequalities [34,35].

Definition 2. *Given $p \geq 1$ and a Polish space $(\mathcal{X}, c)$, the L_p-Wasserstein distance is defined as*

$$W_p(P_X, P_Y) = \inf \left(\mathbb{E}[c^p(X, Y)]\right)^{\frac{1}{p}},$$

where the infimum is over all jointly distributed random variables $(X, Y) \in \mathrm{Prob}(\mathcal{X} \times \mathcal{X})$.

For each $p \geq 1$, $W_p(,)$ defines a metric on $\mathrm{Prob}(\mathcal{X})$. In practice, W_1 and W_2 are most widely used.

2.2.4. Common Assumptions

In the more general case, several assumptions are made regarding perceptual measures across different settings, which we briefly discuss here.

Assumption 1 (Non-negativity). *For arbitrary distributions P_X and P_Y defined on the σ-algebra $(\mathcal{X}, \mathcal{F})$, the perceptual measure satisfies*

$$\mathcal{D}(P_X, P_Y) \geq 0 \text{ and } \mathcal{D}(P_X, P_Y) = 0 \text{ if and only if } P_X \stackrel{d}{=} P_Y.$$

Assumption 2 (Convexity in the second argument). *For $\lambda_1, \lambda_2, \ldots, \lambda_n \in \mathbb{R}_{\geq 0}$ such that $\sum_i \lambda_i = 1$,*

$$\mathcal{D}(P, \sum_{i=1}^{n} \lambda_i Q_i) \leq \sum_{i=1}^{n} \lambda_i \mathcal{D}_{\mathrm{TV}}(P, Q_i). \tag{4}$$

This convexity is a property satisfied by the f-divergence family, including the TV distance and the KL divergence, as well as the 1-Wasserstein distance.

Some members of the f-divergence family, such as the Hellinger distance and the χ^2-divergence, exhibit tensorization. This means that, for product distributions, these divergences can be easily expressed in terms of the marginal distributions. Tensorization, or additivity under products, is crucial for establishing converse proofs.

Assumption 3 (Tensorization).

$$\mathcal{D}(\otimes_{i=1}^{n} P_{X_i}, P_{Y^n}) \geq \sum_{i=1}^{n} \mathcal{D}(P_{X_i}, P_{Y_i}). \tag{5}$$

Notably, the KL divergence and W_2 distance are tensorizable, in the sense that

$$\mathcal{D}_{\mathrm{KL}}(\otimes_{i=1}^{n} P_{X^i} \| \otimes_{i=1}^{n} P_{Y^n}) = \sum_{i=1}^{n} \mathcal{D}_{\mathrm{KL}}(P_{X_i} \| P_{Y_i}), \tag{6}$$

$$W_2(\otimes_{i=1}^{n} P_{X^i} \| \otimes_{i=1}^{n} P_{Y^n}) = \sum_{i=1}^{n} W_2(P_{X_i} \| P_{Y_i}). \tag{7}$$

The TV distance, however, is not tensorizable.

We may also consider a sequence of perceptual measures to analyze performance over coding blocks. The sub-decomposable assumption introduced in [32] ensures that coding over longer sequences is advantageous.

Assumption 4 (Sub-decomposability). *A sequence of perception measures* $\mathcal{D}_n(\cdot,\cdot) : \mathrm{Prob}(\mathcal{X}^n) \times \mathrm{Prob}(\mathcal{X}^n) \mapsto \mathbb{R}$ *is called sub-decomposable if*

$$\mathcal{D}_n(\otimes_{i=1}^{k} P_{X_{l_{i-1}+1}^{l_i}}, \otimes_{i=1}^{k} P_{X_{l_{i-1}+1}^{l_i}}) \leq \sum_{i=1}^{k} \mathcal{D}_{n_i}(P_{X_{l_{i-1}+1}^{l_i}}, P_{Y_{l_{i-1}+1}^{l_i}}) \tag{8}$$

for any positive integers $n_1, n_2, \ldots, n_k$ *such that* $\sum_{i=1}^{k} n_i = n$, *where* $l_i := \sum_{j=1}^{i} n_i$ *with* $l_0 := 0$.

By definition, any tensorizable measure, such as the KL divergence, is also sub-decomposable. The non-tensorizable TV distance is sub-decomposable as well, as shown in Equation (3).

2.3. Interplay Between Distortion and Perception Constraints

Distortion and perception measures, though distinct, are closely intertwined through a series of distance–divergence inequalities. For instance, in the product space $\mathcal{X}^n$, the transportation–cost inequalities pioneered by Marton [34] can be employed to derive concentration results.

A notable bound relates the expected values of bounded functions to the TV distance:

$$|\mathbb{E}_{P_X}[f(X)] - \mathbb{E}_{P_Y}[f(X)]| \leq \sup_x |f(x)| \, \mathcal{D}_{\mathrm{TV}}(P_X, P_Y), \tag{9}$$

which facilitates the analysis of expected values using the TV distance. This relationship is particularly useful in machine learning scenarios where the objective is to minimize loss functions that depend on expected values. In such cases, the optimization problem can be reformulated as minimizing the TV distance. Specifically, given that the distortion is bounded by $d_{\max}$, and assuming that $P_{X^nY^n}$ and $Q_{X^nY^n}$ are i.i.d. distributions, we have the following:

$$|\mathbb{E}_P[D(X^n, Y^n)] - \mathbb{E}_Q[D(X^n, Y^n)]]| \leq d_{\max} \mathcal{D}_{\mathrm{TV}}(P, Q). \tag{10}$$

Similarly, the bounded distortion measure exhibits a property elucidated in Lemma 5 of [36] with respect to the TV distance: if P_{XY}, Q_{XY} are probability mass functions with $\mathbb{E}_{P_{XY}}[\delta(X,Y)] = A$ and $\mathcal{D}_{\mathrm{TV}}(P_{XY}, Q_{XY}) < \epsilon$, then

$$\mathbb{E}_{Q_{XY}}[\delta(X,Y)] \leq A + \epsilon d_{\max}. \tag{11}$$

Perceptual measures can also be related through a set of distance–divergence inequalities. A fundamental relationship between the KL divergence and the TV distance, originally due to Pinsker [37], states the following:

$$\mathcal{D}_{\text{TV}}(P_X, P_Y) \leq \sqrt{\frac{1}{2}\mathcal{D}_{\text{KL}}(P_X, P_Y)}. \tag{12}$$

For a finite alphabet, the reverse Pinsker inequality is available (see Lemma 6.3 in [38]):

$$\mathcal{D}_{\text{KL}}(P_X, P_Y) \leq \frac{\mathcal{D}^2_{\text{TV}}(P_X, P_Y)}{\min_{y\in\mathcal{X}} P_Y(y)}. \tag{13}$$

Moreover, for i.i.d. distributions P_{Y^n} and $P_{X^n} \ll P_{Y^n}$, we have (see Equation (30) in [39])

$$\mathcal{D}_{\text{KL}}(P_{X^n}, P_{Y^n}) = O((n - \log(\mathcal{D}_{\text{TV}}(P_{X^n}, P_{Y^n})))\mathcal{D}_{\text{TV}}(P_{X^n}, P_{Y^n})). \tag{14}$$

Assuming that the diameter of $\mathcal{X}$ is bounded by B, we also have (see Theorem 6.15 in [40]) the following:

$$W_1(P_X, P_Y) \leq B \cdot \mathcal{D}_{\text{TV}}(P_X, P_Y). \tag{15}$$

For coding blocks on $\text{Prob}(\mathcal{X}^n)$, Wasserstein distances in product spaces can be naturally related to the distortion measure:

$$\Delta_{\beta,n}(P_{X^n}, P_{Y^n}) := \inf_{\pi\in\Pi(P_{X^n}, P_{Y^n})} (\mathbb{E}_{\pi}[\sum_{i=1}^{n} \delta^p(X_i, Y_i)])^{\frac{1}{p}},$$

and, according to [35], under certain conditions,

$$W_{1,n}(P_{X^n}, P_{Y^n}) \leq \text{Const.}\sqrt{\frac{1}{2}\mathcal{D}_{\text{KL}}(P_{X^n}, P_{Y^n})}. \tag{16}$$

These relationships connect common perceptual measures to the TV distance, which is frequently considered in information-theoretic settings. The perceptual measures discussed—TV distance, KL divergence, and Wasserstein distance—each offer unique advantages depending on the application context. TV distance provides a straightforward measure of distributional similarity, KL divergence captures directional divergence between distributions, and Wasserstein distance offers a geometrically intuitive measure of the transport cost between probability distributions.

3. Information-Theoretic Results

Having established the theoretical foundations of perceptual measures, we now turn to their implications in information theory. Understanding how these measures interact with rate and distortion constraints requires a rigorous information-theoretic analysis of the RDP trade-off. This section summarizes recent information-theoretic results for the RDP problem. Typically, a set of distortion constraints **(D)** and a set of perceptual constraints **(P)** are enforced to ensure that the distortion and perceptual fidelities are bounded by given constants D and P, respectively.

As in classical information theory, we consider a memoryless source $\{X_i\}_{i=1}^{\infty}$ drawn from finite alphabets $\mathcal{X}$. For continuous sources, Assumption 2 in [26] can be invoked to ensure that distortion and perceptual measures are not overly sensitive to discretizations.

3.1. Realism Constraints

We summarize a spectrum of perceptual constraints **(P)** in Table 1.

Table 1. Taxonomy of realism constraints **(P)**.

Realism Constraint	Definition	References
Weak realism	$\mathcal{D}(\hat{P}_{X^n}, \hat{P}_{Y^n}) \leq P$	[41–43]
Per-symbol realism	$\mathcal{D}(P_X, P_{Y_t}) \leq P,\ \forall t \in [n]$	[26]
Average marginal realism	$\sup_n \frac{1}{n}\sum_{t=1}^{n} \mathcal{D}(P_X, P_{Y_t}) \leq P$	[9]
Strong realism	$\mathcal{D}(P_{X^n}, P_{Y^n}) \leq P$	[43–45]
Perfect strong realism	$Y^n \sim P_{X^n}$	[25,31,39]
Near-perfect per-symbol realism	$\lim_{n\to\infty} \max_{1\leq t\leq n} \mathcal{D}(P_X, P_{Y_t}) = 0$	[26,27]
Near-perfect strong realism	$\lim_{n\to\infty} \mathcal{D}(P_{X^n}, P_{Y^n}) = 0$	[25,27]

3.1.1. Weak and Strong Realism Constraints

The notion of weak realism is inspired by machine learning practices, such as GAN-based image reconstruction schemes [4]. In information theory, weak realism has been studied within the framework of empirical coordination [41,42] using the empirical distribution (type). In contrast, strong realism compares joint distributions over blocks of symbols, thereby imposing stricter constraints. Matsumoto [44,45] investigated the RDP trade-off for general information sources using fixed-length and variable-length coding, suggesting the need for channel resolvability codes. Single-letter expressions can be derived under the assumption of i.i.d. output [31,43].

3.1.2. Perfect and Imperfect Realism Constraints

The concept of perfect realism [25,29] is analogous to the lossless scenario in rate–distortion problems, requiring that the output distribution closely matches the source distribution in terms of a perceptual measure. This aligns closely with lossy coding under distribution constraints [31], where the output sequence must adhere to a specified i.i.d. distribution while also satisfying distortion constraints. The near-perfect realism constraint requires that the reconstruction distribution be asymptotically arbitrarily close to the source distribution. Wagner [25] demonstrated that achievability with perfect realism is equivalent to achievability with near-perfect realism when the distortion–perception pair is uniformly integrable. Specifically, deterministic coding is sufficient when $D > 0$ and $P > 0$ [26].

3.2. *Information-Theoretic System Model*

As an example, we consider the general system model introduced in [27], which incorporates both common randomness and private randomness (see Figure 2). The encoder and the decoder have access to a shared source of randomness J uniformly distributed over $[2^{nR_c}]$. The encoder and decoder also have private randomness sources $L_e \sim P_{L_e}$ and L_d uniformly distributed over $[2^{nR_d}]$, respectively. The encoder observes the source X^n, J, L_e and selects a message $M \in [2^{nR}]$. The decoder observes the message, has access to J and L_d, and attempts to reconstruct the input as Y^n. Hamdi et al. [27] showed that the private randomness of the encoder is not useful under the constraint of near-perfect realism. Other variants of the system model include models with (common) side information [43,46].

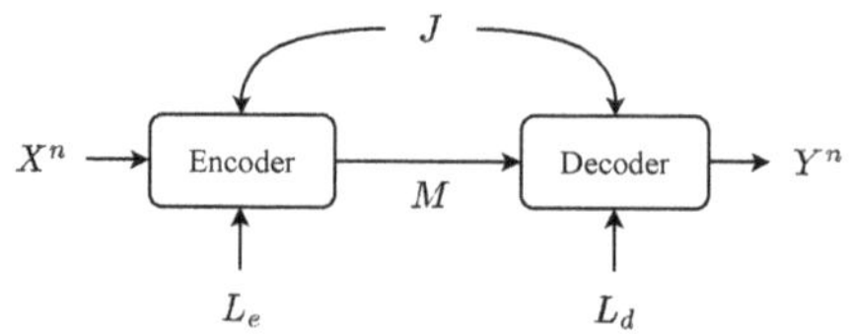

Figure 2. A general system model including common randomness J, encoder private randomness L_e, and decoder randomness L_d as in [27].

Definition 3. *An $(n, 2^{nR}, 2^{nR_c}, 2^{nR_d})$ fixed-length code consists of an encoding function*

$$f_n : \mathcal{X}^n \times [2^{nR_c}] \times \mathcal{L}_d \mapsto [2^{nR}] \qquad \text{(possibly stochastic)}$$

and a decoding function

$$g_n : [2^{nR}] \times [2^{nR_c}] \times [2^{nR_d}] \mapsto \mathcal{X}^n \qquad \text{(possibly stochastic)}.$$

The system presented here is designed for fixed-length codes. For variable-length codes, the uniform distributions of J and L_d are replaced with the following constraints:

$$R \geq \frac{1}{n}H(M), \quad R_c \geq \frac{1}{n}H(J), \quad R_d \geq \frac{1}{n}H(L_d).$$

In stochastic coding, it is assumed that various degrees of common randomness between the encoder and decoder, as well as private randomness, are available [27]. When common or private randomness is not available, the corresponding random variables J, L_e, or L_d are set to constant, and their respective rates become zero. Specifically, when J and L_e are constant, the encoding function f_n becomes deterministic with respect to X^n. Similarly, when J and L_d are constant, the decoding function g_n becomes deterministic with respect to X^n.

3.3. Coding Theorems

Within the RDP framework, two scenarios, the one-shot and the asymptotic, have been extensively studied by Theis and Wagner [47] and Chen et al. [26]. The proofs for the one-shot scenario mainly rely on the strong functional representation lemma [48], whereas the proofs for the asymptotic scenario predominantly utilize techniques in channel synthesis [39,41]. Coding theorems in information theory typically involve both achievability and converse results.

Definition 4 (Achievablility)**.** *The tuple $(R, R_c, R_d, D, P) \in \mathbb{R}_{\geq 0} \times \overline{\mathbb{R}}^4_{\geq 0}$ is achievable if, for any $\epsilon > 0$, there exists a sequence of $(n, 2^{n(R+\epsilon)}, 2^{n(R_c+\epsilon)}, 2^{n(R_d+\epsilon)})$ codes (f_n, g_n) such that the distortion constraint*

$$\mathbb{E}_P[\Delta(X^n, Y^n)] \leq D + \epsilon, \tag{D}$$

and the perceptual constraint(s) **(P)** *are both satisfied, where $Y^n = g_n(f_n(X^n, Z^n, K), Z^n, K)$.*

Definition 5. *The rate region $\mathcal{R}_{D,P}$ is the closure of the set of achievable rates, i.e.,*

$$\mathcal{R}_{D,P} = \mathrm{cl}\Big(\{(R, R_c, R_d) \in \mathbb{R}_{\geq 0} \times \overline{\mathbb{R}}^2_{\geq 0} : (R, R_c, R_d, D, P) \text{ is achievable}\}\Big).$$

Given a rate region $\mathcal{R}_{D,P}$ induced by a coding scheme, the converse theorem asserts that any rate tuples (R, R_c, R_d) outside $\mathcal{R}_{D,P}$ are unachievable. Proofs of the converse often leverage the time-sharing technique (e.g., see [25,31,43]), which relies on the assumption that the output sequence is i.i.d. However, the single-letter characterization can also be derived under tensorizable and decomposable conditions [26], which implicitly imply the optimality of an i.i.d. output sequence.

3.4. The Rate–Distortion–Perception Frontier

The rate–distortion function in the traditional (additive) distortion setting has been successful in characterizing the minimum rate required to describe a source within a specified distortion. For a (not necessarily finite) set of distortion measures $\{\Delta_\lambda(\cdot,\cdot)\}_{\lambda\in\Lambda}$, it is shown in [49] (Exercise 7.14, Page 117) that the rate–distortion function is

$$R(\{D_\lambda\}) = \inf_{P_{\hat{X}|X}} I(X;\hat{X}) \qquad \text{s.t.} \qquad \mathbb{E}[\Delta_\lambda(X,\hat{X})] \le D_\lambda \qquad \forall \lambda \in \Lambda, \tag{17}$$

assuming that $\inf_{D_\lambda \neq 0} D_\lambda > 0$.

The information rate–distortion–perception (I-RDP) function was first proposed in analogy to the traditional RD function within the machine learning community.

Definition 6 (I-RDP). *Given a random variable X that represents the source distribution, the information rate–distortion–perception function [4] is defined as*

$$R^{(I)}(D,P) := \inf_{P_{\hat{X}|X}} I(X;\hat{X}) \qquad s.t. \qquad \mathbb{E}[\Delta(X,\hat{X})] \le D, \quad \mathcal{D}(P_X, P_{\hat{X}}) \le P. \tag{18}$$

When the perceptual constraint **(P)** is relaxed, i.e., when $P = \infty$, the RDP function reduces to the classic RD function $R(D,\infty) = R(D)$. Efficient computation of the I-RDP function has been explored in [50–52].

Based on the I-RDP function, ref. [8] demonstrated that the cost of achieving perfect realism is a doubling of the lowest achievable MSE distortion, i.e.,

$$R^{(I)}(D,0) \le R^{(I)}(\frac{1}{2}D,\infty).$$

Specifically, [53] considered the MSE distortion measure and the 2-Wasserstein distance (see Figure 1b), showing that the distortion–perception function using these measures is quadratic. In [47], the authors first established that the I-RDP function provides a lower bound on the one-shot achievable rate using the Poisson functional representation lemma [48]. Let $R^*(D,P)$ denote the one-shot RDP function. The study in [9] subsequently established the relationship between the information function and the operational functions using the same strategy, resulting in the following upper and lower bounds:

$$R^{(I)}(D,P) \le R^*(D,P) \le R^{(I)}(D,P) + \log(1 + R^{(I)}(D,P)) + 5.$$

In the asymptotic setting, the rate region of the general system illustrated in Figure 2 is given by $\mathcal{R}_{D,0}$ as presented in [27]:

$$\begin{aligned}
\mathcal{R}_{D,0} = \{(R, R_c, R_d, D) :\ \exists\, P_{XVY} \in \mathcal{A} \quad &\text{s.t.}\\
R &\ge I_P(X;V)\\
R + R_c &\ge I_P(Y;V)\\
R_d &\ge H_P(Y|V)\\
D &\ge \mathbb{E}_P[\delta(X,Y)]\},\\
\text{where} \qquad \mathcal{A} := \{P_{XVY} :\ X &\sim P_X,\ Y \sim P_X\\
X &\perp Y \mid V\\
|\mathcal{V}| &\le |\mathcal{X}|^2 + 1\}.
\end{aligned}$$

The RDP function can be derived from the achievability and converse of the coding theorems.

Corollary 1. *When common randomness and decoder randomness are unlimited, the RDP function induced by Equation* (20) *is given by the following:*

$$R(D,P) = \inf_{P_{Y|X}} I(X;Y) \qquad s.t. \qquad \mathbb{E}[\delta(X,Y)] \leq D, \quad Y \sim P_X. \tag{19}$$

This result is obtained by setting $R_c = R_d = \infty$. Consequently, the rate region becomes

$$\begin{aligned}\mathcal{R}_{D,0}^{\infty,\infty} &= \{(R,\infty,\infty,D) : \exists\, P_{XVY} \in \mathcal{A} \quad \text{s.t.} \quad R \geq I_P(X;V), D \geq \mathbb{E}_P[\delta(X,Y)]\} \\ &= \{(R,\infty,\infty,D) : X \sim P_X,\ Y \sim P_X, R \geq I_P(X;Y), D \geq \mathbb{E}_P[\delta(X,Y)]\},\end{aligned} \tag{20}$$

where the equality in Equation (20) follows from the data processing inequality $I_P(X;V) \geq I_P(X;Y)$, given that $X \perp Y \mid V$ in $\mathcal{A}$. Therefore, the rate region $\mathcal{R}_{D,0}^{\infty,\infty}$ is a subset of the RD region $\mathcal{R}_D$, i.e., $\mathcal{R}_{D,0}^{\infty,\infty} \subseteq \mathcal{R}_D$.

In light of these results, we draw the following conclusions regarding the introduction of the realism constraint:

- Common randomness and private randomness are helpful in achieving (near) perfect realism.
- The introduction of the perceptual constraint results in a higher rate requirement, even when common randomness and decoder randomness are unlimited.

As illustrated in Figure 1a, where a Gaussian source is considered, the perceptual constraint modestly increases the bitrate required in theory, suggesting an increase in traffic in communication networks. The red arrows indicate the additional rates needed under conditions of no common randomness and unlimited common randomness, respectively. In practice, decoder randomness can be implemented using a random number generator, while common randomness can be achieved through a shared random seed in end-to-end training, where neural network models are deployed at both the encoder and decoder.

The information-theoretic results presented reveal that incorporating perceptual constraints necessitates a fundamental rethinking of RD analysis. Key findings include the establishment of the RDP function as a lower bound on achievable rates, the demonstration that common and private randomness can improve performance under perceptual constraints, and the characterization of how these constraints affect system design in practical communication scenarios.

4. Generative Modeling as a Distribution Approximation Process

The theoretical framework of RDP provides valuable insights into how generative models can be designed to balance fidelity and perceptual quality. In practice, these models must navigate complex trade-offs between maintaining statistical properties of the source data and ensuring efficient representation and transmission.

The growing demand for machine-generated content has spurred the development of generative models across various domains, including language, image, and video generation. Given that these models aim to produce content that appears realistic to humans, evaluation often relies on perceptual quality metrics, which have been integrated into several benchmarks. For instance, the PyIQA package [54] provides a convenient means of computing distortion and perceptual quality measures for image compression. This section underscores the significance of high perceptual fidelity in downstream machine learning tasks, particularly in generative modeling. By examining architectures such as VAEs, GANs, transformers, and diffusion models, along with their objectives, we demonstrate that generative modeling can be interpreted as a distribution approximation process, where the models are trained to match the distribution of the training data.

4.1. Objectives, Tasks, and Architectures

The objective of generative modeling is to train a neural network P_θ capable of generating new samples $y \in \mathcal{X}$ from random seeds (and conditional samples) that closely resemble those in the training data $\mathcal{S}$. From a frequentist viewpoint, the observations $x \in \mathcal{S}$ are drawn i.i.d. from an unknown true distribution: $\mathcal{S} = \{x_i\}_{i=1}^N \sim P_X$. The goal is to learn a generator g_θ that can produce samples approximating P_X by passing a random variable U with a fixed distribution, typically $\mathcal{N}(0,1)$, through the network. Since these models are trained to minimize specific perceptual objectives, the random seed U can be regarded as private randomness that enhances the perceptual quality of the reconstruction, conditioned on given messages. The decoding process in generative models can be viewed as a sampling procedure. For example, in the context of LLMs, beam search [55] is a common maximum a posteriori (MAP) decoding algorithm. Other sampling algorithms, such as temperature sampling [56], top-k sampling [57], nucleus sampling [58], and typical sampling [59], have been developed to generate content faithfully according to the learned distribution.

A variety of generative model architectures have been proposed, with the most prominent ones including variational auto-encoders (VAEs) [60], generative adversarial networks (GANs) [61], diffusion models [62,63], and transformers [64]. These models have achieved notable success in generating images, videos, and language content. They are trained by minimizing specific loss functions that quantify the similarity between the model distribution P_θ and the data distribution $P_\mathcal{D}$. For instance, VAEs and diffusion models minimize the negative evidence lower bound (ELBO), which effectively reduces the KL divergence, while GANs optimize objectives ranging from the Jensen–Shannon divergence [61] to the Wasserstein distance [65]. At the core of generative modeling are the divergence measures $\mathcal{D}(P_\theta, P_\mathcal{D})$ between the model and data distributions. Building on these foundations, neural networks for specific tasks, such as lossy compression, can be trained to minimize a combined distortion and perception loss with a weighting factor λ:

$$\mathcal{L} = \Delta(X, \hat{X}) + \lambda \mathcal{D}(P_X, P_{\hat{X}}). \tag{21}$$

Variants of this loss function have been applied in numerous settings, including those described in [5–11], to achieve high perceptual quality. These applications underscore the perceptual–distortion trade-off inherent in the training of generative models in practice. As the realism depends heavily on the statistical properties of the training datasets, different dataset statistics may affect the RDP trade-off of generative models.

4.1.1. Variational Auto-Encoder

VAEs can effectively learn the distribution of data $P(x)$ and generate samples $x \sim P(X)$ using latent variables Z from a prior distribution $P(Z)$. The marginal likelihood for inference requires the integration of the latent variable $P(x) = \int P(x,z)\mathrm{d}z$, which is often intractable. Therefore, an inference model $Q_\phi(z|x)$ and generative decoder $P_\theta(x|z)$ are trained end-to-end by maximizing the evidence lower bound (ELBO):

$$\begin{aligned} \log P(x) &= \log \int Q(z|x) \frac{P(x,z)}{Q(z|x)} \mathrm{d}z \geq \int Q(z|x) \log\left(\frac{P(x|z)P(z)}{Q(z|x)}\right) \\ &= \mathbb{E}_{Q_\phi(z|x)}[\log P_\theta(x|z)] - \mathcal{D}_{\mathrm{KL}}(Q_\phi(z|x) \| P_\theta(z)) =: \mathcal{L}_{\mathrm{ELBO}}(x;\theta,\phi) \end{aligned} \tag{22}$$

for continuous z via stochastic gradient descent. Semi-supervised VAEs [66] are capable of incorporating discrete "semantic labels" as additional variables.

4.1.2. Generative Adversarial Network

The objective of a GAN is to minimize the divergence between the real data distribution P_X and the generative model distribution P_G. For example, the vanilla GAN [67] employs the Jensen–Shannon divergence

$$\mathcal{D}_{\mathrm{JS}}(P_X, P_Y) = \frac{1}{2}\mathcal{D}_{\mathrm{KL}}(P_X\|\frac{P_X + P_Y}{2}) + \frac{1}{2}\mathcal{D}_{\mathrm{KL}}(P_Y\|\frac{P_X + P_Y}{2}).$$

The f-GAN [68] has been proposed to minimize a variational objective for different f-divergences:

$$d_f(P_X\|P_Y) = \sum_{T\in\tau}(\mathbb{E}_X[T(X)] - \mathbb{E}_Y[f^*(T(Y))])$$

where f^* is the conjugate function of f. The Wasserstein GAN (WGAN) [65,69] minimizes the 1-Wasserstein distance. A combination of JS divergence and Wasserstein distance is proposed as the training objective in [70].

4.1.3. Transformer

Transformer networks, introduced by [64], consist of a stack of homogeneous layers, including multi-head attention and feed-forward layers. The pre-training process can be interpreted as learning the energy of the data distribution using associative memory [19]. The transformer architecture has been extensively applied to language models, where the alphabet $\mathcal{X}$ comprises tokens that can be understood as codewords. Additionally, a distinguished symbol EOS $\notin \mathcal{X}$ is introduced to signify the end of the sequence. Let $\overline{\mathcal{X}} := \mathcal{X} \cup \{\mathrm{EOS}\}$, a language model, be parametrized by $\theta \in \Theta$, which is a (discrete) distribution p_θ over $\mathcal{X}^*$, such that

$$p_\theta(\mathbf{x}) = \hat{p}(\mathrm{EOS}|\mathbf{x})\prod_{i=1}^{T}\hat{p}(x_i|\mathbf{x}_{<i}) \tag{23}$$

for $\mathbf{x} \in \mathcal{X}^*$ and $T = |\mathbf{x}|$, where the conditional distribution $\hat{p}(x|\mathbf{x})$ is a sequence model for $x \in \mathcal{X}$ and $\mathbf{x} \in \mathcal{X}^*$. During decoding, the next token is sampled according to a sampler $q(p_\theta)$ to generate sequences at the decoder that approximate the distribution of the language model.

The autoregressive modeling of images using convolutional architectures has achieved success for low-resolution images. However, transformers consistently outperform their convolutional counterparts for high-resolution images [71]. Specifically, ref. [72] utilizes transformers to simplify neural video compression.

4.1.4. Diffusion Model

In diffusion models [62,63], particularly score-based diffusion models [73,74], refinement information is obtained by incrementally adding white noise to the signal, thereby transforming the source distribution into a Gaussian shape after a Markov chain of diffusion steps. Compared to other image generation methods, such as generative GANs, diffusion-based image generation exhibits superior image sample quality [75].

The forward diffusion process encodes the refinement information using the following Gaussian transition kernel:

$$p_t(x_t|x_{t-1}) = \mathcal{N}(x_t; \sqrt{1-\beta_t}x_{t-1}, \beta_t I). \tag{24}$$

A learned diffusion process starts at a trivial known distribution, typically $\mathcal{N}(0, I)$. Furthermore, X_t can be sampled directly according to the cumulative kernel [63], such that

$$X_t = \sqrt{\bar{\alpha}_t}X_0 + \sqrt{1-\bar{\alpha}_t}\epsilon, \quad (25)$$

where $\bar{\alpha}_t = \prod_{s=1}^{t}(1-\beta_s)$ and $\epsilon \sim \mathcal{N}(0, I)$. Therefore, the generated samples X_t approximately follow the same distribution as the data distribution.

While diffusion models can be interpreted as a special case of VAEs with a particular choice of inference model and generative decoder, the training objective is the ELBO loss with simple data augmentation [76].

4.2. Practical Distortion and Perceptual Quality Measures

In practical applications such as image quality assessment, two types of metrics focus on pixel quality and statistical properties, respectively. Distortion measures, such as mean squared error (MSE), structural similarity index (SSIM), its multiscale variant (MS-SSIM) [77], and peak signal-to-noise ratio (PSNR), require a ground-truth image for comparative analysis (see Figure 1c). Traditional video codecs are designed to efficiently remove spatial–temporal redundancies. Current coding standards, including H.264/AVC [78], H.265/HEVC [79], and H.266/VVC [80], achieve efficient compression through rate–distortion optimization, where the rate is represented by bits-per-pixel (BPP) and distortion is measured by PSNR.

In contrast, perceptual quality measures focus on the statistical properties of images. For example, the Fréchet Inception distance (FID) [81] uses the Inception Network to assess image quality without a reference image by comparing the distributions of generated and real images used to train the generator. The learned perceptual image patch similarity (LPIPS) [82] computes the distance between features in the latent space of a trained neural network and has been shown to effectively capture the underlying semantics of the data. In [83], an unsupervised perceptual information metric (PIM) is proposed using information-theoretic objectives. It is common practice, especially in the domain of LLMs, to employ a powerful model as a judge of semantic similarities. This judge can be conceptualized as a function, and the optimal rate of lossless functional compression can be determined using graph entropy [84–86].

Learning-based compression methods not only consider pixel-wise signal quality metrics such as PSNR but also emphasize perceptual quality. These methods are increasingly outperforming standard codecs in many cases. Inspired by the information-theoretic setting [31], ref. [3] employs a GAN-based model to optimize the RD trade-off under the constraint that reconstructed samples follow the training data distribution. Source coding based on diffusion models is also gaining prominence [87,88]. In [89], a posterior sampling-based compression (PSC) method using diffusion is proposed, with two configurations: PSC-Perception and PSC-Distortion, focusing on high perceptual quality and low-distortion reconstructions, respectively. With the increasing demand for processing longer contexts, significant research has also been devoted to the RD trade-off in text compression using large language models (LLMs) [90–92].

4.3. Experimental Validation in Image Compression

To demonstrate the practical implications of our theoretical findings, we conducted experiments on image compression using the RDP framework. We implemented several learning-based compression methods that incorporate perceptual measures and compared them against traditional compression codecs.

We evaluated the performance of five compression methods: BPG (baseline), VAE-based compression [93], attention-based compression [15], GAN-based compression [7], and diffusion-based compression [88] at a low bpp regime ($R \approx 0.2$ bpp). We used the

CLIC2020 dataset [94], which contains 428 high-quality color images, for our experiments. The performance metrics include PSNR, MS-SSIM, and the perceptual-oriented LPIPS.

The results are summarized in Table 2. The GAN-based method shows the most significant improvement in perceptual quality metrics while maintaining competitive distortion metrics. The attention-based method provided better PSNR than traditional methods but showed less improvement in perceptual metrics.

Table 2. Comparison of compression methods on the CLIC2020 dataset.

Method ($R \approx 0.2$ bpp)	PSNR (↑)	MS-SSIM (↑)	LPIPS (↓)
BPG	33	0.96	0.20
Attention-based [15]	**34**	**0.97**	0.14
VAE-based [93]	31	0.95	0.20
GAN-based [7]	32	**0.97**	**0.06**

5. AI-Empowered Communication with Perceptual Constraint

The advances in generative modeling discussed thus far have significant implications for communication systems, particularly in scenarios where high perceptual quality is essential for downstream tasks. These models can be deployed at various points in the communication pipeline to enhance both compression efficiency and reconstruction quality.

Recent years have witnessed substantial progress in applying machine learning algorithms, particularly generative modeling, to communication networks, driven by their capacity to enhance perceptual quality. Downstream tasks, ranging from image reconstruction [13] to steganography [51], are highly sensitive to distribution and can be executed at the wireless edge using neural networks. Learning-based methods can more easily account for and optimize perceptual qualities as the training of these neural network models inherently addresses the distribution of the output. Thus, perceptual requirements are both natural and essential for AI-empowered communication systems.

5.1. Source–Channel Coding for Perceptual Oriented Communications

Current digital communication systems are designed based on Shannon's source–channel separation theorem [95], which posits that there is no loss of optimality in applying separate source coding followed by channel coding in the asymptotic infinite block length regime, provided that the source and channel statistics are ergodic and the distortion measure is additive. As shown in Figure 3a, the source-encoded data are transmitted through the wireless channel after channel coding and modulation. The receiver reverses these procedures by first demodulating and decoding the channel code, followed by decompression to reconstruct the original data.

While the optimality of separation holds for distortion–perception measures under assumptions of perceptual measures, including sub-decomposability, it has been demonstrated that separation is no longer optimal when common randomness between the encoder and decoder is unavailable [32]. Moreover, in practice, idealized assumptions, such as memorylessness, are rarely met [96], rendering separation-based digital communication systems suboptimal [97]. This motivates the adoption of joint source–channel coding (JSCC) to enhance end-to-end performance in practical communication systems (see Figure 3b). Recently, in the context of semantic communications [98], deep-learning-based JSCC methods, such as DeepJSCC [13], have achieved remarkable results by learning mappings directly from training data (both source and channel) [13,99–104]. Furthermore, a hybrid scheme that combines SSCC and JSCC has been proposed in [105] (see Figure 3c), demonstrating significant potential in mediating between the two systems.

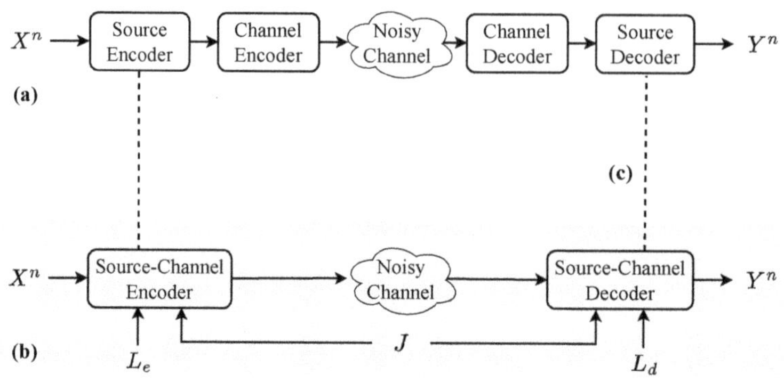

Figure 3. (**a**) Separate source and channel coding (SSCC) in current communication system. (**b**) Joint source–channel coding (JSCC) scheme as in [13]. (**c**) The dashed lines link SSCC and JSCC to form a hybrid communication scheme, as in [105].

5.2. AI-Empowered Semantic Communication

Driven by advances in machine learning, there has been a significant increase in interest in semantic communication systems [98,106,107], with intelligent network architectures being progressively integrated into existing communication standards [108–113]. Broadly, the objective of communication is to transmit meaningful information. In the context of generative models, the term "meaningful" is contingent upon the semantic meaning of the information, which represents a fundamentally different global property compared to traditional average distortion measures, such as Hamming distance and MSE. The notions of semantic and pragmatic communication problems are addressed by drawing parallels to linguistics [107]. By integrating machine learning algorithms, particularly generative modeling, into the widely deployed digital communication infrastructure, semantic communication aims to deliver content with higher perceptual quality more robustly over wireless channels, which are frequently influenced by environmental factors such as weather conditions, buildings, and device activities.

5.2.1. Theoretical Foundation and Practical Motivation

In the RDP framework, common and private randomness have been shown to play crucial roles in improving perceptual fidelity while maintaining efficient communication. Theoretically, common randomness (shared between the transmitter and receiver) and private randomness (available only to one node) provide additional degrees of freedom that can be leveraged to optimize the trade-off between rate, distortion, and perception. In practical systems, this can be implemented through several methods.

Shared Random Seeds in End-to-End Training

In learning-based communication systems, common randomness can be implemented by sharing random seeds between the transmitter and receiver during the training phase. For example, in systems using VAEs or GANs, the encoder and decoder can be trained with a shared random seed that initializes their respective random number generators. This ensures that both ends of the communication system can generate correlated random variations, which can be used to improve perceptual quality.

Pilot Signals and Synchronization

In wireless communication systems, common randomness can be established through pilot signals transmitted from the base station to user equipment. These pilot signals can be used to synchronize random number generators at both ends of the communication link. For instance, in massive MIMO systems, the base station can transmit reference signals that user equipment uses to align its random seed with the base station's generator.

Implementation of Private Randomness

Both transmitters and receivers can incorporate local random number generators that do not require coordination with the other end of the communication system. These generators can be based on physical phenomena (such as thermal noise) or algorithmic approaches (such as pseudorandom number generators with locally maintained seeds).

In the following, we identify three use cases where generative models can be deployed on user equipment (UE), base stations (BSs), and the core network (CN), as illustrated in Figure 4.

5.2.2. Generative Modeling in User Equipment

Due to the increasing hardware computing capability, UE such as smartphones is increasingly capable of performing intelligent tasks involving generative models. In wireless communications, UE encompasses a wide range of devices, including smartphones, tablets, specialized Internet of Things (IoT) devices, and industrial sensors, all of which are capable of transmitting and receiving reliable and efficient communication services. UE features software-defined encoders and decoders for audio, video, and other data formats, as well as support for wireless communication protocols such as LTE and 5G NR. More recently, LLMs have been deployed on edge devices, such as smartphones. Applications like prompt compression [92] enable extended model inference (EMI) and native model inference (NMI), which apply prompt compression and inference on the same devices and facilitate interactions between edge devices and cloud servers, respectively.

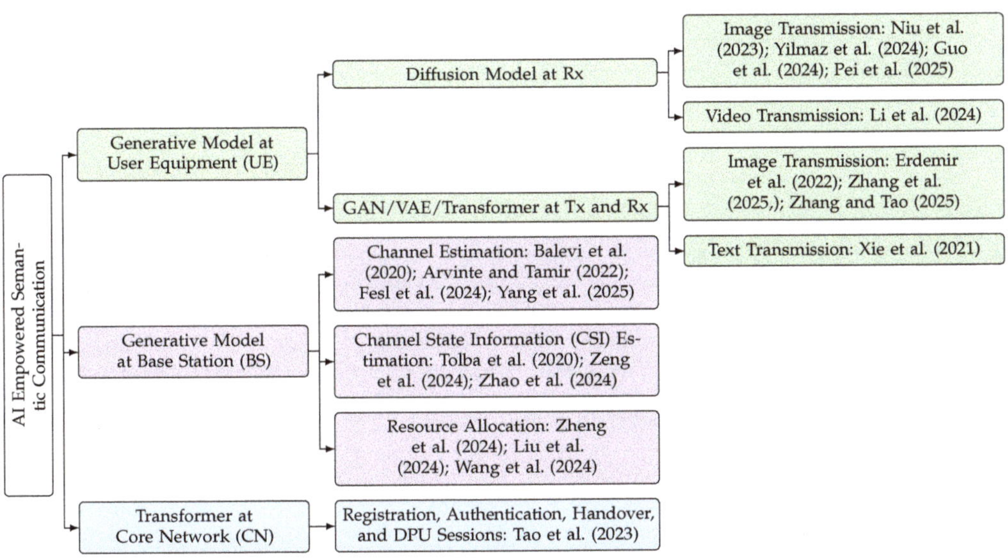

Figure 4. Generative models deployed on user equipment (UE), base stations (BSs), and core network (CN) in AI-empowered communication [105,114–133].

Recent research indicates that the joint source–channel coding (JSCC) scheme, combined with a generative model for reconstruction, can achieve substantial reductions in bandwidth while significantly enhancing the perceptual quality of the reconstruction. Utilizing VAEs, ref. [12] reimagines communication systems as a joint optimization of the transmitter (Tx) and receiver (Rx) in an end-to-end manner for reconstruction tasks. The source node (Tx) encodes the data using neural networks that create compact representations while ensuring reliability. For example, a pre-trained generative model based on GANs is employed in [126], and the destination node (Rx) utilizes a generative model to reconstruct the data. In [131], a diffusion model is deployed at the receiver to achieve high-perceptual-quality wireless image transmission. In [134], common modulation schemes are incorporated into the encoded representation as well. In [100], a JSCC video transmission scheme is proposed using deep neural networks. Additionally, Rx may provide feedback to the source node, enabling dynamic adjustments to enhance communication quality [135].

5.2.3. Generative Modeling in Base Station

As part of the radio Access Network (RAN), the BS possesses powerful Tx and Rx capabilities to communicate simultaneously with multiple UE. Generative models have been applied to the BS for channel estimation, channel state information (CSI) acquisition, and resource allocation.

The BS features encoders and decoders to process both uplink (from UE to the BS) and downlink (from the BS to UE) data streams. Modern cellular networks typically operate in full-duplex mode [136], enabling simultaneous bidirectional communication between UE and the BS for concurrent transmission and reception. Antenna arrays in the BS are used to send and receive radio signals, employing sophisticated beamforming techniques. The BS can estimate the current state of the channel, thereby optimizing downlink data transmission. In frequency division duplexing systems, the CSI is fed back to the BS for beamforming. In [118], a GAN-based CSI feedback approach is proposed, where the encoder learns a compressed codeword of the CSI and passes it to the generator for reconstruction in the BS. In [119], a CSI-GPT framework is proposed to efficiently acquire downlink CSI information in massive MIMO systems. In [137], the generalization ability of multi-modal large models across diverse base station environments is explored for various CSI-based tasks. Intelligent algorithms [115–117] can be applied to resource allocation and scheduling to dynamically allocate frequency, time, and power resources, thereby meeting real-time user needs and maximizing overall system performance.

5.2.4. Generative Modeling in Core Network

The core network may include multiple types of encoders and decoders to handle data from different protocol stack layers, such as voice encoding and video encoding, to meet diverse service requirements and quality of service (QoS) standards. In [114], two models, 5GCSeq2Seq and 5GC-former, are proposed based on the vanilla Seq2Seq model and the transformer, respectively, to accurately replicate the principal functionalities of the 5G core network control plane, including registration, authentication, handover, and DPU sessions.

5.2.5. Basic Unit for AI-Empowered Communications

In contemporary communication networks, formatted blocks of data are transmitted across various layers of the protocol stack. For instance, in the physical layer of 5G networks, binary digits (bits) are modulated and transmitted over the air interface. In the transport layer, messages from applications are encapsulated into segments such as TCP segments, which include headers, source and destination port numbers, and checksums. This segmentation focuses on the accurate transmission of application messages, with the goal of minimizing the average distortion measure, which is additive in terms of segmental distortion.

In DeepJSCC-like systems, analog signals are employed for end-to-end uncoded transmission [13,135]. Ref. [134] further integrates uncoded signals into a digital modulation system, which is then transmitted and received by the decoder. In the context of low-latency transmission, where information freshness is crucial, short packets serve as the basic unit [138], and the age–distortion trade-off has been studied [139]. Ref. [105] combines analog signals for JSCC with conventional digital signals to form a hybrid communication scheme.

In many generative modeling architectures, tokens function as the fundamental unit. Ref. [140] introduces a token-domain multiple-access scheme, which allows multiple devices to transmit over the same multiple-access channel in a non-orthogonal manner. In the realm of source coding, ref. [141] utilizes 1D tokenization to project 2D images into variable-length, ordered 1D token sequences. This method describes images in a coarse-to-fine manner, thereby achieving a trade-off between the number of tokens (rate) and perceptual quality. The SoTA tokenizer FlowMo is a transformer-based diffusion autoencoder that combines mode matching pre-training and mode seeking post-training [142]. In [143], a video tokenizer is developed for both videos and images using a common token vocabulary. These systems are trained end-to-end using losses that incorporate perceptual quality. Furthermore, technologies such as chunking and the semantic compression of token chunks have been developed in [90], leveraging the parallel computational power of GPUs. In this approach, chunks of tokens serve as the fundamental unit. Given the diverse representation of information, the integration of signals such as tokens and architectures such as tokenizers into intelligent communication systems is necessitated through the lens of the RDP framework.

The integration of generative models into communication systems demonstrates substantial potential for improving perceptual quality while maintaining efficient transmission. Joint source–channel coding approaches like DeepJSCC have shown particular promise by directly optimizing for end-to-end reconstruction quality rather than treating source and channel coding as separate problems. However, practical implementation faces challenges related to computational complexity, training data requirements, and the need for robustness against varying channel conditions.

6. Conclusions and Future Direction

6.1. Conclusions

This paper has explored the critical role of perceptual constraints in information theory and their impact on practical generative modeling scenarios. We have demonstrated that incorporating perceptual constraints into the RD framework, resulting in the RDP framework, offers a novel and comprehensive perspective for evaluating the performance of AI-empowered systems in compression and communication. We have discussed the implications of the perceptual constraint on the design and deployment of generative models, which is particularly relevant in intelligent communication systems, where downstream tasks demand high perceptual fidelity, such as interactive AI agents and visually pleasing content. By highlighting the importance of perceptual constraints and demonstrating their impact on system design and performance, we project an increase in expected traffic in intelligent communication networks with consideration of perceptual quality. While our theoretical analysis suggests that incorporating perceptual constraints generally requires additional rate, we acknowledge that intelligent compression techniques can significantly mitigate this traffic growth.

6.2. Future Direction

6.2.1. Information-Theoretic Directions

In [31,43], it is assumed that the output follows the i.i.d. distribution for i.i.d. sources. When imposing the perfect realism constraint, the i.i.d. condition is naturally imposed on the output. However, it is unclear whether this assumption is valid or redundant. Therefore, we pose the following conjecture for further investigation.

Conjecture 1. *Consider the system model in Figure 2 and the* $(n, 2^{nR}, 2^{nR_c}, 2^{nR_d})$ *fixed-length code with encoder and decoder* (f_n, g_n)*. For i.i.d. source* $\{X_i\}_{i=1}^{\infty}$*, suppose that the distortion and perceptual constraints are*

$$\mathbb{E}_P[\Delta(X^n, Y^n)] \leq D, \quad \textbf{(D)}$$
$$\mathcal{D}(P_{X^n}, P_{Y^n}) \leq P, \quad \textbf{(P)}$$

where $Y^n = g_n(f_n(X^n, Z^n, K), Z^n, K)$*. Then, the capacity achieving* Y^n *is also i.i.d. when* $n \to \infty$ *for perception measures* $\mathcal{D}(\cdot, \cdot)$ *that belong to the* f*-divergence family.*

Analogously to the RD function with the multiple-distortion constraint, we pose the following conjecture.

Conjecture 2. *For a (not necessarily finite) set of distortion measures* $\{\Delta_\lambda(\cdot, \cdot)\}_{\lambda \in \Lambda}$ *and a (not necessarily finite) set of* f*-divergences* $\{D_{f_\gamma}(\cdot, \cdot)\}_{\gamma \in \Gamma}$*, suppose that the source* $\{X_i\}_{i=1}^{\infty}$ *and reconstruction* Y *are from the same discrete alphabet* $\mathcal{X}$*. Consider the (possibly stochastic) code* (f_n, g_n)*; then, the RDP function with unlimited common randomness and unlimited private randomness is*

$$\begin{aligned} R(\{D_\lambda\}, \{P_\gamma\}) = &\inf_{P_{Y|X}} I(X;Y) \\ \text{s.t.} \quad &\mathbb{E}[\Delta_\lambda(X, Y)] \leq D_\lambda, \quad \forall \lambda \in \Lambda \\ &D_{f_\gamma}(P_{X^n}, P_{Y^n}) \leq P_\gamma, \quad \forall \gamma \in \Gamma \end{aligned} \tag{26}$$

where $\inf_{D_\lambda \neq 0} D_\lambda > 0$ *and* $\inf_{P_\gamma \neq 0} P_\gamma > 0$.

When the realism constraint is defined in terms of weak realism, the conjecture can be proven using the method of types [42]. However, it remains unclear whether the conjecture holds under other realism constraints, such as strong realism, or under a combination of different constraints.

6.2.2. Architectural Improvement for Intelligent Communication Systems

Future architectural designs for semantic communications have been discussed in [144–147]. The integration of perceptual fidelity into the design of intelligent communication architectures represents a paradigm shift from traditional communication systems optimized solely for distortion. The development of systems that better align with human-centric quality assessments and support emerging applications requiring high perceptual fidelity is a promising direction for future research and development, particularly as applications increasingly demand high perceptual quality in transmitted data. By bridging the gap between theoretical advances in information theory and practical deployment considerations, the RDP framework can guide intelligent communication architectures that better serve human-centric needs.

Interactive AI Agents

In interactive AI agent scenarios, communication systems must support real-time decision making while maintaining perceptual consistency with human expectations. RDP trade-off provides a theoretical foundation for balancing the rate requirements against both distortion and perceptual constraints in these dynamic environments. The deployment of generative models at both transmitter and receiver nodes allows for the incorporation of common and private randomness, which has been shown to improve perceptual fidelity in RDP frameworks. For interactive agents, this translates to more natural human–AI interactions where the AI can generate responses that are not only factually accurate but also perceptually coherent with the user's expectations. Architecturally, this requires communication systems that can dynamically adjust their rate allocation based on the perceptual importance of different components of the transmitted information. For example, in multi-modal communication systems involving text, image, and video data, the RDP function can guide the allocation of bandwidth to prioritize perceptually critical features across different data types.

Perceptually Optimized Data Transmission

RDP frameworks enable the design of communication systems that explicitly optimize for perceptual quality rather than just fidelity to the original data. This is particularly important in applications where the end-user experience depends on how natural/realistic the reconstructed data appear rather than on strict pixel-wise accuracy. In image and video transmission, for example, RDP-informed architectures can prioritize the preservation of distributions that contribute significantly to human perception of quality, even if this requires slightly higher bitrates. Conversely, they can allocate fewer bits to components that have minimal impact on perceptual quality, achieving more efficient compression. For example, systems employing generative models like GANs can achieve high perceptual quality with manageable increases in bitrate by leveraging the models' ability to capture the underlying data distribution.

Reinforcement learning has emerged as a potentially transformative approach for developing agent-based systems, including embodied AI, as downstream tasks for intelligent communications. Recently, the rate–reward trade-off has been introduced [148]. Moreover, the remote coordination problem has been introduced [149], driven by the necessity to develop coordinated policies among distributed agents [150]. In this context, exploring the fundamental limits of coordination under rate-constrained communication emerges as a significant area of investigation.

Human-Centric Quality Systems

Communication systems prioritizing human-centric quality should account for the subjective nature of human perception, which often differs from objective distortion metrics in current system design. This requires the development of communication architectures that can adapt to the specific perceptual requirements of different applications and user contexts. For example, in tele-medicine applications, the communication system might prioritize the accurate transmission of fine details in medical images that are critical for diagnosis, while, in video conferencing, the system might focus on maintaining smooth motion and natural facial expressions. From an implementation perspective, future design should consider adaptability through modular architectures where different perceptual quality modules can be activated based on the application requirements. These modules could employ specialized generative models trained on task-specific data to optimize the perceptual quality for particular use cases.

6.2.3. Implementation Challenges in Deploying Generative Models for Intelligent Communications

While generative models offer significant theoretical advantages for intelligent communication systems, practical implementation presents several challenges that must be addressed for successful deployment in real-world scenarios.

Computational Complexity

The computational requirements for training and deploying generative models represent a significant implementation challenge. VAEs, GANs, and diffusion models each have distinct computational profiles. VAEs typically require substantial computational resources for training, particularly when dealing with high-dimensional data such as images or video. The encoding and decoding processes involve complex neural network operations that can be computationally intensive. The adversarial training process for GANs between generator and discriminator networks can lead to increased computational complexity. The need for careful balancing between the two networks adds to the computational burden during training. Diffusion models generally require the most computational resources due to their iterative denoising process. The multiple forward and backward passes during both training and inference phases result in higher computational demands compared to VAEs and GANs. The following directions are important for addressing these challenges.

- Model architecture simplification through techniques like depthwise separable convolutions and reduced latent space dimensions.
- Knowledge distillation methods where smaller models are trained to mimic the behavior of larger, more complex generative models.
- The quantization of model weights and activations to reduce precision requirements and computational intensity.

Latency Considerations

Real-time communication systems often have strict latency requirements that must be met for effective operation. The latency introduced by generative models can impact system performance in end-to-end latency, model inference time, and transmission delay: the total delay from the input to output must be minimized, especially in interactive applications like video conferencing or augmented reality; the time required to generate or reconstruct data at the receiver must be compatible with the system's real-time constraints; the additional bits required for perceptual quality may increase transmission time, creating a trade-off between quality and latency. Future directions include model architecture design specifically targeting low-latency inference, such as using lightweight models.

Hardware Constraints

The hardware limitations of communication devices significantly impact the deployment of generative models. Many communication systems rely on edge devices with limited computational capabilities, memory, and power. Deploying generative models on these devices requires careful optimization. While specialized hardware can mitigate some computational limitations, it introduces additional design considerations and potential costs. Moreover, in wireless communication networks, energy consumption is a critical concern. Generative models should be optimized to operate within the power constraints of battery-powered devices. Future research exploring various solutions to these hardware constraints include:

- On-device model compression techniques, including pruning and quantization.
- Federated learning approaches where model training is distributed across multiple devices.
- Hybrid architectures that perform partial processing at the edge and partial processing in the cloud.

Author Contributions: Conceptualization, X.N. and B.B.; methodology, X.N.; validation, X.N., N.G., W.Z. and W.H.; formal analysis, X.N.; investigation, X.N.; resources, B.B., N.G., W.Z. and W.H.; writing—original draft preparation, X.N.; writing—review and editing, X.N., B.B., N.G., W.Z. and W.H.; visualization, X.N.; supervision, B.B., N.G., W.Z. and W.H.; project administration, B.B., N.G., W.Z. and W.H.; funding acquisition, B.B., N.G., W.Z. and W.H. All authors have read and agreed to the published version of the manuscript.

Funding: This research received no external funding.

Institutional Review Board Statement: Not applicable.

Data Availability Statement: The original data presented in the study are openly available in CLIC2020 at [94].

Conflicts of Interest: X.N, B.B., N.G., W.Z., and W.H.are employed by Huawei Technologies Co., Ltd.

References

1. Blau, Y.; Michaeli, T. The perception-distortion tradeoff. In Proceedings of the IEEE Conference on Computer Vision and Pattern Recognition, Salt Lake City, UT, USA, 18–23 June 2018; pp. 6228–6237.
2. Dahl, R.; Norouzi, M.; Shlens, J. Pixel recursive super resolution. In Proceedings of the IEEE International Conference on Computer Vision, Venice, Italy, 22–29 October 2017; pp. 5439–5448.
3. Tschannen, M.; Agustsson, E.; Lucic, M. Deep generative models for distribution-preserving lossy compression. *Adv. Neural Inf. Process. Syst.* **2018**, *31*, 5929–5940.
4. Blau, Y.; Michaeli, T. Rethinking lossy compression: The rate-distortion-perception tradeoff. In Proceedings of the International Conference on Machine Learning. PMLR, Long Beach, CA, USA, 9–15 June 2019; pp. 675–685.
5. Ledig, C.; Theis, L.; Huszár, F.; Caballero, J.; Cunningham, A.; Acosta, A.; Aitken, A.; Tejani, A.; Totz, J.; Wang, Z.; et al. Photo-realistic single image super-resolution using a generative adversarial network. In Proceedings of the IEEE Conference on Computer Vision and Pattern Recognition, Honolulu, HI, USA, 21–26 July 2017; pp. 4681–4690.
6. Agustsson, E.; Tschannen, M.; Mentzer, F.; Timofte, R.; Gool, L.V. Generative adversarial networks for extreme learned image compression. In Proceedings of the IEEE/CVF International Conference on Computer Vision, Seoul, Republic of Korea, 27 October–2 November 2019; pp. 221–231.
7. Mentzer, F.; Toderici, G.D.; Tschannen, M.; Agustsson, E. High-fidelity generative image compression. *Adv. Neural Inf. Process. Syst.* **2020**, *33*, 11913–11924.
8. Yan, Z.; Wen, F.; Ying, R.; Ma, C.; Liu, P. On perceptual lossy compression: The cost of perceptual reconstruction and an optimal training framework. In Proceedings of the International Conference on Machine Learning. PMLR, Virtual, 18–24 July 2021; pp. 11682–11692.
9. Zhang, G.; Qian, J.; Chen, J.; Khisti, A. Universal rate-distortion-perception representations for lossy compression. *Adv. Neural Inf. Process. Syst.* **2021**, *34*, 11517–11529.
10. Yan, Z.; Wen, F.; Liu, P. Optimally Controllable Perceptual Lossy Compression. In Proceedings of the International Conference on Machine Learning. PMLR, Baltimore, MD, USA, 17–23 July 2022; pp. 24911–24928.
11. Salehkalaibar, S.; Phan, T.B.; Chen, J.; Yu, W.; Khisti, A. On the choice of perception loss function for learned video compression. *Adv. Neural Inf. Process. Syst.* **2023**, *36*, 48226–48274.
12. O'shea, T.; Hoydis, J. An introduction to deep learning for the physical layer. *IEEE Trans. Cogn. Commun. Netw.* **2017**, *3*, 563–575. [CrossRef]
13. Bourtsoulatze, E.; Burth Kurka, D.; Gündüz, D. Deep Joint Source-Channel Coding for Wireless Image Transmission. *IEEE Trans. Cogn. Comms. Netw.* **2019**, *5*, 567–579. [CrossRef]
14. Bégaint, J.; Racapé, F.; Feltman, S.; Pushparaja, A. CompressAI: A PyTorch library and evaluation platform for end-to-end compression research. *arXiv* **2020**, arXiv:2011.03029.
15. Cheng, Z.; Sun, H.; Takeuchi, M.; Katto, J. Learned image compression with discretized gaussian mixture likelihoods and attention modules. In Proceedings of the IEEE/CVF conference on Computer Vision and Pattern Recognition, Seattle, WA, USA, 14–19 June 2020; pp. 7939–7948.
16. Gregory, R.L. Perceptions as hypotheses. *Philos. Trans. R. Soc. Lond. B Biol. Sci.* **1980**, *290*, 181–197.
17. Rao, R.P.; Ballard, D.H. Predictive coding in the visual cortex: A functional interpretation of some extra-classical receptive-field effects. *Nat. Neurosci.* **1999**, *2*, 79–87. [CrossRef]

18. Jiang, L.P.; Rao, R.P. Predictive Coding Theories of Cortical Function. 2022. Available online: https://oxfordre.com/neuroscience/display/10.1093/acrefore/9780190264086.001.0001/acrefore-9780190264086-e-328 (accessed on 26 February 2025).
19. Niu, X.; Bai, B.; Deng, L.; Han, W. Beyond Scaling Laws: Understanding Transformer Performance with Associative Memory. *arXiv* **2024**, arXiv:2405.08707.
20. Lin, B.; Ye, Y.; Zhu, B.; Cui, J.; Ning, M.; Jin, P.; Yuan, L. Video-LLaVA: Learning United Visual Representation by Alignment Before Projection. In Proceedings of the 2024 Conference on Empirical Methods in Natural Language Processing, Miami, FL, USA, 12–16 November 2024; pp. 5971–5984.
21. Fei, W.; Niu, X.; Xie, G.; Zhang, Y.; Bai, B.; Deng, L.; Han, W. Retrieval meets reasoning: Dynamic in-context editing for long-text understanding. *arXiv* **2024**, arXiv:2406.12331.
22. Meng, C.; He, Y.; Song, Y.; Song, J.; Wu, J.; Zhu, J.Y.; Ermon, S. SDEdit: Guided Image Synthesis and Editing with Stochastic Differential Equations. In Proceedings of the International Conference on Learning Representations, Online, 25–29 April 2022.
23. Cover, T.M. *Elements of Information Theory*; John Wiley & Sons: Hoboken, NJ, USA, 1999.
24. Theis, L.; Agustsson, E. On the advantages of stochastic encoders. *arXiv* **2021**, arXiv:2102.09270.
25. Wagner, A.B. The Rate-Distortion-Perception Tradeoff: The Role of Common Randomness. *arXiv* **2022**, arXiv:2202.04147.
26. Chen, J.; Yu, L.; Wang, J.; Shi, W.; Ge, Y.; Tong, W. On the Rate-Distortion-Perception Function. *IEEE J. Sel. Areas Inf. Theory* **2022**, *3*, 664–673. [CrossRef]
27. Hamdi, Y.; Wagner, A.B.; Gündüz, D. The Rate-Distortion-Perception Trade-off: The Role of Private Randomness. *arXiv* **2024**, arXiv:2404.01111.
28. Li, M.; Klejsa, J.; Kleijn, W.B. Distribution preserving quantization with dithering and transformation. *IEEE Signal Process. Lett.* **2010**, *17*, 1014–1017. [CrossRef]
29. Li, M.; Klejsa, J.; Kleijn, W.B. On distribution preserving quantization. *arXiv* **2011**, arXiv:1108.3728.
30. Saldi, N.; Linder, T.; Yüksel, S. Randomized quantization and source coding with constrained output distribution. *IEEE Trans. Inf. Theory* **2014**, *61*, 91–106. [CrossRef]
31. Saldi, N.; Linder, T.; Yüksel, S. Output constrained lossy source coding with limited common randomness. *IEEE Trans. Inf. Theory* **2015**, *61*, 4984–4998.
32. Tian, C.; Chen, J.; Narayanan, K. Source-Channel Separation Theorems for Distortion Perception Coding. *arXiv* **2025**, arXiv:2501.17706.
33. Qiu, Y.; Wagner, A.B.; Ballé, J.; Theis, L. Wasserstein distortion: Unifying fidelity and realism. In Proceedings of the 2024 58th Annual Conference on Information Sciences and Systems (CISS), Princeton, NJ, USA, 13–15 March 2024; IEEE: New York, NY, USA, 2024; pp. 1–6.
34. Marton, K. Bounding $\bar{d}$-distance by informational divergence: A method to prove measure concentration. *Ann. Probab.* **1996**, *24*, 857–866.
35. Marton, K. Measure concentration for a class of random processes. *Probab. Theory Relat. Fields* **1998**, *110*, 427–439.
36. Yassaee, M.H.; Aref, M.R.; Gohari, A. Achievability proof via output statistics of random binning. *IEEE Trans. Inf. Theory* **2014**, *60*, 6760–6786.
37. Pinsker, M.S. Information and information stability of random variables and processes. *J. R. Stat. Soc. Ser. Appl. Stat.* **1964**, *13*, 134–135.
38. Csiszár, I.; Talata, Z. Context tree estimation for not necessarily finite memory processes, via BIC and MDL. *IEEE Trans. Inf. Theory* **2006**, *52*, 1007–1016.
39. Cuff, P. Distributed channel synthesis. *IEEE Trans. Inf. Theory* **2013**, *59*, 7071–7096. [CrossRef]
40. Villani, C. *Optimal Transport: Old and New*; Springer: Berlin/Heidelberg, Germany, 2009; Volume 338.
41. Cuff, P.W.; Permuter, H.H.; Cover, T.M. Coordination capacity. *IEEE Trans. Inf. Theory* **2010**, *56*, 4181–4206.
42. Raginsky, M. Empirical processes, typical sequences, and coordinated actions in standard Borel spaces. *IEEE Trans. Inf. Theory* **2012**, *59*, 1288–1301. [CrossRef]
43. Niu, X.; Gündüz, D.; Bai, B.; Han, W. Conditional Rate-Distortion-Perception Trade-Off. In Proceedings of the 2023 IEEE International Symposium on Information Theory (ISIT), Taipei, Taiwan, 25–30 June 2023; IEEE: New York, NY, USA, 2023; pp. 1068–1073.
44. Matsumoto, R. Introducing the perception-distortion tradeoff into the rate-distortion theory of general information sources. *IEICE Commun. Express* **2018**, *7*, 427–431.
45. Matsumoto, R. Rate-distortion-perception tradeoff of variable-length source coding for general information sources. *IEICE Commun. Express* **2019**, *8*, 38–42.
46. Hamdi, Y.; Gündüz, D. The Rate-Distortion-Perception Trade-off with Side Information. In Proceedings of the 2023 IEEE International Symposium on Information Theory (ISIT), Taipei, Taiwan, 25–30 June 2023; IEEE: New York, NY, USA, 2023; pp. 1056–1061.
47. Theis, L.; Wagner, A.B. A coding theorem for the rate-distortion-perception function. *arXiv* **2021**, arXiv:2104.13662.

48. Li, C.T.; El Gamal, A. Strong functional representation lemma and applications to coding theorems. *IEEE Trans. Inf. Theory* **2018**, *64*, 6967–6978. [CrossRef]
49. Csiszár, I.; Körner, J. *Information Theory: Coding Theorems for Discrete Memoryless Systems*, 2nd ed.; Cambridge University Press: Cambridge, UK, 2011.
50. Chen, C.; Niu, X.; Ye, W.; Wu, S.; Bai, B.; Chen, W.; Lin, S.J. Computation of rate-distortion-perception functions with Wasserstein barycenter. In Proceedings of the 2023 IEEE International Symposium on Information Theory (ISIT), Taipei, Taiwan, 25–30 June 2023; IEEE: New York, NY, USA, 2023; pp. 1074–1079.
51. Chen, C.; Niu, X.; Ye, W.; Wu, H.; Bai, B. Computation and Critical Transitions of Rate-Distortion-Perception Functions with Wasserstein Barycenter. *arXiv* **2024**, arXiv:2404.04681.
52. Serra, G.; Stavrou, P.A.; Kountouris, M. Computation of the Multivariate Gaussian Rate-Distortion-Perception Function. In Proceedings of the 2024 IEEE International Symposium on Information Theory (ISIT), Athens, Greece, 7–12 July 2024; IEEE: New York, NY, USA, 2024; pp. 1077–1082.
53. Freirich, D.; Michaeli, T.; Meir, R. A theory of the distortion-perception tradeoff in wasserstein space. *Adv. Neural Inf. Process. Syst.* **2021**, *34*, 25661–25672.
54. Chen, C.; Mo, J. IQA-PyTorch: PyTorch Toolbox for Image Quality Assessment. 2022. Available online: https://github.com/chaofengc/IQA-PyTorch (accessed on 26 February 2025).
55. Graves, A. Sequence transduction with recurrent neural networks. *arXiv* **2012**, arXiv:1211.3711.
56. Ackley, D.H.; Hinton, G.E.; Sejnowski, T.J. A learning algorithm for Boltzmann machines. *Cogn. Sci.* **1985**, *9*, 147–169.
57. Fan, A.; Lewis, M.; Dauphin, Y. Hierarchical Neural Story Generation. In Proceedings of the 56th Annual Meeting of the Association for Computational Linguistics (Volume 1: Long Papers), Melbourne, Australia, 15–20 July 2018; pp. 889–898.
58. Holtzman, A.; Buys, J.; Du, L.; Forbes, M.; Choi, Y. The Curious Case of Neural Text Degeneration. In Proceedings of the International Conference on Learning Representations, Addis Ababa, Ethiopia, 30 April 2020.
59. Meister, C.; Pimentel, T.; Wiher, G.; Cotterell, R. Locally typical sampling. *Trans. Assoc. Comput. Linguist.* **2023**, *11*, 102–121. [CrossRef]
60. Kingma, D.P.; Welling, M. Auto-encoding variational Bayes. In Proceedings of the 2nd International Conference on Learning Representations, Banff, AB, Canada, 14–16 April 2014.
61. Goodfellow, I.; Pouget-Abadie, J.; Mirza, M.; Xu, B.; Warde-Farley, D.; Ozair, S.; Courville, A.; Bengio, Y. Generative adversarial nets. In Proceedings of the Advances in Neural Information Processing Systems, Montreal, QC, Canada, 8–13 December 2014; Volume 27.
62. Sohl-Dickstein, J.; Weiss, E.; Maheswaranathan, N.; Ganguli, S. Deep Unsupervised Learning using Nonequilibrium Thermodynamics. In Proceedings of the International Conference on Machine Learning (ICML), Lille, France, 7–9 July 2015.
63. Ho, J.; Jain, A.; Abbeel, P. Denoising Diffusion Probabilistic Models. In Proceedings of the Advances in Neural Information Processing Systems (NeurIPS), Virtual, 6–12 December 2020.
64. Vaswani, A.; Shazeer, N.; Parmar, N.; Uszkoreit, J.; Jones, L.; Gomez, A.N.; Kaiser, Ł.; Polosukhin, I. Attention is all you need. *Adv. Neural Inf. Process. Syst.* **2017**, *30*, 5998–6008.
65. Arjovsky, M.; Chintala, S.; Bottou, L. Wasserstein generative adversarial networks. In Proceedings of the International Conference on Machine Learning. PMLR, Sydney, NSW, Australia, 6–11 August 2017; pp. 214–223.
66. Kingma, D.P.; Mohamed, S.; Jimenez Rezende, D.; Welling, M. Semi-supervised learning with deep generative models. *Adv. Neural Inf. Process. Syst.* **2014**, *27*, 3581–3589.
67. Goodfellow, I.; Pouget-Abadie, J.; Mirza, M.; Xu, B.; Warde-Farley, D.; Ozair, S.; Courville, A.; Bengio, Y. Generative adversarial networks. *Commun. ACM* **2020**, *63*, 139–144. [CrossRef]
68. Nowozin, S.; Cseke, B.; Tomioka, R. f-GAN: Training generative neural samplers using variational divergence minimization. In Proceedings of the Advances in Neural Information Processing Systems, Barcelona, Spain, 5–10 December 2016; Volume 29.
69. Gulrajani, I.; Ahmed, F.; Arjovsky, M.; Dumoulin, V.; Courville, A.C. Improved training of Wasserstein GANs. In Proceedings of the Advances in Neural Information Processing Systems, Long Beach, CA, USA, 4–9 December 2017.
70. Farnia, F.; Tse, D. A convex duality framework for GANs. In Proceedings of the Advances in Neural Information Processing Systems, Montréal, QC, Canada, 3–8 December 2018.
71. Esser, P.; Rombach, R.; Ommer, B. Taming transformers for high-resolution image synthesis. In Proceedings of the IEEE/CVF Conference on Computer Vision and Pattern Recognition, Nashville, TN, USA, 20–25 June 2021; pp. 12873–12883.
72. Mentzer, F.; Toderici, G.; Minnen, D.; Hwang, S.J.; Caelles, S.; Lucic, M.; Agustsson, E. VCT: A video compression transformer. In Proceedings of the 36th International Conference on Neural Information Processing Systems, New Orleans, LA, USA, 28 November–9 December 2022; pp. 13091–13103.
73. Song, Y.; Ermon, S. Generative Modeling by Estimating Gradients of the Data Distribution. In Proceedings of the Advances in Neural Information Processing Systems (NeurIPS), Vancouver, BC, Canada, 8–14 December 2019.

74. Song, Y.; Ermon, S. Improved Techniques for Training Score-Based Generative Models. In Proceedings of the Advances in Neural Information Processing Systems (NeurIPS), Virtual, 6–12 December 2020.
75. Dhariwal, P.; Nichol, A. Diffusion Models Beat GANs on Image Synthesis. In Proceedings of the Advances in Neural Information Processing Systems (NeurIPS), Online, 6–14 December 2021 ; pp. 8780–8794.
76. Kingma, D.; Gao, R. Understanding diffusion objectives as the elbo with simple data augmentation. *Adv. Neural Inf. Process. Syst.* **2023**, *36*, 65484–65516.
77. Wang, Z.; Simoncelli, E.P.; Bovik, A.C. Multiscale structural similarity for image quality assessment. In Proceedings of the Thrity-Seventh Asilomar Conference on Signals, Systems & Computers, Pacific Grove, CA, USA, 9–12 November 2003; IEEE: New York, NY, USA, 2003; Volume 2, pp. 1398–1402.
78. Wiegand, T.; Sullivan, G.J.; Bjontegaard, G.; Luthra, A. Overview of the H. 264/AVC video coding standard. *IEEE Trans. Circuits Syst. Video Technol.* **2003**, *13*, 560–576. [CrossRef]
79. Sullivan, G.J.; Ohm, J.R.; Han, W.J.; Wiegand, T. Overview of the high efficiency video coding (HEVC) standard. *IEEE Trans. Circuits Syst. Video Technol.* **2012**, *22*, 1649–1668. [CrossRef]
80. Bross, B.; Wang, Y.K.; Ye, Y.; Liu, S.; Chen, J.; Sullivan, G.J.; Ohm, J.R. Overview of the versatile video coding (VVC) standard and its applications. *IEEE Trans. Circuits Syst. Video Technol.* **2021**, *31*, 3736–3764.
81. Heusel, M.; Ramsauer, H.; Unterthiner, T.; Nessler, B.; Hochreiter, S. GANs trained by a two time-scale update rule converge to a local nash equilibrium. *Adv. Neural Inf. Process. Syst.* **2017**, *30*, 6626–6637.
82. Zhang, R.; Isola, P.; Efros, A.A.; Shechtman, E.; Wang, O. The unreasonable effectiveness of deep features as a perceptual metric. In Proceedings of the IEEE Conference on Computer Vision and Pattern Recognition, Salt Lake City, UT, USA, 18–22 June 2018; pp. 586–595.
83. Bhardwaj, S.; Fischer, I.; Ballé, J.; Chinen, T. An unsupervised information-theoretic perceptual quality metric. In Proceedings of the Advances in Neural Information Processing Systems, Virtual, 6–12 December 2020.
84. Alon, N.; Orlitsky, A. Source coding and graph entropies. *IEEE Trans. Inf. Theory* **1996**, *42*, 1329–1339. [CrossRef]
85. Harangi, V.; Niu, X.; Bai, B. Conditional graph entropy as an alternating minimization problem. *IEEE Trans. Inf. Theory* **2023**, *70*, 904–919. [CrossRef]
86. Harangi, V.; Niu, X.; Bai, B. Generalizing Körner's graph entropy to graphons. *Eur. J. Comb.* **2023**, *114*, 103779. [CrossRef]
87. Theis, L.; Salimans, T.; Hoffman, M.D.; Mentzer, F. Lossy compression with Gaussian diffusion. *arXiv* **2022**, arXiv:2206.08889.
88. Yang, R.; Mandt, S. Lossy image compression with conditional diffusion models. *Adv. Neural Inf. Process. Syst.* **2023**, *36*, 64971–64995.
89. Elata, N.; Michaeli, T.; Elad, M. Zero-Shot Image Compression with Diffusion-Based Posterior Sampling. *arXiv* **2024**, arXiv:2407.09896.
90. Fei, W.; Niu, X.; Zhou, P.; Hou, L.; Bai, B.; Deng, L.; Han, W. Extending Context Window of Large Language Models via Semantic Compression. In Proceedings of the Findings of the Association for Computational Linguistics: ACL 2024, Association for Computational Linguistics, Bangkok, Thailand, 11–16 August 2024; pp. 5169–5181.
91. Arda, E.; Yener, A. A Rate-Distortion Framework for Summarization. *arXiv* **2025**, arXiv:2501.13100.
92. Fei, W.; Niu, X.; Xie, G.; Liu, Y.; Bai, B.; Han, W. Efficient Prompt Compression with Evaluator Heads for Long-Context Transformer Inference. *arXiv* **2025**, arXiv:2501.12959.
93. Ballé, J.; Minnen, D.; Singh, S.; Hwang, S.J.; Johnston, N. Variational image compression with a scale hyperprior. In Proceedings of the International Conference on Learning Representations, Vancouver, BC, Canada, 30 April–3 May 2018.
94. Toderici, G.; Theis, L.; Johnston, N.; Agustsson, E.; Mentzer, F.; Ballé, J.; Shi, W.; Timofte, R. CLIC 2020: Challenge on learned image compression. 2020. Available online: https://www.tensorflow.org/datasets/catalog/clic (accessed on 26 February 2025).
95. Shannon, C.E. A mathematical theory of communication. *Bell Syst. Tech. J.* **1948**, *27*, 379–423. [CrossRef]
96. Goldsmith, A. Joint source/channel coding for wireless channels. In Proceedings of the IEEE Vehicular Technology Conference, Chicago, IL, USA, 25–28 July 1995; pp. 614–618.
97. Vembu, S.; Verdu, S.; Steinberg, Y. The source-channel separation theorem revisited. *IEEE Trans. Inf. Theory* **1995**, *41*, 44–54. [CrossRef]
98. Gündüz, D.; Qin, Z.; Aguerri, I.E.; Dhillon, H.S.; Yang, Z.; Yener, A.; Wong, K.K.; Chae, C.B. Beyond Transmitting Bits: Context, Semantics, and Task-Oriented Communications. *IEEE J. Sel. Areas Commun.* **2023**, *41*, 5–41. [CrossRef]
99. Kurka, D.B.; Gündüz, D. Bandwidth-agile image transmission with deep joint source-channel coding. *IEEE Trans. Wirel. Commun.* **2021**, *20*, 8081–8095. [CrossRef]
100. Tung, T.Y.; Gündüz, D. DeepWiVe: Deep-Learning-Aided Wireless Video Transmission. *IEEE J. Sel. Areas Commun.* **2022**, *40*, 2570–2583. [CrossRef]

101. Wang, M.; Zhang, Z.; Li, J.; Ma, M.; Fan, X. Deep Joint Source-Channel Coding for Multi-Task Network. *IEEE Signal Process. Lett.* **2021**, *28*, 1973–1977. [CrossRef]
102. Yang, M.; Bian, C.; Kim, H.S. OFDM-guided Deep Joint Source Channel Coding for Wireless Multipath Fading Channels. *IEEE Trans. Cogn. Commun. Netw.* **2022**, *8*, 584–599. [CrossRef]
103. Shao, Y.; Gunduz, D. Semantic Communications With Discrete-Time Analog Transmission: A PAPR Perspective. *IEEE Wirel. Commun. Lett.* **2023**, *12*, 510–514. [CrossRef]
104. Wu, H.; Shao, Y.; Mikolajczyk, K.; Gündüz, D. Channel-Adaptive Wireless Image Transmission With OFDM. *IEEE Wirel. Commun. Lett.* **2022**, *11*, 2400–2404. [CrossRef]
105. Niu, X.; Wang, X.; Gündüz, D.; Bai, B.; Chen, W.; Zhou, G. A hybrid wireless image transmission scheme with diffusion. In Proceedings of the 2023 IEEE 24th International Workshop on Signal Processing Advances in Wireless Communications (SPAWC), Shanghai, China, 25–28 September 2023; IEEE: New York, NY, USA, 2023; pp. 86–90.
106. Kountouris, M.; Pappas, N. Semantics-empowered communication for networked intelligent systems. *IEEE Commun. Mag.* **2021**, *59*, 96–102. [CrossRef]
107. Gündüz, D.; Chiariotti, F.; Huang, K.; Kalør, A.E.; Kobus, S.; Popovski, P. Timely and massive communication in 6G: Pragmatics, learning, and inference. *IEEE BITS Inf. Theory Mag.* **2023**, *3*, 27–40. [CrossRef]
108. Li, Z.; Wang, Q.; Wang, Y.; Chen, T. The Architecture of AI and Communication Integration towards 6G: An O-RAN Evolution. In Proceedings of the 30th Annual International Conference on Mobile Computing and Networking, Washington, DC, USA, 18–22 November 2024; pp. 2329–2334.
109. Cui, Q.; You, X.; Wei, N.; Nan, G.; Zhang, X.; Zhang, J.; Lyu, X.; Ai, M.; Tao, X.; Feng, Z.; et al. Overview of AI and Communication for 6G Network: Fundamentals, Challenges, and Future Research Opportunities. *arXiv* **2024**, arXiv:2412.14538.
110. Tao, M.; Zhou, Y.; Shi, Y.; Lu, J.; Cui, S.; Lu, J.; Letaief, K.B. *Federated Edge Learning for 6G: Foundations, Methodologies, and Applications*; IEEE: New York, NY, USA, 2024.
111. Park, J.; Ko, S.W.; Choi, J.; Kim, S.L.; Choi, J.; Bennis, M. Towards semantic MAC protocols for 6G: From protocol learning to language-oriented approaches. *IEEE BITS Inf. Theory Mag.* **2024** *4*, 59–72. [CrossRef]
112. Van Huynh, N.; Wang, J.; Du, H.; Hoang, D.T.; Niyato, D.; Nguyen, D.N.; Kim, D.I.; Letaief, K.B. Generative AI for physical layer communications: A survey. *IEEE Trans. Cogn. Commun. Netw.* **2024**, *10*, 706–728. [CrossRef]
113. Han, X.; Wu, Y.; Gao, Z.; Feng, B.; Shi, Y.; Gündüz, D.; Zhang, W. SCSC: A Novel Standards-Compatible Semantic Communication Framework for Image Transmission. *IEEE Trans. Commun.* 2025, *early access*
114. Tao, Z.; Guo, Y.; He, G.; Huang, Y.; You, X. Deep learning-based modeling of 5G core control plane for 5G network digital twin. *IEEE Trans. Cogn. Commun. Netw.* **2023**, *10*, 238–251. [CrossRef]
115. Zheng, J.; Du, B.; Du, H.; Kang, J.; Niyato, D.; Zhang, H. Energy-Efficient Resource Allocation in Generative AI-Aided Secure Semantic Mobile Networks. *IEEE Trans. Mob. Comput.* **2024**, *23*, 11422–11435. [CrossRef]
116. Liu, Z.; Du, H.; Huang, L.; Gao, Z.; Niyato, D. Joint Model Caching and Resource Allocation in Generative AI-Enabled Wireless Edge Networks. *arXiv* **2024**, arXiv:2411.08672.
117. Wang, X.; Feng, L.; Zhou, F.; Li, W. Joint Power Allocation and Reliability Optimization with Generative AI for Wireless Networked Control Systems. In Proceedings of the 2024 IEEE/CIC International Conference on Communications in China (ICCC Workshops), Hangzhou, China, 7–9 August 2024; IEEE: New York, NY, USA, 2024; pp. 197–202.
118. Tolba, B.; Elsabrouty, M.; Abdu-Aguye, M.G.; Gacanin, H.; Kasem, H.M. Massive MIMO CSI feedback based on generative adversarial network. *IEEE Commun. Lett.* **2020**, *24*, 2805–2808. [CrossRef]
119. Zeng, Y.; Qiao, L.; Gao, Z.; Qin, T.; Wu, Z.; Khalaf, E.; Chen, S.; Guizani, M. CSI-GPT: Integrating generative pre-trained transformer with federated-tuning to acquire downlink massive MIMO channels. *IEEE Trans. Veh. Technol.* **2024**, *74*, 5187–5192. [CrossRef]
120. Zhao, Z.; Meng, F.; Li, H.; Li, X.; Zhu, G. Mining Limited Data Sufficiently: A BERT-inspired Approach for CSI Time Series Application in Wireless Communication and Sensing. *arXiv* **2024**, arXiv:2412.06861.
121. Balevi, E.; Doshi, A.; Jalal, A.; Dimakis, A.; Andrews, J.G. High dimensional channel estimation using deep generative networks. *IEEE J. Sel. Areas Commun.* **2020**, *39*, 18–30. [CrossRef]
122. Arvinte, M.; Tamir, J.I. MIMO channel estimation using score-based generative models. *IEEE Trans. Wirel. Commun.* **2022**, *22*, 3698–3713. [CrossRef]
123. Fesl, B.; Strasser, M.B.F.; Joham, M.; Utschick, W. Diffusion-based generative prior for low-complexity MIMO channel estimation. *IEEE Wirel. Commun. Lett.* **2024**, *13*, 3493–3497. [CrossRef]
124. Yang, T.; Zhang, P.; Zheng, M.; Shi, Y.; Jing, L.; Huang, J.; Li, N. WirelessGPT: A Generative Pre-trained Multi-task Learning Framework for Wireless Communication. *arXiv* **2025**, arXiv:2502.06877.
125. Xie, H.; Qin, Z.; Li, G.Y.; Juang, B.H. Deep learning enabled semantic communication systems. *IEEE Trans. Signal Process.* **2021**, *69*, 2663–2675. [CrossRef]

126. Erdemir, E.; Tung, T.Y.; Dragotti, P.L.; Gunduz, D. Generative Joint Source-Channel Coding for Semantic Image Transmission. *arXiv* **2022**, arXiv:2211.13772. [CrossRef]
127. Zhang, G.; Li, H.; Cai, Y.; Hu, Q.; Yu, G.; Qin, Z. Progressive Learned Image Transmission for Semantic Communication Using Hierarchical VAE. *IEEE Trans. Cogn. Commun. Netw.* 2025, *early access*
128. Zhang, M.; Wu, H.; Zhu, G.; Jin, R.; Chen, X.; Gündüz, D. Semantics-Guided Diffusion for Deep Joint Source-Channel Coding in Wireless Image Transmission. *arXiv* **2025**, arXiv:2501.01138.
129. Zhang, H.; Tao, M. SNR-EQ-JSCC: Joint Source-Channel Coding with SNR-Based Embedding and Query. *IEEE Wirel. Commun. Lett.* **2025**, *14*, 881–885.
130. Li, B.; Liu, Y.; Niu, X.; Bait, B.; Han, W.; Deng, L.; Gunduz, D. Extreme Video Compression with Prediction Using Pre-trained Diffusion Models. In Proceedings of the 2024 16th International Conference on Wireless Communications and Signal Processing (WCSP), Hefei, China, 24–26 October 2024; IEEE: New York, NY, USA, 2024; pp. 1449–1455.
131. Yilmaz, S.F.; Niu, X.; Bai, B.; Han, W.; Deng, L.; Gündüz, D. High perceptual quality wireless image delivery with denoising diffusion models. In Proceedings of the IEEE INFOCOM 2024-IEEE Conference on Computer Communications Workshops (INFOCOM WKSHPS), Vancouver, BC, Canada, 20 May 2024; IEEE: New York, NY, USA, 2024; pp. 1–5.
132. Guo, L.; Chen, W.; Sun, Y.; Ai, B.; Pappas, N.; Quek, T. Diffusion-Driven Semantic Communication for Generative Models with Bandwidth Constraints. *arXiv* **2024**, arXiv:2407.18468. [CrossRef]
133. Pei, J.; Feng, C.; Wang, P.; Tabassum, H.; Shi, D. Latent Diffusion Model-Enabled Low-Latency Semantic Communication in the Presence of Semantic Ambiguities and Wireless Channel Noises. *IEEE Trans. Wirel. Commun.* 2025, *early access*
134. Tung, T.Y.; Kurka, D.B.; Jankowski, M.; Gündüz, D. DeepJSCC-Q: Constellation Constrained Deep Joint Source-Channel Coding. *IEEE J. Sel. Areas Inf. Theory* **2022**, *3*, 720–731.
135. Kurka, D.B.; Gündüz, D. DeepJSCC-f: Deep joint source-channel coding of images with feedback. *IEEE J. Sel. Areas Inf. Theory* **2020**, *1*, 178–193.
136. Geng, Y.; Niu, X.; Bai, B.; Han, W. Capacity Bounds of Broadcast Channel with a Full-Duplex Base-User Pair. In Proceedings of the 2024 IEEE Information Theory Workshop (ITW), Shenzhen, China, 24–28 November 2024; IEEE: New York, NY, USA, 2024; pp. 145–150.
137. Jiao, T.; Ye, C.; Huang, Y.; Feng, Y.; Xiao, Z.; Xu, Y.; He, D.; Guan, Y.; Yang, B.; Chang, J.; et al. 6G-Oriented CSI-Based Multi-Modal Pre-Ttaining and Downstream Task Adaptation Paradigm. In Proceedings of the 2024 IEEE International Conference on Communications Workshops (ICC Workshops), Denver, CO, USA, 9–13 June 2024; IEEE: New York, NY, USA, 2024; pp. 1389–1394.
138. Delfani, E.; Pappas, N. Optimizing Information Freshness in Constrained IoT Systems: A Token-Based Approach. *IEEE Trans. Commun.* 2024, *early access*
139. Li, J.; Zhang, W. Asymptotically Optimal Joint Sampling and Compression for Timely Status Updates: Age-Distortion Tradeoff. *IEEE Trans. Veh. Technol.* **2024**, *74*, 2338–2352.
140. Qiao, L.; Mashhadi, M.B.; Gao, Z.; Gündüz, D. Token-Domain Multiple Access: Exploiting Semantic Orthogonality for Collision Mitigation. *arXiv* **2025**, arXiv:2502.06118.
141. Bachmann, R.; Allardice, J.; Mizrahi, D.; Fini, E.; Kar, O.F.; Amirloo, E.; El-Nouby, A.; Zamir, A.; Dehghan, A. FlexTok: Resampling Images into 1D Token Sequences of Flexible Length. *arXiv* **2025**, arXiv:2502.13967.
142. Sargent, K.; Hsu, K.; Johnson, J.; Fei-Fei, L.; Wu, J. Flow to the Mode: Mode-Seeking Diffusion Autoencoders for State-of-the-Art Image Tokenization. *arXiv* **2025**, arXiv:2503.11056.
143. Yu, L.; Lezama, J.; Gundavarapu, N.B.; Versari, L.; Sohn, K.; Minnen, D.; Cheng, Y.; Gupta, A.; Gu, X.; Hauptmann, A.G.; et al. Language Model Beats Diffusion-Tokenizer is key to visual generation. In Proceedings of the International Conference on Learning Representations, Vienna, Austria, 7–11 May 2024.
144. Yang, W.; Du, H.; Liew, Z.Q.; Lim, W.Y.B.; Xiong, Z.; Niyato, D.; Chi, X.; Shen, X.; Miao, C. Semantic communications for future internet: Fundamentals, applications, and challenges. *IEEE Commun. Surv. Tutorials* **2022**, *25*, 213–250.
145. Luo, X.; Chen, H.H.; Guo, Q. Semantic communications: Overview, open issues, and future research directions. *IEEE Wirel. Commun.* **2022**, *29*, 210–219. [CrossRef]
146. Guo, S.; Wang, Y.; Zhang, N.; Su, Z.; Luan, T.H.; Tian, Z.; Shen, X. A survey on semantic communication networks: Architecture, security, and privacy. *IEEE Commun. Surv. Tutor.* 2024, *early access*
147. Chaccour, C.; Saad, W.; Debbah, M.; Han, Z.; Poor, H.V. Less data, more knowledge: Building next generation semantic communication networks. *IEEE Commun. Surv. Tutor.* **2024**, *27*, 37–76. [CrossRef]
148. Wu, H.; Chen, G.; Gunduz, D. Actions Speak Louder Than Words: Rate-Reward Trade-off in Markov Decision Processes. In Proceedings of the The Thirteenth International Conference on Learning Representations, Singapore, 24–28 April 2025.

149. Hamdi, Y.; Niu, X.; Bai, B.; Gunduz, D. Non-interactive Remote Coordination. In Proceedings of the Workshop on Machine Learning and Compression, NeurIPS, Vancouver, BC, Canada, 15 December 2024.
150. Zhang, G.; Yue, Y.; Li, Z.; Yun, S.; Wan, G.; Wang, K.; Cheng, D.; Yu, J.X.; Chen, T. Cut the crap: An economical communication pipeline for LLM-based multi-agent systems. In Proceedings of the International Conference on Learning Representations, Singapore, 24–28 April 2025.

entropy

MDPI

Article

Semantic Arithmetic Coding Using Synonymous Mappings

Zijian Liang [1], Kai Niu [1,2,*], Jin Xu [1] and Ping Zhang [3]

[1] Key Laboratory of Universal Wireless Communications, Ministry of Education, Beijing University of Posts and Telecommunications, Beijing 100876, China; liang1060279345@bupt.edu.cn (Z.L.); xujinbupt@bupt.edu.cn (J.X.)

[2] Department of Broadband Communication, Pengcheng Laboratory, Shenzhen 518055, China

[3] State Key Laboratory of Networking and Switching Technology, Beijing University of Posts and Telecommunications, Beijing 100876, China; pzhang@bupt.edu.cn

* Correspondence: niukai@bupt.edu.cn

Abstract: Recent semantic communication methods explore effective ways to expand the communication paradigm and improve the performance of communication systems. Nonetheless, a common problem with these methods is that the essence of semantics is not explicitly pointed out and directly utilized. A new epistemology suggests that synonymity, which is revealed as the fundamental feature of semantics, guides the establishment of semantic information theory from a novel viewpoint. Building on this theoretical basis, this paper proposes a semantic arithmetic coding (SAC) method for semantic lossless compression using intuitive synonymity. By constructing reasonable synonymous mappings and performing arithmetic coding procedures over synonymous sets, SAC can achieve higher compression efficiency for meaning-contained source sequences at the semantic level and approximate the semantic entropy limits. Experimental results on edge texture map compression show a significant improvement in coding efficiency using SAC without semantic losses compared to traditional arithmetic coding, demonstrating its effectiveness.

Keywords: semantics; arithmetic coding; synonymity; synonymous mappings; semantic lossless compression

1. Introduction

In recent years, research on semantic communications has taken a different development route from traditional communication technologies. While traditional communications separately optimize source compression and data transmission guided by Shannon's classical information theory [1,2], recent works on semantic communications mostly focus on exploring end-to-end performance optimization utilizing deep neural networks. As a typical method, deep joint source-channel coding (JSCC)-based methods effectively improve the end-to-end performance of communication systems for diverse source modalities, whether in point-to-point [3–8] or multi-user transmission scenarios [9–13]. However, these works are empirical in processing semantic information: they often refer to the high-dimensional space representation from neural network processing as "semantic information" [3,14], following expressions in the field of natural language processing (NLP) or computer vision (CV). Additionally, the optimization direction of these works still relies on measures in classical information theory, such as mean-squared error (MSE) [6], cross-entropy [4], and Kullback–Leibler (KL) divergence [7]. They do not deeply explore the concept of semantic information or guide information processing based on specific semantic information viewpoints and theoretical frameworks.

As a critical cornerstone of semantic communication, a complete semantic information theory framework can provide theoretical guidance for evaluating semantic abstraction abilities, measuring semantic processing bounds, and aiding in designing semantic communication methods [15]. In particular, it can help us recognize the problems that still exist in semantic information processing but have been overlooked due to the current trend in the evolution of semantic communication methods, such as how to identify the core of specific semantic information and how to approach its compression limits.

However, compared with the rapid development of semantic communication methods, semantic information theory still lacks a unified viewpoint, which makes the problems hard to solve. Since Weaver discussed three-level communication problems [16] in the 1950s, researchers have explored semantic information theory from various viewpoints, ranging from the perspective of logical probability [17–20] to fuzzy information theory [21–23]. Nevertheless, none of these theories has become a universal guiding theory for semantic communication methods, as these viewpoints face challenges in general scenarios. As theoretical research deepens, some basic viewpoints have gained consensus, including, but not limited to, the existence of background knowledge (referred to as the knowledge base) [20,24–26] and the hiddenness/invisibility of semantic information (referred to as the meaning behind the message) [27,28]. Based on these consensuses, various sub-viewpoints have been proposed to interpret semantic information in different directions. For example, some works suggest that the semantic information of the message can be extracted based on the knowledge base [29], and some works suggest that semantic information is closely tied to the selection of specific downstream tasks [14,30]. Therefore, various mathematical models have been established based on these viewpoints, and different forms of semantic entropy have thus been defined. As a result, there is still no unified definition of semantic entropy (unlike Shannon entropy), and most definitions lack the operational relevance that Shannon entropy has to many engineering problems [31], which makes it difficult to characterize the theoretical bounds of semantic information compression.

Based on the above situation, we recognize that a unified semantic information theory should be simple and highly abstract while guiding engineering exploration, especially in semantic information compression. With the proposal of a semantic information theory framework based on synonymity [32] (The official version was published in the *Journal on Communications*, Volume 6, 2024. Due to issues with the hyperlink provided by its DOI number, please refer to the following web link: https://www.joconline.com.cn/en/article/doi/10.11959/j.issn.1000-436x.2024111/, accessed on 25 June 2024), theoretical unification may become possible. Founded on commonly existing synonymous relationships in source data across diverse modalities and different task-oriented scenarios, this viewpoint establishes the framework based on the "synonymous relationship" between semantic information and syntactic information and constructs a complete semantic information theory system, including basic measures and coding theorems. The basic viewpoint of synonymity aligns with Shannon's 1953 viewpoint [33], which defines the actual information of a stochastic process as "that which is common to all stochastic processes which may be obtained from the original by reversible encoding operations". Additionally, the author believes previous viewpoints can be considered as different synonymous relationships within this theoretical framework and further proves that the proposed semantic information theory is compatible with classical information theory—specifically, that the synonymous set only contains one syntactic message. Such a viewpoint makes it possible to establish a unified semantic entropy measure, design a corresponding semantic entropy algorithm, and improve compression efficiency while maintaining specific semantic information. We observed that similar ideas have appeared in semantic compression methods for tabular data [34–36]; however, we should point out that this methodology should be adaptable to any source data type under the premise of well-designed synonymous mappings.

In this paper, we focus on designing a semantic entropy coding algorithm to improve compression efficiency while maintaining common semantic information determined by synonymous mappings and analyzing their theoretical limits. Specifically, we propose semantic arithmetic coding (SAC), an arithmetic coding (AC) method for semantic lossless compression built on synonymous mappings. The contributions of our work are as follows:

- **A semantic arithmetic coding algorithm built on synonymous mappings.** By constructing reasonable synonymous mappings to partition synonymous sets and determine the common semantic information, SAC performs the arithmetic encoding procedures over the synonymous set corresponding to the coding syntactic symbol, thereby achieving higher compression efficiency under intuitive semantic lossless conditions. Based on the corresponding decoding and post-processing processes, the decoded sequence preserves the common semantic information of the source data while reducing syntactic distortion. The computational complexity analyses of the SAC encoding and decoding procedures are also provided accordingly.
- **Semantic compression limit analysis of bidirectional squeezing.** The theoretical limit approachability to the semantic entropy of our proposed SAC is validated based on an extension of the code length theorem of arithmetic codes. This shows that, with an ideal semantic arithmetic code design, a compression efficiency very close to the semantic entropy limit built on synonymity can be achieved.
- **Performance verification on edge texture map datasets.** By designing appropriate synonymous mapping rules for the processing units on the BIPEDv2 edge texture feature map dataset [37] and using the proposed semantic arithmetic code for compression, we achieve a 20.5% improvement in average compression efficiency over classical arithmetic coding, which strictly requires syntactic losslessness. This is achieved while maintaining consistency with the semantic information of the original edge texture image and ensuring low syntactic distortion.

Herein, we emphasize that our work focuses on using the proposed semantic arithmetic code to approximate the corresponding semantic compression limit under reasonable synonymous mapping. How to construct a more effective synonymous mapping to minimize the semantic compression limit, as another key issue in semantic information theory [32], requires more future work.

The rest of this paper is organized as follows. Section 2 presents the system model of the semantic lossless source coding and introduces semantic entropy based on synonymous mappings. In Section 3, we present semantic arithmetic coding in detail, including its encoding procedure, decoding procedure, optional syntactic post-processing, and corresponding theoretical limit analysis on the average code length. Section 4 uses the edge texture semantics of natural images as the object, applies SAC for semantic lossless encoding and decoding, and verifies SAC's effectiveness through numerical results. Finally, we conclude this paper in Section 5.

2. System Model and Theoretical Limits

In this section, we briefly review the system model of semantic lossless source coding, along with its theoretical compression limit based on a critical feature of synonymous mappings.

2.1. System Model

Semantic lossless source coding is an extension of classic lossless source coding under the guidance of semantic information theory, with its goal still being to compress source data. However, unlike classic lossless source coding, semantic lossless source coding focuses on ensuring no distinctions in implicit meanings between sequences before encoding and after decoding, without strictly requiring complete consistency in their explicit syntactical forms.

As stated in [32], all perceptible messages are syntactic information, and all such syntactic information is presented to illuminate the underlying semantic information. Therefore, we can establish the system model for semantic source coding as follows:

$$\tilde{\boldsymbol{u}} \xrightarrow{f(\cdot)} \boldsymbol{u} \xrightarrow{e(\cdot)} \boldsymbol{b} \xrightarrow{d(\cdot)} \hat{\boldsymbol{u}} \xrightarrow{g(\cdot)} \hat{\tilde{\boldsymbol{u}}}, \tag{1}$$

where $\tilde{\boldsymbol{u}}$ and $\hat{\tilde{\boldsymbol{u}}}$ are the invisible source and reconstructed semantic variable sequences, and $\boldsymbol{u}$ and $\hat{\boldsymbol{u}}$ are the perceptible source and reconstructed syntactic variable sequences, respectively. We assume that m represents the length of the syntactic sequences $\boldsymbol{u}$ and $\hat{\boldsymbol{u}}$. The mapping $f(\cdot)$ and its reverse $g(\cdot)$ represent the invisible conversion relationship between the semantic information and the syntactic information, i.e., the synonymous mappings and synonymous de-mappings presented by [32].

For the main process of the coding, the semantic source encoder $e(\cdot)$ operates on the syntactic sequence $\boldsymbol{u}$, encoding it into a codeword sequence $\boldsymbol{b}$ of length l, and the corresponding semantic source decoder $d(\cdot)$ transforms the codeword sequence $\boldsymbol{b}$ into the reconstructed syntactic sequence $\hat{\boldsymbol{u}}$. Only consistency between the semantic sequences $\tilde{\boldsymbol{u}}$ and $\hat{\tilde{\boldsymbol{u}}}$ needs to be guaranteed in the coding procedures; thus, the lossless constraints between the syntactic sequences $\boldsymbol{u}$ and $\hat{\boldsymbol{u}}$ can be relaxed, which makes the coding a lossy source coding from a syntactic perspective.

Herein, we state that, in general cases, synonymous mappings (constructed from a single piece of semantic information to multiple syntactic representations) must first be applied to the sequence data to build non-overlapping synonymous sets, such as natural languages, images, and audio sequences. This is because when the information sequence is sufficiently long, contextual structures and characteristics such as Markov chains [38] can help determine the unique meaning of polysemous or homonymous words within the sequence. To illustrate this statement, we provide an example using the following English sentence as the data source $\boldsymbol{u}$:

"I walk along a river bank".

In this sentence, most words have a single meaning, while the word "bank" itself has multiple meanings, such as a financial institution and the side of a river. However, when placed in this sentence (especially after the word "river"), the meaning of the word "bank" collapses into a specific interpretation, i.e., "the side of the water".

Based on this simple example, we can summarize a basic principle for determining synonymous mapping relationships: **It should first be considered at the sequence level and then applied to individual elements based on contextual relationships within the sequence for practical implementation**. This principle means the following:

- If a sequence cannot determine a unique meaning for each element, the sequence length must be extended until its context is sufficient to make this determination, and then treating the extended sequence as the processing object;
- Conversely, if a definite meaning can be independently determined for each element in the sequence, the synonymous mappings can be directly applied to each element;
- Furthermore, if all elements in the sequence follow an i.i.d assumption, in which each element represents diverse meanings under the same attribute, then each element in the sequence can be assigned the same synonymous mapping.

We emphasize that the principle of first considering synonymous mappings at the sequence level cannot only be derived from simple examples but can also be rigorously proven based on the semantic asymptotic equipartition property (AEP) proposed in [32] under the assumption of sufficiently long syntactic sequences, providing sufficient theoretical support.

In view of this, the mathematical model and algorithm design for establishing synonymous relationships for each variable in the sequence, as described in the following text, adhere to this principle.

2.2. Synonymous Mappings-Based Semantic Entropy

As remarked in [32], synonymity is a critical source of the relationships between semantic information and syntactic information since, in most instances, single-meaning semantic information has myriad syntactic presentation forms. However, it should be emphasized that directly processing semantic information is not feasible, as semantic information is hidden behind the message (syntactic information) and thus invisible. Thus, semantic information processing must construct entities that can reflect semantic content. Based on the synonymous relationship we previously established, syntactic information with similar meanings can be grouped into synonymous sets, which serve as entities that reflect semantic information. Therefore, processing information at the level of these entities is then equivalent to processing semantic information. In light of this, for semantic information processing, constructing synonymous sets based on synonymous relationships is essential.

Figure 1 shows an example of the synonymous mappings $f_i : \tilde{\mathcal{U}}_i \to \mathcal{U}_i$ between the semantic information set $\tilde{\mathcal{U}}_i$ and the syntactic information set $\mathcal{U}_i$ for the i-th variable in the source sequences $\tilde{\boldsymbol{u}}$ and $\boldsymbol{u}$. From this example, a general rule can be observed: semantic elements can be mapped to an equal number of synonymous sets that represent different meanings and contain all the possible syntactic values without overlap between any two synonymous sets.

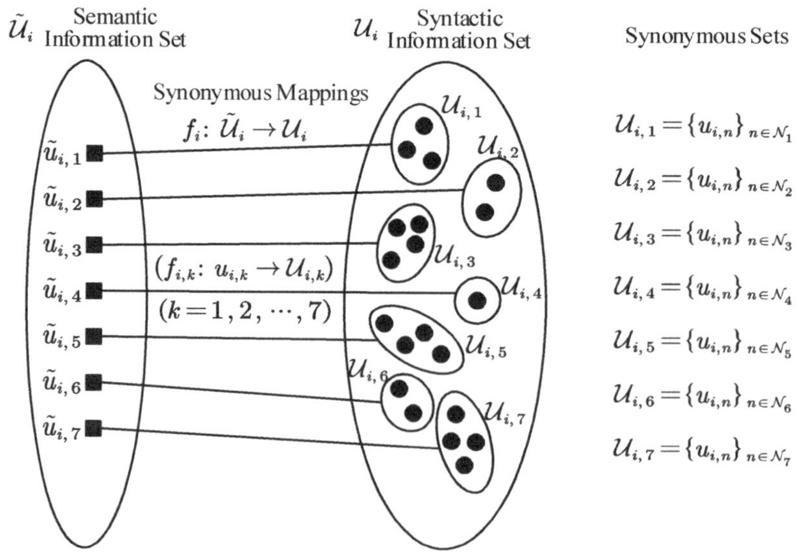

Figure 1. An example of the synonymous mappings and the corresponding synonymous sets.

For an i.i.d semantic sequence $\tilde{\boldsymbol{u}}$ with unified $f : \tilde{\mathcal{U}} \to \mathcal{U}$ for $\forall i = 1, 2, \ldots, m$, the semantic entropy $H_s(\tilde{\mathcal{U}})$ is expressed as

$$H_s(\tilde{\mathcal{U}}) = -\sum_k p(\mathcal{U}_k) \log p(\mathcal{U}_k), \tag{2}$$

where the probability of the k-th synonymous set is

$$p(\mathcal{U}_k) = \sum_{n \in \mathcal{N}_k} p(u_n), \tag{3}$$

where $\mathcal{N}_k$ denotes a set that contains the indices of the syntactic values with the same meaning as the semantic element k. It should be noted that a synonymous relationship itself is a form of a semantic knowledge base, which is consistent with the current consensus: by applying specific prior knowledge or criteria to determine synonymous relationships for actual source information, all syntactic data within the constructed synonymous sets share common information corresponding to that prior knowledge or criteria.

In [32], we demonstrated that for single-symbol semantic source coding, with the semantic prefix code performed over the synonymous sets, the average code length can approach the theoretical semantic entropy limit $H_s(\tilde{\mathcal{U}})$ without semantic losses by providing a theorem based on the semantic Kraft inequality. Naturally, the same effect can be achieved by performing semantic prefix coding on the sequences, leading to our proposed semantic arithmetic coding.

3. Semantic Arithmetic Coding

Consider a sequence compression procedure with arithmetic coding methods for the syntactic sequence $\boldsymbol{u}$, in which each syntactic variable u_i exhibits a similar synonymous relationship to that shown in Figure 1, based on the basic determining principle. Traditional arithmetic coding directly performs the coding procedure on each syntactic variable u_i without considering the implicit meaning, thereby lacking certain compression efficiency due to the sole requirement of semantic losslessness. In this section, we propose semantic arithmetic coding (SAC) using synonymous mappings for efficient semantic compression with intuitive semantic synonymity.

3.1. The Encoding Procedure

Figure 2 shows the general framework of the SAC encoding procedure. Similar to the traditional method [2,39], the SAC encoder uniquely maps the message $\boldsymbol{u}$ to a sub-interval on the $[0, 1)$ interval and outputs the shortest codeword represented by a binary fraction b in this sub-interval as the encoding result. The difference is that, to achieve semantic-oriented compression, the SAC encoder constructs reasonable synonymous mappings to determine the synonymous set $\mathcal{U}_{i,r_i}$ for each syntactic variable u_i and performs the coding interval update procedure over each determined synonymous set $\mathcal{U}_{i,r_i}$.

As a specific description of the process shown in Figure 2, the encoding process of the SAC encoder is detailed in Algorithm 1. With an initialized encoding interval $[L_0, H_0) = [0, 1)$ and an interval length of $R_0 = 1$, the SAC encoder performs semantic compression through a series of iterations, in which each iteration i includes the following:

- *Construct synonymous mappings:* For all the syntactic values $\{u_{i,n}\}$ of the i-th variable, construct synonymous mappings $f_i : \tilde{\mathcal{U}}_i \to \mathcal{U}_i$ under specific semantic criteria to partition synonymous sets $\{\mathcal{U}_{i,k}\}_{k=1,\ldots,|\tilde{\mathcal{U}}_i|}$, in which $\mathcal{U}_{i,k} = \{u_{i,n}\}_{n \in \mathcal{N}_k}$;
- *Determine synonymous sets:* According to the actual value of the syntactic variable u_i, determine a synonymous set $\mathcal{U}_{i,r_i}$ such that $u_i \in \mathcal{U}_{i,r_i}, r_i \in \{1, \ldots, |\tilde{\mathcal{U}}_i|\}$;

- *Calculate probabilities:* For all synonymous sets $\{\mathcal{U}_{i,k}\}$, calculate their probabilities with

$$p(\mathcal{U}_{i,k}) = \sum_{n \in \mathcal{N}_k} p(u_{i,k}). \quad (4)$$

- *Update encoding interval:* According to the determined synonymous set $\mathcal{U}_{i,r_i}$ and the probabilities for all synonymous sets $p(\mathcal{U}_{i,k}), k = 1, \ldots, |\tilde{\mathcal{U}}_i|$, update the encoding interval $[L_i, H_i)$ and its interval length R_i with

$$\begin{cases} L_i = L_{i-1} + \sum_{k=1}^{r_i - 1} p(\mathcal{U}_{i,k}), \\ H_i = L_i + p(\mathcal{U}_{i,r_i}) \cdot R_{i-1}, \\ R_i = p(\mathcal{U}_{i,r_i}) \cdot R_{i-1} = H_i - L_i. \end{cases} \quad (5)$$

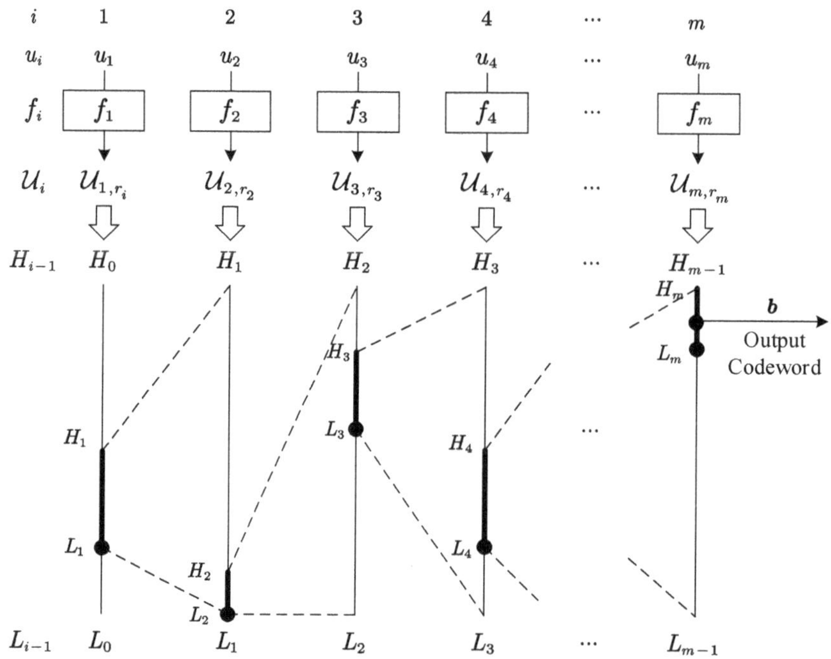

Figure 2. A schematic diagram of the SAC encoding procedure.

Once the encoding interval update process corresponding to the last variable u_m is completed, the SAC encoder concludes its iterations. Then, it determines a shortest binary fraction $\boldsymbol{b} = (b_1, \ldots, b_l)$ as the output codeword such that its corresponding decimal fraction c belongs to the final interval $[L_m, H_m)$ and satisfies

$$c = b_1 \cdot 2^{-1} + b_2 \cdot 2^{-2} + \ldots + b_l \cdot 2^{-l}. \quad (6)$$

Finally, the SAC encoder transmits the output codeword $\boldsymbol{b}$ to the receiver for reconstructing the syntactic sequence. As the necessary information, the length m of the syntactic sequence $\boldsymbol{u}$, along with the synonymous set partitions of each syntactic variable and their corresponding probability information, must be synchronized at the receiving end.

Algorithm 1: Encoding algorithm of SAC encoder

Data: Input syntactic sequence $\boldsymbol{u} = (u_1, \ldots, u_m)$.
Result: Output codeword b.

Initialize: The encoding interval $[L_0, H_0) = [0, 1)$, interval length $R_0 = 1$, variable index $i = 1$.
repeat
  Construct synonymous mappings $f_i : \tilde{\mathcal{U}}_i \to \mathcal{U}_i$.
  Determine synonymous set $\mathcal{U}_{i,r_i}$, s.t., $u_i \in \mathcal{U}_{i,r_i}$.
  Calculate probabilities for all synonymous sets $p(\mathcal{U}_{i,k})$ with Equation (4).
  Update encoding interval based on $\mathcal{U}_{i,r_i}$: $[L_{i-1}, H_{i-1}) \to [L_i, H_i)$ with Equation (5).
until $i \leq m$;
Determine the shortest fractional partial of the binary fraction as the codeword $\boldsymbol{b}$, s.t. its corresponding decimal fraction $c \in [L_i, H_i)$.
return *The output codeword* $\boldsymbol{b}$.

When only the i.i.d. assumption is considered, the possible values of each syntactic variable, the synonymous mappings along with the synonymous set partitions, and the corresponding probabilities are exactly the same. In this case, the process of SAC encoding is equivalent to a simplified procedure that first converts the syntactic sequence into a synonymous set sequence using the predefined synonymous mapping rules, then treats the synonymous subset sequence as a new syntactic sequence and compresses it using traditional arithmetic coding.

Herein, we provide a complexity analysis of the SAC encoding process and compare it with the general arithmetic encoding process.

First, we consider the standard case of SAC encoding. Considering that the number of syntactic values for each variable may be different, as well as the number of synonymous sets, we assume that the average number of syntactic values per variable in the sequence is $|\bar{\mathcal{U}}|$, and the average number of corresponding synonymous sets is $|\bar{\tilde{\mathcal{U}}}|$. These two averages are used to evaluate the encoding complexity.

For a syntactic source sequence with length m, the computational complexity of calculating the probabilities of the synonymous sets for each variable is expressed as $O(|\bar{\mathcal{U}}| \cdot m)$. Additionally, the complexity of updating the coding interval is expressed as $O(|\bar{\tilde{\mathcal{U}}}| \cdot m)$ since only the scale of the synonymous sets is considered. Therefore, the computational complexity of SAC can be summarized as $O((|\bar{\mathcal{U}}| + |\bar{\tilde{\mathcal{U}}}|) \cdot m)$, which is slightly higher than the complexity of general arithmetic encoding $O(|\bar{\mathcal{U}}| \cdot m)$.

However, for a special case when only the i.i.d. assumption is considered, the number of syntactic values is $|\mathcal{U}|$, and the number of corresponding synonymous sets is $|\tilde{\mathcal{U}}|$ for all the variables in the sequence. In this case, the synonymous mappings can be calculated once, regardless of the sequence length m. So, the computational complexity of SAC encoding is reduced to $O(|\mathcal{U}| + |\tilde{\mathcal{U}}| \cdot m) \approx O(|\tilde{\mathcal{U}}| \cdot m)$, which is less than the complexity of general arithmetic encoding $O(|\mathcal{U}| \cdot m)$ since $|\tilde{\mathcal{U}}| \leq |\mathcal{U}|$.

3.2. The Decoding Procedure

As a duality process within SAC encoding, the decoding procedure of the SAC decoder is presented in Algorithm 2. To reconstruct the syntactic sequence from the received codeword $\boldsymbol{b}$, the SAC decoder initializes a decoding interval $[L'_0, H'_0) = [0, 1)$ with an interval length of $R'_0 = 1$ and then utilizes the decimal fraction c corresponding to the codeword $\boldsymbol{b}$ to determine the values of each syntactic variable. The determination process is also performed through a series of iterations, in which each iteration i includes the following:

- *Construct synonymous mappings:* For all the syntactic values $\{\hat{u}_{i,n}\}$ of the i-th reconstructed variable, construct opposite synonymous mappings $g_i : \hat{\mathcal{U}}_i \rightarrow \hat{\hat{\mathcal{U}}}_i$ according to the synchronized synonymous sets information at the sending end, and accordingly partition synonymous sets $\{\hat{\mathcal{U}}_{i,k}\}_{k=1,\ldots,|\tilde{\mathcal{U}}_i|}$, in which $\hat{\mathcal{U}}_{i,k} = \{\hat{u}_{i,n}\}_{n\in\hat{\mathcal{N}}_k}$;
- *Synchronize probabilities:* To guarantee successful semantic decoding, the probabilities of all synonymous sets should be synchronized with the sending end, i.e., $p(\hat{\mathcal{U}}_{i,k}) = p(\mathcal{U}_{i,k})$. The probability of each syntactic value needs to be assigned, satisfying

$$p(\hat{\mathcal{U}}_{i,k}) = \sum_{n\in\hat{\mathcal{N}}_k} p(\hat{u}_{i,k}). \tag{7}$$

- *Determine synonymous sets:* Based on the decimal fraction c and the decoding interval $[L'_{i-1}, H'_{i-1})$, determine the reconstructed synonymous set $\hat{\mathcal{U}}_{i,r_i}, r_i \in \{1,\ldots,|\tilde{\mathcal{U}}_i|\}$ such that

$$\frac{c - L'_{i-1}}{R'_{i-1}} \in \left[\sum_{k=1}^{r_i-1} p(\hat{\mathcal{U}}_{i,k}), \sum_{k=1}^{r_i} p(\hat{\mathcal{U}}_{i,k})\right). \tag{8}$$

- *Export syntactic value:* Select a syntactic value $\hat{u}_{i,n}$ from the determined synonymous set $\hat{\mathcal{U}}_{i,r_i}$ as the reconstructed syntactic value $\hat{u}_i$. It can be selected based on certain rules, such as the maximum probability-based selection within the synonymous set, normalized probability-based random selection based on the normalized probability of each syntactic value in the determined synonymous set

$$p'(\hat{u}_{i,n}) = \frac{p(\hat{u}_{i,n})}{p(\hat{\mathcal{U}}_{i,r_i})}, n \in \mathcal{N}_{r_i}, \tag{9}$$

or context correlation-based selection based on already-reconstructed syntactic sequences.
- *Update decoding interval:* Based on the determined synonymous set $\hat{\mathcal{U}}_{i,r_i}$ and the probabilities for all synonymous sets $p(\hat{\mathcal{U}}_{i,k}), k = 1,\ldots,|\hat{\mathcal{U}}_i|$, update the decoding interval $[L'_i, H'_i)$ and its interval length R'_i with

$$\begin{cases} L'_i = L'_{i-1} + \sum_{k=1}^{r_i-1} p(\hat{\mathcal{U}}_{i,k}), \\ H'_i = L'_i + p(\hat{\mathcal{U}}_{i,r_i}) \cdot R'_{i-1}, \\ R'_i = p(\hat{\mathcal{U}}_{i,r_i}) \cdot R'_{i-1} = H'_i - L'_i. \end{cases} \tag{10}$$

Algorithm 2: Decoding algorithm of SAC decoder

Data: Received codeword $\boldsymbol{b}$, sequence length m.
Result: Output reconstructed syntactic sequence $\hat{\boldsymbol{u}}$.

Initialize: The decoding interval $[L'_0, H'_0) = [0, 1)$, interval length $R'_0 = 1$, variable index $i = 1$.
Recover the decimal fraction c corresponding to the codeword b^l.
repeat
  Construct synonymous mappings $g_i : \hat{\mathcal{U}}_i \rightarrow \hat{\hat{\mathcal{U}}}_i$.
  Synchronize probabilities for all synonymous sets $p(\hat{\mathcal{U}}_{i,k}) = p(\mathcal{U}_{i,k})$.
  Determine synonymous set $\hat{\mathcal{U}}_{i,r_i} \in \{\mathcal{U}_{i,k}\}$, s.t., satisfying Equation (8).
  Export syntactic value $\hat{u}_i$, s.t., $\hat{u}_i \in \hat{\mathcal{U}}_{i,r_i}$.
  Update decoding interval based on $\hat{\mathcal{U}}_{i,r_i}$: $[L'_{i-1}, H'_{i-1}) \rightarrow [L'_i, H'_i)$ with Equation (10).
until $i \leq m$;
Combine output sequence $\hat{\boldsymbol{u}} = (\hat{u}_1, \ldots, \hat{u}_m)$.
return *The output syntactic sequence* $\hat{\boldsymbol{u}}$.

Once the decoding interval update process corresponding to the last reconstructed variable $\hat{u}_m$ is completed, the SAC decoder concludes its iterations and outputs a combination of reconstructed syntactic values $\hat{\boldsymbol{u}} = (\hat{u}_1, \ldots, \hat{u}_m)$ as the reconstructed syntactic sequence.

Similar to the SAC encoder when only the i.i.d. assumption was considered, the synonymous mappings, along with the synonymous set partitions, and the corresponding probabilities are exactly the same. In this case, the process of SAC decoding is equivalent to a simplified procedure that first reconstructs the synonymous set sequence with the traditional arithmetic decoder and determines each syntactic variable based on the unified synonymous set partition rules.

To summarize, SAC implements semantic compression and reconstruction by constructing reasonable synonymous mappings and performing arithmetic coding procedures over synonymous sets.

Herein, we provide a corresponding complexity analysis of the SAC decoding process and compare it with the general arithmetic decoding process.

Similar to the encoding complexity analysis, we first consider the standard case of SAC decoding. we assume that the average number of syntactic values per variable in the sequence is $|\bar{\mathcal{U}}|$, and the average number of corresponding synonymous sets is $|\bar{\tilde{\mathcal{U}}}|$. These two averages are used to evaluate the decoding complexity. However, unlike the encoding side, since the probability and grouping information of the synonymous set can be directly transmitted from the encoding end to the decoding end, the decoding end does not incur additional computational complexity related to the probability calculation of the synonymous sets. Therefore, only the necessary computational complexity for the SAC decoding process should be considered.

For an expected decoded syntactic source sequence with the length m, the computational complexity of updating the coding interval is $O(|\bar{\tilde{\mathcal{U}}}| \cdot m)$. Additionally, the complexity of the normalized probability calculation of each syntactic value should also be considered, which is expressed as $O((|\bar{\mathcal{U}}|/|\bar{\tilde{\mathcal{U}}}|) \cdot m)$, in which the division term indicates that only the syntactic values in the determined synonymous set should be used for the calculation of the conditional probability. Therefore, the computational complexity of SAC can be summarized as $O((|\bar{\tilde{\mathcal{U}}}| + (|\bar{\mathcal{U}}|/|\bar{\tilde{\mathcal{U}}}|)) \cdot m)$, which is slightly lower than the complexity of the general arithmetic encoding $O(|\bar{\mathcal{U}}| \cdot m)$ since not all probability intervals of syntactic elements need to be considered.

As for the special case with i.i.d. assumption, the calculation of the normalized probability can be done only once as a reference for the overall sequence decoding, thus the complexity is expressed as $O(|\mathcal{U}|)$ (rather than the complexity with the division term, since every value should have its normalized probability calculated within its corresponding synonymous sets), regardless of the sequence length m. So, the computational complexity of SAC decoding can be further reduced to $O(|\mathcal{U}| + |\tilde{\mathcal{U}}| \cdot m) \approx O(|\tilde{\mathcal{U}}| \cdot m)$, which is less than the complexity of general arithmetic encoding $O(|\mathcal{U}| \cdot m)$ since $|\tilde{\mathcal{U}}| \leq |\mathcal{U}|$.

Therefore, we conclude that the computational complexity of SAC encoding is generally higher than that of general arithmetic encoding but lower than that in the i.i.d. case, while the computational complexity of SAC decoding is lower than that of general arithmetic decoding in all cases.

3.3. Optional Syntactic Post-Processing

While SAC can achieve semantic-level lossless encoding and decoding based on synonymous mapping, it may not ensure syntactic-level consistency of the reconstructed syntactic sequence with human perception since the syntactic-level accuracy requirement is relaxed. This is mainly because the aforementioned selection rules for reconstructed syntactic values cannot effectively utilize the overall correlation information within the syntactic sequence. Therefore, an effective solution is to utilize syntactic post-processing methods to optimize syntactic-level consistency by utilizing the overall contextual correlation information. The final output of syntactic sequences after post-processing is represented as

$$\tilde{\boldsymbol{u}} = \min_{f_p(\hat{\boldsymbol{u}})} d\big(\boldsymbol{u}, f_p(\hat{\boldsymbol{u}})\big) \text{ s.t. } \forall i, \{\tilde{u}_i, \hat{u}_i\} \in \hat{\mathcal{U}}_{i,r_i}, \tag{11}$$

where $f_p(\cdot)$ denotes a post-processing function and $d(\cdot,\cdot)$ is a specific distortion measure. $\tilde{u}_i$ is the i-th element in the output sequence $\tilde{\boldsymbol{u}} = (\tilde{u}_1, \ldots, \tilde{u}_m)$, which should share the same synonymous set $\hat{\mathcal{U}}_{i,r_i}$ with its input $\hat{u}_i$.

Specifically, the post-processing function $f_p(\cdot)$ can be determined through two types of operations: empirical linear processing and nonlinear processing based on deep neural networks. Empirical linear processing mainly relies on various linear smoothing filters in traditional signal processing to smooth parts of the reconstructed syntactic sequence that do not conform to perception. In contrast, nonlinear processing is mainly based on deep neural networks and various optimal algorithms. By constructing a dataset including the reconstructed syntactic sequences output by the SAC decoder as the input data and their corresponding source syntactic sequences as the labels and training the model to minimize the gap between the post-processing output sequence and the source syntactic sequence, the syntactic post-processing model can be applied after the SAC decoder to reduce syntactic-level distortion. With a hard decision module using suitable judgment criteria, the post-processed sequence can be finally determined.

It should be noted that not all semantic information processing scenarios require syntactic-level consistency. Therefore, syntactic post-processing is optional for SAC and only necessary to meet specific syntactic consistency requirements.

3.4. Theoretical Limit Analysis

Herein, we analyze the theoretical semantic compression limits of our proposed SAC, based on the extension of the code length theorem of the classical arithmetic coding algorithm [2] to the semantic version described below.

Theorem 1. *For a semantic arithmetic coding procedure, given any syntactic sequence $\boldsymbol{u}$ of length m with the probability mass function of its corresponding synonymous set sequence $q(\mathcal{U}_{1,r_1}, \ldots, \mathcal{U}_{m,r_m})$, it enables one to encode $\boldsymbol{u}$ in a code of length $-\log q(\mathcal{U}_{1,r_1}, \ldots, \mathcal{U}_{m,r_m}) + 2$ bits.*

This theorem can be simply proved by replacing the probability mass function for the syntactic sequence in the compression limit of arithmetic coding [2] with the probability mass function for the synonymous set sequence, in which the compression limit of arithmetic coding is fundamentally derived from the corresponding analysis of Shannon–Fano–Elias codes [2,40].

Under an i.i.d. assumption and the assumed distribution q being equal to the true distribution p, the average code length can approach the semantic entropy limit $H_s(\tilde{\mathcal{U}})$ if $m \to \infty$, i.e.,

$$H_s(\tilde{\mathcal{U}}) < \bar{L}_s \leq \lim_{m \to \infty} \frac{-\log p(\mathcal{U}_{1,r_1}, \ldots, \mathcal{U}_{m,r_m}) + 2}{m}, \tag{12}$$

where the upper bound approaches $H_s(\tilde{\mathcal{U}})$, demonstrating the theoretical compression limit of our proposed SAC can be tightly bounded around the semantic entropy, thereby verifying the achievability of the proposed method.

4. Implementations Showcase

In this section, we verify the semantic compression performance of our proposed SAC along with its ability to preserve intuitive semantic synonymity.

4.1. Experimental Setup

We consider a scenario of edge texture-oriented semantic compression for natural images. In our experiments, the edge texture maps and their corresponding natural images are all derived from the BIPEDv2 dataset [37]. We use the edge texture in natural images as a form of semantic information contained in the images and employ the annotated edge texture maps as the syntactic source for semantic compression and reconstruction. The resolutions of the annotated edge texture maps are 1280×720, in which pixels representing objects and the background are labeled as value 0, and those of the edge texture between different objects and between an object and the background are labeled as value 1.

To construct the synonymous mappings, we regard each non-overlapping 2×2-pixel block as a syntactic symbol so that the edge texture maps can be considered a syntactic sequence of length $m = 640 \times 360 = 230,400$. On this basis, we partition the 16 syntactic symbols into seven synonymous subsets based on Figure 3, in which each synonymous set represents a type of local edge texture semantic. For example, the first synonymous set $\mathcal{U}_{i,1}$ ("almost empty texture") includes all the all-zero and single blocks, while the last synonymous set $\mathcal{U}_{i,7}$ ("upper-left (lower-right) direction texture") includes all the blocks that can be regarded as being in the upper-left or lower-right. We assume that syntactic sequences satisfy the i.i.d. assumption and the probabilities of syntactic symbols. The synonymous sets in the encoding and decoding process are directly obtained based on probability statistics and are synchronized at both ends.

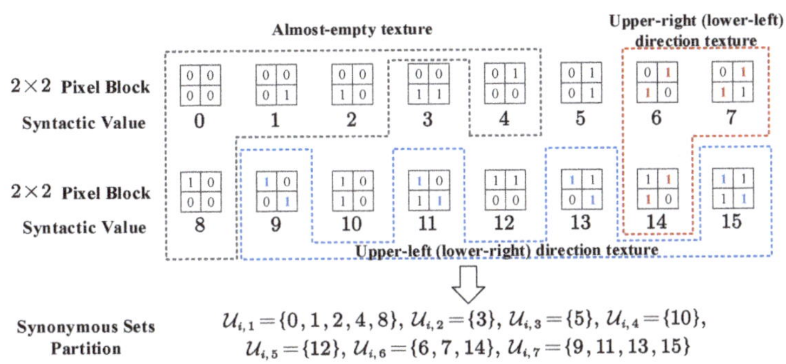

Figure 3. The synonymous set partitions for edge texture maps.

Figure 4 shows the overall SAC processing flow for edge texture maps of natural images. First, the SAC encoder compresses the source edge texture map $\boldsymbol{u}$ at the semantic level instructed by synonymous mappings and produces the output bitstream $\boldsymbol{b}$. Then, the SAC decoder reconstructs the source information $\hat{\boldsymbol{u}}^{(r)}$ using the bit stream $\boldsymbol{b}$ under the guidance of synonymous de-mapping. Finally, a neural network model is used for syntactic post-processing, followed by a hard decision module and an edge texture recovery module to obtain the final post-processed edge texture map $\hat{\boldsymbol{u}}^{(p)}$.

During the SAC decoding process, the selection rules for each reconstructed syntactic value $\hat{u}_i^{(r)}$ are as follows:

- If the decoded synonymous set is $\mathcal{U}_{i,1}$, the maximum probability value of 0 is output;
- If another synonymous set is decoded, the reconstructed syntactic value is randomly output based on the normalized probability within the synonymous set.

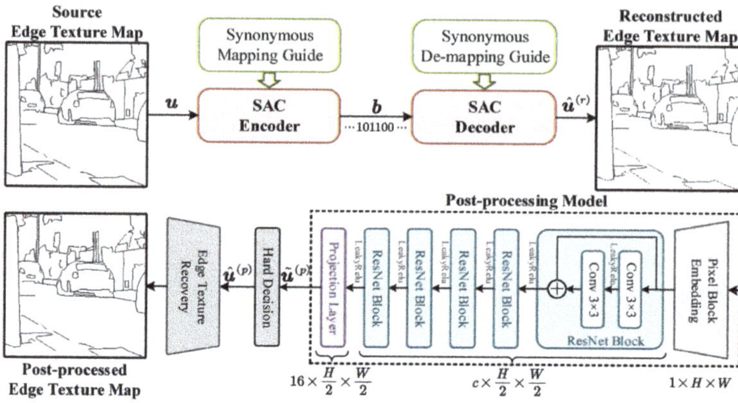

Figure 4. The overall SAC processing flow for edge texture maps of natural images.

Regarding the post-processing model, a convolutional layer with a 2×2 kernel and a stride of 2 is first utilized for pixel block embedding, mapping each 2×2 pixel block to a latent vector with $c = 128$ channels. Then, the model employs five ResNet blocks [41] to capture the overall spatial correlations of the texture map. The final projection layer maps each $c \times 1 \times 1$ vector to a $16 \times 1 \times 1$ vector and uses the softmax function to estimate the probabilities of each syntactic value shown in Figure 3 for u_i, thereby obtaining a probability-estimation sequence $\tilde{\boldsymbol{u}}^{(p)}$ for the syntactic source $\boldsymbol{u}$.

To reduce syntactic errors in the post-processed edge texture map under the given synonymous sets, we conduct a two-stage training process. The first stage optimizes the standard cross-entropy (CE) loss between the projection layer output $\tilde{\boldsymbol{u}}^{(p)}$ and the original syntactic source $\boldsymbol{u}$ to capture its spatial correlation, i.e.,

$$\mathcal{L}_1 = \mathrm{CE}\left(\boldsymbol{u}, \tilde{\boldsymbol{u}}^{(p)}\right), \tag{13}$$

while the second stage further adjusts the standard cross-entropy loss to a synonymous cross-entropy (S-CE) loss with a constraint on the decoded synonymous set sequence, i.e.,

$$\mathcal{L}_2 = \text{S-CE}\left(\boldsymbol{u}, \tilde{\boldsymbol{u}}^{(p)}\right). \tag{14}$$

The calculations of the CE and S-CE losses are almost identical, except for the probability estimation methods for each syntactic value. For the standard CE loss, the probability estimation for the syntactic value $\tilde{u}_i^{(p)}$ equals $n \in \{0, 1, \ldots, 15\}$ (denoted as $\tilde{u}_{i,n}^{(p)}$), and it is presented using the softmax function, i.e.,

$$\mathrm{Softmax}\left(\tilde{u}_{i,n}^{(p)}\right) = \frac{\exp\left(\tilde{u}_{i,n}^{(p)}\right)}{\sum_{n=0}^{15} \exp\left(\tilde{u}_{i,n}^{(p)}\right)}, \tag{15}$$

while the probability estimation, under the constraints of a given synonymous set, is presented using an adjusted synonymous softmax (s-softmax) function, i.e.,

$$\text{S-Softmax}\left(\tilde{u}_{i,n}^{(p)}\right) = \frac{\exp\left(\tilde{u}_{i,n}^{(p)}\right)}{\sum_{n \in \hat{\mathcal{U}}_{i,r_i}} \exp\left(\tilde{u}_{i,n}^{(p)}\right)}. \tag{16}$$

This S-SE function, along with its s-softmax function, follows the requirement of Equation (11), where the output syntactic value belongs to the decoded synonymous set, thereby achieving better syntactic-level consistency while maintaining semantic losslessness.

After training, by determining each value with the highest probability as the value of the syntactic symbol $\hat{u}_i^{(p)}$, we obtain the final post-processed edge texture map $\hat{\boldsymbol{u}}^{(p)}$.

We use the Adam optimizer to train the post-processing model. During training, we first use the loss function L_1 for the first stage, with 100 epochs and a learning rate of $\text{lr} = 1 \times 10^{-5}$, to estimate the probability in Equation (15), then modify the loss function to L_2 for the second stage, with 200 epochs and a learning rate of $\text{lr} = 5 \times 10^{-6}$ to achieve a better estimation of the probability in Equation (16) under the constraints. After training, the average S-CE of each synset symbol on the test set is 0.014, which supports acceptable post-processed syntactic qualities.

4.2. Visualization Results and Numerical Analysis

We employed our proposed SAC method on the test set, which consisted of 50 edge texture maps, along with their corresponding natural images, to verify the semantic compression effect, and utilized the traditional AC method as the comparison scheme. As a representative result, Figure 5 shows an example of the compression and reconstruction effects for semantic compression of edge texture maps using our proposed SAC method, in which the source, reconstructed, and post-processed edge texture maps are all labeled on the corresponding natural image to verify the semantic accuracy of the edge texture semantics. From the perspective of the reconstruction effect, although the syntactic form of the reconstructed and post-processed edge texture maps differed from the original edge texture, they did not affect the accuracy of their edge texture semantics in this natural image. This observation is consistent with the effects seen in the other samples in the test set, indicating that no semantic losses exist on the reconstructed edge texture map with our proposed method.

Additionally, by comparing the reconstructed and post-processed edge feature maps, we found that the syntactic consistency of the reconstructed map with the source one was relatively poor. However, with the syntactic post-processing model, the syntactic distortion between the post-processed map and the source map was effectively reduced, translating to better consistency at the syntactic level. This confirms the effectiveness of our proposed syntactic post-processing model.

Based on these results, it is evident that compression efficiency was significantly improved using SAC. From the perspective of the actual code length, SAC provided effective compression efficiency improvements compared with the traditional method. For the example edge texture map shown in Figure 5, SAC saved 26,515 sebits [32] compared with traditional arithmetic coding, equivalent to a 12.9% improvement in compression efficiency. As for the entire test set, SAC saved an average of 29,085.1 sebits of code length compared to traditional methods, equivalent to a 20.5% improvement in the average compression efficiency. This demonstrates that SAC significantly improves compression efficiency compared to traditional arithmetic coding with semantic losslessness.

From another perspective, the averaged code length calculated by SAC can exceed the Shannon entropy of the classical information theory, and further approximate the theoretical semantic compression limits, i.e., semantic entropy. Specifically, for both the single example test edge texture map and the entire test set, the gap between the average code sequence length after SAC encoding and the corresponding ideal code length was within 2 bits, which confirms the analysis results in Section 3.4.

These results effectively demonstrate the performance of our proposed SAC method, i.e., it can achieve an effective compression efficiency improvement and approximate the semantic entropy with intuitive semantic losslessness.

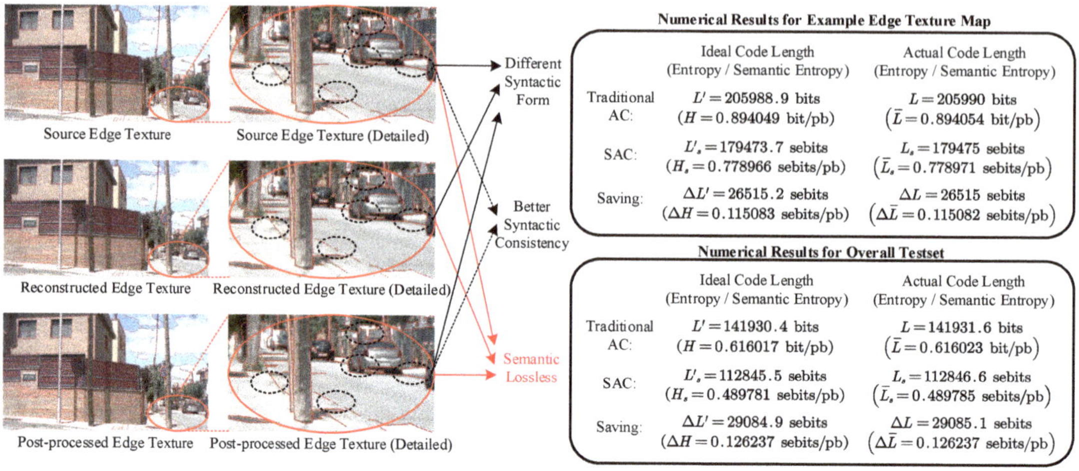

Figure 5. An example of compression and reconstruction effects for edge texture map semantic compression, in which "sebits" denotes the semantic bits for the resulting unit of semantic source coding, as presented in [32]. Additionally, "bit/pb" and "sebit/pb", respectively, denote the bit per pixel block and the sebit per pixel block, acting as the units of entropy and the average code length of traditional AC and our proposed SAC based on our coding configuration.

5. Conclusions

In this paper, we propose a semantic source coding method called semantic arithmetic coding. By constructing reasonable synonymous mappings and performing arithmetic coding procedures over synonymous sets, the compression efficiency can be significantly improved compared with traditional arithmetic codes under intuitive semantic lossless conditions. Additionally, we provide a theoretical limit analysis of our proposed method based on an extension of the code length theorem of arithmetic codes, along with experimental verification, to confirm its convergence to semantic entropy. Future work will focus on theories and methods for constructing more effective synonymous mappings while ensuring intuitive semantic losslessness, thereby minimizing the semantic compression limit. In addition, integrating semantic arithmetic coding algorithms with neural network compression coding and extending the idea to the design of corresponding semantic communication methods are important directions for future work.

6. Patents

The work presented in this paper is related to a Chinese Patent [42] and a corresponding US patent [43].

Author Contributions: Conceptualization, K.N. and P.Z.; methodology, Z.L. and J.X.; software, Z.L.; validation, Z.L.; formal analysis, Z.L.; investigation, Z.L. and J.X.; resources, Z.L.; data curation, Z.L.; writing—original draft preparation, Z.L.; writing—review and editing, Z.L., K.N., and J.X.; visualization, Z.L.; supervision, K.N. and P.Z.; project administration, K.N.; funding acquisition, K.N. and P.Z. All authors have read and agreed to the published version of the manuscript.

Funding: This research was funded by the National Natural Science Foundation of China (No. 62293481, No. 62471054).

Institutional Review Board Statement: Not applicable.

Data Availability Statement: The data that support the findings of this study are available from the corresponding author upon reasonable request.

Conflicts of Interest: The authors declare no conflicts of interest.

Abbreviations

The following abbreviations are used in this manuscript:

AC	arithmetic coding
SAC	semantic arithmetic coding
AEP	asymptotic equipartition property
i.i.d.	independent and identically distributed
BIPED	Barcelona Images for Perceptual Edge Detection
CE	cross-entropy
S-CE	synonymous cross-entropy
S-Softmax	synonymous softmax

References

1. Shannon, C.E. A mathematical theory of communication. *Bell Syst. Tech. J.* **1948**, *27*, 379–423. [CrossRef]
2. Cover, T.M. *Elements of Information Theory*, 2nd ed.; John Wiley & Sons: Hoboken, NJ, USA, 2006. [CrossRef]
3. Farsad, N.; Rao, M.; Goldsmith, A. Deep learning for joint source-channel coding of text. In Proceedings of the 2018 IEEE International Conference on Acoustics, Speech and Signal Processing (ICASSP), Calgary, AB, Canada, 15–20 April 2018; pp. 2326–2330. [CrossRef]
4. Xie, H.; Qin, Z.; Li, G.Y.; Juang, B.H. Deep learning enabled semantic communication systems. *IEEE Trans. Signal Process.* **2021**, *69*, 2663–2675. [CrossRef]
5. Weng, Z.; Qin, Z. Semantic communication systems for speech transmission. *IEEE J. Sel. Areas Commun.* **2021**, *39*, 2434–2444. [CrossRef]
6. Bourtsoulatze, E.; Kurka, D.B.; Gündüz, D. Deep joint source-channel coding for wireless image transmission. *IEEE Trans. Cogn. Commun. Netw.* **2019**, *5*, 567–579. [CrossRef]
7. Dai, J.; Wang, S.; Tan, K.; Si, Z.; Qin, X.; Niu, K.; Zhang, P. Nonlinear transform source-channel coding for semantic communications. *IEEE J. Sel. Areas Commun.* **2022**, *40*, 2300–2316. [CrossRef]
8. Jiang, P.; Wen, C.K.; Jin, S.; Li, G.Y. Wireless Semantic Communications for Video Conferencing. *IEEE J. Sel. Areas Commun.* **2023**, *41*, 230–244. [CrossRef]
9. Mu, X.; Liu, Y. Exploiting Semantic Communication for Non-Orthogonal Multiple Access. *IEEE J. Sel. Areas Commun.* **2023**, *41*, 2563–2576. [CrossRef]
10. Zhang, W.; Bai, K.; Zeadally, S.; Zhang, H.; Shao, H.; Ma, H.; Leung, V.C.M. DeepMA: End-to-End Deep Multiple Access for Wireless Image Transmission in Semantic Communication. *IEEE Trans. Cogn. Commun. Netw.* **2024**, *10*, 387–402. [CrossRef]
11. Mu, X.; Liu, Y.; Guo, L.; Al-Dhahir, N. Heterogeneous semantic and bit communications: A semi-NOMA scheme. *IEEE J. Sel. Areas Commun.* **2022**, *41*, 155–169. [CrossRef]
12. Xie, H.; Qin, Z.; Tao, X.; Letaief, K.B. Task-Oriented Multi-User Semantic Communications. *IEEE J. Sel. Areas Commun.* **2022**, *40*, 2584–2597. [CrossRef]
13. Feng, Y.; Shen, H.; Shan, Z.; Yang, Q.; Shi, X. Semantic Communication for Edge Intelligence Enabled Autonomous Driving System. *IEEE Netw.* **2025**, *39*, 149–157. [CrossRef]
14. Qin, Z.; Tao, X.; Lu, J.; Tong, W.; Li, G.Y. Semantic communications: Principles and challenges. *arXiv* **2021**, arXiv:2201.01389. [CrossRef]
15. Lu, K.; Zhou, Q.; Li, R.; Zhao, Z.; Chen, X.; Wu, J.; Zhang, H. Rethinking Modern Communication from Semantic Coding to Semantic Communication. *IEEE Wirel. Commun.* **2023**, *30*, 158–164. [CrossRef]
16. Weaver, W. Recent contributions to the mathematical theory of communication. *ETC Rev. Gen. Semant.* **1953**, *10*, 261–281.
17. Carnap, R.; Bar-Hillel, Y. An outline of a theory of semantic information. *J. Symb. Log.* **1954**, *19*, 230–232.
18. Bar-Hillel, Y.; Carnap, R. Semantic information. *Br. J. Philos. Sci.* **1953**, *4*, 147–157. [CrossRef]
19. Floridi, L. Outline of a theory of strongly semantic information. *Minds Mach.* **2004**, *14*, 197–221. [CrossRef]
20. Bao, J.; Basu, P.; Dean, M.; Partridge, C.; Swami, A.; Leland, W.; Hendler, J.A. Towards a theory of semantic communication. In Proceedings of the 2011 IEEE Network Science Workshop, West Point, NY, USA, 22–24 June 2011; pp. 110–117. [CrossRef]
21. De Luca, A.; Termini, S. A definition of a nonprobabilistic entropy in the setting of fuzzy sets theory. *Inf. Control* **1972**, *20*, 301–312. [CrossRef]
22. De Luca, A.; Termini, S. Entropy of L-fuzzy sets. *Inf. Control* **1974**, *24*, 55–73. [CrossRef]

23. Al-Sharhan, S.; Karray, F.; Gueaieb, W.; Basir, O. Fuzzy entropy: A brief survey. In Proceedings of the 10th IEEE International Conference on Fuzzy Systems (Cat. No. 01CH37297), Melbourne, Australia, 2–5 December 2001; Volume 3, pp. 1135–1139. [CrossRef]
24. Niu, K.; Dai, J.; Yao, S.; Wang, S.; Si, Z.; Qin, X.; Zhang, P. A paradigm shift toward semantic communications. *IEEE Commun. Mag.* **2022**, *60*, 113–119. [CrossRef]
25. Shao, Y.; Cao, Q.; Gündüz, D. A theory of semantic communication. *IEEE Trans. Mob. Comput.* **2024**, *23*, 12211–12228. [CrossRef]
26. Ma, S.; Zhang, C.; Qi, H.; Li, H.; Bi, Y.; Shi, G.; Al-Dhahir, N. A Theory for Semantic Channel Coding With Many-to-one Source. *IEEE Trans. Cogn. Commun. Netw.* **2025**, *Early Access*. [CrossRef]
27. Zhong, Y. A theory of semantic information. *China Commun.* **2017**, *14*, 1–17. [CrossRef]
28. Zhang, H.; Shao, S.; Tao, M.; Bi, X.; Letaief, K.B. Deep Learning-Enabled Semantic Communication Systems With Task-Unaware Transmitter and Dynamic Data. *IEEE J. Sel. Areas Commun.* **2023**, *41*, 170–185. [CrossRef]
29. Luo, X.; Chen, H.H.; Guo, Q. Semantic Communications: Overview, Open Issues, and Future Research Directions. *IEEE Wirel. Commun.* **2022**, *29*, 210–219. [CrossRef]
30. Huang, J.; Li, D.; Huang, C.; Qin, X.; Zhang, W. Joint Task and Data-Oriented Semantic Communications: A Deep Separate Source-Channel Coding Scheme. *IEEE Internet Things J.* **2024**, *11*, 2255–2272. [CrossRef]
31. Gündüz, D.; Qin, Z.; Aguerri, I.E.; Dhillon, H.S.; Yang, Z.; Yener, A.; Wong, K.K.; Chae, C.B. Beyond Transmitting Bits: Context, Semantics, and Task-Oriented Communications. *IEEE J. Sel. Areas Commun.* **2023**, *41*, 5–41. [CrossRef]
32. Niu, K.; Zhang, P. A mathematical theory of semantic communication. *J. Commun.* **2024**, *45*, 7–59. [CrossRef]
33. Shannon, C. The lattice theory of information. *Trans. IRE Prof. Group Inf. Theory* **1953**, *1*, 105–107. [CrossRef]
34. Jagadish, H.; Madar, J.; Ng, R.T. Semantic compression and pattern extraction with fascicles. In Proceedings of the VLDB, Edinburgh, UK, 7–10 September 1999; Volume 99, pp. 186–197.
35. Babu, S.; Garofalakis, M.; Rastogi, R. Spartan: A model-based semantic compression system for massive data tables. *ACM SIGMOD Rec.* **2001**, *30*, 283–294. [CrossRef]
36. Jagadish, H.; Ng, R.T.; Ooi, B.C.; Tung, A.K. Itcompress: An iterative semantic compression algorithm. In Proceedings of the Proceedings, 20th International Conference on Data Engineering, Boston, MA, USA, 2 April 2004; pp. 646–657. [CrossRef]
37. Soria, X.; Sappa, A.; Humanante, P.; Akbarinia, A. Dense extreme inception network for edge detection. *Pattern Recognit.* **2023**, *139*, 109461. [CrossRef]
38. Xu, J.; Du, T.; Liang, Z.; Niu, K.; Zhang, P. Semantic Markov Chain using Synonymous Mapping. *Tsinghua Sci. Technol.* **2025**, *Accepted*.
39. Witten, I.H.; Neal, R.M.; Cleary, J.G. Arithmetic coding for data compression. *Commun. ACM* **1987**, *30*, 520–540. [CrossRef]
40. Cover, T. Enumerative source encoding. *IEEE Trans. Inf. Theory* **1973**, *19*, 73–77. [CrossRef]
41. He, K.; Zhang, X.; Ren, S.; Sun, J. Deep residual learning for image recognition. In Proceedings of the IEEE Conference on Computer Vision and Pattern Recognition, Las Vegas, NV, USA, 27–30 June 2016; pp. 770–778. [CrossRef]
42. Niu, K.; Liang, Z.; Xu, J.; Zhang, P. Arithmetic encoding and decoding method based on semantic information source and related equipment. CN118118033B, 16 August 2024.
43. Niu, K.; Liang, Z.; Xu, J.; Zhang, P. Arithmetic encoding and decoding method based on semantic source and related device. US12192467B1, 7 January 2025.

entropy

MDPI

Review

A Survey on Semantic Communications in Internet of Vehicles

Sha Ye [1], Qiong Wu [1,*], Pingyi Fan [2] and Qiang Fan [3]

[1] School of Internet of Things Engineering, Jiangnan University, Wuxi 214122, China; shaye@stu.jiangnan.edu.cn
[2] State Key Laboratory of Space Network and Communications, Department of Electronic Engineering, Beijing National Research Center for Information Science and Technology, Tsinghua University, Beijing 100084, China; fpy@tsinghua.edu.cn
[3] Qualcomm, San Jose, CA 95110, USA; qf9898@gmail.com
* Correspondence: qiongwu@jiangnan.edu.cn; Tel.: +86-0510-8591-0633

Abstract: The Internet of Vehicles (IoV), as the core of intelligent transportation system, enables comprehensive interconnection between vehicles and their surroundings through multiple communication modes, which is significant for autonomous driving and intelligent traffic management. However, with the emergence of new applications, traditional communication technologies face the problems of scarce spectrum resources and high latency. Semantic communication, which focuses on extracting, transmitting, and recovering some useful semantic information from messages, can reduce redundant data transmission, improve spectrum utilization, and provide innovative solutions to communication challenges in the IoV. This paper systematically reviews state-of-the-art semantic communications in the IoV, elaborates the technical background of the IoV and semantic communications, and deeply discusses key technologies of semantic communications in the IoV, including semantic information extraction, semantic communication architecture, resource allocation and management, and so on. Through specific case studies, it demonstrates that semantic communications can be effectively employed in the scenarios of traffic environment perception and understanding, intelligent driving decision support, IoV service optimization, and intelligent traffic management. Additionally, it analyzes the current challenges and future research directions. This survey reveals that semantic communications have broad application prospects in the IoV, but it is necessary to solve the real existing problems by combining advanced technologies to promote their wide application in the IoV and contributing to the development of intelligent transportation systems.

Keywords: internet of vehicles; semantic communication; semantic information; semantic encoding and decoding; resource optimization

1. Introduction

In today's digital era, the Internet of Vehicles (IoV) [1] and semantic communications [2–4], as cutting-edge technologies in the field of intelligent transportation and communication, are gradually changing the way we travel and are transforming traffic management. The IoV realizes real-time sharing and interaction of traffic information through vehicle-to-vehicle (V2V), vehicle-to-infrastructure (V2I), and vehicle-to-pedestrian (V2P) communications. It greatly improves traffic efficiency and safety. Semantic communications, on the other hand, are an emerging communication paradigm that significantly improves the efficiency and reliability of communications by directly transmitting the semantic content of information instead of the traditional sequence of bits.

However, with the continuous emergence of new applications in the IoV, such as autonomous driving [5], vehicle remote monitoring and diagnostics [6], and IoV entertainment services [7], the mobile data traffic between vehicles and roadside units (RSUs), as well as between vehicles, has shown an explosive growth trend. This surge in data volume has extremely stringent demands on the communication infrastructure of the IoV, particularly highlighting the issue of scarce spectrum resources. When facing massive amounts of data, traditional IoV communication technologies often reveal limitations such as limited spectrum resources, high latency, and insufficient capabilities for processing semantic information. These issues significantly restrict the further enhancement of IoV performance and hinder the development of intelligent transportation systems.

Against this background, semantic communication becomes a promising communication technology to address the IoV communication bottleneck. Unlike traditional communication that primarily focuses on the accurate transmission of data, semantic communication concentrates on extracting, transmitting, and recovering the semantic information contained within messages, enabling the receiver to understand the intent and content of the sender. The integration of the IoV and semantic communication can effectively improve the efficiency of data transmission and ensure the accuracy and reliability of information transfer in complex traffic environments. The concealment of semantic communication provides a new approach for privacy protection in the Internet of Vehicles, making information transmission more secure. At the same time, it can flexibly adjust information content and services according to the specific needs and scenarios of users, providing more precise support for applications such as autonomous driving and intelligent traffic management.

This combination also faces some challenges. For example, in dynamic and changeable traffic scenarios, how to accurately understand and process contextual information and how to ensure the efficient decoding and comprehension of information while maintaining its concealment are all issues that require further research. Despite these challenges, the combination of the IoV and semantic communication undoubtedly paves a new way for the development of future intelligent transportation, and its potential and value are worthy of in-depth exploration.

In recent years, researchers have paid attention to the application of semantic communication in the field of the IoV. A substantial amount of research has been conducted on how to integrate the advantages of semantic communication into the IoV. In light of this, this survey provides a comprehensive and systematic review of the current research related to semantic communications in the IoV. We summarize these studies from two perspectives: key technologies and specific applications, as shown in Table 1. To the best of our knowledge, this is the first comprehensive study discussing the IoV based on semantic communication.The rest of the paper is organized as follows: Section 2 begins with an overview of the architecture and key technologies of the IoV, as well as the fundamental principles, system architecture, and classification of semantic communication, providing the theoretical background for subsequent research. Section 3 delves into the key technologies of semantic communication in the IoV, covering the core technical areas of semantic information extraction, semantic communication architecture, resource allocation and management, and details regarding current research progress. Section 4 demonstrates the significant achievements of semantic communication in practical application scenarios such as traffic environment perception and understanding, intelligent driving decision support, IoV service optimization, and intelligent traffic management through specific case studies, further validating the potential of semantic communication in the IoV. Section 5 provides an in-depth analysis of the current challenges and a prospective outlook on future research directions. Finally, in Section 6, we present the conclusions of this survey. Additionally, the organization and structure of the survey are shown in Figure 1.

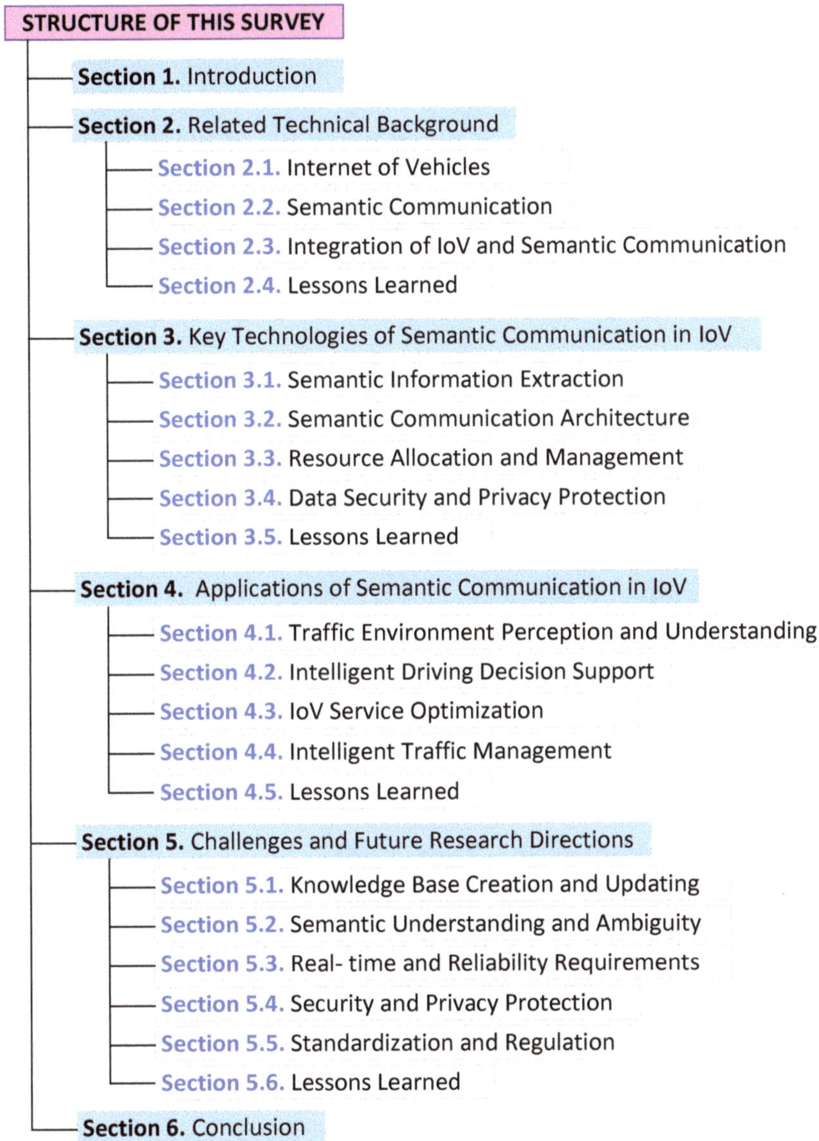

Figure 1. Structure of this survey.

Table 1. Studies related to semantic communication in IoV.

	Category	Literatures	Core Content
Key Technologies	Semantic Information Extraction	[8–15]	Extract semantic information from multimodal data.
	Semantic Communication Architecture	[12,14–29]	Diverse semantic communication architectures covering multitask and multiuser collaboration, image transmission, generative AI, etc.
	Resource Allocation and Management	[24,30–38]	Resource allocation methods based on reinforcement learning, optimization theory, and federated learning.
Specific Applications	Traffic Environment Perception and Understanding	[39,40]	Enhance the coverage and accuracy of environmental perception.
	Intelligent Driving Decision Support	[41,42]	Extract key semantic information to support real-time decision making.
	IoV Service Optimization	[43–45]	Optimize service performance through semantic communication.
	Intelligent Traffic Management	[46–49]	Improve traffic management efficiency and emergency response capabilities.

2. Related Technical Background

2.1. Internet of Vehicles

The Internet of Vehicles (IoV) is an intelligent transportation system that connects vehicles with other vehicles, infrastructure, pedestrians, and roadside units via advanced communication technologies. Essentially, it is a deep integration of vehicular ad hoc networks (VANETs) and the Internet of Things (IoT) [50,51]. It aims to enhance traffic safety, improve transportation efficiency, and optimize the driving experience through real-time information sharing and collaborative interaction [52,53]. It can be primarily categorized as follows:

- Vehicle-to-Vehicle (V2V) [54]: Vehicles directly exchange information with each other, such as speed, direction, and emergency braking signals. This mode enables vehicles to anticipate potential collision risks in advance, thereby enhancing driving safety.
- Vehicle-to-Infrastructure (V2I) [54]: Vehicles communicate with roadside units, such as traffic lights and road sensors, to obtain information on traffic conditions and traffic signal status. V2I communication helps optimize traffic flow and reduce congestion.
- Vehicle-to-Pedestrian (V2P) [55]: Vehicles interact with pedestrian devices, such as smartphones and smartwatches, to alert pedestrians to the approach of vehicles or to provide vehicles with pedestrian location information.
- Vehicle-to-Roadside Unit (V2R) [56]: Vehicles communicate with roadside units (RSUs), which are devices installed along roadsides to provide local traffic information, weather conditions, and other relevant data.
- Vehicle-to-Device (V2D) [57]: Vehicles communicate with various mobile devices to offer personalized services, such as vehicle status monitoring and remote control.
- Vehicle-to-Grid (V2G) [58]: Vehicles interact with the power grid, functioning as mobile energy storage units that can exchange energy with the grid. For example, vehicles can charge during periods of low grid load and discharge during periods of high grid load, thereby improving the stability and efficiency of the power grid.

Through these communications, the IoV can achieve a smarter, safer, and more efficient transportation system. A mature IoV system typically incorporates all of the above communication modes.

2.1.1. IoV Architectures

To address the diverse requirements of IoV scenarios, researchers have proposed various IoV architectural frameworks. The most common classifications include the three-tier architecture, the in-vehicle and intervehicle network architecture, and the vehicle–road–cloud integrated architecture.

The typical three-tier IoV architecture consists of the perception layer, network layer, and application layer [59–61], as shown in Figure 2. The perception layer acts as the nerve endings of the IoV, utilizing technologies such as sensors, RFID, and GPS to collect information on vehicle status, road environment parameters, and surrounding vehicle dynamics, providing foundational data for the IoV, such as vehicle speed and tire pressure. The network layer serves as the hub for information exchange, leveraging cloud computing, virtualization, and other technologies to integrate various communication networks, such as 4G/5G, Wi-Fi, Bluetooth, and DSRC, enabling information sharing and interconnectivity between vehicles, roads, people, and the cloud. The application layer is the core value realization for the IoV, developing and optimizing functions such as intelligent traffic management, vehicle safety control, and traffic event warning based on cloud computing platforms, offering users services like vehicle information queries, information subscriptions, and event alerts. In addition to the three-tier architecture, researchers also proposed more detailed four-tier [51,62,63], five-tier [1], and seven-tier [64,65] architectures for IoV scenarios.

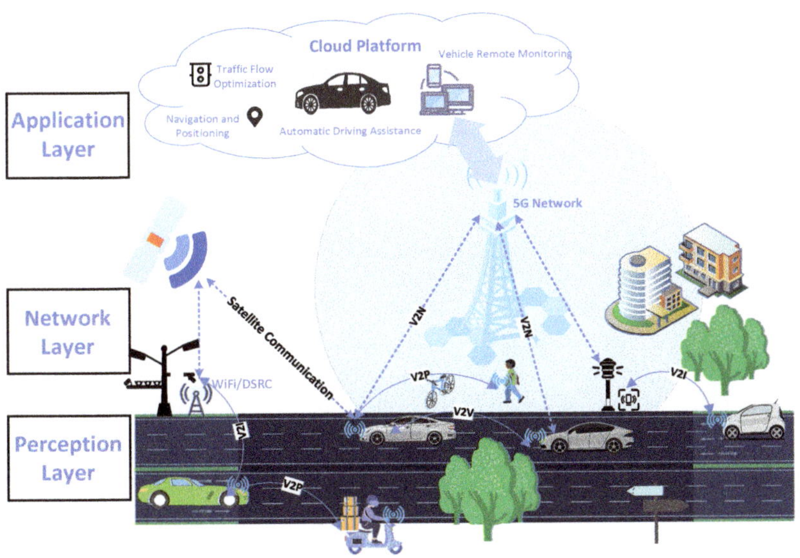

Figure 2. IoV scenario architecture diagram.

In terms of subnetwork division, IoV can be categorized into two main subnetworks: the in-vehicle network and intervehicle network [66–69]. The in-vehicle network utilizes bus technologies such as the Controller Area Network (CAN), the Local Interconnect Network (LIN), FlexRay, MOST, and Ethernet to construct the internal network of the vehicle, connecting sensors and Electronic Control Units (ECUs) within the vehicle to enable functions like vehicle status monitoring, fault diagnosis, and intelligent control.

The intervehicle network consists of four entities: the onboard unit, roadside users, roadside units (RSUs), and cloud servers. It leverages technologies such as GPS, wireless local area networks, and cellular networks to build an open, dynamic mobile communication network, facilitating real-time information exchange between vehicles, vehicles and road infrastructure, and vehicles and pedestrians, thereby enhancing traffic safety and efficiency.

Furthermore, the IoV can also be divided according to the vehicle–road–cloud integrated architecture [70,71], which primarily consists of three components: the onboard unit, road facility unit, and cloud control platform. Specifically, the onboard unit integrates sensors, control units, and communication devices within the vehicle to perceive vehicle status and environmental information and transmit it to the cloud. The road facility unit includes traffic lights, roadside cameras, and sensors, collecting traffic and environmental information from the road and communicating with the onboard unit to enable data exchange and sharing. The cloud control platform, composed of multiple cloud systems, undertakes tasks such as data storage, processing, and analysis, providing vehicles with real-time traffic information, road condition data, and navigation guidance. Simultaneously, it receives data uploaded by vehicles while offering a wide range of applications and services and maintaining end-to-end Quality of Service (QoS) for users [72,73].

2.1.2. Communication Technologies

Communication technologies in the IoV include V2X communication technology, 4G/5G mobile communication technology, Dedicated Short-Range Communication (DSRC) [74], Bluetooth, Wi-Fi, and others, enabling efficient information interaction between vehicles and the external environment. In [51], three types of wireless communication technologies are summarized: vehicular communication, cellular mobile communication, and short-range static communication:

- Vehicular communication: In VANETs, On-Board Units (OBUs) and roadside units (RSUs) often use DSRC for communication. For example, vehicles transmit collected data such as speed, acceleration, and fuel levels to nearby RSUs or other vehicles via OBUs based on the IEEE 802.11p standard. RSUs also use DSRC to communicate with OBUs, enabling functions such as information forwarding, local communication, and road safety information provision. Continuous Air-interface for Long and Medium range (CALM) is another important vehicular communication standard in IoV, providing specifications and support for communication, ensuring compatibility and stability between vehicles and other devices.
- Cellular mobile communication: Vehicles can communicate with other networks through 4G/LTE, WiMax, and other cellular network technologies, enabling V2I connectivity, thereby extending communication range and accessing more comprehensive traffic and environmental information [75,76]. Among these, 5G NR V2X, as a new-generation cellular IoV technology, offers ultra-low latency, high reliability, and high data transmission rates, significantly enhancing the performance and safety of IoV applications. It supports advanced V2X scenarios such as platooning, remote driving, and sensor extension. Satellite communication also plays a role in special scenarios or remote areas, ensuring vehicle connectivity. For instance, in mountainous regions or areas with poor signal coverage, satellite communication can maintain the vehicle's connection with the outside world.
- Short-range static communication: This includes technologies such as Zigbee, Bluetooth, and Wi-Fi. Zigbee can be used for short-range communication between vehicles and sensors, enabling environmental perception and data collection, such as vehicle status monitoring and environmental parameter detection. Bluetooth is primarily used for connecting vehicles with personal devices (e.g., smartphones, tablets, etc.), facili-

tating device interaction and information sharing within the vehicle. Wi-Fi provides high-speed network access for vehicles in specific areas (e.g., parking lots, service stations, etc.), meeting the demand for large data transmission and real-time information acquisition. For example, vehicles in parking lots can download maps or access service information via Wi-Fi.

2.2. Semantic Communication

Semantic communication is a method of encoding, transmitting, and decoding information based on its meaning and intent, aiming to achieve efficient communication by extracting and conveying the essential semantic content of the information. For instance, in an autonomous driving scenario where a vehicle needs to quickly identify and react to obstacles ahead, traditional communication methods might require the transmission of large amounts of image data. In contrast, semantic communication would simply transmit the critical message that "there is an obstacle ahead," thereby saving time and bandwidth.

2.2.1. Semantic Communication System Architectures

Weaver [77] proposed three levels of communication, including technical issues, semantic issues, and effectiveness issues. The technical layer focuses on the precise transmission of information between the sender and receiver; the semantic layer focuses on the meaning that the receiver understands and the meaning that the sender wants to express; and the effectiveness layer focuses on the effectiveness of the information to achieve the expected impact on the receiver's behavior. Traditional communication mainly focuses on the technical layer, pursuing the accurate transmission of data bits [78–80]. However, with the explosive growth of data volume in the era of big data, the transmission of a large amount of raw data by traditional communication methods leads to problems such as inefficient transmission and waste of resources [81]. Semantic communication, on the other hand, focuses on the latter two layers and aims to accurately transmit semantic meanings rather than mere bit information [82]. Semantic communication systems include components such as a semantic encoder, channel encoder, channel decoder, semantic decoder, and knowledge base [83], as shown in Figure 3. These components are described in the following:

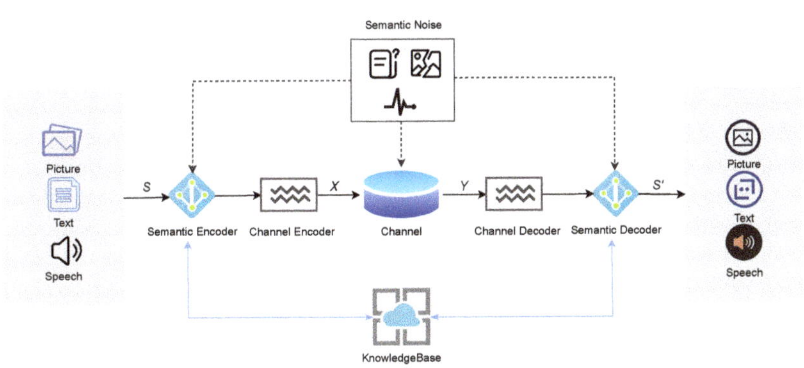

Figure 3. Semantic communication system architectures.

- Semantic encoder: The semantic encoder accurately extracts semantic information from the source message and effectively compresses it through a series of complex algorithms and techniques.

- Channel encoder: The channel encoder encodes and modulates the semantic features processed by the semantic encoder and maps the semantic features into a signal form suitable for transmission over the channel.
- Channel decoder: The channel decoder uses a decoding algorithm corresponding to the channel encoder to restore the encoded semantic features from the received signal.
- Semantic decoder: The semantic decoder converts the signal output from the channel decoder into a format that the user can understand.
- Knowledge base: The knowledge base provides the semantic understanding basis for the encoder and decoder. It further analyzes and transforms the recovered semantic features based on pre-established semantic rules and the knowledge system within the knowledge base. Depending on the scope of knowledge sharing and the user, it can be divided into local knowledge bases and public knowledge bases.
- Semantic noise: Semantic noise is an interfering factor that leads to wrong recognition and interpretation of semantic information in the whole process of semantic communication. Semantic noise includes semantic and physical channel noise, such as text semantic ambiguity, image antagonistic samples, and so on.

In a semantic communication system, assume that the input raw data are S, which can be text, image, etc. After passing through the semantic encoder and the channel encoder, we can obtain the encoded data as

$$X = ch_{\beta}(se_{\alpha}(S)), \tag{1}$$

where $se_{\alpha}(\cdot)$ and $ch_{\beta}(\cdot)$ are the semantic and channel encoder networks with parameters α and β, respectively.

After passing through the channel, we can obtain

$$Y = HX + N, \tag{2}$$

where H and N represent the channel gain and noise, respectively. The specific formula expression usually needs to be calculated according to the specific scenario.

Then, after passing through the channel decoder and the semantic decoder, we can reconstruct the data as

$$S' = se_{\mu}^{-1}(ch_{v}^{-1}(Y)), \tag{3}$$

where $se_{\mu}^{-1}(\cdot)$ and $ch_{v}^{-1}(\cdot)$ are the networks of the semantic and channel decoders with parameters μ and v, respectively.

Unlike the traditional communication paradigm of "transmit first, then understand", semantic communication adopts a "understand first, then transmit" paradigm, ensuring that it can overcome the limitations of traditional communication. Semantic information extraction is the foundation of semantic communication, which can extract semantic information from raw data and reduce the amount of transmitted data. This requires the precise extraction of key semantic elements from various complex data sources, such as text, speech, images, and sensor data. This relies on advanced technical methods, such as the artificial intelligence method [84]. For example, in the semantic extraction of textual information, Natural Language Processing (NLP) techniques can determine the core semantics of text through lexical and syntactic analysis, as well as semantic role labeling. For image data, computer vision techniques such as object detection, image classification, and semantic segmentation algorithms can identify objects and their relationships within images, thereby extracting corresponding semantic information. As for speech signals, they are first converted into text using speech recognition technology, and then their semantic connotations are further explored.

In the design of semantic communication systems, the encoding process is crucial for achieving efficient semantic transmission. Similar to traditional communication systems, semantic communication systems also involve source coding and channel coding, but their design goals and methods differ significantly from those of traditional communication. In semantic communication, the source coding is primarily responsible for extracting semantic information from raw data, removing redundancy, and improving transmission efficiency. Channel coding, on the other hand, focuses on addressing noise and interference in the channel to ensure the reliability of semantic information during transmission. Traditional communication systems typically employ separate source coding and channel coding approaches. Source coding is responsible for redundancy removal, while channel coding enhances anti-interference capabilities. However, this separated design may not fully leverage the characteristics of semantic information in semantic communication. Therefore, semantic communication systems tend to adopt Joint Source–Channel Coding (JSCC), which jointly optimizes source and channel coding to meet the transmission requirements of semantic information.

In recent years, the JSCC technology based on deep learning has shown significant advantages in semantic communication. For example, Deep JSCC technology [85] employs Convolutional Neural Networks (CNNs) to achieve end-to-end semantic information encoding and decoding for wireless image transmission, exhibiting excellent performance under low signal-to-noise ratios (SNRs) and limited bandwidth conditions. Further optimized Deep JSCC-f [86] introduces a channel output feedback mechanism and adopts a hierarchical autoencoder structure, showing progressive improvement and robust performance in low-SNR scenarios. In the field of text transmission, DeepSC [87] extracts semantic information from text based on the Transformer model and achieves efficient transmission through joint semantic–channel coding, outperforming traditional methods under low-SNR conditions. For speech signal transmission, DeepSC-S [88] combines attention mechanisms and Squeeze-and-Excitation (SE) networks to effectively extract semantic information from speech, significantly improving the relevant indicators in telephony and multimedia systems. Additionally, the MU-DeepSC system [89], designed for multiuser and multimodal data transmission, jointly designs the transmitter and receiver using Deep Neural Networks (DNNs), focusing on transmitting and recovering task-relevant semantic information and providing a novel solution for semantic communication in complex scenarios.

2.2.2. Semantic Communication Types

Based on the roles of semantics in the communication process, communication objectives, and application scenarios, semantic communication can be categorized into three types: semantics-oriented communication, goal-oriented communication, and semantics-aware communication [90].

Semantics-oriented communication: In this communication design, the key lies in the accuracy of the semantic content of the source data. Unlike traditional content-blind source coding, semantic communication introduces a semantic representation module before encoding, which is responsible for extracting the core information and filtering redundancy, and semantic encoding and semantic decoding are similar to source coding and source decoding, respectively, in traditional communication. In practical scenarios, such as image transmission, irrelevant image details are filtered before transmission according to different tasks to reduce the network burden without affecting system performance. At the same time, the communication parties need to share local knowledge in real time; otherwise, semantic noise will be generated, resulting in semantic ambiguity, even if the physical transmission is free of syntactic errors.

Goal-oriented communication: This type needs to capture the semantic information, where the communication goal plays an important role in the semantic extraction process and thus helps to further filter the irrelevant semantic information in each transmission. For example, image transmission tasks are different and require different image features to be transmitted. In contrast to semantics-oriented communication, the outputs are direct action execution instructions aimed at accomplishing the task with limited network resources rather than focusing only on semantic accuracy. Similarly, the local knowledge of the communicating parties and the goal of the communication need to be consistent, otherwise semantic noise may lead to task failure.

Semantic-aware communication: Semantic-aware communication plays a role in task-oriented communication in scenarios such as autonomous driving and drone swarms. In these scenarios, multiple intelligent agents accomplish tasks through centralized or distributed collaboration, and semantic-aware communication establishes multiple explicit or implicit connections between different endpoints to enhance knowledge sharing among agents. Its semantic information is obtained by analyzing the behavior of intelligent agents and current environment in which the task is performed rather than extracting from data sources. Unlike the above two types, there is no generalized system model, and it is not part of traditional connection-oriented communication.

2.2.3. Semantic Metrics

Semantic metrics mainly depended on the similarity, which can be divided into two aspects: the semantic level and effectiveness level. The semantic level focuses on the accurate understanding and transmission of information, while the effectiveness emphasizes the performance and functional achievement of the system in practical applications [82].

Semantic-level metrics: The measurement of semantic similarity often serves to evaluate the similarity between the previously mentioned original input data S and the reconstructed output data S′. For different types of media such as text, images, and speech, there are various semantic similarity measurement methods. For example, text has average semantic distortion [91] and Bilingual Evaluation Understudy (BLEU) [92]; for images, metrics such as the peak signal-to-noise ratio (PSNR) [85] and Structural Similarity Index (SSIM) [93] are used; for speech, metrics like the Signal-to-Distortion Ratio (SDR) [94] and Perceptual Evaluation of Speech Quality (PESQ) [95] are employed, where each one has it pros and cons. Additionally, there are metrics for evaluating data compression ratios, such as the bit reduction rate [96] and average bits [97].

Effectiveness-level metrics: These include metrics based on Age of Information (AoI) [98] and Value of Information (VoI) [99]. The core of AoI-based metrics lies in measuring the time interval from the generation of information to its reception, while VoI-related metrics focus on the contribution of information to the completion of specific tasks. These metrics are used to assess the contribution of information to task completion, with different metrics being suitable for different scenarios and tasks.

2.3. *Integration of IoV and Semantic Communication*

The IoV imposes stringent requirements on communication technologies in terms of reliability, low latency, high bandwidth, and security [100–102]. For instance, in autonomous driving scenarios, vehicles need to acquire real-time and accurate traffic information to make safe decisions, which demands extremely low latency and high reliability in communication. In applications such as remote vehicle monitoring and diagnostics, the large volume of data transmission necessitates a high bandwidth. With the increasing number of vehicle smart sensors, growing IoV communication demands, and diversification of user needs, the data volume transmitted and processed in IoV has surged dramatically [103].

Traditional communication technologies, such as cellular networks and DSRC, face limitations in meeting IoV communication requirements, including limited spectrum resources, increased latency during network congestion, and insufficient capability to process semantic information. Therefore, how to improve spectrum utilization efficiency, real-time performance, and accuracy in IoV communication, while ensuring communication security and privacy protection, are urgent challenges to address.

Semantic communication offers several significant advantages [104]. First, it reduces the transmission of redundant data, improving spectrum utilization and enabling efficient information exchange. Second, it enhances communication effectiveness and accuracy through contextual information, particularly in environments with limited bandwidth or low signal-to-noise ratios. Third, semantic communication can obscure information, ensuring that only individuals with specific background knowledge can understand the transmitted content. Finally, it focuses on the meaning of information and user needs, allowing flexible adaptation to diverse communication scenarios. These characteristics provide vast potential for IoV applications, optimizing data transmission, enhancing driving safety, protecting user privacy, and supporting intelligent decision making, thereby advancing the development of intelligent transportation systems.

In recent years, the application of semantic communication technology in the IoV has received extensive attention. By extracting, transmitting, and restoring the semantic content in information, semantic communication significantly improves the efficiency and reliability of communication. The Telecommunication Standardization Sector of the International Telecommunication Union (ITU-T) released a technical report [105] in November 2023, which thoroughly explored the application potential of the Semantic-Aware Network (SAN) in future networks, including the Internet of Vehicles. The report states that by adopting semantic terms and grammars shared by machines and humans, the SAN can effectively represent, annotate, analyze, and interpret network and user-generated data, thus supporting automatic data processing, learning, and analysis. From a vehicular network perspective, the SAN enhances interoperability by translating heterogeneous data (e.g., LiDAR, camera feeds, etc.) into unified semantic domains, supports real-time decision making through semantic cognition, and ensures reliability via distributed semantic resource provisioning.

The integration of the IoV and semantic communication has extensive application scenarios, including autonomous driving, intelligent traffic management, remote vehicle diagnostics and maintenance, and connected entertainment. Autonomous driving refers to the technology that enables vehicles to perform various driving tasks without continuous human intervention. The IoV provides the necessary technical support for autonomous driving by enabling real-time communication between vehicles and between vehicles and infrastructure. This allows autonomous vehicles to acquire information about their surroundings, make more accurate decisions, and improve driving safety and comfort. Semantic communication in the IoV can further enhance the efficiency and accuracy of information transmission, enabling vehicles to better understand and respond to complex traffic scenarios. In intelligent traffic management, IoV technology connects vehicles with traffic infrastructure to enable smart traffic management, such as traffic signal control, road condition monitoring, and electronic toll collection, thereby improving traffic efficiency and alleviating urban congestion. Semantic communication can provide personalized traffic information and services based on vehicle needs and user preferences. For example, it can offer customized navigation suggestions, traffic updates, and information about nearby facilities based on the vehicle's route and destination, thus supporting the efficient operation and optimized management of intelligent transportation systems. Additionally, a semantic IoV can be applied to remote vehicle diagnostics and maintenance, as well as connected entertainments. In remote diagnostics and maintenance, vehicles can transmit data in real time to service centers to accurately identify faults, provide remote repair guidance, or schedule on-site services, thereby reducing troubleshooting time and maintenance costs. For connected entertainments, it allows passengers to enjoy online music and videos and interact with users in other vehicles, enhancing travel enjoyment and social experiences, as well as making the driving process more engaging and less monotonous.

2.4. Lessons Learned

This chapter provides the technical background for the combination of the IoV and semantic communication. We discuss the basic architecture and key communication modes of the IoV, as well as the system architecture and types of semantic communication. Through this chapter, we gain an understanding of the communication challenges faced by the IoV and how semantic communication can enhance communication efficiency and security by extracting and transmitting the semantic content of information. In addition, we also explore the potential of integrating the IoV with semantic communication and how this integration can promote the development of intelligent transportation systems.

3. Key Technologies of Semantic Communication in IoV

Based on the technical background discussed above, the following section will delve into the key technologies of semantic communication in the IoV, including semantic information extraction, communication architecture, and resource allocation, which are critical for realizing efficient and reliable semantic communication.

The IoV aims to build an intelligent transportation ecosystem where vehicles, infrastructure, and people are interconnected. This imposes extremely high demands on communication technologies. In the pursuit of higher transmission efficiency, stronger information comprehension capabilities, and more reliable collaborative interactions, semantic communication has emerged as a breakthrough. It goes beyond the traditional signal transmission level of conventional communication, delving into the dimensions of semantic understanding and knowledge sharing. Compared to the traditional three-layer architecture of the IoV, the semantic communication-based IoV introduces an additional semantic layer to facilitate the acquisition and processing of semantic information. For instance, ref. [106] proposed a four-layer semantic V2X architecture comprising the device layer, network layer, semantic layer, and application layer. The newly added semantic layer extracts key semantic features and compresses redundant information with a semantic encoder and then restores the semantic content via a semantic decoder, ensuring that the receiver accurately understands the sender's intent. The semantic layer also relies on a shared knowledge base to provide a unified foundation for semantic understanding and achieves collaborative optimization between semantic encoding and channel encoding, as well as semantic decoding and channel decoding. This enhances transmission efficiency, reduces data redundancy, overcomes the limitations of traditional communication, and meets the requirements for efficient communication in complex scenarios [107]. Figure 4 shows the system architecture combining the IoV and semantic communication.

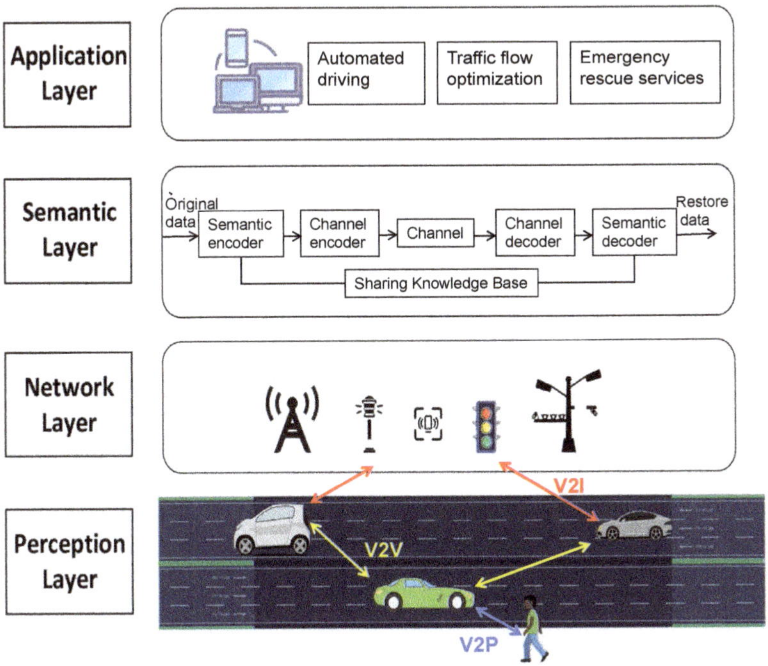

Figure 4. The system architecture combining the IoV and semantic communication.

To comprehensively evaluate the performance of integrated IoV and semantic communication technologies, we propose a multidimensional unified evaluation framework. This framework covers critical metrics such as semantic accuracy and real-time capability, enabling systematic quantitative comparisons across methodologies. These metrics are described as follows:

- Semantic accuracy: This measures the precision of semantic information extraction and reconstruction. It includes general metrics (e.g., BLEU for text, PSNR/SSIM for images, etc.) and task-specific metrics (e.g., IoU for object detection, F1-score for classification, etc.).
- End-to-end latency: This defines the total time from data generation to application reception (encoding + transmission + decoding). This directly impacts real-time-sensitive scenarios like V2V collision warnings.
- Resource efficiency: This includes computational overhead (FLOPs/memory usage) and bandwidth efficiency (data compression ratio), determining feasibility for edge device deployment.

Table 2 summarizes the complete metric definitions and typical application scenarios. Subsequent sections will analyze the strengths and limitations of each technology based on this framework.

Table 2. A summary of three major categories of evaluation metrics.

Category	Metric	Definition	Applicable Scenarios
Semantic Accuracy	IoU	Intersection over Union (overlap between predicted and ground-truth regions)	Environmental perception, object detection
	mIoU	Mean IoU across multiple classes	Complex scene perception
	PSNR	Peak signal-to-noise ratio (pixel-level difference between original and reconstructed data)	Image transmission quality
	F1-score	Harmonic mean of precision and recall for classification tasks	Object classification, anomaly detection
Real-Time Capability	End-to-End Latency	Total time from data generation to application (encoding + transmission + decoding) in ms	V2V collision alerts, autonomous driving
Resource Efficiency	Computational Overhead (FLOPs)	Floating-point operations per semantic encoding/decoding cycle	Edge device deployment feasibility
	Bandwidth Efficiency	Compression ratio (original data size/transmitted data size)	Image/video transmission

3.1. Semantic Information Extraction

Semantic information extraction is the foundation of semantic communication and a critical component for efficient information interaction in the IoV. Vehicles need to extract key semantic information from massive sensor data to support real-time perception and intelligent decision making. The development of semantic information extraction technology has evolved from processing single-sensor data to multimodal data fusion. With the rise of deep learning techniques in recent years, the efficiency and accuracy of semantic information extraction have been significantly improved.

In the IoV domain, semantic information extraction predates that of semantic communication. Early studies focused on extracting useful semantic information from single-sensor data or multimodal data (e.g., vision, radar, LiDAR, etc.) to support vehicle perception and decision making. Initial approaches relied on computer vision or multisensor fusion techniques to extract semantic information about the vehicle's surrounding environment (e.g., object detection, road conditions, etc.), thereby enhancing the performance of autonomous driving systems.

3.1.1. Single-Modal Extraction

In the semantic communication system of the IoV, computer vision-based methods dominate the processing of single-modal data. Semantic segmentation techniques are widely used to extract key features, and different methods exhibit distinct advantages. Semantic segmentation is a pixel-level image classification task, aiming to assign each pixel in an image to a predefined category. This process usually relies on deep learning models. The process from image input to semantic information extraction mainly includes the following steps. Firstly, the input image needs to be pre-processed, such as resizing the image and normalizing pixel values, so that the model can process it better. Secondly, feature extraction is performed on the image through convolutional neural networks (such as UNet, DeepLab, etc.). These networks extract high-level semantic features of the image step by step through multiple convolutional operations. For example, the UNet network extracts and fuses image features through the downsampling and upsampling processes. Then, based on the extracted features, the network classifies each pixel to determine its category. This step is usually achieved through a classification layer, such as a fully connected layer or a convolutional layer. Finally, after obtaining the preliminary segmentation result, post-processing is required, such as noise reduction and boundary smoothing, to improve the accuracy and consistency of the segmentation result. The process of semantic information extraction for other data, such as text data, is similar to that of image data, generally involving steps such as text pre-processing, lexical analysis, syntactic analysis, and semantic understanding.

In the IoV scenario, semantic information extraction technology can be used to extract key information in the road environment, such as vehicles, pedestrians, and traffic signs. For example, ref. [8] employed a deep convolutional model for the semantic segmentation of aerial images and achieved vehicle detection and classification through pixel-level semantic mapping. Their architecture based on SegNet achieved an Intersection over Union (IoU) of 82.4% and an F1-score of 95.7% in their vehicle segmentation task. However, the segmentation accuracy of its pyramid pooling module for small targets (such as traffic signs) decreased by approximately 15%, indicating that this type of method is more suitable for extracting macroscopic objects. Ref. [9] conducted a comparative study to evaluate the effects of U-Net, Seg-Net, and Fully Convolutional Networks (FCNs) for road segmentation. U-Net achieved a mean Intersection over Union (mIoU) of 94% on the Camvid dataset, while Seg-Net prioritized computational efficiency in real-time applications. Ref. [10] combined semantic segmentation with learned image compression, focusing on the preservation of regions of interest (ROIs). At 0.25 bits per pixel (bpp), their method achieved a peak signal-to-noise ratio (PSNR) of 24.25 decibels (dB) in the ROIs, which is 1.19 dB higher than traditional compression methods. The latest research by [12] introduced a multiscale feature extractor based on Swin Transformer, which increased the mIoU by 75% on the Cityscapes dataset compared to traditional methods. Ref. [13] used computer vision algorithms such as RealtimeSeg to extract semantic information from images. Experimental results show that SemCom can significantly increase the load supported by the network, reduce latency, and also perform well in energy consumption.

From the above methods, it can be seen that different semantic information extraction methods have their own characteristics and advantages. Semantic segmentation methods based on deep convolutional models perform well in vehicle detection and classification tasks and can accurately extract vehicle semantic information. Road detection methods based on U-Net, Seg-Net, and FCNs have their own advantages in distinguishing between road and non-road areas and are suitable for different application scenarios. Methods based on learned image compression can not only extract semantic information but also effectively reduce the amount of data and improve transmission efficiency, especially in enhancing the image quality within the region of interest. The method based on the Swin Transformer has significant advantages in multiscale feature capture and target recognition accuracy in complex traffic scenarios. The semantic segmentation technology in semantic communication performs well in solving the bandwidth bottleneck problem of IoV image transmission and can significantly improve network performance and energy consumption efficiency.

3.1.2. Multimodal Fusion

Multimodal fusion integrates heterogeneous sensor data (such as LiDAR, cameras, and Global Positioning System—GPS) to enhance the environmental perception ability. The semantic communication framework further optimizes this process through task-aware feature extraction and transmission.

Ref. [11] used PSPNet for semantic segmentation and the Random Sample Consensus (RANSAC) algorithm for geometric feature alignment, fusing visual, GPS, and map data. Their Bird's-Eye-View (BEV) registration achieved a feature matching accuracy of over 90%, effectively eliminating blind spots. Ref. [14] designed a hybrid Convolutional Neural Network–Graph Neural Network–Long Short-Term Memory Network (CNN-GNN-LSTM) encoder to unify multimodal features (images, point clouds, and radar) into a semantic space. This method maintained an F1-score of 0.93 at an SNR of 0 dB, demonstrating strong noise resistance. Ref. [15] combined Bird's-Eye-View (BEV) fusion with a Diffusion Model (DM) for noise suppression. At an SNR of 0 dB, the DM-enhanced decoding increased the IoU from 0.65 to 0.80, with further improvements at higher SNR levels.

In the field of multimodal data fusion, different methods have their unique advantages and applicable scenarios. Ref. [11] significantly expanded the vehicle's perception range by integrating multisource data such as visual, GPS, and digital maps, especially excelling in eliminating blind spots with a feature point matching accuracy of over 90%. The semantic communication in [14] focused on efficiently extracting key semantic information from multimodal data through a semantic encoder. It used multiple neural network architectures to process different modal data, not only significantly reducing the amount of data transmission but also maintaining an F1-score as high as 0.93 under low-SNR conditions. The work of [15] integrates multisensor data through technologies such as BEV fusion and uses generative AI technology for noise reduction and enhancement. Its IoU has been significantly improved under different SNR conditions, especially under low-SNR conditions, where the IoU value increased from 0.65 to 0.80, and it can effectively predict future scenarios. Overall, these methods have different emphases in expanding the perception range, reducing data redundancy, enhancing robustness, and improving prediction capabilities, providing diverse solutions for autonomous driving systems.

From the current research, semantic information extraction technology shows a trend toward more efficient and accurate models. With the increasing requirements for real-time performance and accuracy in the Internet of Vehicles, future research will pay more attention to the lightweight and fast-processing capabilities of models to meet the real-time processing requirements of a large amount of data during high-speed vehicle driving. At the same time, the accuracy and real-time performance of multimodal data fusion will also be a key research direction. Through more advanced fusion algorithms and technologies, the quality and efficiency of semantic information extraction from multimodal data will be further improved.

3.2. Semantic Communication Architecture

In practical application scenarios of the IoV, such as autonomous driving and intelligent traffic coordination management, the realization of complex functionalities not only relies on accurate semantic information extraction but also imposes stringent requirements on the subsequent transmission and interaction modes of information. The design of semantic communication architectures must meet the demands of the IoV for real-time performance, reliability, and efficiency. This section categorizes and summarizes existing semantic communication architectures in the IoV, highlighting their applications and optimization strategies in different scenarios. Table 3 summarizes the semantic communication architecture in the IoV.

Table 3. Classification and characteristics of semantic communication architectures in IoV.

Category	Architecture	Characteristics
Multitask and Multiuser	Co-SC Architecture [16]	Multiuser collaboration, with the semantic codec (Sem-Codec) and joint source–channel codec (JSC-Codec) working together to improve semantic reconstruction performance.
	Unified Multiuser Semantic Communication System [14]	Integration of multiuser semantic information, dynamic update of shared and private knowledge bases, and support for joint training of multiple tasks.
	Multitask-Oriented Semantic Communication Framework [17]	Multitask processing combining the semantic encoder with task-oriented decoders to support image reconstruction and classification tasks.
	SemHARQ Framework [18]	Semantic-aware hybrid automatic repeat request (HARQ), feature importance ranking, and distortion evaluation to enhance transmission robustness.
Image Transmission	ISSC System [12]	Multiscale semantic feature extraction based on Swin Transformer to reduce data transmission volume while ensuring image quality.
	VIS-SemCom System [19]	Importance-aware image segmentation, multiscale semantic extraction, and importance-aware loss function to improve the segmentation accuracy of important objects.
	SEECAD System [20]	Deep learning-based semantic encoder and decoder, combined with LDPC codes, to transmit semantic information instead of original pixel data.
	MTDSC Method [21]	Multiscene object detection, combined with spatial pyramid pooling and long-short-term memory network to optimize semantic label assignment and transmission.
	Combination of Low-latency Routing and Semantic Communication [22]	Low-latency routing algorithm combined with semantic communication to optimize image data transmission and reduce latency.
Based on Generative AI	AIGC Encoder–Decoder Architecture [23]	Image-to-text conversion and reinforcement learning optimization to reduce data transmission volume while ensuring image quality.
	Multimodal Semantic-aware Generative AI Framework [24]	Extracts semantic text information and image skeletons and reconstructs images in combination with a generative AI model.
	G-MSC Framework [15]	Multimodal alignment and fusion, with a generative AI-enhanced semantic encoder to improve data quality and communication reliability.
	Generative AI-Driven Semantic Communication Framework [25]	Lightweight MSAM extracts key semantic information, combined with GAN to reconstruct images, reducing data transmission volume.
	Agent-Driven Generative Semantic Communication Framework (A-GSC) [26]	Generative AI combined with reinforcement learning to dynamically adjust the semantic sampling strategy, improving information interpretability and transmission efficiency.
Other Architectures	Blockchain-based Edge-assisted Knowledge Base Management System [27]	Blockchain technology ensures data security and consistency, and semantic segmentation reduces data transmission volume.
	PreCMTS Strategy [28]	Task-driven knowledge-graph-assisted semantic communication; dynamically adjusts semantic unit allocation and relay selection.
	SCKS Framework [29]	Knowledge sharing of neural network models, with a generative adversarial network (GAN) decoding semantic information to update the vehicle model.

3.2.1. Multiuser Collaboration and Multitask Driving

In the IoV, multiuser collaboration and multitask driving are two closely related semantic communication scenarios. Multiuser collaboration focuses on semantic information sharing between vehicles, while multitask driving focuses on optimizing the processing and transmission of semantic information for different tasks.

Ref. [16] proposed a multiuser collaborative semantic communication architecture (Co-SC), which comprises components such as semantic codecs (Sem-Codec), joint source–channel codecs (JSC-Codec), and task-related modules. The Co-SC architecture significantly enhances semantic reconstruction performance and recognition accuracy under low-SNR conditions. By leveraging multiuser collaboration, Co-SC effectively exploits the semantic correlation among users, reducing the transmission of redundant information and thereby significantly improving communication efficiency. However, the performance improvement of this architecture is limited under high-SNR conditions, and it has a high dependence on channel state information (CSI), requiring accurate channel estimation. Moreover, the performance of the architecture is highly reliant on the pre-trained knowledge base and offline-trained models, and its adaptability to the dynamically changing VANET environment needs further investigation. Overall, the Co-SC architecture provides an effective solution for semantic communication in VANETs, but a trade-off between computational resources and real-time requirements is necessary in practical deployment.

Ref. [14] presented a unified multiuser semantic communication system that integrates semantic information from multiple users to achieve collaborative processing. This framework significantly reduces the amount of data transmission through semantic encoding. For instance, in the task of object classification, it achieved performance comparable to or even better than traditional methods with a compression rate of only about 8.4%. The F1-score reached 0.9880 under high-SNR conditions and remained above 0.93 under low-SNR conditions, demonstrating good robustness. The system not only supports multitask processing but also ensures semantic understanding and vehicle privacy by constructing shared and private knowledge bases. However, the system complexity is relatively high, requiring substantial computational resources to support joint training of multiple tasks, which may pose a challenge to the real-time processing capabilities of vehicles in VANETs. Moreover, the adaptability of the system under dynamic channel conditions needs further improvement.

Ref. [17] proposed a multitask semantic communication framework for autonomous vehicles. It employs convolutional autoencoders for semantic encoding of traffic sign images and utilizes satellite communication for information sharing among vehicles. The image reconstruction quality is assessed using the structural similarity index measure (SSIM), and the results show that it outperformed the traditional 16-QAM scheme under low-SNR conditions, indicating good performance in semantic similarity. Additionally, the framework significantly improved data transmission efficiency by reducing the amount of transmitted data by up to 89%, indirectly reducing transmission latency. However, the paper does not provide a detailed discussion on computational overhead. Considering its implementation based on deep learning, it may face certain computational resource demands in real-time deployment.

Ref. [18] introduced a semantic-aware hybrid automatic repeat request (SemHARQ) framework for multitask semantic communication in VANETs. This framework significantly enhances the efficiency and robustness of semantic feature transmission through feature importance ranking (FIR) and feature distortion evaluation (FDE) networks. The study demonstrates excellent performance under low-SNR conditions. For example, in the task of vehicle reidentification, the rank-1 accuracy was improved by more than 20% compared to existing methods, and the vehicle color classification accuracy was increased by 10%. However, despite its superior performance in multitask scenarios, the computational overhead may limit its real-time deployment in VANETs, especially on resource-constrained edge devices. Moreover, the study mainly focuses on the transmission efficiency and accuracy of semantic features, with less discussion on key indicators for practical deployment such as transmission delay and computational overhead. Therefore, although SemHARQ has significant theoretical advantages, further optimization is needed in practical applications to reduce computational complexity and meet real-time requirements.

In the research on multiuser collaboration and multitask-driven semantic communication frameworks, these studies have proposed various distinctive solutions. The Co-SC architecture significantly improves semantic reconstruction performance through multiuser collaboration under low-SNR conditions but has a high dependence on CSI and limited performance improvement under high-SNR conditions. The system in [14] significantly reduces data transmission through semantic encoding and supports multitask processing, but it has high system complexity and a large demand for computational resources. The framework in [17] improves image reconstruction quality and transmission efficiency through semantic encoding in the autonomous driving scenario, but the issue of computational overhead needs to be clarified. The SemHARQ framework significantly enhances the efficiency and accuracy of semantic feature transmission through feature importance ranking under low SNR conditions, but its computational overhead may limit real-time deployment. These studies each have their own advantages, but in practical VANET applications, it is necessary to comprehensively consider factors such as computational resources, real-time performance, and adaptability to channel conditions to achieve more efficient and practical semantic communication solutions. Future work may explore the integration of the advantages of these methods to optimize computational overhead and real-time performance, thereby further enhancing the overall performance of semantic communication in VANETs.

3.2.2. Oriented to Image Transmission

Image transmission is one of core tasks in the IoV for environmental perception and decision making. Efficient image transmission requires not only reducing data volume but also ensuring that image quality meets the real-time demands of autonomous driving and intelligent transportation systems. For specific tasks such as image segmentation and object detection, researchers have proposed various optimized semantic communication architectures to address the needs of different application scenarios.

Ref. [12] proposed an Image Segmentation Semantic Communication (ISSC) system for the IoV. This system utilizes a multiscale semantic feature extractor and a semantic feature aggregator based on the Swin Transformer to achieve an efficient transformation from the input image to semantic features. Additionally, it accurately reconstructs the image segmentation at the receiving end through a semantic feature decoder and a reconstructor. Experimental results show that the ISSC system performs excellently in a low-SNR environment, with its mean Intersection over Union (mIoU) increased by 75% compared to traditional coding methods, indicating that the system has a significant advantage in semantic similarity. Furthermore, although the paper does not explicitly mention the specific values of transmission delay and computational overhead, considering its deep learning-based architecture, the computational overhead may be high, especially in real-time deployment scenarios.

Ref. [19] proposed a semantic communication system for autonomous driving based on importance-aware image segmentation (VIS-SemCom). Through multiscale semantic feature extraction and an importance-aware loss function, it significantly improves the accuracy of image segmentation and communication efficiency. Experiments show that under the requirement of an average mIoU of 60%, this system can achieve a coding gain of nearly 6 dB compared to traditional solutions and performs well under low-SNR conditions, with the maximum reduction of the transmitted data volume reaching 70%. The system improved the segmentation accuracy of key objects (such as vehicles and pedestrians) by approximately 4%, but its generalization ability in complex environments still needs to be further verified.

Ref. [20] proposed a semantic end-to-end communication system named SEECAD, which is specifically designed for image transmission in autonomous driving scenarios. By constructing a semantic encoder and decoder through a deep learning architecture and combining with Low-Density Parity-Check (LDPC) codes, it efficiently transmits the semantic information of images instead of the original pixel data, thus significantly reducing the amount of transmitted data and improving the transmission efficiency. At the receiving end, the system reconstructs the image segmentation mask using a shared knowledge base, enhancing its robustness in noisy environments. Experimental results show that under 4QAM modulation and LDPC (16, 32) coding, it achieved a segmentation accuracy of 97.4% and an IOU value of 0.75 at an SNR of 12 dB, demonstrating high semantic similarity and anti-noise ability. However, the training and real-time inference of the deep learning model require high computational resources, which may limit its real-time deployment in the IoV.

Ref. [21] proposed a semantic communication method for multiscene object detection in intelligent vehicle networks (MTDSC), aiming to improve the processing efficiency of image data through semantic encoding and transmission. This method uses a convolutional neural network and a region proposal network for object detection, combines Spatial Pyramid Pooling (SPP) with a long short-term memory network (LSTM) for semantic label assignment, and finally achieves reliable transmission through a variational autoencoder. In terms of model performance evaluation, MTDSC performs well in semantic similarity. Experiments have verified its high mIoU values in different road scenes (such as 83.276% in highway scenes), indicating that it can accurately understand and transmit key semantic information. In terms of transmission delay, this method reduces the amount of data through efficient semantic encoding, thus reducing the communication delay. However, its limitation lies in the high computational overhead, especially in the training and inference stages of the deep learning model, which may pose a challenge to the real-time deployment in the IoV.

Ref. [22] combined low-latency routing and semantic communication to optimize the transmission of image data in the IoV. In this method, the low-latency routing algorithm takes into account factors such as the distance between vehicle nodes, the packet loss probability of candidate nodes, remaining energy, and load, and it selects the optimal routing node to ensure the rapid transmission of image data. At the same time, semantic communication technology uses a convolutional neural network to extract image features, obtains a semantic sequence through a feature-semantic transformation function, compresses the feature map according to the task importance, and then transmits it. The receiving end performs the inverse operation to restore the image for classification and recognition. This method mainly addresses the problem of high transmission latency of image data in the IoV caused by the high-speed movement of vehicles and the dynamic changes of the network topology. Experiments have proven that compared with traditional methods, this method can significantly reduce the transmission latency and has little impact on the accuracy of image classification. Its advantage lies in significantly reducing the transmission latency and maintaining a high image classification accuracy. However, the high computational overhead and the lack of detailed evaluation limit its feasibility for real-time deployment in resource-constrained environments.

In the research on semantic communication for image transmission in the IoV, different methods have shown their unique advantages and limitations. The ISSC system demonstrates excellent semantic similarity in a low-SNR environment through efficient semantic feature extraction and transformation, with a significant increase in the average mIoU. However, the high computational overhead brought by the deep learning architecture may restrict real-time deployment. The VIS-SemCom system performs excellently in terms of image segmentation accuracy and communication efficiency, with obvious coding gain and a significant reduction in the transmitted data volume. However, its generalization ability in complex environments, as well as the detailed information about computational overhead and transmission delay, remains unclear. The SEECAD system has excellent semantic similarity and anti-noise ability at high SNRs, but it has a certain dependence on the SNR, and the training and inference of the deep learning model require high computational resources. The MTDSC method performs well in semantic similarity for multiscene object detection and reduces the consumption of computational resources through reinforcement learning optimization, but the computational overhead is still high. Combining low-latency routing and semantic communication to optimize image data transmission significantly reduces the transmission latency and maintains a high image classification accuracy, but it also faces the problems of high computational overhead and lack of detailed evaluation. These methods have their own focuses in improving semantic similarity, reducing the transmitted data volume, and decreasing the transmission latency, but there are still challenges to varying degrees in terms of computational overhead, real-time performance, generalization ability, and adaptability to the SNR. Further research is needed in the future to balance these factors to better meet the actual needs of image transmission in the IoV.

3.2.3. Generative AI-Based Semantic Communication Architectures

Generative AI technologies, such as generative adversarial networks (GANs) and large language models (LLMs), have shown significant potential in optimizing data processing and transmission efficiency in semantic communication, particularly in the context of the IoV. By transforming complex data (e.g., images, text, etc.) into concise semantic representations and leveraging multimodal fusion and reconstruction techniques, generative AI substantially reduces data volume while enhancing the intelligence and accuracy of communication. Current generative AI-based semantic communication architectures in the IoV primarily focus on image transmission. Unlike traditional image transmission architectures, these approaches emphasize the use of generative AI to intelligently process complex data. By converting images, text, and other data types into compact semantic representations and integrating multimodal fusion and reconstruction, these architectures not only reduce data transmission but also significantly improve communication intelligence, thus offering new perspectives and methods for semantic communication in the IoV. Below are several generative AI-based semantic communication architectures and their applications.

Ref. [23] proposed an scalable Artificial Intelligence Generated Content (AIGC) encoder–decoder architecture. The encoder leverages large language models to convert images into concise text prompts. Before transmission, the text information is optimized by a reinforcement learning module. The decoder then converts the optimized text back into images and decides whether to transmit semantically important image regions based on bandwidth conditions. The system demonstrates excellent performance in semantic similarity. Experiments have validated its advantages in image reconstruction quality while significantly reducing the amount of transmitted data, with a compression ratio of several times. This is highly beneficial for bandwidth-constrained VANET environments.

Ref. [24] proposed a multimodal semantic-aware framework based on generative AI. It achieves efficient data transmission and reconstruction by extracting semantic text information and image skeletons. The framework first extracts semantic text information and image skeletons from real-time road images and then combines them into small data packets for V2V communication. The receiving end uses a generative AI model to generate road condition images that match reality and reconstructs them for display to intelligent assistants. This significantly reduces data volume and effectively reduces transmission delay. However, although the framework emphasizes data privacy protection, it does not provide detailed explanations on how to ensure data security in practical deployment. Therefore, while the framework excels in improving semantic similarity and transmission efficiency, it still needs further optimization in terms of computational overhead and privacy security.

Ref. [15] proposed a Generative AI-Enhanced Multimodal Semantic Communication (G-MSC) framework enhanced by generative AI. It reduces data redundancy through multimodal alignment and fusion and performs denoising and semantic inference on noisy data at the receiver. In the G-MSC framework, generative AI technology enhances the capabilities of the semantic encoder, enabling it to better handle multimodal data. The optimization of channel transmission and the semantic decoder also improves the reliability and stability of communication. Experimental results show that diffusion models significantly improve image clarity and IoU. Particularly under low-SNR conditions, it effectively mitigates the impact of channel noise on performance. The framework's strengths lie in its efficient processing of multimodal data and adaptability to dynamic environments. However, its limitation is the high demand for computational resources, which may restrict its real-time deployment in resource-constrained VANET environments. Future research directions include hybrid digital–analog transmission, multivehicle semantic information scheduling, and cross-task coordination, which are expected to further optimize the performance and application scope of the G-MSC framework.

Ref. [25] proposed a GAI-driven semantic communication framework for next-generation wireless networks (such as 6G). The framework extracts key semantic information from images using the lightweight Mobile Segment Anything Model (MSAM) and reconstructs and denoises images at the receiver using a generative adversarial network (GAN), achieving high-quality image reconstruction under different SNR conditions. Experimental results show that models trained under specific SNR conditions can achieve high PSNRs. Moreover, the framework further reduces data transmission by periodically updating background information. Experimental results indicate that the framework achieved a significant reduction in data transmission volume, up to 93.45%, while maintaining the integrity of the original content. However, the framework is sensitive to the SNR during training, with limited robustness. The real-time and feasibility of its deployment in VANETs still need further investigation.

Ref. [26] proposed an Agent-Driven Generative Semantic Communication (A-GSC) framework based on reinforcement learning. It seamlessly integrates semantic extraction and semantic sampling using generative AI. By transmitting the semantic information of a scene in text form, it reduces data volume while improving information interpretability. Moreover, the semantic sampling agent based on reinforcement learning can dynamically adjust sampling strategies according to channel conditions and changes in source data, ensuring optimal semantic information transmission under limited energy consumption. The framework performs well in terms of semantic similarity, transmission delay, and computational overhead. Its strengths are high semantic similarity, low transmission delay, and small computational overhead, making it suitable for real-time applications in VANETs. However, its limitations include insufficient adaptability to complex communication environments, and the feasibility of real-time deployment on resource-constrained devices still needs further verification.

In summary, these generative AI-based semantic communication frameworks each have their own characteristics. The AIGC architecture excels in data compression but lacks sufficient evaluation of real-time performance and computational overhead, with its deployment feasibility remaining to be verified. The multimodal framework has high data transmission efficiency but demands substantial computational resources and lacks clear privacy security guarantees. The G-MSC framework has strong capabilities in processing multimodal data and adapting to dynamic environments, but its high demand for computational resources restricts real-time deployment. The framework in [25] achieves high semantic similarity and significant reduction in data transmission under specific SNR conditions, but it is sensitive to the SNR, with limited robustness, and the real-time and feasibility of its deployment in VANETs need further investigation. The A-GSC framework performs well in semantic similarity, transmission delay, and computational overhead, making it suitable for real-time applications in VANETs, but it has insufficient adaptability to complex communication environments, and the feasibility of real-time deployment on resource-constrained devices remains to be verified.

Overall, these methods have their own advantages in terms of data transmission efficiency and semantic similarity, but they also have varying degrees of shortcomings in computational overhead, real-time performance, robustness, privacy security, and deployment feasibility. Future research needs to balance and optimize these aspects to better meet the practical needs of integrating VANETs and semantic communication.

3.2.4. Other Architectures

In addition to the mainstream semantic communication architectures mentioned above, several innovative architectures have demonstrated unique advantages in the IoV. These architectures expand the application scenarios of semantic communication and enhance communication efficiency and intelligence by integrating technologies such as blockchain, knowledge graphs, and neural network sharing.

The fusion of blockchain and edge computing technologies brings multiple benefits to semantic communication, including data security, privacy protection, and improved system efficiency. Ref. [27] proposed a blockchain-based edge-assisted knowledge base management system for semantic communication in the IoV. This system extracts key information through semantic segmentation and utilizes blockchain sharding technology to enhance the efficiency and security of knowledge base management. Experiments show that the proposed semantic communication method has lower transmission latency compared with traditional communication methods under low-SNR conditions and performs better in terms of transmission efficiency. Its advantages lie in effectively reducing communication costs, improving data transmission efficiency, and ensuring the consistency and security of the knowledge base with the help of blockchain technology. However, the limitation of this study is that it does not discuss in detail the computational overhead in the real-time deployment of the IoV, as well as the scalability issues in large-scale networks, which may affect its widespread application in practical scenarios.

Ref. [28] proposed a task-driven semantic-aware green cooperative transmission strategy (PreCMTS) that is suitable for intermittently connected IoV scenarios. This strategy employs a weighted directed graph to achieve semantic-aware transmission by analyzing parameters such as the remaining dwell time of vehicles at RSUs, encounter time with target vehicles, and lifetime of V2V links. It derives an expression for achievable throughput that meets delay requirements and formulates the coupled problem of semantic unit allocation and predictive relay selection as a combinatorial optimization problem. A low-complexity algorithm based on Markov approximation is designed to solve this problem. PreCMTS primarily addresses the intermittent connectivity caused by the high deployment costs and energy consumption of the infrastructure in vehicular networks, as well as the limited applicability of existing semantic communication research in dynamic and complex vehicle networks. The strategy aims to achieve both semantic and green communication. Experimental results show that PreCMTS effectively reduces energy consumption, improves the reliability of semantic transmission, and enhances semantic energy efficiency, thus outperforming baseline methods under various conditions.However, this strategy has deficiencies in terms of the analysis of computational overhead and feasibility for real-time deployment, and it fails to thoroughly explore the computational complexity and resource consumption of the deep learning model in the IoV environment.

In the integration of the IoV and semantic communication, besides transmitting IoV data through semantic communication systems, neural network models can also be shared. Ref. [29] proposed a deep semantic communication framework, SCKS, to address the efficiency issues of knowledge sharing of neural network models in the IoV. This architecture extracts semantic features of neural network models using a dataset distillation algorithm and designs a semantic decoding algorithm based on GANs. By leveraging the deep semantic communication system, RSUs extract semantic information from neural network models, encode it into semantic feature vectors, and transmit it to vehicles. Upon receiving the vectors, vehicles decode them into synthetic datasets using a semantic decoder and then update their neural network models. This enables efficient knowledge sharing from RSUs to multiple vehicles. The experimental results demonstrate that the framework exhibits remarkable performance in semantic similarity, effectively extracting the semantic features of neural network (NN) models. Under low-SNR conditions, the framework outperformed traditional methods in terms of transmission delay. However, the framework incurs a high computational overhead, particularly during the training phase, which poses limitations on the feasibility of real-time deployment. Despite these challenges, the framework, referred to as SCKS, performs well on high-resolution datasets. Further investigation is required to assess its performance when the number of categories increases.

These innovative architectures, through task-driven approaches, knowledge graph optimization, and neural network sharing, further expand the application scenarios of semantic communication in the IoV. However, they also demonstrate their respective advantages and limitations. The blockchain-based edge-assisted knowledge base management system performs excellently in terms of data security and transmission efficiency. However, the issues of computational overhead in the real-time deployment of the IoV and scalability in large-scale networks have not been resolved yet. The PreCMTS effectively reduces energy consumption and improves the reliability of semantic transmission, but it lacks a detailed analysis of the computational complexity and resource consumption of the deep learning model. The deep semantic communication framework SCKS enhances semantic similarity and transmission efficiency through the knowledge sharing of the neural network model. However, the relatively high computational overhead, especially during the training phase, limits its feasibility for real-time deployment. Although these architectures are innovative in their own ways, in practical applications, various factors such as computational overhead, scalability, and energy consumption need to be comprehensively considered to better adapt to the complex and changeable environmental requirements of the IoV and achieve efficient and reliable semantic communication.

3.3. Resource Allocation and Management

In intelligent networking scenarios, semantic-oriented resource allocation methods have significant advantages [108]. Similarly, in the context of the IoV, the high mobility of vehicles and the diverse semantic communication tasks make resource allocation and management critically important. Different tasks have time-varying demands for resources such as spectrum, power, and computing. For instance, road condition information transmission requires low latency and high bandwidth, while vehicle diagnostics emphasize data accuracy and completeness. This subsection reviews relevant research progress and categorizes resource allocation and management strategies based on different technical approaches. Table 4 summarizes existing research on resource allocation and management in the IoV based on semantic communication.

Table 4. Resource allocation and management methods in IoV based on semantic communication.

Category	Methodology	Characteristics	Application Scenario
Reinforcement Learning	SARADC Framework [30]	Significantly improves HSSE and semantic throughput, adapting to high-resolution and low-signal-to-noise-ratio conditions.	5G-V2X heterogeneous networks
	SSS Algorithm [31]	Dynamically optimizes spectrum sharing, improving semantic transmission efficiency and spectrum utilization.	Spectrum sharing in vehicle networking
	DDQN Method [24]	Ensures efficient semantic information transmission and supports multiagent collaborative resource allocation.	Generative AI-empowered V2V communication in IoV
	SAMRA Algorithm [32]	Adapts to multiscenario changes, improving resource allocation efficiency and task success rate.	C-V2X platoon communication
	VSRAA-SM Algorithm [33]	Improves video semantic understanding accuracy, reducing the CUE outage probability and V2V transmission rate.	In-vehicle video semantic resource allocation
Optimization Theory	Lyapunov Optimization Method [34]	Features fast convergence, improving system robustness and power consumption efficiency.	D2D in-vehicle networks
	Two-stage Suboptimal Solution Method [35]	Maximizes semantic detection accuracy, minimizes wireless resource costs, and ensures communication link quality.	Vehicle platoon collaboration
	Two-stage Stochastic Integer Programming (SSTS) [36]	Optimizes resource allocation, reduces transmission costs, and supports immersive experiences.	Virtual transportation network in the meta-verse
Federated Learning	MSFTL Framework [37]	Reduces vehicle computational costs, improves resource utilization efficiency, and supports distributed training.	In-vehicle semantic communication
	FVSCom Framework [38]	Improves computational efficiency and semantic extraction accuracy, enhancing robustness to vehicle departure or withdrawal.	In-vehicle semantic communication

3.3.1. Reinforcement Learning-Based Resource Allocation Methods

In the context of integrating VANETs with semantic communication, reinforcement learning (RL)-based resource allocation methods have garnered significant attention due to their strong dynamic adaptability and optimization capabilities. These methods can dynamically adjust resource allocation strategies in real time according to the dynamic environment and task requirements in VANETs, thereby significantly enhancing system performance.

Ref. [30] proposed a Semantic-Aware Resource Allocation and Decision-making Framework (SARADC) specifically for the complex scenario of spectrum sharing between vehicles and Wi-Fi users in 5G-V2X heterogeneous networks. This research introduces innovative metrics such as high-speed semantic transmission rate (HSR) and high-speed semantic spectrum efficiency (HSSE). The near-policy optimization (PPO) algorithm is employed to optimize parameters, including channel allocation, power allocation, duty cycle, and semantic symbol length. Experimental results demonstrate that the framework significantly improves the HSSE and semantic throughput (ST) under high-resolution and low-SNR conditions, effectively enhancing resource utilization efficiency and system performance. However, the discussion on computational overhead and transmission delay is insufficient, which may limit its real-time deployment in VANETs.

Similarly, ref. [31] proposed a Semantic-Aware Spectrum Sharing (SSS) algorithm based on Deep Reinforcement Learning (DRL) to address the spectrum sharing problem in the IoV. This algorithm redefines spectrum sharing metrics such as HSSE and the HSR by incorporating semantic information and utilizes the soft actor-critic (SAC) method to optimize decisions to maximize HSSE and improve the success rate of effective semantic information transmission (SRS). Simulation results show that the SSS algorithm outperforms traditional bit-based spectrum sharing methods in terms of HSSE and SRS. However, the limitation of this algorithm is its potentially high computational overhead, especially considering the computational capabilities and resource constraints of vehicles in real-time deployment.

Ref. [24] started from the perspective of generative AI and used a deep reinforcement learning (DRL) algorithm to design a resource allocation strategy for V2V communication in the IoV. The study uses the double deep Q-network (DDQN) method to optimize parameters such as channel selection, transmission power, and diffusion steps, ensuring efficient semantic information transmission in VANETs. Additionally, the method designs action space, state space, and reward functions adapted to semantic communication to accommodate the dynamically changing channel conditions and transmission requirements in VANETs. Its advantage lies in dynamically adjusting resource allocation using DRL to adapt to the dynamics of vehicular networks, effectively reducing transmission delay and improving semantic similarity. However, the study lacks in-depth discussion on the quantification of computational overhead and lacks discussion on the weight allocation of multimodal data fusion, which may affect its robustness in complex scenarios and scalability of practical applications.

Ref. [32] aimed at the difficult problem of C-V2X platoon communication resource management and proposed a Semantic-Aware Multimodal Resource Allocation (SAMRA) algorithm using Multiagent Reinforcement Learning (MARL). The study defines metrics and quality of experience (QoE) concepts suitable for semantic and multimodal data in the system model, with maximizing the QoE and the success rate of V2V semantic information transmission as joint optimization objectives. By optimizing channel allocation, power allocation, and semantic symbol length using MARL, experimental results show that the algorithm outperformed baseline methods in multiple scenarios. Its advantage is the enhanced scalability and adaptability of the system through distributed decision making, effectively improving the QoE and the success rate of semantic information transmission

(SRS). However, similar to the previous studies, this research lacks in-depth discussion on computational overhead in real-time deployment and lacks quantitative comparison among different methods, making it difficult to comprehensively assess its feasibility in practical VANET scenarios.

Finally, ref. [33] aimed at the dilemma of in-vehicle video semantic resource allocation and built a model based on the multiagent deep Q-network (MADQN) for optimization according to the tasks between vehicles, base stations, and vehicles. Experimental results show that compared to traditional algorithms, the VSRAA-SM achieved higher accuracy in video semantic understanding under different vehicle transmission power and bandwidth conditions and also performed better in terms of the CUE outage probability and V2V transmission rate, making it more suitable for spectrum reuse scenarios. However, the limitation of this study is the lack of detailed analysis on computational overhead, with the feasibility of real-time deployment remaining unclear. Moreover, the paper does not construct a unified evaluation framework, posing certain difficulties for quantitative comparison with other methods.

In summary, these RL-based resource allocation methods have demonstrated significant advantages in enhancing semantic communication performance. However, they still have shortcomings in terms of computational overhead, the feasibility of real-time deployment, and multimodal data fusion. Future research needs to further optimize these methods to reduce computational overhead and improve their adaptability and scalability in practical VANET scenarios. Additionally, constructing a unified evaluation framework to quantitatively compare the performance of different methods will be crucial for advancing this field.

3.3.2. Optimization Theory-Based Resource Allocation Methods

Optimization algorithms are also widely used in resource allocation to enable efficient resource distribution through mathematical modeling and optimization techniques. Compared to reinforcement learning methods, optimization algorithms often provide more precise solutions for resource allocation problems under specific constraints, demonstrating superior performance in system stability and robustness. For example, ref. [109] proposed an RSU caching incentive scheme based on the Stackelberg game and optimized the content caching strategy and pricing mechanism by establishing a game model between the base station (BS) and RSU. In the field of the combination of vehicle networking and semantic communication, researchers have also proposed some resource allocation schemes based on optimization theory, significantly improving the efficiency and performance of semantic communication in scenarios such as Device-to-Device (D2D) communication and vehicle platooning in the IoV.

Ref. [34] proposed a long-term robust resource allocation scheme for D2D in-vehicle networks. The scheme also considers the semantic access control of the application layer and the power control of the physical layer. The Lyapunov optimization method is used to transform the long-term constraints into queue stability conditions. Then, successive convex approximation and the Karush–Kuhn–Tucker (KKT) condition are used to solve the subproblem, while Bernstein approximation is used to deal with uncertain probability constraints. Simulation results show that the algorithm enables rapid convergence of metrics such as the semantic access rate and power. Under different interruption probability thresholds, the algorithm demonstrates the trade-off between the transmission rate and delay. Compared to traditional methods, it exhibited superior performance in system robustness and power consumption. Simulation results show that this algorithm performs excellently in terms of system robustness and power consumption. However, there is relatively little discussion on the computational overhead and real-time performance in practical deployment, which limits the feasibility of its application in an IoV environment with limited resources.

Beyond resource allocation in D2D vehicular networks, optimization theory has also been extensively applied in vehicle platooning scenarios. Ref. [35] proposed an innovative resource allocation scheme based on semantic communication for the collaborative data processing scenario between autonomous vehicle platoons and base stations in the IoV. The scheme aims to maximize semantic detection accuracy and minimize wireless resource costs while incorporating constraints such as bandwidth, transmission power, and SNR. Given the NP-hard nature of the optimization problem, a two-stage suboptimal solution is adopted. In the first stage, a bipartite graph is used to transform the communication mode selection problem into a maximum weight matching problem, and the Hungarian algorithm is applied to determine the matching relationship between vehicles and task processing units, ensuring communication link quality and reliability. In the second stage, based on the results of the first stage, the resource allocation problem is transformed into a convex optimization problem, which is solved using Matlab's fmincon function to achieve reasonable allocation of resources such as bandwidth and transmission power. Simulation results show that, compared to the scheme that only used V2I communication, this method significantly improved the accuracy of video semantic detection, especially showing obvious advantages when the distance between vehicles is large. However, the paper does not provide specific data on key indicators such as semantic similarity, transmission delay, and computational overhead, which limits the comprehensive evaluation of the performance of the scheme.

Additionally, ref. [36] proposed a Stochastic Semantic Transmission Scheme (SSTS) based on two-stage Stochastic Integer Programming (SIP) to address resource allocation problems in virtual traffic networks within the metaverse. By introducing semantic communication technology, the scheme leverages the sensing capabilities of edge devices to transmit data from the physical world to the virtual world, providing immersive experiences for Virtual Service Providers (VSPs). The SSTS scheme considers the demand uncertainty of VSPs and optimizes resource allocation through a combination of reservation and on-demand plans, reducing transmission costs. Experiments have verified the advantages of the SSTS in energy consumption optimization. The energy consumption of semantic data transmission is significantly lower than that of non-semantic data transmission, which indicates that it has significant advantages in reducing energy consumption. However, the limitation of this study is that it mainly focuses on the transmission cost of semantic data and the subscription strategy, and the analysis of the computational overhead and complexity in real-time deployment is not in-depth enough.

In these studies on resource allocation for semantic communication in the IoV, methods based on optimization theory exhibit diverse characteristics and advantages, but they also have their own limitations. The D2D in-vehicle network resource allocation scheme proposed in reference [34] uses methods such as Lyapunov optimization, which significantly enhances the system's robustness in high-speed mobile scenarios. However, it lacks sufficient discussion on computational overhead and real-time performance. In reference [35], for the scenario of vehicle platoon collaboration, technologies such as bipartite graph matching are employed, effectively improving the accuracy of semantic detection. Nevertheless, there is a lack of comprehensive evaluation of key indicators such as semantic similarity and transmission delay. The SSTS scheme, on the other hand, focuses on energy consumption optimization and demonstrates the advantage of semantic data transmission in reducing energy consumption. But the analysis of computational overhead and complexity in real-time deployment is not in-depth enough.

These methods have different focuses in terms of objectives, technical means, and application scenarios. However, in practical applications, various factors such as system stability, resource utilization efficiency, real-time performance, and computational overhead need to be comprehensively considered to achieve a more optimal resource allocation strategy.

3.3.3. Federated Learning-Based Resource Allocation Methods

Federated learning, as a distributed machine learning paradigm, has demonstrated unique advantages in semantic communication for the IoV. By enabling distributed training and knowledge sharing, federated learning optimizes resource allocation and enhances system efficiency while preserving data privacy.

Ref. [37] proposed a Mobility-Aware Split Federated Transfer Learning (MSFTL) framework, offering a novel approach to resource optimization in IoV semantic communication. The framework divides model training into four parts, leveraging split federated learning to reduce computational costs for vehicles. By incorporating a Stackelberg game-based resource optimization mechanism, it considers factors such as vehicle dwell time, computational load, and communication overhead to fairly select the most suitable training data volume for each vehicle and the entire network. This approach effectively reduces training costs and improves resource utilization efficiency. Experiments show that MSFTL outperformed traditional Federated Learning (FL) in terms of convergence speed and final accuracy, with lower computational overhead. In the scenario of few-shot learning, it also has an advantage in terms of communication cost. However, its communication efficiency during large-scale data transmission still needs to be improved.

Ref. [38] introduced the Federated Vehicular Semantic Communication (FVSCom) framework, which also focuses on resource optimization. This framework employs federated learning for semantic extraction and proposes a semantic utility metric to evaluate performance. The problem of maximizing semantic utility is transformed into a stochastic optimization problem, which is solved using a deep reinforcement learning-driven dynamic semantic-aware algorithm. This approach achieves efficient semantic extraction and resource allocation, improving computational efficiency and semantic extraction accuracy while enhancing robustness to scenarios where vehicles leave or drop out. However, the limitation of this study is that, although a semantic utility index is proposed, in the actual IoV scenarios, key performance indicators such as the specific transmission delay and computational overhead under different channel conditions are not taken into account.

Through comparative analysis, it can be found that although [37,38] both focus on the resource optimization problem in semantic communication of the IoV, they have different emphases.The MSFTL framework, through split federated learning and a resource optimization mechanism based on the Stackelberg game, performs excellently in reducing the computational cost of vehicles and improving the efficiency of resource utilization. Especially in the scenario of few-shot learning, it has an obvious advantage in communication cost. However, its communication efficiency is insufficient during large-scale data transmission.The FVSCom framework, by introducing a semantic utility index and a dynamic semantic-aware algorithm driven by deep reinforcement learning, achieves efficient semantic extraction and resource allocation, improves computational efficiency and the accuracy of semantic extraction, and also enhances the robustness in the situation of vehicles leaving or exiting. However, it does not adequately consider key performance indicators such as transmission delay and computational overhead under different channel conditions.These two methods each have their own advantages in terms of resource allocation optimization, but they also have certain limitations. Future research can consider combining the advantages of the two while making up for their respective deficiencies so as to further improve the efficiency and performance of resource allocation in semantic communication of the IoV.

3.4. Data Security and Privacy Protection

The application of semantic communication in the IoV has significantly improved communication efficiency and intelligence levels. However, it has also introduced new security and privacy challenges. The sensitivity of semantic information (such as vehicle trajectories, driving intentions, passenger preferences, etc.) requires the system to ensure confidentiality, integrity, and reliability during the transmission process. This section systematically analyzes the security risks faced by semantic communication in the IoV and summarizes the existing countermeasures.

3.4.1. Security Risk Analysis

The security threats to semantic communication systems mainly manifest as adversarial attacks, privacy leakage, man-in-the-middle attacks, model poisoning attacks, etc. Their risk characteristics and attack mechanisms show significant differences:

1. Adversarial attacks: Existing research shows that semantic communication systems are significantly vulnerable to adversarial attacks. Tiny perturbations generated based on algorithms such as Auto-PGD, FSGM, and DeepFool can lead to a substantial decline in the accuracy of semantic segmentation [110]. Of particular concern is the new type of covert attack mechanism. For example, the Covert Semantic Backdoor Attack (CSBA) can achieve the directional elimination of target semantics (such as traffic signs) without explicit triggers by analyzing the self-contained semantic features of the transmitted images [111]. Experiments show that even under high SNRs, the CSBA can still successfully remove the target semantics, and the restored image is visually indistinguishable from the original image. In addition, the Semantic Noise Attack (SNA) can inject semantic-level interference into the transmitted data, causing cascading error propagation in the encoding and decoding stages and leading to the failure of system decision making [112].
2. Privacy leakage risk: The deep correlation characteristics of semantic information enable attackers to reverse-derive users' sensitive data through multidimensional semantic analysis. For example, by analyzing the spatio-temporal patterns of vehicle trajectory semantics, users' resident areas and travel patterns can be inferred. Continuous monitoring of driving intention semantics may expose confidential information such as commercial transportation routes.
3. Man-in-the-middle attack threat: In V2V/V2I communication links, attackers can take advantage of the vulnerabilities of semantic protocols to conduct data eavesdropping and tampering. Typical attack scenarios include forging emergency braking commands, tampering with the semantic state of traffic lights, and hijacking path planning semantic data to induce vehicles to enter a preset area. Since such attacks directly operate on semantic layer information, traditional encryption mechanisms are difficult to effectively detect them.
4. Model poisoning attack: During the construction of a distributed semantic knowledge base, malicious vehicles can carry out covert poisoning by uploading contaminated data (such as distorted semantic features of traffic signs). More seriously, the poisoning attack may trigger systematic deviations in the semantic rule system, resulting in the failure of the Vehicle-to-Everything (V2X) collaborative decision-making mechanism.

The current defense mechanisms mainly focus on single-point protection, and a security system covering the entire chain of semantic generation, transmission, and processing has not been formed yet. In particular, there are still significant technical gaps in detection algorithms for semantic-level covert attacks and dynamic privacy protection solutions, which urgently require systematic breakthroughs through the design of cross-layer defense architectures and lightweight cryptographic primitives.

3.4.2. Countermeasures

To effectively address the numerous security risks faced by semantic communication in the IoV, researchers have proposed a series of comprehensive countermeasures and key technologies. These can be addressed through methods such as semantic information encryption, federated learning, blockchain, edge intelligence, and adversarial sample detection, which are defined below:

1. Semantic information encryption: Semantic information encryption is an important means to protect the confidentiality of semantic data in the Internet of Vehicles. By designing lightweight semantic-aware encryption algorithms, such as semantic feature obfuscation technology based on lattice cryptography, end-to-end confidentiality can be achieved while ensuring semantic decodability. This encryption method can effectively prevent data from being illegally stolen and tampered with during data transmission and storage, ensuring the security of semantic information.
2. Federated learning and differential privacy: Federated learning is a distributed machine learning framework that enables distributed training of semantic models without sharing the original data. Combined with differential privacy technology, by adding controllable noise to semantic features, the leakage of original data can be further prevented. This combined approach can not only protect data privacy but also improve the robustness and generalization ability of semantic models. For example, refs. [37,38] have elaborated on the application of federated learning in semantic communication of the Internet of Vehicles, demonstrating its remarkable effects in privacy protection and model performance improvement.
3. Blockchain and edge intelligence: The introduction of blockchain technology provides new ideas for data security and privacy protection in semantic communication of the Internet of Vehicles. Using blockchain to record the update operations of the semantic knowledge base can ensure the consistency and immutability of semantic rules. For example, the blockchain sharding technology proposed in [27] reduces the verification delay of the knowledge base by dividing the knowledge base into multiple small pieces for verification while effectively resisting tampering attacks. In addition, the application of edge intelligence also provides strong support for privacy protection. Ref. [14] achieved a balance between semantic understanding and vehicle privacy by building shared and private knowledge bases on edge servers. The shared library stores the background knowledge of autonomous driving on the edge server, while the private library stores the unique information of vehicles. The private library can be transmitted to the edge server according to the travel plan and updated by the vehicle itself when updated, and the edge server aggregates multisource information to update the shared library. This hierarchical architecture allows vehicles to only update and maintain their own private knowledge bases without uploading all data to the shared knowledge base, thus greatly reducing the risk of data leakage.

4. Adversarial sample detection: Adversarial sample detection is an important technology to deal with potential attacks in semantic communication of the Internet of Vehicles. The semantic anomaly detection module constructed based on the generative adversarial network (GAN) can identify adversarial semantic features in real time. Ref. [112] proposed a defense mechanism based on Semantic Distance Minimization (SDM). SDM generates adversarial samples during the training process and optimizes the model to enable it to extract correct semantic information from adversarial samples. This method not only improves the model's robustness against adversarial attacks but also enhances the model's semantic understanding ability to a certain extent, ensuring the accuracy and reliability of semantic communication.

In conclusion, through the comprehensive application of key technologies such as semantic information encryption, federated learning and differential privacy, blockchain and edge intelligence, and adversarial sample detection, the issues of data security and privacy protection in the combination of the Internet of Vehicles and semantic communication can be effectively addressed. These methods are not only innovative in theory but also show good effects in practical applications, providing a solid technical guarantee for the further development of semantic communication in the Internet of Vehicles.

3.5. Lessons Learned

Semantic information extraction and communication architectures must balance computational efficiency with accuracy. Deep learning-based methods (e.g., Swin Transformer, GANs, etc.) excel in multimodal fusion and noise resistance but face deployment challenges due to high resource demands. Reinforcement learning and federated learning show promise in dynamic resource allocation but require optimization for real-time IoV constraints. Blockchain integration enhances security but introduces scalability issues. Future work should prioritize lightweight models, edge-compatible algorithms, and hybrid optimization strategies to address these trade-offs.

4. Applications of Semantic Communication in IoV

In Section 3, we delved deep into the key technologies of semantic communication in the IoV, including semantic information extraction, communication architecture design, and resource allocation and management. These technologies form the foundation for achieving efficient and reliable semantic communication. They involve how to extract crucial semantic information from raw data, how to design the communication architecture to support the transmission of semantic information, and how to manage and allocate resources to optimize communication performance.The design of the semantic communication architecture needs to take into account the requirements of different application scenarios. For example, intelligent driving decision support may require communication with low latency and high reliability, while traffic management may place more emphasis on the comprehensiveness and accuracy of data. In this chapter, we will demonstrate how these key technologies function in practical application scenarios and how they support key applications in the IoV, such as intelligent traffic management, driving decision support, and service optimization. Through these application cases, we will further verify the potential of semantic communication in the IoV and explore its advantages and challenges in actual deployment. Table 5 summarizes several application scenarios of semantic communication in the IoV.

Table 5. Application scenarios of semantic communication in IoV.

Application Scenarios	Representative Research	Advantages
Traffic Environment Perception	Environmental Semantic Communication [39]	Reduces data transmission volume, improves system response ability, and is suitable for millimeter-wave and terahertz communication systems.
	Cooperative Perception Semantic Communication [40]	Improves perception accuracy and throughput in low-signal-to-noise-ratio environments and avoids the "cliff effect".
Intelligent Driving Decision Support	Dynamic Roadblock Semantic Traffic Control [41]	Improves decision-making accuracy and real-time performance, and reduces communication overhead.
	High-altitude Platform Semantic Communication [42]	Reduces communication costs; improves overall system performance and decision-making accuracy.
IoV Service Optimization	SemCom-empowered Service Provisioning Scheme [43]	Significantly reduces queuing delay and improves the throughput of semantic data packets.
	Receiver-demand-centered Semantic Communication System [44]	Greatly reduces data transmission volume and improves users' personalized experience.
	6G Semantic Communication Scheme [45]	Improves communication efficiency and service quality in in-vehicle scenarios.
Intelligent Traffic Management	Vehicle Quantity Prediction Model [46]	Improves the decision-making support ability for traffic signal control and congestion alleviation.
	Scalable Multitask Semantic Communication System (SMSC-FIR) [47]	Improves adaptability under dynamic channel conditions and significantly improves multitask processing efficiency.
	Diffusion Model-based Channel Enhancer (DMCE) [48]	Improves the channel interference suppression ability of multiuser semantic communication systems and enhances the quality of semantically segmented images.
	Emergency Vehicle Dispatching Semantic Communication [49]	Improves the passage efficiency of emergency vehicles and reduces interference with other traffic flows.

4.1. Traffic Environment Perception and Understanding

In the IoV, vehicles need to perceive and understand the surrounding traffic environment in real time, including road conditions, traffic signs, and the dynamics of other vehicles and pedestrians. This is crucial for enhancing traffic safety, optimizing traffic flow, and enabling advanced applications such as autonomous driving. Traditional data transmission methods struggle to meet the demands of massive, real-time, and dynamically changing traffic information. Semantic communication, with its deep mining and precise transmission of data semantics, offers a novel solution for traffic environment perception and understanding in IoV. The following research cases demonstrate the effectiveness of semantic communication in this field.

The deployment of distributed sensing nodes in the IoV can significantly enhance the coverage and accuracy of environmental perception. Ref. [39] proposed an environmental semantic communication method to support distributed sensing-assisted networks, particularly in millimeter-wave (mmWave) and terahertz (THz) communication systems. By deploying multiple distributed sensing nodes, the study extracts environmental semantic information (e.g., bounding boxes and masks of targets) using RGB cameras and transmits this information to base stations to predict optimal beams. This approach significantly reduces the storage and transmission requirements of raw image data while improving the system's adaptability to dynamic environments. The experiment was conducted based on the DeepSense 6G dataset, and the results show that the proposed solution can accurately predict the optimal beam in the real communication environment while reducing the transmission overhead of sensing data.

In autonomous driving scenarios, collaborative perception among vehicles can provide more comprehensive environmental information, thereby enhancing driving safety. Ref. [40] proposed a semantic communication framework that combines Joint Source–Channel Coding (JSCC) and Hybrid Automatic Repeat Request (HARQ) technologies. The framework extracts critical semantic features through importance maps and optimizes transmission. By employing intermediate fusion, sensor data (e.g., LiDAR point clouds) from vehicles are semantically processed and transmitted using Orthogonal Frequency Division Multiplexing (OFDM) in time-varying multipath fading channels. The OPV2V dataset was used in the study. Simulation results show that, compared to the traditional separate source–channel coding method, the proposed model has significantly improved in terms of sensing performance and throughput. In addition, this study also introduced a new semantic error detection method, SimCRC, and combined it with Hybrid Automatic Repeat Request (HARQ) to enhance the transmission reliability in scenarios with low SNRs.

Both of the above two experimental studies verify the effectiveness of the proposed methods through specific experimental designs. The work of Ref. [39] performed outstandingly in reducing data transmission overhead and beam prediction, and it is more suitable for optimizing communication resources. However, as the amount of data increases, this requires a higher processing capacity of the base station. The work of Ref. [40] has obvious advantages in sensing performance, and indicators such as AP@0.5 and AP@0.7 are superior to traditional methods. It is also more suitable for scenarios of precise target recognition. However, as the amount of data increases, it may face the problem of insufficient computing resources.

Through the above discussion on traffic environment perception and understanding, we can see the importance of the semantic information extraction techniques proposed in Section 3 in practical applications. These techniques not only improve the accuracy of environmental perception but also optimize communication efficiency by reducing the amount of data transmitted. In addition, the design of the semantic communication architecture ensures the reliable transmission of information in dynamic and complex traffic environments. The resource allocation and management strategies further optimize the transmission of semantic information, ensuring that critical information can be preferentially processed and transmitted under limited bandwidth and computing resources. The integrated application of these techniques demonstrates the potential of semantic communication in enhancing the performance of the IoV.

In the scenarios of achieving traffic environment perception and understanding, vehicles must be capable of processing and integrating information from different sensors and data sources in real time. The challenge in this process lies in the fact that the data formats and accuracies of different sensors vary, and the traffic environment itself is dynamically changing, including constantly changing weather conditions and traffic flows. These factors not only increase the complexity of data fusion but also require the perception system to have a high degree of adaptability and accuracy to ensure that it can still provide reliable environmental understanding in a changeable environment.

4.2. Intelligent Driving Decision Support

In intelligent driving scenarios, vehicles need to perceive the surrounding environment in real time and make rational decisions, which relies on accurate and efficient information transmission and processing. Semantic communication technology can precisely extract key semantic information from massive traffic data, avoiding the transmission of redundant data in traditional communication methods, thereby significantly improving data transmission efficiency and decision-making speed. Below are several research cases that utilize semantic communication to enhance intelligent driving decisions.

In autonomous driving scenarios, vehicles need to perceive dynamic changes in the environment, such as sudden road obstacles (e.g., road maintenance, accidents, or vehicle breakdowns). In such cases, vehicles must quickly decide whether to change lanes or maintain their current lane to ensure safe and efficient driving. Ref. [41] proposed a deep learning-based semantic traffic control system that assigns semantic encoding tasks to vehicles themselves rather than relying on server processing, thereby alleviating resource constraints. Specifically, autonomous vehicles (AVs) collect critical driving dynamics (e.g., speed, acceleration, and position) through sensors and use the deep Q-network (DQN) algorithm for decision making. The system converts complex driving environment information into compact semantic representations through semantic encoding and transmits them to the traffic monitoring module. The traffic monitoring module receives the encoded information and processes it using the DQN algorithm to derive appropriate driving decisions. In the experiment, the researchers used the KUL traffic sign classification dataset from Belgium, the MASTIF dataset from Croatia, and the German Traffic Sign Recognition Benchmark dataset to train the object detection model through a custom framework. The experimental results show that, compared to directly transmitting images, when the semantic system transmits a single image, 900 images equivalent to a 30 s video, and 1800 images equivalent to a 60 s video, the file transmission time is significantly shortened, and the file size is also greatly reduced. In addition, the accuracy rate of the traffic optimization model of this system reached 92%. Although affected by the noise added in the simulation (such as changes in vehicle speed), this result still indicates that the system has a high degree of reliability in intelligent driving decision making.

In more complex traffic scenarios, such as fully connected autonomous vehicle networks involving High-Altitude Platforms (HAPs), semantic communication also plays a crucial role. Ref. [42] proposed an AI-driven semantic communication framework for this scenario. In this framework, the traffic infrastructure (TI) extracts semantic concepts from traffic signs using a convolutional autoencoder (CAE) and transmits these concepts to macro base stations (MBSs). Upon receiving the semantic concepts, the MBS uses the Proximal Policy Optimization (PPO) algorithm to make decisions for CAVs. For example, when the TI observes a "left turn ahead" sign, it extracts the corresponding semantic concept and transmits it to the MBS. The MBS analyzes the concept using the PPO algorithm and generates appropriate driving instructions, such as "turn left", for the CAVs. In the experiment, 12 traffic signs from the TSRD dataset were used, and the proposed framework was compared with the Augmented Random Search (ARS) baseline. The results show that the deep Q-network (DQN) outperform ARS in terms of training convergence and received rewards, with the total reward increased by 37.11%. In addition, as the size of the Resource Block (RB) increased, the total reward received by the Connected and Automated Vehicle (CAV) also increased, which indicates that more complete semantic information helps to improve the accuracy of decision making. This framework was able to reduce the communication cost by up to 90.81%, demonstrating great potential in improving communication efficiency.

Overall, both semantic communication methods have achieved positive results in the experiments, but some key factors still need to be considered in actual deployment. The method in [41] shows high real-time performance and decision-making accuracy when dealing with sudden roadblock scenarios, making it suitable for autonomous driving scenarios with high requirements for response speed. However, its stability may be affected by the quality of model training data and the network environment. The framework in [42] has significant advantages in reducing communication costs and improving resource utilization, and it is suitable for large-scale data transmission and decision support in the Internet of Vehicles. But in practical applications, it is necessary to address the resource requirements for deep Q-network (DQN) training and improve the system's adaptability to complex traffic environments.

In the context of exploring decision support for intelligent driving, the semantic communication architecture discussed in Section 3 demonstrates its core role in handling real-time decision-making information. Semantic information extraction technology can filter out key information from the massive data generated by vehicles and their environments, such as the positions and speed changes of potential obstacles, which are crucial for the immediate response of vehicles. In addition, through optimized resource allocation and management strategies, it is ensured that these key pieces of information can be transmitted and processed in the shortest possible time, thereby supporting vehicles in making quick and accurate driving decisions. The combination of this technology and application not only improves the reliability of intelligent driving systems but also provides strong technical support for the development of future autonomous driving technologies.

In the scenario of intelligent driving decision support, vehicles need to quickly and accurately extract key semantic information from complex traffic data and make timely driving decisions based on it. The challenge in this process is how to ensure that in a dynamic and unpredictable traffic environment the decision-making system can not only accurately understand environmental information but also respond quickly to avoid potential collisions and improve driving safety. In addition, how to effectively utilize vehicle data while protecting personal privacy is also an issue that needs to be addressed.

4.3. IoV Service Optimization

In the field of the IoV, leveraging semantic communication technology to enhance service performance has become a critical research direction. Semantic communication, with its advantages of reducing data volume and improving real-time performance and accuracy, offers users more efficient and personalized service experiences. Below, specific research cases are analyzed to delve into its applications in IoV service optimization.

The demand for next-generation ultra-reliable low-latency communication (xURLLC) in the IoV is growing, necessitating the optimization of semantic data packet transmission to reduce queuing delays and enhance user experience. Ref. [43] addressed the challenges posed by resource scarcity and xURLLC requirements by proposing a SemCom-empowered Service Supplying Solution. Based on queuing theory, the study derives a formula for queuing delays of semantic data packets based on knowledge base matching. An optimization problem is formulated to minimize queuing delays, which is subject to reliability constraints in knowledge base construction (KBC) and vehicle service pairing (VSP). Using the Lagrangian dual method, the original problem is decomposed into two subproblems: in the first stage, a heuristic algorithm is applied to solve the KBC subproblem for potential vehicle pairs while identifying the optimal knowledge base construction strategy; in the second stage, based on the results of the first stage, a greedy algorithm is used to determine the optimal pairing strategy for the VSP subproblem. This solution significantly reduces queuing delays, improves the throughput of semantic data packets, and enhances user satisfaction. While the theoretical advantages of this approach are evident through precise mathematical derivations and algorithm design, its practical application may incur high computational costs and require advanced hardware performance, limiting its use in low-configuration vehicles.

Traditional semantic communication often fails to meet users' personalized needs due to the loss of critical receiver information. Ref. [44] proposed a receiver-centric semantic communication system where the received component can request specific semantic information from senders. The sender utilizes the natural language processing capabilities of large language models (e.g., GPT-4) to understand the request, combined with tools such as object detection and license plate detection, to analyze video or image data. Through an attention mechanism-based semantic extraction algorithm, relevant semantic information is accurately extracted and fed back in text form. If task planning is unreasonable, a task reflection module replans or selects the most relevant video frames for transmission. This system emphasizes user-centric personalized demands, leveraging advanced language models and intelligent algorithms to address the shortcomings of traditional semantic communication. However, reliance on large language models introduces challenges, such as high training costs and potential delays in real-time scenarios due to model processing speed limitations, affecting service immediacy.

In in-vehicle scenarios, efficient perception and interaction are essential to enhance user experience. Ref. [45] proposed a 6G semantic communication solution integrated with smart fabrics. Smart fabrics perceive the position, movements, and environmental conditions (e.g., temperature and humidity) of individuals inside the vehicle through principles such as electromagnetic induction, collecting raw data. The semantic sensing terminal designs a deep network based on recurrent neural networks (RNNs) and their variants (e.g., LSTM, GRU, etc.) to extract environmental data from time-series features of the data stream, thus reducing transmission data volume through dimensionality reduction techniques. Semantic information is transmitted via an integrated space–air–ground network to a remote AI platform, where technologies like GANs enable semantic recovery and advanced deep learning services. This solution achieves high-quality signal reconstruction and advanced services under different SNR conditions, effectively improving communication efficiency and service quality in in-vehicle scenarios. While this solution is specifically designed for in-vehicle scenarios, where 6G technologies and smart fabrics are leveraged to provide high-quality communication and service experiences, its applicability is limited to other IoV scenarios, such as vehicle-to-vehicle or vehicle-to-infrastructure communication.

By comparing the experimental results of the three literature sources, it can be seen that the S4 scheme in [43] performs excellently in the service optimization of the Internet of Vehicles. It has significant advantages, especially in reducing latency and increasing throughput, and is suitable for Internet of Vehicles scenarios with high real-time requirements. The system in [44] performs well in reducing the amount of data transmission and meeting the semantic information needs of the receiving end, and it is suitable for scenarios that require efficient transmission of key information. However, there is still room for improvement in its performance when dealing with complex requests. The DL-SCMT model in [45] performs outstandingly in terms of signal reconstruction and classification accuracy and has good robustness, especially in environments with a low signal-to-noise ratio. It is suitable for 6G application scenarios that require high reliability and intelligent interaction.

The discussion on the service optimization of the IoV further confirms the potential of semantic communication in enhancing the service quality and user experience. Through identifying the true intentions behind user requests, semantic information extraction technology enables service providers to more accurately meet user needs. The optimized strategies for resource allocation and management ensure the efficient transmission of semantic information between users and service providers, reducing unnecessary data transmission and improving the service response speed. This user-centered service optimization approach not only enhances user satisfaction but also provides a new direction for the innovation and development of IoV services.

In the scenario of IoV service optimization, the challenge lies in how to meet users' demands for personalized services while maintaining the efficiency and consistency of services. As users' expectations for IoV services continue to rise, service providers need to optimize resource allocation under limited network resources to support services with different quality of service requirements. In addition, integrating diverse services into a unified platform while ensuring service interoperability and an excellent user experience is also a technical challenge.

4.4. Intelligent Traffic Management

In the field of intelligent traffic management, semantic communication has demonstrated significant potential and value. Numerous research papers have focused on this area, providing rich insights and practical outcomes for the application of semantic communication. Below, we explore the specific applications of semantic communication in intelligent traffic management, including vehicle count prediction, multitask communication, and emergency vehicle scheduling.

Vehicle count prediction is a critical component of intelligent traffic management to provide decision-making support for traffic signal control and congestion mitigation. Ref. [46] proposed a vehicle count prediction model based on semantic communication. This model employs a joint convolutional neural network (CNN) and long short-term memory network (LSTM) to construct a semantic encoder–decoder architecture. Raw images captured by cameras are first processed by the semantic encoder to extract key semantic information, such as vehicle density maps, which are then converted into symbols and transmitted to the central traffic controller (CTC). The CTC utilizes the received semantic information, combined with the LSTM's ability to handle temporal correlations in image sequences, to achieve accurate vehicle count predictions for various road segments. Based on these predictions, scientifically effective traffic management strategies are formulated. The experiment utilized the TRANCOS dataset, which consists of 1244 images, and a total of 46,796 cars were labeled. The results show that, compared to the traditional source encoder/decoder method, this model reduced the communication overhead by 54.42%. In terms of the Mean Absolute Error (MAE) and Mean Squared Error (MSE), this model outperformed the existing methods based on GRU, LSTM, and FCN-rLSTM respectively. The MAE was reduced by 90.71%, 73.03%, and 19.1%, respectively, and the MSE was reduced by 103.91%, 77.74%, and 13.45%, respectively. This result indicates that semantic communication technology can significantly improve the accuracy of vehicle number prediction while reducing the amount of data transmission, providing strong support for real-time traffic management.

As the complexity of intelligent transportation systems increases, multitask processing capabilities have become increasingly important. Ref. [47] discussed a scalable multitask semantic communication system (SMSC-FIR) that focuses on tasks such as vehicle reidentification (ReID), vehicle color classification, and vehicle type classification. The system prioritizes the transmission of critical semantic features using a Feature Importance Ranking (FIR) method. The experiment made use of the VeRi-776 dataset, which contains more than 50,000 images of 776 vehicles. The results demonstrate that under low-SNR conditions, the SMSC-FIR outperformed the existing state-of-the-art methods in various tasks. For instance, at 0 dB, compared to the sequential selection and random selection methods, the performance of vehicle reidentification (ReID) was improved by 40.0% and 212.2%, respectively, the performance of color classification was enhanced by 11.0% and 9.8%, respectively, and the performance of type classification was increased by 6.9% and 7.0%, respectively. This result indicates that through feature importance ranking and dynamic coding rate adjustment, SMSC-FIR can effectively improve task performance in complex multitask scenarios, especially when the channel conditions are poor.

In multiuser semantic communication systems, channel interference remains a critical issue affecting communication quality. Ref. [48] proposed a Diffusion Model-based Channel Enhancer (DMCE) to address channel interference in multiuser semantic communication systems for intelligent traffic management. The DMCE improves channel equalization performance by learning the specific data distribution of channel effects on transmitted semantic features, thereby suppressing noise in channel state information (CSI) estimation. In the system model, multiple users transmit semantic features of multisource images (e.g., RGB and infrared images) of the same traffic scene through a MIMO channel to a centralized receiver. The receiver then recovers and fuses the semantic features using channel equalization and DMCE-enhanced CSI estimation while ultimately generating a semantic segmentation image of the traffic scene. The experiment used a multisource image dataset containing 1569 pairs of RGB-IR urban traffic scene images. The results show that under low-SNR conditions, the DMCE could increase the mean Intersection over Union (mIoU) by more than 25%. In addition, the DMCE significantly reduced the Normalized Mean Squared Error (NMSE) of the channel state information (CSI) estimation, with an average reduction of 14 dB. This result indicates that the DMCE can effectively improve the accuracy of semantic feature recovery in complex wireless channel environments, providing strong support for the practical application of multiuser semantic communication systems.

Efficient scheduling of emergency vehicles is crucial for improving emergency response capabilities. Ref. [49] explored the application of semantic communication in 6G networks, particularly for resource optimization in emergency vehicle scheduling. Through semantic encoding and decoding, data from emergency vehicles (e.g., GPS location, speed, and medical equipment information) are converted into semantic information and sent to a traffic infrastructure that dynamically adjusts traffic signal durations to prioritize emergency vehicles. This semantic communication-based scheduling method not only improves the efficiency of emergency vehicles but also minimizes disruption to other traffic flows, thus significantly enhancing emergency response capabilities. However, the scalability of this solution in large-scale urban traffic networks poses challenges, because how to ensure efficient operation and rapid response in increasingly complex and high-traffic environments remains a key focus for future research.

In these four studies, ref. [46] verified the advantages of the semantic communication model based on CNN-LSTM in reducing overhead and improving prediction accuracy by constructing the model and conducting training and testing on the TRANCOS dataset. Ref. [47] proposed the SMSC-FIR system and carried out multitask learning experiments on the VeRi-776 dataset. Through comparison with existing methods, it demonstrated the performance improvement of the system under low-SNR conditions. Ref. [48] proposed the DMCE scheme. By introducing a diffusion model into the multiuser semantic communication system to enhance the estimation of channel state information, it improves the accuracy of semantic feature recovery.

In the application scenarios of intelligent traffic management, the key technologies of semantic communication introduced in Section 3 have demonstrated their significant value in improving the overall efficiency and safety of the traffic system. Semantic information extraction technology enables the traffic management system to quickly identify key events, such as traffic accidents or congestion situations, from complex traffic data. The semantic communication architecture supports the rapid and reliable transmission of this information, while the resource allocation and management strategies ensure the real-time nature and accuracy of traffic management decisions. The integrated application of these technologies not only enhances the intelligent level of traffic management but also provides technical support for the sustainable development of urban traffic.

In the scenario of intelligent traffic management, the system needs to handle large-scale data from an entire city or region, which poses challenges to data storage, processing, and analysis capabilities. Moreover, in order to achieve effective traffic control, the collaborative work among different traffic management systems is of vital importance. This requires the systems to be able to achieve effective coordination among different management platforms. At the same time, the implementation of intelligent traffic management may be restricted by existing policies and regulations. It is necessary to cooperate with the government and regulatory authorities to promote the necessary updates of regulations so as to adapt to the development and application of new technologies.

4.5. Lessons Learned

Semantic communication significantly improves IoV applications like traffic perception and emergency response by reducing data redundancy and enhancing decision accuracy. Case studies demonstrate that task-oriented semantic frameworks (e.g., HARQ-enhanced perception and generative AI-driven scheduling) outperform traditional methods in low-SNR scenarios. However, generalization to complex environments (e.g., extreme weather) remains a challenge. Collaborative systems leveraging edge computing and distributed knowledge sharing are critical for scalability, while privacy-preserving mechanisms (e.g., federated learning) must be prioritized in sensitive applications like remote diagnostics.

5. Challenges and Future Research Directions

5.1. Knowledge Base Creation and Updating

In the semantic communication-based IoV, the knowledge base plays an indispensable role as the foundation for achieving accurate semantic understanding and effective communication. However, the construction and updating of knowledge bases still face significant challenges. In terms of construction, the complexity of data sources is a primary obstacle. In the IoV, vehicles generate massive amounts of data through various onboard sensors, while external data sources such as traffic management centers and map service providers continuously contribute additional data. These data are often heterogeneous in format and lack unified standards, making integration highly challenging. Moreover, the inherent complexity and ambiguity of traffic-related knowledge pose difficulties in knowledge representation. For instance, describing traffic congestion is not a simple binary state of "congested" or "clear"; it involves multiple degrees of congestion influenced by factors such as time, location, and traffic flow. Accurately representing such complex knowledge in a machine-understandable form remains a major challenge. Selecting appropriate knowledge representation methods, such as semantic networks, ontologies, or production rules, is crucial for transforming complex traffic knowledge into a usable format. In semantic communication, the knowledge base must be dynamically updated based on data from sources, channels, and tasks. The dynamic nature of IoV also imposes stringent real-time requirements on knowledge base updates. However, current update mechanisms often suffer from delays and cannot meet the real-time demands of the IoV.

To address these challenges, future research can explore multidimensional approaches by integrating cutting-edge technologies. On the one hand, incorporating AI large models can leverage their powerful natural language processing and knowledge understanding capabilities to deeply analyze and integrate heterogeneous traffic data, efficiently constructing knowledge graphs. The continuous learning capabilities of large models can also facilitate real-time updates to the knowledge base, enabling them to promptly capture changes in the traffic environment. On the other hand, federated learning can be employed to enable collaborative training of distributed data while preserving data privacy, thereby enriching the knowledge base and enhancing its generalizability. Additionally, blockchain technology can be introduced to ensure the security and consistency of the updating process. By leveraging its tamper-proof and decentralized characteristics, blockchain can record update operations, ensuring reliable knowledge transmission. These combined efforts can drive the advancement of knowledge base technologies in the IoV.In addition, the uncertainty of user behavior brings additional challenges to the update of the knowledge base. Users' personalized needs and behavior patterns change over time, which requires the system to be able to continuously learn and adapt to these changes to ensure that the relevant information in the knowledge base can reflect users' latest preferences and demands.

5.2. *Semantic Understanding and Ambiguity*

The IoV involves multisource heterogeneous data from various vehicles, sensors, and infrastructure, which differ in format, semantics, and precision. For example, sensors from different manufacturers may use varying measurement units and data formats, while data exchange between roadside infrastructure and vehicles often encounters semantic mismatches. Integrating and accurately understanding the semantics of such heterogeneous data is a significant challenge, requiring the development of universal data models and semantic transformation methods to achieve seamless integration and effective utilization. Additionally, natural language descriptions of traffic scenarios and instructions often contain ambiguities. For instance, the phrase "slow down at the upcoming intersection" lacks a clear definition of what constitutes "slow", leading to potential differences in interpretation among drivers or vehicle systems. In semantic communication, resolving such ambiguities is critical. This can be achieved by establishing precise semantic models, incorporating contextual information, and leveraging knowledge base reasoning to ensure accurate transmission and understanding of semantic information.In the process of multisource data fusion, the heterogeneity of data and the dynamic changes of the environment may lead to ambiguities and misunderstandings of semantic information. Therefore, the development of advanced data fusion technologies capable of handling these complexities is the key to achieving accurate semantic understanding.

To address these challenges, future research can focus on integrating advanced technologies to achieve seamless data integration and accurate semantic understanding. On the one hand, efforts should be directed toward developing universal data models and semantic transformation methods, including cross-domain unified models, dynamic semantic conversion, and international standardization. On the other hand, research should emphasize ambiguity resolution through context-aware semantic understanding, multimodal semantic fusion, and human–machine collaborative semantic interaction. Advanced technologies such as deep learning, reinforcement learning, and generative AI can be utilized for feature extraction, autonomous decision making, and data augmentation of heterogeneous data. Knowledge graph construction and fusion can provide background knowledge and reasoning support for semantic understanding. Additionally, edge computing can be employed to decentralize semantic processing, enabling intelligent decision making at the edge and enhancing the real-time performance and efficiency of semantic communication.

5.3. *Real-Time and Reliability Requirements*

In the IoV, vehicles are in constant high-speed motion, which leads to rapidly changing network topologies and unstable communication channels. This demands that semantic communication achieves real-time performance in highly dynamic environments to achieve timely transmission and processing of semantic information. For example, in scenarios such as emergency braking or lane changes, relevant semantic information (e.g., braking intent or lane change direction) must be quickly transmitted to surrounding vehicles to prevent collisions. Therefore, vehicles need to rapidly encode and decode large amounts of road condition and driving intent information during operation. When multiple vehicles communicate simultaneously, encoding and decoding delays may occur, affecting the timeliness and accuracy of information transmission. The dynamically changing traffic environment poses higher requirements for the real-time performance of the system. The system must be able to quickly adapt to environmental changes, such as fluctuations in traffic flow and sudden road conditions, to ensure the continuity of communication and the timeliness of decision making.

In order to meet the real-time and reliability requirements, it is necessary to optimize the communication protocol, adopt efficient channel access technology and resource allocation algorithms, and reduce the communication delay. For example, ref. [113] proposed the TDMA-based Capture-Aware MAC protocol (CT-MAC), which effectively improves broadcast reliability and channel utilization efficiency by optimizing frame length and utilizing capture effect. This shows that optimization combined with the MAC protocol can better cope with the challenges of high vehicle dynamics in the vehicle networking environment, thus improving real-time performance and reliability and providing a useful reference for the combination of vehicle networking and semantic communication. Meanwhile, semantic information in the IoV is critical for traffic safety, necessitating reliable transmission. Interference, fading, and noise in wireless channels can lead to data loss or errors. To enhance reliability, error control techniques (e.g., ARQ and FEC), multipath transmission, and redundancy mechanisms should be employed to ensure accurate and error-free delivery of semantic information under adverse channel conditions. Future research can focus on low-latency, high-accuracy semantic encoding and decoding algorithms, such as those based on the Transformer architecture, to improve information processing speed and meet the real-time and reliability requirements of the IoV.

5.4. Security and Privacy Protection

Semantic communication involves sensitive semantic information such as vehicle trajectories, driving behaviors, and passenger details, the leakage of which could pose significant threats to user privacy. For instance, attackers could analyze semantic communication data to infer a vehicle's travel routes and stop locations, thereby violating user privacy. If semantic information is intercepted or tampered, this could lead to erroneous vehicle decisions that may jeopardize driving safety. Additionally, the IoV encompasses numerous communication links, including vehicle-to-vehicle (V2V) and vehicle-to-infrastructure (V2I) connections. These links are vulnerable to security threats such as hacking, interference, and attacks like semantic message forgery, tampering, and man-in-the-middle attacks. Malicious actors could send false traffic condition information to mislead vehicles or alter semantic communication commands between vehicles and infrastructure, causing traffic disruptions or even accidents. While intelligent connected vehicles can alleviate spectrum pressure through semantic communication, deep learning-based semantic communication is susceptible to adversarial attacks [110], backdoor attacks [111], and other security threats. The IoV based on semantic communication also faces risks such as eavesdropping attacks, adversarial attacks, and poisoning attacks [112].

To address these challenges, it is essential to develop encryption algorithms specifically designed for semantic information, integrating digital signatures and identity authentication technologies to ensure the confidentiality, integrity, and authenticity of semantic communication. Dedicated security communication protocols for the IoV should be established, leveraging technologies such as blockchain and federated learning [114], to build distributed trust mechanisms, preventing communication link attacks and data theft. Existing encryption and detection algorithms, such as homomorphic encryption, often introduce high latency and are difficult to meet the millisecond response requirements of the IoV. It is necessary to design lightweight security protocols, such as dynamic key distribution mechanisms based on edge computing. And existing detection methods are mostly targeted at specific attack patterns (such as FGSM or PGD), with insufficient generalization ability for unknown attack types. Combining meta-learning with online adaptive mechanisms may be a potential solution. The acceptance of new technologies by users also affects the effectiveness of privacy protection. By enhancing users' trust in the system, making the data processing procedures transparent and strengthening data security measures, we can boost users' confidence in privacy protection.

5.5. Standardization and Regulation

Currently, different enterprises and institutions in the IoV industry may have different definitions and encoding methods for semantics, making seamless semantic communication between vehicles and infrastructure challenging. Moreover, the IoV involves multiple industries, including automotive, telecommunications, and transportation, each of which has its own semantic standards and business requirements, and this thus complicates the harmonization of semantic standards.

Therefore, stakeholders such as automotive manufacturers, communication companies, and research institutions should collaborate to develop unified semantic standards for the IoV, clarifying semantic definitions, encoding rules, and data formats to ensure compatibility across different devices and systems. Active participation in international standardization efforts is also crucial to align domestic standards with global ones, fostering the coordinated development of the worldwide IoV industry.

5.6. Lessons Learned

The semantic IoV ecosystem faces unresolved challenges in security (e.g., adversarial attacks), real-time knowledge base updates, and standardization. Dynamic environments demand adaptive semantic models with low-latency processing, while cross-domain semantic alignment requires unified ontologies. Future research should focus on AI-driven solutions (e.g., large language models for knowledge fusion), lightweight encryption for resource-constrained devices, and global standardization efforts to ensure interoperability. Collaborative frameworks integrating academia, industry, and policymakers will accelerate practical adoption.

6. Conclusions

This paper provides a comprehensive and in-depth review of semantic communication technologies in the IoV that covers key aspects ranging from foundational technical backgrounds to specific applications, challenges, and future directions. As the core of intelligent transportation systems, the IoV integrates multiple communication modes to achieve comprehensive connectivity between vehicles and their environment. However, traditional communication technologies face numerous bottlenecks in IoV applications. Semantic communication, with its unique advantages such as reducing redundant transmissions, enhancing communication efficiency and accuracy, and ensuring information security, offers innovative solutions to IoV communication challenges while demonstrating broad application prospects in the field. By enabling efficient extraction, transmission, and understanding of semantic information, semantic communication can significantly improve the communication efficiency, data processing capabilities, and intelligent decision-making support of the IoV, providing robust technical support for safer, more efficient, and smarter transportation systems.

Nevertheless, the application of semantic communication in the IoV still faces many challenges. Future research needs to further explore these critical issues and propose more effective solutions by integrating advanced technologies such as artificial intelligence, edge computing, and blockchain. Additionally, strengthening interdisciplinary collaboration and fostering close ties between academia, industry, and application will accelerate the practical implementation of semantic communication technologies in the IoV and promote the comprehensive development of intelligent transportation systems.

Author Contributions: Conceptualization, S.Y. and Q.W.; methodology, S.Y.; investigation, S.Y.; data curation, S.Y.; writing—original draft preparation, S.Y. and Q.W.; writing—review and editing, P.F. and Q.F.; visualization, S.Y.; supervision, Q.W. All authors have read and agreed to the published version of the manuscript.

Funding: This work was supported in part by the National Natural Science Foundation of China under Grant No. 61701197, in part by the National Key Research and Development Program of China under Grant No. 2021YFA1000500(4), and in part by the 111 project under Grant No. B23008.

Institutional Review Board Statement: Not applicable.

Informed Consent Statement: Not applicable.

Data Availability Statement: No new data were created or analyzed in this study. Data sharing is not applicable to this article.

Conflicts of Interest: The author Qiang Fan was employed by the company Qualcomm. The remaining authors declare that this research was conducted in the absence of any commercial or financial relationships that could be construed as a potential conflicts of interest.

References

1. Kaiwartya, O.; Abdullah, A.H.; Cao, Y.; Altameem, A.; Prasad, M.; Lin, C.T.; Liu, X. Internet of vehicles: Motivation, layered architecture, network model, challenges, and future aspects. *IEEE Access* **2016**, *4*, 5356–5373. [CrossRef]
2. Luo, X.; Chen, H.H.; Guo, Q. Semantic communications: Overview, open issues, and future research directions. *IEEE Wirel. Commun.* **2022**, *29*, 210–219. [CrossRef]
3. Gündüz, D.; Qin, Z.; Aguerri, I.E.; Dhillon, H.S.; Yang, Z.; Yener, A.; Wong, K.K.; Chae, C.B. Beyond transmitting bits: Context, semantics, and task-oriented communications. *IEEE J. Sel. Areas Commun.* **2022**, *41*, 5–41. [CrossRef]
4. Shi, G.; Xiao, Y.; Li, Y.; Gao, D.; Xie, X. Semantic communication networking for the intelligence of everything. *Chin. J. Internet Things* **2021**, *5*, 26–36.
5. Duan, W.; Gu, J.; Wen, M.; Zhang, G.; Ji, Y.; Mumtaz, S. Emerging technologies for 5G-IoV networks: Applications, trends and opportunities. *IEEE Netw.* **2020**, *34*, 283–289. [CrossRef]
6. Maksimychev, O.; Matiukhina, E.; Ostroukh, A.; Vasiliev, Y. Connected Vehicle Remote Diagnostic System. In Proceedings of the 2021 Systems of Signals Generating and Processing in the Field of on Board Communications, Moscow, Russia, 16–18 March 2021; IEEE: Piscataway, NJ, USA, 2021; pp. 1–5.
7. Ang, L.M.; Seng, K.P.; Ijemaru, G.K.; Zungeru, A.M. Deployment of IoV for smart cities: Applications, architecture, and challenges. *IEEE Access* **2018**, *7*, 6473–6492. [CrossRef]
8. Audebert, N.; Le Saux, B.; Lefèvre, S. Segment-before-detect: Vehicle detection and classification through semantic segmentation of aerial images. *Remote Sens.* **2017**, *9*, 368. [CrossRef]
9. Dewangan, D.K.; Sahu, S.P. Road Detection Using Semantic Segmentation-Based Convolutional Neural Network for Intelligent Vehicle System. In *Data Engineering and Communication Technology*; Reddy, K.A., Devi, B.R., George, B., Raju, K.S., Eds.; Springer: Singapore, 2021; pp. 629–637.
10. Löhdefink, J.; Bär, A.; Schmidt, N.M.; Hüger, F.; Schlicht, P.; Fingscheidt, T. Focussing Learned Image Compression to Semantic Classes for V2X Applications. In Proceedings of the 2020 IEEE Intelligent Vehicles Symposium (IV), Las Vegas, NV, USA, 19 October–13 November 2020; pp. 1641–1648. [CrossRef]

11. Xiao, Z.; Mo, Z.; Jiang, K.; Yang, D. Multimedia Fusion at Semantic Level in Vehicle Cooperactive Perception. In Proceedings of the 2018 IEEE International Conference on Multimedia & Expo Workshops (ICMEW), San Diego, CA, USA, 23–27 July 2018; pp. 1–6. [CrossRef]
12. Pan, Q.; Tong, H.; Lv, J.; Luo, T.; Zhang, Z.; Yin, C.; Li, J. Image Segmentation Semantic Communication over Internet of Vehicles. In Proceedings of the 2023 IEEE Wireless Communications and Networking Conference (WCNC), Glasgow, UK, 26–29 March 2023; pp. 1–6. [CrossRef]
13. Gimenez-Guzman, J.M.; Leyva-Mayorga, I.; Popovski, P. Semantic V2X Communications for Image Transmission in 6G Systems. *IEEE Netw.* **2024**, *38*, 48–54. [CrossRef]
14. Feng, Y.; Shen, H.; Shan, Z.; Yang, Q.; Shi, X. Semantic Communication for Edge Intelligence Enabled Autonomous Driving System. *arXiv* **2024**, arXiv:2406.10606. [CrossRef]
15. Lu, J.; Yang, W.; Xiong, Z.; Xing, C.; Tafazolli, R.; Quek, T.Q.; Debbah, M. Generative AI-Enhanced Multi-Modal Semantic Communication in Internet of Vehicles: System Design and Methodologies. *arXiv* **2024**, arXiv:2409.15642.
16. Xu, W.; Zhang, Y.; Wang, F.; Qin, Z.; Liu, C.; Zhang, P. Semantic Communication for the Internet of Vehicles: A Multiuser Cooperative Approach. *IEEE Veh. Technol. Mag.* **2023**, *18*, 100–109. [CrossRef]
17. Eldeeb, E.; Shehab, M.; Alves, H. A Multi-Task Oriented Semantic Communication Framework for Autonomous Vehicles. *arXiv* **2024**, arXiv:2403.12997. [CrossRef]
18. Hu, J.; Wang, F.; Xu, W.; Gao, H.; Zhang, P. SemHARQ: Semantic-Aware HARQ for Multi-task Semantic Communications. *arXiv* **2024**, arXiv:2404.08490.
19. Lv, J.; Tong, H.; Pan, Q.; Zhang, Z.; He, X.; Luo, T.; Yin, C. Importance-Aware Image Segmentation-based Semantic Communication for Autonomous Driving. *arXiv* **2024**, arXiv:2401.10153.
20. Ribouh, S.; Hadid, A. SEECAD: Semantic End-to-End Communication for Autonomous Driving. In Proceedings of the 2024 IEEE Intelligent Vehicles Symposium (IV), Jeju Island, Republic of Korea, 2–5 June 2024; pp. 1808–1813. [CrossRef]
21. Wan, Z.; Liu, S.; Xu, Z.; Ni, W.; Ye, S.; Wang, F. A Semantic Communication Approach for Multiscene Target Detection in Intelligent Vehicle Networks. *IEEE Internet Things J.* **2024**, *11*, 35877–35890. [CrossRef]
22. Wan, Z.; Liu, S.; Xu, Z.; Zou, J. A Low Latency Routing for Telematics Combined with Image Semantic Communication. In Proceedings of the 2023 IEEE 3rd International Conference on Software Engineering and Artificial Intelligence (SEAI), Xiamen, China, 16–18 June 2023; pp. 229–234. [CrossRef]
23. Feng, H.; Yang, Y.; Han, Z. Scalable AI Generative Content for Vehicular Network Semantic Communication. *arXiv* **2023**, arXiv:2311.13782.
24. Zhang, R.; Xiong, K.; Du, H.; Niyato, D.; Kang, J.; Shen, X.; Poor, H.V. Generative AI-Enabled Vehicular Networks: Fundamentals, Framework, and Case Study. *IEEE Netw.* **2024**, *38*, 259–267. [CrossRef]
25. Raha, A.D.; Munir, M.S.; Adhikary, A.; Qiao, Y.; Hong, C.S. Generative ai-driven semantic communication framework for nextg wireless network. *arXiv* **2023**, arXiv:2310.09021.
26. Yang, W.; Xiong, Z.; Yuan, Y.; Jiang, W.; Quek, T.Q.; Debbah, M. Agent-driven Generative Semantic Communication with Cross-Modality and Prediction. *IEEE Trans. Wirel. Commun.* **2024**, *24*, 2233–2248. [CrossRef]
27. Lin, Y.; Murase, T.; Ji, Y.; Bao, W.; Zhong, L.; Li, J. Blockchain-based knowledge-aware semantic communications for remote driving image transmission. *Digit. Commun. Netw.* 2024, *in press*. [CrossRef]
28. Yang, W.; Chi, X.; Zhao, L.; Xiong, Z.; Jiang, W. Task-Driven Semantic-Aware Green Cooperative Transmission Strategy for Vehicular Networks. *IEEE Trans. Commun.* **2023**, *71*, 5783–5798. [CrossRef]
29. Wang, Z.; Leng, S.; Zhang, H.; Yuen, C. Deep Semantic Communication for Knowledge Sharing in Internet of Vehicles. *IEEE Internet Things J.* **2025**. [CrossRef]
30. Shao, Z.; Wu, Q.; Fan, P.; Cheng, N.; Fan, Q.; Wang, J. Semantic-Aware Resource Allocation Based on Deep Reinforcement Learning for 5G-V2X HetNets. *IEEE Commun. Lett.* **2024**, *28*, 2452–2456. [CrossRef]
31. Shao, Z.; Wu, Q.; Fan, P.; Cheng, N.; Chen, W.; Wang, J.; Ben Letaief, K. Semantic-Aware Spectrum Sharing in Internet of Vehicles Based on Deep Reinforcement Learning. *IEEE Internet Things J.* **2024**, *11*, 38521–38536. [CrossRef]
32. Shao, Z.; Wu, Q.; Fan, P.; Wang, K.; Fan, Q.; Chen, W.; Letaief, K.B. Semantic-Aware Resource Management for C-V2X Platooning via Multi-Agent Reinforcement Learning. *arXiv* **2024**, arXiv:2411.04672.
33. Zhu, M.; Feng, C.; Chen, J.; Guo, C.; Gao, X. Video Semantics based Resource Allocation Algorithm for Spectrum Multiplexing Scenarios in Vehicular Networks. In Proceedings of the 2021 IEEE/CIC International Conference on Communications in China (ICCC Workshops), Xiamen, China, 28–30 July 2021; pp. 31–36. [CrossRef]
34. Su, J.; Liu, Z.; Xie, Y.a.; Ma, K.; Du, H.; Kang, J.; Niyato, D. Semantic Communication-Based Dynamic Resource Allocation in D2D Vehicular Networks. *IEEE Trans. Veh. Technol.* **2023**, *72*, 10784–10796. [CrossRef]
35. Ma, X.; Yang, X. V2X Wireless Resource Optimization for Vehicle Road Collaboration in Vehicle Platoons. In Proceedings of the 2024 IEEE/CIC International Conference on Communications in China (ICCC), Hangzhou, China, 7–9 August 2024; pp. 203–207. [CrossRef]

36. Ng, W.C.; Du, H.; Lim, W.Y.B.; Xiong, Z.; Niyato, D.; Miao, C. Stochastic Resource Allocation for Semantic Communication-Aided Virtual Transportation Networks in the Metaverse. In Proceedings of the 2024 IEEE Wireless Communications and Networking Conference (WCNC), Dubai, United Arab Emirates, 21–24 April 2024; pp. 1–6. [CrossRef]
37. Zheng, G.; Ni, Q.; Navaie, K.; Pervaiz, H.; Min, G.; Kaushik, A.; Zarakovitis, C. Mobility-Aware Split-Federated with Transfer Learning for Vehicular Semantic Communication Networks. *IEEE Internet Things J.* **2024**, *11*, 17237–17248. [CrossRef]
38. Liu, J.; Lu, Y.; Wu, H.; Dai, Y. Efficient Resource Allocation and Semantic Extraction for Federated Learning Empowered Vehicular Semantic Communication. In Proceedings of the 2023 IEEE 98th Vehicular Technology Conference (VTC2023-Fall), Hong Kong, China, 10–13 October 2023; pp. 1–5. [CrossRef]
39. Imran, S.; Charan, G.; Alkhateeb, A. Environment Semantic Communication: Enabling Distributed Sensing Aided Networks. *arXiv* **2024**, arXiv:2402.14766. [CrossRef]
40. Sheng, Y.; Liang, L.; Ye, H.; Jin, S.; Li, G.Y. Semantic Communication for Cooperative Perception using HARQ. *arXiv* **2024**, arXiv:2409.09042.
41. Figetakis, E.; Bello, Y.; Refaey, A.; Shami, A. Decentralized Semantic Traffic Control in AVs Using RL and DQN for Dynamic Roadblocks. In Proceedings of the ICC 2024—IEEE International Conference on Communications, Denver, CO, USA, 9–13 June 2024; pp. 5449–5454. [CrossRef]
42. Deb Raha, A.; Shirajum Munir, M.; Adhikary, A.; Qiao, Y.; Park, S.B.; Seon Hong, C. An Artificial Intelligent-Driven Semantic Communication Framework for Connected Autonomous Vehicular Network. In Proceedings of the 2023 International Conference on Information Networking (ICOIN), Bangkok, Thailand, 11–14 January 2023; pp. 352–357. [CrossRef]
43. Xia, L.; Sun, Y.; Niyato, D.; Feng, D.; Feng, L.; Imran, M.A. xURLLC-Aware Service Provisioning in Vehicular Networks: A Semantic Communication Perspective. *IEEE Trans. Wirel. Commun.* **2024**, *23*, 4475–4488. [CrossRef]
44. Liu, X.; Sun, Y.; Wang, Z.; You, L.; Pan, H.; Wang, F.; Cui, S. Receiver-Centric Generative Semantic Communications. *arXiv* **2024**, arXiv:2411.03127. Available online: http://arxiv.org/abs/2411.03127 (accessed on 25 February 2025).
45. Tang, Y.; Zhou, N.; Yu, Q.; Wu, D.; Hou, C.; Tao, G.; Chen, M. Intelligent Fabric Enabled 6G Semantic Communication System for In-Cabin Scenarios. *IEEE Trans. Intell. Transp. Syst.* **2023**, *24*, 1153–1162. [CrossRef]
46. Kadam, S.; Kim, D.I. Semantic Communication-Empowered Vehicle Count Prediction for Traffic Management. In Proceedings of the 2024 IEEE Wireless Communications and Networking Conference (WCNC), Dubai, United Arab Emirates, 21–24 April 2024; pp. 1–6. [CrossRef]
47. Hu, J.; Wang, F.; Xu, W.; Gao, H.; Zhang, P. Scalable Multi-Task Semantic Communication System with Feature Importance Ranking. In Proceedings of the ICASSP 2023—2023 IEEE International Conference on Acoustics, Speech and Signal Processing (ICASSP), Rhodes Island, Greece, 4–10 June 2023; pp. 1–5. [CrossRef]
48. Zeng, Y.; He, X.; Chen, X.; Tong, H.; Yang, Z.; Guo, Y.; Hao, J. DMCE: Diffusion Model Channel Enhancer for Multi-User Semantic Communication Systems. *arXiv* **2024**, arXiv:2401.16017.
49. Sharif, S.; Khandaker, F.; Ejaz, W. Semantic Communication: Implication for Resource Optimization in 6G Networks. In Proceedings of the 2024 IEEE International Conference on Advanced Telecommunication and Networking Technologies (ATNT), Johor Bahru, Malaysia, 9–10 September 2024; Volume 1, pp. 1–4. [CrossRef]
50. Bhardwaj, I.; Khara, S. Research trends in Architecture, Security, Services and Applications of Internet of Vehicles (IOV). In Proceedings of the 2018 International Conference on Computing, Power and Communication Technologies (GUCON), Greater Noida, India, 28–29 September 2018; pp. 91–95. [CrossRef]
51. Sharma, S.; Kaushik, B. A survey on internet of vehicles: Applications, security issues & solutions. *Veh. Commun.* **2019**, *20*, 100182.
52. Wu, Q.; Wang, W.; Fan, P.; Fan, Q.; Zhu, H.; Letaief, K.B. Cooperative Edge Caching Based on Elastic Federated and Multi-Agent Deep Reinforcement Learning in Next-Generation Networks. *IEEE Trans. Netw. Serv. Manag.* **2024**, *21*, 4179–4196. [CrossRef]
53. Zhang, C.; Zhang, W.; Wu, Q.; Fan, P.; Fan, Q.; Wang, J.; Letaief, K.B. Distributed Deep Reinforcement Learning Based Gradient Quantization for Federated Learning Enabled Vehicle Edge Computing. *IEEE Internet Things J.* **2025**, *12*, 4899–4913. [CrossRef]
54. Al-Sultan, S.; Al-Doori, M.M.; Al-Bayatti, A.H.; Zedan, H. A comprehensive survey on vehicular Ad Hoc network. *J. Netw. Comput. Appl.* **2014**, *37*, 380–392. [CrossRef]
55. Tahmasbi-Sarvestani, A.; Mahjoub, H.N.; Fallah, Y.P.; Moradi-Pari, E.; Abuchaar, O. Implementation and evaluation of a cooperative vehicle-to-pedestrian safety application. *IEEE Intell. Transp. Syst. Mag.* **2017**, *9*, 62–75. [CrossRef]
56. Wu, C.; Yoshinaga, T.; Ji, Y.; Zhang, Y. Computational intelligence inspired data delivery for vehicle-to-roadside communications. *IEEE Trans. Veh. Technol.* **2018**, *67*, 12038–12048. [CrossRef]
57. Jomaa, D.; Yella, S.; Dougherty, M. A comparative study between vehicle activated signs and speed indicator devices. *Transp. Res. Procedia* **2017**, *22*, 115–123. [CrossRef]
58. Endo, M.; Tanaka, K. Evaluation of Storage Capacity of Electric Vehicles for Vehicle to Grid Considering Driver's Perspective. In Proceedings of the 2018 IEEE International Conference on Environment and Electrical Engineering and 2018 IEEE Industrial and Commercial Power Systems Europe (EEEIC/I&CPS Europe), Palermo, Italy, 12–15 June 2018; IEEE: Piscataway, NJ, USA, 2018; pp. 1–5.

59. Sadiku, M.N.; Tembely, M.; Musa, S.M. Internet of vehicles: An introduction. *Int. J. Adv. Res. Comput. Sci. Softw. Eng.* **2018**, *8*, 11. [CrossRef]
60. Agbaje, P.; Anjum, A.; Mitra, A.; Oseghale, E.; Bloom, G.; Olufowobi, H. Survey of Interoperability Challenges in the Internet of Vehicles. *IEEE Trans. Intell. Transp. Syst.* **2022**, *23*, 22838–22861. [CrossRef]
61. Panigrahy, S.K.; Emany, H. A survey and tutorial on network optimization for intelligent transport system using the internet of vehicles. *Sensors* **2023**, *23*, 555. [CrossRef] [PubMed]
62. Yang, F.; Li, J.; Lei, T.; Wang, S. Architecture and Key Technologies for Internet of Vehicles: A Survey. *J. Commun. Inf. Netw.* **2017**, *2*, 1–17. [CrossRef]
63. Liu, K.; Xu, X.; Chen, M.; Liu, B.; Wu, L.; Lee, V.C.S. A Hierarchical Architecture for the Future Internet of Vehicles. *IEEE Commun. Mag.* **2019**, *57*, 41–47. [CrossRef]
64. Contreras-Castillo, J.; Zeadally, S.; Guerrero Ibáñez, J.A. A seven-layered model architecture for Internet of Vehicles. *J. Inf. Telecommun.* **2017**, *1*, 4–22. [CrossRef]
65. Contreras-Castillo, J.; Zeadally, S.; Guerrero-Ibañez, J.A. Internet of Vehicles: Architecture, Protocols, and Security. *IEEE Internet Things J.* **2018**, *5*, 3701–3709. [CrossRef]
66. Yang, F.; Wang, S.; Li, J.; Liu, Z.; Sun, Q. An overview of Internet of Vehicles. *China Commun.* **2014**, *11*, 1–15. [CrossRef]
67. Alnasser, A.; Sun, H.; Jiang, J. Cyber security challenges and solutions for V2X communications: A survey. *Comput. Netw.* **2019**, *151*, 52–67. [CrossRef]
68. Taslimasa, H.; Dadkhah, S.; Neto, E.C.P.; Xiong, P.; Ray, S.; Ghorbani, A.A. Security issues in Internet of Vehicles (IoV): A comprehensive survey. *Internet Things* **2023**, *22*, 100809. [CrossRef]
69. Guo, J.; Bilal, M.; Qiu, Y.; Qian, C.; Xu, X.; Raymond Choo, K.K. Survey on digital twins for Internet of Vehicles: Fundamentals, challenges, and opportunities. *Digit. Commun. Netw.* **2024**, *10*, 237–247. [CrossRef]
70. Wan, J.; Zhang, D.; Zhao, S.; Yang, L.T.; Lloret, J. Context-aware vehicular cyber-physical systems with cloud support: Architecture, challenges, and solutions. *IEEE Commun. Mag.* **2014**, *52*, 106–113. [CrossRef]
71. Ji, B.; Zhang, X.; Mumtaz, S.; Han, C.; Li, C.; Wen, H.; Wang, D. Survey on the Internet of Vehicles: Network Architectures and Applications. *IEEE Commun. Stand. Mag.* **2020**, *4*, 34–41. [CrossRef]
72. Ji, M.; Wu, Q.; Fan, P.; Cheng, N.; Chen, W.; Wang, J.; Letaief, K.B. Graph Neural Networks and Deep Reinforcement Learning Based Resource Allocation for V2X Communications. *IEEE Internet Things J.* **2025**, *12*, 3613–3628. [CrossRef]
73. Qi, K.; Wu, Q.; Fan, P.; Cheng, N.; Chen, W.; Letaief, K.B. Reconfigurable Intelligent Surface Aided Vehicular Edge Computing: Joint Phase-Shift Optimization and Multi-User Power Allocation. *IEEE Internet Things J.* **2025**, *12*, 764–778. [CrossRef]
74. Zhou, H.; Xu, W.; Chen, J.; Wang, W. Evolutionary V2X Technologies Toward the Internet of Vehicles: Challenges and Opportunities. *Proc. IEEE* **2020**, *108*, 308–323. [CrossRef]
75. Wang, X.; Wu, Q.; Fan, P.; Fan, Q.; Zhu, H.; Wang, J. Vehicle Selection for C-V2X Mode 4-Based Federated Edge Learning Systems. *IEEE Syst. J.* **2024**, *18*, 1927–1938. [CrossRef]
76. Zhang, Z.; Wu, Q.; Fan, P.; Cheng, N.; Chen, W.; Letaief, K.B. DRL-Based Optimization for AoI and Energy Consumption in C-V2X Enabled IoV. *IEEE Trans. Green Commun. Netw.* **2025**. [CrossRef]
77. Shannon, C.E. A mathematical theory of communication. *Bell Syst. Tech. J.* **1948**, *27*, 379–423. [CrossRef]
78. Jiang, R.; Xiong, K.; Fan, P.; Zhou, L.; Zhong, Z. Outage probability and throughput of multirelay SWIPT-WPCN networks with nonlinear EH model and imperfect CSI. *IEEE Syst. J.* **2019**, *14*, 1206–1217. [CrossRef]
79. Di, X.; Xiong, K.; Fan, P.; Yang, H.C.; Letaief, K.B. Optimal Resource Allocation in Wireless Powered Communication Networks With User Cooperation. *IEEE Trans. Wirel. Commun.* **2017**, *16*, 7936–7949. [CrossRef]
80. Li, T.; Fan, P.; Chen, Z.; Letaief, K.B. Optimum Transmission Policies for Energy Harvesting Sensor Networks Powered by a Mobile Control Center. *IEEE Trans. Wirel. Commun.* **2016**, *15*, 6132–6145. [CrossRef]
81. Zhou, H.; Fan, P.; Li, J. Global Proportional Fair Scheduling for Networks With Multiple Base Stations. *IEEE Trans. Veh. Technol.* **2011**, *60*, 1867–1879. [CrossRef]
82. Lu, Z.; Li, R.; Lu, K.; Chen, X.; Hossain, E.; Zhao, Z.; Zhang, H. Semantics-Empowered Communications: A Tutorial-Cum-Survey. *IEEE Commun. Surv. Tutor.* **2024**, *26*, 41–79. [CrossRef]
83. Xin, G.; Fan, P.; Letaief, K.B. Semantic Communication: A Survey of Its Theoretical Development. *Entropy* **2024**, *26*, 102. [CrossRef]
84. Zhang, P.; Liu, Y.; Song, Y.; Zhang, J. Advances and challenges in semantic communications: A systematic review. *Natl. Sci. Open* **2024**, *3*, 20230029. [CrossRef]
85. Bourtsoulatze, E.; Burth Kurka, D.; Gündüz, D. Deep Joint Source-Channel Coding for Wireless Image Transmission. *IEEE Trans. Cogn. Commun. Netw.* **2019**, *5*, 567–579. [CrossRef]
86. Kurka, D.B.; Gündüz, D. DeepJSCC-f: Deep Joint Source-Channel Coding of Images with Feedback. *IEEE J. Sel. Areas Inf. Theory* **2020**, *1*, 178–193. [CrossRef]
87. Xie, H.; Qin, Z.; Li, G.Y.; Juang, B.H. Deep Learning Enabled Semantic Communication Systems. *IEEE Trans. Signal Process.* **2021**, *69*, 2663–2675. [CrossRef]

88. Weng, Z.; Qin, Z. Semantic Communication Systems for Speech Transmission. *IEEE J. Sel. Areas Commun.* **2021**, *39*, 2434–2444. [CrossRef]
89. Xie, H.; Qin, Z.; Li, G.Y. Task-Oriented Multi-User Semantic Communications for VQA. *IEEE Wirel. Commun. Lett.* **2022**, *11*, 553–557. [CrossRef]
90. Yang, W.; Du, H.; Liew, Z.Q.; Lim, W.Y.B.; Xiong, Z.; Niyato, D.; Chi, X.; Shen, X.; Miao, C. Semantic Communications for Future Internet: Fundamentals, Applications, and Challenges. *IEEE Commun. Surv. Tutor.* **2023**, *25*, 213–250. [CrossRef]
91. Guler, B.; Yener, A. Semantic index assignment. In Proceedings of the 2014 IEEE International Conference on Pervasive Computing and Communication Workshops (PERCOM WORKSHOPS), Budapest, Hungary, 24–28 March 2014; pp. 431–436. [CrossRef]
92. Papineni, K.; Roukos, S.; Ward, T.; Zhu, W.J. Bleu: A method for automatic evaluation of machine translation. In Proceedings of the 40th Annual Meeting of the Association for Computational Linguistics, Philadelphia, PA, USA, 6–12 July 2002; pp. 311–318.
93. Sara, U.; Akter, M.; Uddin, M.S. Image quality assessment through FSIM, SSIM, MSE and PSNR—A comparative study. *J. Comput. Commun.* **2019**, *7*, 8–18. [CrossRef]
94. Vincent, E.; Gribonval, R.; Févotte, C. Performance measurement in blind audio source separation. *IEEE Trans. Audio Speech Lang. Process.* **2006**, *14*, 1462–1469. [CrossRef]
95. Rix, A.; Beerends, J.; Hollier, M.; Hekstra, A. Perceptual evaluation of speech quality (PESQ)-a new method for speech quality assessment of telephone networks and codecs. In Proceedings of the 2001 IEEE International Conference on Acoustics, Speech, and Signal Processing. Proceedings (Cat. No. 01CH37221), Salt Lake City, UT, USA, 7–11 May 2001; Volume 2, pp. 749–752. [CrossRef]
96. Wang, Y.; Chen, M.; Luo, T.; Saad, W.; Niyato, D.; Poor, H.V.; Cui, S. Performance Optimization for Semantic Communications: An Attention-Based Reinforcement Learning Approach. *IEEE J. Sel. Areas Commun.* **2022**, *40*, 2598–2613. [CrossRef]
97. Jiang, P.; Wen, C.K.; Jin, S.; Li, G.Y. Deep Source-Channel Coding for Sentence Semantic Transmission with HARQ. *IEEE Trans. Commun.* **2022**, *70*, 5225–5240. [CrossRef]
98. Yates, R.D.; Sun, Y.; Brown, D.R.; Kaul, S.K.; Modiano, E.; Ulukus, S. Age of Information: An Introduction and Survey. *IEEE J. Sel. Areas Commun.* **2021**, *39*, 1183–1210. [CrossRef]
99. Molin, A.; Esen, H.; Johansson, K.H. Scheduling networked state estimators based on value of information. *Automatica* **2019**, *110*, 108578. [CrossRef]
100. Qi, K.; Wu, Q.; Fan, P.; Cheng, N.; Chen, W.; Wang, J.; Letaief, K.B. Deep-Reinforcement-Learning-Based AoI-Aware Resource Allocation for RIS-Aided IoV Networks. *IEEE Trans. Veh. Technol.* **2024**, *74*, 1365–1378. [CrossRef]
101. Qi, K.; Wu, Q.; Fan, P.; Cheng, N.; Fan, Q.; Wang, J. Reconfigurable Intelligent Surface Assisted VEC Based on Multi-Agent Reinforcement Learning. *IEEE Commun. Lett.* **2024**, *28*, 2427–2431. [CrossRef]
102. Gu, X.; Wu, Q.; Fan, P.; Fan, Q.; Cheng, N.; Chen, W.; Letaief, K.B. Drl-based resource allocation for motion blur resistant federated self-supervised learning in iov. *IEEE Internet Things J.* **2024**, *12*, 7067–7085. [CrossRef]
103. Gu, X.; Wu, Q.; Fan, P.; Cheng, N.; Chen, W.; Letaief, K.B. DRL-based federated self-supervised learning for task offloading and resource allocation in ISAC-enabled vehicle edge computing. *Digit. Commun. Netw.* 2024, *in press*. [CrossRef]
104. Sun, P. Semantic Communication Technologies. In *A Guidebook for 5GtoB and 6G Vision for Deep Convergence*; Springer Nature: Singapore, 2023; pp. 301–313. [CrossRef]
105. ITU-T. *Requirements and Reference Architecture of Semantic Aware Networking in Future Networks*; Technical Report TR.Reqts SAN; ITU-T: Geneva, Switzerland, 2023.
106. Lan, Q.; Wen, D.; Zhang, Z.; Zeng, Q.; Chen, X.; Popovski, P.; Huang, K. What is Semantic Communication? A View on Conveying Meaning in the Era of Machine Intelligence. *J. Commun. Inf. Netw.* **2021**, *6*, 336–371. [CrossRef]
107. Liu, Y.; Wang, X.; Ning, Z.; Zhou, M.; Guo, L.; Jedari, B. A survey on semantic communications: Technologies, solutions, applications and challenges. *Digit. Commun. Netw.* **2024**, *10*, 528–545. [CrossRef]
108. Chen, J.; Guo, C.; Feng, C.; Liu, C. Resource allocation for the semantic communication in the intelligent networked environment. *Chin. J. Internet Things* **2022**, *6*, 47–57. [CrossRef]
109. Wang, Y.; Lin, Y.; Chen, L.; Shi, J. A Stackelberg game-based caching incentive scheme for roadside units in VANETs. *Sensors* **2020**, *20*, 6625. [CrossRef]
110. Ribouh, S.; Hadid, A. Is Semantic Communication for Autonomous Driving Secured against Adversarial Attacks? In Proceedings of the 2024 IEEE 6th International Conference on AI Circuits and Systems (AICAS), Abu Dhabi, United Arab Emirates, 22–25 April 2024; pp. 139–143. [CrossRef]
111. Xu, X.; Chen, Y.; Wang, B.; Bian, Z.; Han, S.; Dong, C.; Sun, C.; Zhang, W.; Xu, L.; Zhang, P. CSBA: Covert Semantic Backdoor Attack Against Intelligent Connected Vehicles. *IEEE Trans. Veh. Technol.* **2024**, *73*, 17923–17928. [CrossRef]
112. Kang, J.; He, J.; Du, H.; Xiong, Z.; Yang, Z.; Huang, X.; Xie, S. Adversarial Attacks and Defenses for Semantic Communication in Vehicular Metaverses. *IEEE Wirel. Commun.* **2023**, *30*, 48–55. [CrossRef]

113. Wang, Y.; Shi, J.; Chen, L.; Lu, B.; Yang, Q. A novel capture-aware TDMA-based MAC protocol for safety messages broadcast in vehicular ad hoc networks. *IEEE Access* **2019**, *7*, 116542–116554. [CrossRef]
114. Zheng, G.; Ni, Q.; Navaie, K.; Pervaiz, H.; Zarakovitis, C. A Distributed Learning Architecture for Semantic Communication in Autonomous Driving Networks for Task Offloading. *IEEE Commun. Mag.* **2023**, *61*, 64–68. [CrossRef]

entropy

MDPI

Review

A Semantic Generalization of Shannon's Information Theory and Applications

Chenguang Lu [1,2]

[1] Intelligence Engineering and Mathematics Institute, Liaoning Technical University, Fuxin 123000, China; survival99@gmail.com
[2] School of Computer Engineering and Applied Mathematics, Changsha University, Changsha 410022, China

Abstract: Does semantic communication require a semantic information theory parallel to Shannon's information theory, or can Shannon's work be generalized for semantic communication? This paper advocates for the latter and introduces a semantic generalization of Shannon's information theory (G theory for short). The core idea is to replace the distortion constraint with the semantic constraint, achieved by utilizing a set of truth functions as a semantic channel. These truth functions enable the expressions of semantic distortion, semantic information measures, and semantic information loss. Notably, the maximum semantic information criterion is equivalent to the maximum likelihood criterion and similar to the Regularized Least Squares criterion. This paper shows G theory's applications to daily and electronic semantic communication, machine learning, constraint control, Bayesian confirmation, portfolio theory, and information value. The improvements in machine learning methods involve multi-label learning and classification, maximum mutual information classification, mixture models, and solving latent variables. Furthermore, insights from statistical physics are discussed: Shannon information is similar to free energy; semantic information to free energy in local equilibrium systems; and information efficiency to the efficiency of free energy in performing work. The paper also proposes refining Friston's minimum free energy principle into the maximum information efficiency principle. Lastly, it compares G theory with other semantic information theories and discusses its limitation in representing the semantics of complex data.

Keywords: semantic information theory; semantic information measures; information rate–distortion; information rate–fidelity; variational Bayes; free energy principle; maximum information efficiency; portfolio; information value; constraint control

1. Introduction

Although Shannon's information theory [1] has achieved remarkable success, it faces three significant limitations that restrict its applications to semantic communication and machine learning. First, it cannot measure semantic information. Second, it relies on the distortion function to evaluate communication quality, but the distortion function is subjectively defined and lacks an objective standard. Third, it is challenging to incorporate model parameters into Shannon's entropy and information formulas. In contrast, machine learning often uses cross-entropy and cross-mutual information involving model parameters. Moreover, the minimum distortion criterion resembles the philosophy of the "absence of fault is a virtue", whereas a more desirable principle might be "merit outweighing fault is a virtue". Why does Shannon's information theory use the distortion criterion instead of the information criterion? This is intriguing.

The study of semantic information gained attention soon after Shannon's theory emerged. Weaver initiated research on semantic information and information utility [2], and Carnap and Bar-Hillel proposed a semantic information theory [3]. Thirty years ago, the author of this article generalized Shannon's theory to a semantic information theory [4–6]. Now, we call it G theory for short [7]. Earlier contributions to semantic information theories include works by Carnap and Bar-Hillel [3], Dretske [8], Wu [9], and Zhong [10], while contributions after the author's generalization include those by Floridi [11,12] and others [13]. These theories primarily address natural language information and semantic information measures for daily semantic communication, involving the philosophical foundation of semantic information.

In the past decade, research on semantic communication and semantic information theory has developed rapidly in the following two fields. One field is electronic communication. The demand for the sixth generation high-speed internet has led to the emergence of some new semantic information theories or methods [14–16], which pay more attention to electronic semantic communication, especially semantic compression and distortion [17–19]. These studies have a high practical value. However, they mainly address electronic semantic information without considering how to measure the information in daily semantic communication, such as information conveyed by a prediction, a GPS pointer, a color perception, or a label. (All the abbreviations with original texts are listed in the back matter).

The other field is machine learning. Now, cross-entropy, posterior cross-entropy $H(X \mid Y_\theta)$ (roughly speaking, it is Variational Free Energy (VFE) [20–22]), semantic similarity, estimating mutual information (MI) [23–25], regularization distortion [26], etc., are widely used in the field of machine learning. These information or entropy measures are used to optimize model parameters and latent variables [27–29], achieving significant successes. However, machine learning researchers rarely talk about "semantic information theory". An important reason is that these authors have not found that estimating MI is a special case of semantic MI, and source entropy $H(X)$ minus VFE equals semantic MI. So, they also did not propose a general measure of semantic information. Machine learning researchers are still unclear about the relationship between estimating MI and Shannon MI. For example, there is controversy over which type of MI needs to be maximized or minimized [23,30–32]. Although significant progress has been made in applying deep learning methods to electronic semantic communication and semantic compression [17,18,33], the theoretical explanation is still unclear, resulting in many different methods.

Thirty years ago, the author extended the information rate–distortion function to obtain the information rate–fidelity function $R(G)$ (where R is the minimum Shannon's MI for the given semantic MI, G). The $R(G)$ has already been applied to image data compression according to visual discrimination [5,7]. Over the past 10 years, the author has incorporated model parameters into the truth function and used it as the learning function [7,32,34], optimizing it with the sample distribution. Machine learning applications include multi-label learning and classification, the maximum MI classification of unseen instances, mixture models [8], Bayesian confirmation [35,36], semantic compression [37], and solving latent variables. Semantic communication urgently requires semantic compression theories like the information rate–distortion theory [38–40]. The $R(G)$ function can intuitively display the relationship between Shannon MI and semantic MI and seems to have universal significance.

Due to the above reasons, the first motivation for writing this article is to combine the above three fields to introduce G theory and its applications, demonstrating that different fields can use the same semantic information measures and optimization methods.

On the other hand, researchers hold two extreme viewpoints on semantic information theory. One view argues that Shannon's theory suffices, rendering a dedicated semantic information theory unnecessary; at most, semantic distortion needs consideration. This is a common practice in the field of electronic semantic communication. The opposite viewpoint advocates for a parallel semantic information theory alongside Shannon's framework. Among parallel approaches, some researchers (e.g., Carnap and Bar-Hillel) use only logical probability without statistical probability; others incorporate semantic sources, semantic channels, semantic destinations, and semantic information rate distortion [16].

G theory offers a compromise between these extremes. It fully inherits Shannon's information theory, including its derived theories. Only the semantic channel composed of truth functions is newly added. Based on Davidson's truth-conditional semantics [41], truth functions represent the extensions and semantics of concepts or labels. By leveraging the semantic channel, G theory can

- Derive the likelihood function from the truth function and source, enabling semantic probability predictions, thereby quantifying semantic information;
- Replace the distortion constraint in Shannon's theory with semantic constraints, which include semantic distortion, semantic information quantity, and semantic information loss constraints.

The semantic information measure (i.e., the G measure) does not replace Shannon's information measure but supplants the distortion metric used to evaluate communication quality. Truth functions can be derived from sample distributions using machine learning techniques with the maximum semantic information criterion, addressing the challenges of defining classic distortion functions and optimizing Shannon channels with an information criterion. A key advantage of generalization over reconstruction is that semantic constraint functions can be treated as new and negative distortion functions, allowing the use of existing coding methods without additional coding considerations for electronic semantic communication.

Because of the above reasons, the second motivation for writing this article is to point out that based on Shannon's information theory, we only need to replace the distortion constraint with the semantic constraints for semantic communication optimization.

G theory has been continuously improved in recent years, and many conclusions are scattered across about ten articles. Therefore, the author wants to provide a comprehensive introduction so that later generations can avoid detours. This is the third motivation for writing this article.

The existing literature reviews of semantic communication theory mainly introduce the progress of electronic semantic communication [14,15,42,43]. However, this article mainly involves daily semantic communication with its philosophical foundation and machine learning. Although this article mainly introduces G theory, it also compares its differences and similarities with other semantic information theories. Electronic semantic communication theory is different from semantic information theory. The former focuses on one task and involves many theories, whereas the latter focuses on a fundamental theory that involves many tasks. They are complementary, but one cannot replace the other.

The novelty of this article also lies in the introduction of philosophical thoughts behind G theory. In addition to Shannon's idea, G theory integrates Popper's views on semantic information, logical probability, and factual testing [44,45], as well as Fisher's maximum likelihood criterion [46] and Zadeh's fuzzy set theory [47,48].

The primary purposes of this article are to

- Introduce G theory and its applications for exchanging ideas with other researchers in different fields related to semantic communication;

- Show that G theory can become a fundamental part of future unified semantic information theory.

The main contributions of this article are as follows:

1. It systematically introduces G theory from a new perspective (replacing distortion constraints with semantic constraints) and points out its connections with Shannon information theory and its differences and similarities with other semantic information theories.
2. It systematically introduces the applications of G theory in semantic communication, machine learning, Bayesian confirmation, constraint control, and investment portfolios.
3. It links many concepts and methods in information theory and machine learning for readers to better understand the relationship between semantic information and machine learning.

G theory is also limited, as it is not a complete or perfect semantic information theory. For example, its semantic representation and data compression of complex data cannot keep up with the pace of deep learning.

The remainder of this paper is organized as follows: Section 2 introduces G theory; Section 3 discusses the G measure for electronic semantic communication; Section 4 explores goal-oriented information and information value (in conjunction with portfolio theory); and Section 5 examines G theory's applications to machine learning. The final section provides discussions and conclusions, including comparing G theory with other semantic information theories, exploring the concept of information, and identifying G theory's limitations and areas for further research.

2. From Shannon's Information Theory to G Theory

2.1. *Semantics and Semantic Probabilistic Predictions*

Popper pointed out, in his 1932 book, "*The Logic of Scientific Discovery*" [44] (p. 102): the significance of scientific hypotheses lies in their predictive power, and predictions provide information; the smaller the logical probability and the more it can withstand testing, the greater the amount of information it provides. Later, he proposed a logical probability axiom system. He emphasized that a hypothesis has two types of probabilities, statistical and logical probabilities, at the same time [39] (pp. 252–258). However, he had not established a probability system that included both. In Popper's book, "*Conjectures and Refutations*" [45] (p. 294), he affirmed more clearly that the value of scientific theory lies in the information. We can say that Popper is the earliest researcher of semantic information theory.

The semantics of a word or label encompass both its connotation and extension. Connotation refers to an object's essential attribute, while extension denotes the range of objects the term refers to. For example, the extension of "adult" includes individuals aged 18 and above, while its connotation is "over 18 years old". Extensions for some concepts, like "adult", may be explicitly defined by regulations, whereas others, such as "elderly", "heavy rain", "excellent grades", or "hot weather", are more subjective and evolve through usage. Connotation and extension are interdependent; we can often infer one from the other.

According to Tarski's truth theory [49] and Davidson's truth-conditional semantics [41], a concept's semantics can be represented by a truth function, which reflects the concept's extension. For a crispy set, the truth function acts as the characteristic function of the set. For example, if x is age, and y_1 is the label of the set {adult}, we denote the truth function as $T(y_1 \mid x)$, which is also the characteristic function of the set {adult}.

The truth function serves as the tool for semantic probability predictions (illustrated in Figure 1). The formula is

$$P(x|y_1 \text{ is true}) = P(x)T(y_1|x)/\sum_i P(x_i)T(y_1|x_i). \tag{1}$$

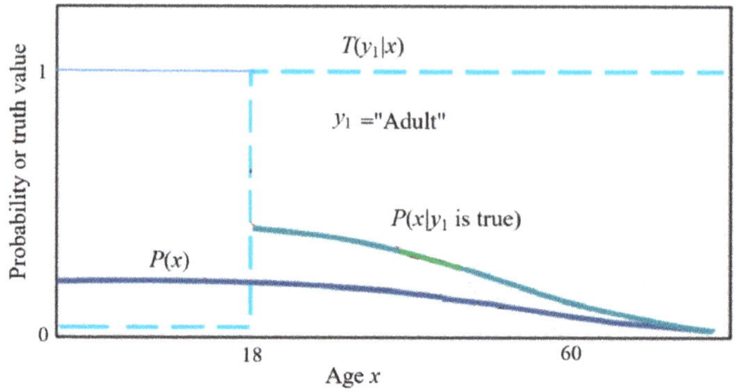

Figure 1. The semantic probability prediction, according to that "*x* is adult" is true.

If "adult" is changed to "elderly", the crispy set becomes a fuzzy set, so the truth function is equal to the membership function of the fuzzy set, and the above formula remains unchanged.

The extension of a sentence can be regarded as a fuzzy range in a high-dimensional space. For example, an instance described by a sentence with a subject, object, and predicate structure can be regarded as a point in the Cartesian product of three sets, and the extension of a sentence is a fuzzy subset in the Cartesian product. For example, the subject and the predicate are two people in the same group, and the predicate can be one of "bully", "help", etc. The extension of "Tom helps Jone" is an element in the three-dimensional space, and the extension of "Tom helps an old man" is a fuzzy subset in the three-dimensional space. The extension of a weather forecast is a subset in the multidimensional space with time, space, rainfall, temperature, wind speed, etc., as coordinates. The extension of a photo or a compressed photo can be regarded as a fuzzy set, including all things with similar characteristics.

Floridi affirms that all sentences or labels that may be true or false contain semantics and provide semantic information [12]. The author agrees with this view and suggests converting the distortion function and the truth function $T(y_j \mid x)$ to each other. To this end, we define

$$T(y_j \mid x) \equiv \exp[-d(y_j \mid x)],\ d(y_j \mid x) \equiv -\log T(y_j \mid x). \tag{2}$$

where exp and log are a pair of inverse functions; $d(y_j \mid x)$ means the distortion when y_j represents x_i. We use $d(y_j \mid x)$ instead of $d(x, y_j)$ because the distortion may be asymmetrical.

For example, the pointer on a Global Positioning System (GPS) map has relative deviation or distortion; the distortion function can be converted to a truth function or similarity function:

$$T(y_j \mid x) = \exp[-d(y_j \mid x)] = \exp[-(x - x_j)^2/(2\sigma^2)], \tag{3}$$

where σ is the standard deviation; the smaller it is, the higher the precision. Figure 2 shows the mobile phone positioning seen by someone on a train.

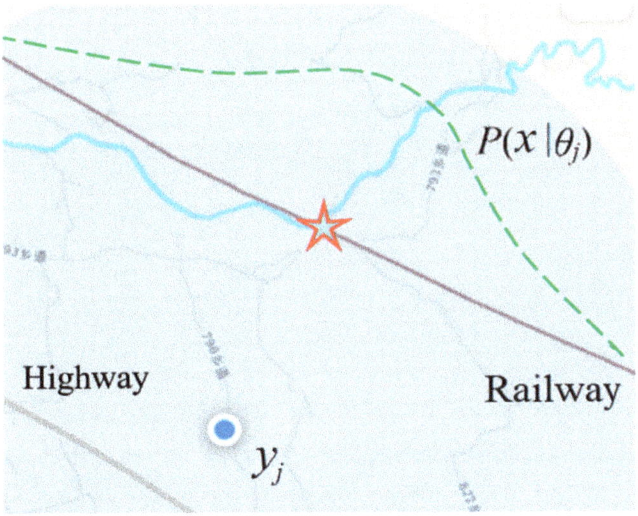

Figure 2. A GPS device's positioning with a deviation. The round point is the pointed position with a deviation, and the place with the star is the most likely position.

According to the semantics of the GPS pointer, we can predict that the actual position is an approximate normal distribution on the high-speed rail, and the red pentagram indicates the maximum possible position. If a person is on a specific highway, the prior probability distribution, $P(x)$, is different, and the maximum possible position is the place closest to the small circle on the highway.

Clocks, scales, thermometers, and various economic indices are similar to the positioning pointers and can all be regarded as estimates ($y_j = \hat{x}_j$) with error ranges or extensions, so they can all be used for semantic probability prediction and provide semantic information. A color perception can also be regarded as an estimate of color or color light. The higher the discrimination of the human eye (expressed by a smaller σ), the smaller the extension. A Gaussian function can also be used as a truth function or discrimination function.

2.2. The P-T Probability Framework

Carnap and Bar-Hillel only use logical probability. In the above semantic probability prediction, we use the statistical probability, $P(x)$; the logical probability; and the truth value, $T(y_1 \mid x)$, which can be regarded as the conditional logical probability. G theory is based on the P-T probability framework, which is composed of Shannon's probability framework, Kolmogorov's probability space [50], and Zadeh's fuzzy sets [47,48].

Next, we introduce the P-T probability framework by its construction process.

Step 1: We use Shannon's probability framework (see the left part of Figure 3). The two random variables, X and Y, take two values from two domains, $\boldsymbol{U} = \{x_1, x_2, \ldots\}$ and $\boldsymbol{V} = \{y_1, y_2, \ldots\}$, respectively. The probability is the limit of the frequency, as defined by Mises [51]. We call it statistical probability. The statistical probability is defined by "=", such as $P(y_j \mid x_i) = P(Y = y_j \mid X = x_i)$. Shannon's probability framework can be represented by a triple $(\boldsymbol{U}, \boldsymbol{V}, P)$.

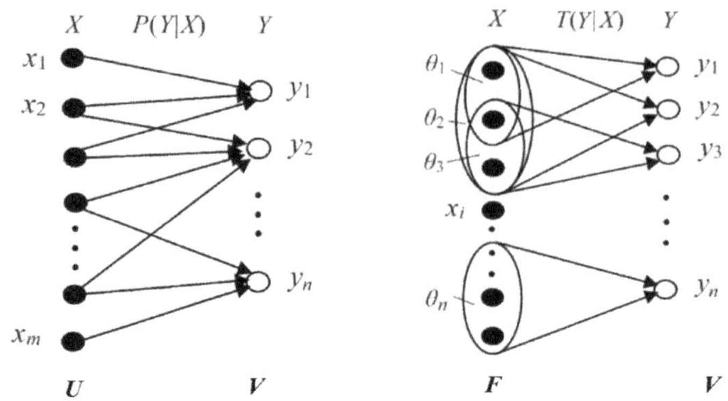

Figure 3. Shannon's probability framework and the P-T probability framework.

Step 2: We use domain $\boldsymbol{U}$ to define the Kolmogorov's probability of a set (see the right side of Figure 3). Kolmogorov's probability space can be represented by a triple ($\boldsymbol{U}$, $\boldsymbol{B}$, P), where $\boldsymbol{B}$ is the Borel field on $\boldsymbol{U}$, and its element, θ_j, is a subset of $\boldsymbol{U}$. If we only consider a discrete $\boldsymbol{U}$, then $\boldsymbol{B}$ is the power set of $\boldsymbol{U}$. The probability, P, is the probability of a subset of $\boldsymbol{U}$. It is defined by "$\in$", that is, $P(\theta_j) = P(X \in \theta_j)$. To distinguish it from the probability of elements, we use T to denote the probability of a set, so the triple becomes ($\boldsymbol{U}$, $\boldsymbol{B}$, T).

Step 3: Let y_j be the label of θ_j, that is, define that there is a bijection between $\boldsymbol{B}$ and $\boldsymbol{V}$ (one-to-one correspondence between their elements), and y_j is the image of θ_j. Hence, we obtain the quintuple ($\boldsymbol{U}$, $\boldsymbol{V}$, P, $\boldsymbol{B}$, T).

Step 4: We generalize $\theta_1, \theta_2, \ldots$ to fuzzy sets to obtain the P-T probability framework, which is represented by the same quintuple ($\boldsymbol{U}$, $\boldsymbol{V}$, P, $\boldsymbol{B}$, T).

Because of y_j = "X is in θ_j", $T(\theta_j)$ equals $P(X = \in \theta_j) = P(y_j \text{ is true})$ (according to Tarsiki's truth theory [49]). So, $T(\theta_j)$ equals the logical probability of y_j, that is, $T(y_j) \equiv T(\theta_j)$.

Given $X = x_i$, the conditional logical probability of y_j becomes the truth value $T(\theta_j \mid x_i)$ of the proposition $y_j(x_i)$, and the truth function $T(\theta_j \mid x)$ is also the membership function of θ_j. That is,

$$T(y_j \mid x) \equiv T(\theta_j \mid \mathrm{x}) \equiv m_{\theta j}(x). \tag{4}$$

We also treat θ_j as the model parameter in the parameterized truth function. This makes it easier to establish the connection between the truth function and the likelihood function. According to Davidson's truth conditional semantics [41], $T(\theta_j \mid x)$ reflects the semantics of y_j.

The only problem with the P-T probability framework is that the fuzzy set algebra on $\boldsymbol{B}$ may not follow Boolean algebra operations. The author used fuzzy quasi-Boolean algebra [52] to establish the mathematical model of the color vision mechanism, which can solve this problem to a certain extent. Because, in general, we do not need complex fuzzy set functions $f(\theta_1, \theta_2, \ldots)$, so this problem can be temporarily ignored.

According to the above definition, y_j has two probabilities: $P(y_j)$, meaning how often y_j is selected, and $T(\theta_j)$, meaning how true y_j is. The two are generally not equal. The logical probability of a tautology is one, while its statistical probability is close to zero. We have $P(y_1) + P(y_2) + \ldots + P(y_n) = 1$, but it is possible that $T(y_1) + T(y_2) + \ldots + T(y_n) > 1$. For example, the age labels include "adult", "non-adult", "child", "youth", "elderly", etc., and the sum of their statistical probabilities is one. In contrast, the sum of their logical probabilities is greater than one because the sum of the logical probabilities of "adult" and "non-adult" alone is equal to one.

According to the above definition, we have

$$T(y_j) \equiv T(\theta_j) \equiv P(X \in \theta_j) = \sum_i P(x_i)T(\theta_j|x_i). \tag{5}$$

This is the probability of a fuzzy event, as defined by Zadeh [48].

We can put $T(\theta_j \mid x)$ and $P(x)$ into the Bayes' formula to obtain the semantic probability prediction formula:

$$P(x|\theta_j) = \frac{T(\theta_j|x)P(x)}{T(\theta_j)}, T(\theta_j) = \sum_i T(\theta_j|x_i)P(x_i). \tag{6}$$

$P(x \mid \theta_j)$ is the likelihood function $P(x \mid y_j, \theta)$ in the popular method. We use $P(x \mid \theta_j)$ here because θ_j is bound to y_j. We call the above formula the semantic Bayes' formula.

Because the maximum value of $T(y_j \mid x)$ is 1, from $P(x)$ and $P(x \mid \theta_j)$, we derive a new formula:

$$T(\theta_j|x) = \frac{P(x|\theta_j)}{P(x)} / \max_x [\frac{P(x|\theta)}{P(x)}]. \tag{7}$$

2.3. Semantic Channel and Semantic Communication Model

Shannon calls $P(X)$, $P(Y \mid X)$, and $P(Y)$ the source, the channel, and the destination. Just as a set of transition probability functions $P(y_j \mid x)$ (j = 1, 2, ...) constitutes a Shannon channel, a set of truth value functions $T(\theta_j \mid x)$ (j = 1, 2, ...) constitutes a semantic channel. The comparison of the two channels is shown in Figure 3. For convenience, we also call $P(x)$, $P(y \mid x)$, and $P(y)$ the source, the channel, and the destination, and we call $T(y \mid x)$ the semantic channel.

The semantic channel reflects the semantics or extensions of labels, while the Shannon channel indicates the usage of labels. The comparison between the Shannon and the semantic communication models is shown in Figure 4. The distortion constraint is usually not drawn, but it actually exists.

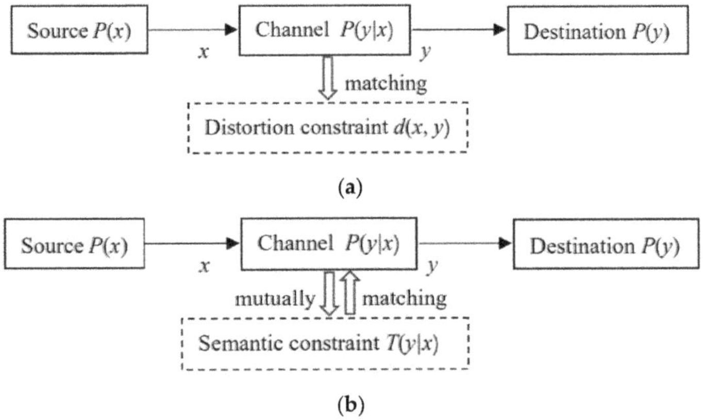

Figure 4. Communication models. (**a**) The Shannon communication model, where the channel needs to match the distortion function. (**b**) The semantic communication model, where two channels need to match mutually.

The semantic channel contains information about the distortion function, and the semantic information represents the communication quality, so there is no need to define a distortion function anymore. The purpose of optimizing the model parameters is to make the semantic channel match the Shannon channel, that is, $T(\theta_j \mid x) \propto P(y_j \mid x)$ or

$P(x \mid \theta_j) = P(x \mid y_j)$ ($j = 1, 2, \ldots$), so that the semantic MI reaches its maximum value and is equal to the Shannon MI. Conversely, when the Shannon channel matches the semantic channel, the information difference reaches the minimum, or the information efficiency reaches the maximum.

2.4. Generalizing Shannon's Information Measure to the Semantic Information G Measure

Shannon MI can be expressed as

$$I(X;Y) = \sum_j \sum_i P(x)P(x|y_j) \log \frac{P(x_i|y_j)}{P(x_i)} = H(X) - H(X|Y), \tag{8}$$

where $H(X)$ is the entropy of X, reflecting the minimum average code length. $H(X \mid Y)$ is the posterior entropy of X, reflecting the minimum average code length after predicting x based on y. Therefore, the Shannon MI means the average code length saved due to the prediction $P(x \mid y)$.

Replacing $P(x_i \mid y_j)$ on the right side of the log with the likelihood function $P(x_i \mid \theta_j)$, we obtain the following semantic MI:

$$\begin{aligned} I(X;Y_\theta) &= \sum_j \sum_i P(x_i)P(x_i|y_j) \log \frac{P(x_i|\theta_j)}{P(x_i)} \\ &= \sum_j \sum_i P(x_i)P(x_i|y_j) \log \frac{T(\theta_j|x_i)}{T(\theta_j)} \\ &= H(X) - H(X|Y_\theta) = H(Y_\theta) - H(Y_\theta|X) = H(Y_\theta) - \bar{d}, \end{aligned} \tag{9}$$

where $H(X \mid Y_\theta)$ is the semantic posterior entropy of x:

$$H(X|Y_\theta) = -\sum_j \sum_i P(x_i, y_j) \log P(x_i|\theta_j). \tag{10}$$

Roughly speaking, $H(X \mid Y_\theta)$ is the free energy, F, in the Variational Bayes method (VB) [27,28] and the minimum free energy (MFE) principle [20–22]. The smaller it is, the greater the amount of semantic information. $H(Y_\theta \mid X)$ is called the fuzzy entropy, equal to the average distortion, $\bar{d}$. According to Equation (2), there is

$$H(Y_\theta|X) = -\sum_j \sum_i P(x_i, y_j) \log T(\theta_j|x_i) = \bar{d}. \tag{11}$$

$H(Y_\theta)$ is the semantic entropy:

$$H(Y_\theta) = -\sum_i P(y_j) \log T(\theta_j). \tag{12}$$

Note that $P(x \mid y_j)$ on the left side of the log is used for averaging and represents the sample distribution. It can be a relative frequency and may not be smooth or continuous. $P(x \mid \theta_j)$ and $P(x \mid y_j)$ may differ, indicating that obtaining information needs factual testing. It is easy to see that the maximum semantic MI criterion is equivalent to the maximum likelihood criterion and similar to the Regularized Least Squares (RLS) criterion. Semantic entropy is the regularization term. Fuzzy entropy is a more general average distortion than the average square error.

Semantic entropy has a clear coding meaning. Assume that the sets $\theta_1, \theta_2, \ldots$ are crispy sets; the distortion function is

$$d(y_j|x_i) = \begin{cases} \infty, & x_i \notin \theta_j, \\ 0, & x_i \in \theta_j. \end{cases} \tag{13}$$

If we regard $P(Y)$ as the source and $P(X)$ as the destination, then the parameter solution of the information rate–distortion function is [38]

$$\begin{aligned} &R(D) = sD(s) - \sum_j P(y_j) \log \lambda_j, \\ &\lambda_j = \sum_i P(x_i) \exp[-d(x_i, y_j)] = \sum_i P(x_i) T(\theta_j|x_i) = T(\theta_j). \end{aligned} \tag{14}$$

It can be seen that the minimum Shannon MI is equal to the semantic entropy, that is, $R(D = 0) = H(Y_\theta)$.

The following formula indicates the relationship between the Shannon MI and the semantic MI and the encoding significance of the semantic MI:

$$\begin{aligned} &I(X;Y) = \sum_j \sum_i P(x_i, y_j) \log \frac{P(x_i|y_j)}{P(x_i)} = \\ &\sum_j \sum_i P(x_i, y_j) \log \frac{P(x_i|\theta_j)}{P(x_i)} + \sum_j \sum_i P(x_i, y_j) \log \frac{P(x_i|y_j)}{P(x_i|\theta_j)} \\ &= I(X; Y_\theta) + \sum_j P(y_j) KL(P(x|y_j)||P(x|\theta_j)), \end{aligned} \tag{15}$$

where $KL(\ldots)$ is the Kullbak–Leibler (KL) divergence [53] with a likelihood function, which Akaike [54] first used to prove that the minimum KL divergence criterion is equivalent to the maximum likelihood criterion. The last term in the above formula is always greater than 0, reflecting the average code length of the residual coding. Therefore, the semantic MI is less than or equal to the Shannon MI; it indicates the lower limit of the average code length saved due to semantic prediction.

From the above formula, the semantic MI reaches its maximum value when the semantic channel matches the Shannon channel. According to Equation (15), by letting $P(x \mid \theta_j) = P(x \mid y_j)$, we can obtain the optimized truth function from the sample distribution:

$$T*(\theta_j|x) = \frac{P(x|y_j)}{P(x)} / \max_x \left(\frac{P(x|y)}{P(x)} \right) = \frac{P(y_j|x)}{\max_x (P(y_j|x))}. \tag{16}$$

When $Y = y_j$, the semantic MI becomes semantic KL information or semantic side information:

$$I(X;\theta_j) = \sum_i P(x_i|y_j) \log \frac{P(x_i|\theta_j)}{P(x_i)} = \sum_i P(x_i|y_j) \log \frac{T(\theta_j|x_i)}{T(\theta_j)}. \tag{17}$$

The KL divergence cannot usually be interpreted as information because the smaller it is, the better. But the $I(X; \theta_j)$ above can be regarded as information because the larger it is, the better.

Solving $T^*(\theta_j \mid x)$ with Equation (16) requires that the sample distributions, $P(x)$ and $P(x \mid y_j)$, are continuous and smooth. Otherwise, by using Equation (17), we can obtain

$$T*(\theta_j|x) = \underset{\theta_j}{\operatorname{argmax}} \sum_i P(x_i|y_j) \log \frac{T(\theta_j|x_i)}{T(\theta_j)}. \tag{18}$$

The above method for solving $T^*(\theta_j \mid x)$ is called Logical Bayes' Inference (LBI) [7] and can be called the random point falling shadow method. This method inherits Wang's idea of the random set falling shadow [55,56].

Suppose the truth function in (10) becomes a similarity function. In that case, the semantic MI becomes the estimating MI [32], which has been used by deep learning researchers for Mutual Information Neural Estimation (MINE) [23] and Information Noise Contrast Estimation (InfoNCE) [24].

In the semantic KL information formula, when $X = x_i$, $I(X; \theta_j)$ becomes the semantic information between a single instance x_i and a single label y_j,

$$I(x_i;\theta_j) = \log\frac{T(\theta_j|x_i)}{T(\theta_j)} = \log\frac{P(x_i|\theta_j)}{P(x_i)}. \tag{19}$$

$I(x_i; \theta_j)$ is called the G measure. This measure reflects Popper's idea about factual testing. Figure 5 illustrates the above formula. It shows that the smaller the logical probability, the greater the absolute value of the information; the greater the deviation, the less the information; wrong hypotheses convey negative information.

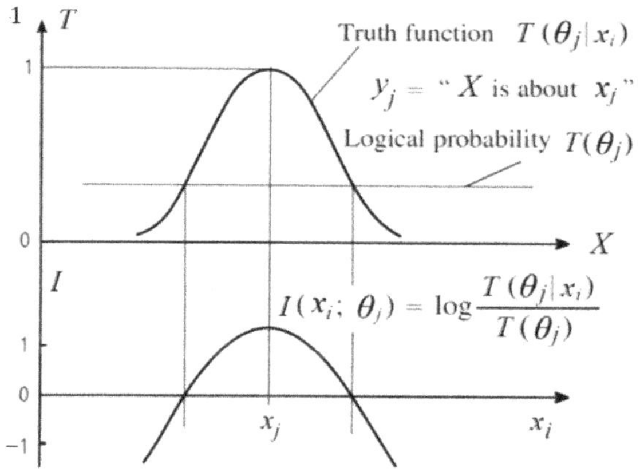

Figure 5. The semantic information y_j conveys about x_i decreases with the deviation increasing.

Bringing Equation (2) into (19), we have

$$I(x_i; \theta_j) = \log[1/T(\theta_j)] - d(y_j \mid x), \tag{20}$$

which means that $I(x_i; \theta_j)$ equals Carnap and Bar-Hillel's semantic information minus distortion.

2.5. From the Information Rate–Distortion Function to the Information Rate–Fidelity Function

Shannon defines that given a source, $P(x)$, a distortion function, $d(x, y)$, and the upper limit, D, of the average distortion, $\bar{d}$, we change the channel, $P(y \mid x)$, to find the minimum MI, $R(D)$. $R(D)$ is the information rate–distortion function, which can guide us in using Shannon information economically.

Now, we use $d(y_j \mid x) = \log[1/T(\theta_j \mid x)]$ as the asymmetrical distortion function, meaning the distortion when y_j is used as the label of x. We replace $d(y_j \mid x_i)$ with $I(x_i; \theta_j)$, replace $\bar{d}$ with $I(X; Y_\theta)$, and replace D with the lower limit, G, of the semantic MI to find the minimum Shannon MI, $R(G)$. $R(G)$ is the information rate–fidelity function. Because G reflects the average codeword length saved due to semantic prediction, using G as the constraint is more consistent in shortening the codeword length, and G/R can represent the information efficiency.

The author uses the word "fidelity" because Shannon originally proposed the information rate–fidelity criterion [1] and later used minimum distortion to express maximum fidelity [38]. The author has previously called $R(G)$ "the information rate of keeping precision" [6] or "information rate–verisimilitude" [34].

The $R(G)$ function is defined as

$$R(G) = \min_{P(Y|X):I(X;\theta)\geq G} I(X;Y). \tag{21}$$

We use the Lagrange multiplier method to find the minimum MI and the optimized channel $P(y \mid x)$. The Lagrangian function is

$$L(P(y|x), P(y)) = I(X;Y) - sI(X;Y_\theta) - \mu_j \sum_j P(y_j|x_i) - \alpha \sum_j P(y_j). \tag{22}$$

Using $P(y \mid x)$ as a variation, we let $\partial L / \partial P(y_j|x_i) = 0$. Then, we obtain

$$P(y_j|x_i) = P(y_j) m_{ij}^s / \lambda_i,\ \lambda_i = \sum_j P(y_j) m_{ij}^s, i = 1, 2, \ldots; j = 1, 2, \ldots \tag{23}$$

where $m_{ij} = P(x_i \mid \theta_j)/P(x_i) = T(\theta_j \mid x_i)/T(\theta_j)$. Using $P(y)$ as a variation, we let $\partial L / \partial P(y_j) = 0$. Then, we obtain

$$P^{+1}(y_j) = \sum_i P(x_i) P(y_j|x_i), \tag{24}$$

where $P^{+1}(y_j)$ means the next $P(y_j)$. Because $P(y \mid x)$ and $P(y)$ are interdependent, we can first assume a $P(y)$ and then repeat the above two formulas to obtain the convergent $P(y)$ and $P(y \mid x)$ (see [40] (P. 326)). We call this method the Minimum Information Difference (MID) iteration.

The parameter solution of the $R(G)$ function (as illustrated in Figure 6) is

$$\begin{aligned} G(s) &= \sum_i \sum_j P(x_i) P(y_j|x_i) I_{ij} = \sum_i \sum_j I_{ij} P(x_i) P(y_j) m_{ij}{}^s / Z_i, \\ R(s) &= sG(s) - \sum_i P(x_i) \log Z_i,\ Z_i = \sum_k P(y_k) m_{ij}{}^s. \end{aligned} \tag{25}$$

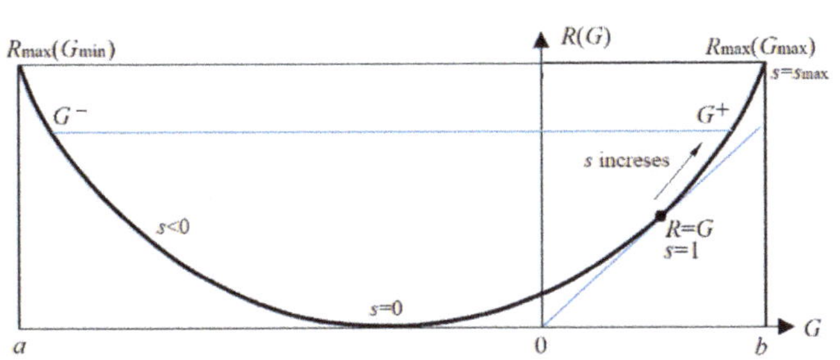

Figure 6. The information rate–fidelity function, $R(G)$, for binary communication. Any $R(G)$ function is a bowl-like function. There is a point at which $R(G) = G$ ($s = 1$). Two anti-functions, $G^-(R)$ and $G^+(R)$, exist for a given R.

Any $R(G)$ function is bowl-shaped (possibly not symmetrical [6]), with the second derivative being greater than zero. The $s = \mathrm{d}R/\mathrm{d}G$ is positive on the right. When $s = 1$, G equals R, meaning the semantic channel matches the Shannon channel. G/R represents the information efficiency; its maximum is one. G has a maximum value of G^+ and a minimum value of G^- for a given R. G^- means how small the semantic information the receiver receives can be when the sender intentionally lies.

It is worth noting that, given a semantic channel $T(y \mid x)$, matching the Shannon channel with the semantic channel, i.e., letting $P(y_j \mid x) \propto T(y_j \mid x)$ or $P(x \mid y_j) = P(x \mid \theta_j)$, does not maximize the semantic MI, but minimizes the information difference between

R and G or maximizes the information efficiency, G/R. Then, we can increase G and R simultaneously by increasing s. When $s \rightarrow \infty$ in Equation (23), $P(y_j \mid x)$ ($j = 1, 2, \ldots, n$) only takes the value zero or one, becoming a classification function.

We can also replace the average distortion with fuzzy entropy, $H(Y_\theta \mid X)$ (using semantic distortion constraints), to obtain the information rate-truth function, $R(\Theta)$ [35]. In situations where information rather than truth is more important, $R(G)$ is more appropriate than $R(D)$ and $R(\Theta)$. The $P(y)$ and $P(y \mid x)$ obtained for $R(\Theta)$ are different from those obtained for $R(G)$ because the optimization criteria are different. Under the minimum semantic distortion criterion, $P(y \mid x)$ becomes

$$P(y_j|x_i) = P(y_j)[T(\theta_{xi} \mid y_j)]^s / \sum_j P(y_j)[T(\theta_{xi} \mid y_j)]^s, i = 1, 2, \ldots; j = 1, 2, \ldots \quad (26)$$

where $T(\theta_{xi} \mid y)$ is a constraint function, so the distortion function $d(x_i \mid y) = -\log T(\theta_{xi} \mid y)$. $R(\Theta)$ becomes $R(D)$. If $T(\theta_j)$ is small, the $P(y_j)$ required for $R(G)$ will be larger than the $P(y_j)$ required for $R(D)$ or $R(\Theta)$.

2.6. Semantic Channel Capacity

Shannon calls the maximum MI obtained by changing the source, $P(x)$, for the given Shannon channel, $P(y \mid x)$, the channel capacity. Because the semantic channel is also inseparable from the Shannon channel, we must provide both the semantic and the Shannon channels to calculate the semantic MI. Therefore, after the semantic channel is given, there are two cases: (1) the Shannon channel is fixed; (2) we must first optimize the Shannon channel using a specific criterion.

When the Shannon channel is fixed, the semantic MI is less than the Shannon MI, so the semantic channel capacity is less than or equal to the Shannon channel capacity. The difference between the two is shown in Equation (15).

If the Shannon channel is variable, we can use the MID iteration to find the Shannon channel for $R = G$ after each change of the source, $P(x)$, and then use $s \rightarrow \infty$ to find the Shannon channel, $P(y \mid x)$, that makes R and G reach their maxima simultaneously. At this time, $P(y \mid x) \in \{0, 1\}$ becomes the classification function. Then, we calculate semantic MI. For a different $P(x)$, the maximum semantic MI is the semantic channel capacity. That is

$$C_{T(y|x)} = \underset{P(x);P(y|x) \text{ for } R(G,s\rightarrow\infty)}{\operatorname{argmax}} I(X; Y_\theta) = \underset{P(x)}{\operatorname{argmax}} G_{\max}, \quad (27)$$

where $G_{\max}$ is G^+ when $s \rightarrow \infty$ (see Figure 6). Hereafter, the semantic channel capacity only means $C_{T(y \mid x)}$ in the above formula.

Practically, to find $C_{T(Y \mid X)}$, we can look for $x^{(1)}, x^{(2)}, \ldots, x^{(j)} \in \boldsymbol{U}$, which are instances under the highest points of $T(y_1 \mid x), T(y_2 \mid x), \ldots, T(y_n \mid x)$, respectively. Let $P(x^{(j)}) = 1/n$, $j = 1, 2, \ldots, n$, and the probability of any other x equals zero. Then we can choose the Shannon channel: $P(y_j \mid x^{(j)}) = 1, j = 1, 2, \ldots, n$. At this time, $I(X; Y)) = H(Y) = \log n$, which is the upper limit of $C_{T(Y \mid X)}$. If there is x_i among the n $x^{(j)}$s, which makes more than one truth function true, then either $T(y_j) > P(y_j)$ or the fuzzy entropy is not zero. $C_{T(Y \mid X)}$ will be slightly less than $\log n$ in this case.

According to the above analysis, the encoding method to increase the capacity of the semantic channel is

- Try to choose x that only makes one label's truth value close to one (to avoid ambiguity and reduce the logical probability of y);
- Encoding should make $P(y_j \mid x_j) = 1$ as much as possible (to ensure that Y is used correctly).
- Choose $P(x)$ so that each Y's probability and logical probability are as equal as possible (close to $1/n$, thereby maximizing the semantic entropy).

3. Electronic Semantic Communication Optimization

3.1. The Electronic Semantic Communication Model

The previous discussion of semantic communication did not consider conveying semantic information by electronic communication. Assuming that the time and space distance between the sender and the receiver is very far, we must transmit information through cables or disks. At this time, we need to add an electronic channel to the previous communication model, as shown in Figure 7:

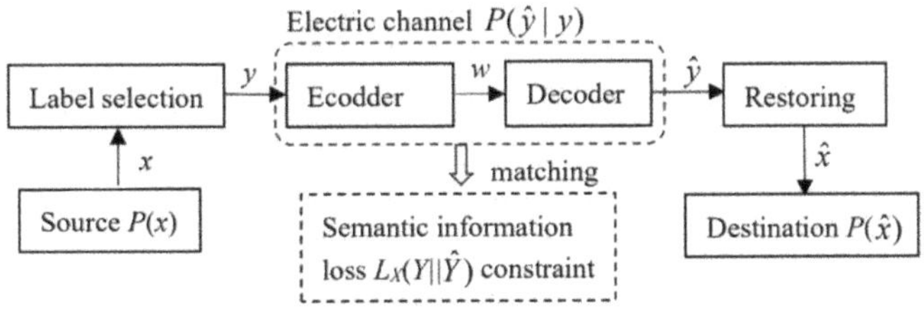

Figure 7. The electronic semantic communication model. The distortion constraint is replaced with the semantic information loss constraint. The $\hat{x}$ and $\hat{y}$ are estimates of x and y, and w is the electronic code to be transmitted.

There are two optimization tasks:

- Task 1: optimizing $P(y\,|\,x)$.
- Task 2: optimizing $P(\hat{y}\,|\,y)$.

With the optimized $P(y\,|\,x)$ and $P(\hat{y}\,|\,y)$, we can obtain $P(\hat{x}\,|\,\hat{y})$ and restore $\hat{x}$ according to $P(\hat{x}\,|\,\hat{y})$. The $\hat{x}$ will be quite different from x, but the basic feature information will be retained. The restoration quality depends on the feature extraction method.

Task 1 is a machine learning task. Assuming we have selected feature y, we can use the previous method to optimize the encoding with semantic information constraints. For example, the overall task is to transmit fruit image information. In Task 1, x is a high-dimensional feature vector of the fruit, which contains color and shape information; y is the low-dimensional feature vector of a fruit, which contains the fruit variety information. The steps are

(1) Extract the feature vector, y, from x using machine learning methods (this is a task beyond G theory);
(2) Obtain the sample distribution $P(y_j\,|\,x)$ ($j = 1, 2, \ldots$) from the sample;
(3) Obtain $T(\theta_j\,|\,x) \propto P(y_j\,|\,x)$ using LBI and further obtain $I(x; y_j) = \log[T(\theta_j\,|\,x)/T(\theta_j)]$ and G;
(4) Use the method of solving the $R(G)$ function to obtain the R (to ensure that G or G/R is large enough) and the $P(y\,|\,x)$ that reflect the encoding rule.

We also need to optimize step (1) according to the classification error between $\hat{x}$ and x).

Task 2 is to optimize the electronic channel. Electronic semantic communication is still electronic communication, in essence. The difference is that we need to use semantic information loss instead of distortion as the optimization criterion.

3.2. Optimization of Electronic Semantic Communication with Semantic Information Loss as Distortion

Consider electronic semantic communication. If $\hat{y}_j \neq y_j$, there is semantic information loss. Farsad et al. call it a semantic error and propose the corresponding formula [57,58]. Papineni et al. also proposed a similar formula for translation [59]. Gündüz et al. [17] used a method to reduce the loss of semantic information by preserving data features. For more discussion, see [60]. G theory provides the following method for comparison.

According to G theory, the semantic information loss caused by using $\hat{y}_j$ instead of y_j is

$$L_X(y_j||\hat{y}_j) = I(X;Y_\theta) - I(X;\hat{Y}_\theta) = \sum_i P(x_i|y_j) \log \frac{P(x_i|\theta_j)}{P(x_i|\hat{\theta}_j)}. \tag{28}$$

$L_X(y_j||\hat{y}_j)$ is a generalized KL divergence because there are three functions. It represents the average codeword length of residual coding.

Since the loss is generally asymmetric, there may be $L_X(y_j||\hat{y}_j) \neq L_X(\hat{y}_j||y_j)$. For example, when "motor vehicle" and "car" are substituted for each other, the information loss is asymmetric. The reason is that there is a logical implication relationship between the two. Using "motor vehicle" to replace "car", although it reduces information, it is not wrong; while using "car" to replace "motor vehicle" may be wrong, because the actual may be a truck or a motorcycle. When an error occurs, the semantic information loss is enormous. An advantage of using the truth function to generate the distortion function is that it can reflect concepts' implications or similarity relationships.

Assuming y_j is a correctly used label, it comes from sample learning, so $P(x \mid \theta_j) = P(x \mid y_j)$, and $L_X(y_j||\hat{y}_j) = KL(P(x \mid \theta_j)||P(x \mid \hat{\theta}_j))$. The average semantic information loss is

$$L_X(Y||\hat{Y}) = \sum_j \sum_k P(y_j)P(\hat{y}_k|y_j)KL(P(x|\theta_j)||P(x|\hat{\theta}_j)). \tag{29}$$

Consider using $P(Y)$ as the source and $P(\hat{Y})$ as the destination to encode y. Let $d(\hat{y}_k \mid y_j) = L_X(y_j||\hat{y}_k)$; we can obtain the information rate–distortion function $R(D)$ for replacing Y with $\hat{Y}$. We can code Y for data compression according to the parameter solution of the $R(D)$ function.

In the electronic communication part (from Y to $\hat{Y}$), other problems can be resolved by classical electronic communication methods, except for using semantic information loss as distortion.

If finding $I(x; \hat{\theta}_j)$ is not too difficult, we can also use $I(x; \hat{\theta}_j)$ as a fidelity function. Minimizing $I(X; \hat{y})$ for a given $G = I(X; \hat{y}_\theta)$, we can obtain the $R(G)$ function between X and $\hat{Y}$ and compress the data accordingly.

3.3. Experimental Results: Compress Image Data According to Visual Discrimination

The simplest visual discrimination is the discrimination of human eyes to different colors or gray levels. The next is the spatial discrimination of points. If the movement of a point on the screen is not perceived, the fuzzy movement range can represent spatial discrimination, which can be represented by a truth function (such as the Gaussian function). What is more complicated is to distinguish whether two figures are the same person. Advanced image compression methods, such as the Autoencoder, need to extract image features and use features to represent images. The following methods need to be combined with the feature extraction methods in deep learning to obtain better applications.

Next, we use the simplest gray-level discrimination as an example to illustrate digital image compression.

(1) Measuring Color Information

A color can be represented by a vector (B, G, R). For convenience, we assume that the color is one-dimensional (or we only consider the gray level), expressed in x, and the color sense, y, is the estimation of x, similar to the GPS indicator. The universes of x and y are the same, and y_j = "x is about x_j". If the color space is uniform, the distortion function can be defined by distance, that is, $d(y_j \mid x) = \exp[-(x - x_j)^2/(2\sigma^2)]$. Then there is the average information of color perception, $I(X; Y_\theta) = H(Y_\theta) - \overline{d}$.

Given the source $P(x)$ and the discrimination function $T(y \mid x)$, we can solve $P(y \mid x)$ and $P(y)$ using the Semantic Variational Basyes (SVB) method [61]. The Shannon channel is matched with the semantic channel to maximize the information efficiency.

(2) Gray Level Compression

We used an example to demonstrate color data compression. It was assumed that the original gray level was 256 (8-bit pixels) and needed to be compressed into 8 (3-bit pixels). We defined eight constraint functions, as shown in Figure 8a.

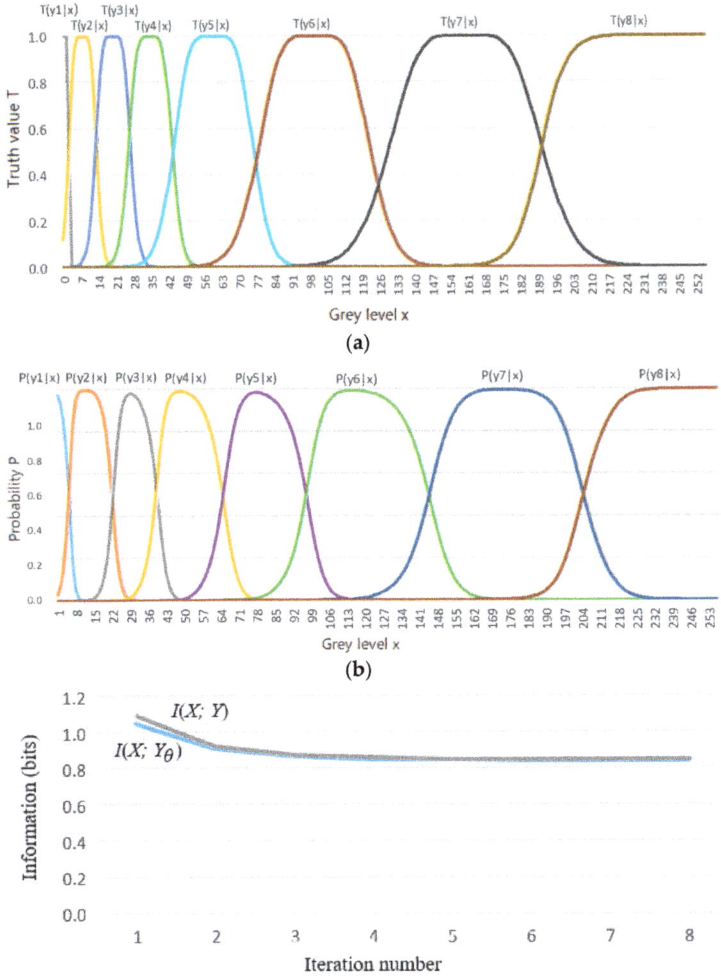

Figure 8. The gray level compression. (**a**) Eight truth functions form a semantic channel $T(y \mid x)$ (see Appendix C in [37] for the data generation method). (**b**) Convergent Shannon channel $P(y \mid x)$. (**c**) The variation of $I(X; Y_\theta)$ and $I(X; Y)$ during the iteration process.

Considering that human visual discrimination varies with the gray level (the higher the gray level, the lower the discrimination), we used the eight truth functions shown in Figure 8a, representing eight fuzzy ranges. Appendix C in Reference [37] shows how these curves are generated. The task was to use the maximum information efficiency (MIE) criterion to find the Shannon channel $P(y \mid x)$ that made R close to G ($s = 1$).

The convergent $P(y \mid x)$ is shown in Figure 8b. Figure 8c shows that the Shannon MI and the semantic MI gradually approach in the iteration process. Comparing Figure 8a,b, we find it easy to control $P(y \mid x)$ by $T(y \mid x)$. However, defining the distortion function without using the truth function is difficult. Predicting the convergent $P(y \mid x)$ by $d(y \mid x)$ is also difficult.

If we use s to strengthen the constraint, we obtain the parametric solution of the $R(G)$ function. As $s \to \infty$, $P(y_j \mid x)$ ($j = 1, 2, \ldots$) display as rectangles and become classification functions.

(3) The Influence of Visual Discrimination and the Quantization Level on the $R(G)$ Function

The author performed some experiments to examine the influence of the discrimination function and the quantization level $b = 2^n$ (n is the number of quantization bits) on the $R(G)$ function. Figure 9 shows that when the quantization level was enough, the R and G variation range increased with the discrimination increasing (i.e., with σ decreasing). The result explains how the discrimination determines the semantic channel capacity.

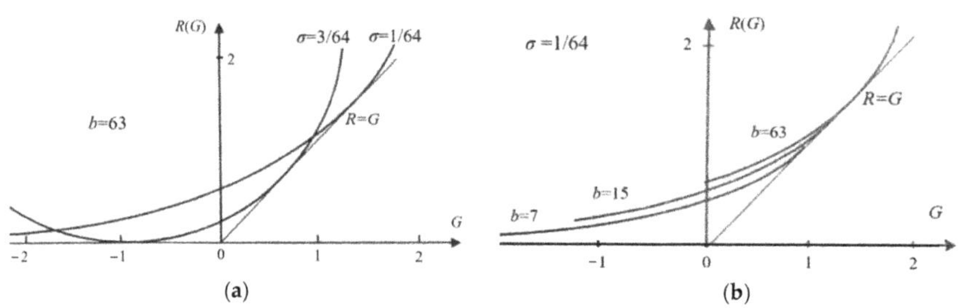

Figure 9. The variations of the $R(G)$ function with discrimination (**a**) and quantization level (**b**).

Figure 9a indicates that higher discrimination can convey more semantic information for a given quantization level ($b = 63$). Figure 9b shows that for a given discrimination ($\sigma = 1/64$), less b will waste the semantic channel capacity. For more discussion on visual information, see Section 6 in [6].

4. Goal-Oriented Information, Information Value, Physical Entropy, and Free Energy

4.1. Three Kinds of Information Related to Value

We call the increment of utility the value. Information involves utility and value in three aspects:

(1) Information about utility. For example, the information about university admissions or the bumper harvest of grain is about utility. The measurement of this information is the same as in the previous examples. Before providing information, we have the prior probability distribution, $P(x)$, of grain production. The information is provided by ranges, such as "about 2000 kg per acre", which can be expressed by a truth function. The previous semantic information formula is also applicable.

(2) Goal-oriented information [61]. This is also purposeful information or constraint control feedback information.

For example, a passenger and a driver watch a GPS map in a taxi. Assume that the probability distribution of the taxi position without looking at the positioning map (or without some control) is $P(x)$, and the destination is a fuzzy range, which is represented by a truth function. The actual position is the probability distribution, $P(x \mid a_j)$ (a_j is an action). The positioning map provides information. For the passenger, this is purposeful information (about how the control result comforts the purpose); for the driver, this is the control feedback information. We call both types goal-oriented information. This information involves constraint control and reinforcement learning. Section 3.2 discusses the measurement and optimization of this information.

(3) Information that brings value. For example, Tom made money by buying stocks based on John's prediction of stock prices. The information provided by John brings Tom increased utility, so John's information is valuable to Tom.

The value of information is relative. For example, weather forecast information is different for workers and farmers, and prediction information about stock markets is worth zero to people who do not buy stocks. Information value is often difficult to judge. For example, value losses due to missed reporting and false reporting are difficult regarding medical cancer tests. In most cases, the missed reporting of low-probability events often causes more loss than false reporting, such as medical tests and earthquake forecasts. In these cases, the semantic information criterion can be used to reduce the missed reporting of low-probability events.

For investment portfolios, the quantitative analysis of the information value is possible. Section 4.3 focuses on the information values of portfolios.

4.2. Goal-Oriented Information

4.2.1. Similarities and Differences Between Goal-Oriented Information and Prediction Information

Previously, we used the G measure to measure prediction information, requiring the prediction, $P(x \mid \theta_j)$, to conform to the fact, $P(x \mid y_j)$. Goal-oriented information is the opposite, requiring the fact to conform to the purpose.

An imperative sentence can be regarded as a control instruction. We need to know whether the control result conforms to the control purpose. The more consistent the result is, the more information there is.

A truth function or a membership function can represent a control target. For example, there are the following targets:

- "Workers' wages should preferably exceed 5000 dollars";
- "The age of death of the population had better exceed 80 years old";
- "The cruising distances of electric vehicles should preferably exceed 500 km";
- "The error of train arrival time had better be less than one minute".

The semantic KL information formula can measure purposeful information:

$$I(X; a_j/\theta_j) = \sum_i P(x_i|a_j) \log \frac{T(\theta_j|x_i)}{T(\theta_j)}. \tag{30}$$

In the formula, θ_j is a fuzzy set, indicating that the control target is a fuzzy range. Here, y_j becomes a_j, indicating the action corresponding to the j-th control task, y_j. If the control result is a specific x_i, the above formula becomes the semantic information $I(x_i; a_j/\theta_j)$.

If there are several control targets, $y_1, y_2, \ldots$, we can use the semantic MI formula to express the purposeful information:

$$I(X; A/\theta) = \sum_j P(a_j) \sum_i P(x_i|a_j) \log \frac{T(\theta_j|x_i)}{T(\theta_j)}, \tag{31}$$

where A is a random variable taking a value a or a_j. Using SVB, the control ratio, $P(a)$, can be optimized to minimize the control complexity (i.e., Shannon MI) for given fuzzy range constraints.

4.2.2. The Optimization of Goal-Oriented Information

Goal-oriented information can be regarded as the cumulative reward in constraint control. However, the goal here is a fuzzy range, which is expressed by a plan, command, or imperative sentence. The optimization task is similar to the active inference task using the MFE principle [22].

The semantic information formulas of imperative and descriptive (or predictive) sentences are the same, but the optimization methods differ (see Figure 10). For descriptive sentences, the fact is unchanged, and we hope that the predicted range conforms to the fact, that is, we fix $P(y_j \mid x)$ so that $T(\theta_j \mid x) \propto P(y_j \mid x)$, or we fix $P(x \mid y_j)$ so that $P(x \mid \theta_j) = P(x \mid y_j)$. For imperative sentences, we hope that the fact conforms to the purpose, that is, we fix $T(\theta_j \mid x)$ or $P(x \mid \theta_j)$ and minimize the information difference or maximize the information efficiency G/R by changing $P(y_j \mid x)$ or $P(x \mid y_j)$, or we balance between the purposiveness and the efficiency.

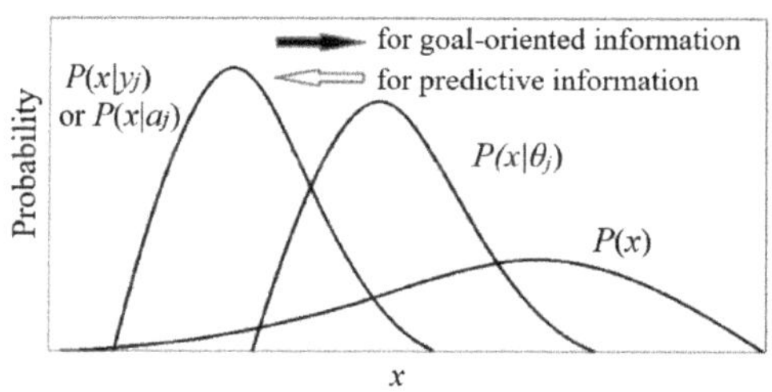

Figure 10. The optimization methods of the two types of semantic information are different. For predictive information, we hope that $P(x \mid \theta_j)$ is close to $P(x \mid y_j)$ (see the white arrow), while for goal-oriented information, we hope that $P(x \mid a_j)$ is close to $P(x \mid \theta_j)$ (see the black arrow).

For multi-target tasks, the objective function to be minimized is

$$f = I(X; A) - sI(X; A/\theta). \tag{32}$$

When the actual distribution, $P(x \mid a_j)$, is close to the constrained distribution, $P(x \mid \theta_j)$, the information efficiency (not information) reaches its maximum value of one. To further increase the two types of information, we can use the MID iteration formula to obtain

$$P(a_j|x) = P(a_j)m_{ij}^s/\lambda_i, \tag{33}$$

$$P(x_i|a_j) = P(a_j|x_i)P(x_i)/P(a_j) = P(x_i)m_{ij}^s/\sum_k P(x_k)m_{kj}^s. \tag{34}$$

Compared with VB [20,27–29] for active inference, the above method is simpler and can change the constraint strength by s.

Because the optimized $P(x \mid a_j)$ is a function of θ_j and s, we write $P^*(x \mid a_j) = P(x \mid \theta_j, s)$. It is worth noting that many distributions, $P(x \mid a_j)$, satisfy the constraint and maximize $I(X; a_j/\theta_j)$, but only $P^*(x \mid a_j)$ minimizes $I(X; a_j)$.

4.2.3. Experimental Results: Trade-Off Between Maximizing Purposiveness and MIE

Figure 11 shows a two-objective control task, with the objectives represented by the truth functions $T(\theta_0 \mid x)$ and $T(\theta_1 \mid x)$. We can imagine these as two pastures with fuzzy boundaries where we need to herd sheep. Without control, the density distribution of the sheep is $P(x)$. We need to solve an appropriate distribution, $P(a)$.

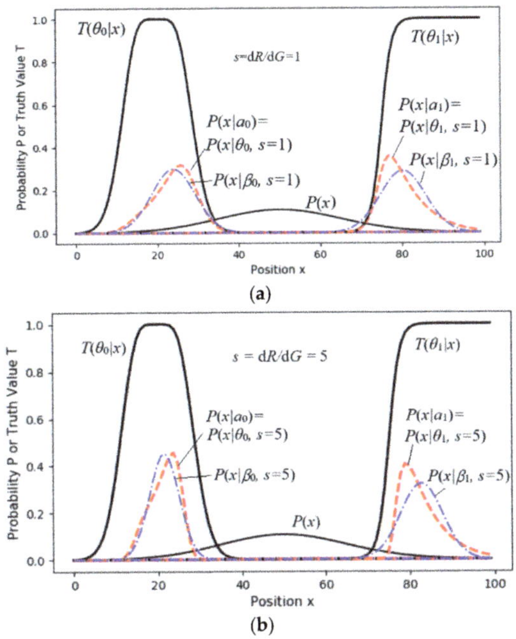

Figure 11. A two-objective control task. Dashed lines show $P(x \mid a_j) = P(x \mid \theta_j, s)$ $(j = 0, 1)$, and dash–dotted lines represent $P(x \mid \beta_j, s)$ $(j = 0, 1)$. (**a**) The case with s = 1; (**b**) The case with s = 5. $P(x \mid \beta_j, s)$ is a normal distribution produced by action a_j (See [61] for details).

For a different s, we set the initial proportions: $P(a_0) = P(a_1) = 0.5$. Then, we used Equations (23) and (24) for the MID iteration to obtain the proper $P(a_j \mid x)$ $(j = 0, 1)$. Then, we obtained $P(x \mid a_j) = P(x \mid \theta_j, s)$ by using Equation (34). Finally, we obtained $G(s)$, $R(s)$, and $R(G)$ by using Equation (25).

The dashed line for $R_1(G)$ in Figure 12 indicates that if we replace $P(x \mid a_j) = P(x \mid \theta_j, s)$ with a normal distribution, $P(x \mid \beta_j, s)$, G, and G/R_1 do not obviously become worse.

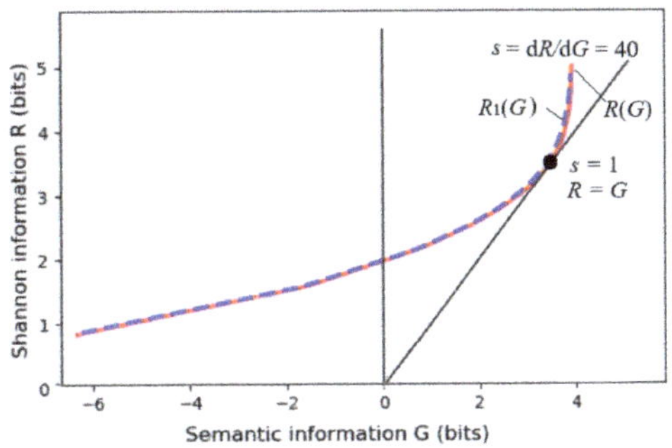

Figure 12. The $R(G)$ for constraint control. G slightly increases when s increases from 5 to 40, meaning $s = 5$ is good enough.

4.3. Investment Portfolios and Information Values

4.3.1. Capital Growth Entropy

Markowitz's portfolio theory [62] uses a linear combination of expected income and standard deviation as the optimization criterion. In contrast, the compound interest theory of portfolios uses compound interest, i.e., geometric mean income, as the optimization criterion.

The compound interest theory began from Kelley [63], followed by Latanne and Tuttle [64], Arrow [65], Cover [66], and the author of this paper. The famous American information theory textbook "*Elements of Information Theory*" [67], co-authored by Cover and Thomas, introduced Cover's research. Arrow, Cover, and the author of this article also discussed information value. The author published a monograph, "*Entropy Theory of Portfolios and Information Value*" [68] in 1997 and obtained many different conclusions.

The following is a brief introduction to the capital growth entropy proposed by the author.

Assuming that the principal is A, the profit is B, and the sum of principal plus profit is C. The investment income is $r = B/A$, and the rate of return on investment (i.e., output ratio: output/input) is $R = C/A = 1 + r$.

N security prices form an N-dimensional vector, and the price of the k-th security has n_k possible prices, $k = 1, 2, \ldots, N$. There are $W = n_1 \times n_2 \times \ldots \times n_N$ possible price vectors. The i-th price vector is $x_i = (x_{i1}, x_{i2}, \ldots x_{iN})$, $i = 1, 2, \ldots, W$; the current price vector is $x_0 = (x_{01}, x_{02}, \ldots, x_{0N})$. Assuming that one year later, the price vector x_i occurs, then the rate of return of the k-th security is $R_{ik} = x_{ik}/x_{0k}$, and the total rate of return is

$$R_i = \sum_{k=0}^{N} q_k R_{ik} \tag{35}$$

where q_k is the investment proportion in the k-th security, q_0 is the proportion of cash (or risk-free assets) held by the investor. There is $R_{0k} = R_0 = (1 + r_0)$, where r_0 is the risk-free interest rate.

Suppose we conduct m investment experiments to obtain the price vectors, and the number of times x_i or r_i occurs is m_i. The average multiple of the capital growth after each investment period or the geometric mean output ratio is

$$R_g = \prod_{i=1}^{W} R_i^{m_i/m}. \tag{36}$$

When $m \to \infty$, we have $m_i/m = P(x_i)$ and the capital growth entropy

$$H_g = \log R_g = \sum_{i=1}^{W} P(x_i) \log R_i = \sum_{i=1}^{W} P(x_i) \log \sum_{k=0}^{N} q_k R_{ik}. \tag{37}$$

If the log is base 2, H_g represents the doubling rate.

If the investment turns into betting on horse racing, where only one horse (the k-th horse) wins each time, the winner's return rate is R_k, and the others lose their wagers. Then, the above formula becomes

$$H_g = \log R_g = \sum_{k} P(x_k) \log[q_0 + q_k R_k - (1 - q_0 - q_k)], \tag{38}$$

where q_0 is the proportion of funds not betted, and $1 - q_0 - q_k$ is the proportion of funds paid.

4.3.2. The Generalization of Kelley's Formula

Kelley, a colleague of Shannon, found that the method used by Shannon's information theory can be used to optimize betting, so he proposed the Kelley formula [63].

Assume that in a gambling game, if you lose, you will lose $r_1 = 1$ times; if you win, you will earn $r_2 > 0$ times. If the probability of winning is P, then the optimal ratio is

$$q^* = P - (1 - P)/r_2. \tag{39}$$

Using capital growth entropy can lead to more general conclusions. Let $r_1 < 0$. The capital growth entropy is

$$q* = \underset{q}{\operatorname{argmax}}\, H_g = P_1 \log(1 - qr_1) + P_2 \log(1 + qr_2). \tag{40}$$

Letting $\mathrm{d}H_g/\mathrm{d}q = 0$, we derive

$$q^* = E/(r_1 r_2), \tag{41}$$

where E is the expected income. For example, for a coin toss bet, if one wins, he earns twice as much; if he loses, he loses one times; the probabilities of winning and losing are equal. Therefore, E is 0.5, and the optimal investment ratio is $q^* = 0.5/(1 \times 2) = 0.25$.

We assume $r_0 = 0$ above. If we consider the opportunity cost or the risk-free income, then $r_0 > 0$. At this time, the optimal ratio is

$$\begin{aligned} q* &= \underset{q}{\operatorname{argmax}}\, H_g \\ &= \underset{q}{\operatorname{argmax}} \{P_1 \log[r_0(1-q) + q - qr_1] + P_2 \log[r_0(1-q) + q + qr_2]\}. \end{aligned} \tag{42}$$

Letting $\mathrm{d}H_g/\mathrm{d}q = 0$, we can obtain

$$q* = \frac{P_2 d_2 - P_1 d_1}{d_1 d_2} R_0, \tag{43}$$

where $R_0 = 1 + r_0$, $d_1 = r_1 + r_0$, and $d_2 = r_2 - r_0$.

The author's abovementioned book [68] also discusses optimizing the investment ratio when short selling and leverage are allowed (see Section 3.3 in [68]) and optimizing the investment ratio for multi-coin betting. The book derives the limit theorem of diversified investment: if the number of coins increases infinitely, the geometric mean income equals the arithmetic mean income.

4.3.3. Risk Measures, Investment Channels, and Investment Channel Capacity

Markowitz uses the expected income, E, and the standard deviation, σ, to represent the income and the risk of a portfolio. Similarly, we use R_g and R_r to represent the return and risk of a portfolio. R_r is defined in the following formula:

$$R_r^2 = R_a^2 - R_g^2, \tag{44}$$

where $R_a = 1 + E$. Assuming that the geometric mean return of any portfolio is equivalent to the geometric mean return of a coin toss bet with an equal probability of gain or loss, then

$$H_g = \log R_g = 0.5\log(R_a - R_r) + 0.5\log(R_a + R_r). \tag{45}$$

Let $\sin\alpha = R_r/R_a \in [0, 1]$, which represents the bankruptcy risk better. When $\sin\alpha$ is close to one, the investment may go bankrupt (see Figure 13).

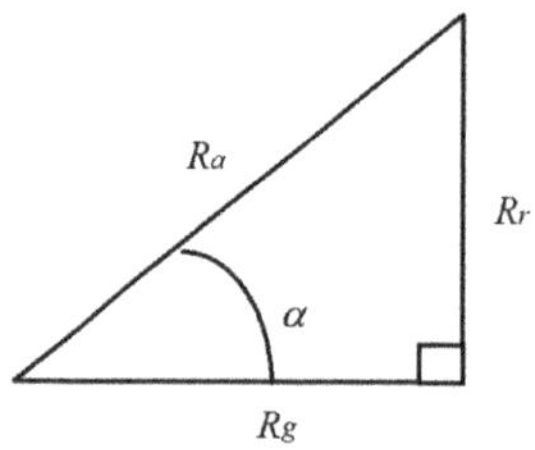

Figure 13. Relationship between the relative risk, sinα, and R_r, R_a, and R_g.

We call the pair ($\boldsymbol{P}$, $\boldsymbol{R}$) the investment channel, where $\boldsymbol{P} = (P_1, P_2, \ldots P_M)$ is the future price vector, $\boldsymbol{R} = (R_{ik})$ is the return matrix, and the set of all possible investment ratio vectors is $\boldsymbol{q}_C$. Then, the capacity of the investment channel (abbreviated as investment capacity) is defined as

$$H_C* = \max_{q \in q_C} H(\boldsymbol{P}, \boldsymbol{R}, \boldsymbol{q}) = \boldsymbol{H}(\boldsymbol{P}, \boldsymbol{R}, \boldsymbol{q}*), \tag{46}$$

where $\boldsymbol{q}^* = \boldsymbol{q}^*(\boldsymbol{R}, \boldsymbol{P})$ is the optimal investment ratio.

For example, for a typical coin toss bet (with equal probabilities of winning and losing, and $r_0 = 0$), $q^* = E/(r_1 r_2)$, the investment capacity is

$$H_C* = \frac{1}{2} \log \frac{1}{1 - E^2/{R_r}^2}. \tag{47}$$

Since $1/(1 - x) = 1 + x + x^2 + \ldots \approx 1 + x$, when $E/R_r << 1$, there is an approximate formula:

$$H_C* \approx \frac{1}{2} \log(1 + \frac{E^2}{{R_r}^2}). \tag{48}$$

In comparison with the Gaussian channel capacity formula for communication,

$$C = \frac{1}{2} \log(1 + \frac{P}{N}), \tag{49}$$

we can see that the investment capacity formula is very similar to the Gaussian channel capacity formula. This similarity means that investment needs to reduce risk, just as communication needs to reduce noise.

4.3.4. The Information Value Formula Based on Capital Growth Entropy

Weaver, who co-authored the book "*A Mathematical Theory of Communication*" [2] with Shannon, proposed three communication levels related to Shannon's information, semantic information, and information value.

According to the common usage of "information value", the information value mentioned in the academic community does not refer to the value of information on markets but to the utility or utility increment generated by information. We define the information value as the increment of capital growth entropy.

Assume that the prior probability distribution of different returns is $P(x)$, and the return matrix is (R_{ik}), then the expected capital growth entropy is $H_g(X)$. The optimal investment ratio vector $\boldsymbol{q}^*$ is $\boldsymbol{q}^* = \boldsymbol{q}^*(P(x), (R_{ik}))$. When the probability distribution of the predicted return becomes $P(x \mid \theta_j)$, the capital growth entropy becomes

$$H_g * (X|\theta_j) = \sum_i P(x_i|\theta_j) \log R_i(\boldsymbol{q}*), R_i(\boldsymbol{q}*) = \sum_k q_k * R_{ik}. \tag{50}$$

The optimal investment ratio becomes $\boldsymbol{q}^{**} = \boldsymbol{q}^{**}(P(x \mid \theta_j), (R_{ik}))$. We define the increment of the capital growth entropy due to the semantic KL information $I(X; \theta_j)$ as the information value

$$V(X;\theta_j) = \sum_i P(x_i|y_j) \log \frac{R_i(\boldsymbol{q}**)}{R_i(\boldsymbol{q}*)}. \tag{51}$$

$V(X; \theta_j)$ and $I(X; \theta_j)$ have similar structures. For the above formula, when x_i is determined to occur, the information value of y_j becomes

$$v_{ij} = v(x_i;\theta_j) = \log \frac{R_i(\boldsymbol{q}**)}{R_i(\boldsymbol{q}*)}. \tag{52}$$

The information value also needs to be verified by facts; wrong predictions may bring a negative information value. In contrast, Cover and Thomas [67] do not distinguish $P(x \mid \theta_j)$ and $P(x \mid y_j)$.

4.3.5. Comparison with Arrow's Information Value Formula

The utility function defined by Arrow [65] is

$$U = \sum_i P_i U(q_i R_i) = \sum_i P_i \log(q_i R_i) = \sum_i P_i \log q_i + \sum_i P_i \log R_i, \tag{53}$$

where $U(q_iR_i)$ is the utility obtained by the investor when the i-th return occurs.

Under the restriction of $\sum_i q_i = 1$, $q_i = P_i$ $(i = 1, 2, \ldots)$ maximizes U so that

$$U* = \sum P_i \log P_i + \sum_i P_i \log R_i. \tag{54}$$

After receiving the information, the investor knows which income will occur and thus invests all his funds in it. Hence, there is

$$U** = \sum_i P_i \log R_i. \tag{55}$$

The information value is defined as the difference in utility between investment with and without information and is equal to Shannon entropy, that is

$$V = U** - U* = -\sum_i P_i \log P_i = H(X). \tag{56}$$

The optimal investment ratio obtained from the above formula is inconsistent with the Kelley formula and common sense. For example, according to the Kelley formula, the optimal ratio is 25% for the coin toss bet above. According to common sense, if we know the result of the coin toss, the return will depend on the odds.

According to Arrow's theory, profit and loss have nothing to do with odds. How does one bet? Should one bet by using $q_i = P_i$ or by putting all in the profit? Arrow seems to confuse the k-th security with the i-th return. He uses $U(q_iR_i) = \log(q_iR_i)$, while the author uses

$$U(q_k R_k) = \log[q_0 + q_k R_k - (1 - q_0 - q_k)]. \tag{57}$$

Arrow does not consider the non-bet proportion, q_0, nor the paid proportion, $1 - q_0 - q_k$. Calculating the utility in this way is puzzling.

Cover and Thomas inherited Arrow's method and concluded that when there is information, the optimal investment doubling rate increment equals the Shannon MI [67] (see Section 6.2). Their conclusion has the same problem.

4.4. Information, Entropy, and Free Energy in Thermodynamic Systems

To clarify the relationship between information and free energy in physics, we discuss information, entropy, and free energy in thermodynamic systems.

Jaynes [69] used Stirling's formula, ln$N$! = Nln$N$ − N (when $N \rightarrow \infty$), to prove there is a simple connection between Boltzmann's microscopic sate number W (of N molecules) and Shannon entropy:

$$S = \mathrm{k} \ln W = \mathrm{k} \ln \frac{N!}{\prod_i N_i!} = -\mathrm{k}N \sum_i P(x_i|T) \ln P(x_i|T) = \mathrm{k}NH(X|T), \tag{58}$$

where S is entropy, k is the Boltzmann constant, N is the number of molecules, x_i is the i-th microscopic state of one molecule, and T is the absolute temperature, which equals a molecule's average translational kinetic energy. $P(x_i | T)$ represents the probability density of molecules in state x_i at temperature T. The Boltzmann distribution for a given energy constraint is

$$P(x_i|T) = \exp(-\frac{e_i}{\mathrm{k}T})/Z', Z' = \sum_i \exp(-\frac{e_i}{\mathrm{k}T}), \tag{59}$$

where Z' is the partition function.

Considering the information between temperature and molecular energy, we use Maxwell–Boltzmann statistics. In this case, we replace x_i with energy e_i and let G_i denote the number of microscopic states of one molecule with energy e_i and let G denote the number of all states of one molecule. Then $P(e_i) = G_i/G$ is the prior probability of e_i. So, Equation (58) becomes

$$\begin{aligned} S &= \mathrm{k} \ln \frac{N!}{\prod_i N_i!/G_i^{N_i}} = -\mathrm{k}N \sum_i P(e_i|T) \ln \frac{P(e_i|T)}{G_i} \\ &= -\mathrm{k}N \sum_i P(e_i|T) \ln \frac{P(e_i|T)}{P(e_i)} + \mathrm{k}N \ln G \\ &= \mathrm{k}N[\ln G - KL(P(e|T)||P(e)]. \end{aligned} \tag{60}$$

Under the energy constraint, when the system reaches equilibrium, Equation (59) becomes

$$P(e_i|T) = P(e_i) \exp(-\frac{e_i}{kT})/Z, Z = \sum_i P(e_i) \exp(-\frac{e_i}{kT}), \tag{61}$$

Now, we can interpret $\exp[-e_i/(kT)]$ as the truth function $T(\theta_j | x)$, Z as the logical probability $T(\theta_j)$, and Equation (61) as the semantic Bayes' formula.

Consider a local non-equilibrium system. Different regions y_j (j = 1, 2, ...) of the system have different temperatures, T_j (j = 1, 2, ...). Hence, we have $P(y_j) = P(T_j) = N_j/N$ and $P(x | y_j) = P(x | T_j)$. From Equation (60), we obtain

$$\begin{aligned} I(E;Y) &= \sum_j P(y_j) KL(P(e|y_j)||P(e) = \sum_j P(y_j)[\ln G_m - S_j/(\mathrm{k}N_j)] \\ &= \ln G_m - S(kN), \end{aligned} \tag{62}$$

where E is a random variable taking a value e, and lnG_m is the prior entropy $H(X)$ of X. Since e is certain for a given x, there are $H(E | X) = 0$ and $H(X, E) = H(X) = \ln G_m$. From Equations (60) and (62), we derive

$$I(E;Y) = \ln G_m - S/(kN) = H(X) - H(X|Y) = I(X;Y). \tag{63}$$

This formula indicates that the information about E provided by Y or T is equal to the information about X, and $S/(kN)$ equals $H(X \mid Y)$. The above formula shows that the entropy increase law in physics can be equivalently expressed as the MI decrease law.

According to Equations (61)–(63), when the local equilibrium is reached, there is

$$\begin{aligned} I(X;Y) &= I(E;Y) = \sum_j \sum_i P(e_i, y_j) \ln \frac{\exp[-e_i/(\mathrm{k}T_j)]}{Z_j} \\ &= -\sum_j P(y_j) \log Z_j - \mathrm{E}(e/T)/(\mathrm{k}N) = H(Y_\theta) - H(Y_\theta|X) = I(X;Y_\theta), \end{aligned} \tag{64}$$

where $\mathrm{E}(e/T)$ is the average of e/T, which is similar to relative square error. It can be seen that in local equilibrium systems, minimum Shannon MI can be expressed by the semantic MI formula. Since $H(X \mid Y)$ becomes $H(X \mid Y_\theta)$, there is

$$S = \mathrm{k}NH(X|Y_\theta) = \mathrm{k}NF, \tag{65}$$

which means that VFE, F, is proportional to thermodynamic entropy.

Helmholtz's free energy formula is

$$F^* = U - TS, \tag{66}$$

where F^* is free energy, and U is the system's internal energy. When the internal energy remains unchanged, the increase in free energy is

$$\Delta F* = -\Delta(TS) = TS - \sum_j T_j S_j = \mathrm{k}NTH(X) - \mathrm{k}N\sum_j T_j H(X|Y). \tag{67}$$

Comparing the above equation with Equation (63), we can find that the Shannon MI is analogous to the increase in free energy; the semantic MI is analogous to the increase in free energy in a local equilibrium system, which is smaller than the Shannon MI, just as work is smaller than costed free energy. We can also regard $\mathrm{k}NT$ and $\mathrm{k}NT_j$ as the unit information values [5], so the increase in free energy is equivalent to the increase in the information value.

5. G Theory's Applications in Machine Learning

5.1. Basic Methods of Machine Learning: Learning Functions and Optimization Criteria

The most basic machine learning method has two steps:

- First, we use samples or sample distributions to train the learning functions with a specific criterion, such as the maximum likelihood or RLS criterion;
- Then, we make probability predictions or classifications utilizing the learning function with the minimum distortion, minimum loss, or maximum likelihood criterion.

We use the maximum likelihood or RLS criterion when training learning functions. We may use different criteria when using learning functions for classifications. We generally use maximum likelihood and RLS criteria for prediction tasks where information is important. To judge whether a person is guilty or not, where correctness is essential, we may use the minimum distortion (or loss) criterion. The maximum semantic information criterion is equivalent to the maximum likelihood criterion and is a Regularized Least Distortion (RLD) criterion, including the partition function's logarithm. Compared with the minimum distortion criterion, the maximum semantic information criterion can reduce the under-reporting of small probability events.

We generally do not use $P(x \mid y_j)$ to train $P(x \mid \theta_j)$ because if $P(x)$ changes, the originally trained $P(x \mid \theta_j)$ will become invalid. A parameterized transition probability function,

$P(\theta_j \mid x)$, as a learning function, is still valid even if $P(x)$ is changed. However, using $P(\theta_j \mid x)$ as a learning function also has essential defects. When class number $n > 2$, it is challenging to construct $P(\theta_j \mid x)$ ($j = 1, 2, \ldots$) because of the normalization restriction, that is, $\sum_j P(\theta_j \mid x) = 1$ (for each x). As we will see below, there is no restriction when using truth or membership functions as learning functions.

The following sections introduce G theory's applications to machine learning. If we use existing methods, every task is not easy. Either the solution is complicated, or the convergence proof is difficult.

5.2. For Multi-Label Learning and Classification

Consider multi-label learning, a supervised learning task. From the sample $\{(xk, yk), k = 1, 2, \ldots, N\}$, we can obtain the sample distribution, $P(x, y)$. Then, we use Formula (16) or (18) for the optimized truth functions.

Assume that a truth function is a Gaussian function, there should be

$$T(\theta_j|x) \propto \frac{P(x|y_j)}{P(x)} \propto P(y_j|x). \tag{68}$$

So, we can use the expectation and standard deviation of $P(x \mid y_j)/P(x)$ or $P(y_j \mid x)$ as the expectation and the standard deviation of $T(\theta_j \mid x)$. If the truth function is like a dam cross-section (see Figure 14), we can obtain it through some transformation.

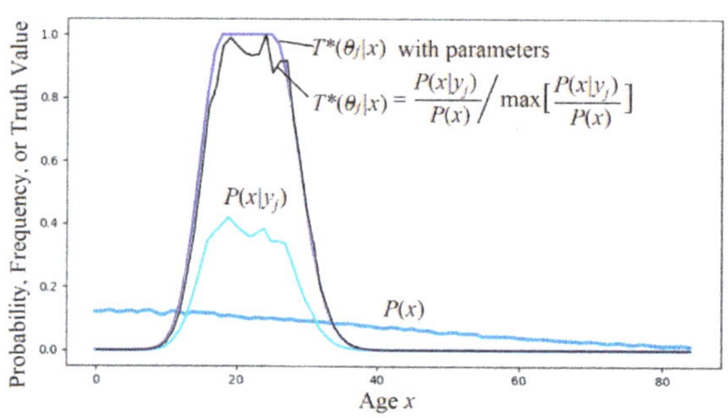

Figure 14. Using prior and posterior distributions, $P(x)$ and $P(x \mid y_j)$, to obtain the optimized truth function, $T^*(\theta_j \mid x)$. For details, see Appendix B in [7].

If we only know $P(y_j \mid x)$ but not $P(x)$, we can assume that $P(x)$ is equally probable, that is, $P(x) = 1/\mid \boldsymbol{U} \mid$, and then optimize the membership function using the following formula:

$$I(X;\theta_j) = \sum_i P(x_i|y_j) \log \frac{T(\theta_j|x_i)}{T(\theta_j)} = \sum_i \frac{P(y_j|x_i)}{\sum_k P(y_j|x_k)} \log \frac{T(\theta_j|x_i)}{\sum_k T(\theta_j|x_k)} + \log|\boldsymbol{U}|. \tag{69}$$

For multi-label classification, we can use the classifier

$$y_j* = \underset{y_j}{\text{argmax}}\ I(x;\theta_j) = \underset{y_j}{\text{argmax}}\ \log \frac{T(\theta_j|x)}{T(\theta_j)}. \tag{70}$$

If the distortion criterion is used, we can use $-\log T(\theta_j \mid x)$ as the distortion function or replace $I(X; \theta_j)$ with $T(\theta_j \mid x)$.

The popular Binary Relevance [70] for multi-label classification converts an n-label learning task into an n-pair label learning task. In comparison, the above method is much simpler.

5.3. Maximum MI Classification of Unseen Instances

This classification belongs to semi-supervised learning. We take the medical test and the signal detection as examples (see Figure 15).

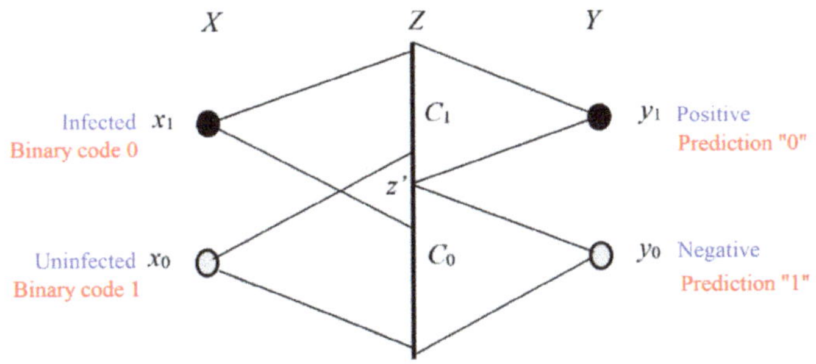

Figure 15. The medical test and the signal detection. We choose y_j according to $z \in C_j$. The task is to find the dividing point, z', that results in maximum MI between X and Y.

The following algorithm is not limited to binary classifications. Let C_j be a subset of C and $y_j = f(z \mid z \in C_j)$; hence, $S = \{C_1, C_2, \ldots\}$ is a partition of C. Our task is to find the optimal S, which is

$$S* = \underset{S}{\text{argmax}}\ I(X;Y_\theta|S) = \underset{S}{\text{argmax}} \sum_j \sum_i P(C_j)P(x_i|C_j) \log \frac{T(\theta_j|x_i)}{T(\theta_j)}. \quad (71)$$

First, we initiate a partition. Then, we do the following iterations.

Matching I: Let the semantic channel match the Shannon channel and set the reward function. First, for given S, we obtain the Shannon channel:

$$P(y_j|x) = \sum_{z_k \in C_j} P(z_k|x),\ j = 1, 2, \ldots, n. \quad (72)$$

Then we obtain the semantic channel, $T(y \mid x)$, from the Shannon channel and $T(\theta_j)$ (or $m_\theta(x, y) = m(x, y)$). Then we have $I(x_i; \theta_j)$. For a given z, we have conditional information as the reward function:

$$I(X;\theta_j|z) = \sum_i P(x_i|z) I(x_i;\theta_j),\ j = 0, 1, \ldots, n, \quad (73)$$

Matching II: Let the Shannon channel match the semantic channel by the classifier

$$y_j* = f(z) = \underset{y_j}{\text{argmax}}\ I(X;\theta_j|z),\ j = 0, 1, \ldots, n. \quad (74)$$

Repeat **Matching I** and **Matching II** until S does not change. Then, the convergent S is the S^* we seek. The author explained the convergence with the $R(G)$ function (see Section 3.3 in [7]).

Figure 6 shows an example. The detailed data can be found in Section 4.2 of [7]. The two lines in Figure 16a represent the initial partition. Figure 16d shows that the convergence is very fast.

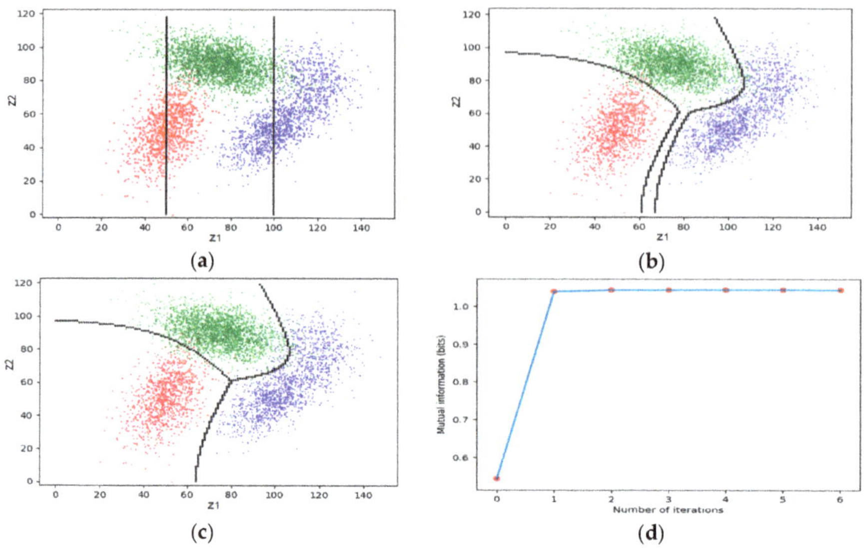

Figure 16. The maximum MI classification. Different colors represent different classes. (**a**) A very bad initial partition; (**b**) after the first iteration; (**c**) after the second iteration; (**d**) the MI changes with the iteration number.

However, this method is unsuitable for the maximum MI classification in a high-dimensional space. We need to combine neural network methods to explore more effective approaches.

5.4. The Explanation and Improvement of the EM Algorithm for Mixture Models

The EM algorithm [71,72] is usually used for mixure models (clustering), an unsupervised learning method.

We know that $P(x) = \sum_j P(y_j)P(x \mid y_j)$. Given a sample distribution, $P(x)$, we use $P_\theta(x) = \sum_j P(y_j)P(x \mid \theta_j)$ to approximate $P(x)$ so that the relative entropy or KL divergence, $KL(P||P_\theta)$, is close to zero. $P(y)$ is the probability distribution of the latent variable to be sought.

The EM algorithm first presets $P(x \mid \theta_j)$ and $P(y_j)$, $j = 1, 2, \ldots, n$. The E-step obtains

$$P(y_j|x) = P(y_j)P(x|\theta_j)/P_\theta(x),\ P_\theta(x) = \sum_k P(y_k)P(x|\theta_k). \tag{75}$$

Then, in the M-step, the log-likelihood of the complete data (usually represented by Q) is maximized. The M-step can be divided into two steps: M1-step for

$$P^{+1}(y_j) = \sum_i P(x_i)P(y_j|x_i) \tag{76}$$

and M2-step for

$$P(x|\theta_j{}^{+1}) = P(x)P(y_j|x)/P^{+1}(y_j) = P(x)\frac{P(x|\theta_j)}{P_\theta(x)}\frac{P(y_j)}{P^{+1}(y_j)}, \tag{77}$$

which optimizes the likelihood function. For Gaussian mixture models, we can use the expectation and standard deviation of $P(x)P(y_j \mid x)/P^{+1}(y_j)$ as the expectation and standard deviation of $P(x \mid \theta_j{}^{+1})$.

From the perspective of G theory, the M2-step is to make the semantic channel match the Shannon channel or minimize the VFE, $H(X \mid Y_\theta)$, and the E-step and M1-step are to match the Shannon channel with the semantic channel. Repeating the above three steps can make the mixture model converge. The converged $P(y)$ is the required probability distribution of the latent variable. According to the derivation process of the $R(G)$ function, the E-step and M1-step minimize the information difference, R–G; the M-step maximizes the semantic MI. Therefore, the optimization criterion used by the EM algorithm is the MIE criterion.

However, there are two problems with the above method to find the latent variable: (1) $P(y)$ may converge slowly; (2) if the likelihood functions are also fixed, how do we solve $P(y)$?

Based on the $R(G)$ function analysis, the author improved the EM algorithm to the EnM algorithm [7]. The EnM algorithm includes the E-step for $P(y \mid x)$, the n-step for $P(y)$, and the M-step for $P(x \mid \theta_j)$ (j = 1, 2, …). The n-step repeats the E-step and the M1-step in the EM algorithm n times so that $P^{+1}(y) \approx P(y)$. The EnM algorithm also uses the MIE criterion. The n-step can speed up the solution of $P(y)$. The M2-step only optimizes the likelihood functions. Because $P(y_j)/P^{+1}(y_j)$ is approximately equal to one, we can use the following formula to optimize the following model parameters:

$$P(x|\theta_j{}^{+1}) = P(x)P(x|\theta_j)/P_\theta(x). \tag{78}$$

Without the n-step, there will be $P(y_j) \neq P^{+1}(y_j)$, and $\sum_i P(x_i)P(x \mid \theta_j)/P_\theta(x_i) \neq 1$. When solving mixure models, we can choose a smaller n, such as n = 3. When solving $P(y)$ specifically, we can select a larger n until $P(y)$ converges. When n = 1, the EnM algorithm becomes the EM algorithm.

The following mathematical formula proves that the EnM algorithm converges. After the M-step, the Shannon MI becomes

$$R = \sum_i \sum_j P(x_i) \frac{P(x_i|\theta_j)}{P_\theta(x_i)} P(y_j) \log \frac{P(y_j|x_i)}{P^{+1}(y_j)}, \tag{79}$$

We define

$$R'' = \sum_i \sum_j P(x_i) \frac{P(x_i|\theta_j)}{P_\theta(x_i)} P(y_j) \log \frac{P(x_i|\theta_j)}{P_\theta(x_i)}. \tag{80}$$

Then, we can deduce that after the E-step, there is

$$KL(P||P_\theta) = R'' - G = R - G + KL(P_Y{}^{+1}||P_Y), \tag{81}$$

where $KL(P||P_\theta)$ is the relative entropy or KL divergence between $P(x)$ and $P_\theta(x)$; the right KL divergence is

$$KL(P_Y{}^{+1}||P_Y) = \sum_j P^{+1}(y_j) \log[P^{+1}(y_j)/P(y_j)]. \tag{82}$$

It is close to zero after the n-step.

Equation (81) can be used to prove that the EnM algorithm converges. Because the M-step maximizes G, and the E-step and the n-step minimize R–G and $KL(P_Y{}^{+1}||P_Y)$, $H(P||P_\theta)$ can be close to zero. We can also use the above method to prove that the EM algorithm converges.

In most cases, the EnM algorithm performs better than the EM algorithm, especially when $P(y)$ is hard to converge.

Some researchers believe that EM makes the mixture model converge because the complete data log-likelihood $Q = -H(X, Y_\theta)$ continues to increase [72], or the negative free energy $F' = H(Y) + Q$ continues to increase [21]. However, we can easily find counterexamples where R–G continues to decrease, but Q and F' do not necessarily continue to increase.

The author used the example used by Neal and Hinton [21] (see Figure 17), but the mixture proportion in the true model was changed from 0.7:0.3 to 0.3:0.7.

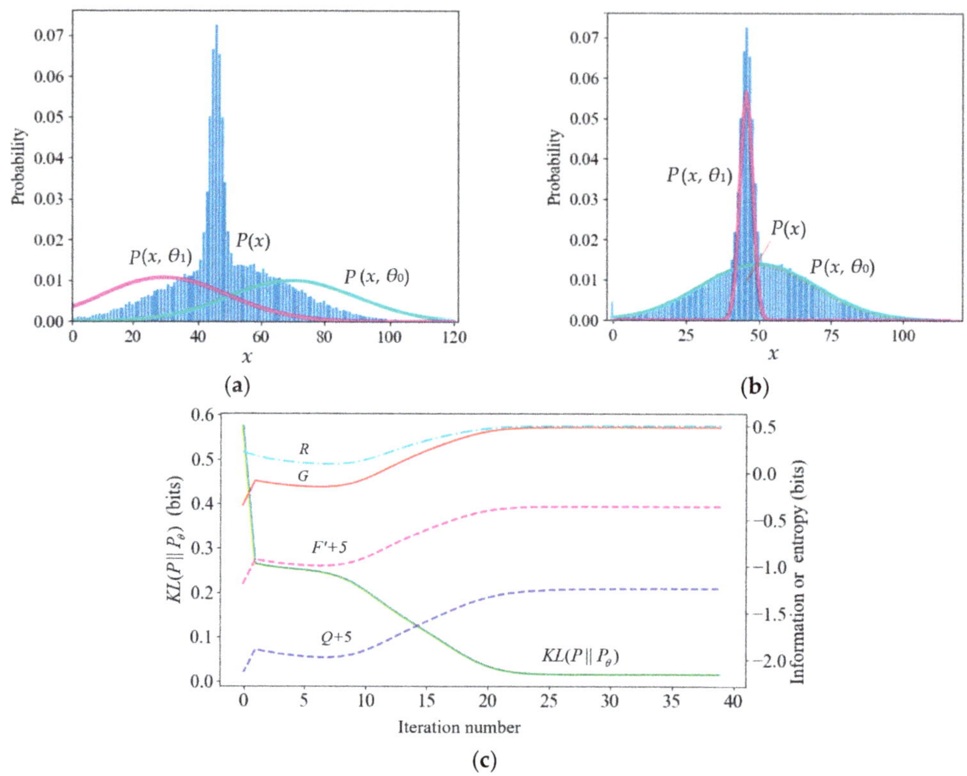

Figure 17. The convergent process of the mixture model from Neal and Hinton [21]. The mixture proportion was changed from 0.7:0.3 to 0.3:0.7. (**a**) The iteration starts; (**b**) the iteration converges; (**c**) the iteration process. $P(x, \theta_j)$ equals $P(y_j)P(x\,|\,\theta_j)$ (j = 0, 1). See Appendix A for the Python source program.

This experiment shows that the decrease in R–G, not the increase in Q or F', is the reason for the convergence of the mixture model.

The free energy of the true mixture model (with true parameters) is the Shannon conditional entropy $H(X\,|\,Y)$. If the standard deviation of the true mixture components is large, $H(X\,|\,Y)$ is also large. If the initial standard deviation is small, F is small initially. After the mixture model converges, F must approach $H(X\,|\,Y)$. Therefore, F increases (i.e., F' decreases) during the convergence process. For example, a true mixture model with two components with two standard deviations of 15. If two initial standard deviations are 5, F must continue increasing during the iteration. Many experiments have shown that this is indeed the case.

Equation (81) can also explain pre-training in deep learning, where we need to maximize the model's predictive ability and minimize the information difference, *R–G* (or compress data).

5.5. Semantic Variational Bayes: A Simple Method for Solving Hidden Variables

Given $P(x)$ and constraints $P(x \mid \theta_j)$, $j = 1, 2, \ldots$, we need to solve $P(y)$ that produces $P(x) = \sum_j P(y_j)P(x \mid \theta_j)$. $P(y)$ is the probability distribution of the latent variable y, sometimes called the latent variable. The popular method is the Variational Bayes method (VB for short) [27–29]. This method originated from the article by Hinton and Camp [20]. It was further discussed and applied in the articles by Neal and Hinton [21], Beal [28], and Koller [29] (ch. 11). Gottwald and Braun's article, "Two Free Energy and the Bayesian Revolution" [73], discusses the relationship between the MFE principle and Maximum Entropy (ME) principle in detail.

VB uses $P(y)$ (usually written as $g(y)$) as a variation to minimize the following function:

$$F = \sum_y g(y) \log \frac{g(y)}{P(x, y|\theta)} = -\sum_y g(y) \log P(x|y, \theta) + KL(g(y)||P(y)) \tag{83}$$

Using the semantic information method, we express F as

$$F = \sum_i P(x_i) \sum_i P(y_j|x_i) \log \frac{P^{+1}(y_j)}{P(x_i, y_j|\theta)} = H(X|Y_\theta) + KL({P_Y}^{+1}||P_Y). \tag{84}$$

Since F is equal to the semantic posterior entropy $H(X \mid Y_\theta)$ of X after the M1-step of the EM algorithm, we can treat F as $H(X \mid Y_\theta)$. Since $I(X; Y_\theta)) = H(X) - H(X \mid Y_\theta) = F - H(X \mid Y)$, the smaller the F, the larger the semantic MI.

It is easy to prove that when the semantic channel matches the Shannon channel, that is, $T(\theta_j \mid x) \propto P(y_j \mid x)$ or $P(x \mid \theta_j) = P(x \mid y_j)$ $(j = 1, 2, \ldots)$, F is minimized, and the semantic MI is maximized. Minimizing F can optimize the prediction model, $P(x \mid \theta_j)$ $(j = 1, 2, \ldots)$, but it cannot optimize $P(y)$. For optimizing $P(y)$, the mean-field approximation [27,28] is used; that is, $P(y \mid x)$ instead of $P(y)$ is used as the variation. Only one $P(y_j \mid x)$ is optimized at a time, and the other $P(y_k \mid x)$ $(k \neq j)$ remains unchanged. Minimizing F in this way is actually maximizing the log-likelihood of x or minimizing $KL(P||P_\theta)$. In this way, optimizing $P(y \mid x)$ also indirectly optimizes $P(y)$.

Unfortunately, when optimizing $P(y)$ and $P(y \mid x)$, F may not continue to decrease (see Figure 17). So, VB is suitable as a tool but imperfect as a theory.

Fortunately, it is easier to solve $P(y \mid x)$ and $P(y)$ using the MID iteration in solving $R(D)$ and $R(G)$ functions. The MID iteration plus LBI for optimizing the prediction model is SVB [61]. It uses the MIE criterion.

When the constraint changes from likelihood functions to truth functions or similarity functions, $P(y_j \mid x_i)$ in the MID iteration formula is changed from

$$P(y|x_i) = P(y)\left[\frac{P(x_i \mid \theta_j)}{P_\theta(x_i)}\right]^s / \sum_k P(y_k)\left[\frac{P(x_i \mid \theta_j)}{P_\theta(x_i)}\right]^s \tag{85}$$

to

$$P(y|x_i) = P(y)\left[\frac{T(\theta_j \mid x_i)}{T(\theta_j)}\right]^s / \sum_k P(y_k)\left[\frac{T(\theta_k \mid x_i)}{T(\theta_k)}\right]^s. \tag{86}$$

From $P(x)$ and the new $P(y \mid x)$, we can obtain the new $P(y)$. Repeating the formulas for $P(y \mid x)$ and $P(y)$ will lead to the convergence of $P(y)$. Using s allows us to tighten the constraints for increasing R and G. Choosing proper s enables us to balance between maximizing semantic information and maximizing information efficiency.

The main tasks of SVB and VB are the same: using variational methods to solve latent variables according to observed data and constraints. The differences are

- **Criteria**: In the definition of VB, it adopts the MFE criterion, whereas, for solving $P(y)$, it uses $P(y \mid x)$ as the variation and hence actually uses the maximum likelihood criterion that makes the mixture model converge. In contrast, SVB uses the MID criterion.
- **Variational method**: VB only uses $P(y)$ or $P(y \mid x)$ as a variation, while SVB alternatively uses $P(y \mid x)$ and $P(y)$ as variations.
- **Computational complexity**: VB uses logarithmic and exponential functions to solve $P(y \mid x)$ [27]; the calculation of $P(y \mid x)$ in SVB is relatively simple (for the same task, i.e., when $s = 1$).
- **Constraints**: VB only uses likelihood functions as constraint functions. In contrast, SVB allows using various learning functions (including likelihood, truth, membership, similarity, and distortion functions) as constraints. In addition, SVB can use the parameter s to enhance constraints.

Because SVB is more compatible with the maximum likelihood criterion and the ME principle, it should be more suitable for many applications in machine learning. However, because it does not consider the probability of parameters, it may not be as applicable as VB on some occasions.

5.6. Bayesian Confirmation and Causal Confirmation

Logical empiricism was opposed by Popper's falsificationism [44,45], so it turned to confirmation (i.e., Bayesian confirmation) instead of induction or positivism [74,75]. Bayesian confirmation was previously a field of concern for researchers in the philosophy of science [76,77], and now many researchers in natural sciences have also begun to study it [78,79]. The reason is that uncertain reasoning requires major premises, which need to be confirmed.

The main reasons why researchers have different views on Bayesian confirmation are

- There are no suitable mathematical tools; for example, statistical and logical probabilities are not well distinguished.
- Many people do not distinguish between the confirmation of the relationship (i.e., $\rightarrow$) in the major premise $y \rightarrow x$ and the confirmation of the consequent (i.e., x occurs);
- No confirmation measure can reasonably clarify the raven paradox [74].

To clarify the raven paradox, the author wrote the article "Channels' confirmation and predictions' confirmation: from medical tests to the Raven paradox" [35].

In the author's opinion, the task of Bayesian confirmation is to evaluate the support of the sample distribution for the major premise. For example, for the medical test (see Figure 15), a major premise is "If a person tests positive (y_1), then he is infected (x_1)", abbreviated as $y_1 \rightarrow x_1$. For a channel's confirmation, a truth (or membership) function can be regarded as a combination of a clear truth function, $T(y_1 \mid x) \in \{0,1\}$, and a tautology's truth function (always one):

$$T(\theta_1 \mid x) = b_1 T(y_1 \mid x) + b_1'. \tag{87}$$

A tautology's proportion, b_1', is the degree of disbelief. The credibility is b_1, and its relationship with b_1' is $b_1' = 1 - \mid b_1 \mid$. See Figure 18.

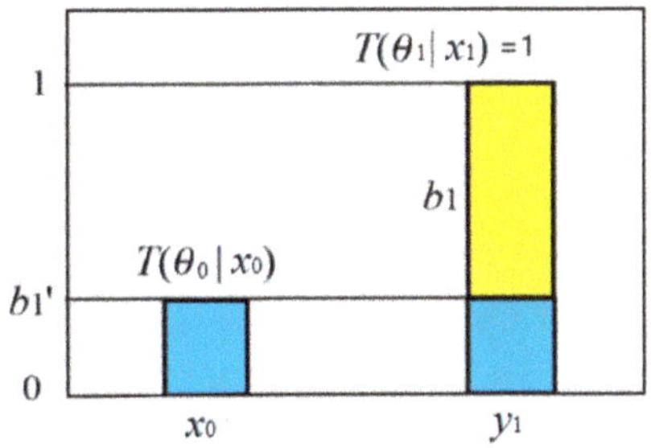

Figure 18. A truth function includes a believable proportion, b_1', and unbelievable proportion, $b_1' = 1 - |b_1|$.

We change b_1 to maximize the semantic KL information, $I(X; \theta_1)$; the optimized b_1, denoted as b_1*, is the confirmation degree:

$$b_1* = b*(y_1 \to x_1) = \frac{P(y_1|x_1) - P(y_1|x_0)}{\max(P(y_1|x_1), P(y_1|x_0))} = \frac{R^+ - 1}{\max(R^+, 1)}, \tag{88}$$

where $R^+ = P(y_1 | x_i)/P(y_1 | x_0)$ is the positive likelihood ratio, indicating the reliability of the tested positive. This conclusion is compatible with medical test theory.

Considering the prediction confirmation degree, we assume that $P(x | \theta_1)$ is a combination of the 0–1 part and the probability-equal part. The ratio of the 0–1 part is the prediction credibility, and the optimized credibility is the prediction confirmation degree:

$$c_1* = c*(y_1 \to x_1) = \frac{P(x_1|y_1) - P(x_0|y_1)}{\max(P(x_1|y_1), P(x_0, y_1))} = \frac{a - c}{\max(a, c)}, \tag{89}$$

where a is the number of positive examples, and c is the number of negative examples.

Both confirmation degrees can be used for probability predictions, i.e., calculating $P(x | \theta_1)$.

Hemple proposed the confirmation paradox, namely the raven paradox [74]. According to the equivalence condition in classical logic, "If x is a raven, then x is black" (Rule 1) is equivalent to "If x is not black, then x is not a raven" (Rule 2). According to this, white chalk supports Rule 2; therefore, it also supports Rule 1. However, according to common sense, a black crow supports Rule 1, and a non-black raven opposes Rule 1; something that is not a raven, such as a black cat or a white chalk, is irrelevant to Rule 1. Therefore, there is a paradox between the equivalence condition and common sense. Using the confirmation measure c_1*, we can ensure that common sense is correct and the equivalence condition for fuzzy major premises is wrong, thus eliminating the raven paradox. However, other confirmation measures cannot eliminate the raven paradox [35].

Causal probability is used in causal inference theory [80]:

$$P_d = \max[0, \frac{P(y_1|x_1) - P(y_1|x_0)}{P(y_1|x_1)}] = \max(0, \frac{R^+ - 1}{R^+}). \tag{90}$$

It indicates the necessity of the cause, x_1, replacing x_0 to lead to the result, y_1, where $P(y_1 | x) = P(y_1 | \mathrm{do}(x))$ is the posterior probability of y_1 caused by intervention x. The author uses the semantic information method to obtain the channel causal confirmation degree [36]:

$$Cc(x_1/x_0 => y_1) = b_1* = \frac{P(y_1|x_1) - P(y_1|x_0)}{\max(P(y_1|x_1), P(y_1|x_0))} = \frac{R^+ - 1}{\max(R^+, 1)}. \tag{91}$$

It is compatible with the above causal probability but can express negative causal relationships, such as the necessity of vaccines inhibiting infection because it can be negative.

5.7. Emerging and Potential Applications

(1) About self-supervised learning.

Applications of estimating MI have emerged in the field of self-supervised learning. The estimating MI is a special case of semantic MI. Both MINE, proposed by Belghazi et al. [23], and InfoNCE, proposed by Oord et al. [24], use the estimating MI. MINE and InfoNCE are essentially the same as the semantic information methods. Their common features are

- The truth function, $T(\theta_j \mid x)$, or similarity function, $S(x, y_j)$, proportional to $P(y_j \mid x)$ is used as the learning function. Its maximum value is generally one, and its average is the partition function, Z_j.
- The estimating information or semantic information between x and y_j is $\log[T(\theta_j \mid x)/Z_j]$ or $\log[S(x, y_j)/Z_j]$.
- The statistical probability distribution, $P(x, y)$, is still used when calculating the average information.

However, many researchers are still unclear about the relationship between the estimating MI and the Shannon MI. G theory's $R(G)$ function can help readers understand this relationship.

(2) About reinforcement learning.

The goal-oriented information introduced in Section 4.2 can be used as a reward for reinforcement learning. Assuming that the probability distribution of x in state s_k is $P(x \mid a_{k-1})$, which becomes $P(x \mid a_k)$ in state s_{k+1}, the reward of a_k is

$$r_k = I(X; a_k/\theta_j) - I(X; a_{k-1}/\theta_j) = \sum_i [P(x_i|a_k) - P(x_i|a_{k-1})] \log \frac{T(\theta_j|x_i)}{T(\theta_j)}. \quad (92)$$

Reinforcement learning is to find the optimal action sequence $a_1, a_2, \ldots$, so that the sum of rewards $r_1 + r_2 + \ldots$ is maximized. Like constraint control, reinforcement learning also needs the trade-off between the maximum purposefulness and the minimum control cost. The $R(G)$ function should be helpful.

(3) About the truth function and fuzzy logic for neural networks.

When we use the truth, distortion, or similarity function as the weight parameter of the neural network, the neural network contains semantic channels. Then, we can use semantic information methods to optimize the neural network. Using the truth function, $T(\theta_j \mid x)$, as the weight is better than using the parameterized inverse probability function, $P(\theta_j \mid x)$, because there is no normalization restriction when using truth functions.

However, unlike the clustering of points on the plane, points become images for image clustering, and the similarity function between images needs different methods. A common method is to regard an image as a vector and use the cosine similarity between vectors. However, the cosine similarity may have negative values, which require activation functions and biases to make necessary conversions. Combining existing neural network methods and channel-matching algorithms needs further exploration.

Fuzzy logic, especially fuzzy logic compatible with Boolean algebra [52], seems to be useful in neural networks; for example, the activation function, *Relu*(a–b) = max(0, a–b), which is commonly used in neural networks, is the logical difference operation, $f(a\bar{b})$ = max(0, a–b), used in the author's color vision mechanism model. Truth functions, fuzzy logic, and the semantic information method used in neural networks should make neural networks easier to understand.

(4) Explaining data compression in deep learning.

To explain the success of deep neural networks, such as AutoEncoders [33] and Deep Belief Networks [81], Tishby et al. [31] proposed the information bottleneck explanation, affirming that when optimizing deep neural networks, we maximize the Shannon MI between some layers and minimize the Shannon MI between other layers. However, from the perspective of the $R(G)$ function, each coding layer of the Autoencoder needs to maximize the semantic MI and minimize the Shannon MI; pre-training is to let the semantic channel match the Shannon channel so that $G \approx R$ and $KL(P||P_\theta) \approx 0$ (as if for mixture models to converge). Fine-tuning increases R and G at the same time by increasing s (making the partition boundaries steeper).

Not long ago, researchers at OpenAI [82,83] explained General Artificial Intelligence by lossless (actually, loss-limited) data compression, similar to the explanation of using MIE.

6. Discussion and Summary

6.1. Core Idea and Key Methods of Generalizing Shannon's Information Theory

In order to overcome the three shortcomings of Shannon's information theory (it is not suitable for semantic communication, lacks the information criterion, and cannot bring model parameters or likelihood functions into the MI formula), the core idea for the generalization is to replace distortion constraints with semantic constraints. Semantic constraints include semantic distortion constraints (using $\log[1/T(\theta_j \mid x)]$ as the distortion function), semantic information quantity constraints, and semantic information loss constraints (for electronic semantic communication). In this way, the shortcomings can be overcome, and existing coding methods can be used.

One key method is using the P-T probability framework with the truth function. The truth function can represent semantics, form a semantic channel, and link likelihood and distortion functions so that sample distributions can be used to optimize learning functions (likelihood function, truth function, similarity function, etc.).

The second key method is to define semantic information as the negative regularized distortion. In this way, the semantic MI equals the semantic entropy minus the average distortion, i.e., $I(X; Y_\theta) = H_\theta(Y) - \bar{d}$. The MI between temperature and molecular energy also has this form in a thermodynamic local equilibrium system. The logarithm of the softmax function, which is widely used in machine learning, also has this form [37]. This regularization's characteristic is that the term has the form of semantic entropy, which contains the logarithm of the logical probability, $T(\theta_j)$, or the partition function, Z_j. We call it "partition regularization" to distinguish it from other forms of regularization. Why can this semantic information measure also measure the information in local equilibrium systems? The reason is that the semantic constraint is similar to the energy constraint; both are fuzzy range constraints and can be represented by negative exponential functions.

Because the MFE criterion is equivalent to the Partition-Regularized Least Distortion (PRLD) criterion, the successful applications of VB and the MFE principle also support the PRLD criterion.

Because $T(\theta_j)$ represents the average of the true value, $\log[T(\theta_j \mid x)/T(\theta_j)]$ represents the progress from not so true to true. Comparing the core part of the Shannon MI, $\log[P(x \mid y_j)/P(x)]$, we can say that Shannon information comes from the improvement of probability. In contrast, semantic information comes from the improvement of truth. Furthermore, because $\log[T(\theta_j \mid x)/T(\theta_j)] = \log[P(x \mid \theta_j)/P(x)]$, the PRLD criterion is equivalent to the maximum likelihood criterion. Machine learning researchers always believe that regularization can reduce overfitting. Now, we find that, more importantly, it is compatible with the maximum likelihood criterion.

Because of the above two key methods, the three shortcomings of Shannon information theory no longer exist in G theory. Moreover, the success of VB and the MFE principle prompted Shannon information theory researchers to use the minimum VFE criterion or the maximum semantic information criterion to minimize the residual coding length of predictive coding.

Semantic constraints include semantic information loss constraints for electronic communication (see Section 3.2). Using this constraint, we can use classic coding methods to achieve electronic semantic communication.

6.2. Some Views That Are Different from Those G Theory Holds

View 1: We can measure the semantic information of language itself.

Some people want to measure the semantic information provided by a sentence (such as Carnap and Bar-Hillel), and others measure the semantic information between two sentences, regardless of the facts. In the author's opinion, these practices ignore the source of information: the real world. G theory follows Popper's idea and affirms that information comes from factual testing; if a hypothesis conforms to the facts and has a small prior logical probability, there is more information; if it is wrong, there is less or negative information. Some people may say that the translation between two sentences transmits semantic information. In this regard, we must distinguish between actual translation and the formulation of translation rules. Actual translation does provide semantic information, while translation rules do not provide semantic information, but they determine semantic information loss. Therefore, the actual translation should use the maximum semantic information criterion, while optimizing translation rules should use the minimum semantic information loss criterion. Optimizing electronic semantic communication is similar to optimizing translation rules, and the minimum semantic information loss criterion should be used.

View 2: Semantic communication needs to transmit semantics.

Because the transmission of Shannon information requires a physical channel, some people believe that the transmission of semantic information also requires a corresponding physical channel or utilizes the physical channel to transmit semantics. In fact, generally speaking, the semantic channel already exists in the brain or knowledge of the sender and the receiver, and there is no need to consider the physical channel. Only when the knowledge of both parties is inconsistent do we need to consider such a physical channel. The picture–text dictionary is a good physical channel for transmitting semantics. However, the receiver only needs to look at it once, and it will not be needed in the future.

View 3: Semantic information also needs to be minimized.

In Shannon's information theory, the MI, R, should be minimized when the distortion limit, D, is given to improve communication efficiency. The information rate–distortion function, $R(D)$, provides the theoretical basis for data compression. Therefore, some people imitated the information rate–distortion function and proposed the semantic information rate–distortion function, $R_s(D)$, where R_s is the minimum semantic MI. However, from the perspective of G theory, although we consider semantic communication, the communication cost is still Shannon's MI, which needs to be minimized. Therefore, G theory replaces the average distortion with the semantic MI to evaluate communication quality and uses the $R(G)$ function.

View 4: Semantic information measures do not require encoding meaning.

Some people believe that the concept of semantic information has nothing to do with encoding and that constructing a semantic information measure does not require considering its encoding meaning. However, the author holds the opposite view. The reasons are (1) semantic information is related to uncertainty, and thus also to encoding; (2) many successful machine learning methods have used cross-entropy to reflect the encoding length and VFE (i.e., posterior cross-entropy $H(X \mid Y_\theta)$) to indicate the lower limit of residual encoding length or reconstruction cost.

The G measure is equal to $H(X) - F$, reflecting the encoding length saved because of semantic predictions. The encoding length is an objective standard, and a semantic information measure without an objective standard makes it hard to avoid subjectivity and arbitrariness.

6.3. What Is Information? Is the G Measure Compatible with the Daily Information Concept?

Is the G measure, a technical information measure, compatible with the daily information concept? This cannot be ignored.

What is information? This question has many different answers, as summarized by Mark Burgin [84]. According to Shannon's definition, information is uncertainty reduced. Shannon information is the uncertainty reduced due to the increase of probability. In contrast, semantic information is the uncertainty reduced due to narrowing concepts' extensions or improving truth.

From a common-sense perspective, information refers to something previously unknown or uncertain, which encompasses

(1) **Information from natural language:** information provided by answers to interrogative sentences (e.g., sentences with "Who?", "What?", "When?", "Where?", "Why?", "How?", or "Is this?").
(2) **Perceptual or observational information:** information obtained from material properties or observed representations.
(3) **Symbolic information:** information conveyed by symbols like road signs, traffic lights, and battery polarity symbols [12].
(4) **Quantitative indicators' information: information provided by** data, such as time, temperature, rainfall, stock market indices, inflation rates, etc.
(5) **Associated information:** information derived from event associations, such as the rooster's crowing signaling dawn and a positive medical test indicating disease.

Items 2, 3, and 4 can also be viewed as answers to the questions in item 1, thus providing information. These forms of information involve concept extensions and truth–falsehood and should be semantic information. The associated information in item 5 can be measured using Shannon's or semantic information formulas. When probability predictions are inaccurate (i.e., $P(x \mid \theta_j) \neq P(x \mid y_j)$), the semantic information formula is more appropriate. Thus, G theory is consistent with the concept of information in everyday life.

In computer science, information is often defined as useful, structured data. What qualifies as "useful"? This utility arises because the data can answer questions or provide associated information. Therefore, the definition of information in data science also ties back to reduced uncertainty and narrowed concept extensions.

6.4. Relationships and Differences Between G Theory and Other Semantic Information Theories

6.4.1. Carnap and Bar-Hillel's Semantic Information Theory

The semantic information measure of Carnap and Bar-Hillel is [3]

$$Ip = \log(1/m_p], \tag{93}$$

where I_p is the semantic information provided by the proposition set, p, and m_p is the logical probability of p. This formula reflects Popper's idea that smaller logical probabilities convey more information. However, as Popper noted, this idea requires the hypothesis to withstand factual testing. The above formula does not account for such tests, implying that correct and incorrect hypotheses provide the same information.

Additionally, G theory differs in calculating logical probability with statistical probability, unlike Carnap and Bar-Hillel's approach.

6.4.2. Dretske's Knowledge and Information Theory

Dretske [9] emphasized the relationship between information and knowledge, viewing information as content tied to facts and knowledge acquisition. Though he did not propose a specific formula, his ideas about information quantification include

- The information must correspond to facts and eliminate all other possibilities.
- The amount of information relates to the extent of the uncertainty eliminated.
- Information used to gain knowledge must be true and accurate.

G theory is compatible with these principles by providing the G measure to implement Dretske's idea mathematically.

6.4.3. Florida's Strong Semantic Information Theory

Florida's theory [12] emphasizes

- The information must contain semantic content and be consistent with reality.
- False or misleading information cannot qualify as true information.

Floridi elaborated on Dretske's ideas and introduced a strong semantic information formula. However, this formula is more complex and less effective at reflecting factual testing than the G measure. For instance, Floridi's approach ensures that tautologies and contradictions yield zero information but fails to penalize false predictions with negative information.

6.4.4. Other Semantic Information Theories

In addition to the semantic information theories mentioned above, other well-known ones include the theory based on fuzzy entropy proposed by Zhong [10] and the theory based on synonymous mapping proposed by Niu and Zhang [16]. Zhong advocated for the combination of information science and artificial intelligence, which greatly influenced China's semantic information theory research. He employed fuzzy entropy [85] to define the semantic information measure. However, this approach yielded identical maximum values (1 bit) for both true and false sentences [10], which is not what we expect. Other people's semantic information measures using DeLuca and Termini's fuzzy entropy also encounter similar problems.

Other authors who discussed semantic information measures and semantic entropy include D'Alfonso [13], Basu et al. [86], and Melamed [87]. These authors improved semantic information measures by improving Carnap and Bar-Hillel's logical probability. The form of semantic entropy is similar to the form of Shannon entropy. The semantic entropy, $H(Y_\theta)$, in G theory differs from these semantic entropies. It contains statistical and logical probabilities and reflects the average codeword length of lossless coding (see Section 2.3).

Liu et al. [88] and Guo et al. [89] used the dual-constrained rate distortion function, $R(D_s, D_x)$, which is meaningful. In contrast, $R(G)$ already contains dual constraints because the semantic constraints include distortion and semantic information constraints.

In addition, some fuzzy information theories [90,91] and generalized information theories [92] also involve semantics more or less. However, most of them are far away from Shannon's information theory.

6.5. Relationship Between G Theory and Kolmogorov's Complexity Theory

Kolmogorov [93] defined the complexity of a set of data as the shortest program length required to restore the data without loss:

$$K(\text{data}) = \min\{|p|\ |U(p) = \text{data}\}. \tag{94}$$

where $U(p)$ is the output of program p. It defines the information provided by knowledge as the complexity reduced due to knowledge [84].

The information measured by Shannon can be understood as the average information provided by y about x, while Kolmgorov's information is the information provided by knowledge about the co-occurring data. Shannon's information theory does not consider the complexity of an individual datum, while Kolmogorov's theory does not consider statistical averages. It can be said that Kolmogorov defines the amount of information in microdata, while Shannon provides a formula to measure the average information in macrodata. The two theories are complementary.

The semantic information measure, $I(X; Y_\theta)$, is related to Kolmogorov complexity in the following two aspects:

- Because knowledge includes the extensions of concepts, the logical relationship between concepts, and the correlation between things (including causality), the information Kolmogorov said contains semantic information.
- Because VFE means the reconstruction cost due to the prediction, and the G measure equals $H(X)$ minus VFE, the G measure is similar to Kolmogorov's information measure. Both mean the saved reconstruction cost.

Some people have proposed complexity distortion [94], the shortest coding length with an error limit. It is possible to extend complexity distortion to the shortest coding length with the semantic constraint to obtain a function similar to the $R(G)$ function. This direction is worth exploring.

6.6. Comparing the MIE Principle and the MFE Principle

Friston proposed the MFE principle, which he believed was a universal principle that bio-organisms use to perceive the world and adapt to the environment (including transforming the environment). The core mathematical method he uses is VB. A better-understood principle in G theory is the MIE principle.

The main differences between the two are

- G theory regards Shannon's MI $I(X; Y)$ as free energy's increment, while Friston's theory considers the semantic posterior entropy, $H(X \mid Y_\theta)$, as free energy.
- The methods for finding the latent variable, $P(y)$, and the Shannon channel, $P(y \mid x)$, are different. Friston uses VB, and G theory uses SVB.

When optimizing the prediction model, $P(x \mid \theta_j)$ ($j = 1, 2, \ldots$), the two are consistent; when optimizing $P(y)$ and $P(y \mid x)$, the results of the two are similar, but the methods are different. SVB is simpler. The reason why the results are similar is that VB uses the mean-field approximation when optimizing $P(y \mid x)$, which is equivalent to using $P(y \mid x)$ instead of $P(y)$ as a variation and actually uses the MID criterion. Figure 18 shows that the information difference, R–G, instead of VFE continuously decreases in a mixture model's convergence process.

In physics, free energy can be used to do work; the more, the better. Why should it be minimized? In physics, there are two situations in which free energy is reduced. One is passive reduction because of the increase in entropy. The other reason is to save the consumed free energy while doing work due to considering thermal efficiency. Reducing the consumed free energy conforms to Jaynes' maximum entropy principle. Therefore, from a physics perspective, it is not easy to understand that one would actively minimize free energy.

MIE is like the maximum doing-work efficiency, $W/\Delta F^*$, when using free energy to perform work, W. The MIE principle is easier to understand.

The author will discuss these two principles further in other articles.

6.7. Limitations and Areas That Need Exploration

G theory is still a basic theory. It has limitations in many aspects, which need improvements.

(1) Semantics and the distortion of complex data.

Truth functions can represent the semantic distortion of labels. However, it is difficult to express the semantics, semantic similarity, and semantic distortion of complex data (such as a sentence or an image). Many researchers have made valuable explorations [14,15,17,95–97]. The author's research is insufficient.

The semantic relationship between a word and many other words is also very complex. Innovations like Word2Vec [98,99] in deep learning have successfully modeled these relationships, paving the way for advancements like Transformer [100] and ChatGPT. Future work in G theory should aim to integrate such developments to align with the progress in deep learning.

(2) Feature extraction.

The features of images encapsulate most semantic information. There are many efficient feature extraction methods in deep learning, such as Convolutional Neural Networks [101] and AutoEncoders [33]. These methods are ahead of G theory. Whether G theory can be combined with these methods to obtain better results needs further exploration.

(3) The channel-matching algorithm for neural networks.

Establishing neural networks to enable the mutual alignment of Shannon and semantic channels appears feasible. Current deep learning practices, relying on gradient descent and backpropagation, demand significant computational resources. If the channel-matching algorithm can reduce reliance on these methods, it would save computational power and physical free energy.

(4) Neural networks utilizing fuzzy logic.

Using truth functions or their logarithms as network weights facilitates the application of fuzzy logic. The author previously used a fuzzy logic method [52] compatible with Boolean algebra for setting up a symmetrical color vision mechanism model: the 3–8 decoding model. Combining G theory with fuzzy logic and neural networks holds promise for further exploration.

(5) Optimizing economic indicators and forecasts.

Forecasting in weather, economics, and healthcare domains provides valuable semantic information. Traditional evaluation metrics, such as accuracy or the average error, can be enhanced by converting distortion into fidelity. Using truth functions to represent semantic information offers a novel method for evaluating and optimizing forecasts, which merits further exploration.

6.8. Conclusions

The semantic information G theory is a generalized Shannon's information theory. Its validity has been supported by its broad applications across multiple domains, particularly in solving problems related to daily semantic communication, electronic semantic communications, machine learning, Bayesian confirmation, constraint control, and investment portfolios with information values.

Particularly, G theory allows us to utilize the existing coding methods for semantic communication. The core idea is to replace distortion constraints with semantic constraints, for which the information rate–distortion function was extended to the information rate–fidelity function. The key methods are (1) to use the P-T probability framework with truth functions and (2) to define the semantic information measure as the negative partition-regularized distortion.

However, G theory's primary limitation lies in the semantic representation of complex data. In this regard, it has lagged behind the advancements in deep learning. Bridging this gap will require learning from and integrating insights from other studies and technologies.

Funding: This research received no external funding.

Informed Consent Statement: Not applicable.

Data Availability Statement: Not applicable.

Acknowledgments: The author thanks the two reviewers for their comments, which significantly helped the author improve the manuscript. The author also thanks the guest editors, Xiaomei Tao and Kai Niu, and the assistant editor for their suggestions. In addition, the author thanks his friend Zedong Yao for his suggestion about defining the P-T probability framework.

Conflicts of Interest: The author declares no conflicts of interest.

Abbreviations

Abbreviation	Original Text
EM	Expectation–Maximization
EnM	Expectation–n–Maximization
GPS	Global Positioning System
G theory	semantic information G theory (G means generalization)
InfoNCE	Information Noise Contrast Estimation
KL	Kullback–Leibler
LBI	Logical Bayes' Inference
ME	maximum entropy
MI	mutual information
MIE	maximum information efficiency
MID	Minimum Information Difference
MINE	Mutual Information Neural Estimation
PRLD	Partition-Regularized Least Distortion
RLD	Regularized Least Distortion
RLS	Regularized Least Squares
SVB	Semantic Variational Bayes
VB	Variational Bayes

Appendix A. Python Source Codes Download Address

Python 3.6 source codes for Figure 17 in this paper is Figure 4 in the file that can be downloaded from http://www.survivor99.com/lcg/Lu-py2025-2.zip (accessed on 20 April 2025).

References

1. Shannon, C.E. A mathematical theory of communication. *Bell Syst. Tech. J.* **1948**, *27*, 379–423. [CrossRef]
2. Weaver, W. Recent contributions to the mathematical theory of communication. In *The Mathematical Theory of Communication*, 1st ed.; Shannon, C.E., Weaver, W., Eds.; The University of Illinois Press: Urbana, IL, USA, 1963; pp. 93–117.
3. Carnap, R.; Bar-Hillel, Y. *An Outline of a Theory of Semantic Information*; Tech. Rep. No. 247; Research Laboratory of Electronics, MIT: Cambridge, MA, USA, 1952.

4. Lu, C. Shannon equations reform and applications. *BUSEFAL* **1990**, *44*, 45–52. Available online: https://projects.listic.univ-smb.fr/busefal/papers/44.zip/44_11.pdf (accessed on 5 March 2019).
5. Lu, C. *A Generalized Information Theory*; China Science and Technology University Press: Hefei, China, 1993; ISBN 7-312-00501-2. (In Chinese)
6. Lu, C. A generalization of Shannon's information theory. *Int. J. Gen. Syst.* **1999**, *28*, 453–490. [CrossRef]
7. Lu, C. Semantic Information G Theory and Logical Bayesian Inference for Machine Learning. *Information* **2019**, *10*, 261. [CrossRef]
8. Dretske, F. *Knowledge and the Flow of Information*; The MIT Press: Cambridge, MA, USA, 1981; ISBN 0-262-04063-8.
9. Wu, W. General source and general entropy. *J. Beijing Univ. Posts Telecommun.* **1982**, *5*, 29–41. (In Chinese)
10. Zhong, Y. A Theory of Semantic Information. *Proceedings* **2017**, *1*, 129. [CrossRef]
11. Floridi, L. Outline of a theory of strongly semantic information. *Minds Mach.* **2004**, *14*, 197–221. [CrossRef]
12. Floridi, L. Semantic conceptions of information. In *Stanford Encyclopedia of Philosophy*; Stanford University: Stanford, CA, USA, 2005. Available online: http://seop.illc.uva.nl/entries/information-semantic/ (accessed on 17 June 2020).
13. D'Alfonso, S. On Quantifying Semantic Information. *Information* **2011**, *2*, 61–101. [CrossRef]
14. Xin, G.; Fan, P.; Letaief, K.B. Semantic Communication: A Survey of Its Theoretical Development. *Entropy* **2024**, *26*, 102. [CrossRef]
15. Strinati, E.C.; Barbarossa, S. 6G networks: Beyond Shannon towards semantic and goal-oriented communications. *Comput. Netw.* **2021**, *190*, 107930. [CrossRef]
16. Niu, K.; Zhang, P. A mathematical theory of semantic communication. *J. Commun.* **2024**, *45*, 8–59.
17. Gündüz, D.; Wigger, M.A.; Tung, T.-Y.; Zhang, P.; Xiao, Y. Joint source–channel coding: Fundamentals and recent progress in practical designs. *Proc. IEEE* **2024**, 1–32. [CrossRef]
18. Saad, W.; Chaccour, C.; Thomas, C.K.; Debbah, M. *Foundation of Semantic Communication Networks*; Wiley-IEEE Press: Hoboken, NJ, USA, 2024.
19. Chaccour, C.; Saad, W.; Debbah, M.; Han, Z.; Poor, H.V. Less data, more knowledge: Building next-generation semantic communication networks. *IEEE Commun. Surv. Tutor.* **2025**, *27*, 37–76. [CrossRef]
20. Hinton, G.E.; van Camp, D. Keeping the neural networks simple by minimizing the description length of the weights. In Proceedings of the COLT, Santa Cruz, CA, USA, 26–28 July 1993; pp. 5–13.
21. Neal, R.; Hinton, G. A view of the EM algorithm that justifies incremental, sparse, and other variants. In *Learning in Graphical Models*; Michael, I.J., Ed.; MIT Press: Cambridge, MA, USA, 1999; pp. 355–368.
22. Friston, K. The free-energy principle: A unified brain theory? *Nat. Rev. Neurosci.* **2010**, *11*, 127–138. [CrossRef] [PubMed]
23. Belghazi, M.I.; Baratin, A.; Rajeswar, S.; Ozair, S.; Bengio, Y.; Courville, A.; Hjelm, R.D. MINE: Mutual information neural estimation. In Proceedings of the 35th International Conference on Machine Learning, Stockholm, Sweden, 10–15 July 2018; pp. 1–44. [CrossRef]
24. Oord, A.V.D.; Li, Y.; Vinyals, O. Representation Learning with Contrastive Predictive Coding. Available online: https://arxiv.org/abs/1807.03748 (accessed on 10 January 2023).
25. Hjelm, R.D.; Fedorov, A.; Lavoie-Marchildon, S.; Grewal, K.; Trischler, A.; Bengio, Y. Learning Deep Representations by Mutual Information Estimation and Maximization. Available online: https://arxiv.org/abs/1808.06670 (accessed on 22 December 2022).
26. Bozkurt, A.; Esmaeili, B.; Tristan, J.-B.; Brooks, D.H.; Dy, J.G.; van de Meent, J.-W. Rate-regularization and generalization in VAEs. *arXiv* **2019**, arXiv:1911.04594.
27. Wikipedia. Variational Bayesian Methods. Available online: https://en.wikipedia.org/wiki/Variational_Bayesian_methods (accessed on 22 December 2024).
28. Beal, M.J. Variational Algorithms for Approximate Bayesian Inference. Ph.D. Thesis, University College London, London, UK, May 2003.
29. Koller, D. *Probabilistic Graphical Models: Principles and Techniques*; The MIT Press: Cambridge, MA, USA, 2009.
30. Tschannen, M.; Djolonga, J.; Rubenstein, P.K.; Gelly, S.; Luci, M. On Mutual Information Maximization for Representation Learning. Available online: https://arxiv.org/pdf/1907.13625.pdf (accessed on 23 February 2023).
31. Tishby, N.; Zaslavsky, N. Deep learning and the information bottleneck principle. In Proceedings of the Information Theory Workshop (ITW), Jerusalem, Israel, 26 April–1 May 2015; pp. 1–5.
32. Lu, C. Reviewing evolution of learning functions and semantic information measures for understanding deep learning. *Entropy* **2023**, *25*, 802. [CrossRef]
33. Hinton, G.E.; Salakhutdinov, R.R. Reducing the dimensionality of data with neural networks. *Science* **2006**, *313*, 504–507. [CrossRef]
34. Lu, C. The P–T probability framework for semantic communication, falsification, confirmation, and Bayesian reasoning. *Philosophies* **2020**, *5*, 25. [CrossRef]
35. Lu, C. Channels' confirmation and predictions' confirmation: From the medical test to the raven paradox. *Entropy* **2020**, *22*, 384. [CrossRef]
36. Lu, C. Causal Confirmation Measures: From Simpson's Paradox to COVID-19. *Entropy* **2023**, *25*, 143. [CrossRef]

37. Lu, C. Using the semantic information G measure to explain and extend rate-distortion functions and maximum entropy distributions. *Entropy* **2021**, *23*, 1050. [CrossRef] [PubMed]
38. Shannon, C.E. Coding theorems for a discrete source with a fidelity criterion. *IRE Nat. Conv. Rec.* **1959**, *4*, 142–163.
39. Berger, T. *Rate Distortion Theory*; Prentice-Hall: Enklewood Cliffs, NJ, USA, 1971.
40. Zhou, J.P. *Fundamentals of Information Theory*; People's Posts and Telecommunications Press: Beijing, China, 1983. (In Chinese)
41. Davidson, D. Truth and meaning. *Synthese* **1967**, *17*, 304–323. [CrossRef]
42. Tao, M.; Zhou, Y.; Shi, Y.; Lu, J.; Cui, S.; Lu, J.; Letaief, K.B. Federated Edge Learning for 6G: Foundations, methodologies, and Applications. *Proc. IEEE* **2024**. [CrossRef]
43. Gündüz, D.; Qin, Z.; Aguerri, I.E.; Dhillon, H.S.; Yang, Z.; Yener, A.; Wong, K.T.; Chae, C.-B. Beyond transmitting bits: Context, semantics, and task-oriented communications. *IEEE J. Sel. Areas Commun.* **2022**, *41*, 5–41. [CrossRef]
44. Popper, K. *The Logic of Scientific Discovery*; Routledge Classic: London, UK; New York, NY, USA, 2002.
45. Popper, K. *Conjectures and Refutations*, 1st ed.; Routledge: London, UK; New York, NY, USA, 2002.
46. Fisher, R.A. On the mathematical foundations of theoretical statistics. *Philos. Trans. R. Soc.* **1922**, *222*, 309–368.
47. Zadeh, L.A. Fuzzy sets. *Inf. Control* **1965**, *8*, 338–353. [CrossRef]
48. Zadeh, L.A. Probability measures of fuzzy events. *J. Math. Anal. Appl.* **1986**, *23*, 421–427. [CrossRef]
49. Tarski, A. The semantic conception of truth: And the foundations of semantics. *Philos. Phenomenol. Res.* **1994**, *4*, 341–376. [CrossRef]
50. Kolmogorov, A.N. *Foundations of Probability*; Dover Publications: New York, NY, USA, 1950.
51. von Mises, R. *Probability, Statistics and Truth*, 2nd ed.; George Allen and Unwin Ltd.: London, UK, 1957.
52. Lu, C. Explaining color evolution, color blindness, and color recognition by the decoding model of color vision. In Proceedings of the 11th IFIP TC 12 International Conference, IIP 2020, Hangzhou, China, 3–6 July 2020; Shi, Z., Vadera, S., Chang, E., Eds.; Springer: Cham, Switzerland, 2020; pp. 287–298. Available online: https://link.springer.com/chapter/10.1007/978-3-030-46931-3_27 (accessed on 21 April 2025).
53. Kullback, S.; Leibler, R. On information and sufficiency. *Ann. Math. Stat.* **1951**, *22*, 79–86. [CrossRef]
54. Akaike, H. Anew look at the statistical model identification. *IEEE Trans. Autom. Control* **1974**, *19*, 716–723. [CrossRef]
55. Wang, P.Z. From the fuzzy statistics to the falling random subsets. In *Advances in Fuzzy Sets, Possibility Theory and Applications*; Wang, P.P., Ed.; Plenum Press: New York, NY, USA, 1983; pp. 81–96.
56. Wang, P.Z. *Fuzzy Sets and Falling Shadows of Random Set*; Beijing Normal University Press: Beijing, China, 1985. (In Chinese)
57. Farsad, N.; Rao, M.; Goldsmith, A. Deep learning for joint source-channel coding of text. In Proceedings of the 2018 IEEE International Conference on Acoustics, Speech and Signal Processing (ICASSP), Calgary, AB, Canada, 15–20 April 2018; IEEE: New York, NY, USA, 2018; pp. 2326–2330.
58. Güler, B.; Yener, A.; Swami, A. The semantic communication game. *IEEE Trans. Cogn. Commun. Netw.* **2018**, *4*, 787–802. [CrossRef]
59. Papineni, K.; Roukos, S.; Ward, T.; Zhu, W.J. Bleu: A method for automatic evaluation of machine translation. In Proceedings of the 40th Annual Meeting of the Association for Computational Linguistics, Philadelphia, PA, USA, 6–12 July 2002; pp. 311–318.
60. Xie, H.; Qin, Z.; Li, G.Y.; Juang, B.H. Deep learning enabled semantic communication systems. *IEEE Trans. Signal Process.* **2021**, *69*, 2663–2675. [CrossRef]
61. Lu, C. Semantic Variational Bayes Based on a Semantic Information Theory for Solving Latent Variables. Available online: https://arxiv.org/abs/2408.13122 (accessed on 1 January 2025).
62. Markowitz, H.M. Portfolio selection. *J. Financ.* **1952**, *7*, 77–91. [CrossRef]
63. Kelly, J.L. A new interpretation of information rate. *Bell Syst. Tech. J.* **1956**, *35*, 917–926. [CrossRef]
64. Latané, H.A.; Tuttle, D.A. Criteria for portfolio building. *J. Financ.* **1967**, *22*, 359–373. [CrossRef]
65. Arrow, K.J. The economics of information: An exposition. *Empirica* **1996**, *23*, 119–128. [CrossRef]
66. Cover, T.M. Universal portfolios. *Math. Financ.* **1991**, *1*, 1–29. [CrossRef]
67. Cover, T.M.; Thomas, J.A. *Elements of Information Theory*; John Wiley & Sons: New York, NY, USA, 2006.
68. Lu, C. *The Entropy Theory of Portfolios and Information Values*; China Science and Technology University Press: Hefei, China, 1997; ISBN 7-312-00952-2F.36. (In Chinese)
69. Jaynes, E.T. *Probability Theory: The Logic of Science*; Bretthorst, G.L., Ed.; Cambridge University Press: Cambridge, UK, 2003.
70. Zhang, M.L.; Li, Y.K.; Liu, X.Y.; Geng, X. Binary relevance for multi-label learning: An overview. *Front. Comput. Sci.* **2018**, *12*, 191–202. [CrossRef]
71. Dempster, A.P.; Laird, N.M.; Rubin, D.B. Maximum Likelihood from Incomplete Data via the EM Algorithm. *J. R. Stat. Soc. Ser. B.* **1997**, *39*, 1–38. [CrossRef]
72. Ueda, N.; Nakano, R. Deterministic annealing EM algorithm. *Neural Netw.* **1998**, *11*, 271–282. [CrossRef] [PubMed]
73. Gottwald, S.; Braun, D.A. The Two Kinds of Free Energy and the Bayesian Revolution. Available online: https://arxiv.org/abs/2004.11763 (accessed on 20 January 2025).
74. Hempel, C.G. Studies in the logic of confirmation. *Mind* **1945**, *54*, 1–26. [CrossRef]

75. Carnap, R. *Logical Foundations of Probability*, 1st ed.; University of Chicago Press: Chicago, IL, USA, 1950.
76. Scheffler, I.; Goodman, N.J. Selective confirmation and the ravens: A reply to Foster. *J. Philos.* **1972**, *69*, 78–83. [CrossRef]
77. Fitelson, B.; Hawthorne, J. How Bayesian confirmation theory handles the paradox of the ravens. In *The Place of Probability in Science*; Eells, E., Fetzer, J., Eds.; Springer: Dordrecht, The Netherlands, 2010; pp. 247–276.
78. Crupi, V.; Tentori, K.; Gonzalez, M. On Bayesian measures of evidential support: Theoretical and empirical issues. *Philos. Sci.* **2007**, *74*, 229–252. [CrossRef]
79. Greco, S.; Slowinski, R.; Szczech, I. Properties of rule interestingness measures and alternative approaches to normalization of measures. *Inf. Sci.* **2012**, *216*, 1–16. [CrossRef]
80. Pearl, J. Causal inference in statistics: An overview. *Stat. Surv.* **2009**, *3*, 96–146. [CrossRef]
81. Hinton, G.E. Deep belief networks. *Scholarpedia* **2009**, *4*, 5947. [CrossRef]
82. Rae, J. Compression for AGI, Stanford MLSys Seminar. Available online: https://www.youtube.com/watch?v=dO4TPJkeaaU (accessed on 18 January 2025).
83. Sutskever, L. An observation on Generalization, Bekeley: Simons Institute. Available online: https://simons.berkeley.edu/talks/ilya-sutskever-openai-2023-08-14 (accessed on 18 January 2025).
84. Burgin, M. *Theory of Information: Fundamentality, Diversity And Unification, World Science*; Knowledge Copyright Publishing: Beijing, China, 2015; ISBN 978-7-5130-3095-3. (In Chinese)
85. De Luca, A.; Termini, S. A definition of a non-probabilistic entropy in setting of fuzzy sets. *Inf. Control* **1972**, *20*, 301–312. [CrossRef]
86. Basu, P.; Bao, J.; Dean, M.; Hendler, J. Preserving quality of information by using semantic relationships. *Pervasive Mobile Comput.* **2014**, *11*, 188–202. [CrossRef]
87. Melamed, D. Measuring Semantic Entropy. 1997. Available online: https://api.semanticscholar.org/CorpusID:7165973 (accessed on 20 January 2025).
88. Guo, T.; Wang, Y.; Han, J.; Wu, H.; Bai, B.; Han, W. Semantic Compression with Side Information: A Rate-Distortion Perspective. Available online: https://arxiv.org/pdf/2208.06094 (accessed on 20 January 2025).
89. Liu, J.; Zhang, W.; Poor, H.V. A rate-distortion framework for characterizing semantic information. In Proceedings of the 2021 IEEE International Symposium on Information Theory (ISIT), Online, 12–20 July 2021; IEEE Press: Piscataway, NJ, USA, 2021; pp. 2894–2899.
90. Kumar, T.; Bajaj, R.K.; Gupta, B. On some parametric generalized measures of fuzzy information, directed divergence and information Improvement. *Int. J. Comput. Appl.* **2011**, *30*, 5–10.
91. Ohlan, A.; Ohlan, R. Fundamentals of fuzzy information measures. In *Generalizations of Fuzzy Information Measures*; Springer: Cham, Switzerland, 2016. [CrossRef]
92. Klir, G. Generalized information theory. *Fuzzy Sets Syst.* **1991**, *40*, 127–142. [CrossRef]
93. Kolmogorov, A.N. Three approaches to the quantitative definition of information. *Probl. Inf. Transm.* **1965**, *1*, 1–7. [CrossRef]
94. Li, M.; Vitanyi, P. *An Introduction to Kolmogorov Complexity and Its Applications*; Springer: Berlin, Germany, 2008.
95. Wikipedia. Semantic Similarity. Available online: https://en.wikipedia.org/wiki/Semantic_similarity (accessed on 20 January 2025).
96. Letaief, K.B.; Chen, W.; Shi, Y.; Zhang, J.; Zhang, Y.A. The Rodmap to 6G: AI-empowered wireless networks. *IEEE Commun. Mag.* **2019**, *57*, 84–90. [CrossRef]
97. Niu, K.; Dai, J.; Yao, S.; Wang, S.; Si, Z.; Qin, X. A Paradigm Shift toward Semantic Communications. *IEEE Commun. Mag.* **2022**, *60*, 113–119. [CrossRef]
98. Mikolov, T.; Chen, K.; Corrado, G.; Dean, J. Efficient estimation of word representations in vector space. *arXiv* **2013**, arXiv:1301.3781.
99. Mikolov, T.; Sutskever, I.; Chen, K.; Corrado, G.S.; Dean, J. Distributed representations of words and phrases and their compositionality. *arXiv* **2013**, arXiv:1310.4546.
100. Vaswani, A.; Shazeer, N.; Parmar, N.; Uszkoreit, J.; Jones, L.; Gomez, A.N.; Kaiser, L.; Polosukhin, I. Attention Is All You Need. Available online: https://arxiv.org/abs/1706.03762 (accessed on 18 January 2025).
101. LeCun, Y.; Bengio, Y.; Hinton, G. Deep learning. *Nature* **2015**, *521*, 436–444. [CrossRef]

entropy

MDPI

Article

Importance-Aware Resource Allocations for MIMO Semantic Communication

Yue Cao [1], Youlong Wu [1,*], Lixiang Lian [1] and Meixia Tao [2]

[1] School of Information Science and Technology, ShanghaiTech University, Shanghai 201210, China; caoyue@shanghaitech.edu.cn (Y.C.); lianlx@shanghaitech.edu.cn (L.L.)

[2] Department of Electronic Engineering and the Cooperative Medianet Innovation Center (CMIC), Shanghai Jiao Tong University, Shanghai 200240, China; mxtao@sjtu.edu.cn

* Correspondence: wuyl1@shanghaitech.edu.cn

Abstract: This study proposes a separate source-channel coding (SSCC) framework to address semantic communication challenges in MIMO systems, overcoming the limitations of joint source-channel coding (JSCC) in channel adaptation and model reusability. Traditional systems suffer from bit-level redundancy in 6G, while JSCC struggles with complex channel variations. Our solution decouples semantic processing from channel coding through a three-tier architecture: (1) Variational autoencoder (VAE)-based semantic encoder and decoder for source coding, (2) A communication-informed bottleneck attribution (CIBA) mechanism quantifying feature importance for learning tasks, and (3) An importance-aware resource allocation scheme aligning communication objectives with deep learning tasks. Systematic experiments validate CIBA's effectiveness in deriving importance scores that bridge learning tasks and communication optimization. Comparisons of feature perturbation schemes confirm the necessity of importance-aware resource allocation, with the proposed allocation strategy outperforming conventional methods in task performance metrics. The SSCC design enhances model reusability while maintaining adaptability to diverse MIMO configurations. By integrating interpretable AI with resource management, this work establishes a foundation for SSCC semantic communication systems in resource-constrained environments, prioritizing semantic fidelity and task efficacy over bit-level redundancy. The methodology highlights the critical role of importance awareness in optimizing both communication efficiency and learning task performance.

Keywords: semantic communication; separate source-channel coding (SSCC); attribution; MIMO

1. Introduction

Traditional communication systems are designed following Shannon's coding theory, aiming to transmit information bits as accurately as possible over noisy channels without considering the semantic information contained within the data. In fact, with the development of artificial intelligence (AI) technologies, practical application scenarios such as semantic communications [1] have demonstrated that accurate transmission of semantic-level information alone can achieve task objectives. In such cases, traditional communication systems' pursuit of lossless bit-level transmission strategies would introduce significant information redundancy. Emerging 6G applications, including autonomous driving, remote robotics, meta-universe, smart healthcare, etc., involve massive data transmission demands driven by large-scale connected intelligent machines, while requiring ultra-low communication latency. It is foreseeable that in the 6G era, conventional communication systems will reach their limits in supporting future ubiquitous-connectivity and machine-intelligence services [2]. This urgency necessitates a fundamental shift in communication system design from traditional bit-level transmission to semantic or effectiveness-level considerations. As a novel communication paradigm, semantic communication focuses on information transmission at semantic or effectiveness levels, significantly reducing communication overhead through semantic extraction and transmission. Current research progress in semantic communication has demonstrated higher communication efficiency, improved reliability, and better compatibility with emerging AI applications compared to traditional systems, particularly in text [3], image [4,5], speech [6], and video [7] transmission scenarios.

The ultimate goal of semantic communication is to leverage intrinsic semantic information from sources to convey the sender's intended meaning to receivers. Historically, the lack of a unified theoretical framework for representing semantics across different sources made semantic information difficult to represent and quantify. However, the powerful representation and generalization capabilities of deep neural networks (DNNs) have enabled semantic extraction. In the current research [8], semantic communication systems typically employ DNN-parameterized feature encoders and decoders to extract and decode semantic representations. Through end-to-end training with incorporated communication constraints, these systems achieve joint design of source-channel coding. The semantic encoder integrates source and channel coding functions, enabling extracted representations to preserve semantic information while maintaining excellent communication performance. This deep learning-based joint source-channel coding (JSCC) approach, implemented through neural network parameterization and end-to-end training, has been extensively studied and validated in SISO scenarios [9–12].

However, unlike the simple model structure in SISO scenarios, MIMO systems face more complex channel conditions. The high dimensionality of MIMO channel matrices leads to exponential growth in potential channel state combinations. End-to-end JSCC semantic communication networks require parameter learning based on task datasets and the entire distribution of wireless channels, resulting in substantial training overhead and unpredictable complexity [13]. Training end-to-end networks to adapt to diverse communication environments often proves impractical. Existing MIMO semantic communication systems, such as the speech-to-text system proposed in [14], employ JSCC but lack CSI adaptive design. The work in [15] utilized vision transformer models for semantic encoder and decoder with JSCC, training separate models for different Signal-to-Noise Ratio (SNR). Their results show optimal performance only when training and testing SNRs match. Although they propose a stochastic SNR training scheme for channel adaptation, this compromises performance compared to non-adaptive approaches. Parameters in JSCC models typically cannot be reused under different channel conditions, necessitating additional training resources and specialized designs for channel adaptation.

The fundamental issue in JSCC stems from semantic encoders being burdened with channel coding tasks, forcing semantic encoder and decoder to memorize complex MIMO channel conditions during training. By decoupling channel coding from source coding through separated design, we can eliminate channel dependence during training, reducing training complexity and overhead. However, a critical challenge emerges in separated designs: how to establish connections between learning tasks and communication objectives through channel coding schemes. In limited related work, Cai et al. [16] proposed a separate source-channel coding (SSCC) design using the maximal coding rate reduction (MCR2) principle to train the source encoder and optimize the precoding matrices. This approach maximizes separation between different classes of encoded representations in feature space, enabling Maximum A Posteriori (MAP) classification at the receiver. Although it addresses channel adaptation and improves model reusability, their method is restricted to the classification task.

Building on [16] that established clustered semantic representations in feature space for non-deep-learning-based channel coding design, we extend this concept; if we can understand how semantic representations influence task performance through their intrinsic properties, we could establish task-communication connections free from deep learning constraints. To realize this vision, we require both highly interpretable DNN models and reliable AI interpretability techniques. The Variational Autoencoder (VAE) [17], which introduced a probabilistic latent space assuming standard normal distribution of latent variables, achieves high interpretability and structured control in generative models. Its latent variables can be disentangled into independent semantic features, enabling the generation of smoothly interpolated samples through continuous interpolation. In AI interpretability research, attribution mechanisms aim to assign relevance scores (importance metrics) to features, quantifying their impact on model outputs. By strategically aligning these importance metrics with communication resource allocation, we can effectively bridge communication objectives with learning tasks.

Based on this rationale, we propose a novel SSCC framework in this paper, the semantic encoder and decoder exclusively handle source coding, while an attribution mechanism provides importance scores for semantic representations extracted by the semantic encoder. The channel coding scheme is then designed by integrating importance scores with communication scenarios. Under this architecture, no additional design is required for the semantic encoder's output, and appropriate models for the semantic encoder and decoder can be flexibly chosen depending on task requirements. This approach enables adaptation to various downstream task types while improving model reusability.

In current research on importance-aware communication, the definition and measurement of importance depend on specific task scenarios. Existing studies employ diverse methods to measure importance for optimizing communication processes and ensuring task performance. For example, Weng et al. [14] directly linked semantic importance to text recovery accuracy in speech-to-text transmission tasks, enhancing semantic fidelity by precisely protecting critical information. Wang et al. [18] evaluated the impact weights of encoder neuron activation values through backpropagation of prediction errors in semantic prediction tasks to reduce waste of communication resources. At the data level, a data importance indicator [19] was proposed to dynamically quantify the effective value of samples in wireless channel environments by integrating the received SNR with data uncertainty. Another study [20] addressed communication resource constraints in edge machine learning scenarios by designing importance discrimination mechanisms under centralized frameworks (prioritizing misclassified data) and distributed frameworks (emphasizing local model data trained on large-scale datasets). Furthermore, Guo et al. [21] utilized pre-trained language modelto generate word importance rankings and implemented differentiated transmission protection, while Liu et al. [22] defined semantic importance by analyzing the correlation between semantic features and task performance, as well as inter-feature relationships, guiding resource allocation in digital semantic communications. These studies employ different approaches to define and utilize importance, yet all adopt task-oriented importance evaluation to optimize resource allocation, thus enhancing the efficiency and performance of communication systems. Although existing research covers various communication scenarios, the problem of importance-aware resource allocation in MIMO semantic communication has not been fully explored.

In our work, we investigate importance-aware resource allocation for MIMO semantic communication within the SSCC framework. We quantify importance based on each feature's influence on the deep learning model's inference performance, leveraging attribution mechanisms to derive importance scores for efficient resource allocation. We propose a communication-aware attribution method applicable to the VAE model, whose results can directly reflect the relative communication resource requirements for each feature, providing explicit guidance for resource allocation.

Our main contributions can be summarized as follows:

1. We propose an SSCC framework that addresses critical challenges in JSCC designs: parameter reusability limitations and adaptive channel condition handling. This paradigm enables flexible model deployment across diverse scenarios by decoupling semantic processing from channel optimization.
2. We propose a communication-inspired attribution method for VAE models by injecting controlled noise into semantic representations. Grounded in information bottleneck theory, our approach minimizes retained information while preserving task-critical features and perturbing non-essential ones. To characterize the importance score, we model the noise injection process as a communication channel, thereby endowing the derived importance scores with physical interpretability in communication contexts. Specifically, we establish a theoretical link between feature importance scores and channel capacity. This connection facilitates an importance-aware resource allocation strategy, bridging communication principles with deep learning objectives.
3. Systematic experiments validate both the effectiveness of the importance scores generated by our attribution method and their pivotal role in bridging learning tasks and communication optimization. Comparisons of resource allocation schemes demonstrate that our importance-aware approach achieves superior performance in learning tasks, highlighting the advantages of integrating importance awareness into communication resource management. This work provides valuable insights for SSCC semantic communication system design while expanding the applicability of explainable AI techniques in communication scenarios.

2. System Model

As shown in Figure 1, we consider an SSCC MIMO image transmission system with N transmit antennas and M receive antennas. At the transmitter side, the DNN-based semantic encoder encodes the source image I into a low-dimensional semantic representation $X \in \mathbb{R}^{m \times n}$. Distinct from JSCC designs, in our system, channel coding is decoupled from the semantic encoder and is not implemented via deep neural networks. After the DNN-free channel coding processing, the obtained symbols suitable for transmission are sent through the channel. At the receiver side, channel decoding is performed to obtain the estimated original semantic representation $\hat{X} \in \mathbb{R}^{m \times n}$, followed by source decoding to reconstruct the transmitted image $\hat{\mathrm{I}}$, completing the entire image transmission process.

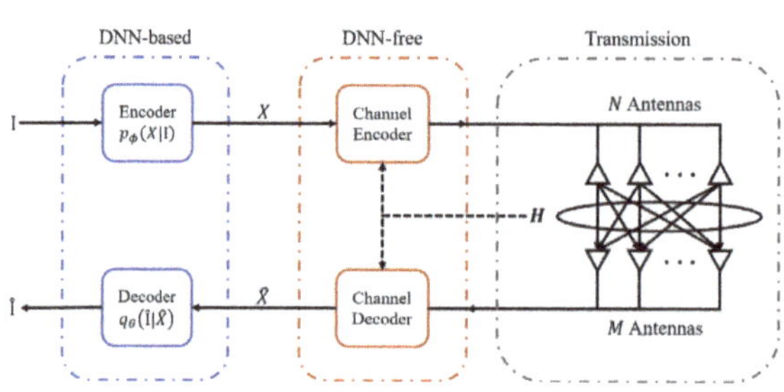

Figure 1. The framework of SSCC MIMO image transmission system.

2.1. Semantic Encoder and Decoder

In this paper, we adopt VAE as our semantic encoder and decoder. VAE is a generative framework based on probabilistic graphical models, learning latent space representations through variational inference. At the transmitter side, the input image I is encoded into a low-dimensional semantic representation X using a probabilistic encoder $p_\phi(X|I)$ parameterized by adjustable parameters. After channel transmission and signal recovery processes, $\hat{X}$ is obtained. The receiver employs the inference model $q_\theta(\hat{I}|\hat{X})$ to reconstruct the image $\hat{I}$.

VAE assumes that latent variables $X \in \mathbb{R}^{m\times n}$ follow a centered isotropic multivariate Gaussian prior, with the parametric encoder modeled as $p_\phi(X|I) = \mathcal{N}(\mu_X, \sigma_X^2 \boldsymbol{I})$. To enable differentiable sampling, VAE introduces a reparameterization trick:

$$X = \mu_\phi(I) + \sigma_\phi(I) \odot \epsilon, \quad (1)$$

where $\mu_\phi(I) \in \mathbb{R}^{m\times n}$ and $\sigma_\phi(I) \in \mathbb{R}^{m\times n}$ are the outputs of the encoder, $\odot$ denotes the Hadamard product, $\epsilon \in \mathbb{R}^{m\times n}$, and each element ϵ_{ij} is independently drawn from a standard normal distribution $\mathcal{N}(0,1)$. This operation shifts stochasticity to the input noise ϵ, allowing gradients to propagate to encoder parameters ϕ.

2.2. Channel Coding

Following the extraction of semantic representations, the transmitter maps these representations to channel inputs. This mapping mechanism ensures reliable delivery of semantic information to the receiver even under channel uncertainty, a procedure we conceptualize as wide-sense channel coding. Specifically, the extracted semantic representation X is modeled as a continuous multivariate Gaussian signal, leading us to consider an analog communication system scenario. Unlike conventional channel coding in digital communication systems, the primary role of the channel coding module in this paper is to transform semantic representations into transmission-suitable symbols, while enhancing the robustness of the entire communication system via precoding, resource allocation, modulation, and demodulation. The process of channel coding is illustrated in Figure 2.

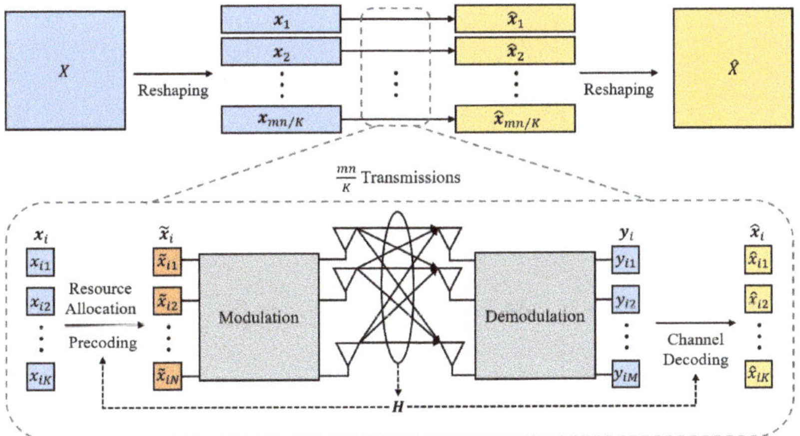

Figure 2. Channel coding process: the semantic representation is transformed into transmission-suitable symbols.

2.2.1. Channel Encoder

Instead of developing new modulation components, we implemented the Amplitude Modulation (AM) scheme. In this paper, our research focuses on the design of precoding and resource allocation processes. Let the MIMO channel matrix be denoted as $\boldsymbol{H} \in \mathbb{C}^{M\times N}$, and let $K = \min(M, N)$, based on Singular Value Decomposition (SVD), $\boldsymbol{H}$ can be decomposed as:

$$\boldsymbol{H} = \boldsymbol{U}\boldsymbol{\Sigma}\boldsymbol{V}^H, \tag{2}$$

where $\boldsymbol{U} \in \mathbb{C}^{M\times K}$ and $\boldsymbol{V} \in \mathbb{C}^{N\times K}$ are unitary matrices, and $\boldsymbol{\Sigma} \in \mathbb{C}^{K\times K}$ is a diagonal matrix with non-negative singular values arranged in descending order along its main diagonal. We denote $\boldsymbol{\Sigma}$ as $\mathrm{diag}(\sigma_1, \ldots, \sigma_j, \ldots, \sigma_K)$, where $\sigma_1 \geq \sigma_2 \geq \cdots \geq \sigma_K$.

To adapt X for transmission and match the number of transmit antennas, X is reshaped into $\boldsymbol{x} \in \mathbb{R}^{K\times \frac{m\cdot n}{K}}$, which means that all available channels are utilized, with K symbols transmitted at a time, requiring $\frac{m\cdot n}{K}$ transmissions to complete sending X (or $\boldsymbol{x}$). Let the i-th transmitted symbols be $\boldsymbol{x}_i = [x_{i1}, \ldots, x_{ij}, \ldots, x_{iK}]^T$.

Let $\boldsymbol{p}_i$ denote the power allocation matrix for the i-th transmission, where $\boldsymbol{p}_i \in \mathbb{R}^{K\times K}$ is a diagonal matrix is defined as $\mathrm{diag}(\sqrt{p_{i1}}, \ldots, \sqrt{p_{ij}}, \ldots, \sqrt{p_{iK}})$, where $p_{ij} (j = 1, 2, \ldots, K)$ denotes the power allocated to the j-th channel. To simplify the optimization conditions, we introduce the vector $\overrightarrow{x_i} = [x_{i1}^2, \ldots, x_{ij}^2, \ldots, x_{iK}^2]$ for pre-processing $\boldsymbol{x}_i$. After pre-processing and resource allocation, x_i is transformed into transmission-ready symbols $\tilde{\boldsymbol{x}}_i = [\tilde{x}_{i1}, \tilde{x}_{i2}, \ldots, \tilde{x}_{iN}]^T$, which is then distributed across the N antennas for transmission. The transformation from $\boldsymbol{x}_i$ to $\tilde{\boldsymbol{x}}_i$ can be expressed as:

$$\tilde{\boldsymbol{x}}_i = \boldsymbol{V}\boldsymbol{p}_i \frac{\boldsymbol{x}_i}{\sqrt{\| \overrightarrow{x_i} \|_2}}. \tag{3}$$

We assume that each transmission has the same total power limit P_{total}, which requires:

$$\mathbb{E}\left[\|\tilde{\boldsymbol{x}}_i\|_2^2\right] = \mathrm{tr}\left(\tilde{\boldsymbol{x}}_i^T \tilde{\boldsymbol{x}}_i\right) \leq P_{\text{total}}. \tag{4}$$

To simplify the power constraint, we introduce the vector $\overrightarrow{p_i} = [p_{i1}, \ldots, p_{ij}, \ldots, p_{iK}]$. Based on the Cauchy–Schwarz Inequality, we derive:

$$\begin{aligned}
\mathbb{E}\left[\|\tilde{\boldsymbol{x}}_i\|_2^2\right] &= \mathrm{tr}\left(\tilde{\boldsymbol{x}}_i^H \tilde{\boldsymbol{x}}_i\right) &(5)\\
&= \mathrm{tr}\left(\left(V\boldsymbol{p}_i \frac{\boldsymbol{x}_i}{\sqrt{\| \overrightarrow{x_i} \|_2}}\right)^H V\boldsymbol{p}_i \frac{\boldsymbol{x}_i}{\sqrt{\| \overrightarrow{x_i} \|_2}}\right) &(6)\\
&= \frac{1}{\| \overrightarrow{x_i} \|_2} \langle \overrightarrow{p_i}, \overrightarrow{x_i} \rangle &(7)\\
&\leq \| \overrightarrow{p_i} \|_2. &(8)
\end{aligned}$$

This implies that by setting $\| \overrightarrow{p_i} \|_2 = P_{\text{total}}$, i.e., $\sum_{j=1}^K p_{ij}^2 = P_{\text{total}}^2$, we can satisfy the power constraint $\mathbb{E}[\|\tilde{\boldsymbol{x}}_i\|_2^2] \leq \| \overrightarrow{p_i} \|_2 = P_{\text{total}}$.

2.2.2. Channel Decoder

At the receiver, the M antennas receive the symbols $\boldsymbol{y}_i = [y_{i1}, y_{i2}, \ldots, y_{iM}]^T$ and $\boldsymbol{y}_i = \boldsymbol{H}\tilde{\boldsymbol{x}}_i + \boldsymbol{w}$. Following transmission of $\tilde{\boldsymbol{x}}_i$, the received signal $\boldsymbol{y}_i$ undergoes SVD post-processing with $\tilde{\boldsymbol{y}}_i = \boldsymbol{U}^H \boldsymbol{y}_i$. The transmission process is derived as:

$$\tilde{y}_i = U^H y_i \tag{9}$$

$$= U^H \left(U \Sigma V^H V p_i \frac{x_i}{\sqrt{\| \overrightarrow{x_i} \|_2}} + w \right) \tag{10}$$

$$= \Sigma p_i \frac{x_i}{\sqrt{\| \overrightarrow{x_i} \|_2}} + U^H w, \tag{11}$$

where $w \in \mathbb{C}^{M \times 1}$ is a noise vector indicating independent and identically distributed (i.i.d.) Gaussian noise following $w \sim \mathcal{CN}(0, \sigma_w^2 I)$.

The recovered information $\hat{x}_i$ can be obtained from $\tilde{y}_i$ as:

$$\hat{x}_i = \sqrt{\| \overrightarrow{x_i} \|_2} p_i^{-1} \Sigma^{-1} \tilde{y}_i \tag{12}$$

$$= \sqrt{\| \overrightarrow{x_i} \|_2} p_i^{-1} \Sigma^{-1} \left(\Sigma p_i \frac{x_i}{\sqrt{\| \overrightarrow{x_i} \|_2}} + U^H w \right) \tag{13}$$

$$= x_i + \sqrt{\| \overrightarrow{x_i} \|_2} p_i^{-1} \Sigma^{-1} U^H w. \tag{14}$$

After channel encoding and decoding processes are repeated $\frac{m \cdot n}{K}$ times until all x_i are transmitted and the receiver obtains the complete recovered information $\hat{x} = [\hat{x}_1, \ldots, \hat{x}_i, \ldots, \hat{x}_{\frac{m \cdot n}{K}}]$. Then, $\hat{x}$ is reshaped into $\hat{X}$.

2.3. Optimization Objective

Since we consider an image transmission system as illustrated in Figure 1, the overall optimization objective of the system is to enhance the image reconstruction quality through communication optimization via power allocation. The optimization problem of the whole system can be formulated as follows:

$$\min \ \mathbb{E}\left[\mathcal{D}(\mathrm{I}, \hat{\mathrm{I}})\right] \tag{15}$$

$$\text{s.t.} \ \mathbb{E}\left[\|\tilde{x}_i\|_2^2\right] \leq P_{\text{total}} \tag{16}$$

where $\mathcal{D}$ represents the distortion between the original image and the reconstructed image. We can measure this distortion in various ways, such as the Mean Squared Error (MSE) between the original and reconstructed images, the Peak Signal-to-Noise Ratio (PSNR) of the reconstructed image, or through downstream task evaluation.

Furthermore, by selecting different deep learning models to construct the semantic encoder and decoder, our proposed SSCC semantic communication system can be extended to various downstream tasks, such as classification, clustering, etc. Relevant experiments and discussions can be found in Section 4.4.

3. Methodology

The global optimization of resource allocation strategies constitutes a core challenge in achieving semantic communication efficiency maximization within SSCC system design. In the JSCC architecture, the system obtains parameter-fixed models through end-to-end joint training, whose performance ceiling is entirely determined by the neural network's feature extraction and channel adaptation capabilities. In contrast, the SSCC architecture requires the semantic encoder to undergo an independent pre-training convergence process, with deployment in communication links only after stabilizing its basic task performance. Here, channel transmission quality governed by resource allocation strategies becomes the critical bottleneck constraining end-to-end semantic fidelity. This paradigm divergence leads SSCC systems to confront unique optimization propositions: given the established capability boundaries of semantic models, how to design adaptive communication resource allocation mechanisms that compensate for semantic distortion induced by channel distortion through establishing mapping relationships between communication conditions and learning task.

To address this challenge, we propose an importance-aware semantic communication framework shown in Figure 3 that establishes connections between learning tasks and communication resource allocation. The image I is encoded into semantic representations X through a semantic encoder. An attribution mechanism analyzes the importance of each feature in X according to the learning task objective (15), generating importance scores S. The resource allocation strategy then combines these importance scores with the learning task objective to influence the feature transmission process, ensuring that the reconstructed image $\hat{\mathrm{I}}$ recovered from $\hat{X}$ achieves the best possible quality, making the learning task objective as optimal as possible. We innovatively propose an attribution mechanism specifically designed for VAE models to establish connections between communication conditions and learning task performance. This framework establishes resource optimization equations with constrained conditions through quantitative evaluation of importance differences in semantic representations, providing SSCC system design with theoretical decision-making models that integrate both interpretability and adaptability.

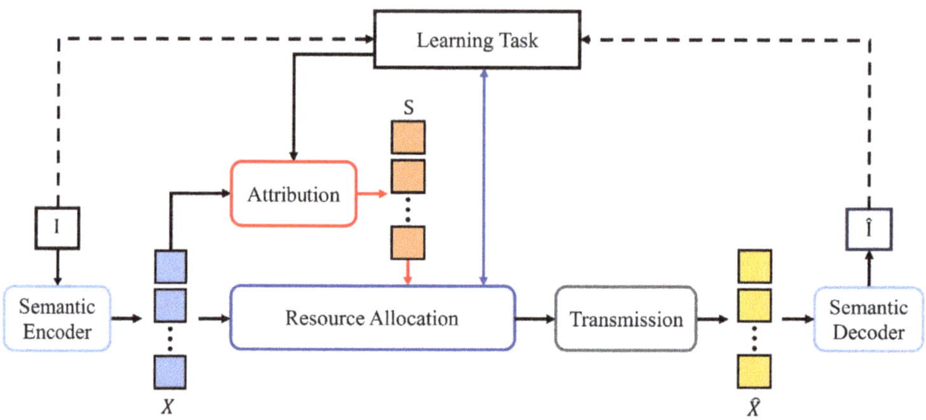

Figure 3. Illustration of importance-aware semantic communication framework.

3.1. Communication-Informed Bottleneck Attribution (CIBA)

In this paper, inspired by IBA [23], we propose a novel perspective to establish the connection between feature importance and communication. As discussed in Section 2.1, VAE assumes that latent variables $X \in \mathbb{R}^{m \times n}$ follow a centered isotropic multivariate Gaussian prior, with the parametric encoder modeled as $p_\phi(X|\mathrm{I}) = \mathcal{N}(\mu_X, \sigma_X^2 \boldsymbol{I})$. Through the reparameterization trick, variables X can be viewed as a series of independent Gaussian signals. To estimate the importance of these Gaussian signals, we can add specific noise to each Gaussian signal to constrain the overall information flow, then feed the perturbed signals into the decoder to observe their impact on task performance.

Figure 4 depicts the framework of the proposed CIBA method. We aim to find appropriate noise distributions that minimally affect the learning task, which implies that more important signals for the task will receive weaker noise (preserving information) while unimportant ones will be completely corrupted, thereby revealing the importance degree of each feature. Let $X \in \mathbb{R}^{m \times n}$ be a feature matrix where each element X_{ij} denotes the feature element at row i and column j. We assume that each X_{ij} follows a normal distribution, i.e., $X_{ij} \sim \mathcal{N}(\mu_{X_{ij}}, \sigma^2_{X_{ij}})$. We can represent the entire matrix X using reparameterization. We have $X = \mu_X + \sigma_X \odot \epsilon$ and $X_{ij} = \mu_{X_{ij}} + \sigma_{X_{ij}}\epsilon_{ij}$, where $\odot$ denotes the Hadamard product, $\epsilon \in \mathbb{R}^{m \times n}$ and each element ϵ_{ij} is independently drawn from a standard normal distribution $\mathcal{N}(0,1)$.

Assuming independence between feature elements, we model the information flow constraint process as an analog additive white Gaussian noise (AWGN) channel communication process. In this process, $m \times n$ feature elements transmit through $m \times n$ parallel AWGN channels. For each element, the relationship is given by $Z_{ij} = X_{ij} + \Lambda_{ij}\tilde{\epsilon}_{ij} = X_{ij} + N_{ij}$, where $\tilde{\epsilon}_{ij} \sim \mathcal{N}(0,1)$ for all $i = 1, \cdots, m$ and $j = 1, \cdots, n$, and N_{ij} represents the analog additive white Gaussian noise at position (i,j).

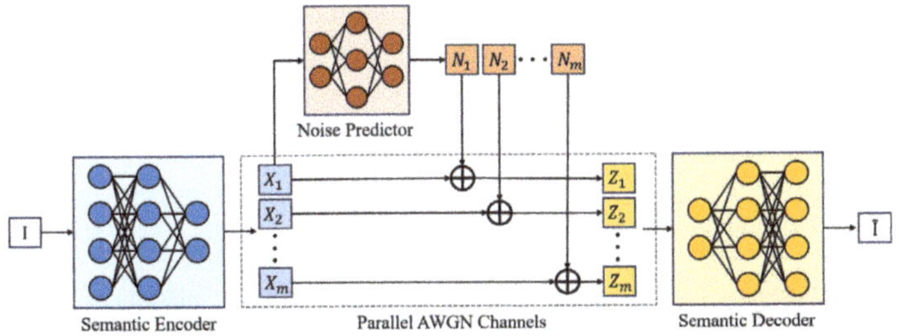

Figure 4. The framework of communication-informed bottleneck attribution method. For the convenience of presentation, we set $n = 1$ and $X \in \mathbb{R}^{m \times 1}$.

The noise predictor, which is a neural network parameterized by α, adjusts Λ_{ij} to control the power of the analog additive white Gaussian noise. We fix the parameters ϕ and θ of the semantic encoder and decoder, and only optimize the parameter α of the noise predictor through the information bottleneck objective.

$$\max \quad I(\mathrm{I};Z) - \beta I(X;Z). \tag{17}$$

This optimization objective aims to preserve more I-relevant information in Z while reducing the mutual information between Z and X. The hyperparameter β is used to control the relative importance of $I(\mathrm{I};Z)$ and $I(X;Z)$. For a small β, more bits of information are flowing and less for a higher value.

In this paper, we focus on image transmission, hence employing a VAE for the image reconstruction task, the reconstructed image denoted as $\tilde{\mathrm{I}}$. $\tilde{\mathrm{I}}$ is generated by the semantic decoder $q_\theta(\hat{\mathrm{I}}|Z)$. We optimize $I(\mathrm{I};Z)$ by minimizing the MSE between $\tilde{\mathrm{I}}$ and I:

$$\mathcal{L}_1(\alpha) = \mathbb{E}_\alpha\left[\|\mathrm{I} - \tilde{\mathrm{I}}\|_2^2\right]. \tag{18}$$

Considering X_{ij} as a Gaussian signal, the AWGN channel capacity C_{ij} becomes:

$$C_{ij} = \max I(X_{ij};Z_{ij}) = \frac{1}{2}\log\left(1 + \frac{\mu^2_{X_{ij}} + \sigma^2_{X_{ij}}}{\Lambda^2_{ij}}\right). \tag{19}$$

Under feature independence assumptions:

$$I(X;Z) = \sum_{i=1}^{m}\sum_{j=1}^{n} I(X_{ij};Z_{ij}) \le \sum_{i=1}^{m}\sum_{j=1}^{n} \frac{1}{2}\log\left(1 + \frac{\mu^2_{X_{ij}} + \sigma^2_{X_{ij}}}{\Lambda^2_{ij}}\right). \tag{20}$$

Letting $\mathcal{L}_2(\alpha) = \mathbb{E}_\alpha\left[\sum_{i=1}^{m}\sum_{j=1}^{n}\frac{1}{2}\log\left(1+\frac{\mu_{X_{ij}}^2+\sigma_{X_{ij}}^2}{\Lambda_{ij}^2}\right)\right]$, we formulate the composite optimization objective:

$$\mathcal{L}(\alpha) = \mathcal{L}_1(\alpha) + \beta\mathcal{L}_2(\alpha). \tag{21}$$

The noise predictor model is optimized to minimize the loss function (21). We use stochastic gradient descent to train the model parameters to search for the optimal parameters α^* with a minimal $\mathcal{L}(\alpha)$ as: $\alpha^* = \arg\min \mathbb{E}[\mathcal{L}(\alpha)]$, where the expectation is taken over the training datasets. It should be noted that during the training process, the parameters of the semantic encoder and decoder are fixed, and only the parameters of the noise predictor are updated. The loss function (21) is calculated through the original images, generated images, outputs of the semantic encoder, and outputs of the noise predictor.

This framework produces attribution results through the trained "noise power" predictor, specifically revealing the minimum channel capacity required to transmit each feature element X_{ij} in the AWGN channel while minimally impacting learning task performance. Defining the importance score $\mathrm{S}_{ij} = \frac{1}{2}\log\left(1+\frac{\mu_{X_{ij}}^2+\sigma_{X_{ij}}^2}{\Lambda_{ij}^2}\right)$, this metric indicates that higher importance features demand higher channel capacity. The importance score bridges learning task with communication objective, enabling rational communication resource planning that prioritizes high-importance features through enhanced resource allocation, thereby fully unleashing model potential.

3.2. Weighted Minimum Mean Squared Error (WMMSE)

As demonstrated in Section 3.1, each feature possesses distinct importance scores. To ensure alignment between communication objective and learning task, features with higher importance scores require prioritized fulfillment of their communication demands through enhanced resource allocation.

Minimum Mean Squared Error (MMSE) serves as a statistical estimation criterion aiming to minimize MSE between estimated and true values. Widely adopted in channel equalization, multi-user detection, and MIMO signal detection, it constitutes an indispensable tool in communication algorithm design. For MIMO communication scenarios, we formulate the power allocation optimization problem based on MMSE as follows:

$$\min \ \mathbb{E}\left[\|\boldsymbol{x}_i - \hat{\boldsymbol{x}}_i\|_2^2\right] \tag{22}$$

$$\text{s.t.} \ \sum_{j=1}^{K} p_{ij}^2 = P_{\text{total}}^2. \tag{23}$$

Despite the widespread application of MMSE, its optimization objective is solely anchored to communication goals, which complicates its integration with learning tasks. We, therefore, enhance the MMSE scheme by incorporating importance scores into the optimization objective, proposing the WMMSE formulation:

$$\min \ \sum_{j=1}^{K} \mathbb{E}\left[\mathrm{S}_{ij}^{\gamma}\|x_{ij} - \hat{x}_{ij}\|_2^2\right] \tag{24}$$

$$\text{s.t.} \ \sum_{j=1}^{K} p_{ij}^2 = P_{\text{total}}^2. \tag{25}$$

The hyperparameter γ controls the magnitude of importance weights, with its value being empirically determined through systematic tuning.

Leveraging results from Equation (14), the optimization objective (24) simplifies to:

$$\sum_{j=1}^{K} \mathbb{E}\left[S_{ij}^{\gamma}\|x_{ij}-\hat{x}_{ij}\|_2^2\right] = \sum_{j=1}^{K} \frac{S_{ij}^{\gamma}\|\overrightarrow{x_i}\|_2\sigma_w^2}{\sigma_j^2 p_{ij}^2}. \tag{26}$$

This leads to the refined optimization problem:

$$\min \sum_{j=1}^{K} \frac{S_{ij}^{\gamma}\|\overrightarrow{x_i}\|_2\sigma_w^2}{\sigma_j^2 p_{ij}^2} \tag{27}$$

$$\text{s.t.} \sum_{j=1}^{K} p_{ij}^2 = P_{\text{total}}^2. \tag{28}$$

Introducing the Lagrange multiplier $\lambda \geq 0$, we construct the Lagrangian:

$$L(p_{i1},\ldots,p_{iK},\lambda) = \sum_{j=1}^{K} \frac{S_{ij}^{\gamma}\|\overrightarrow{x_i}\|_2\sigma_w^2}{\sigma_j^2 p_{ij}^2} + \lambda\left(\sum_{j=1}^{K} p_{ij}^2 - P_{\text{total}}^2\right). \tag{29}$$

Setting $\nabla_{p_{ij}} L(p_{i1},\ldots,p_{iK},\lambda) = 0$ yields optimal power allocation for the j-th subchannel during i-th transmission:

$$p_{ij}^* = \sqrt[4]{\frac{S_{ij}^{\gamma}\|\overrightarrow{x_i}\|_2\sigma_w^2}{\lambda^*\sigma_j^2}}. \tag{30}$$

Substitution into the constraint gives:

$$\lambda^* = \left(\sum_{j=1}^{K}\sqrt{\frac{S_{ij}^{\gamma}\|\overrightarrow{x_i}\|_2\sigma_w^2}{\sigma_j^2}}\right)^2 \Big/ P_{\text{total}}^4. \tag{31}$$

The resultant transmission MSE per symbol becomes the following:

$$\mathbb{E}\left[\|x_{ij}-\hat{x}_{ij}\|_2^2\right]^* = \sqrt{\frac{\lambda^*\|\overrightarrow{x_i}\|_2\sigma_w^2}{S_{ij}^{\gamma}\sigma_j^2}}. \tag{32}$$

WMMSE explicitly incorporates importance scores S_{ij}, making MSE inversely proportional to both channel gain σ_j and importance score S_{ij}. This dual dependency ensures that high-importance features receive superior communication conditions, effectively aligning communication objectives with learning tasks. Additionally, since the optimization objective (26) are inversely proportional to channel gains, we can introduce subchannel allocation to adjust the channel gain of each feature during transmission, thereby making the optimization objective (26) as small as possible. To achieve this goal, we adopt the following subchannel allocation scheme:

Sort features $\boldsymbol{x}_i = [x_{i1},\ldots,x_{iK}]^T$ by descending importance scores S_{ij}^* to obtain $\boldsymbol{x}_i^* = [x_{i1}^*,\ldots,x_{iK}^*]$ with $S_{i1}^* \geq \cdots \geq S_{iK}^*$. Given SVD-derived subchannel gains σ_j ordered as $\sigma_1 \geq \cdots \geq \sigma_K$, we implement pairwise matching (x_{ij}^*,σ_j), establishing allocation configuration $\{(x_{i1}^*,\sigma_1),\ldots,(x_{iK}^*,\sigma_K)\}$. This configuration minimizes the weighted optimization objective $\sum_{j=1}^{K}\mathbb{E}\left[S_{ij}^{\gamma}\left\|x_{ij}^*-\hat{x}_{ij}^*\right\|_2^2\right]^*$.

The WMMSE framework achieves systematic trade-offs between communication efficiency and learning performance by prioritizing high-importance features through joint power allocation and subchannel matching, thereby fully unleashing model inference potential. Even if the optimal subchannel allocation is not adopted, the introduction of the importance score factor can slightly counterbalance the effects of channel gain.

In our proposed scheme, compared with the JSCC approach, the channel coding is decoupled and implemented through SVD precoding combined with solving the WMMSE optimization problem. This design ensures that under given channel state information conditions, the channel coding scheme yields a unique closed-form solution. Consequently, our proposed SSCC framework can adapt to channel variations while keeping model parameters fixed, thereby enhancing the reusability of DNN models and effectively addressing channel adaptation challenges.

4. Experiments and Discussion

In this section, we present a comparative analysis of the resource allocation schemes outlined in Section 3.2 and Appendix B within a 4×4 MIMO communication scenario. Specifically, each element of the channel matrix $\boldsymbol{H}$ is modeled to follow a complex normal distribution, denoted as $H(i,j) \sim \mathcal{CN}(0,1)$. To quantify the signal quality, we define the average received SNR using the following formula:

$$\mathrm{SNR} = 10\log_{10}\frac{\mathbb{E}[\|\boldsymbol{H}\tilde{\boldsymbol{x}}_i\|_F^2]}{\mathbb{E}[\|\boldsymbol{w}\|_F^2]}\ (\mathrm{dB}). \tag{33}$$

We conduct experiments to demonstrate the impact of semantic importance scores. We investigate the effect of parameter β on attribution performance, and explore the configuration of parameter γ in WMMSE. To evaluate the quality of the generated images, we adopt the PSNR metric. Simultaneously, we train an image classifier neural network termed the "evaluation model", which classifies generated images to provide complementary quality assessment through classification accuracy. These experiments are conducted under various SNR scenarios using the MNIST dataset [24], which comprises 60,000 training images and 10,000 test grayscale images of handwritten digits (0–9). Detailed information about the experiments can be found in Appendix A.

4.1. Resource Allocation Schemes Comparison

In the Appendix B, we also introduce two baseline power allocation schemes named MMSE and Equal Power Allocation (EPA) that do not consider feature importance, along with their corresponding subchannel allocation strategies. Let WMMSE-M, MMSE-M, and EPA-M represent the proposed WMMSE, MMSE, and EPA with subchannel matching.

We experimentally test and obtain the Empirical Upper Bound (EUB) of the performance of the semantic encoder and decoder without communication processes. We use PSNR metrics and the evaluation model for comparative analysis of all six schemes.

As shown in Figure 5, we observe that WMMSE-M achieves superior performance in both evaluation dimensions, and compared to other schemes, it maximizes the potential of the semantic encoder and decoder across various SNRs, which aligns with our design principles. The outperformance of WMMSE over MMSE and EPA stems from its incorporation of semantic importance scores to bridge learning tasks and communication objectives, whereas MMSE and EPA completely neglect learning task considerations. The enhanced performance of WMMSE-M, MMSE-M, and EPA-M compared to their counterparts demonstrates the effectiveness of our subchannel matching scheme: by assigning higher-importance features to channels with stronger gains, we ensure more accurate transmission of critical features, thereby improving learning task performance.

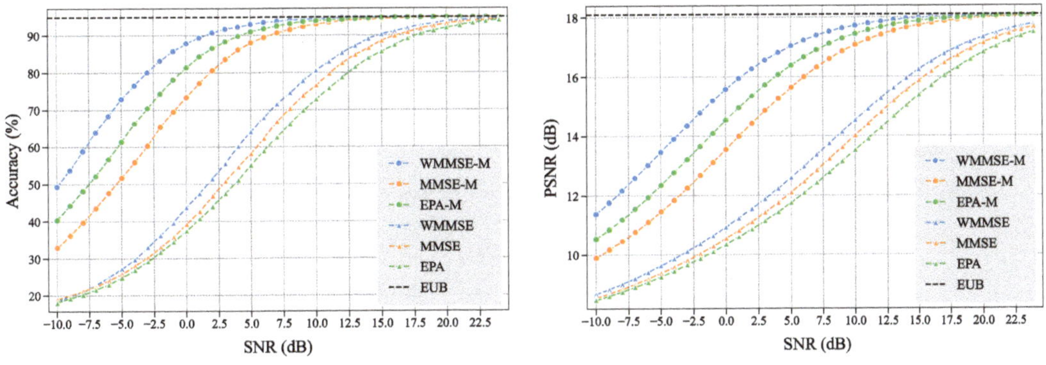

Figure 5. Performance comparison of resource allocation schemes: (**a**) Classification accuracy of evaluation model; (**b**) Reconstruction quality measured by PSNR.

Notably, while EPA-M outperforms MMSE-M, EPA underperforms MMSE. This phenomenon reflects the amplified impact of channel gain variations in EPA-based schemes, consistent with our theoretical analysis in Appendix B.2. These experimental results collectively validate that our proposed CIBA attribution method effectively evaluates importance levels of the features.

4.2. Semantic Importance Score Validation

In Section 3.1, we know the noise predictor provides the maximum tolerable noise power Λ_{ij} for each feature X_{ij}, thus we can derive the importance score, denoted by S_{ij}, for each feature X_{ij} as:

$$\mathrm{S}_{ij} = \frac{1}{2}\log\left(1 + \frac{\mu_{X_{ij}}^2 + \sigma_{X_{ij}}^2}{\Lambda_{ij}^2}\right). \tag{34}$$

The physical meaning of the importance score S_{ij} can be understood as the required channel capacity for the feature X_{ij} in an AWGN channel. When the actual channel capacity of X_{ij} during communication falls below S_{ij}, it will impact the performance of the deep learning task. To validate this perspective, after obtaining feature importance scores, we select a threshold S_T and designate features with $\mathrm{S}_{ij} \geq \mathrm{S}_\mathrm{T}$ as important features, while those with $\mathrm{S}_{ij} < \mathrm{S}_\mathrm{T}$ are considered unimportant. Regarding the selection of S_T, we will provide further details later. We posit that important features are more critical for model inference and exhibit lower tolerance to Gaussian noise perturbations, whereas unimportant features show the opposite behavior. To verify this hypothesis, we propose two perturbation modes as shown in Figure 6: Perturbing High-Importance Features (PHIF) and Perturbing Low-Importance Features (PLIF). PHIF and PLIF, respectively, apply Gaussian noise perturbations to important and unimportant features. Under both perturbation modes, the perturbed features are fed into the semantic decoder to observe how changes in important versus unimportant features affect model inference.

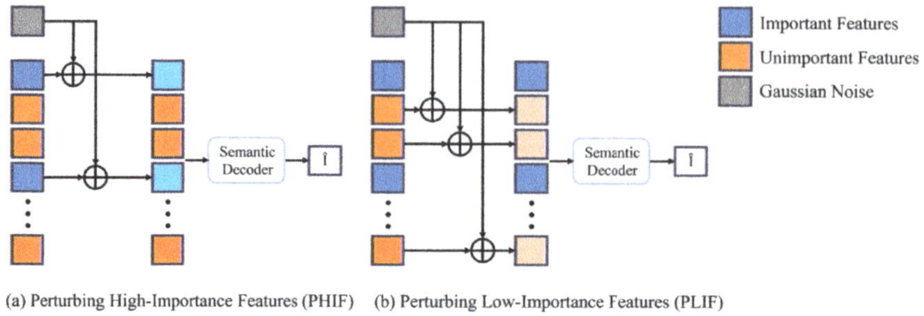

Figure 6. Illustration of two perturbation modes.

We visually demonstrate the different impacts of high- and low-importance features by observing changes in generated images under these two perturbation modes. Figure 7 presents three groups of comparisons between PLIF and PHIF when S_T is set to 3. The leftmost images in red boxes show the original input images, followed by generated results with progressively increasing Gaussian noise power (from left to right). We use the signal-to-noise ratio SNR_{test} between features and added noise to represent perturbation intensity. The upper three rows show PHIF perturbations, while the lower three rows show PLIF perturbations. Increasing progressively SNR_{test}, we observe that distortion in important features causes significant changes in generated images, whereas distortion in unimportant features has minimal impact on generated images.

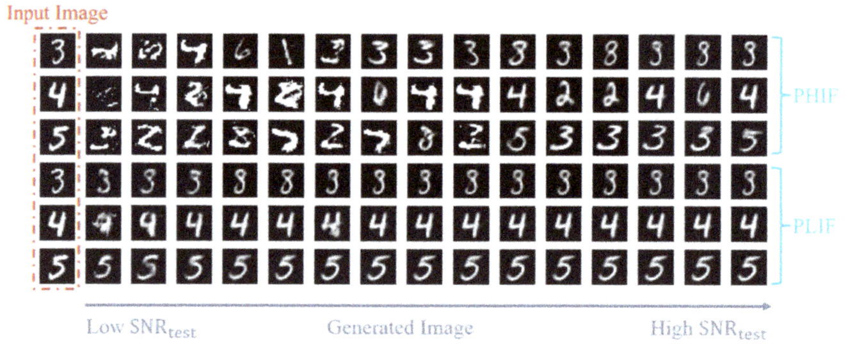

Figure 7. Comparison of PLIF and PHIF perturbations under varying SNR_{test} conditions. PHIF perturbations induce more severe distortion than PLIF under increasing SNR_{test}

Subsequently, we investigate the impact of two perturbation modes on the model's performance under the dynamic change of S_T. Across a range of different importance score thresholds S_T, PHIF and PLIF apply Gaussian noise perturbations with a fixed SNR_{test} to important and unimportant features, respectively, resulting in distinct effects on model inference performance. The experimental results are shown in Figure 8. It can be observed that, under both perturbation modes, the model inference performance begins to change when $S_T \geq 3$. This suggests that features with importance scores $S_{ij} \geq 3$ are more critical for model inference and exhibit lower tolerance to noise, requiring better transmission conditions. Thus, $S_T = 3$ can be a suitable threshold for separating important and unimportant features.

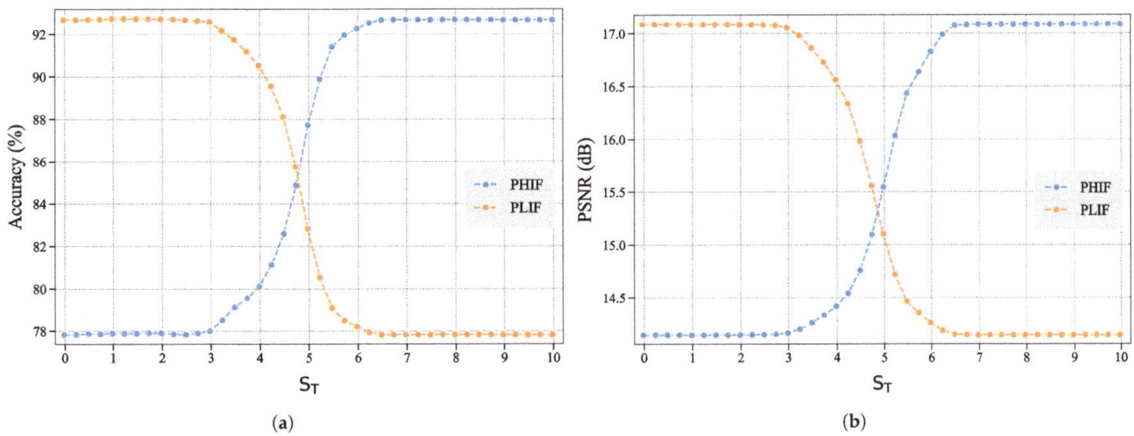

Figure 8. Effects of two perturbation modes on model performance at different S_T (**a**) Classification accuracy of evaluation model; (**b**) Reconstruction quality measured by PSNR. The experimental results indicate that low-importance features have negligible impact on learning task performance, while high-importance features dominate model decision-making.

Furthermore, in the PHIF mode, where perturbations are applied to features satisfying $S_{ij} \geq S_T$, model performance gradually improves as S_T increases because fewer high-importance features are perturbed. Similarly, in the PLIF mode, where perturbations target features with $S_{ij} < S_T$, model performance progressively deteriorates as S_T increases, because more features of high importance are perturbed.

These experimental results demonstrate that low-importance features have negligible impacts on task performance, whereas high-importance features dominate model decision-making. High-importance features (which are fewer in quantity) preserve more critical information, exert greater influence on model decisions, and require better communication conditions for transmission. Therefore, incorporating considerations of feature importance is essential when designing resource allocation schemes in SSCC strategies.

4.3. Hyperparameter Selection

4.3.1. Hyperparameter β Selection

The hyperparameter $\beta \in [10^{-3}, 10^2]$ is determined through grid search to identify the optimal β. We train our noise predictor under different β values with identical training epochs, and evaluate the performance of the EPA-M scheme using predicted importance scores from different predictors on the same task. Since EPA-M's learning performance solely depends on subchannel allocation results where features are only affected by channel gains, this setup effectively reveals the connection between communication resources and feature importance.

Figure 9 demonstrates the performance variation in the EPA-M scheme across different β values. Superior EPA-M performance indicates more accurate importance score predictions by the noise predictor. Experimental results reveal that when $\beta \in [10^{-3}, 10]$, the EPA-M performance remains stable with satisfactory outcomes. However, as β increases beyond this range, excessive information flow constraints lead to significant dilution of task-relevant information, resulting in degraded prediction accuracy of the noise predictor and, consequently, diminished EPA-M performance. This empirical evidence suggests that setting $\beta \in [10^{-3}, 10]$ enhances the attribution effectiveness of the noise predictor.

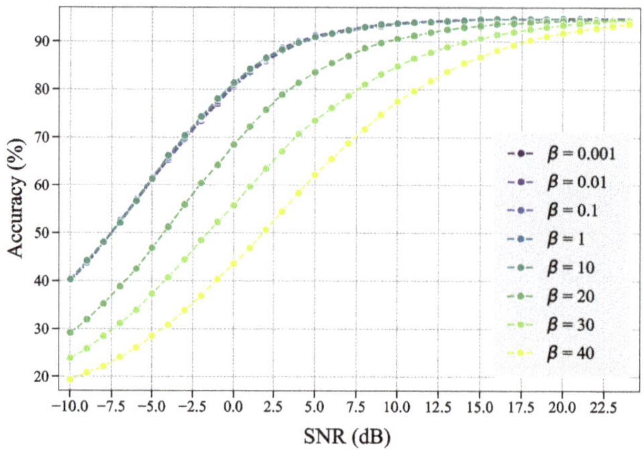

Figure 9. Performance variation in the EPA-M scheme under different β values. Stable performance is observed for $\beta \in [10^{-3}, 10]$.

4.3.2. Hyperparameter γ Selection

Similarly, we determine the optimal hyperparameter $\gamma \in [0, 10]$ through grid search. We evaluate the performance of the WMMSE-M scheme under different γ values, with experimental results shown in Figure 10. Experimental results demonstrate that the WMMSE-M scheme achieves peak performance when γ approaches 2, while values below or beyond this range degrade scheme performance. When $\gamma = 0$, the influence of S_{ij} is eliminated, and WMMSE-M becomes equivalent to the MMSE-M scheme. When the value of γ is excessively large, due to limited allocatable communication resources, the highest-importance features may be allocated more communication resources than required, thereby preempting the resources intended for secondary-importance features. This ultimately leads to performance degradation of the entire communication system in learning tasks. Therefore, selecting an appropriate γ is crucial in importance-aware resource allocation schemes.

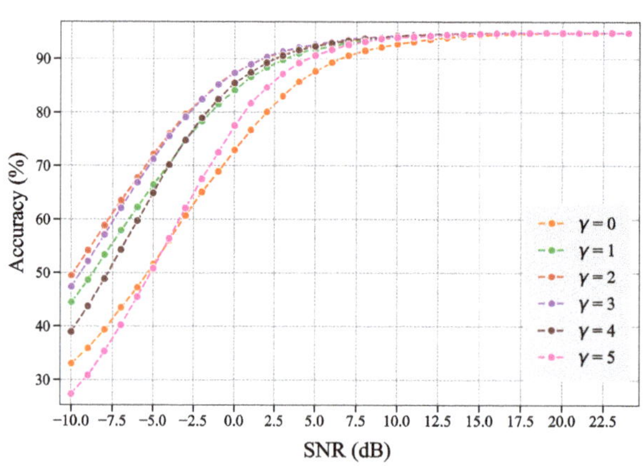

Figure 10. Performance variation in the WMMSE-M scheme under different γ values. Optimal performance occurs at $\gamma = 2$.

4.4. Extension to Classification Task

The proposed SSCC semantic communication framework can construct semantic encoders and decoders using different deep learning models, thus the framework is not limited to image reconstruction task and can be extended to other applications. To validate this capability, we select a deep learning model for the image classification task to build the semantic encoder and decoder, with model parameters detailed in Table A2. The experimental setup is consistent with that in Section 4.1, and we use classification accuracy as the evaluation metric. Experimental results shown in Figure 11 demonstrate that our proposed WMMSE-M achieves the best performance, with schemes that incorporate subchannel matching outperforming those without. These findings confirm the applicability of our proposed method to image classification task, demonstrating that the proposed framework can be extended to classification task.

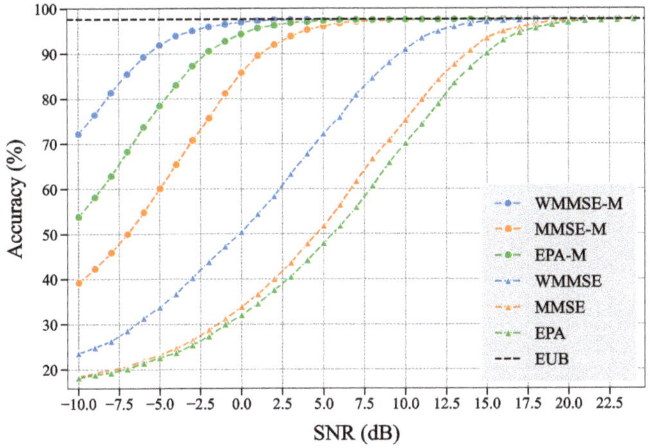

Figure 11. Performance comparison of resource allocation schemes for the image classification task.

5. Conclusions

In this paper, we design and investigate an SSCC framework for semantic communication to address the pain points in JSCC design: low model reusability and channel adaptation issues. We propose a novel AI interpretability method called CIBA for VAE models, along with an importance-aware resource allocation strategy based on significance scores, to enable effective feature transmission in semantic communication systems and fully unleash the performance potential of semantic encoders and decoders. Through systematic experiments and analysis, we validate the effectiveness of the significance scores obtained by CIBA and their crucial role in bridging learning tasks and communication optimization. Comparative experimental results of two feature perturbation schemes (PHIF and PLIF) confirm the necessity of importance-aware resource allocation in semantic communication systems. By comprehensively comparing resource allocation schemes, we demonstrate that the importance-aware allocation scheme outperforms conventional approaches in learning task performance, highlighting the advantages of integrating importance awareness into communication resource management.

The proposed method opens up new possibilities for designing semantic communication systems, particularly in resource-constrained environments where intelligent resource allocation is crucial for maintaining semantic fidelity and task performance. Currently, our framework has only been validated on simple datasets, and future work will extend it to more complex datasets. While our CIBA interpretability scheme is currently specific to VAE models and simple communication scenarios (AWGN channels), future research should extend it to support more DNN architectures and sophisticated communication processes. Our importance-aware resource allocation scheme currently focuses on single-user MIMO power allocation and subchannel allocation, leaving the design of more complex resource allocation schemes for advanced communication scenarios as a valuable future work.

Author Contributions: Conceptualization, Y.C., Y.W., L.L. and M.T.; methodology, Y.C., Y.W., L.L. and M.T.; software, Y.C.; validation, Y.C.; formal analysis, Y.C. and Y.W.; investigation, Y.C. and Y.W.; resources, Y.C.; data curation, Y.C.; writing—original draft preparation, Y.C.; writing—review and editing, Y.C., Y.W., L.L. and M.T.; supervision, Y.W., L.L. and M.T.; project administration, Y.W.; funding acquisition, Y.W. and M.T. All authors have read and agreed to the published version of the manuscript.

Funding: The experiments of this work were supported by the a core facility Platform of Core Facility Platform of Computer Science and Communication, SIST, ShanghaiTech University. The work by M. Tao was supported by National Science and Technology Major Project—Mobile Information Networks under Grant No.2024ZD1300700.

Institutional Review Board Statement: Not applicable.

Informed Consent Statement: Not applicable.

Data Availability Statement: Publicly available datasets were utilized in this study. The MNIST dataset can be accessed from Yann LeCun's official website (http://yann.lecun.com/exdb/mnist/, accessed on 28 February 2025). Additionally, the dataset is available on Kaggle (https://www.kaggle.com/datasets/hojjatk/mnist-dataset, accessed on 28 February 2025).

Acknowledgments: The authors appreciate the special contributions of School of Information Science and Technology, ShanghaiTech University.

Conflicts of Interest: The authors declare no conflicts of interest.

Appendix A. Experimental Details

Appendix A.1. Model Training and Neural Network Architecture

We employ a VAE model to provide the semantic encoder and decoder required for the semantic communication process. The model parameters of the semantic encoder and decoder are listed in Tables A1 and A2. The semantic encoder and decoder for image reconstruction task, trained on the MNIST dataset using the same training loss function in [17], handle image encoding and generation. The semantic encoder and decoder for classification task, trained on the MNIST dataset using cross-entropy loss, handle image encoding and classification. We adopt the PSNR metric to evaluate the quality of generated images. Simultaneously, we train an image classifier neural network termed the "evaluation model", which classifies generated images to provide complementary quality assessment through classification accuracy. The parameters of the evaluation model are shown in Table A4. The evaluation model is trained on the MNIST dataset using cross-entropy loss.

After training the semantic encoder-decoder, we proceed to train the noise predictor. The parameters of the noise predictor are presented in Table A3. With the semantic encoder-decoder parameters fixed, the noise predictor takes the semantic encoder's input as its input and produces outputs that feed into the semantic decoder. The loss function (21) is computed based on the decoder's output, enabling gradient backpropagation to update the noise predictor's parameters.

Table A1. The Neural Network Architecture for Semantic Encoder and Decoder (Image Reconstruction).

	Layer	Outputs
Encoder	Dense + ReLU	400
	Dense + ReLU	400
	[Dense → 32 (μ_X) / Dense → 32 (σ_X)]	32 ($\mu_X + \sigma_X \odot \epsilon$)
Decoder	Dense + ReLU	400
	Dense + ReLU	400
	Dense + Sigmoid	28×28

Table A2. The Neural Network Architecture for Semantic Encoder and Decoder (Classification).

	Layer	Outputs
Encoder	Dense + ReLU	400
	Dense + ReLU	400
	[Dense → 32 (μ_X) / Dense → 32 (σ_X)]	32 ($\mu_X + \sigma_X \odot \epsilon$)
Decoder	Dense + ReLU	400
	Dense + ReLU	400
	Dense + Softmax	10

Table A3. The Neural Network Architecture for Noise Predictor.

	Layer	Outputs
Predictor	Dense + ReLU	128
	Dense + ReLU	256
	Dense + ReLU	128
	Dense + ReLU	32

Table A4. The Neural Network Architecture of Evaluation Model for MNIST Classification Task.

	Layer	Outputs
Encoder	Flatten + Dense	400
Inference	Dense + ReLU	1024
	Dense + ReLU	256
	Dense + Softmax	10

Appendix A.2. Evaluation Metrics

Appendix A.2.1. Peak Signal-to-Noise Ratio (PSNR)

The PSNR between a reference image I and a processed image $\hat{\mathrm{I}}$ is defined as:

$$\mathrm{PSNR} = 10 \cdot \log_{10}\left(\frac{\mathrm{MAX}_{\mathrm{I}}^2}{\mathrm{MSE}}\right) \quad (\mathrm{dB}), \tag{A1}$$

where:

- $\mathrm{MSE} = \frac{1}{HW}\sum_{h=1}^{H}\sum_{w=1}^{W}[\mathrm{I}(h,w) - \hat{\mathrm{I}}(h,w)]^2$
- $H \times W$ is the image resolution
- $\mathrm{MAX}_{\mathrm{I}}$ denotes the maximum possible pixel value (typically 255 for 8-bit images)

Appendix A.2.2. Classification Accuracy

Classification accuracy is a fundamental metric for evaluating the performance of classification models, defined as the proportion of correctly predicted instances over the total number of samples. For the MNIST handwritten digit recognition benchmark, classification accuracy is computed as:

$$\text{Accuracy} = \frac{1}{N_{\text{test}}} \sum_{i=1}^{N_{\text{test}}} \mathbb{I}(\hat{y}_i = y_i) \tag{A2}$$

where:

- N_{test} is the standard test set size
- $\hat{y}_i$ denotes the predicted class label
- y_i is the true label
- $\mathbb{I}(\cdot)$ is the indicator function

This can be practically implemented using the confusion matrix for the 10-class problem:

$$\text{Accuracy} = \frac{\sum_{k=0}^{9} C_{kk}}{\sum_{i=0}^{9}\sum_{j=0}^{9} C_{ij}}, \tag{A3}$$

where C_{ij} represents the count of samples with true label i predicted as class j.

Appendix B. Power Allocation Strategy

Appendix B.1. Minimum Mean Squared Error (MMSE)

For MIMO communication scenarios, we formulate the power allocation optimization problem based on MMSE as follows:

$$\min \ \mathbb{E}\left[\|\boldsymbol{x}_i - \hat{\boldsymbol{x}}_i\|_2^2\right] \tag{A4}$$

$$\text{s.t.} \ \sum_{j=1}^{K} p_{ij}^2 = P_{\text{total}}^2. \tag{A5}$$

Leveraging results from Equation (14), the optimization objective (A4) simplifies to:

$$\mathbb{E}\left[\|\boldsymbol{x}_i - \hat{\boldsymbol{x}}_i\|_2^2\right] = \mathbb{E}\left[\left\|\sqrt{\|\overrightarrow{x_i}\|_2}\boldsymbol{p}_i^{-1}\boldsymbol{\Sigma}^{-1}\boldsymbol{U}^H\boldsymbol{w}\right\|_2^2\right] \tag{A6}$$

$$= \sum_{j=1}^{K} \frac{\|\overrightarrow{x_i}\|_2\sigma_w^2}{\sigma_j^2 p_{ij}^2}. \tag{A7}$$

This reduces to the optimization problem:

$$\min \ \sum_{j=1}^{K} \frac{\|\overrightarrow{x_i}\|_2\sigma_w^2}{\sigma_j^2 p_{ij}^2} \tag{A8}$$

$$\text{s.t.} \ \sum_{j=1}^{K} p_{ij}^2 = P_{\text{total}}^2. \tag{A9}$$

Introducing Lagrange multiplier $\lambda \geq 0$, we construct the Lagrangian:

$$L(p_{i1}, \ldots, p_{iK}, \lambda) = \sum_{j=1}^{K} \frac{\|\overrightarrow{x_i}\|_2\sigma_w^2}{\sigma_j^2 p_{ij}^2} + \lambda\left(\sum_{j=1}^{K} p_{ij}^2 - P_{\text{total}}^2\right). \tag{A10}$$

Setting $\nabla_{p_{ij}} L(p_{i1}, \ldots, p_{iK}, \lambda) = 0$ yields optimal power allocation for the j-th subchannel during i-th transmission:

$$p_{ij}^* = \sqrt[4]{\frac{\| \overrightarrow{x_i} \|_2 \sigma_w^2}{\lambda^* \sigma_j^2}}. \tag{A11}$$

Substitution into the constraint gives:

$$\lambda^* = \left(\sum_{j=1}^{K} \sqrt{\frac{\| \overrightarrow{x_i} \|_2 \sigma_w^2}{\sigma_j^2}} \right)^2 \bigg/ P_{\text{total}}^4. \tag{A12}$$

Under optimal power allocation, the transmission MSE per symbol becomes:

$$\mathbb{E}\left[\|x_{ij} - \hat{x}_{ij}\|_2^2 \right]^* = \sqrt{\frac{\lambda^* \| \overrightarrow{x_i} \|_2 \sigma_w^2}{\sigma_j^2}}. \tag{A13}$$

Notably, MMSE-optimized power allocation and transmission MSE depend solely on subchannel gain σ_j, with MSE inversely proportional to channel gain. This implies high-importance features assigned to low-gain subchannels receive fewer resources, potentially compromising task performance. To address this, we design subchannel allocation strategies prioritizing high-importance features through ordered matching:

Sort features $\boldsymbol{x}_i = [x_{i1}, \ldots, x_{iK}]^T$ by descending importance scores S_{ij}^* to obtain $\boldsymbol{x}_i^* = [x_{i1}^*, \ldots, x_{iK}^*]$ with $S_{i1}^* \geq \cdots \geq S_{iK}^*$. Given SVD-derived subchannel gains σ_j ordered as $\sigma_1 \geq \cdots \geq \sigma_K$, we implement pairwise matching (x_{ij}^*, σ_j), establishing allocation configuration $\{(x_{i1}^*, \sigma_1), \ldots, (x_{iK}^*, \sigma_K)\}$. This strategy optimally aligns MMSE power allocation with learning task requirements.

Appendix B.2. Equal Power Allocation (EPA)

We also design an equal power allocation scheme where equal power is allocated to all subchannels, satisfying $p_{i1}^2 = \cdots = p_{ij}^2 = \cdots = p_{iK}^2 = \frac{P_{\text{total}}^2}{K}$. The transmission MSE for each symbol x_{ij} can be derived as:

$$\mathbb{E}\left[\|x_{ij} - \hat{x}_{ij}\|_2^2 \right] = \frac{K \| \overrightarrow{x_i} \|_2 \sigma_w^2}{P_{\text{total}}^2 \sigma_j^2}. \tag{A14}$$

It can be observed that under the EPA scheme, the transmission MSE for each symbol only relates to the channel gain and is inversely proportional to σ_j^2. Subchannels with higher channel gains provide better communication conditions. Similar to MMSE, to balance both learning and communication tasks, subchannel allocation is required to assign high-importance features to subchannels with higher channel gains. The allocation strategy is as follows:

Sort features x_i by descending S_{ij}^* to obtain x_i^*, then pair with ordered subchannels σ_j through $\{(x_{i1}^*, \sigma_1), \ldots, (x_{iK}^*, \sigma_K)\}$.

The transmission MSE of EPA scheme is inversely proportional to σ_j^2, while that of MMSE scheme is inversely proportional to σ_j. Therefore, under subchannel allocation strategy, the EPA scheme can provide smaller MSE for high-importance features, resulting in better learning task performance. Without this subchannel allocation strategy, if high-importance features are assigned to low-gain subchannels, EPA would introduce larger MSE for these features, leading to inferior learning performance compared to the MSE scheme.

References

1. Shi, Y.; Zhou, Y.; Wen, D.; Wu, Y.; Jiang, C.; Letaief, K.B. Task-Oriented Communications for 6G: Vision, Principles, and Technologies. *IEEE Wirel. Commun.* **2023**, *30*, 78–85. [CrossRef]
2. Wu, Y.; Shi, Y.; Ma, S.; Jiang, C.; Zhang, W.; Letaief, K.B. Toward Effective and Interpretable Semantic Communications. *IEEE Netw.* **2024**, *38*, 55–62. [CrossRef]
3. Xie, H.; Qin, Z.; Li, G.Y.; Juang, B.H. Deep Learning Enabled Semantic Communication Systems. *IEEE Trans. Signal Process.* **2021**, *69*, 2663–2675. [CrossRef]
4. Yang, K.; Wang, S.; Dai, J.; Tan, K.; Niu, K.; Zhang, P. WITT: A Wireless Image Transmission Transformer for Semantic Communications. In Proceedings of the ICASSP 2023—2023 IEEE International Conference on Acoustics, Speech and Signal Processing (ICASSP), Rhodes Island, Greece, 5 May 2023; pp. 1–5. [CrossRef]
5. Hu, Q.; Zhang, G.; Qin, Z.; Cai, Y.; Yu, G.; Li, G.Y. Robust Semantic Communications With Masked VQ-VAE Enabled Codebook. *IEEE Trans. Wirel. Commun.* **2023**, *22*, 8707–8722. [CrossRef]
6. Weng, Z.; Qin, Z. Semantic Communication Systems for Speech Transmission. *IEEE J. Sel. Areas Commun.* **2021**, *39*, 2434–2444. [CrossRef]
7. Jiang, P.; Wen, C.K.; Jin, S.; Li, G.Y. Wireless Semantic Communications for Video Conferencing. *IEEE J. Sel. Areas Commun.* **2023**, *41*, 230–244. [CrossRef]
8. Ma, S.; Qiao, W.; Wu, Y.; Li, H.; Shi, G.; Gao, D.; Shi, Y.; Li, S.; Al-Dhahir, N. Task-Oriented Explainable Semantic Communications. *IEEE Trans. Wirel. Commun.* **2023**, *22*, 9248–9262. [CrossRef]
9. Farsad, N.; Rao, M.; Goldsmith, A. Deep learning for joint source-channel coding of text. In Proceedings of the 2018 IEEE International Conference on Acoustics, Speech and Signal Processing (ICASSP), Calgary, AB, Canada, 15–20 April 2018; IEEE: Piscataway Township, NJ, USA, 2018; pp. 2326–2330.
10. Bourtsoulatze, E.; Kurka, D.B.; Gündüz, D. Deep joint source-channel coding for wireless image transmission. *IEEE Trans. Cogn. Commun. Netw.* **2019**, *5*, 567–579. [CrossRef]
11. Kurka, D.B.; Gündüz, D. Deepjscc-f: Deep joint source-channel coding of images with feedback. *IEEE J. Sel. Areas Inf. Theory* **2020**, *1*, 178–193. [CrossRef]
12. Huang, D.; Gao, F.; Tao, X.; Du, Q.; Lu, J. Toward Semantic Communications: Deep Learning-Based Image Semantic Coding. *IEEE J. Sel. Areas Commun.* **2023**, *41*, 55–71. [CrossRef]
13. Jiang, P.; Wen, C.K.; Jin, S.; Li, G.Y. Wireless Semantic Transmission via Revising Modules in Conventional Communications. *IEEE Wirel. Commun.* **2023**, *30*, 28–34. [CrossRef]
14. Weng, Z.; Qin, Z.; Xie, H.; Tao, X.; Letaief, K.B. Semantic MIMO Systems for Speech-to-Text Transmission. *IEEE Trans. Wirel. Commun.* **2024**, *23*, 18697–18710. [CrossRef]
15. Wu, H.; Shao, Y.; Bian, C.; Mikolajczyk, K.; Gündüz, D. Deep Joint Source-Channel Coding for Adaptive Image Transmission Over MIMO Channels. *IEEE Trans. Wirel. Commun.* **2024**, *23*, 15002–15017. [CrossRef]
16. Cai, C.; Yuan, X.; Angela Zhang, Y.J. Multi-Device Task-Oriented Communication via Maximal Coding Rate Reduction. *IEEE Trans. Wirel. Commun.* **2024**, *23*, 18096–18110. [CrossRef]
17. Kingma, D.P.; Welling, M. Auto-Encoding Variational Bayes. *arXiv* **2022**, arXiv:1312.6114.
18. Wang, Y.; Han, S.; Xu, X.; Liang, H.; Meng, R.; Dong, C.; Zhang, P. Feature Importance-Aware Task-Oriented Semantic Transmission and Optimization. *IEEE Trans. Cogn. Commun. Netw.* **2024**, *10*, 1175–1189. [CrossRef]
19. Liu, D.; Zhu, G.; Zhang, J.; Huang, K. Data-Importance Aware User Scheduling for Communication-Efficient Edge Machine Learning. *IEEE Trans. Cogn. Commun. Netw.* **2021**, *7*, 265–278. [CrossRef]
20. Liu, Y.; Zeng, Z.; Tang, W.; Chen, F. Data-Importance Aware Radio Resource Allocation: Wireless Communication Helps Machine Learning. *IEEE Commun. Lett.* **2020**, *24*, 1981–1985. [CrossRef]
21. Guo, S.; Wang, Y.; Li, S.; Saeed, N. Semantic Importance-Aware Communications Using Pre-Trained Language Models. *IEEE Commun. Lett.* **2023**, *27*, 2328–2332. [CrossRef]
22. Liu, C.; Guo, C.; Yang, Y.; Ni, W.; Quek, T.Q.S. OFDM-Based Digital Semantic Communication With Importance Awareness. *IEEE Trans. Commun.* **2024**, *72*, 6301–6315. [CrossRef]

23. Schulz, K.; Sixt, L.; Tombari, F.; Landgraf, T. Restricting the Flow: Information Bottlenecks for Attribution. In Proceedings of the 8th International Conference on Learning Representations, ICLR 2020, Addis Ababa, Ethiopia, 26–30 April 2020.
24. LeCun, Y.; Bottou, L.; Bengio, Y.; Haffner, P. Gradient-based learning applied to document recognition. *Proc. IEEE* **1998**, *86*, 2278–2324. [CrossRef]

entropy

Article

Soft Classification in a Composite Source Model

Yuefeng Cao, Jiakun Liu and Wenyi Zhang *

Department of Electronic Engineering and Information Science, University of Science and Technology of China, Hefei 230026, China; yf980515@mail.ustc.edu.cn (Y.C.); liujk@mail.ustc.edu.cn (J.L.)
* Correspondence: wenyizha@ustc.edu.cn

Abstract: A composite source model consists of an intrinsic state and an extrinsic observation. The fundamental performance limit of reproducing the intrinsic state is characterized by the indirect rate–distortion function. In a remote classification application, a source encoder encodes the extrinsic observation (e.g., image) into bits, and a source decoder plays the role of a classifier that reproduces the intrinsic state (e.g., label of image). In this work, we characterize the general structure of the optimal transition probability distribution, achieving the indirect rate–distortion function. This optimal solution can be interpreted as a "soft classifier", which generalizes the conventionally adopted "classify-then-compress" scheme. We then apply the soft classification to aid the lossy compression of the extrinsic observation of a composite source. This leads to a coding scheme that exploits the soft classifier to guide reproduction, outperforming existing coding schemes without classification or with hard classification.

Keywords: composite source; indirect rate–distortion function; rate–distortion theory; semantic information; soft classification

1. Introduction

In [1,2], information transmission with additional noise is studied. In this setting, the encoder has access only to a noise-corrupted version of the original signal, while the goal is to minimize the expected distortion between the original signal and the final output. Under the mean-squared error (MSE) distortion criterion, the optimality of an estimate-then-compress scheme is proved. This indirect compression model shares similarities with the semantic communication problem, which has recently attracted much attention. A common model for studying semantic communication is the composite source model [3], which consists of an intrinsic state and an extrinsic observation. The intrinsic state corresponds to the semantic aspect of information, while the encoder observes only the extrinsic observation. In classification tasks, the states are discrete, and a scheme similar to the one mentioned above is the hard-classify-then-compress (HCTC) scheme, i.e., first performing optimal classification based on the observation, then compressing the classification result.

As will be shown in this paper, in general, however, this HCTC scheme is suboptimal due to the inherent "ambiguity" of the states. In a typical composite source, some observations correspond to multiple states with similar posterior probabilities. In this case, losslessly transmitting the classification result offers limited performance gains. The HCTC scheme, however, compresses the classification results indifferently, without accounting for the "ambiguity" of the observations. In [4,5], a soft classification scheme is investigated in a binary classification model. Unlike the HCTC scheme, the soft classification scheme directly compresses the observation and leverages the "ambiguity" of the source. In this paper, the study is further conducted and generalized to multi-class classification.

The value of the knowledge of semantic information in reconstructing observations has also received much attention. In most cases, a codebook precisely matched to the source statistics is hard to obtain. In contrast, the Gaussian codebook is well studied and commonly used. In this work, the role of the classification results obtained through the soft classification scheme in aiding the reconstruction of observations is investigated. We propose a classification-aided-compression (CAC) scheme and study its rate–distortion properties. An achievable upper bound proposed in [6], where the codebook precisely matched to the source statistics is available, is used for comparison. Our work compares the rate–distortion performance achievable using Gaussian codebooks, assisted by different classifiers when the matched codebook is unavailable, with the performance achievable when the matched codebook is available. Numerical results show the benefit of soft classification in improving the rate–distortion performance when only Gaussian codebooks are available, especially at high rates.

1.1. Related Works

In his landmark work [7,8], Shannon excluded the semantic aspects of information from the framework of his classical rate–distortion theory, asserting that the semantic information is irrelevant to the engineering problem. This viewpoint that communication systems should focus on symbol transmission has since become a foundational paradigm in source coding. However, in many practical scenarios, the encoder has only indirect access to the target signal (e.g., through observations corrupted by channel noise or measurement errors). Such indirect source coding problems have been studied in [1,2], but largely limited to simple cases involving AWGN.

To enhance the performance of communication systems in such scenarios, there has been ongoing consideration of how to leverage the semantic aspects of information in communication [9–12]. These works aim to establish a universal, task-independent definition of semantic information. In recent years, with the development of 5G and the growing interest in post-5G technologies, some researchers have taken the semantic aspects of information into account when designing communication systems [13–16], to enable new applications in emerging scenarios. Compared to the former works, in these studies, the semantic aspects of information are associated with specific goals. Our work aligns with the latter. Task-oriented compression has been investigated in several works, with quantization being the primary method [17–20]. In such works, classification [21,22], detection [23], and inferring a latent variable from compressed data [24] are common tasks.

A commonly used model for studying semantic communication is the composite source model [3], which consists of an intrinsic state and multiple sub-sources. Different values of the intrinsic state correspond to different sub-sources and output symbol distributions. The source coding problem for composite sources is studied in [25]. The rate–distortion problems of composite sources under various distortion metrics and constraints are investigated in [4,26], where the composite source model is also connected to the semantic aspects of information. Such rate–distortion problems involving an intrinsic state or noisy observations are referred to as "indirect rate–distortion problems" [1–3,27,28]. Two cases have been studied in [4]. In the first case, the state and the observation obey a joint Gaussian distribution, which is further explored in [27]. The second case involves binary classification, and the corresponding solution implies a soft classification scheme. In our work, this case is extended to multi-class classification settings.

The concept of semantic information and the composite source model has also drawn attention in real-world signal processing tasks such as image and speech processing. In certain machine vision tasks, only specific semantic features are required, and the bitrate needed to represent these features is often much lower than that required to encode the entire image. In [29], a scalable image compression scheme is proposed, which simultaneously satisfies the requirements of both human vision and machine vision tasks. The composite source model has also been used to characterize image and speech signals [30–33]. A widely used model in speech signal processing, the Hidden Markov Model (HMM), is essentially a type of composite source model [34]. In image classification tasks, the label of an image can be viewed as the intrinsic state, with the image generated by its corresponding sub-source. The classification task thus becomes equivalent to inferring the intrinsic state from the image [35]. Other tasks such as recognition [36] and anomaly detection [37] can be modeled in a similar manner. Recently developed generative models, such as the variational auto-encoder [38] and the diffusion model [39], are also related to the composite source model. Taking the variational auto-encoder as an example, different latent variables correspond to different output distributions, similar to how different intrinsic states correspond to different observation distributions in the composite source model. Beyond signal processing, composite sources have also been applied to other practical applications. In [40], a multi-source or composite source information fusion method is studied in the context of the failure mode and effects analysis (FEMA) problem, where assessments from different experts are treated as different sources. The model is also well-suited for capturing ambiguity in classification tasks, where observations do not correspond to unique labels but instead map to multiple possible states with different probabilities. In such scenarios, soft classification is employed [41–43].

Despite the numerous studies on semantic information and composite sources, several important issues remain to be addressed. For the composite source classification, studies such as [4,5] have only investigated the case of symmetric binary classification. Nevertheless, many practical tasks involve more general scenarios, such as multi-class classification. In these cases, the soft classification scheme that achieves the classification rate–distortion function is difficult to obtain. In [44], the authors propose a classification-based approach to reconstruct sparse sources, indicating the value of classification when the codebook matched to the source statistics is unavailable. However, only hard classification is considered therein. To the best of our knowledge, no existing work has considered the tradeoff between the classification rate and the effectiveness of classification in reducing the reconstruction rate under this kind of scenarios.

1.2. Contribution and Organization of Paper

Our main contributions include:

- We characterize the classification rate–distortion function for general multi-class composite sources under classification distortion constraint only.
- Based on this setting, we study two schemes: the HCTC scheme and the soft classification scheme. We convert the rate–distortion performance of the HCTC scheme into the rate–distortion function of a discrete source. We also identify sufficient conditions for the rate–distortion optimality of both schemes and analyze the rate–distortion properties of the soft classification scheme. Our analysis shows that, by allowing only a small additional distortion compared to the minimum achievable distortion, the upper bound of the rate of the soft classification scheme can decrease rapidly. Through numerical results, we compare the performance of the two schemes and show that each has different strengths and weaknesses under different scenarios.
- When the reconstruction distortion is constrained, we derive an achievable upper bound of the reconstruction rate–distortion function and propose the CAC scheme using only Gaussian codebooks. Numerical results show that, with proper classification before compression, the rate–distortion performance of the CAC scheme can approach that of the scheme with a matched codebook. We also find that, under

high-resolution conditions, the total bitrate of the CAC scheme can be minimized by separately optimizing the classifier and each sub-encoder.

The remainder of the paper is organized as follows.

Section 2 introduces and describes the composite source model and formulates the problem as an indirect rate–distortion problem. In Section 3, the classification rate–distortion function is characterized. We further study two achievable upper bounds of the rate–distortion function and, based on these, propose two classification schemes. Section 4 derives an upper bound of the rate–distortion function under reconstruction distortion constraint, and based on this, proposes the CAC scheme. Section 5 presents the numerical results. For cases with only the classification distortion constraint, we compare the performance of the two schemes. For cases with the reconstruction distortion constraint, we evaluate the performance of the proposed CAC scheme under classifiers of different levels. Finally, Section 6 concludes the paper.

2. Problem Formulation

The composite source consists of two parts: the intrinsic state S and the extrinsic observation X. Within the composite source, different states correspond to different sub-sources of observation X, each with a distinct distribution.

In the composite source coding, the encoder and decoder do not have access to the state S, while the observation X is available to the encoder [4]. The state can only be inferred from the extrinsic observation. Assume that the source has L states, with prior probabilities $P_1, \cdots, P_L$.

For state S, the conditional distribution of the observation X is denoted as $P(X|S)$. In the following work, we assume that the state S is a discrete label. Let $\mathcal{X}$ and $\mathcal{S}$ denote the alphabets of X and S, respectively. The conditional probability density function (pdf) corresponding to the t-th state is denoted as $f_t(x)$. The pdf of the entire source is denoted by $f(x)$, given by,

$$f(x) = \sum_{t=1}^{L} P_t f_t(x). \tag{1}$$

Let the block length be denoted by n. When encoding a sequence of source observations X^n, it is first mapped to an index $\mathcal{W}$ in the codebook. Here $\mathcal{W}$ takes value from $\{1, 2, \cdots, 2^{nR}\}$, where R is the rate. On the decoder side, $\mathcal{W}$ is mapped to either the reconstruction of the states (classification result) $\hat{S}$ or the reconstruction of the observation $\hat{X}$. The model for this coding problem is illustrated in Figure 1. In all of the schemes described in this work, we assume $n \to +\infty$.

Figure 1. System model.

In different scenarios, the primary concern varies. In some cases, the emphasis is on classification distortion [21,22]. In some other cases, reconstruction distortion is the focus [44]. Consider two distortion measures: classification distortion measure d_s and the reconstruction distortion measure d_o. Let D_s and D_o denote the distortion constraints on classification and reconstruction, respectively. The rate–distortion problem can then be formulated as an optimization problem that minimizes the mutual information between X and $\hat{S}$ (or $\hat{X}$), subject to the corresponding distortion constraint [4]:

$$\begin{aligned} R(D_s) &= \min I(X; \hat{S}), \\ s.t. \mathbb{E}\{\hat{d}_s(X, \hat{S})\} &\leq D_s, \end{aligned} \tag{2}$$

or

$$R(D_o) = \min I(X;\hat{X}),\\ s.t.\mathbb{E}\{d_o(X,\hat{X})\} \le D_o, \tag{3}$$

where $S, X, \hat{S}$, and $\hat{X}$ form a Markov chain $S \leftrightarrow X \leftrightarrow \hat{S}/\hat{X}$ and $\hat{d}_s(x,\hat{s}) = \mathbb{E}\{d_s(S,\hat{s})|X=x\}$. Equation (2) describes the rate–distortion formulation for tasks concerned solely with classification distortion, while (3) corresponds to scenarios where reconstruction distortion is the main focus. In this work, we adopt the Hamming distortion metric to characterize classification distortion, i.e., $d_S(s,\hat{s}) = \mathbb{1}(s \neq \hat{s})$ and use the MSE to measure the reconstruction distortion.

In the following sections, the rate–distortion function is referred to as the classification rate–distortion function when only classification distortion is constrained, and as the reconstruction rate–distortion function when only reconstruction distortion is constrained.

3. Rate–Distortion Analysis for Classification in Composite Sources

3.1. Classification Rate–Distortion Function

In this section, we consider the case where only the classification distortion is constrained. The corresponding optimization problem is formulated by (2).

Let the transition probability from $X = x$ to $\hat{S} = t$ be denoted as $g_t(x)$, i.e., $g_t(x) = P(\hat{S} = t|X = x)$. The expected distortion can be expressed as

$$\begin{aligned}\mathbb{E}\{\hat{d}_S(X,\hat{S})\} &= \mathbb{E}\{d_S(S,\hat{S})\}\\ &= \sum_{t=1}^{L} P_t \mathbb{E}\{d_S(t,\hat{S})|S=t\}\\ &= \sum_{t=1}^{L} P_t \int_{\mathcal{X}} f_t(x) \sum_{u=1}^{L} g_u(x)\mathbb{1}(t \neq u)dx\\ &= 1 - \sum_{t=1}^{L} P_t \int_{\mathcal{X}} f_t(x) \sum_{u=1}^{L} g_u(x)\mathbb{1}(t = u)dx\\ &= 1 - \int_{\mathcal{X}} \sum_{t=1}^{L} P_t f_t(x) g_t(x)dx,\end{aligned} \tag{4}$$

while the rate (mutual information) is given by [45]

$$I(X;\hat{S}) = H(\hat{S}) - H(\hat{S}|X). \tag{5}$$

The two terms $H(\hat{S})$ and $H(\hat{S}|X)$ in the equation above can also be expressed with $g_t(x)$. Therefore, the optimization problem can be solved by optimizing the transition probability $g_t(x)$. As a result, the classification rate–distortion function can be characterized based on the optimization result.

Theorem 1. *The classification rate–distortion function of a composite source is given by*

$$R(D_s) = \sum_{t=1}^{L} \int_{\mathcal{X}} f(x) g_t(x) \log_2 \frac{g_t(x)}{\int_{\mathcal{X}} f(x) g_t(x) dx} dx, \tag{6}$$

where

$$g_t(x) = \frac{P(\hat{S}=t)e^{\frac{\lambda P_t f_t(x)}{f(x)}}}{\sum\limits_{w=1}^{L} P(\hat{S}=w)e^{\frac{\lambda P_w f_w(x)}{f(x)}}}, \tag{7}$$

$$P(\hat{S}=t)=\int_{\mathcal{X}} f(x)g_t(x)dx, \tag{8}$$

and the parameter λ is chosen such that

$$1-\int_{\mathcal{X}}\sum_{t=1}^{L} P_t f_t(x) g_t(x)dx = D_s. \tag{9}$$

Proof. See Appendix A. □

Remark 1. *In Theorem 1, $g_t(x)$ represents the transition probability $P(\hat{S}=t|X=x)$. The theorem shows that, for a fixed $X=x$, the transition probability from $X=x$ to $\hat{S}=t$ satisfies*

$$g_t(x) \propto P(\hat{S}=t)e^{\lambda P(S=t|X=x)}. \tag{10}$$

The result aligns with the intuition that, for a fixed $X=x$, the transition probability $g_t(x)$ increases with the posterior probability $P(S=t|X=x)$.

The form of $g_t(x)$ implies a soft classification scheme. In this scheme, as λ increases, $g_t(x)$ approaches a step function, indicating that the classification becomes "harder". At the same time, the rate increases and the distortion decreases. When $\lambda \to +\infty$, we have

$$g_t(x) \to \begin{cases} 1 & t=t^*(x) \\ 0 & \text{otherwise}, \end{cases} \tag{11}$$

for all x where the most probable state $t^*(x)=\arg\max_t P(S=t \mid X=x)$ is unique. In this case, the classification reduces to hard classification. Thus, at the far left of the RD curve, the rate approaches the entropy of the hard classification results.

Conversely, as λ decreases towards 0, the functions $g_t(x)$ for $t=[1:L]$ become smoother, making the classification more "random". As a result, the distortion increases while the rate decreases. By adjusting λ, the functions $g_t(x)$ can be tuned to satisfy the distortion constraint.

Equation (7) also involves the marginal probability of $\hat{S}$, assigning larger weights to the states with higher marginal probabilities. This helps reduce the first term $H(\hat{S})$ in (5).

3.2. Two Classification Schemes

Next, two achievable upper bounds of the classification rate–distortion function are introduced and analyzed, along with the corresponding classification–compression schemes.

3.2.1. Hard-Classify-Then-Compress

The first scheme is called the hard-classify-then-compress (HCTC) scheme. In this scheme, a hard classification is first performed on the observation X, and the resulting classification outcome is denoted as $\bar{S}$. This hard classification result $\bar{S}$ is then compressed into $\hat{S}$.

The procedure of the HCTC scheme is illustrated in Figure 2. As shown in the figure, the following Markov chain is formed:

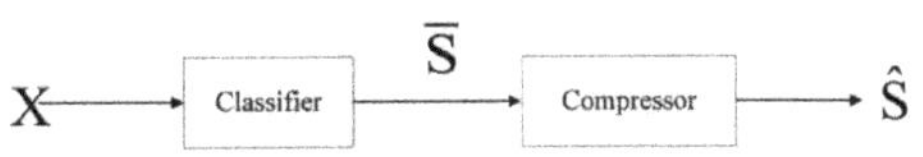

Figure 2. The procedure of the HCTC scheme.

$$S \longleftrightarrow X \longleftrightarrow \bar{S} \longleftrightarrow \hat{S}. \tag{12}$$

Define

$$\begin{aligned}\tilde{d}_s(\bar{s},\hat{s}) &= \mathbb{E}_S\{d_s(S,\hat{s})|\bar{S}=\bar{s}\}\\ &= \mathbb{E}_S\{\mathbb{1}(S\neq\hat{s})|\bar{S}=\bar{s}\}\\ &= 1-\mathbb{E}_S\{\mathbb{1}(S=\hat{s})|\bar{S}=\bar{s}\}\\ &= 1-P(S=\hat{s}|\bar{S}=\bar{s}).\end{aligned} \tag{13}$$

Since the joint distribution of S and $\bar{S}$ is known, $\tilde{d}(\bar{s},\hat{s})$ can be calculated for each pair $(\bar{S},\hat{S})$.

Theorem 2. *The rate–distortion behavior of the HCTC scheme is equivalent to the rate–distortion function of the hard classification result $\bar{S}$ using the distortion metric defined in (13).*

Proof. See Appendix B. □

Remark 2. *Theorem 2 shows that the rate–distortion performance of the HCTC scheme can be reduced to the rate–distortion function of a discrete source, enabling numerical computation using the Blahut–Arimoto (BA) algorithm [46] and its variants such as [47].*

Corollary 1. *A sufficient condition for the optimality of the HCTC scheme is as follows: $\forall x_1, x_2 \in \mathcal{X}_u, t=[1:L]$, $P(S=t|X=x_1)=P(S=t|X=x_2)$, where $\mathcal{X}_u=\{x|P(S=u|X=x)\geq P(S=i|X=x), \forall i=[1:L]\}$.*

Proof. See Appendix C. □

Remark 3. *The condition in Corollary 1 implies that all the observations X leading to the same hard classification result convey identical information about the intrinsic state S. Consequently, compressing the hard classification result $\bar{S}$ introduces no additional distortion compared to directly compressing the original observation X.*

3.2.2. Symmetric Cases and Soft Classification

Based on Theorem 1, the classification rate–distortion function can be computed by alternatively optimizing $g_t(x)$ and $P(\hat{S}=t), t=[1:L]$, in a manner similar to the BA algorithm [48].

When $\lambda>0$, if all $P(\hat{S}=t), t=1,2,\cdots$ are initialized as $\frac{1}{L}$ and remain unchanged after the first iteration, then in all subsequent iterations, we have

$$\begin{aligned} g_t(x)^{(i)} &= \frac{P(\hat{S}=t)^{(i-1)}e^{\frac{\lambda P_t f_t(x)}{f(x)}}}{\sum\limits_{w=1}^{L} P(\hat{S}=w)^{(i-1)}e^{\frac{\lambda P_w f_w(x)}{f(x)}}}\\ P(\hat{S}=t)^{(i)} &= \frac{1}{L}, \forall t\in[1:L], \end{aligned} \tag{14}$$

thus achieving convergence. For such composite sources, the optimal transition functions are given by

$$g_t(x) = \frac{e^{\frac{\lambda P_t f_t(x)}{f(x)}}}{\sum\limits_{w=1}^{L} e^{\frac{\lambda P_w f_w(x)}{f(x)}}}, \forall t\in[1:L]. \tag{15}$$

Equation (15) shows that $g_t(x)$ takes the form of a softmax function with coefficient λ applied to the conditional probability $P(S=t|X=x)$. Unlike (7), this expression does not involve the marginal probability of $\hat{S}$. Consequently, $g_t(x)$ can be directly derived from the joint distribution of S and X using (15), without the need to solve any nonlinear equations. This significantly simplifies the computation.

Lemma 1. *The optimal transition probability functions take the form of (15), if and only if*

$$\int_{\mathcal{X}} f(x) \frac{e^{\frac{\lambda P_t f_t(x)}{f(x)}}}{\sum_{w=1}^{L} P e^{\frac{\lambda P_w f_w(x)}{f(x)}}} dx = \frac{1}{L}, \forall t \in [1:L]. \tag{16}$$

Proposition 1. *One type of composite source that satisfies the condition in Lemma 1 is as follows (assume the source has L states):*

- *The number of states is finite, and the observation space satisfies $\mathcal{X} \subseteq \mathbb{R}^K$.*
- *The probability distributions of the sub-sources are distinct.*
- $P_t = \frac{1}{L}, \forall t \in [1:L]$.
- *Let μ_t denote the mean of the t-th sub-source. There exists a point μ_0 such that $||\mu_t - \mu_0||_2^2$ is equal for all t. For simplicity and without loss of generality, assume $\mu_0 = 0$ in the following discussion.*
- *For any two sub-sources indexed by a and b, there exists an orthonormal matrix H such that*
  (1) $\mu_b = H\mu_a$.
  (2) $\forall t \in [1:L], \exists u \in [1:L], s.t.$

$$f_u(Hx) = f_t(x), \forall x \in \mathcal{X}, \tag{17}$$

specifically,

$$f_b(Hx) = f_a(x), \forall x \in \mathcal{X} \tag{18}$$

  (3) *If $x \in \mathcal{X}$, $Hx \in \mathcal{X}$.*

Proof. See Appendix D. □

Unfortunately, many practical scenarios do not satisfy the conditions in Proposition 1. Nevertheless, (15) can still be employed to obtain an achievable upper bound of the classification rate–distortion function in cases where the rate–distortion function itself is difficult to solve. Moreover, (15) induces a simplified soft classification scheme, in which the conditional probabilities $P(\hat{S} = t|X = x)$ follow the transition functions $g_t(x)$ in (15). In the remainder of this paper, the soft classification scheme refers to this simplified version.

Assume a length-n sequence of observation X^n (with n sufficiently large). The steps of the soft-classification are as follows:

- Calculate the transition probabilities from observation X to the classification result $\hat{S}$ using (20).
- Calculate the marginal distribution $P(\hat{S})$ and the mutual information $I(X;\hat{S})$.
- $\forall R > I(X;\hat{S})$, randomly generate a codebook $\mathcal{C}$ containing 2^{nR} i.i.d. sequences $\hat{S}^n$ drawn according to $P(\hat{S})$. Each sequence is a codeword, indexed by $\mathcal{W} \in \{1, 2, \cdots, 2^{nR}\}$.
- When encoding, select the codeword that is distortion typical [45] with X^n. If there is more than one such $\hat{S}^n$, choose the one with the smallest index $\mathcal{W}$. If no such codeword exists for a given X^n, encode it using $\mathcal{W} = 1$.
- At the decoder, recover the sequence $\hat{S}^n$ from the received index $\mathcal{W}$ using the codebook $\mathcal{C}$. Due to the properties of the distortion-typical set, the rate–distortion pair (R, D) is achievable for any $R > I(X;\hat{S})$.

Theorem 3. *An achievable upper bound on the classification rate–distortion function is given by*

$$\begin{aligned} R(D_s) &\leq I(\tilde{g}_t) \\ &\leq \log L + \int_{\mathcal{X}} f(x) \sum_{t=1}^{L} \tilde{g}_t(x) \log_2 \tilde{g}_t(x) dx, \end{aligned} \tag{19}$$

where

$$\tilde{g}_t(x) = \frac{e^{\frac{sP_t f_t(x)}{f(x)}}}{\sum_{w=1}^{L} e^{\frac{sP_w f_w(x)}{f(x)}}}, \tag{20}$$

and s is set to satisfy

$$1 - \int_{\mathcal{X}} \sum_{t=1}^{L} P_t f_t(x) \tilde{g}_t(x) dx = D_s. \tag{21}$$

$$I(\tilde{g}_t) = \sum_{t=1}^{L} \int_{\mathcal{X}} f(x) \tilde{g}_t(x) \log_2 \frac{\tilde{g}_t(x)}{\int f(x) \tilde{g}_t(x) dx} dx \tag{22}$$

is the rate required by this scheme. Its upper bound, denoted as $R_{ub}(\tilde{g}_t)$, is given in the last line of (19).

Proposition 2. *The slope of the upper bound $R_{ub}(\tilde{g}_t)$ is $-s \log_2 e$, and s varies from 0 to $+\infty$, with the classification changing from "soft" to "hard". As $s \to +\infty$, $\forall x$ with unique t^*, the classification becomes the hard classification, corresponding to the optimal Bayesian classification. Conversely, When $s = 0$, the classifier performs classification completely randomly.*

Proof. See Appendix E. □

Remark 4. *Denote the rate of the soft classifier as R_s. Let $R_s(s)$ and $D_s(s)$ denote the rate and distortion, respectively, of the classifier parameterized by a fixed s. The corresponding upper bound on the rate is denoted as $R_{ub}(s)$.*

Proposition 2 can be expressed as

$$\frac{dR_{ub}}{dD_s} = -s \log_2 e. \tag{23}$$

Consider the upper bound R_{ub}. Let $D_{s,min}$ denote the minimum achievable distortion, attained by the Bayesian optimal classifier, (i.e., the hard classification). Now suppose a small additional distortion Δ_D beyond $D_{s,min}$ is acceptable. In this scenario, since the classifier is almost a hard one, we have $s \to +\infty$. When the distortion increases by Δ_D, R_{ub} can be reduced by $\delta_{R_{ub}} \approx s \log_2 e \Delta_D$. This indicates that even a slight relaxation in the distortion constraint can significantly reduce the rate upper bound of the soft classification scheme.

Equation (20) gives the form of transition probability from the observation X to the classification result $\hat{S}$. Consider the following example of a four-class classification problem. Assume a composite source with state S and observation X. When $S = t$, $X \sim \mathcal{N}(\mu_t, I)$, where I is the identity matrix and $\mu_1 = (1,0), \mu_2 = (0,1), \mu_3 = (-1,0), \mu_4 = (0,-1)$. Figure 3a–c illustrate $\tilde{g}_1(x)$ for $s = 0, 1$, and 100, respectively.

When $s = 0$, the transition probability $\tilde{g}_1(x)$ is 0.25 for all $X = x$, indicating completely random classification. Comparing the cases where $s = 1$ and $s = 100$, the latter case is very close to the hard classification since s is very large. As shown in Figure 3c, the transition probability function is almost 0-1 binary.

In the HCTC scheme, the classification results are compressed without considering the posterior probabilities $P(S = t|X = x)$ for different x. Such compression can cause significant distortion since the classification results of X with "clear" states are also compressed. In contrast, in the soft classification scheme (Figure 3b), for $X = x$ with "ambiguous" states (e.g., the point $(0,0)$), $H(\hat{S}|X = x)$ is significantly greater than 0. Consequently, the rate allocated to these classification results is much lower than that allocated to X with more certain states. Therefore, compression mainly occurs in these "ambiguous" regions. In these regions, the optimal classification already introduces non-negligible distortion. As a result, saving bits for these observations does not lead to significant additional distortion.

When the classification distortion constraint is tight, the rate that can be saved is limited. Therefore, the soft classification scheme, by concentrating bit savings primarily on X with "ambiguous" states, can achieve a smaller distortion than the HCTC scheme.

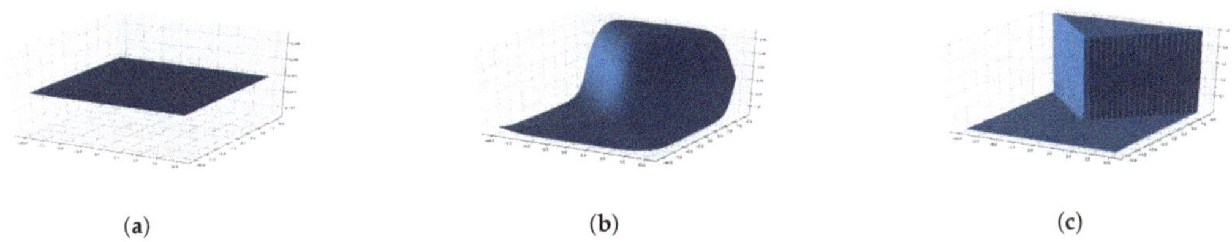

Figure 3. $\tilde{g}_1(x)$ when s is set to 0, 1 and 100. **(a)** $\tilde{g}_1(x)$ when $s = 0$, **(b)** $\tilde{g}_1(x)$ when $s = 1$, **(c)** $\tilde{g}_1(x)$ when $s = 100$.

As shown in Corollary 1, when the "ambiguity" of observations with the same hard classification result is identical, the performance of the HCTC scheme is no worse than that of the soft classification scheme. When the prior probabilities of the states are different and the classification distortion constraint is loose, the performance of the HCTC scheme can even surpass that of the soft classification. In the soft classification scheme, as $s \to 0$, $\tilde{g}_t(x) \to \frac{1}{L}, \forall t = [1 : L], x \in \mathcal{X}$. Thus, when $R = 0$, $D = 1 - \frac{1}{L}$, the classification becomes completely random, regardless of the prior distribution of the states. In contrast, the HCTC scheme classifies all observations into the class with the highest prior probability, resulting in a smaller distortion compared to the soft classification scheme.

It is also noteworthy that, unlike deep neural networks with the output of the softmax results, our soft classification scheme does not output the posterior distribution of the states. In practical applications, the observations are first compressed into an index $\mathcal{W}$. Then the classification results are decoded based on $\mathcal{W}$. Therefore, the soft classification scheme directly outputs a reconstruction of the state. Its difference from the hard classification is that, when the rate is constrained, by incorporating the source statistics and applying stronger compression to the "ambiguous" observations, the soft classification can reduce the expected distortion.

4. Classification-Aided Reconstruction of Composite Sources

In this section, we consider the case where the reconstruction distortion is constrained. The metric of the reconstruction distortion is the MSE distortion.

Consider an achievable upper bound of $R(D_o)$. This problem can be formulated as the optimization problem (3). One approach is to perform direct lossy compression on the observation. Nevertheless, for most sources, the matched codebook is difficult to obtain. In contrast, for Gaussian sources, which are widely adopted in signal processing tasks, the codebook is easy to obtain. Therefore, in such cases, the codebook of a Gaussian source with the same variance (covariance matrix), can be used as a substitute. However, some sources have large variances, leading to poor rate–distortion performance when compressed directly. In [44], the magnitude classifying quantization (MCQ) scheme is proposed. In this scheme, the observation is first classified according to its amplitude. Then the observations are compressed by sub-encoders corresponding to the classification result. The study shows that classification changes the variance of the input to each sub-encoder. Hence when using Gaussian codebooks, although an additional rate is introduced for classification, the overall rate of the MCQ scheme can still be lower than that of direct compression in some cases.

In this section, the soft classification introduced in Section 3.2.2 is adopted, and the classification-aided-compression (CAC) scheme is proposed. Based on this scheme, an achievable upper bound of $R(D_o)$ is also derived.

Another upper bound of $R(D_o)$ is as follows:

$$\begin{aligned} R(D_o) &\leq I(X;\hat{X}) \\ &\leq I(X;\hat{S},\hat{X}) \\ &= I(X;\hat{S}) + I(X;\hat{X}|\hat{S}). \end{aligned} \tag{24}$$

Inequality (24) implies the CAC scheme to encode the observation of an L-state composite source X under the reconstruction distortion D_o. The first term represents classification, while the second term represents compression using the corresponding encoder according to the classification result.

The specific steps of the scheme are as follows:

- Select a distortion level D and perform the soft classification. Denote the result as $\hat{S}$.
- Encode X using the corresponding Gaussian encoder based on the soft classification result.

Figure 4 illustrates the steps of the CAC scheme.

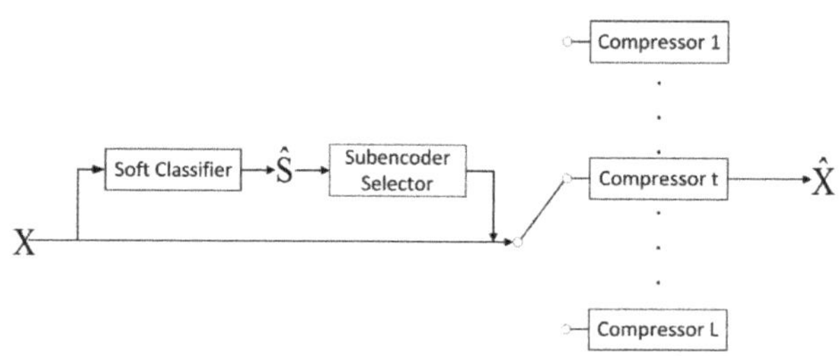

Figure 4. The procedure of the CAC scheme.

An upper bound of $R(D_o)$ can be derived from the scheme described above.

Theorem 4. *An achievable upper bound of $R(D_o)$ is*

$$R(D_o) \leq \min_{D \in [D_{s,min}, D_{s,max}]} \{R_s(D) + \sum_{u=1}^{L} P(\hat{S}=u) R_{\tilde{X}_u,g}\}, \tag{25}$$

where $D_{s,min}$ and $D_{s,max}$ are the minimum and maximum classification distortions that can be achieved by the soft classifier, $R_s(D)$ is the rate at the classification distortion D when using the soft classification scheme in Section 3.2.2, $P(\hat{S}=u)$ is obtained from (8), and

$$R_{\tilde{X}_u,g} = \frac{1}{2}\sum_{i=1}^{K} \log_2 \frac{\sigma_{ui}^2}{D_{ui}}. \tag{26}$$

In (26), K denotes the dimension of X. σ_{ui}^2 is the i-th eigenvalue of Σ_u, where

$$\Sigma_u = \frac{\int_{\mathcal{X}} f(x) g_{D,u}(x)(x-\gamma_u)(x-\gamma_u)^T dx}{\int_{\mathcal{X}} f(x) g_{D,u}(x) dx}, \tag{27}$$

$$\gamma_u = \frac{\int_{\mathcal{X}} x f(x) g_{D,u}(x) dx}{\int_{\mathcal{X}} f(x) g_{D,u}(x) dx}, \tag{28}$$

and $g_{D,u}(x)$ is the transition probability function of the soft classification scheme that satisfies (21) with the right-hand side replaced by D. For D_{ui}, we have

$$D_{ui} = \min\{\alpha, \sigma_{ui}^2\}, \tag{29}$$

where α is chosen to satisfy

$$\sum_{u=1}^{L} \sum_{i=1}^{K} P(\hat{S} = u) D_{ui} = D_o. \tag{30}$$

Proof. See Appendix F. □

For the CAC scheme, in the compression step, X is compressed using a Gaussian encoder. Define

$$R_{ub}(D_o) \triangleq R_s(D) + \sum_{u=1}^{L} P(\hat{S} = u) R_{\tilde{X}_u, g}, \tag{31}$$

where $D \in [D_{s,min}, D_{s,max}]$. We have

$$\begin{aligned} R_{ub}(D_o) &= R_s(D) + \frac{1}{2} \sum_{u=1}^{L} P(\hat{S} = u) \sum_{i=1}^{K} \log_2 \frac{\sigma_{ui}^2}{D_{ui}} \\ &= R_s(D) + \frac{1}{2} \sum_{u=1}^{L} P(\hat{S} = u) \log_2(\det(\Sigma_u)) - \frac{1}{2} \sum_{u=1}^{L} \sum_{i=1}^{K} P(\hat{S} = u) \log_2 D_{ui}. \end{aligned} \tag{32}$$

Consider two special cases where $s = 0$ and $s \to +\infty$. When $s = 0$, (20) becomes $\tilde{g}_t = 1/L$. Thus $P(\hat{S} = u) = 1/L, \forall u = [1 : L]$. Hence $\forall u = [1 : L]$, the pdf of X given the condition that $\hat{S} = u$ is

$$\begin{aligned} f(x|\hat{S} = u) &= \frac{P(X = x, \hat{S} = u)}{P(\hat{S} = u)} \\ &= \frac{f(x)\frac{1}{L}}{\frac{1}{L}} \\ &= f(x). \end{aligned} \tag{33}$$

From (33), we can see that when $s = 0$, the input to each sub-encoder obeys the same distribution as the composite source. It is also evident that, in this case, the rate required for the classification part is 0. Hence when $s = 0$, the CAC scheme reduces to the direct compression. As $s \to +\infty$, the classification becomes hard classification. In this case, the scheme is similar to the MCQ method proposed in [44], where a pre-compression classification based on amplitude is performed.

In the compression step, X is first subtracted by the mean of the corresponding sub-encoder input, resulting in a zero-mean vector for encoding. Then, orthogonal transformations are applied separately to the vectors to be encoded by each sub-encoder, ensuring their components are mutually uncorrelated. After the transformation, the distortion allocation D_{ui} to each component of different classification results follows the classical reverse water-filling strategy. The only difference is that each D_{ui} is weighted by its corresponding probability $P(\hat{S} = u)$.

When $D_o \leq K\sigma_{ui}^2, \forall u = [1:L], i = [1:K]$, according to (29), all D_{ui} are equal. Hence, $D_{ui} = \alpha$ and (32) can be rewritten as

$$\begin{aligned} R_{ub}(D_o) &= R_s(D) + \frac{1}{2}\sum_{u=1}^{L} P(\hat{S}=u)\log_2(\det(\Sigma_u)) - \frac{1}{2}\sum_{u=1}^{L}\sum_{i=1}^{K} P(\hat{S}=u)\log_2\alpha \\ &= R_s(D) + \frac{1}{2}\sum_{u=1}^{L} P(\hat{S}=u)\log_2(\det(\Sigma_u)) - \frac{K}{2}\log_2\alpha. \end{aligned} \tag{34}$$

In (34), the third term depends solely on α. According to (30), we have

$$D_{ui} = \alpha = \frac{D_o}{K}, \tag{35}$$

Hence the third term in (34) is solely determined by D_o. Denote $D_T = K\sigma^{*2}$, where σ^{*2} denotes the minimum eigenvalue among all Σ_u across classifiers with $s \geq 0$ (with s being the coefficient in (20) that controls the softness of the classifier). It can also be observed that in (34), the first two terms depend only on the classification operation and are independent of D_o. Thus, when $D_o \leq D_T$, the effects of the classifier and D_o on R_{ub} can be completely decoupled, which is convenient for further analysis. Therefore, the optimal classifier can be obtained by optimizing s to minimize the first two terms when $D_o \leq D_T$.

In the high-resolution case, D_o is very small, thus satisfying the condition above. Denote the first two terms in (34) as $RC(s)$, i.e., $RC(s) = R_s(D) + \frac{1}{2}\sum_{u=1}^{L} P(\hat{S} = u)\log_2(\det(\Sigma_u))$. Let $D_o(s,R)$ denote the reconstruction distortion achieved by the CAC scheme when the coefficient of the classifier is s and the total rate is R. From (34), we have

$$\begin{aligned} D_o(s,R) &= K2^{\frac{2}{K}(RC(s)-R)} \\ &= K2^{\frac{2}{K}RC(s)}2^{-\frac{2}{K}R}. \end{aligned} \tag{36}$$

Hence in the high-resolution case, the achievable distortion of this scheme exhibits an exponential decay with respect to the rate R. By selecting a proper classifier, the coefficient of the function can be minimized, thus minimizing the reconstruction distortion.

As the reconstruction distortion constraint becomes more relaxed, the reverse water-filling scheme allows for completely omitting the bits used to reconstruct components corresponding to small eigenvalues in the covariance matrices of each classification result.

5. Numerical Result

In this section, we present and compare numerical results of the schemes developed in the previous sections.

5.1. Soft Classification and HCTC

This section presents and compares the performance of the schemes proposed in Section 3.2 under various settings. The procedures of the two schemes are detailed in Sections 3.2.1 and 3.2.2, respectively.

First, we consider the Gaussian mixture (GM) source model with equal prior probabilities for all states. The distributions of the composite sources in the first seven settings are given as follows. For each setting, let μ_t denote the mean of the t-th state, and Σ_t its covariance matrix.

In the first two settings, the sources are 4-state GM sources. In both settings, $\mu_1 = (1,0)$, $\mu_2 = (0,1)$, $\mu_3 = (-1,0)$, $\mu_4 = (0,-1)$. In the first setting, $\Sigma_t = \mathbf{I}_{2\times 2}, t = 1,2,3,4$. In the second setting, $\Sigma_t = 2\mathbf{I}_{2\times 2}, t = 1,2,3,4$.

In the next two settings, the sources remain 4-state GM sources, and the covariance matrices of all states are again identity matrices. In the third setting, the mean points of the states are $\mu_1 = (1,1)$, $\mu_2 = (-1,1)$, $\mu_3 = (-1,-1)$, $\mu_4 = (1,-1)$. In the fourth setting, the mean points of the states are $\mu_1 = (3,3)$, $\mu_2 = (-3,3)$, $\mu_3 = (-3,-3)$, $\mu_4 = (3,-3)$.

These four settings perfectly satisfy the conditions in Proposition 1. Hence in these settings, the rate–distortion function $R(D_s)$ attains the value of the upper bound $R_{ub}(\tilde{g}_t)$.

In the fifth setting, the number of states is increased to 9, with the mean points of the different states illustrated in Figure 5a. Furthermore, the number of states is further increased to 16 and 32 as shown in Figures 5b and 5c, respectively. In these three settings, the covariance matrix of each state remains the identity matrix. The performance of the soft classification scheme and the HCTC scheme is compared under these seven settings as depicted in Figure 6.

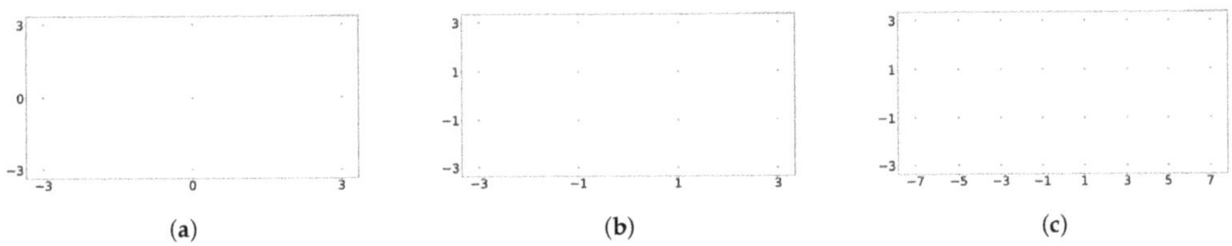

Figure 5. The mean points distribution of the fifth, sixth and seventh settings. (**a**) The mean points distribution of the fifth setting. (**b**) The mean points distribution of the sixth setting. (**c**) The mean points distribution of the seventh setting.

As shown in Figure 6, the soft classification scheme consistently outperforms the HCTC scheme in all seven settings. In some cases, such as the sources depicted in Figures 6e–g, the conditions in Proposition 1 are not satisfied, indicating that the transition probability functions in (15) are not optimal. In Figures 6e,f, the performance of both schemes is compared with the rate–distortion function obtained from the constrained BA (CBA) algorithm [47]. In these cases, even with the suboptimal transition probability functions (20), the soft classification scheme still outperforms the HCTC scheme, and its performance is close to the rate–distortion function, especially when the distortion is near the minimum. As analyzed in Section 3.2.2, the soft classification scheme can better exploit the "ambiguity" in a composite source, thus reducing the rate without significantly increasing the distortion.

It is also noteworthy that in some sources, the gap between the two schemes is significant, while in some others, it is not. Figure 7 shows how the ratio of the bits required for the soft classification and the HCTC schemes changes as the extra classification distortion allowed beyond the Bayesian minimum classification distortion increases in different sources. In this figure, D_s denotes the distortion constraint, and $D_{s,min}$ denotes the Bayesian minimum distortion. The classification distortion constraint D_s takes the value from $D_{s,min}$ to 0.5 for all sources. The second setting is not shown in this figure since in this setting, the Bayesian minimum distortion is greater than 0.5.

As shown in Figure 7, the ratio of the bits required by the two schemes decreases dramatically as the distortion constraint D_s increases slightly compared to the Bayesian minimum distortion in all sources, except for the fourth setting. In the fourth setting, the distances between the states are large relative to their variances, resulting in a very small probability of "ambiguity" for the state corresponding to the observation. As mentioned in Section 3.2.2, the soft classification scheme primarily exploits the "ambiguity" of the states. Hence in this setting, there is no significant difference between the two schemes.

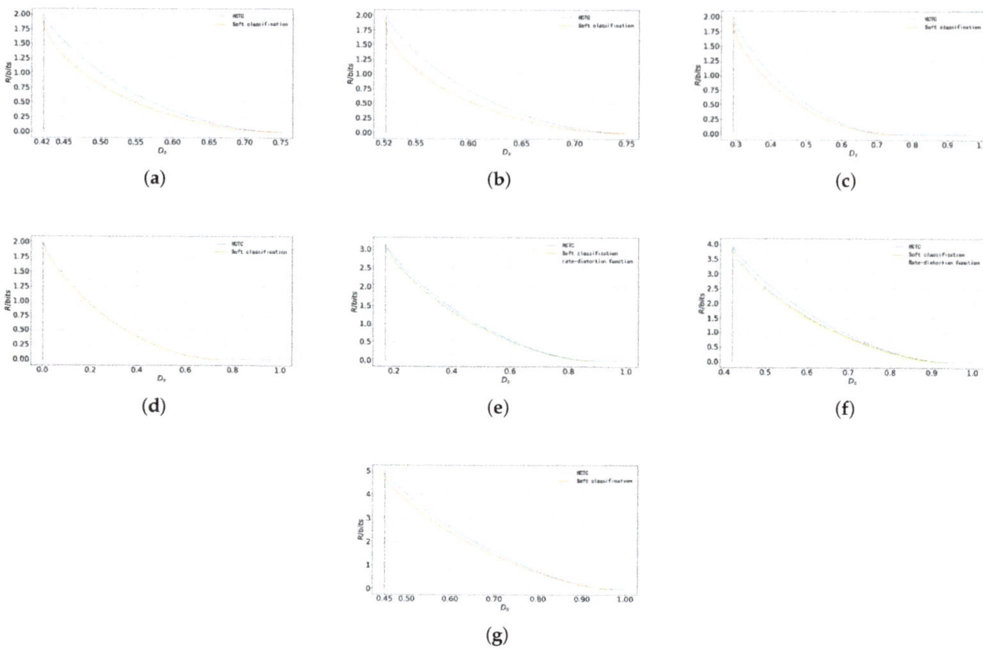

Figure 6. The classification rate–distortion performance of the soft classification scheme versus the HCTC scheme for the 4-state, 16-state, and 32-state composite sources. (a) The classification rate–distortion performance of the soft classification scheme versus the HCTC scheme for the first setting. (b) The classification rate–distortion performance of the soft classification scheme versus the HCTC scheme for the second setting. (c) The classification rate–distortion performance of the soft classification scheme versus the HCTC scheme for the third setting. (d) The classification rate–distortion performance of the soft classification scheme versus the HCTC scheme for the fourth setting. (e) The classification rate–distortion performance of the soft classification scheme versus the HCTC scheme for the fifth setting. (f) The classification rate–distortion performance of the soft classification scheme versus the HCTC scheme for sixth setting. (g) The classification rate–distortion performance of the soft classification scheme versus the HCTC scheme for seventh setting.

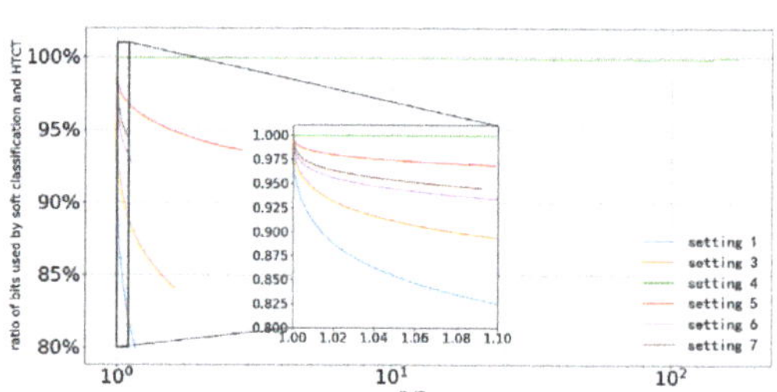

Figure 7. The change in the ratio of the bits required for the soft classification and the HCTC as the extra classification distortion constraint beyond the Bayesian minimum classification distortion increases in different sources.

Now, we compare the first, third, and fourth settings. All three settings have four states, and the covariance matrices of the states are identity matrices. As shown in Figure 7, in the sources where the states are closer to each other, the soft classification scheme achieves more significant bit savings. This still holds when comparing the fourth, fifth, and sixth settings, where the number of states varies. In these three settings, the outermost mean points are located at the same positions. Thus, as the number of states increases, the distances between the states decrease, and the performance gap between the two schemes becomes larger.

An interesting finding emerges from the comparison among the third, sixth, and seventh settings. Although the minimum distances between the mean points are the same across these three sources, the ratio of the bits required by the two schemes approaches one as the number of states increases. A straightforward explanation is that adding more states in this manner does not introduce significant additional "ambiguity" to the source, since, for most observations, only a few (at most 4) states have non-negligible posterior probabilities. Nevertheless, as the number of states increases, both schemes require more bits. Thus the relative gap between the two schemes narrows.

In some other cases, however, the degree of "ambiguity" is consistent across all parts of the source. In such scenarios, the advantages of soft classification become less evident. Consider a 4-class composite source where the observation X is also discrete when $S = i(i = [1:4]), P(X = i) = 0.7, P(X = j) = 0.1, \forall j = [1:4], j \neq i$.

Figure 8 shows the rate–distortion performance of the HCTC scheme and soft classification scheme in this discrete composite source. Figure 8a illustrates the cases where the prior probabilities of the states are all equal. The result shows that the performance of the two schemes is identical. Figure 8b shows the case where the prior probabilities of the states are unequal, with $P(S = 1) = 0.4, P(S = 2) = P(S = 3) = P(S = 4) = 0.2$. In this setting, the performance of the soft classification scheme is inferior to that of the HCTC scheme, which aligns with the analysis presented in Section 3.2.2.

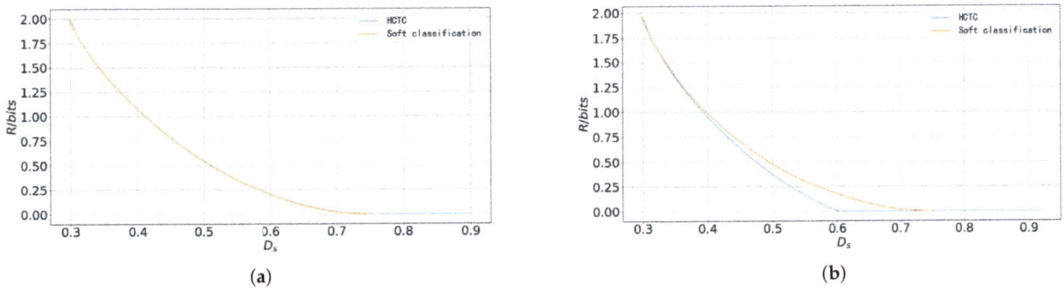

Figure 8. The rate–distortion performance of the composite sources with discrete observation. (**a**) The rate–distortion performance of the composite source with discrete observation with equal prior probabilities of states, (**b**) The rate–distortion performance of the composite source with discrete observation with unequal prior probabilities of states.

In Figure 9, the performance of the soft classification scheme, the HCTC scheme, and the rate–distortion function (obtained via the CBA algorithm) is compared in a four-component composite source, where the sub-sources are the same as those in the first setting. The difference lies in the prior probabilities of the states: $P(S = 1) = 0.4$, $P(S = 2) = 0.2$, $P(S = 3) = 0.2, P(S = 4) = 0.2$. This setting clearly illustrates the strengths and weaknesses of the two schemes. When the distortion constraint is very loose, the HCTC scheme performs better since the soft classification tends to classify observations with an almost uniform distribution, while the HCTC scheme tends to classify the observations into the state with higher prior probability, leading to lower distortion. However, when the distortion constraint is tight, the soft classification outperforms the HCTC scheme by better saving bits in the "ambiguous" regions without significantly increasing the distortion.

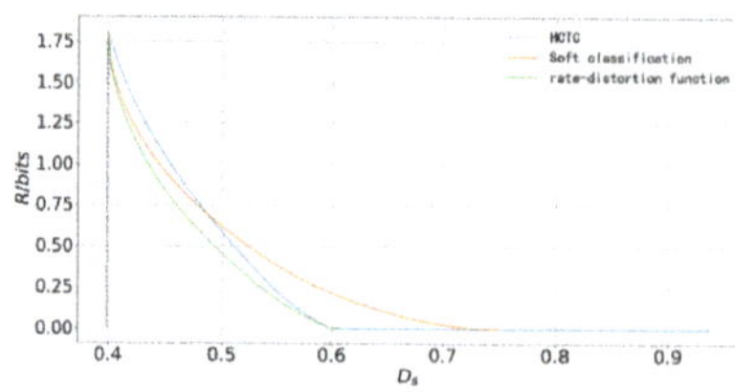

Figure 9. The rate–distortion performance of soft classification scheme and HCTC scheme in the composite source where the prior distribution of states in the first setting is changed to be non-uniform.

5.2. Upper Bound of Reconstruction Rate–Distortion Function

In this part, the achievable upper bounds of $R(D_o)$ and their properties are shown in five cases.

The first setting is the same as the four-class Gaussian mixture source in Section 5.1. In the second setting, the distances between different sub-sources are increased, with $\mu_1 = (3,0)$, $\mu_2 = (0,3)$, $\mu_3 = (-3,0)$, $\mu_4 = (0,-3)$. The covariance matrices of all sub-sources remain identity matrices. The third setting considers a two-component composite source, where X is a scalar. Specifically, $X \sim \mathcal{N}(0,1)$ when $S = 1$, and $X \sim \mathcal{N}(0,25)$ when $S = 2$. The fourth setting is also a one-dimensional two-component GM source, where $X \sim \mathcal{N}(-1,1)$ when $S = 1$, and $X \sim \mathcal{N}(1,25)$ when $S = 2$. The fifth setting involves a four-component two-dimensional GM source. When $S = t$, $X \sim \mathcal{N}(0,\Sigma_t)$. We have

$$\Sigma_1 = \begin{pmatrix} 1 & 0 \\ 0 & 1 \end{pmatrix}, \Sigma_2 = \begin{pmatrix} 1 & 0 \\ 0 & 25 \end{pmatrix}, \Sigma_3 = \begin{pmatrix} 25 & 0 \\ 0 & 1 \end{pmatrix}, \Sigma_4 = \begin{pmatrix} 5 & 0 \\ 0 & 5 \end{pmatrix}. \quad (37)$$

In all of these settings, the distribution of the state S is uniform.

As mentioned in Section 4, the influence of D_s and D_o on R_{ub} can be decoupled, and the optimal classifier can be obtained by minimizing $RC(s)$ when the reconstruction distortion constraint satisfies $D_o \leq D_T$. The function $RC(s)$ in the first three settings is shown in Figure 10.

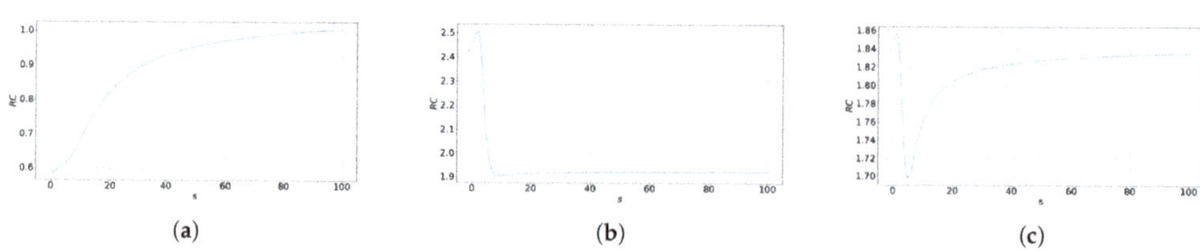

Figure 10. The plot of $RC(s)$ in different settings. (**a**) $RC(s)$ in the first setting, (**b**) $RC(s)$ in the second setting, and (**c**) $RC(s)$ in the third setting.

As s increases, the classification rate $R_s(D)$ also increases. Nevertheless, changing s also changes the conditional covariance matrices Σ_u corresponding to each classification result. Thus, a tradeoff arises between the classification rate and the determinants of these covariance matrices.

In the first setting, the distributions of different states are close to each other, leading to a small determinant for the overall covariance matrix. Consequently, classification does not significantly reduce the determinants of the conditional covariance matrices. On the contrary, it introduces additional code length. Since the classification rate dominates in $RC(s)$, the value of $RC(s)$ increases as the classification becomes harder.

In other cases where the determinant of the initial covariance matrix is large, such as in the second setting, applying a harder classification before compression can make the conditional distributions of the observation corresponding to each classification result more "concentrated", thus reducing the determinants. Therefore, harder classification can help save bits as illustrated in Figure 10b.

In some cases, however, proper soft classification can help save bits as shown in Figure 10c. Specifically, in the third setting, it can be explained as follows. The weighted average of the input variances of the two sub-encoders, weighted by the probabilities of the classification results, remains unchanged after classification. Since the logarithmic function is concave, the corresponding weighted average of the log-variances of the sub-encoders after classification is smaller than that of the entire composite source, thereby reducing $RC(s)$. Nevertheless, when hard classification is applied, the weighted log-variance cannot be further reduced significantly, while the classification rate R_s increases.

The curves of the achievable upper bounds $R_{ub}(D_o)$ in the first two settings are shown in Figure 11. The performance is compared with the achievable upper bound $R_1(D_o)$ of the rate–distortion function proposed in [6]. The bound $R_1(D_o)$ characterizes the achievable rate–distortion pairs when a codebook matched to the source statistics is available and is asymptotically tight at high rates. In addition, the CAC scheme with a hard classifier is similar to the MCQ scheme in [44].

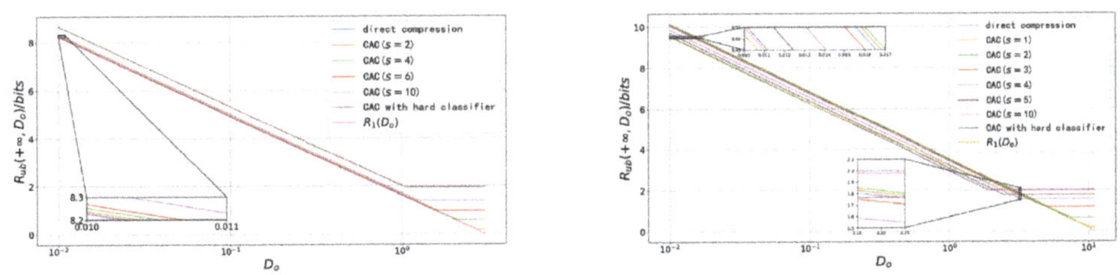

(a) (b)

Figure 11. The plot of $R_{ub}(+\infty, D_o)$ in different settings. (**a**) $R_{ub}(+\infty, D_o)$ in the first setting, (**b**) $R_{ub}(+\infty, D_o)$ in the second setting.

The results align with the $RC(s)$ curve in Figure 10. At high rates, classifiers with smaller $RC(s)$ values lead to lower distortion. In the first setting, direct compression performs better, while in the second setting, the CAC scheme with a hard classifier achieves better performance. In Figure 11b, the CAC scheme with a properly chosen classifier performs closely to the $R_1(D_o)$ bound at high rates. This indicates that when the codebook matched to the source statistics is unavailable and only Gaussian codebooks can be used, classification before compression can reduce the variance and thus lower the rate in this setting. Moreover, the performance of this scheme can approach that of using a matched codebook.

For a fixed classifier, when $D_o > D_T$, a series of inflection points appear as D_o increases. When $D_o > \sum_{u=1}^{L} P(\hat{S} = u) tr(\Sigma_u)$, reconstructing every observation as the mean of the input to the corresponding sub-encoder satisfies the constraint. In this case, no coding is needed for reconstruction, and the overall code length equals the classification code length. Therefore, when D_o is sufficiently large, a "softer" classifier can save bits. It can also be observed from Figure 11 that in these two settings, the "harder" the classifier, the smaller the values of D_o corresponding to the turning points. This is because in both cases, a "harder" classifier results in smaller eigenvalues and trace values of the covariance matrices.

Figure 11b further shows that for some composite sources, the optimal classifier varies with the reconstruction distortion constraint. Denote the optimal s as s^*. At high rates, $s^* = 10$, whereas when $D_o = 3.2$, $s^* = 4$.

Next, the high-rate scenario is studied in the last three settings.

Figure 12 compares the distortion–rate performance of three schemes—direct compression, CAC with a soft classifier, and CAC with a hard classifier—along with $D_1(R)$, the distortion–rate function corresponding to $R_1(D_o)$, under high rate conditions in the last three settings. It can be observed that, with a properly chosen soft classifier, the CAC scheme significantly outperforms the other two schemes in all settings. In the third setting, the CAC scheme with a soft classifier can achieve approximately a 15% reduction in distortion at the same rate compared to both direct compression and the CAC scheme with a hard classifier. In the fourth and fifth settings, the distortion reductions are approximately 21% and 25%, respectively. These numerical results are consistent with the analysis in Section 4, which shows that, under high-rate conditions and with a fixed classifier, the achievable distortion of the three schemes decays exponentially with the rate R. Under this condition, when the rate is the same for all three schemes, the ratio of the distortions remains constant, and this constant does not vary with the rate. Therefore, optimizing s in the classifier effectively minimizes the coefficient of the exponential function in (36), thereby minimizing the distortion. The comparison between the performance of the CAC scheme with a soft classifier and the $D_1(R)$ curve further demonstrates that, with a properly selected classifier and Gaussian codebooks, the CAC scheme can approach the rate–distortion performance of the scheme using codebook matched to the source statistics.

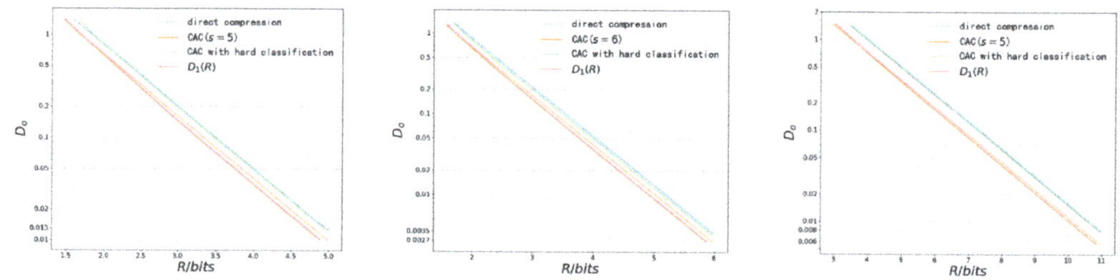

(a) (b) (c)

Figure 12. The distortion–rate performance of different schemes in the 3rd, 4th, and 5th settings. (**a**) The distortion–rate performance of different schemes in the third setting. (**b**) The distortion–rate performance of different schemes in the fourth setting. (**c**) The distortion–rate performance of different schemes in the fifth setting.

6. Conclusions

We have generalized the classification problem in [4,5] into the multi-class classification scenario. In the case where only the classification distortion is constrained, we have characterized the rate–distortion function and proposed two classification schemes based on two upper bounds. We have also studied the scenario where the reconstruction distortion is constrained and evaluated the performance of the CAC scheme. In our future work, we plan to explore methods for implementing soft classification or compression methods that asymptotically approach the information-theoretic performance limits. In addition, investigating data-driven methods for estimating the rate–distortion behaviors of composite sources under both constraints is also an interesting direction for future research.

Author Contributions: Conceptualization, W.Z.; Methodology, Y.C., W.Z. and J.L.; Software, Y.C. and J.L.; Validation, Y.C.; Formal Analysis, Y.C.; Investigation, Y.C. and W.Z.; Resources, W.Z.; Data Curation, Y.C. and J.L.; Writing—Original Draft Preparation, Y.C.; Writing—Review and Editing, W.Z. and Y.C.; Visualization, Y.C.; Supervision, W.Z.; Project Administration, W.Z.; Funding Acquisition, W.Z. All authors have read and agreed to the published version of the manuscript.

Funding: This work has been supported in part by the National Natural Science Foundation of China under Grant 62231022.

Institutional Review Board Statement: Not applicable.

Data Availability Statement: The data that support the findings of this study are available from the corresponding author upon reasonable request.

Conflicts of Interest: The authors declare no conflicts of interest.

Abbreviations

The following abbreviations are used in this manuscript:

MSE	Mean-Squared Error
HCTC	Hard-Classify-Then-Compress
CAC	Classification-Aided-Compression
AWGN	Additive White Gaussian Noise
HMM	Hidden Markov Model
MCQ	Magnitude Classifying Quantization
GM	Gaussian Mixture

Appendix A. Proof of Theorem 1

When encoding X, the state S cannot be observed. So the classification process can be simplified as a coding problem from X to $\hat{S}$. For $X = x$ and $\hat{S} = t$, the distortion $\hat{d}_s(x,t)$ is

$$\begin{aligned}\hat{d}_s(x,t) &= \mathbb{E}\{d_s(S,t)|X=x\}\\ &= 1 - P_{t|x},\end{aligned}$$

where $P_{t|x} = P(S = t|X = x)$. For convenience, such a shorthand will be used in the rest of this paper.

Hence the indirect rate–distortion problem is transformed into a direct one. The optimal transition function $g_t(x)$ can be derived from Section 4.2 of [3].

$$\begin{aligned}g_t(x) &= \frac{P(\hat{S}=t)e^{-\lambda(1-P_{t|x})}}{\sum\limits_{w=1}^{L} P(\hat{S}=w)e^{-\lambda(1-P_{w|x})}}\\ &= \frac{P(\hat{S}=t)e^{\lambda P_{t|x}}}{\sum\limits_{w=1}^{L} P(\hat{S}=w)e^{\lambda P_{w|x}}}\\ &= \frac{P(\hat{S}=t)e^{\frac{\lambda P_t f_t(x)}{f(x)}}}{\sum\limits_{w=1}^{L} P(\hat{S}=w)e^{\frac{\lambda P_w f_w(x)}{f(x)}}},\end{aligned}$$

where $P(\hat{S} = t)$ is the marginal probability of $\hat{S} = t$:

$$P(\hat{S}=t) = \int_{\mathcal{X}} f(x)g_t(x)dx.$$

The parameter λ is chosen to satisfy the constraint on classification distortion:

$$1 - \int_{\mathcal{X}} \sum_{t=1}^{L} P_t f_t(x) g_t(x) dx = D_s.$$

With the transition probability function, the rate (mutual information) can be obtained:

$$R(D_s) = \sum_{t=1}^{L} \int_{\mathcal{X}} f(x) g_t(x) \log_2 \frac{g_t(x)}{\int_{\mathcal{X}} f(x) g_t(x) dx} dx.$$

Appendix B. Proof of Theorem 2

From the chain rule of entropy, we have

$$\begin{aligned} H(\bar{S}, \hat{S}|X) &= H(\bar{S}|X) + H(\hat{S}|\bar{S}, X) \\ &= H(\hat{S}|X) + H(\bar{S}|X, \hat{S}). \end{aligned}$$

In the HCTC scheme, $\bar{S}$ is a function of X, which indicates that $H(\bar{S}|X) = 0$. Also we have $H(\bar{S}|X, \hat{S}) \leq H(\bar{S}|X) = 0$. Hence $H(\bar{S}|X, \hat{S}) = 0$.

From (12), we also have $H(\hat{S}|\bar{S}, X) = H(\hat{S}|\bar{S})$. Hence, we have $H(\hat{S}|\bar{S}) = H(\hat{S}|X)$. Therefore

$$\begin{aligned} I(X; \hat{S}) &= H(\hat{S}) - H(\hat{S}|X) \\ &= H(\hat{S}) - H(\hat{S}|\bar{S}) \\ &= I(\hat{S}; \bar{S}). \end{aligned}$$

For the distortion, the classification distortion constraint is $\mathbb{E}\{d_s(S, \hat{S})\} \leq D_s$. Since

$$\begin{aligned} \mathbb{E}_{\bar{S},\hat{S}}\{\tilde{d}_s(\bar{S}, \hat{S})\} &= \mathbb{E}_{\bar{S},\hat{S}}\{\mathbb{E}_S\{d_s(S, \hat{S})|\bar{S}\}\} \\ &= \mathbb{E}\{d_s(S, \hat{S})\}, \end{aligned}$$

the distortion constraint is equivalent to

$$\mathbb{E}_{\bar{S},\hat{S}}\{\tilde{d}_s(\bar{S}, \hat{S})\} \leq D_s.$$

Hence the rate–distortion property of the HCTC scheme can be transformed into the rate–distortion problem of compressing the hard classification result $\bar{S}$.

Appendix C. Proof of Corollary 1

For $x \in \mathcal{X}_u$, denote $P_{t|x} = P_{t|u}$.

$$\begin{aligned} P(S = t|\bar{S} = u) &= \frac{P(S = t, \bar{S} = u)}{P(\bar{S} = u)} \\ &= \frac{P_t \int_{\mathcal{X}_u} f_t(x) dx}{\int_{\mathcal{X}_u} f(x) dx} \\ &= \frac{\int_{\mathcal{X}_u} f(x) P_{t|x} dx}{\int_{\mathcal{X}_u} f(x) dx} \\ &= P_{t|u}. \end{aligned}$$

According to Theorem 2, we have

$$d(\hat{S} = t, \bar{S} = u) = 1 - P_{t|u}.$$

As the rate–distortion performance of the HCTC scheme is the rate–distortion function of $\bar{S}$, the transition probabilities from $\bar{S}$ to $\hat{S}$ are the same as the conditional probabilities in the rate–distortion function of discrete source $\bar{S}$. Denote the conditional probabilities $P(\hat{S}=t|\bar{S}=u)$ as $g_t(u)$, and it satisfies [3]

$$g_t(u) = \frac{P(\hat{S}=t)e^{\lambda P_{t|u}}}{\sum_{w=1}^{L} P(\hat{S}=w)e^{\lambda P_{w|u}}}$$
$$P(\hat{S}=t) = \sum_{u=1}^{L} P(\bar{S}=u)g_t(u).$$

Now consider the transition probability functions $g_t(x)$ that achieves the rate–distortion function $R(D_s)$. From Theorem 1, it satisfies

$$g_t(x) = \frac{P(\hat{S}=t)e^{\lambda P_{t|x}}}{\sum_{w=1}^{L} P(\hat{S}=w)e^{\lambda P_{w|x}}} \tag{A1}$$

$$P(\hat{S}=t) = \int_{\mathcal{X}} f(x)g_t(x)dx. \tag{A2}$$

Since $\forall x1, x2 \in \mathcal{X}_u$, the posterior probability distributions of the states are equal, we have $g_t(x_1) = g_t(x_2), \forall t = [1:L]$. Hence for $x \in \mathcal{X}_u$, $g_t(x)$ is a constant for each $t = 1, \ldots, L$. Denote the constant as Q_{tu}. (A1) can be rewritten as

$$Q_{tu} = \frac{P(\hat{S}=t)e^{\lambda P_{t|u}}}{\sum_{w=1}^{L} P(\hat{S}=w)e^{\lambda P_{w|u}}}$$

(A2) can be rewritten as

$$\begin{aligned} P(\hat{S}=t) &= \int_{\mathcal{X}} f(x)g_t(x)dx \\ &= \sum_{u=1}^{L} \int_{\mathcal{X}_u} f(x)Q_{tu}dx \\ &= \sum_{u=1}^{L} Q_{tu} \int_{\mathcal{X}_u} f(x)dx \\ &= \sum_{u=1}^{L} P(\bar{S}=u)Q_{tu} \end{aligned} \tag{A3}$$

So for $x \in \mathcal{X}_u$, $g_t(x) = g_t(u)$ satisfies the conditions of achieving the rate–distortion function $R(D_s)$. Hence the HCTC scheme has the optimal rate–distortion performance under this condition.

Appendix D. Proof of Proposition 1

In this section, we assume that $\mu_0 = \mathbf{0}$ for simplicity without loss of generality.

First, assume that the sub-source t_1 and t_2 both satisfy

$$f_{t_1}(x) = f_u(Hx)$$
$$f_{t_2}(x) = f_u(Hx).$$

This contradicts the second condition. Hence the orthonormal transformation transformation in Proposition 1 is one-to-one.

For the pdf of the entire source $f(x)$, we have

$$\begin{aligned} f(Hx) &= \frac{1}{L}\sum_{u=1}^{L} f_u(Hx) \\ &= \frac{1}{L}\sum_{t=1}^{L} f_t(x) \\ &= f(x). \end{aligned} \tag{A4}$$

The second equation stands because of the one-to-one property of the transformation. For the prior probability of classification result b, we have

$$\begin{aligned} P(\hat{S}=b) &= \int_{\mathcal{X}} f(x)\frac{e^{\lambda P(S=b|X=x)}}{\sum_{w=1}^{L} e^{\lambda P(S=w|X=x)}}dx \\ &= \int_{\mathcal{X}} f(Hx)\frac{e^{\lambda P(S=b|X=Hx)}}{\sum_{w=1}^{L} e^{\lambda P(S=w|X=Hx)}}dHx \\ &= \int_{\mathcal{X}} f(x)\frac{e^{\lambda P(S=b|X=Hx)}}{\sum_{w=1}^{L} e^{\lambda P(S=w|X=Hx)}}dHx \\ &= \int_{\mathcal{X}} f(x)\frac{e^{\lambda P(S=b|X=Hx)}}{\sum_{w=1}^{L} e^{\lambda P(S=w|X=Hx)}}dx. \end{aligned}$$

The third equation stands because of (A4). The fourth equation stands because H is an orthonormal matrix. Further, we have

$$\begin{aligned} P(S=b|X=Hx) &= \frac{f_b(Hx)}{Lf(Hx)} \\ &= \frac{f_a(x)}{Lf(x)} \\ &= P(S=a|X=x). \end{aligned}$$

Since the transformation by left-multiplying with H is one-to-one between the states, we can obtain $\sum_{w=1}^{L} e^{\lambda P(S=w|X=Hx)} = \sum_{w=1}^{L} e^{\lambda P(S=w|X=x)}$.

Hence for states a and b, we have $P(\hat{S}=a) = P(\hat{S}=b)$. Since a and b are arbitrary, the prior probabilities of the classification results $\hat{S}$ are equal to $1/L$.

Appendix E. Proof of Proposition 2

Similar to [3], Proposition 2 can be proved as follows:

$$\begin{aligned} D &= \int_{\mathcal{X}} \sum_{t=1}^{L} f(x)\frac{e^{sP_{t|x}}}{\sum_{w=1}^{L} e^{sP_{w|x}}}(1-P_{t|x})dx \\ &= 1 - \int_{\mathcal{X}} \sum_{t=1}^{L} f(x)\frac{e^{sP_{t|x}}}{\sum_{w=1}^{L} e^{sP_{w|x}}}P_{t|x}dx, \end{aligned} \tag{A5}$$

$$\begin{aligned}
R_{ub} &= \log_2 L + \int_{\mathcal{X}} \sum_{t=1}^{L} f(x) \frac{e^{sP_{t|x}}}{\sum_{w=1}^{L} e^{sP_{w|x}}} \log_2 \frac{s^{sP_{t|x}}}{\sum_{w=1}^{L} e^{sP_{w|x}}} dx \\
&= \log_2 e (\ln L + \int_{\mathcal{X}} \sum_{t=1}^{L} f(x) \frac{e^{sP_{t|x}}}{\sum_{w=1}^{L} e^{sP_{w|x}}} sP_{t|x} dx + \int_{\mathcal{X}} \sum_{t=1}^{L} f(x) \frac{e^{sP_{t|x}}}{\sum_{w=1}^{L} e^{sP_{w|x}}} \ln \frac{1}{\sum_{w=1}^{L} e^{sP_{w|x}}} dx) \\
&= \log_2 e (-s + s \int_{\mathcal{X}} \sum_{t=1}^{L} f(x) \frac{e^{sP_{t|x}}}{\sum_{w=1}^{L} e^{sP_{w|x}}} P_{t|x} dx + \ln e^s + \ln L \\
&\quad + \int_{\mathcal{X}} \sum_{t=1}^{L} f(x) \frac{e^{sP_{t|x}}}{\sum_{w=1}^{L} e^{sP_{w|x}}} \ln \frac{1}{\sum_{w=1}^{L} e^{sP_{w|x}}} dx) \\
&= \log_2 e (-sD + \int_{\mathcal{X}} \sum_{t=1}^{L} f(x) \frac{e^{sP_{t|x}}}{\sum_{w=1}^{L} e^{sP_{w|x}}} \ln \frac{Le^s}{\sum_{w=1}^{L} e^{sP_{w|x}}} dx) \\
&= \log_2 e (-sD + \int_{\mathcal{X}} f(x) \ln \frac{Le^s}{\sum_{w=1}^{L} e^{sP_{w|x}}} dx).
\end{aligned} \tag{A6}$$

Denote $\eta(x) = \frac{Le^s}{\sum_{w=1}^{L} e^{sP_{w|x}}}$. Then we have

$$R_{ub} = -\log_2 e (sD + \int_{\mathcal{X}} f(x) \ln \eta(x) dx), \tag{A7}$$

$$\begin{aligned}
\frac{dR_{ub}}{dD} &= -s \log_2 e + \log_2 e (-D \frac{ds}{dD} + \int_{\mathcal{X}} f(x) \frac{1}{\eta(x)} \frac{d\eta(x)}{dD} dx) \\
&= -s \log_2 e + \log_2 e (-D \frac{ds}{dD} + \int_{\mathcal{X}} \frac{f(x)}{\eta(x)} \frac{d\eta(x)}{ds} \frac{ds}{dD} dx) \\
&= -s \log_2 e + \log_2 e (\int_{\mathcal{X}} \frac{f(x)}{\eta(x)} \frac{d\eta(x)}{ds} dx - D) \frac{ds}{dD}.
\end{aligned} \tag{A8}$$

For the marginal probability $P(\hat{S} = t)$, we have

$$P(\hat{S} = t) = \int_{\mathcal{X}} \frac{e^{sP_{t|x}}}{\sum_{w=1}^{L} e^{sP_{w|x}}} f(x) dx. \tag{A9}$$

As $\sum_{t=1}^{L} P(\hat{S} = t) = 1$, we have

$$\begin{aligned}
\sum_{t=1}^{L} P(\hat{S} = t) &= \int_{\mathcal{X}} \sum_{t=1}^{L} f(x) \frac{e^{sP_{t|x}}}{\sum_{w=1}^{L} e^{sP_{w|x}}} dx \\
&= \frac{1}{L} \int_{\mathcal{X}} \sum_{t=1}^{L} f(x) \frac{e^{sP_{t|x}} Le^s e^{-s}}{\sum_{w=1}^{L} e^{sP_{w|x}}} dx \\
&= \frac{1}{L} \int_{\mathcal{X}} \sum_{t=1}^{L} f(x) e^{-s(1-P_{t|x})} \eta(x) dx \\
&= 1.
\end{aligned} \tag{A10}$$

Hence the derivative of the second-to-last line of (A10) with respect to s should be 0. So we have

$$\frac{1}{L} \int_{\mathcal{X}} \sum_{t=1}^{L} f(x) [e^{-s(1-P_{t|x})} (P_{t|x} - 1) \eta(x) + e^{-s(1-P_{t|x})} \frac{d\eta(x)}{ds}] dx = 0, \tag{A11}$$

$$\int_{\mathcal{X}} \sum_{t=1}^{L} f(x) e^{sP_{t|x}} [(P_{t|x} - 1) \eta(x) + \frac{d\eta(x)}{ds}] dx = 0, \tag{A12}$$

$$-\int_{\mathcal{X}} \sum_{t=1}^{L} f(x)(1-P_{t|x}) \frac{e^{sP_{t|x}}}{\sum_{w=1}^{L} e^{sP_{w|x}}} Le^s dx + \int_{\mathcal{X}} f(x) \sum_{t=1}^{L} e^{sP_{t|x}} \frac{d\eta(x)}{ds} dx = 0. \tag{A13}$$

From (A5), the first term on the left-hand side of the above equation is $-Le^s D$. For the second term, from the definition of $\eta(x)$, we have $\sum_{t=1}^{L} e^{sP_{t|x}} = \frac{Le^s}{\eta(x)}$. Hence we have

$$-Le^s D + Le^s \int_{\mathcal{X}} \frac{f(x)}{\eta(x)} \frac{d\eta(x)}{ds} dx = 0. \tag{A14}$$

So

$$\int_{\mathcal{X}} \frac{f(x)}{\eta(x)} \frac{d\eta(x)}{ds} dx - D = 0. \tag{A15}$$

Combined with (A8), we have

$$\frac{dR}{dD} = -s \log_2 e. \tag{A16}$$

Appendix F. Proof of Theorem 4

Consider the case of encoding n observations ($n \to +\infty$), where the reconstruction distortion is constrained. From the scheme described in Section 4, the rate of classification and reconstruction can be considered separately. By selecting a classification distortion D, the classification results can be described by $nR_s(D)$ bits with the soft classification scheme described in Section 3.2.2. Hence an achievable classification rate is $R_s(D)$.

Then, according to the results of the soft classification, the observations are encoded with the corresponding sub-encoders. Since

$$I(X;\hat{X}|\hat{S}) = \sum_{u=1}^{L} P(\hat{S}=u) I(X;\hat{X}|\hat{S}=u),$$

the average rate of each reconstruction encoder can be considered separately.

Consider the u-th sub-encoder. Denote the conditional expectation of the observations conditioned on the classification result u as γ_u. We have

$$\begin{aligned} \gamma_u &= \mathbb{E}\{X|\hat{S}=u\} \\ &= \frac{\int_{\mathcal{X}} x f(x) g_{D,u}(x) dx}{\int_{\mathcal{X}} f(x) g_{D,u}(x) dx}. \end{aligned}$$

Denote the conditioned covariance matrix conditioned on classification result u as Σ_u. We have

$$\begin{aligned} \Sigma_u &= \mathbb{E}\{(X-\gamma_u)(X-\gamma_u)^T|\hat{S}=u\} \\ &= \frac{\int_{\mathcal{X}} (X-\gamma_u)(X-\gamma_u)^T f(x) g_{D,u}(x) dx}{\int_{\mathcal{X}} f(x) g_{D,u}(x) dx}. \end{aligned}$$

Denote $\tilde{X}_u = X - \gamma_u$. We use the u-th sub-encoder to encode $\tilde{X}_u$. An achievable joint distribution between $\tilde{X}_u$ and $\hat{X}$ is shown in Figure A1.

First we diagonalize Σ_u as $\Sigma_u = H_u \Sigma_{Y_u} H_u^T$, where H_u is an orthonormal matrix. Assume $\tilde{X}_u = H_u Y_u$. Σ_{Y_u} is the covariance matrix of Y_u. Hence the components of Y_u are independently conditioned on $\hat{S}$. Denote the dimension of X as K. Denote the i-th component of Y_u as Y_{ui}, with the corresponding variance denoted by σ_{ui}^2. Then assume $\hat{Y}_{ui} = \frac{\sigma_{ui}^2 - D_{ui}}{\sigma_{ui}^2}(Y_{ui} + Z_{ui})$, where $Z_{ui} \sim \mathcal{N}(0, \frac{D_{ui}\sigma_{ui}^2}{\sigma_{ui}^2 - D_{ui}})$. $\forall u \in [1:L], i \in [1:N], Z_{ui}$ is independent of X. Finally, the reconstruction $\hat{X} = H_u \hat{Y}_u + \gamma_u$.

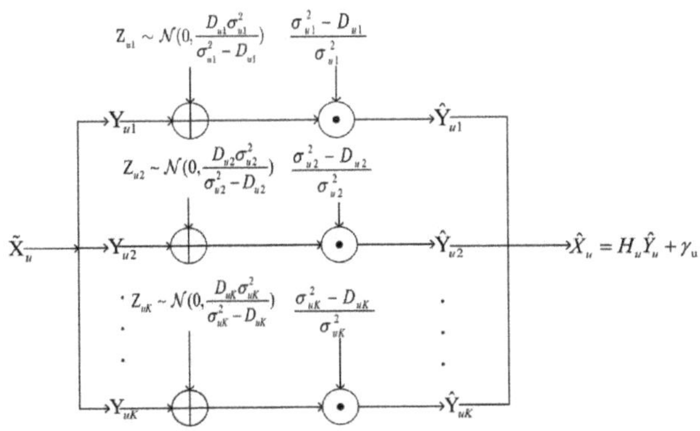

Figure A1. An achievable joint distribution between $\tilde{X}_u$ and $\hat{X}$.

First we consider the distortion

$$\begin{aligned}
\mathbb{E}\{\|X - \hat{X}\|_2^2|\hat{S} = u\} &= \mathbb{E}\{\|\tilde{X}_u - H_u\hat{Y}_u\|_2^2|\hat{S} = u\} \\
&= \mathbb{E}\{\|H_uY_u - H_u\hat{Y}_u\|_2^2|\hat{S} = u\} \\
&= \mathbb{E}\{\|Y_u - \hat{Y}_u\|_2^2|\hat{S} = u\} \\
&= \sum_{i=1}^{K} \mathbb{E}\{(Y_{ui} - \hat{Y}_{ui})^2|\hat{S} = u\}.
\end{aligned}$$

Under the joint distribution described in Figure A1, we have

$$\begin{aligned}
&\mathbb{E}\{(Y_{ui} - \hat{Y}_{ui})^2|\hat{S} = u\} \\
&= \mathbb{E}\{(Y_{ui} - \frac{\sigma_{ui}^2 - D_{ui}}{\sigma_{ui}^2}(Y_{ui} + Z_{ui}))^2|\hat{S} = u\} \\
&= \mathbb{E}\{(\frac{D_{ui}}{\sigma_{ui}^2}Y_{ui} - \frac{\sigma_{ui}^2 - D_{ui}}{\sigma_{ui}^2}Z_{ui})^2|\hat{S} = u\} \\
&= (\frac{D_{ui}}{\sigma_{ui}^2})^2\mathbb{E}\{Y_{ui}^2|\hat{S} = u\} + (\frac{\sigma_{ui}^2 - D_{ui}}{\sigma_{ui}^2})^2\mathbb{E}\{Z_{ui}^2|\hat{S} = u\} \\
&= D_{ui}.
\end{aligned}$$

Hence the overall expected distortion is

$$\mathbb{E}\{\|X - \hat{X}\|_2^2\} = \sum_{u=1}^{L}\sum_{i=1}^{K} P(\hat{S} = u)D_{ui}.$$

Then consider the rate (mutual information) of the u-th sub-encoder

$$I(X; \hat{X}|\hat{S} = u) = h(\hat{X}|\hat{S} = u) - h(\hat{X}|X, \hat{S} = u). \tag{A17}$$

For the first term in (A17),

$$\begin{aligned}
h(\hat{X}|\hat{S} = u) &= h(H_u\hat{Y}_u|\hat{S} = u) \\
&= h(\hat{Y}_u|\hat{S} = u) \\
&= \sum_{i=1}^{K} h(\hat{Y}_{ui}|\hat{S} = u).
\end{aligned}$$

It is obvious that the variance of $\hat{Y}_{ui}$ is $\sigma_{ui}^2 - D_{ui}$. Under variance constraint, Gaussian source has the maximum differential entropy [45]. Hence we have

$$h(\hat{Y}_{ui}|\hat{S}=u) \leq \frac{1}{2}\log_2(2\pi e(\sigma_{ui}^2 - D_{ui})). \tag{A18}$$

For the second term in (A17),

$$\begin{aligned} h(\hat{X}|X,\hat{S}=u) &= h(H_u\hat{Y}_u|X,\hat{S}=u) \\ &= h(\hat{Y}_u|X,\hat{S}=u) \\ &= \sum_{i=1}^{K} h(\hat{Y}_{ui}|X,\hat{S}=u), \end{aligned}$$

$$\begin{aligned} h(\hat{Y}_{ui}|X,\hat{S}=u) &= h(\frac{\sigma_{ui}^2 - D_{ui}}{\sigma_{ui}^2}(Y_{ui}+Z_{ui})|X,\hat{S}=u) \\ &= h(\frac{\sigma_{ui}^2 - D_{ui}}{\sigma_{ui}^2}Z_{ui}|\hat{S}=u) \\ &= \frac{1}{2}\log_2(2\pi e\frac{(\sigma_{ui}^2 - D_{ui})D_{ui}}{\sigma_{ui}^2}). \end{aligned}$$

Combined with (A18), we have

$$I(X;\hat{X}|\hat{S}=u) \leq \frac{1}{2}\sum_{i=1}^{K}\log_2\frac{\sigma_{ui}^2}{D_{ui}}. \tag{A19}$$

Assume $\mathbf{D}$ is an $L \times K$ matrix, with the element in the u-th row and i-th column taking the value of D_{ui}. Denote $R_{\tilde{X}_{u},g} = \frac{1}{2}\sum_{i=1}^{K}\log_2\frac{\sigma_{ui}^2}{D_{ui}}$, which gives the rate of the u-th sub-encoder with the joint distribution described in Figure A1.

From (A19), we can see that for all $\mathbf{D}$ and D that satisfy $\sum_{u=1}^{L}\sum_{i=1}^{K}P(\hat{S}=u)D_{ui} \leq D_o$, and $D \leq D_s$, the classification and reconstruction distortion constraints pair (D, D_o) can be achieved by the overall rate $R_s(D) + \sum_{u=1}^{L}P(\hat{S}=u)R_{\tilde{X}_{u},g}$.

When the classification distortion D is fixed, minimizing the overall rate is equivalent to minimizing the reconstruction rate. Hence we have the following optimization problem:

$$\begin{aligned} \min_{D_{ui},u=[1:L],i=[1:K]} \quad & \sum_{u=1}^{L}\sum_{i=1}^{K}P(\hat{S}=u)\log_2\frac{\sigma_{ui}^2}{D_{ui}} \\ s.t. \quad & \sum_{u=1}^{L}\sum_{i=1}^{K}P(\hat{S}=u)D_{ui} \leq D_o \\ & D_{ui} \leq \sigma_{ui}^2, \forall u=[1:L], i=[1:K] \end{aligned} \tag{A20}$$

Hence we have the following Lagrange function:

$$\begin{aligned} &J(\mathbf{D}) \\ &= \sum_{u=1}^{L}\sum_{i=1}^{K}P(\hat{S}=u)\log_2\frac{\sigma_{ui}^2}{D_{ui}} + \mu\sum_{u=1}^{L}\sum_{i=1}^{K}P(\hat{S}=u)D_{ui}, \end{aligned} \tag{A21}$$

where μ is the Lagrange multiplier. By setting the partial derivative of J with respect to D_{ui} to 0, we obtain

$$D_{ui} = \frac{\log_2 e}{\mu}. \tag{A22}$$

It can be seen from (A22) that under the optimal condition, every D_{ui} is equal to a same constant. Denote the constant as α. We find that the solution to this problem is quite similar to the reverse water-filling method. So combining with the constraint $D_{ui} \leq \sigma_{ui}^2, \forall u = [1:L]$, $i = [1:K]$, the optimal solution to minimize the reconstruction rate is

$$D_{ui} = \min\{\alpha, \sigma_{ui}^2\},$$

where α is chosen to satisfy

$$\sum_{u=1}^{L}\sum_{i=1}^{K} P(\hat{S} = u) D_{ui} = D_o.$$

References

1. Dobrushin, R.; Tsybakov, B. Information transmission with additional noise. *IRE Trans. Inf. Theory* **1962**, *8*, 293–304. [CrossRef]
2. Wolf, J.; Ziv, J. Transmission of noisy information to a noisy receiver with minimum distortion. *IEEE Trans. Inf. Theory* **1970**, *16*, 406–411. [CrossRef]
3. Berger, T. *Rate Distortion Theory*; Prentice-Hall: Englewood Cliffs, NJ, USA, 1971.
4. Liu, J.; Zhang, W.; Poor, H.V. A Rate-Distortion Framework for Characterizing Semantic Information. In Proceedings of the 2021 IEEE International Symposium on Information Theory (ISIT), Melbourne, Australia, 12–20 July 2021; pp. 2894–2899. [CrossRef]
5. Wang, Y.; Guo, T.; Bai, B.; Han, W. The Estimation-Compression Separation in Semantic Communication Systems. In Proceedings of the 2022 IEEE Information Theory Workshop (ITW), Mumbai, India, 1–9 November 2022; pp. 315–320.
6. Gerrish, A.; Schultheiss, P. Information rates of non-Gaussian processes. *IEEE Trans. Inf. Theory* **1964**, *10*, 265–271. [CrossRef]
7. Shannon, C.E. A mathematical theory of communication. *Bell Syst. Tech. J.* **1948**, *27*, 379–423. [CrossRef]
8. Shannon, C.E. Coding theorems for a discrete source with a fidelity criterion. *IRE Nat. Conv. Rec* **1959**, *4*, 1.
9. Bar-Hillel, Y.; Carnap, R. Semantic information. *Br. J. Philos. Sci.* **1953**, *4*, 147–157. [CrossRef]
10. Floridi, L. Outline of a Theory of Strongly Semantic Information. *Minds Mach.* **2004**, *14*, 197–221. [CrossRef]
11. Bao, J.; Basu, P.; Dean, M.; Partridge, C.; Swami, A.; Leland, W.; Hendler, J.A. Towards a theory of semantic communication. In Proceedings of the 2011 IEEE Network Science Workshop, West Point, NY, USA, 22–24 June 2011; pp. 110–117. [CrossRef]
12. Juba, B. *Universal Semantic Communication*; Springer: Berlin/Heidelberg, Germany, 2011.
13. Popovski, P.; Simeone, O.; Boccardi, F.; Gunduz, D.; Sahin, O. Semantic-Effectiveness Filtering and Control for Post-5G Wireless Connectivity. *arXiv* **2019**, arXiv:1907.02441. [CrossRef]
14. Kountouris, M.; Pappas, N. Semantics-Empowered Communication for Networked Intelligent Systems. *IEEE Commun. Mag.* **2021**, *59*, 96–102. [CrossRef]
15. Seo, H.; Kang, Y.; Bennis, M.; Choi, W. Bayesian Inverse Contextual Reasoning for Heterogeneous Semantics- Native Communication. *IEEE Trans. Commun.* **2024**, *72*, 830–844. [CrossRef]
16. Liu, X.; Sun, Y.; Wang, Z.; You, L.; Pan, H.; Wang, F.; Cui, S. User Centric Semantic Communications. *arXiv* **2024**, arXiv:2411.03127.
17. Shlezinger, N.; Eldar, Y.C.; Rodrigues, M.R.D. Hardware-Limited Task-Based Quantization. *IEEE Trans. Signal Process.* **2019**, *67*, 5223–5238. [CrossRef]
18. Ordentlich, O.; Polyanskiy, Y. Optimal Quantization for Matrix Multiplication. *arXiv* **2024**, arXiv:2410.13780.
19. Shlezinger, N.; van Sloun, R.J.G.; Huijben, I.A.M.; Tsintsadze, G.; Eldar, Y.C. Learning Task-Based Analog-to-Digital Conversion for MIMO Receivers. In Proceedings of the ICASSP 2020—2020 IEEE International Conference on Acoustics, Speech and Signal Processing (ICASSP), Barcelona, Spain, 4–8 May 2020; pp. 9125–9129. [CrossRef]
20. Shlezinger, N.; Amar, A.; Luijten, B.; van Sloun, R.J.G.; Eldar, Y.C. Deep Task-Based Analog-to-Digital Conversion. *IEEE Trans. Signal Process.* **2022**, *70*, 6021–6034. [CrossRef]
21. Lexa, M.A.; Johnson, D.H. Joint Optimization of Distributed Broadcast Quantization Systems for Classification. In Proceedings of the 2007 Data Compression Conference (DCC'07), Snowbird, UT, USA, 27–29 March 2007; pp. 363–374. [CrossRef]
22. Dogahe, B.M.; Murthi, M.N. Quantization for classification accuracy in high-rate quantizers. In Proceedings of the 2011 Digital Signal Processing and Signal Processing Education Meeting (DSP/SPE), Sedona, AZ, USA, 4–7 January 2011; pp. 277–282. [CrossRef]
23. Poor, H. Fine quantization in signal detection and estimation. *IEEE Trans. Inf. Theory* **1988**, *34*, 960–972. [CrossRef]
24. Kipnis, A.; Rini, S.; Goldsmith, A.J. The Rate-Distortion Risk in Estimation From Compressed Data. *IEEE Trans. Inf. Theory* **2021**, *67*, 2910–2924. [CrossRef]
25. Fontana, R. Universal codes for a class of composite sources (Corresp.). *IEEE Trans. Inf. Theory* **1980**, *26*, 480–482. [CrossRef]
26. Liu, J.; Poor, H.V.; Song, I.; Zhang, W. A Rate-Distortion Analysis for Composite Sources Under Subsource-Dependent Fidelity Criteria. *arXiv* **2024**, arXiv:2405.11818. [CrossRef]

27. Liu, J.; Shao, S.; Zhang, W.; Poor, H.V. An Indirect Rate-Distortion Characterization for Semantic Sources: General Model and the Case of Gaussian Observation. *IEEE Trans. Commun.* **2022**, *70*, 5946–5959. [CrossRef]
28. Witsenhausen, H. Indirect rate distortion problems. *IEEE Trans. Inf. Theory* **1980**, *26*, 518–521. [CrossRef]
29. Liu, K.; Liu, D.; Li, L.; Ning, Y.; Li, H. Semantics-to-Signal Scalable Image Compression with Learned Revertible Representations. *Int. J. Comput. Vis.* **2021**, *129*, 2605–2621. [CrossRef]
30. Rabiner, L.R.; Schafer, R.W. Introduction to Digital Speech Processing. *Found. Trends® Signal Process.* **2007**, *1*, 1–194. [CrossRef]
31. Kalveram, H.; Meissner, P. Itakura-saito clustering and rate distortion functions for a composite source model of speech. *Signal Process.* **1989**, *18*, 195–216. [CrossRef]
32. Gibson, J.D.; Hu, J. Rate Distortion Bounds for Voice and Video. *Found. Trends® Commun. Inf. Theory* **2014**, *10*, 379–514. [CrossRef]
33. Gibson, J. Rate distortion functions and rate distortion function lower bounds for real-world sources. *Entropy* **2017**, *19*, 604. [CrossRef]
34. Rabiner, L. A tutorial on hidden Markov models and selected applications in speech recognition. *Proc. IEEE* **1989**, *77*, 257–286. [CrossRef]
35. Lu, D.; Weng, Q. A survey of image classification methods and techniques for improving classification performance. *Int. J. Remote Sens.* **2007**, *28*, 823–870. [CrossRef]
36. Lecun, Y.; Bottou, L.; Bengio, Y.; Haffner, P. Gradient-based learning applied to document recognition. *Proc. IEEE* **1998**, *86*, 2278–2324. [CrossRef]
37. Chandola, V.; Banerjee, A.; Kumar, V. Anomaly detection: A survey. *ACM Comput. Surv. (CSUR)* **2009**, *41*, 1–58. [CrossRef]
38. Kingma, D.P. Auto-encoding variational bayes. *arXiv* **2013**, arXiv:1312.6114.
39. Croitoru, F.A.; Hondru, V.; Ionescu, R.T.; Shah, M. Diffusion models in vision: A survey. *IEEE Trans. Pattern Anal. Mach. Intell.* **2023**, *45*, 10850–10869. [CrossRef] [PubMed]
40. Tang, Y.; Fei, Z.; Huang, L.; Zhang, W.; Zhao, B.; Guan, H.; Huang, Y. Failure Mode and Effects Analysis Method on the Air System of an Aircraft Turbofan Engine in Multi-Criteria Open Group Decision-Making Environment. *Cybern. Syst.* **2025**, 1–32. [CrossRef]
41. Popkov, Y.S.; Volkovich, Z.; Dubnov, Y.A.; Avros, R.; Ravve, E. Entropy "2"-Soft Classification of Objects. *Entropy* **2017**, *19*, 178. [CrossRef]
42. Sharma, R.; Garg, P.; Dwivedi, R. A literature survey for fuzzy based soft classification techniques and uncertainty estimation. In Proceedings of the 2016 International Conference System Modeling & Advancement in Research Trends (SMART), Moradabad, India, 25–27 November 2016; pp. 71–75. [CrossRef]
43. Khatami, R.; Mountrakis, G.; Stehman, S.V. Predicting individual pixel error in remote sensing soft classification. *Remote Sens. Environ.* **2017**, *199*, 401–414. [CrossRef]
44. Weidmann, C.; Vetterli, M. Rate Distortion Behavior of Sparse Sources. *IEEE Trans. Inf. Theory* **2012**, *58*, 4969–4992. [CrossRef]
45. Cover, T.M.; Thomas, J.A. *Elements of Information Theory*, 2nd ed.; John Wiley & Sons, Ltd: Hoboken, NJ, USA, 2005.
46. Blahut, R. Computation of channel capacity and rate-distortion functions. *IEEE Trans. Inf. Theory* **1972**, *18*, 460–473. [CrossRef]
47. Chen, L.; Wu, S.; Ye, W.; Wu, H.; Zhang, W.; Wu, H.; Bai, B. A constrained BA algorithm for rate-distortion and distortion-rate functions. *arXiv* **2023**, arXiv:2305.02650.
48. Yeung, R.W. *A First Course in Information Theory*; Springer Science & Business Media: New York, NY, USA, 2012.

entropy

MDPI

Article

Extended Blahut–Arimoto Algorithm for Semantic Rate-Distortion Function

Yuxin Han [1,2], Yang Liu [1,2], Yaping Sun [2,4], Kai Niu [1,2,*], Nan Ma [3,2], Shuguang Cui [4,2] and Ping Zhang [3,2]

1 Key Laboratory of Universal Wireless Communications, Ministry of Education, Beijing University of Posts and Telecommunications, Beijing 100876, China; hanyx@bupt.edu.cn (Y.H.); liuyang@bupt.edu.cn (Y.L.)
2 Department of Broadband Communication, Pengcheng Laboratory, Shenzhen 518055, China; sunyp@pcl.ac.cn (Y.S.)
3 Key Laboratory of Networking and Switching Technology, Beijing University of Posts and Telecommunications, Beijing 100876, China; manan@bupt.edu.cn (N.M.); pzhang@bupt.edu.cn (P.Z.)
4 School of Science and Engineering (SSE) and the Future Network of Intelligent Institute (FNii), The Chinese University of Hong Kong (Shenzhen), Shenzhen 518172, China; shuguangcui@cuhk.edu.cn (S.C.)
* Correspondence: niukai@bupt.edu.cn

Abstract: Semantic communication has recently gained significant attention in theoretical analysis due to its potential to improve communication efficiency by focusing on meaning rather than exact signal reconstruction. In this paper, we extend the Blahut–Arimoto (BA) algorithm, a fundamental method in classical information theory (CIT) for computing the rate-distortion (RD) function, to semantic communication by proposing the extended Blahut–Arimoto (EBA) algorithm, which iteratively updates transition and reconstruction distributions to calculate the semantic RD function based on synonymous mapping in semantic information theory (SIT). To address scenarios where synonymous mappings are unknown, we develop an optimization framework that combines the EBA algorithm with simulated annealing. Initialized with a syntactic mapping, the framework progressively merges syntactic symbols and identifies the mapping with a maximum synonymous number that satisfies objective constraints. Furthermore, by considering the semantic knowledge base (SKB) as a specific instance of synonymous mapping, the EBA algorithm provides a theoretical approach for analyzing and predicting the SKB size. Numerical results validate the effectiveness of the EBA algorithm. For Gaussian sources, the semantic RD function decreases with an increasing synonymous number and becomes significantly lower than its classical counterpart. Additionally, analysis on the CUB dataset demonstrates that larger SKB sizes lead to higher semantic communication compression efficiency.

Keywords: Blahut–Arimoto algorithm; semantic rate-distortion function; semantic information theory; semantic knowledge base

1. Introduction

Recent years have witnessed the rapid development of semantic communication, which has emerged as a promising paradigm for the next-generation communication system [1]. Unlike the traditional communication system that focuses on transmitting symbols, semantic communication aims to recover the message that matches the meaning of the transmitted information [2]. This paradigm enables more efficient data transmission by focusing on transporting and delivering the meaning of messages, potentially reducing communication overhead while maintaining the essential meaning of the information [3–6].

Classical information theory (CIT), established by Shannon in 1948, has served as the cornerstone for modern digital communication [7]. In CIT, the rate-distortion (RD)

theory characterizes the fundamental trade-off between the rate and the distortion in lossy compression systems [8–10]. The Blahut–Arimoto (BA) algorithm has been established as a prevailing numerical method in CIT, which is capable of computing the RD function for arbitrary discrete source models [11,12]. Variants and acceleration techniques of the BA algorithm have been developed [13–17], and a mapping approach has been introduced for continuous sources [18].

Recent research suggests that the RD-perception function plays an important role in semantic communication [19–23]. More recently, Niu and Zhang extended CIT to semantic communication, referred to as the semantic information theory (SIT) [24]. By introducing the synonymous mapping, information measures (such as semantic entropy, which is consistent with that used in large language models [25]) and coding theorems for the semantic communication system were established, thus providing a mathematical foundation for guiding the design of the semantic communication system. In their work, the analytical expression of the semantic RD function for Gaussian sources is derived; however, computing the semantic RD function for other source models remains challenging, which motivates us to extend the classical BA algorithm to the semantic communication system.

In this paper, we propose an extension of the BA algorithm based on the SIT, referred to as the extended Blahut–Arimoto (EBA) algorithm, such that the semantic RD function can be directly calculated with any given source model. The main contributions of this paper are summarized as follows.

- First, based on the synonymous mapping in SIT, the EBA algorithm is proposed by extending the classical BA algorithm to the semantic communication system. Similar to the BA algorithm, the EBA algorithm is also an iterative procedure that converges to the semantic RD function through alternating optimization of the transition and reconstruction distributions. The convergence is guaranteed by the convexity property of the semantic RD function, providing an efficient method for computing the semantic RD function for arbitrary discrete source models.
- Then, starting from a syntactic mapping, an optimization framework is developed for scenarios with unknown synonymous mappings. The framework combines the EBA algorithm with simulated annealing [26] to progressively merge syntactic symbols and identify the mapping with maximum synonymous number that satisfies objective constraints, enabling the discovery of optimal semantic representations that balance compression efficiency and distortion.
- Furthermore, by considering the semantic knowledge base (SKB) as a specific instance of synonymous mapping, the EBA algorithm provides a theoretical approach for analyzing and predicting the SKB size. Using the CUB dataset [27], experimental results indicate that increasing the SKB size directly improves semantic communication compression efficiency, thereby validating the critical role of SKB in enhancing transmission performance.

The remainder of this paper is organized as follows. Section 2 reviews the semantic RD function in SIT and introduces the classical BA algorithm. Section 3 presents the EBA algorithm and details its optimization framework for finding the synonymous mapping with maximum synonymous number. Section 4 describes the application of the EBA to SKB. Simulation results are provided in Section 5, followed by conclusions in Section 6.

2. Preliminaries

2.1. Notation and Conventions

Throughout this paper, calligraphic letters, such as $\mathcal{X}$ and $\mathcal{Y}$, denote sets, while lowercase letters denote elements in these sets. For a syntactic symbol, its reconstruction is denoted by $\hat{\cdot}$, and its associated semantic symbol by $\tilde{\cdot}$. The cardinality of set $\mathcal{X}$ is defined as $|\mathcal{X}|$. Let $f : \mathcal{X} \to \mathcal{Y}$ denote a mapping from set $\mathcal{X}$ to set $\mathcal{Y}$.

2.2. Semantic RD Function

To facilitate understanding, a brief overview of the related concepts is presented first; detailed definitions can be found in [24]. Consider a syntactic information set $\mathcal{X} = \{x_1, \cdots, x_N\}$ and its corresponding semantic information set $\tilde{\mathcal{X}} = \{\tilde{x}_1, \cdots, \tilde{x}_{\tilde{N}}\}$, where $\tilde{N} \leq N$. The synonymous mapping $f_x : \tilde{\mathcal{X}} \to \mathcal{X}$ is a one-to-many mapping that partitions $\mathcal{X}$ into disjoint synonymous sets $\{\mathcal{X}_{i_s}\}$, $i_s = 1, 2, \cdots, \tilde{N}$, where each $\mathcal{X}_{i_s}$ contains syntactic symbols sharing the same semantic meaning and $|\mathcal{X}_{i_s}| = N_{i_s}$. As illustrated in Figure 1, each semantic symbol corresponds to an equivalent set of syntactic symbols, and there is no overlap between any two sets.

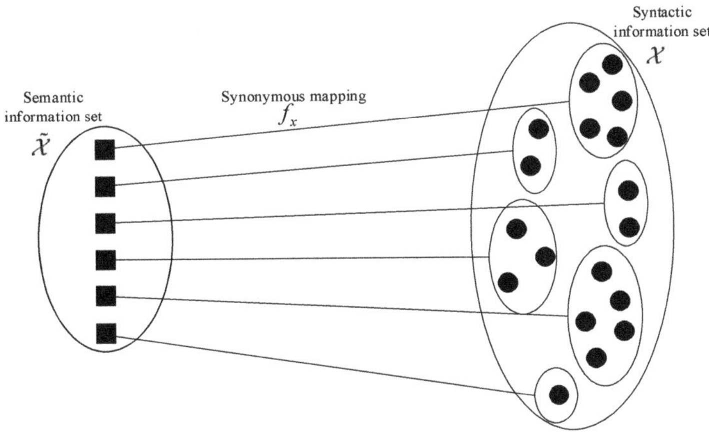

Figure 1. An example of synonymous mapping between semantic and syntactic information sets.

Based on the synonymous mapping, the semantic RD function is obtained by minimizing the semantic mutual information between the source and the reconstruction subject to an average semantic distortion constraint. Assume that given an i.i.d. source $X \in \mathcal{X}$ with its associated semantic source $\tilde{X}$, let $x_{i_s,l}$ denote the l-th syntactic symbol in the i_s-th synonymous set. The corresponding source probability distributions are expressed as $p_{i_sl} = p(x_{i_s,l})$ and $p_{i_s} = p(\tilde{x}_{i_s}) = p(\mathcal{X}_{i_s}) = \sum_{l=1}^{N_{i_s}} p(x_{i_s,l})$. Let $\hat{x}_{j_s,m}$ denote the m-th reconstruction syntactic symbol in the j_s-th synonymous set and $f_{\hat{x}}$ denote the synonymous mapping $f_{\hat{x}} : \hat{\tilde{\mathcal{X}}} \to \hat{\mathcal{X}}$, which is defined analogously to f_x. The test channel is characterized by transition probability $P_{j_sm,i_sl} = p(\hat{x}_{j_s,m}|x_{i_s,l})$ with semantic distortion $\tilde{d}_{i_sj_s} = \tilde{d}_s(\tilde{x}_{i_s}, \hat{\tilde{x}}_{j_s}) = \tilde{d}_s(\mathcal{X}_{i_s}, \hat{\mathcal{X}}_{j_s})$. For the reconstruction, the probability distributions are defined as $q_{j_sm} = p(\hat{x}_{j_s,m}) = \sum_{i_s=1}^{\tilde{N}} \sum_l p_{i_sl} P_{j_sm,i_sl}$ and $q_{j_s} = p(\hat{\tilde{x}}_{j_s}) = p(\hat{\mathcal{X}}_{j_s}) = \sum_{m=1}^{N_{j_s}} \sum_{i_s} \sum_l p_{i_sl} P_{j_sm,i_sl}$. Then, the semantic RD function is defined as follows, and this problem is convex as shown in [24]:

$$R_s(D) = \min_{f_x, f_{\hat{x}}} \min_{P_D} \sum_{i_s} \sum_{j_s} \sum_{l} \sum_{m} p_{i_sl} P_{j_sm,i_sl} \log \frac{p_{i_sl} P_{j_sm,i_sl}}{\sum_{l'} \sum_{m'} p_{i_sl'} q_{j_sm'}} \tag{1}$$

where the test channel set P_D is defined as

$$P_D = \left\{ P_{j_sm,i_sl} : \sum_{i_s} \sum_{j_s} \sum_{l} \sum_{m} p_{i_sl} P_{j_sm,i_sl} \tilde{d}_{i_sj_s} \leq D \right\}. \tag{2}$$

2.3. BA Algorithm

The BA algorithm is an iterative procedure for computing the RD function. Let $p(x)$, $p(\hat{x})$, and $p(\hat{x}|x)$ denote the source distribution, reconstruction distribution, and test channel transition probability, respectively. For each fixed Lagrange multiplier $\lambda \in \mathbb{R}^+$, the algorithm minimizes the RD Lagrangian $L_\lambda = I(X;\hat{X}) + \lambda \mathbb{E}[d(x,\hat{x})]$, where $I(X;\hat{X})$ represents the mutual information and $d(x,\hat{x})$ represents the distortion measure.

Starting with an initial reconstruction distribution $p(\hat{x})$, each iteration alternates between two steps: first, computing the test channel transition probability

$$p(\hat{x}|x) = \frac{p(\hat{x})e^{-\lambda d(x,\hat{x})}}{\sum_{\hat{x}} p(\hat{x})e^{-\lambda d(x,\hat{x})}} \tag{3}$$

and then updating the reconstruction distribution according to

$$p(\hat{x}) = \sum_x p(x)p(\hat{x}|x). \tag{4}$$

This iterative process continues until the change in the reconstruction distribution between consecutive iterations is less than a predetermined threshold. Geometrically, λ represents the slope of the tangent line of the RD curve, and each optimal solution corresponds to a point on the RD curve. By varying λ, the entire RD curve can be swept out. The convergence of this algorithm has been proved by Blahut.

3. Extended BA Algorithm

In this section, the EBA algorithm is presented as a systematic approach for computing the semantic RD function. We first establish the theoretical foundations of the EBA algorithm, followed by an optimization framework for finding the synonymous mapping with maximum synonymous number.

3.1. EBA Algorithm for the Semantic RD Function

Without loss of generality, we consider the case where the synonymous mappings f_x and $f_{\hat{x}}$ are identical. Given a synonymous mapping that partitions the syntactic symbols into disjoint synonymous sets, the semantic RD function can be formulated as the following optimization problem:

$$\min_{P_D} \sum_{i_s}\sum_{j_s}\sum_{l}\sum_{m} p_{i_s l} P_{j_s m, i_s l} \log \frac{p_{i_s l} P_{j_s m, i_s l}}{\sum_{l'}\sum_{m'} p_{i_s l'} q_{j_s m'}} \tag{5}$$

subject to the following constraints:

$$\begin{aligned} P_D = \left\{ P_{j_s m, i_s l} : \sum_{i_s}\sum_{j_s}\sum_{l}\sum_{m} p_{i_s l} P_{j_s m, i_s l} \tilde{d}_{i_s j_s} \le D \right\} \\ \sum_{j_s}\sum_{m} P_{j_s m, i_s l} = 1, \quad \forall i_s = 1,2,\cdots,\tilde{N}, l = 1,2,\cdots,N_{i_s} \\ P_{j_s m, i_s l} \ge 0, \quad \forall i_s, m, j_s, l \end{aligned} \tag{6}$$

The EBA algorithm solves this optimization problem through iterative updates of the transition and reconstruction distributions. The main steps are outlined below, with a detailed pseudo-code provided in Algorithm 1.

(i) For a fixed $q_{j_s m}$, the transition distribution $\check{P}_{j_s m, i_s l}$ is calculated with a multiplier $\lambda \in \mathbb{R}^+$:

$$\check{P}_{j_s m, i_s l} = \frac{\sum_{m'} q_{j_s m'} e^{-\lambda \tilde{d}_{i_s j_s}}}{\sum_{j_s}\sum_{m'} q_{j_s m'} e^{-\lambda \tilde{d}_{i_s j_s}}}. \tag{7}$$

(ii) For a fixed $P_{j_s m, i_s l}$, the reconstruction distribution $\check{q}_{j_s m}$ is calculated as follows:

$$\check{q}_{j_s m} = \sum_{i_s} \sum_{l} p_{i_s l} P_{j_s m, i_s l}. \tag{8}$$

Algorithm 1: EBA algorithm for the semantic RD function.

Input: Semantic distortion measure $\tilde{d}_{i_s j_s}$, distribution $p_{i_s l}$, threshold ϵ, Lagrange multiplier λ

Output: Semantic RD curve

Initialize $P_{j_s m, i_s l}$ and $q_{j_s m}$ with uniform distributions;
for $\lambda \in \mathbb{R}^+$ **do**
    for $\epsilon^* \geq \epsilon$ **do**
        $\check{P}_{j_s m, i_s l} \leftarrow \frac{\sum_{m'} q_{j_s m'} e^{-\lambda \tilde{d}_{i_s j_s}}}{\sum_{j_s} \sum_{m'} q_{j_s m'} e^{-\lambda \tilde{d}_{i_s j_s}}}$;
        $\check{q}_{j_s m} \leftarrow \sum_{i_s} \sum_l p_{i_s l} P_{j_s m, i_s l}$;
        Calculate the distribution error ϵ^*;
    end
    Calculate corresponding $R(\lambda)$ and $D(\lambda)$ values;
    Update $P_{j_s m, i_s l}$ and $q_{j_s m}$;
end
return $R_s(D)$

In the following, a detailed derivation of the EBA algorithm will be provided for the semantic RD function. Similar to CIT, the optimization problem can be solved using the method of Lagrange multipliers, as the convexity of the semantic RD function has been proved in SIT [24]. For a fixed initial distribution $q_{j_s m}$, the problem can be formulated as finding the optimal distribution $\check{P}_{j_s m, i_s l}$ that minimizes the objective function under the constraints:

$$\sum_{i_s} \sum_{j_s} \sum_{l} \sum_{m} p_{i_s l} P_{j_s m, i_s l} \tilde{d}_{i_s j_s} = D \tag{9}$$

and

$$\sum_{j_s} \sum_{m} P_{j_s m, i_s l} = 1, \quad \forall i_s, l. \tag{10}$$

Beginning with a choice of Lagrange multipliers λ and $r_{i_s l}$ corresponding to the above constraints, the objective function is constructed as

$$\begin{aligned} L(\lambda) = & \sum_{i_s} \sum_{j_s} \sum_{l} \sum_{m} p_{i_s l} P_{j_s m, i_s l} \log \frac{p_{i_s l} P_{j_s m, i_s l}}{\sum_{l'} \sum_{m'} p_{i_s l'} q_{j_s m'}} \\ & + \lambda \sum_{i_s} \sum_{j_s} \sum_{l} \sum_{m} p_{i_s l} P_{j_s m, i_s l} \tilde{d}_{i_s j_s} \\ & + \sum_{i_s} \sum_{l} r_{i_s l} \sum_{j_s} \sum_{m} P_{j_s m, i_s l} \end{aligned}. \tag{11}$$

To find the optimal solution, the partial derivative of $L(\lambda)$ with respect to $P_{j_{s1} m_1, i_{s1} l_1}$ is taken and set to zero,

$$\begin{aligned} \frac{\partial L(\lambda)}{\partial P_{j_{s1} m_1, i_{s1} l_1}} & = p_{i_{s1} l_1} \left[\log \frac{p_{i_{s1} l_1} P_{j_{s1} m_1, i_{s1} l_1}}{\sum_{l'} p_{i_{s1} l'}} + 1 \right] - p_{i_{s1} l_1} \log \sum_{m'} q_{j_{s1} m'} + \lambda p_{i_{s1} l_1} \tilde{d}_{i_{s1} j_{s1}} + r_{i_{s1} l_1} \\ & = p_{i_{s1} l_1} \log \frac{p_{i_{s1} l_1} P_{j_{s1} m_1, i_{s1} l_1}}{\sum_{l'} p_{i_{s1} l'} \sum_{m'} q_{j_{s1} m'}} + p_{i_{s1} l_1} + \lambda p_{i_{s1} l_1} \tilde{d}_{i_{s1} j_{s1}} + r_{i_{s1} l_1} = 0 \end{aligned}. \tag{12}$$

Solving for $P_{j_{s1}m_1,i_{s1}l_1}$, thus obtaining

$$P_{j_{s1}m_1,i_{s1}l_1} = p_{i_{s1}l_1}^{-1}\sum_{l'} p_{i_{s1}l'}\sum_{m'} q_{j_{s1}m'}e^{-\lambda\tilde{d}_{i_{s1}j_{s1}}-p_{i_{s1}l_1}^{-1}r_{i_{s1}l_1}-1}. \tag{13}$$

By substituting $(i_{s1}, j_{s1}, l_1, m_1) \to (i_s, j_s, l, m)$ and applying the normalization constraint, we derive

$$\check{P}_{j_sm,i_sl} = \frac{p_{i_sl}^{-1}\sum_{l'} p_{i_sl'}\sum_{m'} q_{j_sm'}e^{-\lambda\tilde{d}_{i_sj_s}-p_{i_sl}^{-1}r_{i_sl}-1}}{\sum_{j_s}\sum_m p_{i_sl}^{-1}\sum_{l'} p_{i_sl'}\sum_{m'} q_{j_sm'}e^{-\lambda\tilde{d}_{i_sj_s}-p_{i_sl}^{-1}r_{i_sl}-1}}. \tag{14}$$

The distribution $\check{P}_{j_sm,i_sl}$ is calculated for the fixed q_{j_sm}, as shown in Equation (7). Subsequently, with the transition probability distribution $\check{P}_{j_sm,i_sl}$ fixed, the reconstruction distribution $\check{q}_{j_sm}$ is calculated according to Equation (8). Based on these updated distributions, the distribution error

$$\epsilon^* = \sum_{i_s,l,j_s,m}\left|\check{P}_{j_sm,i_sl} - P_{j_sm,i_sl}\right| + \sum_{j_s,m}\left|\check{q}_{j_sm} - q_{j_sm}\right| \tag{15}$$

is calculated. If ϵ^* is less than the predetermined threshold ϵ, the EBA algorithm is considered to have converged for the current λ, and the corresponding RD pair $(R(\lambda), D(\lambda))$ is obtained by

$$\begin{aligned} R(\lambda) &= \textstyle\sum_{i_s}\sum_{j_s}\sum_l\sum_m p_{i_sl}\check{P}_{j_sm,i_sl}\log\frac{p_{i_sl}\check{P}_{j_sm,i_sl}}{\sum_{l''}\sum_{m''} p_{i_sl''}\check{q}_{j_sm''}} \\ D(\lambda) &= \sum_{i_s}\sum_{j_s}\sum_l\sum_m p_{i_sl}\check{P}_{j_sm,i_sl}\tilde{d}_{i_sj_s} \end{aligned}. \tag{16}$$

Otherwise, these distributions are updated as the initial distributions for the next iteration, i.e.,

$$\begin{aligned} P_{j_sm,i_sl} &= \check{P}_{j_sm,i_sl} \\ q_{j_sm} &= \check{q}_{j_sm} \end{aligned}. \tag{17}$$

The entire semantic RD function curve can be obtained by sweeping through the value of λ, where each $(R(\lambda), D(\lambda))$ pair corresponds to a point on the curve. The EBA algorithm incorporates synonymous mappings, enabling it to compute the semantic rate-distortion function, while the classical BA algorithm operates solely at the syntactic symbol level and does not account for any semantic structure or synonymous relationships.

3.2. EBA Algorithm for the Optimal Synonymous Mapping

When the synonymous mapping is unknown, an optimization framework that combines the EBA algorithm with simulated annealing is introduced to find the optimal synonymous mapping (i.e., the mapping with maximum synonymous number). To formally characterize the synonymous number, we introduce the following definition.

Definition 1. *The synonymous number L_s is defined by*

$$L_s = \sum_{i_s} p_{i_s}N_{i_s} \tag{18}$$

where N_{i_s} represents the number of syntactic symbols mapped to the i_s-th semantic symbol.

As mentioned in [24], it is worth noting that the semantic RD function is not necessarily non-negative, thus requiring specific objective constraints to ensure meaningful results. In this paper, the distortion value at $R_s = 0$ is considered as the constraint, which represents the maximum achievable distortion when no information is transmitted. For convenience, we denote the synonymous mapping as M. Algorithm 2 describes the optimization process.

Algorithm 2: Optimization framework for finding the optimal synonymous mapping.

Input: Distortion constraint D', initial temperature T, cooling rate α, temperature threshold ϵ_T, maximum iterations N_{max}

Output: Optimal synonymous mapping M_{opt} and corresponding $R_s(D)_{opt}$

Initialize mapping M with a one-to-one syntactic mapping;
Calculate $R_s(D)$ using Algorithm 1;
$R_s(D)_{opt} \leftarrow R_s(D)$ and $M_{opt} \leftarrow M$;
iterations $\leftarrow 0$;
while $T > \epsilon_T$ *or iterations* $< N_{max}$ **do**
    Generate new mapping M_{new} by merging syntactic symbols;
    Calculate $R_s(D)_{new}$ using Algorithm 1;
    if $D_0^{new} \geq D'$ **then**
        if $R_s(D)_{new}$ *curve is below* $R_s(D)_{opt}$ *curve* **then**
            $R_s(D)_{opt} \leftarrow R_s(D)_{new}$;
            $M_{opt} \leftarrow M_{new}$;
            $M \leftarrow M_{new}$;
        end
        else
            Calculate probability $P_u \leftarrow \exp(-(D_0^{new} - D')/T)$;
            Generate random number $P_0 \in [0, 1]$;
            if $P_0 \leq P_u$ **then**
                $M \leftarrow M_{new}$;
            end
        end
    end
    $T \leftarrow \alpha T$;
    iterations $\leftarrow$ iterations + 1;
end
return M_{opt} *and* $R_s(D)_{opt}$

The inputs to the optimization framework include the distortion constraint D', the initial temperature T, the cooling rate α, the temperature threshold ϵ_T, and the maximum number of iterations N_{max}. The outputs are the optimal synonymous mapping M_{opt} (which achieves the maximum L_s under the constraint $D = D'$ when $R_s(D) = 0$) and the corresponding semantic RD function $R_s(D)_{opt}$.

In the proposed optimization framework, a syntactic mapping is considered as the initial synonymous mapping M, where one semantic symbol corresponds to one syntactic symbol. Given a source distribution $p_{i_s l}$ and a distortion measure $\tilde{d}_{i_s j_s}$, the problem is transformed into calculating the semantic RD function under a given synonymous mapping, which can be directly solved using the EBA algorithm as shown in Algorithm 1. Then set $M_{opt} = M$, $R_s(D)_{opt} = R_s(D)$.

Initialize the iteration number to zero. While the current temperature T is larger than the threshold ϵ_T or the number of iterations is less than the maximum limit N_{max}, the following steps are executed:

At each iteration, based on the current mapping and the probability distribution, which determines the probability of merging adjacent syntactic symbols into one semantic symbol, a new semantic mapping M_{new} is generated. The new semantic RD curve $R_s(D)_{new}$ is then computed using the EBA algorithm. The corresponding D_0^{new} is defined as the value of D when $R_s(D)new = 0$. If D_0^{new} is less than the constraint D', indicating that M_{new} does not meet the optimization objective and thus needs to be regenerated. Otherwise, it is checked whether the $R_s(D)_{new}$ curve lies below the current $R_s(D)$ curve. If so, both the optimal mapping M_{opt} and current mapping M are updated. To avoid the local optimum solutions, even if M_{new} yields a higher semantic RD curve, it may still be accepted with probability

$$P_u = e^{-\frac{D_0^{new} - D'}{T}}. \tag{19}$$

The temperature T and the number of iterations are updated after each iteration.

The algorithm terminates when $T \leq \epsilon_T$ or the iterations reach N_{max}, returning the optimal mapping M_{opt} and its corresponding semantic RD function $R_s(D)_{opt}$. Through the combination of the EBA algorithm and simulated annealing, the optimal synonymous mapping M_{opt} under the given constraints can be found.

4. The Application to SKB

SKB is a key concept in the semantic communication system that facilitates the semantic encoding and decoding process between the transmitter and the receiver [28–31]. For each mobile intelligent agent, it defines a set of semantic knowledge vectors corresponding to different classes, which can be obtained from Word2Vec or manually annotated semantic attribute vectors [32]. These vectors not only characterize the attribute features of corresponding classes but also reflect the semantic relationships among different classes. Specifically, we denote $\mathcal{W} \triangleq \{w_1, w_2, \cdots, w_N\}$ as the set of syntactic vectors and $\mathcal{S} \triangleq \{s_1, s_2, \cdots, s_K\}$ as the set of semantic vectors, where semantic vector s_i is referred to as the semantic prototype of the i-th class. It is worth noting that both transmitter and the receiver use the same SKB to ensure the effectiveness of semantic communication.

From the perspective of SIT, the SKB can be considered as a specific instance of synonymous mapping, where each semantic vector s corresponds to a semantic symbol $\tilde{x}$ defined in Section 2, and syntactic vectors w sharing similar semantic vectors can be regarded as syntactic symbols x mapped to the same semantic symbol $\tilde{x}$. Therefore, for a given source, the semantic RD function can be directly computed using the EBA algorithm by considering the SKB as a synonymous mapping. By varying the SKB size, different semantic RD function results can be obtained. Through analyzing the relationship between the semantic RD function and the SKB size, the semantic communication compression efficiency can be quantitatively evaluated, which has theoretical significance for guiding the design of the semantic communication system.

An example is presented in Figure 2 to illustrate the SKB as a synonymous mapping. The left part shows the syntactic samples, the middle part presents the set of syntactic vectors $\mathcal{W}$, and the right part displays the set of semantic vectors $\mathcal{S}$. For this example, a dataset containing 10 uniformly distributed samples from 5 different bird classes is considered, with 2 samples per class (samples of the same class are circled by dashed lines). These images are first converted into vector representations to obtain their corresponding syntactic vectors. Obviously, the probability distribution is given by $p(w) = \{0.1, 0.1, \cdots, 0.1\}$. Assuming that the SKB contains semantic attributes of 4 bird classes, these syntactic vectors can be mapped to the corresponding semantic vector space. Specifically, this mapping can be expressed as: $\{w_1, w_2\} \to s_1$, $\{w_3, w_4\} \to s_2$, $\{w_5, w_6\} \to s_3$, $\{w_7, w_8\} \to s_4$. However, for the remaining bird class whose semantic attributes are not included in the SKB, its two syntactic vectors correspond to distinct semantic vectors in semantic space, i.e., $w_9 \to s_5$ and $w_{10} \to s_6$. Consequently, the probability distribution $p(s) = \{0.2, 0.2, 0.2, 0.2, 0.1, 0.1\}$

is obtained. Based on $p(w)$ and $p(s)$, the semantic RD result can be computed using the EBA algorithm.

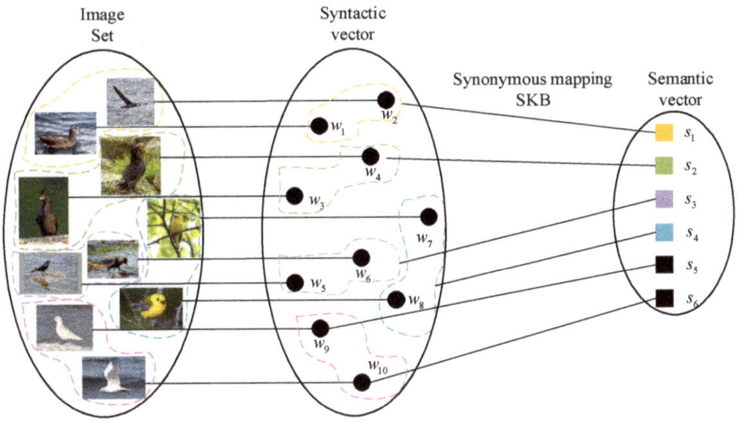

Figure 2. Illustration of the SKB as a synonymous mapping. The left part shows the syntactic samples, the middle part shows the set of syntactic vectors $\mathcal{W}$, and the right part shows the set of semantic vectors $\mathcal{S}$.

5. Experimental Results

In this section, the simulation results of the semantic RD function calculated by the EBA algorithm are presented. The semantic mean squared error (SMSE) distortion is adopted, which is defined as

$$\tilde{d}_{i_s j_s} = \begin{cases} 0, & i_s = j_s \\ \frac{1}{l \cdot m} \cdot \sum_l \sum_m \|x_{i_s,l} - \hat{x}_{j_s,m}\|^2, & i_s \neq j_s \end{cases}. \tag{20}$$

Figure 3a shows the semantic RD function of Gaussian sources with zero mean and variance $\sigma^2 = 1$ computed by the EBA algorithm under the given synonymous mappings f_x, where the blue curve represents the syntactic RD function of a Gaussian source. For the Gaussian source, 201 syntactic points are uniformly sampled in the interval $[-10, 10]$, and their corresponding probability distribution $p(x)$ follows the Gaussian distribution. Based on f_x, $p(\tilde{x})$ can be easily obtained. Figure 3b,c illustrate two synonymous mappings f_x^1 and f_x^2 with $L_s = 1.0809$ and $L_s = 1.4736$, respectively. With the error threshold $\epsilon = 0.0001$, the corresponding semantic RD function can be computed using the EBA algorithm. The simulation results show that the semantic RD function decreases as the synonymous number L_s grows and becomes significantly lower than the classic counterparts. Furthermore, it can be observed that when $L_s = 1$, the semantic RD function is identical to the classic RD function.

Given the distortion constraint D', the optimal synonymous mapping can be obtained using Algorithm 2. The simulated annealing parameters are set as follows: initial temperature $T = 100$, maximum iteration number $N_{max} = 1000$, cooling rate $\alpha = 0.99$, and temperature threshold $\epsilon_T = 10^{-6}$. For the aforementioned Gaussian source, 201 syntactic points are uniformly sampled in the interval $[-10, 10]$. The interval merging is performed as follows: based on the probability distribution (a mixture of two Gaussian distributions centered at -10 and 10), an interval endpoint is first located and extended by δ, where δ ranges from -0.5 to 0.5 with a step size of 0.1. Then, multiple syntactic points within this extended range are merged into a semantic representation. Finally, to maintain symmetry, the same merging process is applied to the corresponding symmetric interval. With $D' = 0.5$, the optimization results are presented in Figure 4. Specifically, Figure 4b shows an intermediate synonymous mapping with $L_s = 1.1328$ during the optimization process, while Figure 4c presents the final optimal synonymous mapping with $L_s = 1.3470$. The results clearly show that the optimization algorithm finds the synonymous mapping with the maximum L_s under the given distortion constraint. Figure 4a illustrates the corresponding semantic RD function, where the blue curve represents the syntactic RD function of a Gaussian source. It should be noted that the optimization problem may yield multiple optimal synonymous mappings under the current constraint setting, and additional constraints would be necessary to ensure uniqueness.

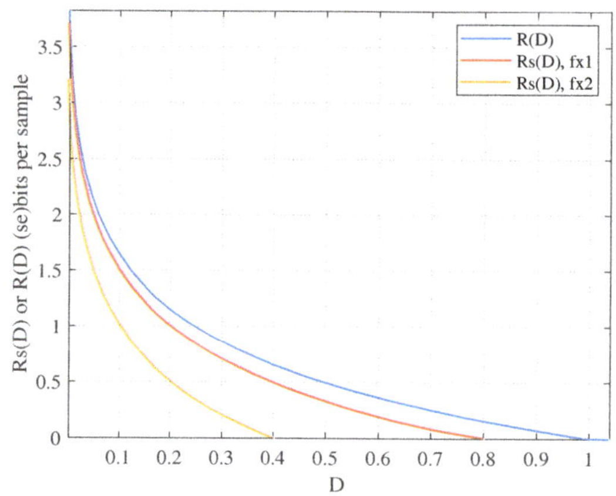

(**a**) Semantic RD function of Gaussian sources

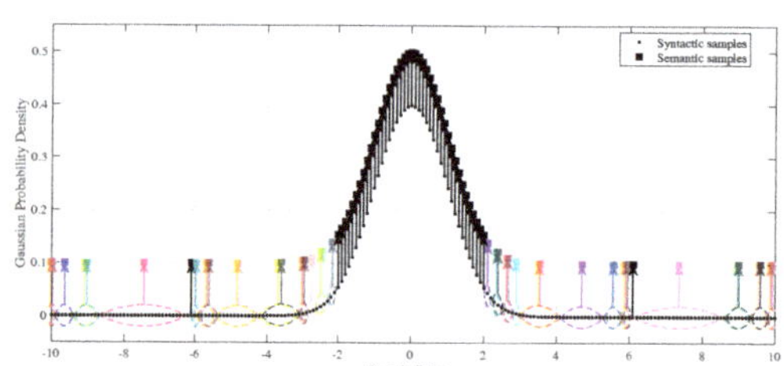

(**b**) Synonymous mapping $f_x^1$with $L_s = 1.0809$

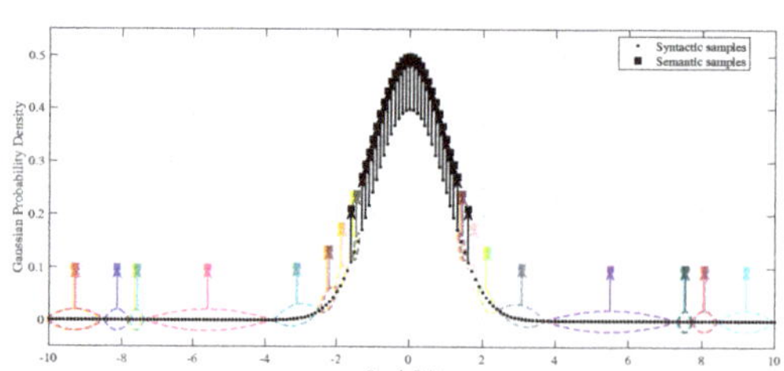

(**c**) Synonymous mapping $f_x^2$with $L_s = 1.4736$

Figure 3. Semantic RD function of Gaussian sources under the given synonymous mappings.

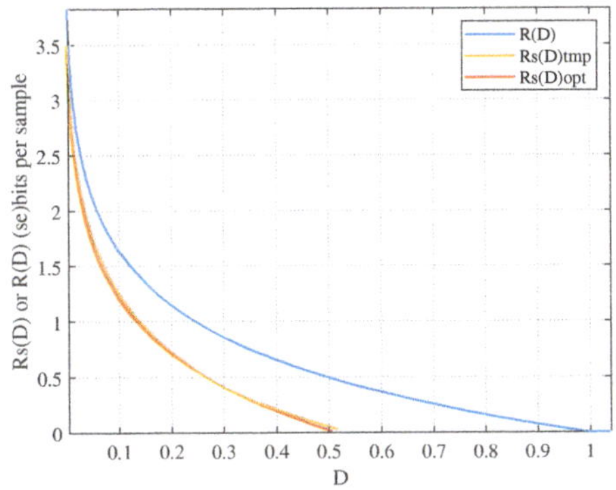

(**a**) Semantic RD function

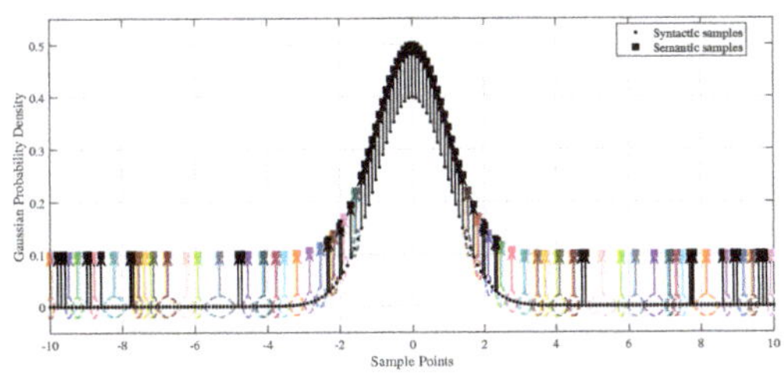

(**b**) Intermediate synonymous mapping with $L_s = 1.1328$

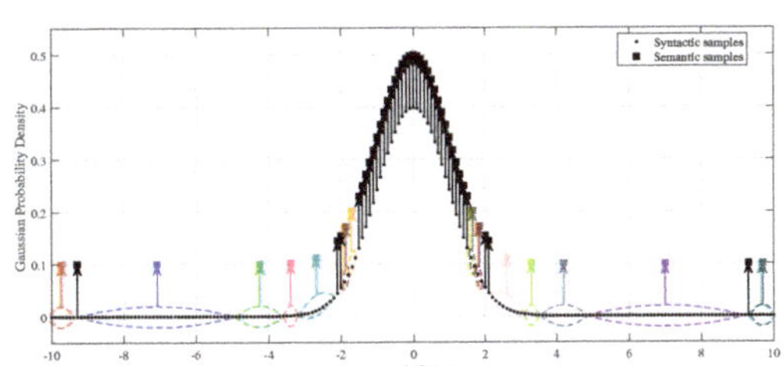

(**c**) Optimal synonymous mapping with $L_s = 1.3470$

Figure 4. Semantic RD function and optimal synonymous mapping obtained by the optimization algorithm.

Using the CUB dataset [27], the test set can be seen as an SKB containing 50 feature vectors; 2 samples are selected from each class, resulting in a total of 100 test samples. To investigate the impact of SKB size on the semantic RD function, the number of test samples is fixed and three SKB configurations are considered: 10 classes, 20 classes, and the complete 50 classes from the CUB test set. Figure 5 shows the semantic RD results under different SKB sizes, where the blue curve represents the syntactic RD function for transmitting 100 samples without the assistance of SKB. The simulation result shows that as the SKB size increases, the semantic RD function decreases significantly, indicating improved compression efficiency. Furthermore, compared with the syntactic RD function, the simulation result demonstrates the effectiveness of the SKB in improving compression performance. In practical applications, the semantic RD function can be computed by the EBA algorithm and then utilized for theoretical analysis to predict the required SKB size and compression limits based on specific task objectives.

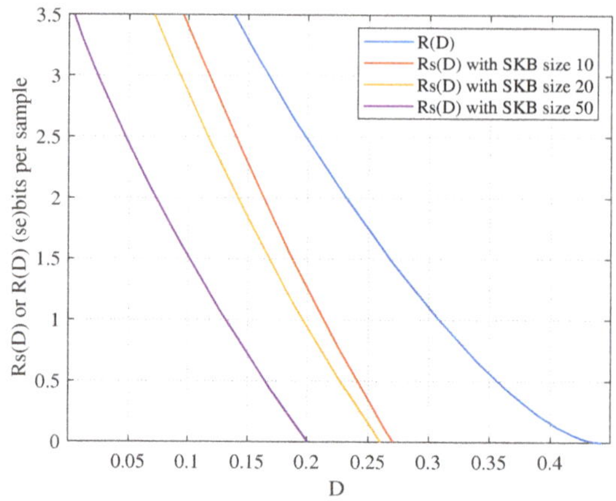

Figure 5. Impact of SKB size on the semantic RD function.

6. Conclusions

In this paper, we extend the classic BA algorithm to semantic communication based on synonymous mapping and propose the EBA algorithm, which can compute the semantic RD function for a given source. Furthermore, by combining it with the optimization algorithm, the optimal synonymous mapping can be obtained under given constraints. From a practical perspective, by considering the SKB as a given synonymous mapping, the EBA algorithm provides an approach for analyzing the SKB size, thereby offering theoretical insights into the trade-off between semantic distortion and compression performance. Future work could explore the application of the EBA algorithm in other scenarios, establishing a more comprehensive theoretical foundation for the semantic communication system.

Author Contributions: Writing—original draft, Y.H.; writing—review and editing, Y.L., Y.S., K.N., N.M., S.C. and P.Z. All authors have read and agreed to the published version of the manuscript.

Funding: This research was funded by the National Natural Science Foundation of China under Grant 62293481, Grant 9246730007, Grant 62471054, Grant 62301471, and Grant 62293482 and the National Science and Technology Major Project-Mobile Information Networks under Grant No.2024ZD1300700.

Institutional Review Board Statement: Not applicable.

Data Availability Statement: The original contributions presented in this study are included in the article. Further inquiries can be directed to the corresponding author.

Conflicts of Interest: The authors declare no conflicts of interest.

Abbreviations

The following abbreviations are used in this manuscript:

BA	Blahut–Arimoto
CIT	classical information theory
CUB	CUB-200-2011 Birds
EBA	extended Blahut–Arimoto
RD	rate-distortion
SIT	semantic information theory
SKB	semantic knowledge base
SMSE	semantic mean squared error

References

1. Gündüz, D.; Qin, Z.; Aguerri, I.E.; Dhillon, H.S.; Yang, Z.; Yener, A.; Wong, K.K.; Chae, C.B. Beyond transmitting bits: Context, semantics, and task-oriented communications. *IEEE J. Sel. Areas Commun.* **2022**, *41*, 5–41. [CrossRef]
2. Weaver, W. The mathematics of communication. In *Communication Theory*; Routledge: London, UK , 2017; pp. 27–38. [CrossRef]
3. Farsad, N.; Rao, M.; Goldsmith, A. Deep learning for joint source-channel coding of text. In Proceedings of the 2018 IEEE International Conference on Acoustics, Speech and Signal Processing (ICASSP), Calgary, AB, Canada, 15–20 April 2018; pp. 2326–2330.
4. Xie, H.; Qin, Z.; Li, G.Y.; Juang, B.H. Deep learning enabled semantic communication systems. *IEEE Trans. Signal Process.* **2021**, *69*, 2663–2675. [CrossRef]
5. Bourtsoulatze, E.; Kurka, D.B.; Gündüz, D. Deep joint source-channel coding for wireless image transmission. *IEEE Trans. Cogn. Commun. Netw.* **2019**, *5*, 567–579. [CrossRef]
6. Weng, Z.; Qin, Z. Semantic communication systems for speech transmission. *IEEE J. Sel. Areas Commun.* **2021**, *39*, 2434–2444. [CrossRef]
7. Shannon, C.E. A mathematical theory of communication. *Bell Syst. Tech. J.* **1948**, *27*, 379–423. [CrossRef]
8. Shannon, C.E. Coding Theorems for a Discrete Source With a Fidelity CriterionInstitute of Radio Engineers, International Convention Record, vol. 7, 1959. In *Claude E. Shannon: Collected Papers*; IEEE Press: Piscataway, NJ, USA, 1993. [CrossRef]
9. Berger, T. Rate-distortion theory. In *Wiley Encyclopedia of Telecommunications*; John Wiley & Sons: Hoboken, NJ, USA, 2003.
10. Cover, T.M. *Elements of Information Theory*; John Wiley & Sons: Hoboken, NJ, USA , 1999. [CrossRef]
11. Arimoto, S. An algorithm for computing the capacity of arbitrary discrete memoryless channels. *IEEE Trans. Inf. Theory* **1972**, *18*, 14–20. [CrossRef]
12. Blahut, R. Computation of channel capacity and rate-distortion functions. *IEEE Trans. Inf. Theory* **1972**, *18*, 460–473. [CrossRef]
13. Dupuis, F.; Yu, W.; Willems, F.M. Blahut-Arimoto algorithms for computing channel capacity and rate-distortion with side information. In Proceedings of the International Symposium onInformation Theory, ISIT 2004, Chicago, IL, USA, 27 June–2 July 2004; p. 179.
14. Lingyi, C.; Wu, S.; Ye, W.; Wu, H.; Zhang, W.; Wu, H.; Bo, B. A Constrained BA Algorithm for Rate-Distortion and Distortion-Rate Functions. *Csiam Trans. Appl. Math.* **2025**, *6*, 350–379. [CrossRef]
15. Matz, G.; Duhamel, P. Information geometric formulation and interpretation of accelerated Blahut-Arimoto-type algorithms. In Proceedings of the Information Theory Workshop, San Antonio, TX, USA, 24–29 October 2004; pp. 66–70.
16. Sayir, J. Iterating the Arimoto-Blahut algorithm for faster convergence. In Proceedings of the 2000 IEEE International Symposium on Information Theory (Cat. No. 00CH37060), Sorrento, Italy, 25–30 June 2000; p. 235.
17. Yu, Y. Squeezing the Arimoto–Blahut algorithm for faster convergence. *IEEE Trans. Inf. Theory* **2010**, *56*, 3149–3157. [CrossRef]
18. Rose, K. A mapping approach to rate-distortion computation and analysis. *IEEE Trans. Inf. Theory* **1994**, *40*, 1939–1952. [CrossRef]
19. Stavrou, P.A.; Kountouris, M. The role of fidelity in goal-oriented semantic communication: A rate distortion approach. *IEEE Trans. Commun.* **2023**, *71*, 3918–3931. [CrossRef]
20. Serra, G.; Stavrou, P.A.; Kountouris, M. Alternating Minimization Schemes for Computing Rate-Distortion-Perception Functions with f-Divergence Perception Constraints. *arXiv* **2024**, arXiv:2408.15015.
21. Serra, G.; Stavrou, P.A.; Kountouris, M. Computation of rate-distortion-perception function under f-divergence perception constraints. In Proceedings of the 2023 IEEE International Symposium on Information Theory (ISIT), Taipei, Taiwan, 25–30 June 2023; pp. 531–536.
22. Li, D.; Huang, J.; Huang, C.; Qin, X.; Zhang, H.; Zhang, P. Fundamental limitation of semantic communications: Neural estimation for rate-distortion. *J. Commun. Inf. Netw.* **2023**, *8*, 303–318. [CrossRef]
23. Liang, Z.; Niu, K.; Wang, C.; Xu, J.; Zhang, P. Synonymous Variational Inference for Perceptual Image Compression. *arXiv* **2025**, arXiv:2505.22438.
24. Niu, K.; Zhang, P. A mathematical theory of semantic communication. *J. Commun.* **2024**, *45*, 7–59. [CrossRef]
25. Farquhar, S.; Kossen, J.; Kuhn, L.; Gal, Y. Detecting hallucinations in large language models using semantic entropy. *Nature* **2024**, *630*, 625–630. [CrossRef]
26. Rose, K. Deterministic annealing for clustering, compression, classification, regression, and related optimization problems. *Proc. IEEE* **1998**, *86*, 2210–2239. [CrossRef]
27. Wah, C.; Branson, S.; Welinder, P.; Perona, P.; Belongie, S. *The Caltech-UCSD Birds-200–2011 Dataset*; Tech. Rep. CNS-TR-2010-001; California Institute of Technology: Pasadena, CA, USA, 2011.
28. Ren, J.; Zhang, Z.; Xu, J.; Chen, G.; Sun, Y.; Zhang, P.; Cui, S. Knowledge base enabled semantic communication: A generative perspective. *IEEE Wirel. Commun.* **2024**, *31*, 14–22. [CrossRef]
29. Ni, F.; Wang, B.; Li, R.; Zhao, Z.; Zhang, H. Interplay of semantic communication and knowledge learning. In *Wireless Semantic Communications: Concepts, Principles and Challenges*; John Wiley & Sons: Hoboken, NJ, USA, 2025; pp. 87–108.

30. Hello, N.; Di Lorenzo, P.; Strinati, E.C. Semantic communication enhanced by knowledge graph representation learning. In Proceedings of the 2024 IEEE 25th International Workshop on Signal Processing Advances in Wireless Communications (SPAWC), Lucca, Italy, 10–13 September 2024; pp. 876–880.
31. Yi, P.; Cao, Y.; Kang, X.; Liang, Y.C. Deep learning-empowered semantic communication systems with a shared knowledge base. *IEEE Trans. Wirel. Commun.* **2023**, *23*, 6174–6187. [CrossRef]
32. Sun, Y.; Chen, H.; Xu, X.; Zhang, P.; Cui, S. Semantic knowledge base-enabled zero-shot multi-level feature transmission optimization. *IEEE Trans. Wirel. Commun.* **2023**, *23*, 4904–4917. [CrossRef]

entropy

MDPI

Article

On the Rate-Distortion Theory for Task-Specific Semantic Communication

Jingxuan Chai [1], Huixiang Zhu [2], Yong Xiao [2,3,4,*], Guangming Shi [1,3,4] and Ping Zhang [5]

1 School of Artificial Intelligence, Xidian University, Xi'an 710126, China; chaijingxuan@stu.xidian.edu.cn (J.C.); gmshi@xidian.edu.cn (G.S.)
2 School of Electronic Information & Communications, Huazhong University of Science & Technology, Wuhan 430074, China; zhuhuixiang@hust.edu.cn
3 Peng Cheng Laboratory, Shenzhen 518055, China
4 Pazhou Laboratory (Huangpu), Guangzhou 510335, China
5 State Key Laboratory of Networking and Switching Technology, Beijing University of Posts and Telecommunications, Beijing 100876, China; pzhang@bupt.edu.cn
* Correspondence: yongxiao@hust.edu.cn

Abstract: Semantic communication has attracted considerable interest due to its potential to support emerging human-centric services, such as holographic communications, extended reality (XR), and human-machine interactions. Different from traditional communication systems that focus on minimizing the symbol-level distortion (e.g., bit error rate, signal-to-noise ratio, etc.), semantic communication targets at delivering the intended meaning at the destination user which is often quantified by various statistical divergences, often referred to as the semantic distances. Currently, there still lacks a unified framework to quantify the rate-distortion tradeoff for semantic communication with different task-specific semantic distance measures. To tackle this problem, we propose the task-specific rate-distortion theory for semantic communication where different task-specific statistic divergence metrics can be considered. To investigate the impact of different semantic distance measures on the achievable rate, we consider two popular tasks, classification and signal generation. We present the closed-form expressions of the semantic rate-distortion functions for these two different tasks and compare their performance under various scenarios. Extensive experimental results are presented to verify our theoretical results.

Keywords: semantic communication; rate-distortion theory; task-specific communication

1. Introduction

The rapidly growing need for human-oriented communication services has led to the emergence of semantic communication, a novel communication paradigm that focuses on effectively transmitting and delivering the meaning of messages [1–5]. Here, the semantic meaning can be the implicit interpretation of the messages, which may not always be directly observable to users.

Instead of ensuring the bit-level accuracy of the message of delivery, in semantic communication, semantic distance quantifying how well the intended meaning is preserved during transmission is often measured by statistical divergence [2,6–9]. Generally speaking, different tasks require different divergences to measure their semantic distances because the choice of metrics depends on the nature of the task, the structure of the data, and the desired semantic fidelity. For example, in classification tasks, the Kullback-Leibler (KL) divergence has been commonly considered as the main metrics for measuring the difference between predicted probability distributions and true labels, or for model comparison in Bayesian inference [10]. Also, in generation tasks, the Wasserstein distance is known to exhibit good performance in capturing the geometric relationships between high-dimensional distributions and providing stable gradient flows for generative adversarial networks (GANs) [11].

Despite its promising potential, most existing work focuses on optimizing the semantic communication system based on a single predefined and fixed semantic distance metric [12,13]. There is still lacking a unified information theoretic framework that quantifies the achievable rate for semantic communication under different tasks with different semantic distance measures. In this paper, we propose a novel task-specific rate-distortion theory for semantic communication in which different task-specific statistic divergence-based distance metrics are considered and compared. We consider two popular tasks, classification and signal generation, to investigate the impact of different types of semantic distances on the minimum achievable rate. We present the closed-form expressions of the semantic rate-distortion functions for both tasks and compare their performance under various scenarios. We summarize the main contribution of this paper as follows:

(1) We propose a novel taks-specific semantic communication architecture that generalizes traditional rate-distortion theory by incorporating a general divergence metrics to quantify semantic distance.
(2) We derive the closed-form expressions for the semantic rate-distortion functions under Gaussian semantic sources, specifically for Wasserstein distance, KL divergence, and reverse KL divergence, revealing fundamental tradeoffs among transmission rate, distortion, and semantic distance.
(3) Extensive experiments are conducted on image-based semantic communication systems for both generation and classification tasks. Our results suggest that the proposed framework significantly outperforms traditional MSE-based approaches, with reverse KL divergence demonstrating superior perceptual quality in generation tasks and KL divergence achieving higher classification accuracy.

The rest of this paper is organized as follows: Section 2 introduces the background and preliminaries. The system model and theoretical results are discussed in Sections 3 and 4, respectively. Section 5 present experimental results and the paper is concluded in Section 6.

2. Background and Preliminary

The rate-distortion theory is a branch of information theory that focuses on characterizing the fundamental limit of lossy data compression by the optimal trade-off between the minimum data rate required between the source and the destination (rate) and the maximum tolerable distortion allowed when reconstructing the source data by the destination user based on the received signal (distortion). More formally, for a given distortion level $D \geq 0$, the fundamental tradeoff between the minimum achievable rate and maximum tolerable distortion is often represented by the rate-distortion function $R(D)$, defined by

$$\begin{aligned} R(D) = \inf_{p_{\hat{S}|S}} & I(S, \hat{S}) \\ \text{s.t. } & E[d(S, \hat{S})] \leq D, \end{aligned} \quad (1)$$

where $d(S, \hat{S})$ is the distortion metric that is adopted by the source and destination users for measuring the difference between the original source signal and the signal recovered by the destination. In traditional Shannon rate-distortion theory, d is often measured by the symbol-level distortion such as Hamming distortion for discrete signal sources and mean squared error (MSE) distortion for continuous signal sources.

Motivated by the fact that human users are more sensitive to the perceptual quality of the recovered signal, instead of symbol-level recovery, the rate-distortion-perception (RDP) theory has been developed by incorporating the constraint on the statistic divergence of the probability distributions, called perception level, between the source and the recovered signal [12,13]. More formally, for a given maximum-tolerable distortion level D and a perception level P, the rate-distortion-perception function $R(D,P)$ is defined as

$$\begin{aligned} R(D,P) = \inf_{p_{\hat{S}|S}} & I(S,\hat{S}) \\ \text{s.t. } & E[d(S,\hat{S})] \le D, \\ & \theta(p_S, p_{\hat{S}}) \le P, \end{aligned} \tag{2}$$

where $\theta(p_S, p_{\hat{S}})$ is the perception metric that measures the statistical divergence between the source signal distribution and the reconstructed signal distribution. Most existing works on RDP focus on a single perception metrics, such as the total variation (TV) distance [14,15]. Recently, some researchers have investigated the RDP problem under other divergence metrics such as Wasserstein distance [16] and f-divergence [17–20].

In this paper, we investigate the rate-distortion theory of task-specific semantic communication. Our key innovation lies in introducing a generalized divergence metric that quantifies the statistical semantic distance between source and reconstructed signals, where the specific metric is adaptively selected based on communication task requirements. We also obtain the closed-from expressions of the semantic rate-distortion function under various task-specific divergence metrics. A comparison between the existing information-theoretic results of the RDP theory and our results under various types of source signals is shown in Table 1, where the columns of "SI" represent whether or not the corresponding result considers side information.

Table 1. A summary of information-theoretic results in RDP theory. For Bernoulli case, the source follows a Bernoulli distribution with parameter π. For Gaussian case, the source follows a Gaussian distribution $\mathcal{N}(0,1)$. Here $D_1 = \frac{P}{1-2\pi-2P}$, $D_2 = 2\pi(1-\pi) - (1-2\pi)P$.

Divergence	Source	$R(D,P)$	SI	Work
TV	Bernoulli	$\begin{cases} H_b(\pi) - H_b(D), & D \in [0, D_1) \\ 2H_b(\pi) + H_b(\pi - P) - H_t(\frac{D-P}{2}, \pi) \\ -H_t(\frac{D+P}{2}, 1-\pi), & D \in [D_1, D_2) \\ 0, & D \in [D_2, \infty] \end{cases}$	✗	[13]
WD	Gaussian	$\begin{cases} \frac{1}{2}\log \frac{1}{1-\left(\frac{(1-\sqrt{P})^2+1-D}{2-2\sqrt{P}}\right)^2}, & \sqrt{P} \le 1-\sqrt{\lvert 1-D \rvert} \\ \max\{\frac{1}{2}\log\frac{1}{D}, 0\}, & \sqrt{P} > 1-\sqrt{\lvert 1-D \rvert} \end{cases}$	✗	[16]
WD, KL, RKL	Gaussian	Equations (15)–(17)	✓	Proposed

3. System Model and Problem Formulation

3.1. System Model

We adopt the system model of semantic communication introduced in [2,5], where the primary objective is to effectively convey implicit semantic information to end users by leveraging background knowledge, as depicted in Figure 1. Formally, let the semantic source signal S^n represent an n-length i.i.d. random variable containing intrinsic information that remains unobservable to the encoder. The encoder accesses only a limited set of k indirect observations U^k about the semantic source, which may comprise noisy samples or partial observations. The relationship between the source and the observations is characterized by the conditional probability $p_{U|S}$ of obtaining observation U given source S. Due to the limited channel capacity, the encoder produces an encoded signal sequence

X^m with its length being m. The decoder then receives a potentially corrupted version $\hat{X}^m$ of this signal through a discrete memoryless channel modeled by $p_{\hat{X}|X}$.

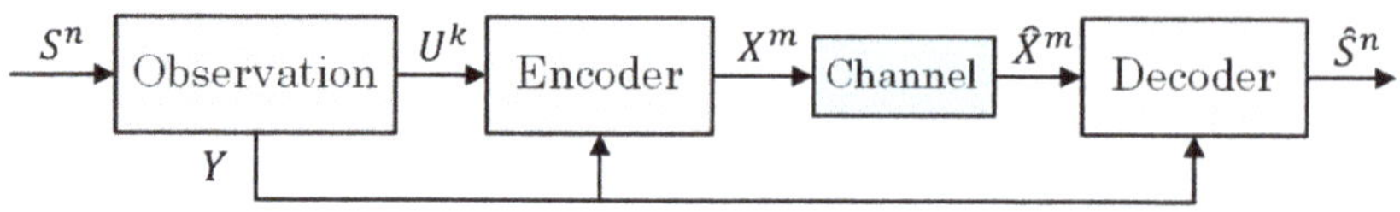

Figure 1. Illustration of the semantic communication model.

Moreover, we assume that both the encoder and the decoder have access to side information, denoted as Y. This may correspond to some background knowledge shared between the source and the destination. For example, in human communication scenarios [5], different users may employ different languages or word sequences to convey the same semantic concept. In such cases, the side information may include the user's language background and lexical preferences when transforming the semantic information source into observable signals. The main objective of the decoder is to infer the implicit semantic source $\hat{S}$ with a certain level of signal fidelity, based on the signal received from the channel and the available side information.

It can be observed that the above model is similar to the indirect source coding problem with side information in the classic information theory setup. In this paper, we extend the above problem to a more general scenario in which, in addition to MSE distortion, we also consider the impact of task-specific semantic distances on the minimum rate required to recover the implicit signal source. We define the semantic distance as a much broader range of signal fidelity measures, including not only classical distribution divergences such as KL and Wasserstein distance but also the state-of-the-art perceptual quality measures such as the Inception score and SSIM.

We should clarify that the semantic source S and its recovery $\hat{S}$ can indeed take traditional forms whether discrete or continuous. Different from traditional communication systems that rely on symbol-level distortion metrics such as Hamming distance and MSE distortion, our proposed semantic communication employs a general task-specific divergence measure to quantify semantic distance. This reflects how effectively the recovered information supports the intended task rather than merely assessing signal-level similarity. Our proposed framework extends classical rate-distortion theory by incorporating the constraint on semantic distance, thereby establishing a theoretical foundation for task-specific communication systems.

Figure 1 illustrates a general semantic communication architecture that encompasses both lossy compression and joint source-channel coding scenarios. In our theoretical analysis, we primarily focus on the lossy compression case with a noiseless channel to clearly demonstrate the fundamental semantic rate-distortion tradeoff.

3.2. Problem Formulation

In this paper, we consider the following two types of constraints to measure the fidelity of the signal recovered by the decoder:

(1) *MSE Distortion:* This corresponds to the signal-level distortion measured by the average squared difference of energy between the source and reconstructed signal, defined as $d : \mathcal{S}^n \times \mathcal{S}^n \to \mathbb{R}$. Denote by $D \geq 0$ the maximum MSE distortion level that can be tolerated by the destination user. We can write the following constraint:

$$C1: \quad E[d(S^n, \hat{S}^n)] \leq D. \tag{3}$$

(2) *Task-relevant Semantic Distance:* This corresponds to the task-specific distribution divergence that measures the semantic dissimilarity between the semantic source and its recovery. Generally speaking, different tasks require different divergence metrics and have different maximum tolerable levels of the recovered signal. For example, KL divergence has been commonly used for signal classification [10,21] and Wasserstein distance has often been adopted for signal generation [11]. In addition to the standard distribution divergence, some novel metrics for measuring the perceptual quality of specific types of signals, such as image and video, including Inception score [22] and SSIM [23], can also be included in our framework. Let $\mathcal{M}$ be the set of supported tasks. Let θ_m and P_m be the task-specific (semantic) distance metric and the maximum tolerable level for task m. We can write the following constraint on the task-relevant semantic distance:

$$\text{C2:} \quad \theta_m(p_{S^n}, p_{\hat{S}^n}) \leq P_m. \tag{4}$$

We then define a semantic code as follows:

Definition 1. *A semantic code (f_n, g_n) consists of a encoder, defined as*

$$f_n : \mathcal{U}^n \times \mathcal{Y}^n \to \{1, 2, ..., 2^{nR}\}, \tag{5}$$

and a decoder, defined as

$$g_n : \{1, 2, ..., 2^{nR}\} \times \mathcal{Y}^n \to \hat{\mathcal{S}}^n. \tag{6}$$

The main objective is to characterize the region of all the achievable tuples $\langle R, D, P_m \rangle$ for each specific task. More formally, we first define the notion of achievability as follows:

Definition 2. *A tuple $\langle R, D, P_m \rangle$ is achievable if there exists a sequence of codes (f_n, g_n) that satisfies both constraints C1 and C2.*

Finally, we define the semantic rate-distortion function as follows:

Definition 3. *The task-specific semantic rate-distortion function with side information is defined as the minimum rate required to achieve a signal fidelity that simultaneously satisfies constraints C1 and C2, when the side information Y is available at both the encoder and the decoder, i.e., for task m, we have*

$$R_m(D, P_m) = \inf\{R : \langle R, D, P_m \rangle \text{ is achievable}\}. \tag{7}$$

In the rest of this paper, we first present some theoretical results in Section 4 and present experimental results in Section 5. We compare achievable rates across different task requirements through both theoretical derivations and empirical evaluations.

4. Theoretical Results

In this section, we first propose the theoretical formulation of the task-specific semantic communication problem to demonstrate how our architecture generalizes generation and classification tasks. We then obtain the closed-form expressions of the Gaussian semantic rate-distortion function under Wasserstein distance, KL divergence and reverse KL divergence.

Since obtaining the exact closed-form solutions of (7) involves a general coding theorem which is out of the scope of this paper, we adopt the following formulation:

$$\begin{aligned} R_m(D, P_m) = &\inf_{p_{\hat{S}|UY}} I(U, \hat{S}|Y) \\ \text{s.t. } &E[d(S^n, \hat{S}^n)] \le D, \\ &\theta_m(p_{S^n}, p_{\hat{S}^n}) \le P_m, \end{aligned} \tag{8}$$

to characterize the task-specific semantic rate-distortion function. This formulation, which uses conditional mutual information between encoder input and decoder output for the rate term, aligns with established approaches in rate-distortion theory [13,15,16].

It is worth noting that our proposed task-specific semantic communication framework can be extended to a range of applications that can be formulated in terms of statistical divergence minimization, such as Bayesian regression [24] and density estimation [25]. There are, however, many other tasks that require novel signal fidelity measures beyond simple distribution divergence minimization. Novel tasks such as reinforcement learning and clustering, for instance, cannot be adequately formulated using divergence minimization approaches. How these alternative measures on codec design and achievable rates is worth further investigation, which will be left for our future work.

4.1. Classification Task

We begin by formalizing our semantic communication framework for the classification task, based on the maximum a posterior probability (MAP) principle [26–28].

The classifier outputs the probability of each class label, given by $q(U)$, where $q(\cdot)$ is the coding function of the classifier. We can write the standard classifier based on the MAP principle as follows:

$$\hat{s} = \arg\max_{s \in \mathcal{S}} p_{S|U}(q(U)|U). \tag{9}$$

We can then apply the following divergence with respect to the output of the classification model to develop the classifier. Formally, the loss function under the MAP approach in (1) of [26] can be reformulated as

$$d_{KL}(p_{\text{data}}, p_{\text{model}}) = d_{KL}(p_S, p_{\hat{S}}) \tag{10}$$

where p_{data} is the distribution of true class labels, which is actually the distribution of semantic source p_S, and p_{model} is the distribution induced by the classifier, which is actually the distribution of the output probability of the semantic decoder $p_{\hat{S}} = p_{q(U)}$.

Consider the tradeoff relationship between the transmission rate, bit-wise distortion, and the classification accuracy; the objective of the semantic rate-distortion problem in (7) specified for the classification task is defined by:

$$\begin{aligned} R_{\text{cls}}(D, P_{\text{cls}}) = &\inf_{p_{\hat{S}|UY}} I(U, \hat{S}|Y) \\ \text{s.t. } &E[d(S^n, \hat{S}^n)] \le D, \\ &d_{KL}(p_{S^n}, p_{\hat{S}^n}) \le P_{\text{cls}}, \end{aligned} \tag{11}$$

where P_{cls} is the parameter that quantifies the maximum tolerable level of misclassification. The distortion term $E[d(S^n, \hat{S}^n)]$ measures the bit-wise fidelity and the semantic distance term $d_{KL}(p_{S^n}, p_{\hat{S}^n})$ measures the classification accuracy. This allows us to characterize the tradeoff relationship between the reconstruction quality and the classification accuracy. Note that the mismatch between the random variables in the mutual information term and the constraint terms is a characteristic of indirect source coding problems [29,30].

This formulation extends our general framework while maintaining consistency with the rate-distortion tradeoff established in previous sections. The KL divergence constraint directly links communication efficiency with classification performance through rate-distortion theory.

4.2. Generation Task

Our proposed semantic communication architecture can also accommodate the generation task. In this context, the semantic source S represents the ground-truth data distribution, while the indirect observation U constitutes a noisy or compressed version of S. For instance, in image generation scenarios, S might correspond to the distribution of high-resolution natural images, while U could represent their quantized or downsampled versions. The decoder learns a mapping function that reconstructs an approximation $\hat{S}$ of the original semantic source, where both S and $\hat{S}$ share the same alphabet $\mathcal{S}$

Inspired by the existing literature on generative models [11,31], we can adopt Wasserstein distance and reverse KL divergence for exact realizations of the semantic distance that measures the perceptual quality of generative samples. Using the above formulation, the semantic rate-distortion problem in (7) for generation task under Wasserstein distance is then specified by:

$$\begin{aligned} R_{\text{gen}}(D, P_{\text{gen}}) = \inf_{p_{\hat{S}|UY}} & \; I(U, \hat{S}|Y) \\ \text{s.t. } & E[d(S^n, \hat{S}^n)] \le D, \\ & d_{WD}(p_{S^n}, p_{\hat{S}^n}) \le P_{\text{gen}}. \end{aligned} \tag{12}$$

Here, P_{cls} is the parameter that quantifies the maximum tolerable statistical difference between p_S and $p_{\hat{S}}$. Similarly, we can also formulate the semantic rate-distortion problem under reverse KL divergence as follows:

$$\begin{aligned} R_{\text{gen}}(D, P_{\text{gen}}) = \inf_{p_{\hat{S}|UY}} & \; I(U, \hat{S}|Y) \\ \text{s.t. } & E[d(S^n, \hat{S}^n)] \le D, \\ & d_{RKL}(p_{S^n}, p_{\hat{S}^n}) \le P_{\text{gen}}. \end{aligned} \tag{13}$$

The operational significance of the above formulations is demonstrated in Section 5 through the following: their direct implementation as training objectives; empirical validation of the predicted tradeoffs; quantitative comparison to baseline approaches. This formulation allows us to systematically analyze the tradeoffs between compression efficiency R, bit-wise reconstruction fidelity D, and perceptual quality P_{gen} in generation-oriented semantic communication systems.

4.3. SRD Function for Gaussian Sources

To explore the semantic rate-distortion tradeoff, we derive the closed-form expressions of the semantic rate-distortion functions by considering a particular continuous semantic source, the Gaussian source. More formally, the semantic source is modeled as a standard Gaussian source $S \in \mathcal{N}(0,1)$. We assume that the side information also follows a Gaussian distribution, denoted as $Y \in \mathcal{N}(0,1)$. The correlation between the semantic source S and the side information Y is characterized as

$$Y = \eta S + \sqrt{1-\eta^2} Z \tag{14}$$

where $\eta \in [0,1]$ and $Z \in \mathcal{N}(0,1)$ is a random variable independent of S.

We now present the main results of the Gaussian semantic rate-distortion functions as stated in the following two theorems:

Theorem 1. *The semantic rate-distortion function for Gaussian semantic source $\mathcal{N}(0,1)$ under Wasserstein distance is*

$$R_{WD}(D,P)=\begin{cases}\frac{1}{2}\log\frac{1-\eta^2}{D}, & \text{if } 0<D<D_1^L\\ \frac{1}{2}\log\frac{1-\eta^2}{1-\left(\frac{1+\sigma_1^2-D}{2\sigma_1}\right)^2}, & \text{if } D_1^L\leq D<D_1^R,\\ 0, & \text{if } D\geq D_1^R\end{cases}\tag{15}$$

where $D_1^L:=\sqrt{P}$, $D_1^R:=1+\sigma_1^2-2\eta\sigma_1$ and $\sigma_1=1-\sqrt{P}$.

Proof. See Appendix A. □

Theorem 2. *The semantic rate-distortion function for Gaussian semantic source $\mathcal{N}(0,1)$ under KL divergence is*

$$R_{KL}(D,P)=\begin{cases}\frac{1}{2}\log\frac{1-\eta^2}{D}, & \text{if } 0<D<D_2^L\\ \frac{1}{2}\log\frac{1-\eta^2}{1-\left(\frac{1+\sigma_2^2-D}{2\sigma_2}\right)^2}, & \text{if } D_2^L\leq D<D_2^R,\\ 0, & \text{if } D\geq D_2^R,\end{cases}\tag{16}$$

and that under reverse KL divergence is

$$R_{RKL}(D,P)=\begin{cases}\frac{1}{2}\log\frac{1-\eta^2}{D}, & \text{if } 0<D<D_3^L\\ \frac{1}{2}\log\frac{1-\eta^2}{1-\left(\frac{1+\sigma_3^2-D}{2\sigma_3}\right)^2}, & \text{if } D_3^L\leq D<D_3^R,\\ 0, & \text{if } D\geq D_3^R,\end{cases}\tag{17}$$

where $D_r^L:=1-\sigma_2^2, D_2^R:=1+\sigma_2^2-2\eta\sigma_2$, and $D_3^L:=1-\sigma_3^2, D_3^R:=1+\sigma_3^2-2\eta\sigma_3$. Here, $\sigma_2,\sigma_3\in[0,1]$ are the unique solutions to

$$\begin{aligned}\ln\sigma_2^2+\frac{1}{\sigma_2^2}-1-2P=0,\\ \ln\sigma_3^2-\sigma_3^2+1+2P=0,\end{aligned}\tag{18}$$

respectively.

Proof. See Appendix A. □

We note that, taking $P\to\infty$, we have

$$R_{WD}(D,\infty)=R_{KL}(D,\infty)=R_{RKL}(D,\infty)=R(D)=\frac{1}{2}\log\frac{1-\eta^2}{D},\tag{19}$$

where $R(D)$ is the classical Gaussian rate-distortion function with side information (see the Wyner–Ziv theorem in [32]). This indicates that, when the constraint on statistical difference is inactive, the semantic rate-distortion functions under Wasserstein distance,

KL divergence, and reverse KL divergence all degenerate into traditional rate-distortion functions. When the side information is independent of the source S (i.e., taking $\eta = 0$), the semantic rate-distortion function $R_W(D, P)$ in Theorem 1 reduces to the rate-distortion-perception function derived in [16]. The above consistency of our results with prior works confirms both the generalization capability and the correctness of our theoretical results.

Based on Theorems 1 and 2, we can quantify the rate difference between the Gaussian semantic rate-distortion function and the traditional rate-distortion function. Formally, taking Wasserstein distance as an example, we have

$$R_{WD}(D, P) - R(D) = \frac{1}{2} \log \frac{D}{1 - \left(\frac{1-(P+D)/2}{1-\sqrt{P}}\right)^2}. \tag{20}$$

We can observe that the above rate difference is always positive. Moreover, this rate difference increases with D and decreases with P. This indicates that, under the same distortion level, the extra rate to satisfy the constraint on semantic distance increases when this constraint becomes tighter. This additional rate requirement decreases when lower bit-wise quality is acceptable.

From Theorem 2, we can derive an inequality relationship between the Gaussian semantic rate-distortion functions under KL divergence and reverse KL divergence:

$$R_{KL}(D, P) \geq R_{RKL}(D, P), \tag{21}$$

where the equality holds if and only if $P = \infty$. This means that, under the same D and P, it generally requires a higher rate to meet the constraint on KL divergence, compared to reverse KL divergence. This also demonstrates that reverse KL divergence is a more rate-efficient metric for preserving the source distribution under the same fidelity requirements. Moreover, the equality condition $P = \infty$ indicates that both divergence metrics converge to the same rate-distortion function when the semantic distance constraint becomes inactive. This aligns with the observation of Theorem 2 that both functions degenerate to the classical Wyner–Ziv rate-distortion function in this limit. The theoretical inequality is further supported by the experimental results in Section 5, where generation tasks using reverse KL divergence achieve better perceptual quality at lower rates.

When $D \leq D_1^L$ (resp. $D \leq D_2^L$, $D \leq D_3^L$), the semantic rate-distortion functions under Wasserstein distance (resp. KL divergence, reverse KL divergence) also coincide with the classical rate-distortion function with side information $R(D)$. This is because, when the distortion constraint is tight, the optimal coding scheme of the classical Shannon rate-distortion problem is able to satisfy the constraint on the distribution-wise semantic distance. Therefore, there is no need to require extra rate to meet the constraints on statistical divergence.

In Figure 2a, we plot the curves of semantic rate-distortion functions using the results of Theorems 1 and 2. We observe a three-way tradeoff among transmission rate, bit-wise distortion, and distribution-wise semantic distance. Specifically, given the distortion level, an increase in transmission rate leads to higher semantic fidelity, i.e., smaller semantic distance. Similarly, given the transmission rate, an increase in semantic fidelity leads to lower bit-wise quality, i.e., higher MSE distortion. This observation is aligned with the existing rate-distortion-perception tradeoff [13].

We further observe that, for a given semantic distance level and MSE distortion level, the semantic rate-distortion function under KL divergence consistently exceeds that under the Wasserstein distance. This suggests that KL divergence imposes a stricter measure of statistical difference than the Wasserstein distance for Gaussian sources. However, the semantic rate-distortion function can only capture one aspect of the difference between these two divergence metrics. A more comprehensive discussion is made in the experiment section by investigating the task performance under different divergence metrics for practical sources of real-world datasets.

Figure 2b illustrates the semantic rate-distortion curves under varying side information conditions. The parameter η represents the covariance between S and Y, serving as a measure of their statistical dependence. A higher η indicates a stronger correlation between the semantic source S and the side information Y, while $\eta = 0$ corresponds to complete independence between them.

As shown in Figure 2b, the semantic rate-distortion function varies significantly with η. Specifically, for a given distortion level D, the required semantic rate decreases as η increases. Furthermore, the maximum achievable distortion diminishes with larger values of η. These observations suggest that side information effectively acts as shared background knowledge between the encoder and the decoder, facilitating more efficient semantic communication. The stronger the correlation, i.e., the higher η, the greater the reduction in the required rate for a given level of reconstruction fidelity.

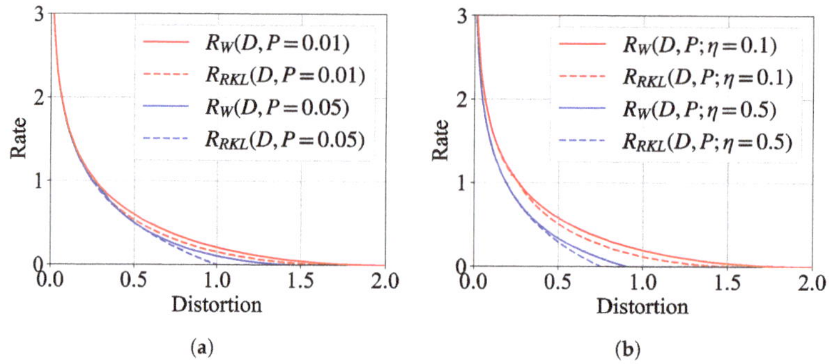

Figure 2. Curve plots of Gaussian semantic rate-distortion functions. (**a**) Rate-distortion curves under some fixed perception level; (**b**) Rate-distortion curves under same perception level and some fixed η values.

5. Experimental Results

In this section, we conduct experiments on practical semantic sources and demonstrate the simulation results for our semantic communication system for generation and classification tasks.

5.1. Experimental Setups

We consider a semantic communication system in which the semantic information source S corresponds to image signals that are uniformly randomly sampled from a given image dataset. The indirect observation U is the quantized version of the semantic source. Specifically, the indirect observation process is represented as $U = Q(S; L_o)$, where $Q(\cdot; L_o)$ denotes a uniform quantizer with L_o quantization levels. The side information is some intrinsic feature of the semantic source, denoted as $Y = f_Y(U)$, where Y denotes the side information of U and f_Y denotes the function that outputs the feature of U, parameterized by deep neural nets (DNNs). The output of the feature extraction net f_Y is a low-dimensional feature vector, which is then concatenated with both the encoder and decoder inputs, serving as side information available to the encoder and the decoder. Denote by d_Y, the dimension of the feature vector of the side information. The encoder maps the indirect observation u into a d-dimensional latent feature vector, whose entries are then uniformly quantized to L_r levels to obtain the output message. The decoder finally recovers the semantic information based on the received message and the side information. The entire process of semantic source coding can be formulated as

$$\hat{S} = f_D(f_E(U,Y),Y), \tag{22}$$

where f_E and f_D denote the encoding and decoding functions. Note that the uniform quantization of the encoder gives an upper bound of $d\log(L_r)$ for rate R. We measure symbol-based signal distortion using the mean-squared-error (MSE), denoted as $E(||S - \hat{S}||^2)$. For a fixed transmission rate, the objective of the semantic rate-distortion function in (12) under Wasserstein distance can be formulated in terms of the following loss function:

$$\mathcal{L}_{\text{gen}} = E(||S - \hat{S}||^2) + \lambda_{\text{gen}} \cdot d_{WD}(p_S, p_{\hat{S}}), \tag{23}$$

where λ_{gen} is a tuning parameter that controls the tradeoff between the bit-wise quality and perceptual quality. Similarly, the loss function for generation under reverse KL divergence is formulated as

$$\mathcal{L}_{\text{gen}} = E(||S - \hat{S}||^2) + \lambda_{\text{gen}} \cdot d_{RKL}(p_S, p_{\hat{S}}), \tag{24}$$

We obtain the experimental SRD curves by evaluating the distortion and perceptual quality of our model on the test set of the image dataset. Different semantic rate-distortion points are obtained by training the model under different desired settings. For the classification task, the objective of the semantic rate-distortion function in (11) for classification can be obtained by minimizing the following loss function:

$$\mathcal{L}_{\text{cls}} = E(||S - \hat{S}||^2) + \lambda_{\text{cls}} \cdot d_{KL}(p_S, p_{\hat{S}}), \tag{25}$$

where λ_{cls} is a tuning parameter that controls the tradeoff between the bit-wise quality and classification performance.

5.2. *Results for Generation Tasks*

In this section, we present the experimental results of generation tasks and investigate the impact of different divergences on perceptual quality. Here, we consider two specific realizations of the divergence function for semantic distance, Wasserstein distance and reverse KL divergence. This choice aligns with our theoretical analysis of Gaussian semantic rate-distortion functions. We also compare our framework with the VAE-based semantic coding paradigm, where a variational codec is optimized for MSE distortion and standard KL divergence.

More specifically, we conduct experiments on two widely used benchmark datasets: MNIST and CIFAR10. The MNIST dataset, consisting of 28 × 28 grayscale handwritten digits, serves as a simple yet effective semantic source to demonstrate the tradeoffs between rate, distortion, and perceptual quality. To further evaluate the scalability of our approach, we also employ the more complex CIFAR10 dataset, which contains 32 × 32 color images across 10 object categories. For both datasets, the semantic source S corresponds to the original images, while the indirect observation U is their quantized version.

5.2.1. Achievable Rates Under Different Distance Measures

Figure 3a illustrates the simulation semantic rate-distortion curves under Wasserstein distance and reverse KL divergence, denoted by R_{WD} and R_{RKL}, respectively. We observe a three-way trade-off among transmission rate, MSE distortion, and semantic distance: For a fixed distortion level, increasing the transmission rate leads to smaller semantic distance. Conversely, under a fixed rate, stricter semantic distance constraints result in higher bit-wise distortion. To obtain a more intuitive understanding of the semantic rate-distortion tradeoff, we also demonstrate a 3D surf plot of the semantic rate-distortion function in Figure 3b.

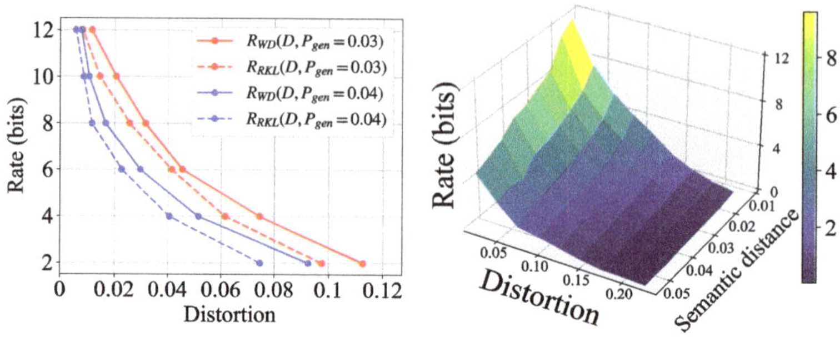

(**a**) (**b**)

Figure 3. Experimental semantic rate-distortion functions for generation task. (**a**) Curve plots of semantic rate-distortion functions under different divergence metrics; (**b**) Surf plot of 3D semantic rate-distortion function.

Moreover, we also note that the rate under Wasserstein distance to achieve the same levels of distortion and semantic distance is always higher than that under reverse KL divergence. This confirms that Wasserstein distance imposes a more stringent measure of statistical dissimilarity, as noted in Section 4.3. The above observations are aligned with the theoretical predictions for Gaussian sources in Theorems 1 and 2.

5.2.2. Impact of Indirect Observation

To investigate the impact of the indirect observation process, we demonstrate the simulation semantic rate-distortion function under different settings of the quantization levels L_o of the indirect observation in Figure 4. Here, "direct observation" corresponds to the case where the encoder directly observes the original samples from semantic source S. From the simulation results on MNIST in Figure 4a and those on CIFAR10 in Figure 4b, we observe that the required rate to achieve the same distortion level increases when the quantization level decreases. This phenomenon can be attributed to the information loss incurred during the quantization process, which forces the system to compensate through higher channel capacity.

Moreover, our experiments reveal a notable difference in how indirect observation affects performance across the MNIST and CIFAR10 datasets. While both datasets exhibit degraded performance under coarser quantization, the impact is significantly more pronounced for CIFAR10. Specifically, for MNIST at 12 bits, direct observation achieves MSE = 0.0061, while quantization degrades performance to 0.0072 ($L_o = 8, +18\%$) and 0.011 ($L_o = 4, +80\%$). For CIFAR10 at equivalent 384 bits (12 × 32), MSE increases from 0.013 (direct) to 0.018 ($L_o = 32, +38\%$) and 0.026 ($L_o = 16, +100\%$). This discrepancy stems from the inherent complexity difference between the two datasets. The CIFAR10 dataset contains more complex visual features and higher-dimensional structures, rendering it more susceptible to information degradation during indirect observation. In contrast, the MNIST dataset's simpler digit patterns and limited variability demonstrate greater resilience to quantization artifacts. This observation suggests that semantic communication systems handling complex, real-world data require more careful design of the observation process compared to those processing simpler, structured data.

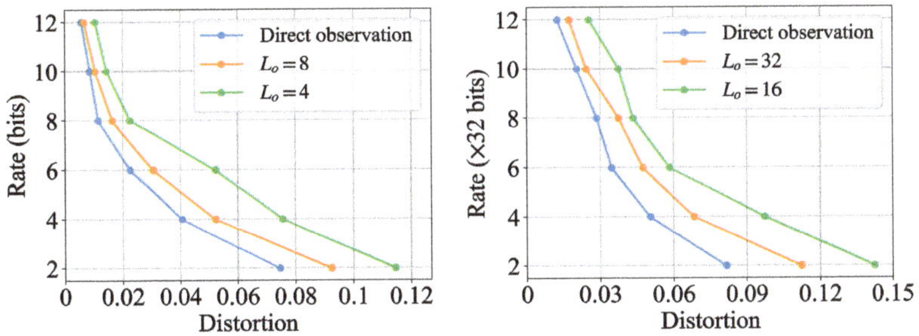

(a) (b)

Figure 4. Experimental semantic rate-distortion functions for generation task under different L_o values. (**a**) Results on MNIST; (**b**) Results on CIFAR10.

5.2.3. Impact of Side Information

In order to observe the role of side information in the proposed semantic communication systems, we also conduct experiments under different settings of side information. Figure 5 demonstrates the simulation semantic rate-distortion curves under different settings of the dimensions of feature vectors of side information, on both MNIST and CIFAR10 datasets. Both the results in Figure 5a and those in Figure 5b show that the required rate can be reduced when side information at the encoder and the decoder is accessible, and the reduced rate increases with the the amount of information in Y, as measured by the value of d_Y. The above observations are aligned with the theoretical results of the Gaussian semantic rate-distortion functions in Theorems 1 and 2. This again justifies the fact that offering side information as the background knowledge of the users can effectively save communication resources.

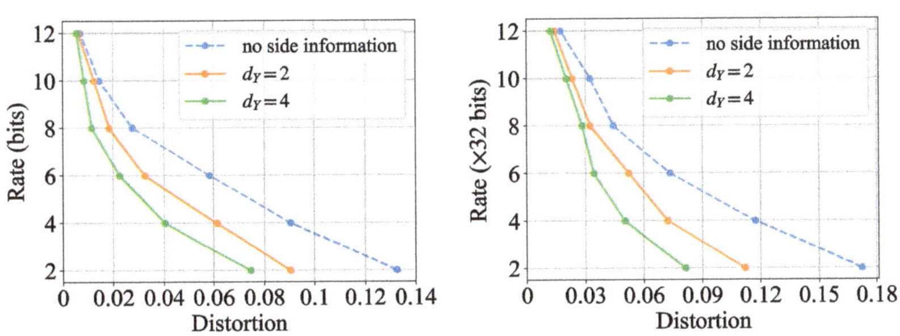

(a) (b)

Figure 5. Experimental semantic rate-distortion functions for generation task under different values of d_Y. (**a**) Results on MNIST; (**b**) Results on CIFAR10.

Moreover, we observe that the reduced rate due to the existence of side information is much higher at low rates than at high rates, demonstrating that side information plays a more crucial role when channel capacity is limited. For the MNIST dataset, at the lowest rate of 2 bits, the MSE distortion decreases significantly from 0.133 (no side information) to 0.091 ($d_Y = 2$, −31.6%) and further to 0.075 ($d_Y = 4$, −43.6%). In contrast, at the highest rate of 12 bits, the distortion only reduces from 0.0075 to 0.0068 (−9.3%) and 0.0061 (−18.7%) for $d_Y = 2$ and $d_Y = 4$, respectively. A similar trend is observed for CIFAR10. At 64 bits, the distortion drops substantially from 0.173 to 0.113 (−34.7%) and 0.082 (−52.6%) when side information is introduced, while at 384 bits (12 × 32) the improvement is more modest, from 0.018 to 0.015 (−16.7%) and 0.013 (−27.8%). These results clearly indicate that side information provides the greatest relative benefit in low-rate regimes where the channel capacity is severely constrained. The additional background knowledge helps compensate for the lack of transmission bandwidth, enabling more efficient semantic communication. As the rate increases, the marginal utility of side information decreases, as the system can rely more on the primary channel to convey necessary information. This observation aligns with theoretical expectations and reveals the importance of incorporating side information, particularly in bandwidth-limited scenarios.

5.2.4. Perceptual Quality Under Different Divergences

In Figure 6, we demonstrate the visual results of generated image samples of our proposed model under Wasserstein distance and reverse KL divergence. We also consider a baseline model where a VAE encoder–decoder pair is adopted for our framework. We see that a higher transmission rate results in increased perceptual quality, which coincides with the theoretical observation of the tradeoff relationship between rate and semantic distance for Gaussian semantic rate-distortion functions.

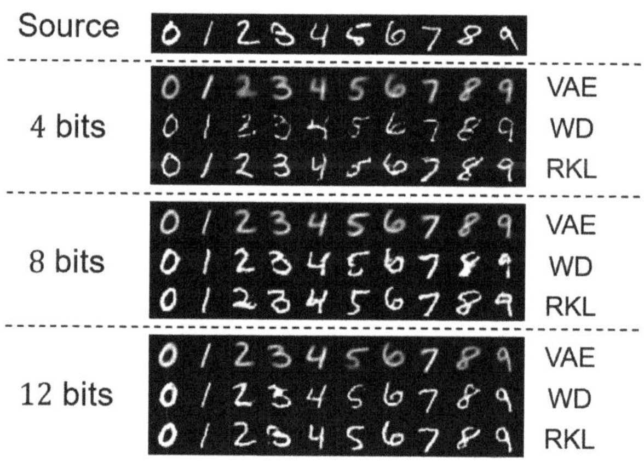

Figure 6. Visual results of the generated image samples under different divergences. The "Source" row displays the ground-truth images available at the encoder. The subsequent rows show reconstructed images at transmission rates of 4 bits, 8 bits, and 12 bits. The columns labeled "WD" and "VAE" demonstrate reconstruction results using our proposed semantic communication architecture optimized for Wasserstein distance and reverse KL divergence respectively.

We also observe that the generative quality of our proposed models consistently outperforms the traditional VAE-based coding scheme. The method optimizing reverse KL divergence produces images with the best perceptual quality. This is aligned with the empirical observation in [31] that leveraging reverse KL divergence can improve the sharpness of generated samples. The inferior perceptual quality of VAE-based approaches can be attributed to their optimization objective: by minimizing standard KL divergence, VAEs prioritize generating easily classifiable samples at the expense of human-oriented perceptual fidelity [31]. This fundamental tradeoff between discriminative performance and perceptual quality underscores the advantages of our proposed divergence metrics for semantic communication.

In order to make a fair comparison between the perceptual quality of generated samples under different divergence constraints, we adopt a widely used metric that quantifies the perceptual quality of generated images, the Inception score (IS) [22]. It provides a way of measuring both the clarity of the generated images and their diversity. Formally, the IS of an image source p_G is calculated using the following formula:

$$\mathrm{IS} = \exp\left(H_p(K) - E_{X\sim p_G}[H_{p_G}(K|\hat{S})]\right) \tag{26}$$

where p is the induced distribution of the Inception-V3 network, $\hat{S}$ is the random variable of generated images, and K is the corresponding class label of $\hat{S}$. The generative quality of generated images increases with IS.

In Figure 7, we present the comparison of Inception scores across the evaluated models at varying transmission rates. Here, "MSE" denotes the model minimizing MSE distortion only, which is realized by taking $\lambda_{\text{gen}} = 0$ in the loss function in (23). Both the results on MNIST in Figure 7a and those on CIFAR10 in Figure 7b demonstrate clear positive correlation between transmission rate and Inception score for all models, which directly corroborate the rate-semantic distance trade-off relationship illustrated in Figure 4a. This observation confirms our theoretical expectation that higher transmission rates enable better preservation of semantic information, as reflected in improved Inception scores. Moreover, we observe that the models with additional divergence constraints produce images with higher perceptual quality with a huge margin, particularly at low-bit regimes, compared to the model that implicitly minimizes the MSE distortion. This means that our proposed architecture is able to obtain much higher human-oriented perceptual quality compared to traditional bit-wise loss function-based models.

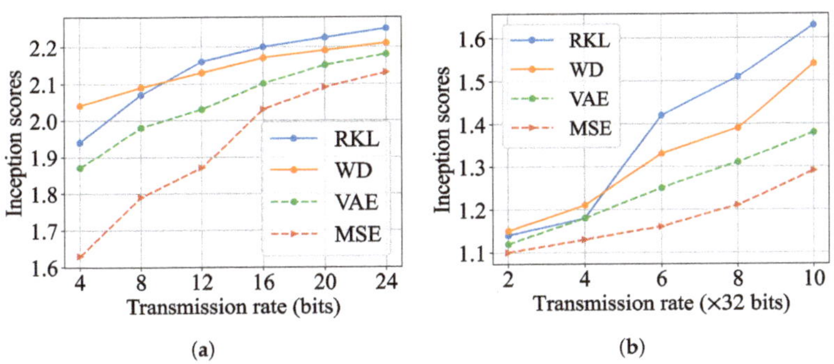

Figure 7. Image quality evaluation of generated samples on MNIST under different divergence metrics. (**a**) Results on MNIST; (**b**) Results on CIFAR10.

Furthermore, the relative performance ranking among models, with KL and WD consistently outperforming the VAE baseline, aligns precisely with the visual comparisons shown in Figure 6. This consistency between quantitative metrics and human perceptual evaluation strengthens the validity of our experimental findings and provides comprehensive evidence for the superiority of our proposed approaches.

5.3. Results for Classification Tasks

To further evaluate the effectiveness of our proposed semantic communication framework across different tasks, we conduct classification experiments using the MNIST dataset under different divergence metrics.

In Figure 8a, we present the classification accuracy of the recovered images under KL divergence and reverse KL divergence. Here, $R(D)$ represents the simulation curves under only MSE distortion, which is obtained by setting $\lambda_{\text{cls}} = 0$ in (25). The results demonstrate that, at any given transmission rate, our proposed models achieve significantly higher classification accuracy compared to conventional bit-wise approaches, highlighting the effectiveness of our task-specific semantic communication architecture. Moreover, the results exhibit the following tradeoff relationship: (1) higher transmission rates consistently lead to improved classification accuracy across all models; (2) a more stringent constraint on semantic distance, i.e., higher P_{gen}, results in higher classification accuracy. This also aligns with the theoretical and empirical findings of the semantic rate-distortion tradeoff, confirming that increased transmission rates enhance the preservation of semantic information. A 3D surf plot of the semantic rate-distortion function for the classification task is shown in Figure 8b.

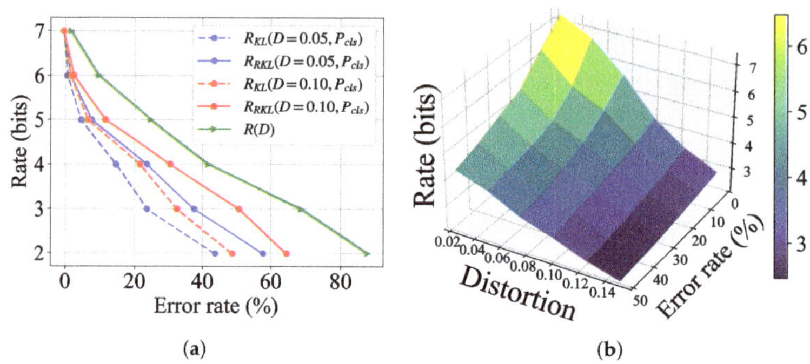

Figure 8. Experimental semantic rate-distortion functions for classification tasks on MNIST dataset. (**a**) Rate-distortion curves; (**b**) Three-dimensional surface plot.

Our experiments also reveal a significant divergence in task performance between the KL-optimized and reverse KL-optimized models. As shown in Figure 8a, the standard KL divergence approach demonstrates superior classification accuracy compared to its reverse KL counterpart, particularly in low-rate regimes ($R \leq 5$ bits) where the performance gap exceeds 11% when $R =$ bits and $P = 0.01$. This empirical observation corroborates fundamental information-theoretic principles: the forward KL divergence directly minimizes the expected negative log-likelihood of the true distribution under the approximated distribution [33], making it theoretically optimal for discriminative tasks like classification.

The performance advantage diminishes at higher transmission rates ($R > 6$ bits), where both divergence metrics achieve comparable accuracy within a 2% margin. This convergence suggests that sufficient channel capacity can compensate for the inherent limitations of reverse KL divergence in classification scenarios. The model minimizing KL divergence to produce distributions with "mode-seeking" behavior [34], while beneficial for perceptual quality, as shown in Figures 6 and 7a, appears less suitable for preserving the complete feature distributions needed for robust classification at low bitrates.

In summary, the classification results validate the practical utility of our semantic communication framework to classification tasks, demonstrating the flexibility of the proposed architecture to different tasks.

6. Conclusions

In this paper, we have investigated the fundamental limits of task-specific semantic communication by extending the traditional rate-distortion theory to incorporate semantic distance constraints, as measured by a general divergence metric. We have considered a semantic communication model where the encoder accesses the semantic information source only through indirect observations, while both the encoder and the decoder utilize available side information. Our framework specifically addresses classification and generation tasks in task-specific semantic communication systems. We have derived the closed-form expressions for Gaussian semantic rate-distortion functions under various divergence metrics, revealing a fundamental three-way tradeoff involving transmission rate, bit-wise distortion, and distribution-wise semantic distance. Experimental validation using image-based semantic sources confirms these theoretical findings.

Author Contributions: Conceptualization, J.C., H.Z., Y.X., G.S., and P.Z.; methodology, Y.X.; software, J.C.; supervision, H.Z., Y.X., G.S., and P.Z.; validation, J.C.; writing—original draft, J.C.; writing—review & editing, Y.X. and J.C. All authors have read and agreed to the published version of the manuscript.

Funding: The work of Y. X., G. S., and P. Z. was supported in part by the Mobile Information Network National Science and Technology Key Project under grant 2024ZD1300700. The work of G. S. was supported in part by the National Natural Science Foundation of China (NSFC) under grant 62293483. The work of P. Z. was supported in part by the NSFC under grants 62293480 and 62293481.

Institutional Review Board Statement: Not applicable.

Data Availability Statement: The MNIST and CIFAR10 datasets used in this study are publicly available through the PyTorch library. The datasets can be accessed via the PyTorch official documentation: https://pytorch.org/vision/stable/datasets.html.

Conflicts of Interest: The authors declare no conflicts of interest.

Appendix A. Proof of Theorems 1 and 2

To begin with, we note that the mutual information between two Gaussian distributions is independent of their means. Therefore, without loss of generality, we may assume that the recovery source $\hat{S}$ and the semantic source S share the same mean. Specifically, we let $\hat{S} \sim \mathcal{N}(0, \sigma^2)$ for analytical convenience.

We first discuss the case where the constraint on Wasserstein distance is not active, i.e.,

$$d_{WD}(p_S, p_{\hat{S}}) = (1-\sigma)^2 < P. \tag{A1}$$

In this case, based on the Wyner–Ziv theorem, we have

$$R_\alpha(D, P) = \frac{1}{2}\log\frac{1-\eta^2}{D}, \tag{A2}$$

with

$$\sigma = 1 - D. \tag{A3}$$

Taking (A3) back into (A1), we have

$$0 \leq D < \sqrt{P} = D_1^L. \tag{A4}$$

When the constraint on Wasserstein distance is active, i.e.,

$$d_{WD}(p_S, p_{\hat{S}}) = (1-\sigma)^2 = P, \tag{A5}$$

we have

$$\sigma = 1 - \sqrt{P} = \sigma_1. \tag{A6}$$

Then, define the following coding schemes

$$(Y, S, \hat{S}) = (\eta S' + \sqrt{1-\eta^2}Y', S', bS' + \sqrt{1-b^2}\hat{S}'), \tag{A7}$$

where $(Y', S', \hat{S}')$ is standard normal and

$$b = \sqrt{\frac{\kappa^2 - \eta^2}{1 + \eta^2\kappa^2 - 2\eta^2}}, \quad \text{(A8)}$$

which gives us $E[E[S|\hat{S}, Y]^2] = \kappa^2$. Let $\hat{S} = \sigma_1\kappa^{-1}E[S|\hat{S}, Y]$ with $\kappa = (1 + \sigma_1^2 - D)/2\sigma_1$, we then have

$$\begin{aligned} &E[d(S, \hat{S})] = E[(S - \kappa^{-1}E[S|\hat{S}, Y])^2] \\ =&E[S^2] + (\sigma_1^2\kappa^{-2} - 2\sigma_1\kappa^{-1})E[E[S|\hat{S}, Y]^2] \\ =&1 + \sigma_1^2 - 2\sigma_1\kappa = D, \end{aligned} \quad \text{(A9)}$$

which is equivalent to $E[d(S, \hat{S})] = D$. The mutual information term is then written as

$$I(S; \hat{S}|Y) = h(S|Y) - h(S|\hat{S}, Y) = \frac{1}{2}\log\frac{1 - \eta^2}{1 - \kappa^2}. \quad \text{(A10)}$$

The mutual information $I(S; \hat{S}|Y)$ equals zero when $\kappa = \eta$, i.e.,

$$\begin{aligned} &(1 + \sigma_1^2 - D)/2\sigma_1 = \eta \\ \Leftrightarrow &D = 1 + \sigma_1^2 - 2\eta\sigma_1 \end{aligned} \quad \text{(A11)}$$

This concludes the proof of Theorem 1. By replacing the constraint on Wasserstein distance with the following KL divergence

$$d_{KL}(p_S, p_{\hat{S}}) = \frac{1}{2}(\ln\sigma^2 + \frac{1}{\sigma^2} - 1) \leq P, \quad \text{(A12)}$$

and reverse KL divergence

$$d_{RKL}(p_S, p_{\hat{S}}) = \frac{1}{2}(-\ln\sigma^2 + \sigma^2 - 1) \leq P, \quad \text{(A13)}$$

and repeating the same steps of the proof of Theorem 1, we conclude the proof of Theorem 2.

References

1. Shi, G.; Xiao, Y.; Li, Y.; Xie, X. From semantic communication to semantic-aware networking: Model, architecture, and open problems. *IEEE Commun. Mag.* **2021**, *59*, 44–50. [CrossRef]
2. Chai, J.; Xiao, Y.; Shi, G.; Saad, W. Rate-distortion-perception theory for semantic communication. In Proceedings of the 2023 IEEE 31st International Conference on Network Protocols (ICNP), Reykjavik, Iceland, 10–13 October 2023; pp. 1–6.
3. Xiao, Y.; Sun, Z.; Shi, G.; Niyato, D. Imitation learning-based implicit semantic-aware communication networks: Multi-layer representation and collaborative reasoning. *IEEE J. Sel. Areas Commun.* **2023**, *41*, 639–658. [CrossRef]
4. Xiao, Y.; Liao, Y.; Li, Y.; Shi, G.; Poor, H.V.; Saad, W.; Debbah, M.; Bennis, M. Reasoning over the air: A reasoning-based implicit semantic-aware communication framework. *IEEE Trans. Wireless Commun.* **2024**, *23*, 3839–3855. [CrossRef]
5. Xiao, Y.; Zhang, X.; Li, Y.; Shi, G.; Başar, T. Rate-distortion theory for strategic semantic communication. In Proceedings of the 2022 IEEE Information Theory Workshop (ITW), Mumbai, India, 1–9 November 2022; pp. 279–284.
6. Weaver, W. Recent contributions to the mathematical theory of communication. *ETC Rev. Gen. Semant.* **1949**, *10*, 261–281.
7. Xie, H.; Qin, Z.; Li, G.Y.; Juang, B.H. Deep learning enabled semantic communication systems. *IEEE Trans. Signal Process.* **2021**, *69*, 2663–2675. [CrossRef]
8. Zhang, H.; Shao, S.; Tao, M.; Bi, X.; Letaief, K.B. Deep learning-enabled semantic communication systems with task-unaware transmitter and dynamic data. *IEEE J. Sel. Areas Commun.* **2022**, *41*, 170–185. [CrossRef]
9. Gündüz, D.; Wigger, M.A.; Tung, T.-Y.; Zhang, P.; Xiao, Y. Joint source–channel coding: Fundamentals and recent Progress in practical designs. *Proc. IEEE* **2024**, 1–32. [CrossRef]
10. Murphy, K.P. *Machine Learning: A Probabilistic Perspective*; MIT Press: Cambridge, MA, USA, 2012.

11. Arjovsky, M.; Chintala, S.; Bottou, L. Wasserstein generative adversarial networks. In Proceedings of the International Conference on Machine Learning, Sydney, Australia, 6–11 August 2017; pp. 214–223.
12. Blau, Y.; Michaeli, T. The perception-distortion tradeoff. In Proceedings of the IEEE Conference on Computer Vision and Pattern Recognition, Salt Lake City, UT, USA, 18–22 June 2018; pp. 6228–6237.
13. Blau, Y.; Michaeli, T. Rethinking lossy compression: The rate-distortion-perception tradeoff. In Proceedings of the International Conference on Machine Learning, Long Beach, CA, USA, 9–15 June 2019; pp. 675–685.
14. Wagner, A.B. The rate-distortion-perception tradeoff: The role of common randomness. *arXiv* **2022**, arXiv:2202.04147.
15. Niu, X.; Gündüz, D.; Bai, B.; Han, W. Conditional Rate-distortion-perception trade-Off. *arXiv* **2023**, arXiv:2305.09318.
16. Zhang, G.; Qian, J.; Chen, J.; Khisti, A. Universal rate-distortion-perception representations for lossy compression. *Adv. Neural Inf. Process. Syst.* **2021**, *34*, 11517–11529. [CrossRef]
17. Serra, G.; Stavrou, P.A.; Kountouris, M. Computation of rate-distortion-perception function under f-divergence perception constraints. In Proceedings of the 2023 IEEE International Symposium on Information Theory (ISIT), Taipei, Taiwan, 25–30 June 2023; pp. 531–536.
18. Serra, G.; Stavrou, P.A.; Kountouris, M. Alternating minimization schemes for computing rate-distortion-perception functions with f-divergence perception constraint. *arXiv* **2024**, arXiv:2408.15015.
19. Serra, G.; Stavrou, P.A.; Kountouris, M. On the computation of the Gaussian rate-distortion-perception function. *IEEE J. Sel. Areas Inf. Theory* **2024**, *5*, 314–330. [CrossRef]
20. Sourla, M.V.; Serra, G.; Stavrou, P.A.; Kountouris, M. Analyzing α-divergence in Gaussian rate-distortion-perception theory. In Proceedings of the IEEE 25th International Workshop on Signal Processing Advances in Wireless Communications (SPAWC), Lucca, Italy, 10–13 September 2024; pp. 856–860.
21. Minka, T.P. Expectation propagation for approximate Bayesian inference. *arXiv* **2013**, arXiv:1301.2294. [CrossRef]
22. Salimans, T.; Goodfellow, I.; Zaremba, W.; Cheung, V.; Radford, A.; Chen, X. Improved techniques for training GANs. In Proceedings of the NIPS 2016 Workshop on Interpretable Machine Learning for Complex Systems, Barcelona, Spain, 9 December 2016; pp. 2234–2242.
23. Wang, Z.; Bovik, A.C.; Sheikh, H.R.; Simoncelli, E.P. Image quality assessment: From error visibility to structural similarity. *IEEE Trans. Image Process.* **2004**, *13*, 600–612. [CrossRef] [PubMed]
24. Wan, N.; Li, D.; Hovakimyan, N. f-divergence variational inference. *Adv. Neural Inf. Process. Syst.* **2020**, *33*, 17370–17379.
25. Beran, R. Minimum Hellinger distance estimates for parametric models. *Ann. Stat.* **1977**, *5*, 445–463. [CrossRef]
26. Novello, N.; Tonello, A.M. f-Divergence based classification: Beyond the use of cross-entropy. In Proceedings of the International Conference on Machine Learning, Vienna, Austria, 21–27 July 2024.
27. Boyd, S.P.; Vandenberghe, L. *Convex Optimization*; Cambridge University Press: Cambridge, UK, 2004.
28. Jeong, M.; Cardone, M.; Dytso, A. Demystifying the optimal performance of multi-class classification. *Adv. Neural Inf. Process. Syst.* **2023**, *36*, 31638–31664.
29. Witsenhausen, H. Indirect rate distortion problems. *IEEE Trans. Inf. Theory* **2003**, *26*, 518–521. [CrossRef]
30. Liu, J.; Shao, S.; Zhang, W.; Poor, H.V. An indirect rate-distortion characterization for semantic sources: General model and the case of gaussian observation. *IEEE Trans. Commun.* **2022**, *70*, 5946–5959. [CrossRef]
31. Zhang, M.; Bird, T.; Habib, R.; Xu, T.; Barber, D. Variational f-divergence minimization. *arXiv* **2019**, arXiv:1907.11891. [CrossRef]
32. Wyner, A.D. The rate-distortion function for source coding with side information at the decoder\3-II: General sources. *Inf. Control* **1978**, *38*, 60–80. [CrossRef]
33. Englesson, E.; Azizpour, H. Generalized Jensen-Shannon divergence loss for learning with noisy labels. In Proceedings of the NeurIPS 2021 Competitions and Demonstrations Track, Online, 6–14 December 2021; pp. 30284–30297.
34. Dieng, A.B.; Tran, D.; Ranganath, R.; Paisley, J.; Blei, D. Variational Inference via χ Upper Bound Minimization. In Proceedings of the NIPS, Long Beach, CA, USA, 4–9 December 2017.

entropy

MDPI

Article

Harnessing the Power of Pre-Trained Models for Efficient Semantic Communication of Text and Images †

Emrecan Kutay * and Aylin Yener

Department of Electrical and Computer Engineering, The Ohio State University, Columbus, OH 43210, USA; yener@ece.osu.edu

* Correspondence: kutay.5@osu.edu

† This paper is an extended version of our paper published in Kutay, E.; Yener, A. Semantic Text Compression for Classification. In Proceedings of the 2023 IEEE International Conference on Communications Workshops (ICC Workshops), Rome, Italy, 28 May–1 June 2023; pp. 1368–1373. doi:10.1109/ICCWorkshops57953.2023.10283705; and Kutay, E.; Yener, A. Classification-Oriented Semantic Wireless Communications. In Proceedings of the ICASSP 2024—2024 IEEE International Conference on Acoustics, Speech and Signal Processing (ICASSP), Seoul, Korea, Republic of Korea, 14–19 April 2024; pp. 9096–9100. doi:10.1109/ICASSP48485.2024.10447549.

Abstract

This paper investigates point-to-point multimodal digital semantic communications in a task-oriented setup, where messages are classified at the receiver. We employ a pre-trained transformer model to extract semantic information and propose three methods for generating semantic codewords. First, we propose semantic quantization that uses quantized embeddings of source realizations as a codebook. We investigate the fixed-length coding, considering the source semantic structure and end-to-end semantic distortion. We propose a neural network-based codeword assignment mechanism incorporating codeword transition probabilities to minimize the expected semantic distortion. Second, we present semantic compression that clusters embeddings, exploiting the inherent semantic redundancies to reduce the codebook size, i.e., further compression. Third, we introduce a semantic vector-quantized autoencoder (VQ-AE) that learns a codebook through training. In all cases, we follow this semantic source code with a standard channel code to transmit over the wireless channel. In addition to classification accuracy, we assess pre-communication overhead via a novel metric we term system time efficiency. Extensive experiments demonstrate that our proposed semantic source-coding approaches provide comparable accuracy and better system time efficiency compared to their learning-based counterparts.

Keywords: semantic communication; semantic compression; multimodal communication; task-oriented efficiency; 6G

1. Introduction

6G is envisioned as AI-native, seamlessly integrating human–machine and machine-to-machine communications to support emerging applications such as digital twins, fully autonomous vehicles, and smart environments, all of which are expected to generate and exchange unprecedented data volumes [1,2]. Conventional communication systems treat information exchange as the precise reconstruction of digital sequences at endpoints, without regard to their semantic content [3] and thus rely exclusively on syntactic error metrics such as bit error rate (BER) and symbol error rate (SER). While this semantic-agnostic framework simplifies design and enables modular optimization, it overlooks the meaning of transmitted data, which can be leveraged for improving efficiency. As 6G applications impose ever-more stringent demands for reliability and latency, there is a growing need to incorporate semantic awareness into communication systems to optimize resource utilization and better serve these requirements.

Semantic communication [4] moves in this direction by shifting the focus from transmitting complete sequences to conveying intended meanings. Paying attention to what messages mean enables the transmission of relevant information. Such efforts can potentially enable more efficient use of spectrum resources in future generations of connectivity.

Efforts towards semantics go back as early as shortly after the seminal work in [3], but have achieved limited adoption in communications design [5–8]. More recently, a decade ago, reference [9] has introduced the concept of *semantic distortion* as an error metric, addressing the transmission of words over noisy channels by optimizing codeword assignments to minimize semantic distortion (loss). The same reference points to the importance of *context* availability at the receiver, which can further improve resource efficiency. Reference [10] builds upon this latter concept and analyzes a system that consists of a transmitter-receiver pair and an external agent that can provide helpful or deceiving context to the receiver. It is important to note that these studies, while fundamental to the concept, were limited to small systems owing to the computational complexity.

Following the machine learning revolution and its entry into the wireless physical layer design [11], efforts in semantic communications were rejuvenated. These efforts adopted deep learning (DL) architectures, structured around four core components: (i) semantic encoder, (ii) channel encoder, (iii) channel decoder, and (iv) semantic decoder [4]. A semantic encoder can extract semantic information from source, generating low-dimensional embeddings using DL models, such as text or vision transformers [12], transmitted over the channel. At the receiver, the semantic decoder processes the reconstructed embeddings to perform tasks from reconstruction to classification, or translation [13,14]. This architecture adopts an autoencoder-based design with end-to-end training with task-specific loss functions [15–18].

This approach, though a clear paradigm shift, is not without its challenges. Notably, the training overhead can be significant, due to large model size, which requires substantial data [19]. In addition, solutions are often case-specific, which necessitates retraining often in dynamic environments. This creates a training overhead in system design that needs to be addressed. In our preliminary conference papers [20,21], we have demonstrated that utilizing pre-trained embedding models can overcome this limitation.

In this paper, building on these initial ideas, we provide a comprehensive framework for harnessing the power of pre-trained models to digitally communicate semantics extracted from text and images. As an example of this framework, we focus on a task-oriented scenario where the receiver is tasked with classification of said text and images. We concatenate these resulting source codewords by a standard channel coder, this is performed to demonstrate that a backward-compatible, modular, i.e., source-channel separation-based approach [3], is sufficient to obtain significant gains. Our contributions are as follows:

- We propose three semantic codebook generation methods: (i) semantic quantization, which forms a fixed codebook from source realizations; (ii) semantic compression, which builds on quantization by exploiting semantic redundancy; and (iii) semantic vector-quantized autoencoder (VQ-AE), which trains a codebook.
- For semantic quantization and compression, we design a neural network-based source code that minimizes end-to-end semantic distortion.
- We introduce a novel performance metric called *system time efficiency* to account for pre-communication overhead in machine-learning aided wireless communication systems. It quantifies task completion given a time budget by jointly accounting for training and transmission phases, enabling fair comparison and penalizing models

with excessive training overhead. Simulations on multiple datasets demonstrate that semantic quantization and compression improve time efficiency over wireless channels, while reducing training cost and enhancing resilience under data scarcity compared to the learning-based semantic VQ-AE.

The rest of the paper is organized as follows. Preliminaries are provided in Section 2, followed by the system model in Section 3. Proposed approaches are presented in Section 4 with numerical results pointing to significant savings against baselines in Section 5. Section 6 concludes the paper.

Notation: Lowercase letters, x, denote scalars, italic uppercase letters, X, denote random variables (RVs), bold lowercase letters, $\mathbf{q}$, denote vectors, and bold uppercase letters, $\mathbf{Q}$, denote matrices. For matrix $\mathbf{Q}$, $\mathbf{Q}[i]$ denotes the ith row vector, $\mathbf{Q}[i,j]$ denotes the element at i^{th} row j^{th} column, and $\mathbf{Q}^T$ denotes the transpose. $\|\cdot\|_2$ and $\|\cdot\|_F$ are the Euclidean and Frobenius norm, respectively. $\mathbf{I}_{t\times t}$ denotes identity matrix of rank t. $\{0,1\}^{a\times b}$ denotes binary matrix of dimensions $a \times b$. $\cdot \mod t$ denotes the modulo operation with respect to t. $\lceil\cdot\rceil$ is the ceiling. $(\cdot)_+$ denotes the $\max(\cdot,0)$. $d_H(\cdot,\cdot)$ is the Hamming distance. $\log_2(\cdot)$ denotes logarithm with base 2. $\mathbb{R}$ and $\mathbb{C}$ denotes the real and complex sets. $\mathcal{U}(a,b)$ denotes uniform RV in range (a,b). $\mathbb{C}\mathcal{N}(\mu,\sigma^2)$ denotes complex Gaussian RV with mean μ and variance σ^2.

2. Preliminaries

In this section, we provide preliminaries of methods we adopt from large language models and unsupervised learning, as these may be less familiar to communications researchers.

Representing text semantics as learned real-valued vectors, i.e., neural embeddings, goes back to *word embeddings*, which capture relationships between words by placing semantically similar words close together in an embedding space [22]. More recently, BERT, one of the first large language models (LLMs), uses the attention mechanism to generate context-aware token embeddings [23], and Sentence-BERT (SBERT) extends this notion to the sentence level by mapping semantically similar sentences to nearby vectors and dissimilar ones to distant vectors [24]. Our preliminary work in references [20,21] utilizes SBERT for semantic text communications.

In this work, our adopted pre-trained model is a recently developed multimodal one. OpenAI CLIP employs transformer-based encoders for both images and text. It uses contrastive learning to jointly train these encoders by predicting the correct (image, text) pairings in a batch. The training objective involves a symmetric loss that equally weights cross-entropies of text-to-image and image-to-text predictions. This ensures consistent embedding properties across both modalities, enabling the unified representation of text and images [25].

Pre-trained embeddings effectively capture semantic information and have demonstrated strong performance across various downstream tasks [26,27]. They serve as compact feature representations, allowing new tasks to be addressed by optimizing only the task-specific block, *without retraining the entire model*. In this work, we use these embeddings to encapsulate message semantics and optimize a classification block for CLIP embeddings.

In unsupervised learning, affinity propagation (AP) is a clustering algorithm that selects centroids from the actual data points, termed "exemplars". The main objective is to assign each sample to an exemplar by optimizing the defined similarity metric. For minimizing the Euclidean distance, the similarity $sim(\mathbf{o}_i,\mathbf{o}_j)$ between points $\mathbf{o}_i$ and $\mathbf{o}_j$ is expressed as follows [28].

$$sim(\mathbf{o}_i,\mathbf{o}_j) = -\|\mathbf{o}_i - \mathbf{o}_j\|_2^2. \tag{1}$$

The algorithm employs message-passing by exchanging "responsibility" and "availability" messages between data points. The "responsibility" message, $r(i,k)$, is sent from each sample i to candidate exemplar k, indicating the suitability of k as an exemplar for i. Correspondingly, the "availability" message, $a(i,k)$, is sent from the candidate exemplar k to sample i, reflecting the level of suitability for i to select k as its exemplar. The equations for these messages are as follows [28].

$$r(i,k) \leftarrow sim(i,k) - \max_{k' s.t. k' \neq k} \left\{ a(i,k') + sim(i,k') \right\}. \tag{2}$$

$$a(i,k) \leftarrow \min\left\{0, r(k,k) + \sum_{i' s.t. i' \notin \{i,k\}} \max\{0, r(i',k)\}\right\}, \tag{3}$$

where for $a(k,k)$, the update reduces to $\sum_{i' s.t. i' \neq k} \max\{0, r(i',k)\}$. A key advantage of AP is that it does not require the number of clusters to be specified beforehand. Instead, it determines the appropriate number dynamically based on the similarities and message-passing. The number of clusters can be adjusted by changing the preference; setting it to the median of the input similarities typically yields a moderate number of clusters [28].

3. System Model

We consider a point-to-point task-oriented communication scenario. The message s at the source may be text, image, or a combination of both. The receiver is tasked to predict a class label, denoted by $\hat{c}$. The goal thus is to transmit the essential semantic information needed for accurate classification. Inspired by the use of pre-trained neural models in inverse problems without additional training [29,30], we adopt the OpenAI CLIP transformer as a semantic encoder. This enables us to extract the semantic information of the message as embeddings, denoted by $\mathbf{q} \in \mathbb{R}^m$, without any further training. The (digitized) CLIP embedding thus becomes the message to be sent to the receiver for classification.

We use semantic distortion [9], denoted as $\delta(\cdot,\cdot)$, to quantify the loss in meaning. For a message s with embedding $\mathbf{q}$, the semantic distortion is

$$\delta(\mathbf{q}, \tilde{\mathbf{q}}) = \|\mathbf{q} - \tilde{\mathbf{q}}\|_2, \tag{4}$$

where $\tilde{\mathbf{q}}$ is the receiver's estimate.

Consider a dataset, denoted as $\mathbf{Q}_{pre}^n$, consisting of embeddings of randomly selected messages. This dataset serves as the initial codebook with n codewords of length m each, where n represents the number of embeddings and m is the embedding dimension. We will investigate several approaches to utilize $\mathbf{Q}_{pre}^n$ for semantic quantization, semantic compression, and semantic VQ AE proposed in Sections 4.1–4.3.

For a channel input $\mathbf{x} \in \mathbb{C}^b$, the channel output $\mathbf{y} \in \mathbb{C}^b$ is as follows.

$$\mathbf{y} = h\mathbf{x} + \mathbf{z}, \tag{5}$$

where $\mathbf{z} \sim \mathcal{CN}(\mathbf{0}, \sigma_{\mathbf{z}}^2 \mathbf{I}_{b \times b})$ denotes the additive noise, and $h \in \mathbb{C}$ represents the fading coefficient.

We employ a neural network (NN) with fully connected layers for the classification block at the receiver. This block takes the reconstructed CLIP embeddings as input for classification.

4. Proposed Methods

In this section, we propose three semantic representations, each using the OpenAI CLIP to generate embeddings from messages and incorporating the available dataset $\mathbf{Q}_{pre}^n$.

4.1. Semantic Quantization

We propose first using $\mathbf{Q}^n_{pre}$ as a shared codebook by arguing that the semantic structure of the source can be inferred from its realizations. This approach encodes messages with actual content (source samples), enabling the interpretability of codeword meanings and their alignment with human understanding, as discussed in Section 5.2. Through semantic quantization, we assign message embeddings to codebook indices that minimize the semantic distortion. In particular, we obtain the codebook index for message embedding $\mathbf{q}$ by the semantic index assignment operation, denoted by $\Pi_{\mathbf{Q}^n_{pre}}(\cdot)$, as follows.

$$\Pi_{\mathbf{Q}^n_{pre}}(\mathbf{q}) = \underset{i' s.t. 0 \leq i' < n}{\text{argmin}}\ \delta\left(\mathbf{q}, \mathbf{Q}^n_{pre}[i']\right). \tag{6}$$

The (source) codeword is then mapped using a standard channel code, that is we have a backward compatible design with existing digital communications systems: a (semantic) source coder followed by a channel coder. At the receiver, the index is reconstructed as $\hat{i}$ and the associated embedding $\hat{\mathbf{q}} = \mathbf{Q}^n_{pre}[\hat{i}]$ is passed to the classifier to obtain the prediction $\hat{c}$. We illustrate this process in Figure 1.

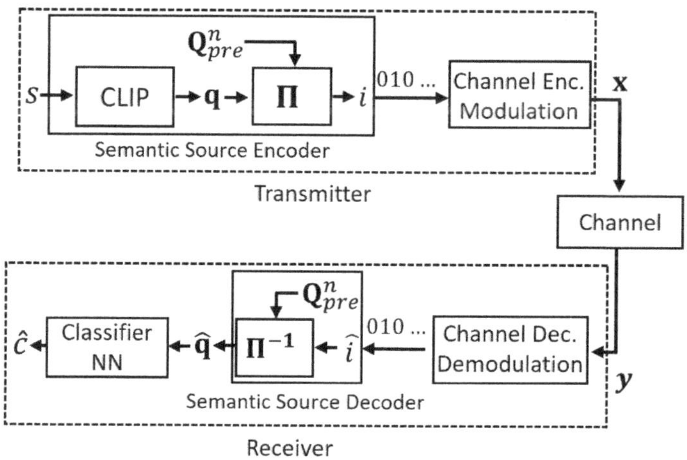

Figure 1. The proposed semantic quantization method.

We explore the fixed-length coding scheme inspired by an early approach that incorporates channel effects into the semantic distortion objective and exploits semantic relationships among source symbols to improve noise robustness [9]. In particular, we investigate the distortion in Equation (4) by incorporating the codeword transition probabilities over the noisy channel. Denote the codewords as $\mathbf{W} \in \{0,1\}^{n \times l_{cw}}$, where j^{th} row contains the codeword assigned to index j, with a fixed length of $l_{cw} = \lceil \log_2 n \rceil$. The expected semantic distortion $\Delta(\cdot)$ is as follows [9]:

$$\Delta(\mathbf{W}) = \sum_{i=0}^{n-1} p(i) \left(\sum_{j=0}^{n-1} p\left(\hat{\mathbf{W}}[j] \mid \mathbf{W}[i]\right) \delta\left(\mathbf{Q}^n_{pre}[i], \mathbf{Q}^n_{pre}[j]\right) \right). \tag{7}$$

In Equation (7), the distortion and index probability terms are fixed. We focus on minimizing the objective by choosing the codewords, which determine the channel transition probabilities $p(\hat{\mathbf{W}}[j] \mid \mathbf{W}[i])$. This makes the problem similar to minimizing a linear function over a probability simplex; it is easy to conclude that we need codewords such that higher transition probabilities correspond to lower semantic distortion. To achieve this goal, we design the codewords by linking transition probabilities to Hamming distances, where smaller Hamming distances indicate higher transition probabilities. This serves as a model-based insight guiding our design. Therefore, the objective is to assign codewords such that the Hamming distance $d_H(\mathbf{W}[i], \mathbf{W}[j])$ reflects the Euclidean distance between their embeddings, ensuring that closer indices have codewords with smaller Hamming distances.

Building on this model-based intuition, we propose the NN-based codeword assignment mechanism to minimize the expected distortion in Equation (7). Specifically, we consider an NN, which takes $\mathbf{Q}^n_{pre}$ as input and aligns codeword Hamming distances with a $tanh(\cdot)$ output activation, as follows.

$$\tilde{\mathbf{W}} = g(\mathbf{Q}^n_{pre}; \boldsymbol{\theta}), \tag{8}$$

where $\boldsymbol{\theta}$ is the learnable parameter vector, and $\tilde{\mathbf{W}} \in \mathbb{R}^{n \times l_{cw}}$ represents the NN soft outputs, which are binarized afterward to form the codewords. To align these assignments with the semantic relationships between indices, we design the loss function $\mathcal{L}_{\text{cw}}$ as a convex combination of multiple components. In particular, we optimize the following loss function through mini-batches of size n_b.

$$\begin{aligned} \mathcal{L}_{\text{cw}} &= \alpha_1 \mathcal{L}_{\text{Triplet}} + \alpha_2 \mathcal{L}_{\text{Diversity}} + \alpha_3 \mathcal{L}_{\text{Orthogonality}} \qquad (9) \\ &= \frac{\alpha_1}{n_b} \sum_{j=0}^{n_b-1} (\|\tilde{\mathbf{W}}_b[j] - \tilde{\mathbf{W}}_b[p_j]\|_2 - \|\tilde{\mathbf{W}}_b[j] - \tilde{\mathbf{W}}_b[n_j]\|_2 + \epsilon)_+ \\ &+ \frac{\alpha_2}{n_b^2} \sum_{i,j=0}^{n_b-1} \left(\sqrt{l_{cw}} - \mathbf{D}_{\tilde{\mathbf{W}}_b}[i,j]\right)_+ \\ &+ \frac{\alpha_3}{n_b^2} \|\tilde{\mathbf{W}}_b \tilde{\mathbf{W}}_b^T - \mathbf{I}_{n_b \times n_b}\|_F^2, \end{aligned} \tag{10}$$

where $\tilde{\mathbf{W}}_b$ is the batch soft output, $p_j = \mathbf{p}_s[j]$ and $n_j = \mathbf{n}_s[j]$ are the positive and negative sample indices of sample j as in Algorithm 1, ϵ is the margin, $\mathbf{D}_{\tilde{\mathbf{W}}_b}$ is the pairwise distance matrix in Algorithm 2. We design codewords by adjusting soft output distances so that outputs with close Euclidean distances are binarized to codewords with small Hamming distances. We use triplet loss to align soft outputs with positions of embeddings in $\mathbf{Q}^n_{pre}$ associated with indices. Specifically, we generate triplets such that positive and negative samples correspond to closer and farther embeddings in a batch, as outlined in Algorithm 1. Instead of generating fixed triplets, we repeatedly generate new ones for each batch, helping the model to align better by adapting to dynamic pairs. As the triplet loss can lead to duplicate assignments, we introduce regularization terms to the loss function to penalize the model for producing outputs that cluster too densely. We provide the training procedure in Algorithm 2.

Algorithm 1 Triplet Generation for Triplet Loss in Each Batch

Inputs: Pairwise distances $\mathbf{D} \in \mathbb{R}^{n_b \times n_b}$
Function `GenerateTriplets()`:
  for *each* $j \in \{0, 1, \ldots, n_b - 1\}$ **do**
    Set anchor $a_s \leftarrow j$
    Positive $p_s \leftarrow \arg\min_{k \neq j} \mathbf{D}[j,k]$
    Negative $n_s \leftarrow \arg\max_k \mathbf{D}[j,k]$
    Append (a_s, p_s, n_s) to triplet list
  end
  Return list of triplets $(\mathbf{a}_s, \mathbf{p}_s, \mathbf{n}_s)$

Algorithm 2 Training Codeword Assignment Model

Inputs: $\mathbf{Q}^n_{pre}$
Function `Train Codeword NN()`:
  Initialize $\boldsymbol{\theta} \sim \textit{Xavier Initialization}$
  for *each batch* $\mathbf{Q}_b \subset \mathbf{Q}^n_{pre}$ **do**
    Compute input pairwise distances $\mathbf{D} \in \mathbb{R}^{n_b \times n_b}$

$$\mathbf{D}[i,j] = \|\mathbf{Q}_b[i] - \mathbf{Q}_b[j]\|_2, \forall i,j \in \{0,\ldots,n_b-1\}$$

    Generate triplets $(\mathbf{a}_s, \mathbf{p}_s, \mathbf{n}_s) = \text{GenerateTriplets}(\mathbf{D})$
    Compute the model output $\tilde{\mathbf{W}}_b = g(\mathbf{Q}_b; \boldsymbol{\theta})$
    Compute output pairwise distances $\mathbf{D}_{\tilde{\mathbf{W}}_b} \in \mathbb{R}^{n_b \times n_b}$

$$\mathbf{D}_{\tilde{\mathbf{W}}_b}[i,j] = \|\tilde{\mathbf{W}}_b[i] - \tilde{\mathbf{W}}_b[j]\|_2, \forall i,j \in \{0,\ldots,n_b-1\}$$

    Compute total loss $\mathcal{L}_{\text{cw}}$ using Equation (10)
    Update params $AdamW(\boldsymbol{\theta}, \mathcal{L}_{\text{cw}})$
  end
  Return $\boldsymbol{\theta}$

After training, we pass $\mathbf{Q}^n_{pre}$ through the model, as in Equation (8), to obtain the soft outputs. We then binarize them based on their sign, resulting in $\tilde{\mathbf{W}}_{bin}$. Although we have designed the loss to encourage distinct assignments, this does not directly ensure unique decodability. To address this, we map $\tilde{\mathbf{W}}_{bin}$ to distinct codewords of the same length by minimizing the Hamming distance, formulating the problem as follows.

$$\mathbf{W}_{opt} = \arg\min_{\mathbf{W}} \sum_{i=0}^{n-1} d_H(\mathbf{W}[i], \tilde{\mathbf{W}}_{bin}[i]) \ s.t. \ \ {}_{\forall i \neq j}^{\mathbf{W}[i] \neq \mathbf{W}[j]}. \tag{11}$$

The problem in Equation (11) is a linear sum assignment problem, which involves minimizing the total assignment cost over one-to-one mappings between agents and tasks [31]. We define the cost by the pairwise Hamming distances between the $\tilde{\mathbf{W}}_{bin}$ and unique codewords to be assigned $\mathbf{W}_{opt}$. In particular, we construct a cost matrix $\mathbf{D}^H$ as given in Algorithm 3. However, when n is not a power of 2, we add dummy rows with a cost greater than the maximum of non-dummy rows. This ensures the use of all distinct codewords of length l_{cw}. Utilizing this cost matrix, we solve the problem using a modified Jonker-Volgenant algorithm [32], an efficient variant of the Hungarian algorithm that improves time complexity. We summarize the complete process in Algorithm 3.

4.2. Semantic Compression

In Section 4.1, increasing n improves resolution in $\mathbb{R}^m$ for quantization, but leads to a larger codebook. Semantics contain inherent redundancies, where the meaning is the same despite variations in sentence structures, or even words [33]. To reduce the codebook size while maintaining resolution, we propose semantic compression, which clusters similar embeddings in $\mathbf{Q}^n_{pre}$, exploiting these semantic redundancies.

In particular, we use the affinity propagation (AP) algorithm for clustering explained in Section 2 which identifies the optimal number of clusters. We assign message embeddings to the resulting clusters by minimizing semantic distortion, as follows.

$$\mathbf{AP}_{\mathbf{Q}^n_{pre}}(\mathbf{q}) = \underset{l' s.t. 0 \leq l' < \tilde{n}}{\text{argmin}} \ \delta\left(\mathbf{q}, \mathbf{Q}^{\tilde{n}}_{pre}[l']\right), \tag{12}$$

where $\mathbf{Q}_{pre}^{\tilde{n}}$ contains $\tilde{n}$ centroids with $\tilde{n} \ll n$. The codeword corresponding to the assigned cluster label, l, is transmitted using the same transmission scheme in Section 4.1. At the receiver, the reconstructed cluster label, $\hat{l}$, is used to retrieve the associated embedding $\hat{\mathbf{q}} = \mathbf{Q}_{pre}^{\tilde{n}}[\hat{l}]$, which is then fed into the classifier to obtain the prediction $\hat{c}$, as illustrated in Figure 2.

Algorithm 3 Codeword Assignment for Codebook Indices

Inputs: $\mathbf{Q}_{pre}^{n}$

Function `Assign Codewords()`:

Train NN $g(\cdot;\boldsymbol{\theta})$ = Train Codeword NN($\mathbf{Q}_{pre}^{n}$)

Get soft outputs $\tilde{\mathbf{W}} = g(\mathbf{Q}_{pre}^{n};\boldsymbol{\theta})$

Binarize

$$\tilde{\mathbf{W}}_{bin}[i,j] = \begin{cases} 1 & \text{if } \tilde{\mathbf{W}}[i,j] > 0 \\ 0 & \text{if } \tilde{\mathbf{W}}[i,j] \leq 0' \end{cases} \quad \forall i,j$$

Project to Distinct Codewords

Initialize distinct codewords $\mathbf{W} \in \{0,1\}^{2^{l_{cw}} \times l_{cw}}$

Compute the Hamming distance matrix

$$\mathbf{D}^{H}[i,j] = d_{H}\left(\tilde{\mathbf{W}}_{bin}[i], \mathbf{W}[j]\right), \quad \forall i,j$$

Define binary decision variable $\mathbf{A} \in \{0,1\}^{n \times 2^{l_{cw}}}$

$$\mathbf{A}[i,j] = \begin{cases} 1 & \text{if index } i \text{ is assigned to codeword } j \\ 0 & \text{otherwise} \end{cases}$$

Minimize with respect to $\mathbf{A}$ s.t. $\sum_{j=0}^{2^{l_{cw}}-1} \mathbf{A}[i,j] = 1, \forall i$ and $\sum_{i=0}^{n-1} \mathbf{A}[i,j] = 1, \forall j$

$$\min_{\mathbf{A}} \sum_{i=0}^{n-1} \sum_{j=0}^{2^{l_{cw}}-1} \mathbf{D}^{H}[i,j]\mathbf{A}[i,j]$$

Return assigned codewords $\mathbf{W}[j], \forall i$ where $\mathbf{A}[i,j] = 1$

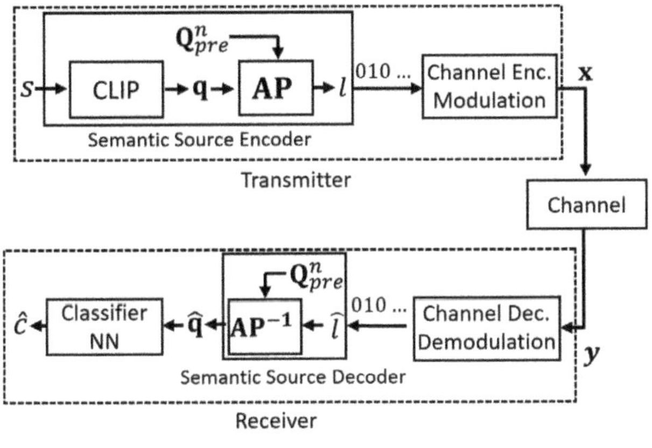

Figure 2. The proposed semantic compression method.

We employ Algorithms 1–3 for a fixed-length coding of cluster labels similar to the Section 4.1. However, instead of utilizing $\mathbf{Q}^{n}_{pre}$ to design codewords of length $l_{cw} = \lceil \log_2 n \rceil$, here we use clustered version $\mathbf{Q}^{\tilde{n}}_{pre}$ to design codewords of length $l'_{cw} = \lceil \log_2 \tilde{n} \rceil$.

4.3. Semantic Vector-Quantized Autoencoder

In this section, we focus on learning-based semantic communication by using $\mathbf{Q}^{n}_{pre}$ as training data instead of directly employing it as a codebook. Drawing inspiration from the vector-quantized variational autoencoder (VQ VAE) [34], we propose the semantic vector-quantized autoencoder (VQ AE) to generate learned discrete representations for message embeddings. The VQ AE consists of an encoder, a decoder, and a codebook $\mathbf{E} \in \mathbb{R}^{d \times k}$, which contains d latent space points for quantizing the encoder's output vectors. In particular, the encoder maps the message embedding to a latent vector, denoted as $\mathbf{v} \in \mathbb{R}^{k}$, expressed as follows.

$$\mathbf{v} = v_{enc}(\mathbf{q}; \gamma_{enc}), \tag{13}$$

where γ_{enc} denotes the learnable parameter vector of the encoder. In the latent space, the vector $\mathbf{v}$ is then quantized by assigning it to one of the elements in the codebook $\mathbf{E}$, as follows.

$$\mathbf{CD}(\mathbf{v}) = \underset{p' s.t. 0 \leq p' < d}{\operatorname{argmin}} ||\mathbf{v} - \mathbf{E}[p']||_2. \tag{14}$$

Equation (14) assigns the codebook element for $\mathbf{v}$, denoted as $\mathbf{e} = \mathbf{E}[p]$, where p is the index of the selected element. We then pass $\mathbf{e}$ through the decoder to reconstruct the embedding, $\hat{\mathbf{q}}$, as

$$\hat{\mathbf{q}} = v_{dec}(\mathbf{e}; \gamma_{dec}), \tag{15}$$

where γ_{dec} is the learnable parameter vector of the decoder. In this architecture, the encoder and decoder constitute an autoencoder, both employing a neural network with fully connected (FC) layers and a parameter α. In the encoder, the initial FC layer maps embeddings to α^{j}-dimensional space, then iteratively scales down dimensions by α^{-1} until reaching $\alpha^{\tilde{j}}$. Here, j and $\tilde{j}$ are chosen such that j represents the largest number where $\alpha^{j} < m$, and $\tilde{j}$ represents the smallest number where $k < \alpha^{\tilde{j}}$. The final FC layer maps directly to $\mathbb{R}^{k}$, i.e., to the latent space. Conversely, the decoder mirrors the encoder's architecture, progressively increasing dimensions to reconstruct the embeddings from the codebook elements. The parameter $\alpha > 1$ determines the model's depth, with smaller values yielding more layers. We illustrate this structure in Figure 3, employing $PReLU(\cdot)$ as the activation function. We optimize the encoder, decoder, and codebook using the VQ-VAE training algorithm, employing the following loss function [34].

$$\mathcal{L}_{\text{AE}} = ||\mathbf{q} - \hat{\mathbf{q}}||_2^2 + ||sg(\mathbf{v}) - \mathbf{e}||_2^2 + \beta||\mathbf{v} - sg(\mathbf{e})||_2^2, \tag{16}$$

where β represents the commitment parameter, and $sg(\cdot)$ denotes the stop gradient operator, preventing parameter updates by ensuring zero partial derivatives. The first term is the reconstruction loss for accurate embedding reconstruction at the decoder. The codebook is learned through the second term, minimizing the distance between $\mathbf{e}$ and $\mathbf{v}$. The final term, i.e., commitment loss, penalizes the encoder for deviating from the codebook elements [34].

In Sections 4.1 and 4.2, we have designed an NN-based codeword assignment mechanism. Here, we utilize adversarial training [35]. This approach provides latent space points that are resilient to channel effects. Specifically, we simulate channel conditions by perturbing selected index p to $\tilde{p}$ and passing the perturbed latent vector, $\tilde{\mathbf{e}} = \mathbf{E}[\tilde{p}]$, through the decoder. Unlike in previous sections, we note that the channel effects here directly modify the discrete representations in the latent space. We provide the details of the perturbation in Algorithm 4 and the training algorithm of the semantic VQ AE in Algorithm 5.

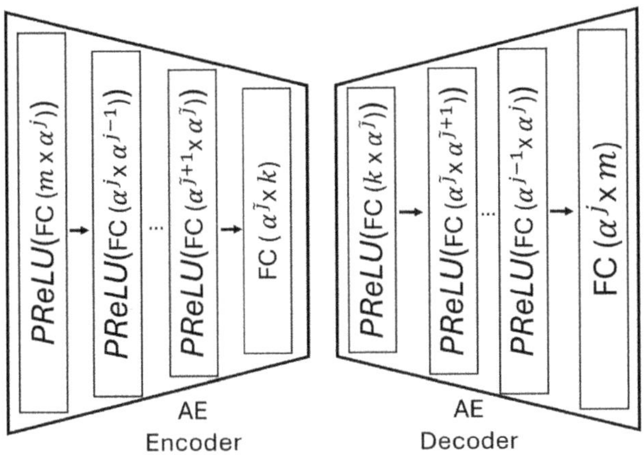

Figure 3. Structure of the AE encoder–AE decoder in semantic VQ AE.

Algorithm 4 Index Perturbation for Adversarial Training

Inputs: Indices $\mathbf{p}$, SNR Range $(\text{SNR}_{\min}, \text{SNR}_{\max})$,
Number of points d, Batch Size $\bar{n}_b$
Function `PerturbIndices()`:
Compute codeword length $\bar{l}_{cw} = \lceil \log_2 d \rceil$
Sample SNR $\xi_{SNR} \sim \mathcal{U}(\text{SNR}_{\min}, \text{SNR}_{\max})$
Compute QPSK bit error prob. $p_b = \text{BER}_{\text{QPSK}}(\xi_{SNR})$
Convert $\mathbf{p}$ to binary, $\mathbf{P}_{bin} \in \{0,1\}^{\bar{n}_b \times \bar{l}_{cw}}$
Define $\mathbf{1}_{p_b} \in \{0,1\}^{\bar{n}_b \times \bar{l}_{cw}}$

$$\mathbf{1}_{p_b}[i,j] = \begin{cases} 1 & \text{with prob. } p_b \\ 0 & \text{o.w.} \end{cases}, \quad \forall i,j$$

Perturb

$$\tilde{\mathbf{P}}_{bin} = \left(\mathbf{P}_{bin} + \mathbf{1}_{p_b}\right) \mod 2$$

Convert the $\tilde{\mathbf{P}}_{bin}$ back to integer indices $\tilde{\mathbf{p}}'$
Apply modulo to handle overflows

$$\tilde{\mathbf{p}} = \tilde{\mathbf{p}}' \mod d$$

Return $\tilde{\mathbf{p}}$

After training the model on the loss in Equation (16), the learned codebook and encoder–decoder components are shared between the transmitter and receiver. We then assign message embeddings to the learned codebook elements by using Equations (13) and (14). The resulting index p is converted to binary and transmitted using the same transmission scheme in Sections 4.1 and 4.2. At the receiver, reconstructed index $\hat{p}$ retrieves $\hat{\mathbf{e}} = \mathbf{E}[\hat{p}]$ which is used to reconstruct $\hat{\mathbf{q}}$ through Equation (15) and then obtain the prediction $\hat{c}$. We illustrate this process in Figure 4.

Algorithm 5 Training Semantic VQ AE Model

Inputs: $\mathbf{Q}^n_{pre}$, Design params. α, d, k
Function `Train Semantic VQ AE()`:
  Initialize $\gamma_{enc}, \gamma_{dec}, \mathbf{E}$
  for *each batch* $\mathbf{Q}_b \subset \mathbf{Q}^n_{pre}$ **do**
    $\mathbf{V} = v_{enc}(\mathbf{Q}_b; \gamma_{enc})$
    $\mathbf{p} = \mathbf{CD}(\mathbf{V})$
    $\tilde{\mathbf{p}} = \text{PerturbIndices}(\mathbf{p})$
    $\hat{\mathbf{Q}}_b = v_{dec}(\mathbf{E}[\tilde{\mathbf{p}}]; \gamma_{dec})$
    Calculate $\mathcal{L}_{\text{AE}}$ using Equation (16)
    Update params $AdamW(\gamma_{enc}, \gamma_{dec}, \mathbf{E}, \mathcal{L}_{\text{AE}})$
  end
  Return $\gamma_{enc}, \gamma_{dec}, \mathbf{E}$

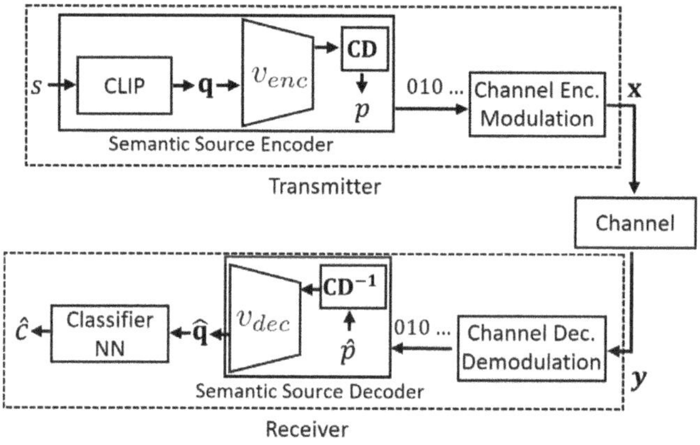

Figure 4. The proposed semantic VQ AE method.

4.4. Performance Metrics

The task in this paper is classification. Naturally, classification accuracy is the performance metric against which to measure the proposed methods. In addition, we introduce a novel performance metric that enables comparing pure deep learning-based approaches and the approaches we propose utilizing pre-trained models. *System time efficiency*, denoted by η_T, quantifies the number of correct task executions in a specified time frame, including the training phase, hence providing a measure for the pre-communication overhead of various machine learning methods. Specifically, for a method that achieves u correct classifications per second following a training phase of t_{train} seconds, we define η_T for a time budget $\tilde{t}$ as follows.

$$\eta_T(\tilde{t}) = (\tilde{t} - t_{train})u. \tag{17}$$

In Equation (17), the higher $\eta_T(\cdot)$ the better the efficiency. This metric addresses a gap often overlooked in recent works, where the computational cost of training is not explicitly included in comparisons with conventional systems.

5. Results

In this section, we present the numerical results for source compression and transmission over wireless channels.

5.1. Datasets and Simulation Settings

We evaluate the proposed methods using four classification datasets: (i) AG's News [36], which contains news articles from 4 categories; (ii) DBPedia 14 [36], consisting of text samples from 14 ontology classes; (iii) CIFAR 10 [37], including 32×32 RGB images of 10 object categories; and (iv) STL 10 [38], with 96×96 RGB images from 10 object categories. We present details of these datasets in Table 1. For consistency, we test on 2000 balanced samples with respect to class labels for each dataset. We employ the `clip-ViT-B-32` as the CLIP model to obtain message embeddings.

Table 1. Summary of AG's News, DBPedia 14, CIFAR 10, and STL 10.

Dataset	Modality	Classes	Train Size
AG's News	Text	4	120,000
DBPedia 14	Text	14	560,000
CIFAR 10	Image	10	50,000
STL 10 *	Image	10	11,000

* The dataset consists of 5000 labeled training and 8000 labeled test samples. Given the limited number of samples, we merge the train and test sets, then extract 2000 samples for the test set, leaving 11,000 samples for training.

The classifier NN involves three layers with 128, 32, and n_{class} hidden units, where n_{class} corresponds to the number of classes in the dataset. We train the NN on the receiver's dataset, which consists of message embeddings, $\mathbf{q}_{train}$, and their corresponding labels, c_{train}.

In the semantic compression method, we use the negative Euclidean distance, defined in Equation (1), as the similarity metric to minimize semantic distortion in Equation (4). To determine the optimal number of clusters, we use the median of sample similarities as the preference, as discussed in Section 2. The codeword neural network (NN) has a simple structure consisting of three fully connected layers with 256, 64, and l_{cw} units (l'_{cw} for semantic compression). We use $PReLU(\cdot)$ activation in the hidden layers and $\tanh(\cdot)$ at the output. For semantic VQ AE, we set d to match the number of clusters determined by the AP algorithm, as given in Table 3. This ensures a fair comparison among methods. We determine the optimal values through grid search $k \in \{16, 64, 256, 512\}$ and $\alpha \in \{2, 3, 4, 5\}$, primarily considering model performance, while also accounting for model size and computational complexity. We set the commitment parameter in Equation (16) to $\beta = 0.25$. To optimize both classification accuracy and expedite the training process, we increase the learning rate and adjust the number of epochs for proper optimization in fewer steps.

Table 2 lists all the parameters used in simulations. We construct $\mathbf{Q}_{pre}^{n}$ by selecting n samples from the shuffled training data. The remaining training samples constitute the receiver dataset, denoted as $\mathbf{Q}_{train}$ and $\mathbf{c}_{train}$. For the classification block training, we split $\mathbf{Q}_{train}$ and $\mathbf{c}_{train}$ into training and validation sets with ratios of 0.85 and 0.15, respectively. We use the model with the minimum validation loss achieved across the training epochs. We simulate the multimodal scenario by combining 2500 samples each from the AG's News and STL 10 datasets, forming $\mathbf{Q}_{pre}^{n}$ with $n = 5000$. We assume the receiver uses separate classifiers for images and text, trained with the same parameters as those used for the original datasets, as given in Table 2. Training procedures of the codeword NN and semantic VQ AE have the same parameters in the AG's News dataset, except for $\gamma_{scheduler} = 0.95$ and $k = 16$ for semantic VQ AE. We simulate the multimodal case using 2000 test samples from each dataset, resulting in 4000 in total, which are also balanced with respect to class labels.

Table 2. Simulation settings.

	Parameter	AG's News	DBPedia 14	CIFAR 10	STL 10
	n	5000	3000		1500
Class. Block	Batch Size	128			
	n_{epochs}	15			
	LR Sched.	Exponential LR			
	$\gamma_{\text{scheduler}}$	0.75			
	Initial LR	0.001			
	Optimizer	$AdamW(\beta_1 = 0.9, \beta_2 = 0.999, w_{\text{decay}} = 0.01)$			
Codeword NN	Batch Size	128			
	n_{epochs}	Semantic Quantization: 6 Semantic Compression: 10			
	LR Sched.	Exponential LR			
	$\gamma_{\text{scheduler}}$	0.97			
	Initial LR	0.001			
	Optimizer	$AdamW(\beta_1 = 0.9, \beta_2 = 0.999, w_{\text{decay}} = 0.01)$			
	ϵ	1			
	$(\alpha_1, \alpha_2, \alpha_3)$	(0.25, 0.5, 0.25)			
Semantic VQ AE	k	64			
	α	4			
	Batch Size	128			
	n_{epochs}	25			
	LR Sched.	Exponential LR			
	$\gamma_{\text{scheduler}}$	0.9	0.98		
	Initial LR	0.005			
	Optimizer	$AdamW(\beta_1 = 0.9, \beta_2 = 0.999)$			
	w_{decay}	0.0001		0.00025	0.0005
	SNR_{min}	0 (dB)			
	SNR_{max}	21 (dB)			

We implement conventional source-coding baselines to investigate the efficacy of the proposed semantic methods. We employ Huffman coding for text compression and JPEG2000 for image compression. We adopt block coding for Huffman, where compression symbols consist group of three characters. We derive empirical probabilities for these blocks from the provided text. Regarding the JPEG2000 algorithm, we use the Python Pillow package (version 9.3.0), adhering to its default parameters, except for configuring the quality layers parameter, set to 20. As these algorithms ensure exact reconstruction, we assess their accuracy using the original embeddings of messages, without any form of quantization or compression.

For wireless channel simulations, $h = 1$ for the AWGN channel and $h \sim \mathbb{C}\mathcal{N}(0, \sigma_h^2)$ for Rayleigh fading channels with $\sigma_h^2 = 1$. We employ an average power constraint of 1 for all transmission methods. Consequently, the channel signal-to-noise ratio (SNR) becomes

$-10 \log_{10}(\sigma_{\mathbf{z}}^2)$ dB. We adjust the noise variance, $\sigma_{\mathbf{z}}^2$, to emulate average channel SNR values. We employ transmit power control (channel inversion) to mitigate the effects of fading.

Table 3. Number of bits required to compress test messages and their classification accuracies for fixed-length coding (mean $\pm$ 1 SD, 10 runs).

Dataset	Method	Number of Bits	Acc. (%)
AG's News	Conventional	1,480,599	92.50 $\pm$ 0.08
	Sem. Quan.	26,000	88.04 $\pm$ 0.65
	Sem. Comp. 501 *	18,000	85.25 $\pm$ 0.87
	Sem. VQ AE 501 +	18,000	84.23 $\pm$ 0.67
DBPedia 14	Conventional	2,160,054	98.60 $\pm$ 0.08
	Sem. Quan.	24,000	90.44 $\pm$ 0.35
	Sem. Comp. 252 *	16,000	85.78 $\pm$ 0.45
	Sem. VQ AE 252 +	16,000	83.51 $\pm$ 0.97
CIFAR 10	Conventional	4,073,328	95.90 $\pm$ 0.08
	Sem. Quan.	24,000	89.08 $\pm$ 0.56
	Sem. Comp. 147 *	16,000	86.13 $\pm$ 0.53
	Sem. VQ AE 147 +	16,000	84.26 $\pm$ 0.94
STL 10	Conventional	22188432	98.55 $\pm$ 0.09
	Sem. Quan.	22,000	97.95 $\pm$ 0.28
	Sem. Comp. 88 *	14,000	97.31 $\pm$ 0.18
	Sem. VQ AE 88 +	14,000	95.39 $\pm$ 1.09
Multi Modal	Conventional	23,659,964	95.67 $\pm$ 0.12
	Sem. Quan.	52,000	92.20 $\pm$ 0.34
	Sem. Comp. 208 *	32,000	89.45 $\pm$ 0.56
	Sem. VQ AE 208 +	32,000	85.60 $\pm$ 1.16

* The number of clusters determined by the AP algorithm. + The size of **E**, i.e., the value of d in semantic VQ AE.

We conduct simulations on a computer equipped with an Intel Core i9-13950HX CPU at 1.6 GHz and an NVIDIA GeForce RTX 4070 GPU, which is employed to accelerate neural model training. To ensure reliable results, we measure the simulation times while the computer is idle and all background applications are disabled. For each method, we repeat the simulations 10 times and present the mean scores with standard deviations (SD) to quantify the uncertainty. In each run, we use a different seed to initialize the neural network parameters and shuffle the data, resulting in distinct $\mathbf{Q}_{pre}^n$ across runs.

5.2. Source Compression

We start by examining the structure of pre-trained embeddings in $\mathbf{Q}_{pre}^n$. To visualize, we project the embeddings into $\mathbb{R}^2$ using uniform manifold approximation and projection (UMAP) [39]. As we have described in Section 3, $\mathbf{Q}_{pre}^n$ consists of random samples without any prior knowledge. However, just for this visualization, we use the class information of embeddings to illustrate their structure. Figure 5 indicates that embeddings from the same class tend to cluster together. This supports the intuition that class-related semantics can be preserved, even after clustering.

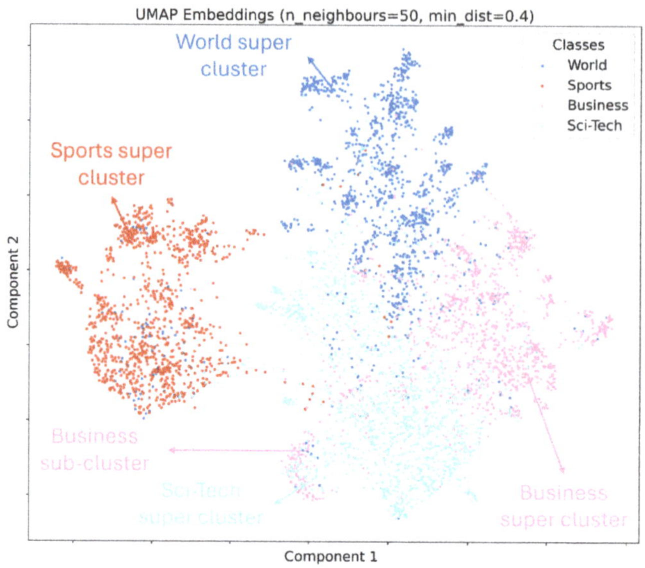

Figure 5. UMAP projection of AG's News $\mathbf{Q}^{n}_{pre}$ embeddings into $\mathbb{R}^2$.

Table 3 presents the source compression results, including the number of bits required to compress test samples and their associated classification accuracies. We observe that the proposed semantic methods improve resource efficiency compared to conventional baselines. Regarding classification accuracies, semantic quantization attains the highest score, likely due to its larger codebook, which offers finer semantic resolution at the cost of higher bit usage. By contrast, semantic compression maintains comparable accuracy while using fewer bits, effectively preserving resolution by removing redundancy. These findings confirm that exploiting semantic redundancy reduces data size without a major accuracy loss. Furthermore, as detailed in Section 5.1, we ensure a fair comparison between semantic compression and semantic VQ AE in terms of resource utilization by having the same codebook size. Under these equal conditions, we observe that semantic compression achieves higher classification accuracies than semantic VQ AE. This suggests that, given the same resource constraints, semantic compression better preserves class-related semantics while utilizing the same amount of resources. These observations are consistent across all datasets, including the custom multimodal dataset. This highlights the feasibility of constructing a unified multimodal codebook consisting of codewords for both image and text messages. Overall, the results demonstrate that semantic quantization and compression methods can generalize across diverse contexts and modalities without requiring separate training for each to obtain learned discrete representations.

The number of clusters determined by the AP algorithm in Table 3 is significantly large. We attribute this to the high dimensionality of the embeddings ($m = 512$) and the existence of small sub-clusters in broader super-clusters. For example, Figure 5 demonstrates a small group from the "Business" class embedded in the "Sci-Tech" class, leading to an additional cluster.

In Table 4, we select a random sample from the AG's News test set denoted as s, and retrieve the messages corresponding to the assigned index and cluster label denoted as s_i and s_l, respectively. A comparison of these messages reveals a strong alignment with human understanding, reinforcing the interpretability discussed in Sections 4.1 and 4.2. This alignment suggests that the semantics required for the classification task are effectively conveyed while enhancing efficiency, which is the aim of this work.

Table 4. Example of assigned messages using AG's News dataset.

Method	Corresponding Message
s	Wiltshire Police warns about "phishing" after its fraud squad chief was targeted.
s_i	Do-it-yourself phishing kits are freely available on the Internet, a security firm said Thursday, and they will lead to more scams sent to online consumers.
s_l	Do-it-yourself phishing kits are being made available for download free of charge from the interest, security watchers have warned.

We examine how the value of n impacts performance. While a larger n demands more computational resources, n needs to be sufficiently large to ensure an adequate number of samples per class for effective codebook construction. Figure 6 provides the accuracy of methods as n varies from 50 to 10,000 for the DBPedia 14 and CIFAR 10 datasets. For $3000 < n$, the accuracy plateaus for all methods, indicating diminishing returns. The proposed semantic quantization and compression methods achieve rapid convergence in accuracy. They perform well even with smaller datasets and demonstrate robustness to varying data sizes. By contrast, semantic VQ AE struggles to achieve high accuracy and converges more slowly. This highlights the data-greedy nature of learning-based approaches, which are sensitive to data size during optimization.

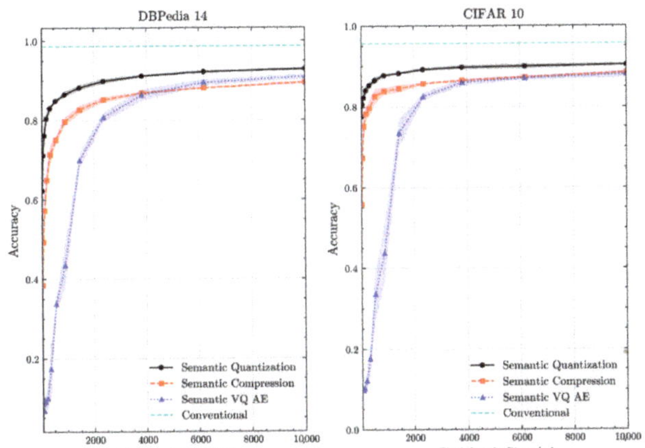

Figure 6. Classification accuracy vs. n for DBPedia 14 and CIFAR 10 datasets (mean $\pm$ 1 SD, 10 runs).

5.3. Wireless Channel Simulations

In this section, we evaluate the proposed methods over wireless channels, assuming the exact channel state for transmit power control, i.e., $\hat{h} = h$. We employ Reed–Solomon coding with rate RS(31, 25) and quadrature phase shift keying (QPSK) modulation. We use the accuracy of the conventional approach at infinite SNR as the upper bound, representing lossless transmission. We examine the convergence of the semantic methods to this limit.

We begin by examining the impact of incorporating codeword transition probabilities. To this end, we establish baselines for semantic quantization and compression. In these baselines, the resulting i and l values are directly encoded into binary format and transmitted with RS(31, 25). For the semantic VQ AE, we train the baseline in a noiseless setup, i.e., without any perturbations to p. In this comparison, we have the same number of channel uses for all schemes, as the codeword lengths and the channel coding rates are the same. Thus, any observed improvement in accuracy is attributed to integrating transition probabilities in the system design.

Figures 7 and 8 illustrate the accuracies of designed codewords over wireless channels for semantic quantization and noisy training in the semantic VQ AE. Figures 9 and 10 further present these accuracies with the full accuracy range $[0, 1]$, as requested by the anonymous reviewer. For the semantic quantization, we observe a significant accuracy improvement in the low SNR region compared to the baseline. This is achieved without adding redundancy and decreasing the rate, making the result promising. The accuracy is the same for high SNR regions, as the proposed codeword assignment mechanism does not interfere with the discrete message representations. For the semantic VQ AE, we observe increased accuracy in low SNR regions, highlighting the benefits of adversarial training. However, a performance gap emerges between noisy and noiseless training in the high SNR region. Unlike semantic quantization, noisy training in semantic VQ AE impacts the discrete representations assigned to codewords. Thus, we interpret this gap as the channel simulation during training acting as a regularizer. Given the small training dataset, the limited number of samples can lead to overfitting. Hence, introducing a regularizer improves performance and ensures more robust discrete representations.

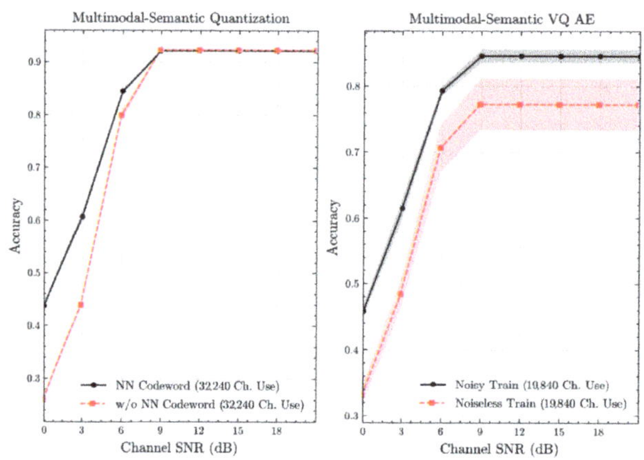

Figure 7. Classification accuracies for the multimodal dataset over AWGN channel (mean ± 1 SD, 10 runs).

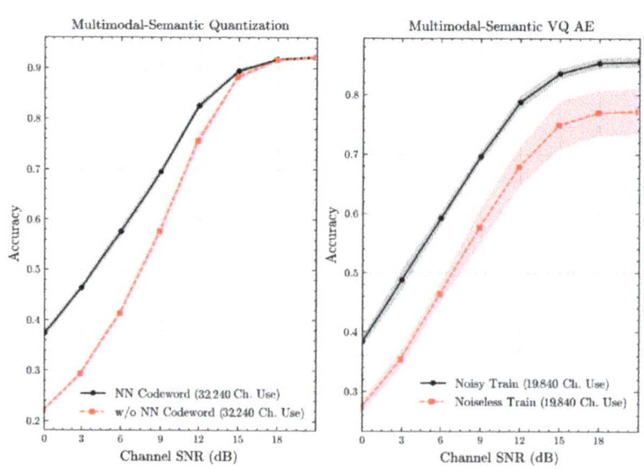

Figure 8. Classification accuracies for the multimodal dataset over Rayleigh channel (mean ± 1 SD, 10 runs).

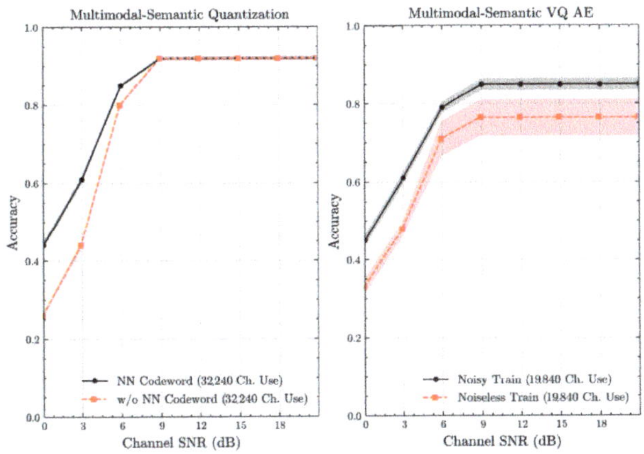

Figure 9. Classification accuracies with full accuracy range for the multimodal dataset over AWGN channel (mean $\pm$ 1 SD, 10 runs).

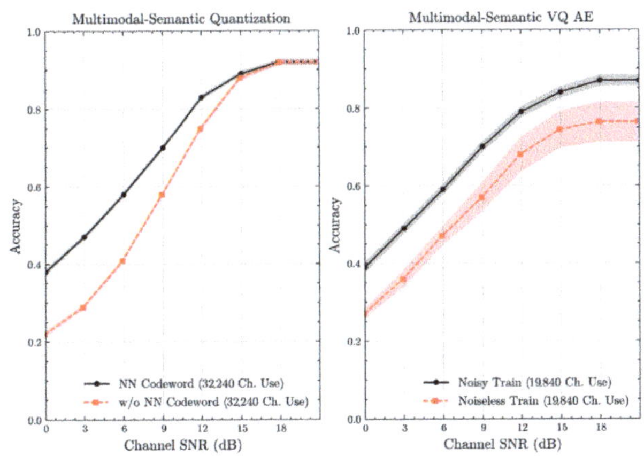

Figure 10. Classification accuracies with full accuracy range for the multimodal dataset over Rayleigh channel (mean $\pm$ 1 SD, 10 runs).

We present the accuracy, time efficiency scores, and corresponding channel uses of the methods for each dataset in Figures 11–14 and 19–22. Figures 15–18 further present these accuracies with the full accuracy range $[0, 1]$, as requested by the anonymous reviewer. The performance over wireless channels is consistent with the source compression results in Table 3, as expected. Notably, we highlight the small n value, representing the scarce data scenario. For larger n values, the methods are expected to converge more closely to the upper limit. Additionally, the variations in convergence across datasets are linked to the semantic structure of the data in the semantic space, which is illustrated for AG's News in Figure 5.

We allocate time budgets based on modalities, message lengths, and training sizes. For example, CIFAR 10 receives more time than STL 10 due to its larger n. Results demonstrate that semantic compression consistently achieves the highest time efficiency, while semantic quantization and semantic VQ AE exhibit inferior performance. We observe that the pre-communication phase of semantic VQ AE, i.e., t_{train}, is significantly longer than that of quantization. However, the smaller codebook of VQ AE helps mitigate this during communication, enabling larger u values compared to quantization.

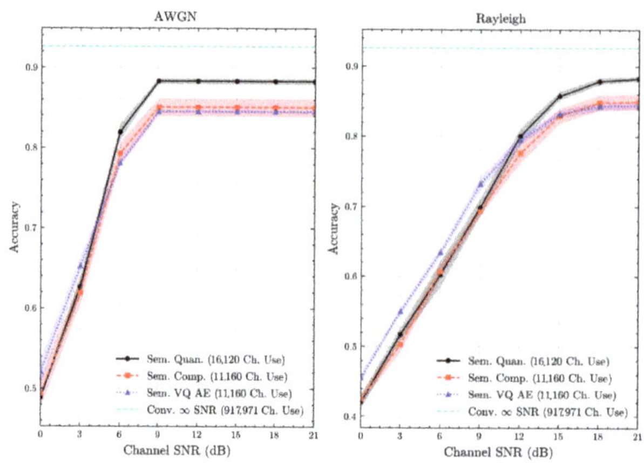

Figure 11. AG's News dataset classification accuracies over AWGN and Rayleigh channels (mean ± 1 SD, 10 runs).

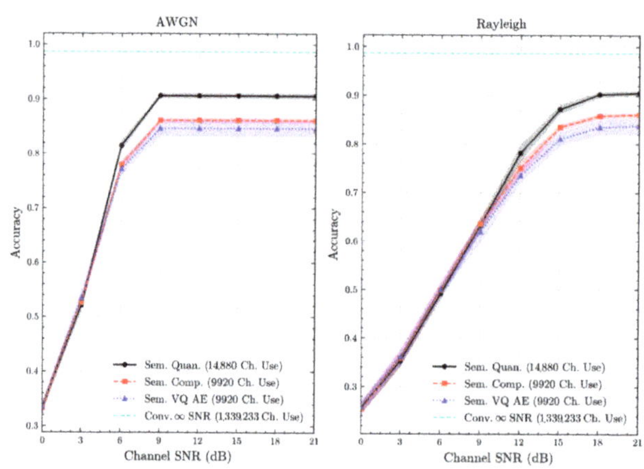

Figure 12. DBPedia 14 dataset classification accuracies over AWGN and Rayleigh channels (mean ± 1 SD, 10 runs).

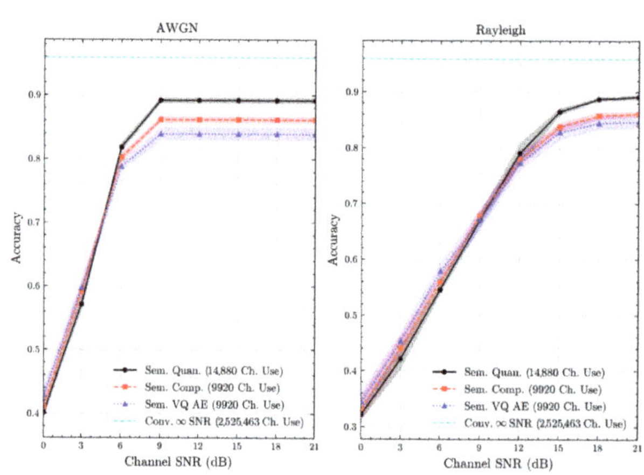

Figure 13. CIFAR 10 dataset classification accuracies over AWGN and Rayleigh channels (mean ± 1 SD, 10 runs).

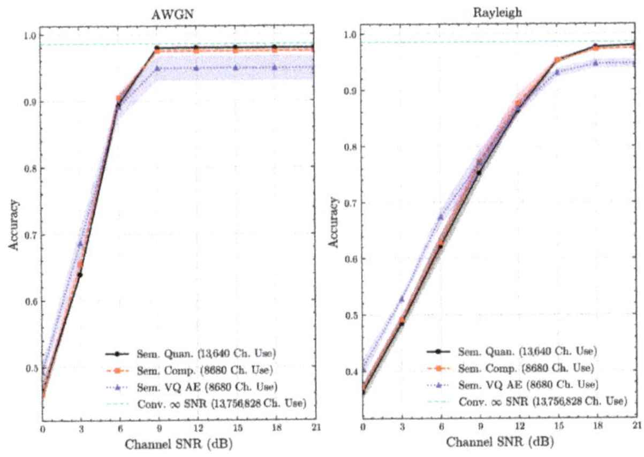

Figure 14. STL 10 dataset classification accuracies over AWGN and Rayleigh channels (mean ± 1 SD, 10 runs).

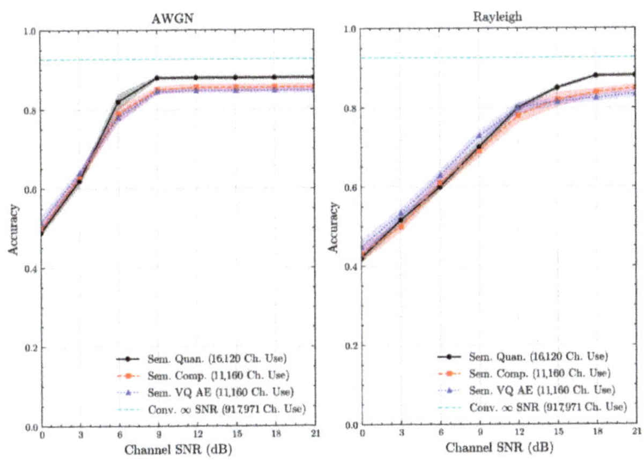

Figure 15. AG's News dataset classification accuracies with full accuracy range over AWGN and Rayleigh channels (mean ± 1 SD, 10 runs).

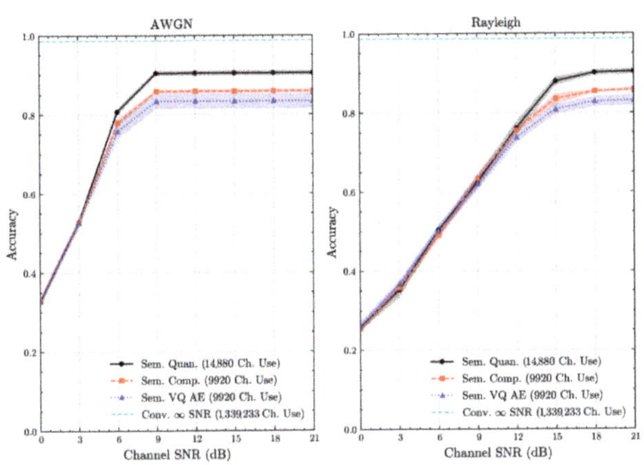

Figure 16. DBPedia 14 dataset classification accuracies with full accuracy range over AWGN and Rayleigh channels (mean ± 1 SD, 10 runs).

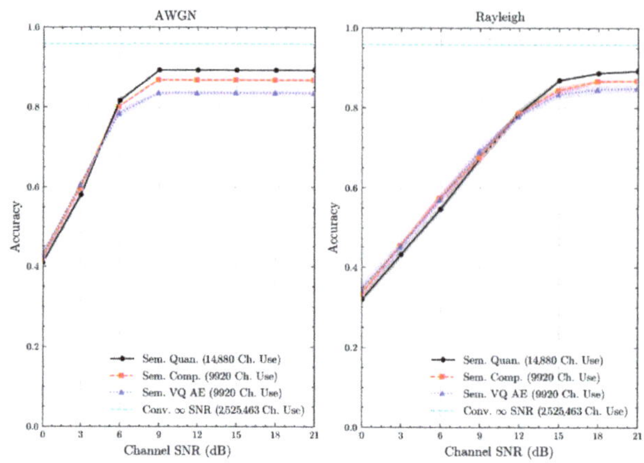

Figure 17. CIFAR 10 dataset classification accuracies with full accuracy range over AWGN and Rayleigh channels (mean $\pm$ 1 SD, 10 runs).

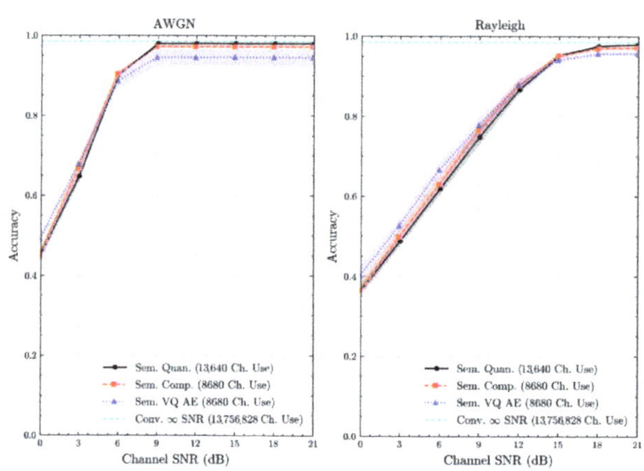

Figure 18. STL 10 dataset classification accuracies with full accuracy range over AWGN and Rayleigh channels (mean $\pm$ 1 SD, 10 runs).

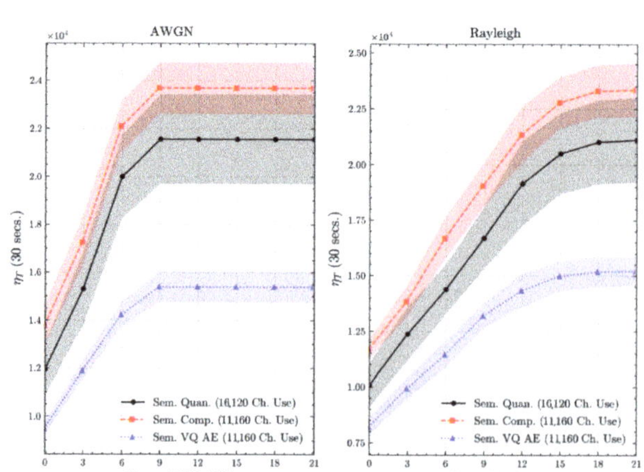

Figure 19. AG's News dataset system time efficiency scores over AWGN and Rayleigh channels (mean $\pm$ 1 SD, 10 runs).

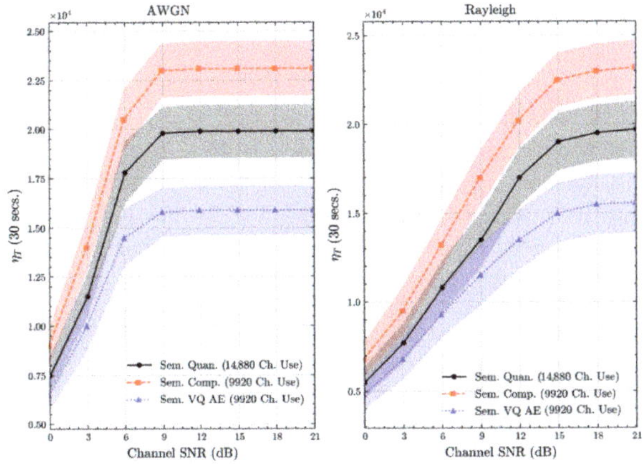

Figure 20. DBPedia 14 dataset system time efficiency scores over AWGN and Rayleigh channels (mean ± 1 SD, 10 runs).

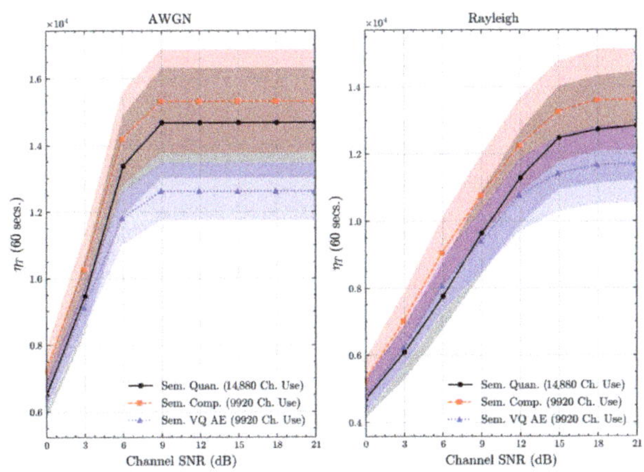

Figure 21. CIFAR 10 dataset system time efficiency scores over AWGN and Rayleigh channels (mean ± 1 SD, 10 runs).

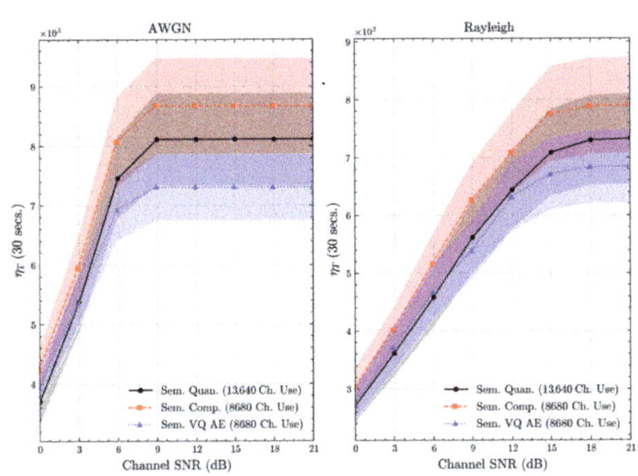

Figure 22. STL 10 dataset system time efficiency scores over AWGN and Rayleigh channels (mean ± 1 SD, 10 runs).

We compare the time efficiency of quantization and compression, focusing on the impact of clustering. Compression involves a clustering step that reduces codebook size. This results in an overhead for clustering but leads to a smaller model and faster training for the codeword NN. During communication, quantization's larger codebook increases computational demands, i.e., the calculation of Equation (4), while compression benefits from a smaller codebook. According to Equation (17), although compression has a similar t_{train}, its larger u enables it to achieve better efficiency scores than quantization.

We observe that integrating model-based insights with pre-trained models simplifies the objective, e.g., aligning codeword Hamming distances with Euclidean distances in the embedding space. In contrast, purely end-to-end approaches, such as semantic VQ-AE, optimize without any structural guidance, making the process more challenging. This highlights the need to combine model-based reasoning with learning-based methods for effective ML-aided communication. Overall, leveraging semantic redundancies reduces computational load and improves the efficiency of wireless resource utilization. We validate performance via 5 different datasets. Proposed semantic methods are compatible with any pre-trained embedding model that shares semantic relation properties, with semantic quantization and compression methods being particularly adaptable due to their lower computational demands. Proposed methods also allow for the change of the classification block with one suited for other tasks using reconstructed embeddings, without requiring changes to their design.

6. Conclusions

In this paper, we have considered classification-oriented multimodal semantic communications. We have used a pre-trained transformer model to extract semantic information, and proposed three different methods for generating their codebooks to minimize semantic distortion. The semantic quantization and compression methods have directly used the available dataset as a codebook, whereas the learning-based method has been trained on the same dataset. We have observed that the proposed methods provide excellent classification accuracy performance, and that pre-training-based methods provide effective compression, resulting in much better system time efficiency with comparable accuracy to their end-to-end learning counterparts. Our study points to the inherent power of utilizing pre-trained models at the edge and demonstrates that with an effective "fine tuning" of codewords, we can have efficient semantic communications.

Future work along these lines include communicating multimodal semantics in multi-node task-oriented networks with personalized tasks.

Author Contributions: Conceptualization, E.K. and A.Y.; methodology, E.K. and A.Y.; software, E.K.; validation, E.K. and A.Y.; writing—original draft preparation, E.K. and A.Y.; writing—review and editing, E.K. and A.Y.; project management, A.Y. All authors have read and agreed to the published version of the manuscript.

Funding: This research received no external funding.

Institutional Review Board Statement: Not applicable.

Data Availability Statement: The raw data supporting the conclusions of this article will be made available by the authors on request.

Acknowledgments: We thank the anonymous reviewer for requesting plots with full accuracy range.

Conflicts of Interest: The authors declare no conflicts of interest.

References

1. Jameel, F.; Chang, Z.; Huang, J.; Ristaniemi, T. Internet of Autonomous Vehicles: Architecture, Features, and Socio-Technological Challenges. *IEEE Wirel. Commun.* **2019**, *26*, 21–29. [CrossRef]
2. Atzori, L.; Iera, A.; Morabito, G. The Internet of Things: A Survey. *Comput. Netw.* **2010**, *54*, 2787–2805. [CrossRef]
3. Shannon, C.E. A mathematical theory of communication. *Bell Syst. Tech. J.* **1948**, *27*, 379–423. [CrossRef]
4. Gündüz, D.; Qin, Z.; Aguerri, I.E.; Dhillon, H.S.; Yang, Z.; Yener, A.; Wong, K.K.; Chae, C.B. Beyond Transmitting Bits: Context, Semantics, and Task-Oriented Communications. *IEEE J. Sel. Areas Commun.* **2023**, *41*, 5–41. [CrossRef]
5. Shannon, C.E.; Weaver, W. *The Mathematical Theory of Communication*; University of Illinois Press: Champaign, IL, USA, 1949.
6. Carnap, R.; Bar-Hillel, Y. *An Outline of a Theory of Semantic Communication*; RLE Technical 522 Reports; Research Laboratory of Electronics, Massachusetts Institute of Technology: Cambridge, MA, USA, 1952; Volume 247.
7. Melamed, I.D. Measuring Semantic Entropy. In Proceedings of the Tagging Text with Lexical Semantics: Why, What, and How? Washington, DC, USA, 4–5 April 1997.
8. Juba, B.; Sudan, M. Universal semantic communication I. In Proceedings of the Fortieth Annual ACM Symposium on Theory of Computing, New York, NY, USA, 17–20 May 2008; STOC '08; pp. 123–132. [CrossRef]
9. Guler, B.; Yener, A. Semantic index assignment. In Proceedings of the IEEE International Conference on Pervasive Computing and Communication Workshops (PerCom), Budapest, Hungary, 24–28 March 2014; pp. 431–436.
10. Güler, B.; Yener, A.; Swami, A. The Semantic Communication Game. *IEEE Trans. Cogn. Commun. Netw.* **2018**, *4*, 787–802. [CrossRef]
11. O'Shea, T.; Hoydis, J. An Introduction to Deep Learning for the Physical Layer. *IEEE Trans. Cogn. Commun. Netw.* **2017**, *3*, 563–575. [CrossRef]
12. Ma, S.; Qiao, W.; Wu, Y.; Li, H.; Shi, G.; Gao, D.; Shi, Y.; Li, S.; Al-Dhahir, N. Task-oriented Explainable Semantic Communications. *IEEE Trans. Wirel. Commun.* **2023**, *22*, 9248–9262. [CrossRef]
13. Sheng, Y.; Li, F.; Liang, L.; Jin, S. A Multi-Task Semantic Communication System for Natural Language Processing. In Proceedings of the 2022 IEEE 96th Vehicular Technology Conference (VTC2022-Fall), London, UK, 26–29 September 2022; pp. 1–5. [CrossRef]
14. Farsad, N.; Rao, M.; Goldsmith, A. Deep Learning for Joint Source-Channel Coding of Text. In Proceedings of the 2018 IEEE International Conference on Acoustics, Speech and Signal Processing (ICASSP), Calgary, AB, Canada, 15–20 April 2018; pp. 2326–2330. [CrossRef]
15. Jankowski, M.; Gündüz, D.; Mikolajczyk, K. Wireless Image Retrieval at the Edge. *IEEE J. Sel. Areas Commun.* **2021**, *39*, 89–100. [CrossRef]
16. Weng, Z.; Qin, Z. Semantic Communication Systems for Speech Transmission. *IEEE J. Sel. Areas Commun.* **2021**, *39*, 2434–2444. [CrossRef]
17. Xie, H.; Qin, Z.; Tao, X.; Letaief, K.B. Task-Oriented Multi-User Semantic Communications. *IEEE J. Sel. Areas Commun.* **2022**, *40*, 2584–2597. [CrossRef]
18. Sagduyu, Y.E.; Erpek, T.; Ulukus, S.; Yener, A. Is Semantic Communication Secure? A Tale of Multi-Domain Adversarial Attacks. *IEEE Commun. Mag.* **2023**, *61*, 50–55. [CrossRef]
19. Kaplan, J.; McCandlish, S.; Henighan, T.; Brown, T.B.; Chess, B.; Child, R.; Gray, S.; Radford, A.; Wu, J.; Amodei, D. Scaling Laws for Neural Language Models. *arXiv* **2020**. [CrossRef]
20. Kutay, E.; Yener, A. Semantic Text Compression for Classification. In Proceedings of the 2023 IEEE International Conference on Communications Workshops (ICC Workshops), Rome, Italy, 28 May–1 June 2023; pp. 1368–1373. [CrossRef]
21. Kutay, E.; Yener, A. Classification-Oriented Semantic Wireless Communications. In Proceedings of the ICASSP 2024—2024 IEEE International Conference on Acoustics, Speech and Signal Processing (ICASSP), Seoul, Republic of Korea, 14–19 April 2024; pp. 9096–9100. [CrossRef]
22. Mikolov, T.; Chen, K.; Corrado, G.; Dean, J. Efficient Estimation of Word Representations in Vector Space. In Proceedings of the 1st International Conference on Learning Representations, ICLR 2013, Scottsdale, AZ, USA, 2–4 May 2013; Workshop Track Proceedings.
23. Devlin, J.; Chang, M.W.; Lee, K.; Toutanova, K. BERT: Pre-training of Deep Bidirectional Transformers for Language Understanding. In Proceedings of the 2019 Conference of the North American Chapter of the Association for Computational Linguistics, Minneapolis, MN, USA, 2–7 June 2019; pp. 4171–4186. [CrossRef]
24. Reimers, N.; Gurevych, I. Sentence-BERT: Sentence Embeddings using Siamese BERT-Networks. In Proceedings of the 2019 Conference on Empirical Methods in NLP, Hong Kong, China, 3–7 November 2019; Association for Computational Linguistics: Stroudsburg, PA, USA, 2019.
25. Radford, A.; Kim, J.W.; Hallacy, C.; Ramesh, A.; Goh, G.; Agarwal, S.; Sastry, G.; Askell, A.; Mishkin, P.; Clark, J.; et al. Learning Transferable Visual Models from Natural Language Supervision. In Proceedings of the 38th International Conference on Machine Learning, PMLR, Virtual, 18–24 July 2021; Volume 139, pp. 8748–8763.

26. Arora, S.; May, A.; Zhang, J.; Ré, C. Contextual Embeddings: When Are They Worth It? In Proceedings of the 58th Annual Meeting of the Association for Computational Linguistics, Online, 5–10 July 2020; Jurafsky, D., Chai, J., Schluter, N., Tetreault, J., Eds.; pp. 2650–2663. [CrossRef]
27. Grollmisch, S.; Cano, E.; Kehling, C.; Taenzer, M. Analyzing the Potential of Pre-Trained Embeddings for Audio Classification Tasks. In Proceedings of the 2020 28th European Signal Processing Conference (EUSIPCO), Amsterdam, The Netherlands, 18–22 January 2021; pp. 790–794. [CrossRef]
28. Frey, B.J.; Dueck, D. Clustering by Passing Messages Between Data Points. *Science* **2007**, *315*, 972–976. [CrossRef] [PubMed]
29. Daras, G.; Dean, J.; Jalal, A.; Dimakis, A. Intermediate Layer Optimization for Inverse Problems using Deep Generative Models. In Proceedings of the 38th International Conference on Machine Learning, PMLR, Virtual, 18–24 July 2021; Volume 139, pp. 2421–2432.
30. Bora, A.; Jalal, A.; Price, E.; Dimakis, A.G. Compressed Sensing using Generative Models. In Proceedings of the 34th International Conference on Machine Learning, PMLR, Sydney, NSW, Australia, 6–11 August 2017; Volume 70, pp. 537–546.
31. Burkard, R.E.; Derigs, U. The Linear Sum Assignment Problem. In *Assignment and Matching Problems: Solution Methods with FORTRAN-Programs*; Springer: Berlin/Heidelberg, Germany, 1980; pp. 1–15. [CrossRef]
32. Crouse, D.F. On implementing 2D rectangular assignment algorithms. *IEEE Trans. Aerosp. Electron. Syst.* **2016**, *52*, 1679–1696. [CrossRef]
33. Liu, X.; Chen, Q.; Wu, X.; Hua, Y.; Chen, J.; Li, D.; Tang, B.; Wang, X. Gated Semantic Difference Based Sentence Semantic Equivalence Identification. *IEEE/ACM Trans. Audio Speech Lang. Process.* **2020**, *28*, 2770–2780. [CrossRef]
34. van den Oord, A.; Vinyals, O.; Kavukcuoglu, K. Neural Discrete Representation Learning. In Proceedings of the Advances in Neural Information Processing Systems, Long Beach, CA, USA, 4–9 December 2017; Guyon, I., Luxburg, U.V., Bengio, S., Wallach, H., Fergus, R., Vishwanathan, S., Garnett, R., Eds.; Curran Associates, Inc.: Red Hook, NY, USA, 2017; Volume 30.
35. Hu, Q.; Zhang, G.; Qin, Z.; Cai, Y.; Yu, G.; Li, G.Y. Robust Semantic Communications with Masked VQ-VAE Enabled Codebook. *IEEE Trans. Wirel. Commun.* **2023**, *22*, 8707–8722. [CrossRef]
36. Zhang, X.; Zhao, J.; LeCun, Y. Character-level Convolutional Networks for Text Classification. In Proceedings of the Advances in Neural Information Processing Systems, Montreal, QC, Canada, 7–12 December 2015; Cortes, C., Lawrence, N., Lee, D., Sugiyama, M., Garnett, R., Eds.; Curran Associates, Inc.: New York, NY, USA, 2015; Volume 28.
37. Krizhevsky, A.; Hinton, G. *Learning Multiple Layers of Features from Tiny Images*; Technical Report 0; University of Toronto: Toronto, ON, Canada, 2009.
38. Coates, A.; Ng, A.; Lee, H. An Analysis of Single-Layer Networks in Unsupervised Feature Learning. In Proceedings of the Fourteenth International Conference on Artificial Intelligence and Statistics, PMLR, Ft. Lauderdale, FL, USA, 11–13 April 2011; Volume 15, pp. 215–223.
39. McInnes, L.; Healy, J.; Melville, J. UMAP: Uniform Manifold Approximation and Projection for Dimension Reduction. *arXiv* **2018**. [CrossRef]

entropy

MDPI

Article

Rate-Distortion Analysis of Distributed Indirect Source Coding

Jiancheng Tang and Qianqian Yang *

College of information Science and Electronic Engineering, Zhejiang University, Hangzhou 310007, China; jianchengtang@zju.edu.cn
* Correspondence: qianqianyang20@zju.edu.cn

Abstract

Motivated by task-oriented semantic communication and distributed learning systems, this paper studies a distributed indirect source coding problem where M correlated sources are independently encoded for a central decoder. The decoder has access to correlated side information in addition to the messages received from the encoders and aims to recover a latent random variable under a given distortion constraint rather than recovering the sources themselves. We characterize the exact rate-distortion function for the case where the sources are conditionally independent given the side information. Furthermore, we develop a distributed Blahut–Arimoto (BA) algorithm to numerically compute the rate-distortion function. Numerical examples are provided to demonstrate the effectiveness of the proposed approach in calculating the rate-distortion region.

Keywords: semantic communication; distributed source coding; rate-distortion theory; side information; Blahut–Arimoto algorithm

1. Introduction

Consider the multiterminal source coding setup as shown in Figure 1. Let $(T, X_1, \dots, X_M, Y) \sim p(t, x_1, \dots, x_M, y)$ be a discrete memoryless source (DMS) taking values in the finite alphabets $\mathcal{T} \times \mathcal{X}_1 \times \cdots \times \mathcal{X}_M \times \mathcal{Y}$ according to a fixed and known probability distribution $p(t, x_1, \dots, x_M, y)$. In this setup, the encoder $m, m \in \mathcal{M} := \{1, \dots, M\}$ has local observations $X_m^n := (X_m^1, \dots, X_m^n)$. The agents independently encode their observations into binary sequences at rates $\{R_1, \dots, R_M\}$ bits per input symbol, respectively. The decoder with side information $Y^n = (Y_1, \dots, Y_n)$ aims to recover some task-oriented latent information $T^n := (T_1, \dots, T_n)$ which is correlated with $(X_1^n, \dots, X_M^n)$, but it is not observed directly by any of the encoders. We are interested in the lossy reconstruction of T^n with the average distortion measured by $\mathbb{E}\left[\frac{1}{n}\sum_{i=1}^n d(T_i, \hat{T}_i)\right]$ for some prescribed single-letter distortion measure $d(\cdot,\cdot)$. A formal $(2^{nR_1}, \dots, 2^{nR_M}, n)$ rate-distortion code for this setup consists of the following:

- M independent encoders, where encoder $m \in \mathcal{M}$ assigns an index $s_m(x_m^n) \in \{1, \dots, 2^{nR_m}\}$ to each sequence $x_m^n \in \mathcal{X}_m^n$;
- A decoder that produces the estimate $\hat{t}^n(s_1, \dots, s_M, y^n) \in \mathcal{T}^n$ to each index tuple $(s_1, \dots, s_M)$ and side information $y^n \in \mathcal{Y}^n$.

A rate tuple $(R_1, \dots, R_M)$ is said to be achievable with the distortion measure $d(\cdot,\cdot)$ and the distortion value D if there exists a sequence of $(2^{nR_1}, \dots, 2^{nR_M}, n)$ codes that satisfy

$$\limsup_{n\to\infty} \mathbb{E}\left[\frac{1}{n}\sum_{i=1}^n d(T_i, \hat{T}_i)\right] \le D. \quad (1)$$

The rate-distortion region $R^*_{X_1,\ldots,X_m|Y}(D)$ for this distributed source coding problem is the closure of the set of all achievable rate tuples $(R_1,\ldots,R_M)$ that permit the reconstruction of the latent variable T^n within the average distortion constraint D.

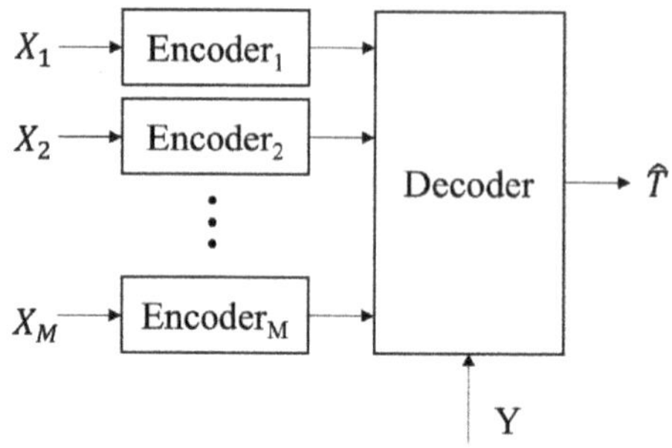

Figure 1. Distributed remote compression of a latent variable with M correlated sources at distributed transmitters and side information at the receiver.

The problem as illustrated in Figure 1 is motivated by semantic/task-oriented communication and distributed learning problems. In semantic/task-oriented communication [1], the decoder only needs to reconstruct some task-oriented information implied by the sources. For instance, it might extract hidden features from a scene captured by multiple cameras positioned at various angles. Here, T_i may also be a deterministic function of the source samples $(X_{1,i},\ldots,X_{M,i})$, which then reduces to the problem of lossy distributed function computation [2–4]. A similar problem also arises in distributed training. Consider Y^n as the global model available at the server at an iteration of a federated learning process and $(X_1^n,\ldots,X_M^n)$ as the independent correlated versions of this model after downlink transmission and local training. The server aims to recover the updated global model, T^n, based on the messages received from all M clients. It is often assumed that the global model is transmitted to the clients intact, but in practical scenarios where downlink communication is limited, the clients may receive noisy or compressed versions of the global model [5–7].

For the case of $M = 1$, the problem reduces to the remote compression in a point-to-point scenario with side information available at the decoder. In [8,9], the authors studied this problem without the correlated side information at the receiver, which is motivated in the context of semantic communication. This problem is known in the literature as the remote rate-distortion problem [10,11], and the rate-distortion trade-off is fully characterized in the general case. The authors studied this trade-off in detail for specific source distributions in [8]. Similarly, the authors of [12] characterized the remote rate-distortion trade-off when correlated side information is available both at the encoder and decoder. Our problem for $M = 1$ can be solved by combining the remote rate-distortion problem with the classical Wyner–Ziv rate-distortion function [13,14].

The rate-distortion region for the multi-terminal version of the remote rate-distortion problem considered here remains open. Wagner et al. developed an improved outer bound for a general multiterminal source model [15]. Sung et al. proposed an achievable rate region for the distributed lossy computation problem without giving an conclusive rate-distortion function [16]. Gwanmo et al. considered a special case in which the sources are independent and derived a single-letter expression for the rate-distortion region [17]. Gastpar [18] considered the lossy compression of the source sequences in the presence of side information at the receiver. He characterized the rate-distortion region for the special case, in which X_i values are conditionally independent given the side information.

To provide a performance reference for practical coding schemes, it is necessary not only to characterize the exact theoretical expression for the rate-distortion region but also to calculate the rate-distortion region for a given distribution and a specific distortion metric. In the traditional single-source direct scenario, determining the rate-distortion function involves solving a convex optimization problem, which can be addressed using the globally convergent iterative Blahut–Arimoto algorithm, as discussed in [17]. In this paper, we are interested in computing the rate-distortion region $R^*_{X_1,\ldots,X_m|Y}(D)$ for the general distributed coding problem. We pay particular attention to the special case in which the sources are conditionally independent given the side information, which is motivated by the aforementioned examples. For the sake of brevity of the presentation, we set $M = 3$ in this paper with the understanding that the results can be readily extended to an arbitrary number of sources. To numerically compute the rate-distortion region, we introduce a distributed iterative optimization framework that generalizes the classical Blahut–Arimoto (BA) algorithm. While the standard BA algorithm is designed for single-source point-to-point settings, our framework extends its alternating minimization structure to a distributed scenario with multiple encoders, indirect source reconstruction, and decoder-side side information. This extension enables the computation of rate-distortion regions in settings that are significantly more general than those considered in the existing literature.

In Section 2, we derive an achievable region $R_a(D) \subseteq R^*_{X_1,X_2,X_3|Y}(D)$. In Section 3, we determine a general outer bound $R_o(D) \supseteq R^*_{X_1,X_2,X_3|Y}(D)$. In Section 4, we show that the two regions coincide and the region is optimal when the sources (X_1, X_2, X_3) are conditionally independent given the side information Y. In Section 5, we develop an alternating minimization framework to calculate the rate-distortion region by generalizing the Blahut–Arimoto (BA) algorithm. In Section 6, we demonstrate the effectiveness of the proposed framework through numerical examples.

2. An Achievable Rate Region

In this section, we introduce an achievable rate region $R_a(D)$, which is contained within the goal rate-distortion region $R_a(D) \subseteq R^*_{X_1,X_2,X_3|Y}(D)$.

Theorem 1. *$R_a(D) \subseteq R^*_{X_1,X_2,X_3|Y}(D)$, where $R_a(D)$ is the set of all rate tuples (R_1, R_2, R_3) such that there exists a tuples (W_1, W_2, W_3) of discrete random variables with $p(w_1, w_2, w_3, x_1, x_2, x_3, y) = p(w_1|x_1)p(w_2|x_2)p(w_3|x_3)p(x_1, x_2, x_3, y)$, for which the following conditions are satisfied*

$$\begin{aligned}
R_1 &\geqslant I(X_1; W_1) - I(W_1; W_2, W_3, Y) &\quad (2a)\\
R_2 &\geqslant I(X_2; W_2) - I(W_2; W_1, W_3, Y) &\quad (2b)\\
R_3 &\geqslant I(X_3; W_3) - I(W_3; W_1, W_2, Y) &\quad (2c)\\
R_1 + R_2 &\geqslant I(X_1; W_1) + I(X_2; W_2) - I(W_1; W_2, W_3, Y)\\
&\quad - I(W_2; W_1, W_3, Y) + I(W_1; W_2|W_3, Y) &\quad (2d)\\
R_1 + R_3 &\geqslant I(X_1; W_1) + I(X_3; W_3) - I(W_1; W_2, W_3, Y)\\
&\quad - I(W_3; W_1, W_2, Y) + I(W_1; W_3|W_2, Y) &\quad (2e)\\
R_2 + R_3 &\geqslant I(X_2; W_2) + I(X_3; W_3) - I(W_2; W_1, W_3, Y)\\
&\quad - I(W_3; W_1, W_2, Y) + I(W_2; W_3|W_1, Y), &\quad (2f)\\
R_1 + R_2 + R_3 &\geqslant I(X_1; W_1) + I(X_2; W_2) + I(X_3; W_3)\\
&\quad - I(W_1; W_2, W_3, Y) - I(W_2; W_1, W_3, Y)\\
&\quad - I(W_3; W_1, W_2, Y) + I(W_1; W_2|W_3, Y)\\
&\quad + I(W_1, W_2; W_3|Y), &\quad (2g)
\end{aligned}$$

and there exist a decoder $g(\cdot)$ such that

$$Ed(T, g(W_1, W_2, W_3, Y)) \leqslant D. \tag{3}$$

The auxiliary random variables W_1, W_2 and W_3 serve as intermediate variables in the encoding process, which was introduced to optimize compression efficiency. Ideally, W_1, W_2 and W_3 should carry information about the source X_1, X_2 and X_3, respectively. But this information should be as independent as possible from the side information Y in order to avoid redundancy and fully exploit the decoder-side knowledge. This helps minimize the required transmission rate R. The rigorous proof of Theorem 1 is provided in Appendix A.

Corollary 1. *The conditions* (25) *of Theorem 1 can be expressed equivalently as*

$$R_1 \geqslant I(X_1, X_2, X_3; W_1 | W_2, W_3, Y) \tag{4a}$$
$$R_2 \geqslant I(X_1, X_2, X_3; W_2 | W_1, W_3, Y) \tag{4b}$$
$$R_3 \geqslant I(X_1, X_2, X_3; W_3 | W_1, W_2, Y) \tag{4c}$$
$$R_1 + R_2 \geqslant I(X_1, X_2, X_3; W_1, W_2 | W_3, Y) \tag{4d}$$
$$R_1 + R_3 \geqslant I(X_1, X_2, X_3; W_1, W_3 | W_2, Y) \tag{4e}$$
$$R_2 + R_3 \geqslant I(X_1, X_2, X_3; W_2, W_3 | W_1, Y) \tag{4f}$$
$$R_1 + R_2 + R_3 \geqslant I(X_1, X_2, X_3; W_1, W_2, W_3 | Y) \tag{4g}$$

Proof. First, we prove $R_1 \geqslant I(X_1; W_1) - I(W_1; W_2, W_3, Y) = I(X_1, X_2, X_3; W_1 | W_2, W_3, Y)$. The bound of (4a) can be written as

$$\begin{aligned} &I(X_1, X_2, X_3; W_1 | W_2, W_3, Y) \\ &= I(X_1; W_1 | W_2, W_3, Y) + \underbrace{I(X_2, X_3; W_1 | X_1, W_2, W_3, Y)}_{=0}, \end{aligned} \tag{5}$$

where $I(X_2, X_3; W_1 | X_1, W_2, W_3, Y) = 0$ because (X_2, X_3, Y) is conditionally independent of W_1 for given X_1. For the first term of the right in (5), we have

$$\begin{aligned} &I(X_1; W_1 | W_2, W_3, Y) + I(W_1; W_2, W_3, Y) \\ &= I(W_1; X_1, W_2, W_3, Y) \\ &= I(W_1; X_1) + \underbrace{I(W_2, W_3, Y; W_1 | X_1)}_{=0}, \end{aligned} \tag{6}$$

where $I(W_2, W_3, Y; W_1 | X_1) = 0$ because (W_2, W_3, Y) is conditionally independent of W_1 given X_1. Then, we have

$$\begin{aligned} &I(X_1, X_2, X_3; W_1 | W_2, W_3, Y) \\ &= I(X_1; W_1 | W_2, W_3, Y) \\ &= I(W_1; X_1) - I(W_1; W_2, W_3, Y) \\ &\leq R_1. \end{aligned} \tag{7}$$

This completes the proof of (4a). (4b) and (4c) can be proved in the same way.

Then, we prove (4d), the bound of the sum rate $R_1 + R_2$ can be written as

$$\begin{aligned} &I(X_1, X_2, X_3; W_1, W_2 | W_3, Y) \\ &= I(X_1; W_1, W_2 | W_3, Y) + I(X_2, X_3; W_1, W_2 | W_3, Y, X_1) \end{aligned} \tag{8a}$$

$$= I(X_1;W_2|W_3,Y) + \underbrace{I(X_1;W_1|W_2,W_3,Y)}_{=I(X_1;W_1)-I(W_1;W_2,W_3,Y)\leq R_1} + \underbrace{I(X_2,X_3;W_1|W_3,Y,X_1)}_{=0} + I(X_2,X_3;W_2|W_1,W_3,Y,X_1), \tag{8b}$$

where (8a) and (8b) are obtained by the chain rule of mutual information, $I(X_2,X_3;W_1|W_3,Y,X_1) = 0$, because (X_2,X_3) is conditionally independent of W_1 given X_1. For the last term in (8b), we have

$$\begin{aligned}
&I(X_2,X_3;W_2|W_1,W_3,Y,X_1) + I(X_1;W_2|W_1,W_3,Y) && \text{(9a)}\\
&= I(X_1,X_2,X_3;W_2|W_1,W_3,Y) && \text{(9b)}\\
&= I(X_2,X_3;W_2|W_1,W_3,Y) + \underbrace{I(X_1;W_2|W_1,W_3,Y,X_2,X_3)}_{=0} && \text{(9c)}\\
&= \underbrace{I(X_2;W_2|W_1,W_3,Y)}_{=I(X_2;W_2)-I(W_2;W_1,W_3,Y)\leq R_2} + \underbrace{I(X_1,X_3;W_2|W_1,W_3,Y,X_2)}_{=0} && \text{(9d)}
\end{aligned}$$

where $I(X_1;W_2|W_1,W_3,Y,X_2,X_3) = 0$ because X_1 is conditionally independent of W_2 given X_2, and $I(X_1,X_3;W_2|W_1,W_3,Y,X_2) = 0$ because (X_1,X_3) is conditionally independent of W_2 given X_2. Thus, the last term in (8b) can be written as

$$\begin{aligned}
&I(X_2,X_3;W_2|W_1,W_3,Y,X_1)\\
&= \underbrace{I(X_2;W_2|W_1,W_3,Y)}_{=I(X_2;W_2)-I(W_2;W_1,W_3,Y)\leq R_2} - I(X_1;W_2|W_1,W_3,Y)
\end{aligned} \tag{10}$$

For the last term in the right-hand side, we have

$$\begin{aligned}
&I(X_1;W_2|W_1,W_3,Y) + I(W_1;W_2|W_3,Y)\\
&= I(X_1,W_1;W_2|W_3,Y)\\
&= I(X_1;W_2|W_3,Y) + \underbrace{I(W_1;W_2|X_1,W_1,W_3,Y)}_{=0},
\end{aligned} \tag{11}$$

thus, the last term in (10) can be written as

$$\begin{aligned}
&I(X_1;W_2|W_1,W_3,Y)\\
&=I(X_1;W_2|W_3,Y) - I(W_1;W_2|W_3,Y)
\end{aligned} \tag{12}$$

By combining (8), (9), (10) and (12), we have

$$\begin{aligned}
R_1 + R_2 \geqslant\ & I(X_1,X_2,X_3;W_1,W_2|W_3,Y)\\
=\ & I(X_1;W_1) + I(X_2;W_2)\\
&- I(W_1;W_2,W_3,Y) - I(W_2;W_1,W_3,Y)\\
&+ I(W_1;W_2|W_3,Y).
\end{aligned} \tag{13}$$

The rest sum rate bounds in (4) can be proved in the same way, which is omitted here. □

3. A General Outer Bound

In this section, we derive a region $R_o(D)$ which contains the goal rate-distortion region $R_o(D) \supseteq R^*_{X_1,X_2,X_3|Y}(D)$.

Theorem 2. *$R_o(D) \supseteq R^*_{X_1,X_2,X_3|Y}(D)$, where $R_o(D)$ is the set of all rate triples (R_1,R_2,R_3) such that there exists a triple (W_1,W_2,W_3) of discrete random variables with $p(w_1|x_1,x_2,x_3,y) =$*

$p(w_1|x_1)$, $p(w_2|x_1,x_2,x_3,y) = p(w_2|x_2)$ and $p(w_3|x_1,x_2,x_3,y) = p(w_3|x_3)$, for which the following conditions are satisfied

$$\begin{aligned} R_1 &\geqslant I(X_1,X_2,X_3;W_1|W_2,W_3,Y) \\ R_2 &\geqslant I(X_1,X_2,X_3;W_2|W_1,W_3,Y) \\ R_3 &\geqslant I(X_1,X_2,X_3;W_3|W_1,W_2,Y) \\ R_1+R_2 &\geqslant I(X_1,X_2,X_3;W_1,W_2|W_3,Y) \\ R_1+R_3 &\geqslant I(X_1,X_2,X_3;W_1,W_3|W_2,Y) \\ R_2+R_3 &\geqslant I(X_1,X_2,X_3;W_2,W_3|W_1,Y) \\ R_1+R_2+R_3 &\geqslant I(X_1,X_2,X_3;W_1,W_2,W_3|Y) \end{aligned} \tag{14}$$

and there exists a decoding function $g(\cdot)$ such that

$$Ed(T, g_1(W_1,W_2,W_3,Y)) \leqslant D, \tag{15}$$

The rigorous proof of Theorem 2 is provided in Appendix B.

While the expressions of the inner bound (4) and the outer bound (14) are the same, these two regions do not coincide because the marginal constrains $p(w_1,w_2,w_3,x_1,x_2,x_3,y) = p(w_1|x_1)p(w_2|x_2)p(w_3|x_3)p(x_1,x_2,x_3,y)$ in Theorem 1 limit the degree of freedom for choosing the auxiliary random variables (W_1,W_2,W_3) compared with the marginal constraints in Theorem 2. In the next section, we will demonstrate that the additional degree of freedom in choosing the auxiliary random variables (W_1,W_2,W_3) in Theorem 2 cannot lower the value of the rate-distortion functions.

4. Conclusive Rate-Distortion Results

Corollary 2. *If X_1,X_2,X_3 are conditionally independent given the side information Y, $R_a(D) \subseteq R^*_{X_1,X_2,|Y}(D)$ where $R_a(D)$ is the set of all rate triples (R_1,R_2,R_3) such that there exists a triple (W_1,W_2,W_3) of random variables with $p(w_1,w_2,w_3,x_1,x_2,x_3,y) = p(w_1|x_1)p(w_2|x_2)p(w_3|x_3)$ $p(x_1|y)p(x_2|y)p(x_3|y)p(y)$, for which the following conditions are satisfied*

$$\begin{aligned} R_1 &\geqslant I(X_1;W_1) - I(W_1;Y) \\ R_2 &\geqslant I(X_2;W_2) - I(W_2;Y) \\ R_3 &\geqslant I(X_3;W_3) - I(W_3;Y) \end{aligned} \tag{16}$$

and there exist decoding functions $g(\cdot)$ such that

$$Ed(T, g(W_1,W_2,W_3,Y)) \leqslant D. \tag{17}$$

Proof. Since the joint distribution can be written as

$$\begin{aligned} &p(w_1,w_2,w_3,x_1,x_2,x_3,y) \\ &= p(w_1,w_2,w_3|x_1,x_2,x_3,y)p(x_1,x_2,x_3|y)p(y) \\ &= p(w_1|x_1)p(w_2|x_2)p(w_3|x_3)p(x_1|y) \\ &\times p(x_2|y)p(x_3|y)p(y), \end{aligned} \tag{18}$$

the terms $I(W_1;W_2|W_3,Y)$ in the sum rate bound (2d) are 0 because W_2 is conditionally independent of W_1. Similarly, the terms $I(W_1;W_3|W_2,Y)$, $I(W_2;W_3|W_1,Y)$ and $I(W_1;W_2|W_3,Y)+I(W_1,W_2;W_3|Y)$ in the sum rate bound (2e)–(2g) are all 0. Therefore, the sum rate bound can be expressed as the combination of the side bounds and hence can be omitted. Meanwhile, the term $I(W_1; W_2, W_3, Y)$ in the side bound in (2a) can be written as

$$I(W_1; W_2, W_3, Y) = I(W_1; Y) + \underbrace{I(W_2, W_3; W_1|Y)}_{=0}. \tag{19}$$

Similarly, we have

$$\begin{aligned} I(W_2; W_1, W_3, Y) &= I(W_2; Y) + \underbrace{I(W_1, W_3; W_2|Y)}_{=0} \\ I(W_3; W_1, W_2, Y) &= I(W_3; Y) + \underbrace{I(W_1, W_2; W_3|Y)}_{=0}. \end{aligned} \tag{20}$$

This completes the proof Corollary 2. □

Corollary 3. *If X_1, X_2, X_3 are conditionally independent given the side information Y, $R_o'(D) \supseteq R_o(D)$, and hence $R_o'(D) \supseteq R^*_{X_1,X_2,W_3|Y}(D)$ where $R_o'(D)$ is the set of all rate triples (R_1, R_2, R_3) such that there exists a triple (W_1, W_2, W_3) of discrete random variables with $p(w_1|x_1, x_2, w_3, y) = p(w_1|x_1)$, $p(w_2|x_1, x_2, w_3, y) = p(w_2|x_2)$ and $p(w_3|x_1, x_2, x_3, y) = p(w_3|x_3)$, for which the following conditions are satisfied*

$$\begin{aligned} R_1 &\geqslant I(X_1; W_1) - I(W_1; Y) \\ R_2 &\geqslant I(X_2; W_2) - I(W_2; Y) \\ R_3 &\geqslant I(X_3; W_3) - I(W_3; Y), \end{aligned} \tag{21}$$

and there exists decoding functions $g(\cdot)$ such that

$$Ed(T, g_1(W_1, W_2, W_3, Y)) \leqslant D, \tag{22}$$

Proof. First, we can enlarge the region $R_o(D)$ by omitting the sum rate bound in (14). Then, the side rate bounds in (14) can be relaxed as

$$\begin{aligned} R_1 &\geqslant I(X_1, X_2, X_3; W_1|W_2, W_3, Y) \\ &\geqslant I(X_1; W_1|W_2, W_3, Y) + I(X_2, X_3; W_1|W_2, W_3, Y, X_1) \\ &\geqslant I(X_1; W_1|W_2, W_3, Y) \\ &= I(X_1; W_1, W_2, W_3|Y) - \underbrace{I(X_1; W_2, W_3|Y)}_{=0}. \end{aligned} \tag{23}$$

According to the conditional independence relations, we have $I(X_1; W_2, W_3|Y) = 0$, and then we have

$$\begin{aligned} R_1 &\geqslant I(X_1; W_1, W_2, W_3|Y) \\ &= I(X_1; W_1|Y) + \underbrace{I(X_1; W_2, W_3|Y, W_1)}_{=0} && \text{(24a)} \\ &= I(X_1, Y; W_1) - I(W_1; Y) && \text{(24b)} \\ &= I(X_1; W_1) - I(W_1; Y) && \text{(24c)} \end{aligned}$$

where (24a) is obtained by the condition that X_1, X_2, X_3 are conditionally independent given the side information Y, (24b) follows from the chain rule of mutual information and (24c) is derived by the Markov chain $Y - X_1 - W_1$. The same derivation can be applied to R_2 and R_3; this proves Corollary 3. □

Theorem 3. *If X_1, X_2, X_3 are conditionally independent given the side information Y,*

$$R_a(D) = R_o(D) = R^*_{X_1,X_2,X_3|Y}(D). \tag{25}$$

Proof. We note that the only difference between $R_a(D)$ and $R_o(D)$ is the degrees of freedom when choosing the auxiliary random variables (W_1, W_2, W_3), and all of the mutual information functions in (16) and (21) only depend on the marginal distribution (X_1, W_1, Y), (X_2, W_2, Y) and (X_3, W_3, Y). Randomly choose a certain rate triple (R_1, R_2, R_3) with a auxiliary random variable triple (W_1, W_2, W_3) meeting the conditions of Corollary 3, and the corresponding joint distribution is given in (18). Then, we construct the auxiliary random variables (W_1', W_2', W_3') such that

$$\begin{aligned} p_{W_1'|X_1}(w_1|s_1) &= \sum_{w_2,s_2,w_3,s_3} p(w_1,w_2,w_3|s_1,s_2,s_3)p(s_2,s_3|s_1) \\ p_{W_2'|X_2}(w_2|s_2) &= \sum_{w_1,s_1,w_3,s_3} p(w_1,w_2,w_3|s_1,s_2,s_3)p(s_1,s_3|s_2) \\ p_{W_3'|X_3}(w_3|s_3) &= \sum_{w_1,s_1,w_2,s_2} p(w_1,w_2,w_3|s_1,s_2,s_3)p(s_1,s_2|s_3). \end{aligned} \tag{26}$$

The joint distribution

$$\begin{aligned} &p(w_1', w_2', w_3', x_1, x_2, x_3, Y) \\ &= p(w_1'|x_1)p(w_2'|x_2)p(w_3'|x_3)p(x_1|y)p(x_2|y)p(x_3|y)p(y) \end{aligned} \tag{27}$$

has the same marginal distributions on (X_1, W_1, Y), (X_2, W_2, Y) and (X_3, W_3, Y). Therefore, the additional degree of freedom for choosing the auxiliary random variables (W_1, W_2, W_3) in Corollary 3 cannot lower the value of rate-distortion functions. This proves Theorem 3. The arguments leading to Theorem 3 indicate that the result extends to the M sources scenario

$$R_i \geq I(X_i; W_i) - I(W_i; Y) \quad \text{for all } l \in \{1, \dots, M\}. \tag{28}$$

□

5. Iterative Optimization Framework Based on BA Algorithm

In this section, we present the iterative optimization framework for calculating the rate distortion region. Starting with the standard Lagrange multiplier method, the problem of calculating the rate-distortion region $R^*_{X_1,\dots,X_m|Y}(D)$ is equivalent to minimize

$$\sum_{i \in \mathcal{M} := \{1,\dots,M\}} I(W_i; X_i) - I(W_i; Y) + \lambda(E[d(T, \hat{T})] - D) \tag{29}$$

By the definition of mutual information, we can rewrite (29) as

$$\begin{aligned} &\mathcal{L}_\lambda(Q, q, q') \\ &= \sum_{y,\hat{t},x_i,w_i,i\in\mathcal{M}} p(y, x_i)q_i(w_i \mid x_i)q'(\hat{t} \mid y, \boldsymbol{w}) \log \frac{q_i(w_i \mid x_i)}{Q_i(w_i \mid y)} \\ &+ \lambda \sum_{\boldsymbol{w},\boldsymbol{x},t,\hat{t},y} d(t, \hat{t})p(t, \boldsymbol{x}, y)q'(\hat{t} \mid y, \boldsymbol{w}) \prod_{i\in\mathcal{M}} q_i(w_i \mid x_i), \end{aligned} \tag{30}$$

where $\boldsymbol{Q}, \boldsymbol{q}, q'$ represent the distributions that need to be iteratively updated, and the vectorized notation $\boldsymbol{Q}$ represents the conditional distribution of the auxiliary variables given Y, i.e., $[Q_i(w_i \mid y) \mid w_i \in \mathcal{W}_i, y \in \mathcal{Y}, i \in \mathcal{M}]$, $\boldsymbol{q}$ represents the conditional distribution of the auxiliary variables given sources X_i, $[q_i(w_i \mid x_i) \mid w_i \in \mathcal{W}_i, x_i \in \mathcal{X}_i, i \in \mathcal{M}]$ and

q' represents the conditional distribution of the indirect variable T given Y and auxiliary variables, $q'(\hat{t} \mid y, w_1, \ldots, w_M)$.

Lemma 1 (Optimization of $\boldsymbol{Q}$). *For a fixed $\boldsymbol{Q}_{\backslash m}, \boldsymbol{q}, q'$, the Lagrangian $\mathcal{L}_\lambda(\boldsymbol{Q}, \boldsymbol{q}, q')$ is minimized by*

$$Q_m^*(w_m \mid y) \triangleq \frac{\sum_{x_m,\hat{t}} p(y, x_m) q(w_m \mid x_m) q'(\hat{t} \mid y, \boldsymbol{w})}{\sum_{x_m,\hat{t},w_m} p(y, x_m) q(w_m \mid x_m) q'(\hat{t} \mid y, \boldsymbol{w})}, \tag{31}$$

where $\boldsymbol{Q}_{\backslash m} = [Q_i(w_i \mid y) \mid w_i \in \mathcal{W}_i, y \in \mathcal{Y}, i \in \mathcal{M} \backslash m]$.

Proof. For any Q_m

$$\begin{aligned}
&\mathcal{L}_\lambda(Q_m^*, \boldsymbol{q}, q') - \mathcal{L}_\lambda(Q_m, \boldsymbol{q}, q') \\
&= \sum_{y,\hat{t},x_m,w_m} p(y, x_m) q_i(w_m \mid x_m) q'(\hat{t} \mid y, \boldsymbol{w}) \log \frac{q_m(w_m \mid x_m)}{Q_m^*(w_m \mid y)} \\
&- \sum_{y,\hat{t},x_m,w_m} p(y, x_m) q_i(w_m \mid x_m) q'(\hat{t} \mid y, \boldsymbol{w}) \log \frac{q_m(w_m \mid x_m)}{Q_m(w_m \mid y)} \\
&= \sum_{y,\hat{t},x_m,w_m} p(y, x_m) q_i(w_m \mid x_m) q'(\hat{t} \mid y, \boldsymbol{w}) \log \frac{Q_m(w_m \mid y)}{Q_m^*(w_m \mid y)} \\
&\overset{(a)}{\leq} \sum_{y,\hat{t},x_m,w_m} p(y, x_m) q_i(w_m \mid x_m) q'(\hat{t} \mid y, \boldsymbol{w}) \left(\frac{Q_m(w_m \mid y)}{Q_m^*(w_m \mid y)} - 1\right) \\
&= 0,
\end{aligned} \tag{32}$$

where (a) follows from the fact that $\log(1 + x) \leq x$, and the equality is achieved if $Q_m^* = Q_m$. This completes the proof of Lemma 1. □

Lemma 2 (Optimization of $\boldsymbol{q}$). *For a fixed $\boldsymbol{Q}, \boldsymbol{q}_{\backslash m}, q'$, the Lagrangian $\mathcal{L}_\lambda(\boldsymbol{Q}, \boldsymbol{q}, q')$ is minimized by*

$$q^*(w_m \mid x_m) = \frac{\exp\left[\sum_y p(y \mid x_m) \log Q(w_m \mid y) - \lambda \sum_{w_{\backslash m}, x_{\backslash m}, t, \hat{t}, y} d(t, \hat{t}) p(t, \boldsymbol{x}, y) q'(\hat{t} \mid y, \boldsymbol{w}) \boldsymbol{q}_{\backslash m}(\boldsymbol{w}_{\backslash m} \mid \boldsymbol{x}_{\backslash m})\right]}{\sum_{w_m} \exp\left[\sum_y p(y \mid x_m) \log Q(w_m \mid y) - \lambda \sum_{w_{\backslash m}, x_{\backslash m}, t, \hat{t}, y} d(t, \hat{t}) p(t, \boldsymbol{x}, y) q'(\hat{t} \mid y, \boldsymbol{w}) \boldsymbol{q}_{\backslash m}(\boldsymbol{w}_{\backslash m} \mid \boldsymbol{x}_{\backslash m})\right]}, \tag{33}$$

and the minimum is given by

$$\begin{aligned}
&\mathcal{L}_\lambda(\boldsymbol{Q}, \boldsymbol{q}_{\backslash m}^*, q') \\
&= \sum_{x_i, i \in \mathcal{M}} p(x_i) \min_{w_i} [\sum_{y,\hat{t}} p(y \mid x_i) q'(\hat{t} \mid y, \boldsymbol{w}) \log \frac{q^*(w_i \mid x_i)}{Q(w_i \mid y)} \\
&+ \lambda \sum_{\boldsymbol{w}, \boldsymbol{x}, t, \hat{t}, y} d(t, \hat{t}) p(t, \boldsymbol{x}, y) q'(\hat{t} \mid y, \boldsymbol{w}) \prod_{i \in \mathcal{M}} q_i(w_i \mid x_i)].
\end{aligned} \tag{34}$$

Proof. For a fixed $\boldsymbol{Q}, \boldsymbol{q}_{\backslash m}, q'$, the Lagrangian $\mathcal{L}_\lambda(\boldsymbol{Q}, \boldsymbol{q}, q')$ is minimized by $q^*(w_m \mid x_m)$ if and only if the following Kuhn–Tucker (KT) conditions are satisfied

$$\left.\frac{\partial \mathcal{L}_\lambda}{\partial q_m}\right|_{q_m^*} = \gamma, \quad \text{if } q^*(w_m \mid x_m) > 0, \tag{35}$$

and

$$\left.\frac{\partial \mathcal{L}_\lambda}{\partial q_m}\right|_{q_m^*} \leq \gamma, \quad \text{if } q_m^*(w_m \mid x_m) = 0. \tag{36}$$

Since

$$
\begin{aligned}
&\frac{\partial \mathcal{L}_\lambda}{\partial q_m}\\
&= \sum_{x_m,y} p(x_m,y)\left(\log \frac{p(w_m \mid x_m)}{p(w_m \mid y)} + 1\right)\\
&+ \lambda \sum_{w,x,t,\hat{t},y} d(t,\hat{t})p(t,x,y)q'(\hat{t} \mid y,w)q_{\setminus m}(u_{\setminus m} \mid x_{\setminus m}),
\end{aligned}
\tag{37}
$$

the first KT condition (35) becomes

$$
\begin{aligned}
&\tilde{\gamma}\\
&= \sum_{x_m,y} p(x_m,y)(\log p(w_m \mid x_m) - \log p(w_m \mid y))\\
&+ \lambda \sum_{w_{\setminus m},x_{\setminus m},t,\hat{t},y} d(t,\hat{t})p(t,x,y)q'(\hat{t} \mid y,w)q_{\setminus m}(w_{\setminus m} \mid x_{\setminus m}),
\end{aligned}
\tag{38}
$$

where

$$
q_{\setminus m}(w_{\setminus m} \mid x_{\setminus m}) = \prod_{i \in \mathcal{M}\setminus m} q_i(w_i \mid x_i) \tag{39}
$$

and we have

$$
\begin{aligned}
&q(w_m \mid x_m)\\
&= \exp\left(\frac{\tilde{\gamma}}{p(x_m)}\right)\exp(\sum_y p(y \mid x_m)\log Q(w_m \mid y)\\
&- \lambda \sum_{w_{\setminus m},x_{\setminus m},t,\hat{t},y} d(t,\hat{t})p(t,x,y)q'(\hat{t} \mid y,w)q_{\setminus m}(w_{\setminus m} \mid x_{\setminus m})).
\end{aligned}
\tag{40}
$$

Then, (33) can be obtained after normalizing $q(w_m \mid x_m)$. □

Lemma 3 (Optimization of q')**.** *For a fixed Q, q, the Lagrangian $\mathcal{L}_\lambda(Q,q,q')$ is minimized by the maximum Bayes detector.*

$$
q'^*(\hat{t} \mid w,y) = \begin{cases} \alpha(w), & \hat{t} \in \arg\min_{\hat{t}\in\hat{\mathcal{T}}} \mathbb{E}[d(t,\hat{t}) \mid W = w],\\ 0, & otherwise \end{cases} \tag{41}
$$

where $\alpha(w)$ is selected to guarantee

$$
\sum_{\hat{t}} q'^*(\hat{t} \mid w,y) = 1 \tag{42}
$$

and $\mathbb{E}[d(t,\hat{t}) \mid W = w]$ denotes

$$
\sum_{w_{\setminus m},x_{\setminus m},t,\hat{t},y} d(t,\hat{t})p(t,x,y)\prod_{i\in\mathcal{M}} q_i(w_i \mid x_i) \tag{43}
$$

Proof. We note that the distortion term in the Lagrangian $\mathcal{L}_\lambda$ that depends on $q'(\hat{t} \mid y,w)$ is the mean distortion, which can be minimized by a Bayes detector.

Based on Lemmas 1–3, we have the iterative algorithm for computing the rate-distortion region for the distributed indirect source with decoder side information. For a given $i \in \mathcal{M}$, we iteratively calculate the following (44) and (45) to alternately update Q_i and q_i

$$
Q_i^{\ell,k_i} = \frac{\sum_{x_i,\hat{t}} p(y,x_i)q^{(\ell,k_i)}(w_i \mid x_i)q'(\hat{t} \mid y,w)}{\sum_{x_i,\hat{t},w_i} p(y,x_i)q^{(\ell,k_i)}(w_i \mid x_i)q'(\hat{t} \mid y,w)} \tag{44}
$$

$$q_i^{(l,k_i+1)} = \frac{\exp\left[\sum_y p(y \mid x_i) \log Q^{(l,k_i)}(w_i \mid y) - \lambda \sum_{w_{\setminus i}, x_{\setminus i}, t, \hat{t}, y} d(t,\hat{t}) p(t,x,y) q'^{(\ell,i)}(\hat{t} \mid y, w) q_{\setminus i}^{(\ell,i)}(w_{\setminus i} \mid x_{\setminus i})\right]}{\sum_{w_i} \exp\left[\sum_y p(y \mid x_i) \log Q^{(\ell,k_i)}(w_i \mid y) - \lambda \sum_{w_{\setminus i}, x_{\setminus i}, t, \hat{t}, y} d(t,\hat{t}) p(t,x,y) q'^{(\ell,i)}(\hat{t} \mid y, w) q_{\setminus i}^{(\ell,i)}(w_{\setminus i} \mid x_{\setminus i})\right]} \tag{45}$$

until the Lagrangian $\mathcal{L}_\lambda$ converges, and the associated q_i is

$$q_i^{(\ell,*)}(w_i \mid x_i) = \lim_{k_i \to \infty} q_i^{(\ell,k_i)}(w_i \mid x_i) =: q_i^{(\ell+1,1)}. \tag{46}$$

Then, we update $q'(\hat{t} \mid w, y)$ according to

$$q'^{\ell',i'} = \begin{cases} \alpha^{\ell',i'}(w), & \hat{t} \in \arg\min_{\hat{t} \in \hat{\mathcal{T}}} J^{(\ell,i)}(\hat{t}, w), \\ 0, & \text{otherwise} \end{cases} \tag{47}$$

with $i' = i+1$ and $\ell' = \ell$ if $i < M$ and $i' = 1$ and $\ell' = \ell + 1$ if $i = M$, and where $\alpha^{\ell',i'}(w)$ is selected to guarantee

$$\sum_{\hat{t}} q'^{(\ell',i')}(\hat{t} \mid w, y) = 1 \tag{48}$$

and

$$\begin{aligned} J^{(\ell,i)}(\hat{t}, w) = &\sum_{x,t,y} d(t,\hat{t}) p(t,x,y) \\ &\times q_{\setminus i}^{(\ell,i)}(w_{\setminus i} \mid x_{\setminus i}) q_i^{(\ell,*)}(w_i \mid x_i). \end{aligned} \tag{49}$$

□

Next, we repeat the process for the next user, i.e., $(i \leftarrow i+1$ if $i < M$ and $i \leftarrow 1, \ell \leftarrow \ell + 1$ if $i = M)$.

Convergence analysis:

The algorithm employs an alternating minimization approach that produces Lagrangian values that are monotonically non-increasing and bounded below, thereby generating a convergent sequence of Lagrangians. Since the rate component of the Lagrangian is convex, and the sum of convex functions remains convex, the Lagrangian will also be convex if the expected distortion is a convex function. As a result, the proposed iterative optimization framework is capable of achieving the global minimum [19].

$$\sum_{w,x,t,\hat{t},y} d(t,\hat{t}) p(t,x,y) q'(\hat{t} \mid y, w) \prod_{i \in \mathcal{M}} q_i(w_i \mid x_i) \tag{50}$$

We note that the expected distortion (50) includes a product of variables in the optimization process, it is not a linear function, and the Lagrangian may exhibit non-convex behavior. Even when the problem is non-convex, the authors in [20] demonstrate that the BA-based iterative algorithm initialized randomly and followed by selecting the minimum Lagrangian among all converged values can still provide highly effective information-theoretic inner bounds for the rate-distortion region, serving as a benchmark for practical quantization schemes.

6. Numerical Examples

In this section, we provide an example to illustrate the proposed iterative algorithms for computing the rate-distortion region of a distributed source coding problem with decoder-side information. As in the problem considered in this paper, distributed edge devices compress their observations $\{X_1, \ldots, X_M\}$ and transmit them to a central server (CEO). The central server then aims to recover the indirect information T from the received data, utilizing side information Y. For the convenience of demonstration, we consider a simple case where $M = 2$ and the sources are binary, i.e., $\mathcal{X}_1 = \mathcal{X}_2 = \mathcal{Y} = \{0,1\}$. The joint distributions, denoted by $Q(x_1, y)$ and $Q(x_2, y)$, are given by

$$\begin{aligned} Q(x_1, y) &= \frac{(1-p_1)}{2}\delta_{x_1,y} + \frac{p_1}{2}(1-\delta_{x_1,y}), \\ Q(x_2, y) &= \frac{(1-p_2)}{2}\delta_{x_2,y} + \frac{p_2}{2}(1-\delta_{x_2,y}), \end{aligned} \tag{51}$$

where the Kronecker delta function $\delta_{x,y}$ equals 1 when $x = y$ and 0 otherwise. We can consider Y as the input to two different binary symmetric channels (BSCs) with crossover probabilities p_1, p_2, respectively, where $0 \leq p_i \leq \frac{1}{2}, i \in \{1,2\}$. The corresponding outputs of these channels are X_1 and X_2. In this example, we set $p_1 = p_2 = 0.3$.

We also assume that the information of interest is directly the combination of the two distributed sources, i.e., $T = \{X_1, X_2\}$. The distortion measure is given by $d(t, \hat{t}) = d(x_1, \hat{x}_1) + d(x_2, \hat{x}_2)$, where

$$d(x_i, \hat{x}_i) = \begin{cases} 0, & x_i = \hat{x}_i, \\ 1, & x_i \neq \hat{x}_i. \end{cases} \tag{52}$$

By applying the proposed iterative optimization framework, we can obtain the optimal transition probability distribution $Q_i^*(w_i \mid y), q_i^*(w_i \mid x_i)$ and $q'^*(\hat{t} \mid w, y)$ that meets a given distortion constraint D on $d(t, \hat{t})$, and the corresponding minimum rate R_i can be calculated by

$$R_i = \sum_{y, x_i, w_i} p(y, x_i) q_i^*(w_i \mid x_i) \log \frac{q_i^*(w_i \mid x_i)}{Q_i^*(w_i \mid y)} \tag{53}$$

The contour plot of the rate-distortion region for this scenario is presented in Figure 2, while Figure 3 displays a surface plot depicting the rate-distortion region. We note that when $M = 1$, the considered problem reduces to the traditional point-to-point Wyner–Ziv problem. In Figure 4, we compare the rate-distortion results computed using the proposed approach with the theoretical analysis by Wyner et al. [13]. We observe that the two rate-distortion function curves coincide, demonstrating the effectiveness of the proposed iterative approach for calculating rate distortion.

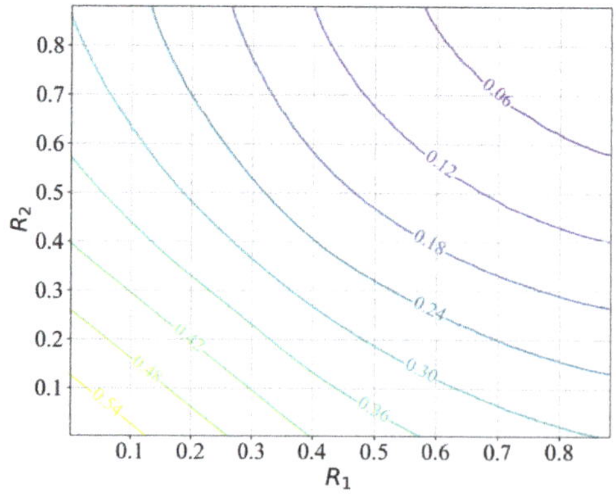

Figure 2. Contour plot of the rate distortion region with two distributed binary sources $\{X_1, X_2\}$, where the labels on the contours represent the distortion values D on $d(t, \hat{t})$.

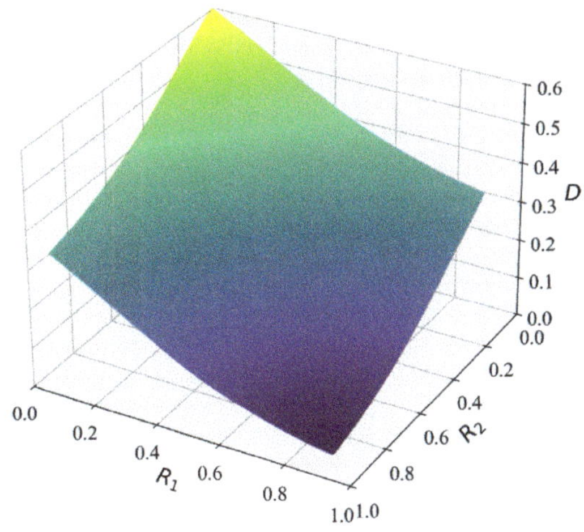

Figure 3. Surface plot of the rate-distortion region.

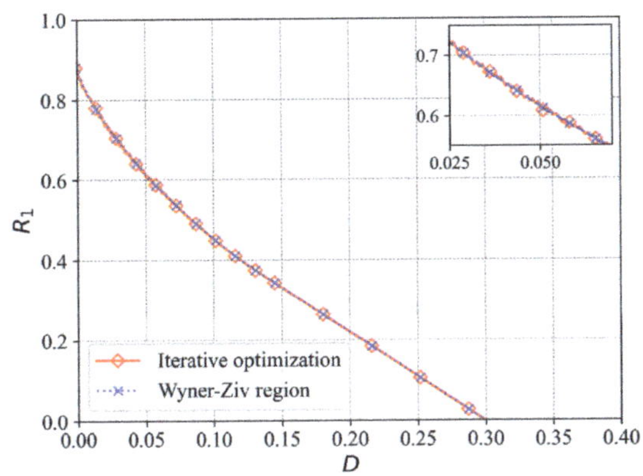

Figure 4. The rate-distortion function for the case when $M = 1$, i.e., the Wyner–Ziv problem.

7. Conclusions

This paper explored a variant of the rate-distortion problem motivated by semantic communication and distributed learning systems, where correlated sources are independently encoded for a central decoder to reconstruct the indirect source of interest. In addition to receiving messages from the encoders, the decoder has access to correlated side information and aims to reconstruct the indirect source under a specified distortion constraint. We derived the exact rate-distortion function for the case where the sources are conditionally independent given the side information. Furthermore, we introduced a distributed iterative optimization framework based on the Blahut–Arimoto (BA) algorithm to numerically compute the rate-distortion function. A numerical example has been provided to demonstrate the effectiveness of the proposed approach.

Author Contributions: Conceptualization, Q.Y.; Methodology, J.T.; Validation, J.T.; Formal analysis, J.T.; Investigation, Q.Y.; Resources, Q.Y.; Writing—original draft, J.T.; Writing—review & editing, Q.Y.; Visualization, J.T.; Project administration, Q.Y.; Funding acquisition, Q.Y. All authors have read and agreed to the published version of the manuscript.

Funding: This work is partly supported by NSFC under grant No. 62293481, No. 62201505, partly by the SUTD-ZJU IDEA Grant (SUTD-ZJU (VP) 202102).

Data Availability Statement: The original contributions presented in this study are included in the article. Further inquiries can be directed to the corresponding author.

Conflicts of Interest: The authors declare no conflicts of interest.

Appendix A

Here, we provide the rigorous proof of Theorem 1.

Lemma A1 (Extended Markov Lemma). *Let*

$$\begin{aligned} &p(w_1, w_2, w_3, x_1, x_2, x_3, y) \\ &= p(w_1|x_1)p(w_2|x_2)p(w_3|x_3)p(x_1, x_2, x_3, y). \end{aligned} \tag{A1}$$

For a fixed $(x_1^n, x_2^n, x_3^n y^n) \in A_\epsilon^{*(n)}$, w_1^n , w_2^n *and* w_3^n *are drawn from* $p(w_1|x_1)$, $p(w_2|x_2)$ *and* $p(w_3|x_3)$, *respectively. Then*

$$\lim_{n\to\infty} Pr\{(w_1^n, w_2^n, w_3^n, x_1^n, x_2^n, x_3^n, y^n) \in A_\epsilon^{*(n)}\} = 1. \tag{A2}$$

Proof. According to (A1), we have several Markov chains $W_1 - X_1 - (X_2, Y)$, $W_2 - X_2 - (X_1, Y)$, $W_1 - (X_1, X_2, Y) - W_2$. We use the Markov lemma three times: first to derive that $((x_2^n, y^n), x_1^n, w_1^n)$ are jointly typical and $((x_1^n, y^n), x_2^n, w_2^n)$ are jointly typical. Then, using the Markov chain $W_1 - (X_1, X_2, Y) - W_2$, we can demonstrate that $(w_1^n, w_2^n, x_1^n, x_2^n, y^n)$ are joint typical. For a fixed $(x_1^n, x_2^n, x_3^n, y^n) \in A_\epsilon^{*(n)}$, W_1^n is drawn from $p(w_1|x_1)$, which implies that $(x_1^n, W_1^n) \in A_\epsilon^{*(n)}$ for sufficiently large n. W_2^n is drawn from $p(w_2|x_2)$, which implies that $(x_2^n, W_2^n) \in A_\epsilon^{*(n)}$ for sufficiently large n; W_3^n is drawn from $p(w_3|x_3)$, which implies that $(x_3^n, W_3^n) \in A_\epsilon^{*(n)}$ for sufficiently large n. Then, with high probability, $(W_1^n, W_2^n, W_3^n, x_1^n, x_2^n, x_3^n, y^n) \in A_\epsilon^{*(n)}$. □

Proof of Theorem 1. For $m = 1, 2, 3$, fix $p(w_m|x_m)$ and $g(W_1, W_2, W_3, Y)$ such that the distortion constraint $Ed(T, \hat{T}) \leqslant D$ is satisfied. Calculate $p(w_m) = \sum_{x_m} p(x_m)p(w_m|x_m)$. □

Generation of codebooks: Generate $2^{nR_m'}$ i.i.d codewords $\mathbf{w_m}^n(s_m) \sim \prod_{i=1}^n p(w_{m,i})$, and index them by $s_m \in \{1, 2, \ldots, 2^{nR_m'}\}$. Provide 2^{nR_m} random bins with indices $t_m \in \{1, 2, \ldots, 2^{nR_m}\}$. Randomly assign the codewords $\mathbf{w_m}^n(s_m)$ to one of 2^{nR_m} bins using a uniform distribution. Let $B_m(t_m)$ denote the set of codeword indices s_m assigned to bin index t_m.

Encoding: Given a source sequence X_m^n, the encoder looks for a codeword $W_m^n(s_m)$ such that $(X_m^n, W_m^n(s_m)) \in A_\epsilon^{*(n)}$. The encoder sends the index of the bin t_m in which s_m belongs.

Decoding: The decoder looks for a pair $(W_1^n(s_1), W_2^n(s_2), W_3^n(s_3))$ such that $s_m \in B_m(t_m)$ and $(W_1^n(s_1), W_2^n(s_2), W_3^n(s_3), Y^n) \in A_\epsilon^{*(n)}$. If the decoder finds a unique triple (s_1, s_2, s_3), he then calculates $\hat{T}^n$, where $\hat{T}_i = g(W_{1,i}, W_{2,i}, W_{3,i}, Y_i)$.

Analysis of the probability of error:

1. The encoders cannot find the codewords $W_m^n(s_m)$ such that $(X_m^n, W_m^n(s_m)) \in A_\epsilon^{*(n)}$. The probability of this event is small if

$$R_m' > I(X_m, W_m) \tag{A3}$$

2. The pair of sequences $(X_1^n, W_1^n(s_1)) \in A_\epsilon^{*(n)}$, $(X_2^n, W_2^n(s_2)) \in A_\epsilon^{*(n)}$ and $(X_3^n, W_3^n(s_3)) \in A_\epsilon^{*(n)}$ but the codewords $\{W_1^n(s_1), W_2^n(s_2), W_3^n(s_3)\}$ are not jointly typical

with the side information sequences Y^n, i.e., $(W_1^n(s_1), W_2^n(s_2), W_3^n(s_3), Y^n) \notin A_\epsilon^{*(n)}$. We have assumed that

$$\begin{aligned} &p(w_1, w_2, w_3, x_1, x_2, x_3, y) \\ &= p(w_1|x_1)p(w_2|x_2)p(w_3|x_3)p(x_1, x_2, x_3, y). \end{aligned} \tag{A4}$$

Hence, by the Markov lemma, the probability of this event goes to zero if n is large enough.

3. There exists another s' with the same bin index that is jointly typical with the side information sequences. The correct codeword indices are denoted by s_1 , s_2 and s_3. We first consider the situation where the codeword index s_1 is in error. The probability that a randomly chosen $W_1^n(s'_1)$ is jointly typical with $(W_2^n(s_2), W_3^n(s_3), Y^n)$ can be bounded as

$$\begin{aligned} &\Pr\left\{ (W_1^n(s_1'), W_2^n(s_2), W_3^n(s_3), Y^n) \in A_\epsilon^{*(n)} \right\} \\ &\leqslant 2^{-n(I(W_1;W_2,W_3,Y)-3\epsilon)}. \end{aligned} \tag{A5}$$

The probability of this error event is bounded by the number of codewords in the bin t_1 times the probability of joint typicality

$$\begin{aligned} &\Pr\{\exists s_1' \in B_1(t_1), s_1' \neq s_1 : \\ &(W_1^n(s_1'), W_2^n(s_2), W_3^n(s_3), Y^n) \in A_\epsilon^{*(n)}\} \\ &\leqslant \sum_{\substack{s_1' \neq s_1, \\ s_1' \in B_1(t_1)}} \Pr\left\{ (W_1^n(s_1'), W_2^n(s_2), W_3^n(s_3), Y^n) \in A_\epsilon^{*(n)} \right\} \\ &\leqslant 2^{n(R_1-R_1')} 2^{-n(I(W_1;W_2,W_3,Y)-3\epsilon)}. \end{aligned} \tag{A6}$$

Similarly, the probability that the codeword index s_2 or s_3 is in error can be bounded by

$$\begin{aligned} &\Pr\{\exists s_2' \in B_2(t_2), s_2' \neq s_2 : \\ &\left(W_1^n(s_1), W_2^n(s_2'), W_3^n(s_3), Y^n\right) \in A_\epsilon^{*(n)}\} \\ &\leqslant 2^{n\left(R_2-R_2'\right)} 2^{-n(I(W_2;W_1,W_3,Y)-3\epsilon)}, \\ &\Pr\{\exists s_3' \in B_3(t_3), s_3' \neq s_3 : \\ &\left(W_1^n(s_1), W_2^n(s_2), W_3^n(s_3'), Y^n\right) \in A_\epsilon^{*(n)}\} \\ &\leqslant 2^{n\left(R_3-R_3'\right)} 2^{-n(I(W_2;W_1,W_3,Y)-3\epsilon)}. \end{aligned} \tag{A7}$$

We then consider the case that two of the three codeword indices are in error. The probability that the randomly chosen $W_1^n(s'_1)$ and $W_2^n(s'_2)$ are jointly typical with $(W_3^n(s_3), Y^n)$ can be bounded as

$$\begin{aligned} &\Pr\left\{ (W_1^n(s_1'), W_2^n(s_2'), W_3^n(s_3), Y^n) \in A_\epsilon^{*(n)} \right\} \\ &= \sum_{(W_1,W_2,W_3,Y) \in A_\epsilon^{*(n)}} p(w_1^n)p(w_2^n)p(w_3^n, y^n) \\ &\leqslant 2^{-n(I(W_1;W_2,W_3,Y)+I(W_2;W_1,W_3,Y)-I(W_1;W_2|W_3,Y)-4\epsilon)}. \end{aligned} \tag{A8}$$

Hence, the error probability can be bounded as

$$\begin{aligned}
&\Pr\{\exists s_1' \in B_1(t_1), s_1' \neq s_1, \exists s_2' \in B_2(t_2), s_2' \neq s_2 : \\
&(W_1^n(s_1'), W_2^n(s_2'), W_2^n(s_3), y^n) \in A_\epsilon^{*(n)}\} \\
&\leqslant 2^{n(R_1 - R_1' + R_2 - R_2')} \\
&\times 2^{-n(I(W_1;W_2,W_3,Y) + I(W_2;W_1,W_3,Y) - I(W_1;W_2|W_3,Y) - 4\epsilon)}.
\end{aligned} \tag{A9}$$

Similarly, we can obtain the probability that the codeword indices (s_1, s_3) or (s_2, s_3) are in error, which we omit here.

For the case where all the codeword indices s_1, s_2 and s_3 are in error, the probability that the randomly chosen $W_1^n(s'_1)$, $W_2^n(s'_2)$ and $W_3^n(s'_3)$ are jointly typical with Y^n can be bounded as

$$\begin{aligned}
&\Pr\{(W_1^n(s_1'), W_2^n(s_2'), W_2^n(s_3'), Y^n) \in A_\epsilon^{*(n)}\} \\
&= \sum_{(W_1,W_2,W_3,Y) \in A_\epsilon^{*(n)}} p(w_1^n)p(w_2^n)p(w_3^n)p(Y^n) \\
&\leqslant 2^{-n(I(W_1;W_2,W_3,Y) + I(W_2;W_1,W_3,Y))} \\
&\times 2^{-n(I(W_3;W_1,W_2,Y) - I(W_1;W_2|W_3,Y) - I(W_1,W_2;W_3|Y) - 5\epsilon)}.
\end{aligned} \tag{A10}$$

The probability of the above error events goes to 0 when

$$\begin{aligned}
R_1' - R_1 &\leqslant I(W_1; W_2, W_3, Y) \\
&\cdots \\
R_1' - R_1 + R_2' - R_2 + R_3' - R_3 &\leqslant I(W_1; W_2, W_3, Y) \\
&+ I(W_2; W_1, W_3, Y) \\
&+ I(W_3; W_1, W_2, Y) \\
&- I(W_1; W_2|W_3, Y) \\
&- I(W_1, W_2; W_3|Y).
\end{aligned} \tag{A11}$$

Therefore, (2) can be obtained by combining (A3) and (A11).

If (s_1, s_2, s_3) are correctly decoded, we have $(X_1^n, X_2^n, X_3^n, W_1^n(s_1), W_2^n(s_2), W_3^n(s_3), Y^n) \in A_\epsilon^{*(n)}$. Therefore, the empirical joint distribution is close to the distribution $p(w_1|x_1)$ $p(w_2|x_2)p(w_3|x_3)p(x_1, x_2, x_3, y)$ that achieves distortion D.

Appendix B

Here, we provide the rigorous proof of Theorem 2. Define a series of encoders $f_m : \mathcal{X}_m^n \to \{1, \ldots, 2^{nR_m}\}$ and decoders $g : \prod_{m \in \mathcal{M}} \{1, \ldots, 2^{nR_m}\} \times \mathcal{Y}^n \to \hat{\mathcal{T}}^n$ that achieve the given distortion D. We can derive the following inequalities

$$\begin{aligned}
&nR_1 \\
&\geq H(f_1(X_1^n)) \\
&\geq H(f_1(X_1^n)|f_2(X_2^n), f_3(X_3^n), Y^n) && \text{(A12a)} \\
&\geq H(f_1(X_1^n)|f_2(X_2^n), f_3(X_3^n), Y^n) \\
&- H(f_1(X_1^n)|f_2(X_2^n), f_3(X_3^n), Y^n, X_1^n, X_2^n, X_3^n) \\
&= I(X_1^n, X_2^n, X_3^n; f_1(X_1^n)|f_2(X_2^n), f_3(X_3^n), Y^n) && \text{(A12b)} \\
&= \sum_{i=1}^n I(X_{1,i}, X_{2,i}, X_{3,i}; f_1(X_1^n)|f_2(X_2^n), f_3(X_3^n), \\
&Y^n, X_{1,1}^{i-1}, X_{2,1}^{i-1}, X_{3,1}^{i-1}) && \text{(A12c)} \\
&= \sum_{i=1}^n H(X_{1,i}, X_{2,i}|f_2(X_2^n), Y^n, X_{1,1}^{i-1}, X_{2,1}^{i-1})
\end{aligned}$$

$$
\begin{aligned}
&- H(X_{1,i}, X_{2,i}|f_1(X_1^n), f_2(X_2^n), Y^n, X_{1,1}^{i-1}, X_{2,1}^{i-1}) && \text{(A12d)}\\
&= \sum_{i=1}^{n} H(X_{1,i}, X_{2,i}|W_{2,i}, Y_i) - H(X_{1,i}, X_{2,i}|W_{1,i}, W_{2,i}, Y_i) && \text{(A12e)}\\
&= \sum_{i=1}^{n} I(X_{1,i}, X_{2,i}; W_{1,i}|W_{2,i}, Y_i),
\end{aligned}
$$

where (A12a) follows from the fact that conditioning reduces entropy, (A12b) and (A12d) are obtained by the definition of conditional mutual information and (A12c) is the chain rule of mutual information. In (A12e), we let $W_{1,i} = \left(f_1(X_1^n), X_{1,1}^{i-1}, X_{2,1}^{i-1}, Y_1^{i-1}, Y_{i+1}^n\right)$, and $W_{2,i} = \left(f_2(X_2^n), X_{1,1}^{i-1}, X_{2,1}^{i-1}, Y_1^{i-1}, Y_{i+1}^n\right)$. Similarly, we have

$$
\begin{aligned}
nR_2 &\geq \sum_{i=1}^{n} I(X_{1,i}, X_{2,i}, X_{3,i}; W_{2,i}|W_{1,i}, W_{3,i}, Y_i),\\
nR_3 &\geq \sum_{i=1}^{n} I(X_{1,i}, X_{2,i}, X_{3,i}; W_{3,i}|W_{2,i}, W_{3,i}, Y_i).
\end{aligned} \tag{A13}
$$

For the sum rate part, we have

$$
\begin{aligned}
&n(R_1 + R_2)\\
&\geq H(f_1(X_1^n), f_2(X_2^n))\\
&\geq H(f_1(X_1^n), f_2(X_2^n)|Y^n) && \text{(A14a)}\\
&\geq H(f_1(X_1^n), f_2(X_2^n)|Y^n)\\
&- H(f_1(X_1^n), f_2(X_2^n)|Y^n, X_1^n, X_2^n)\\
&= I(f_1(X_1^n), f_2(X_2^n); X_1^n, X_2^n|Y^n) && \text{(A14b)}\\
&= \sum_{i=1}^{n} I(f_1(X_{1,i}), f_2(X_{1,i}); X_1^n, X_2^n|Y^n, X_1^{i-1}, X_2^{i-1}) && \text{(A14c)}\\
&= \sum_{i=1}^{n} H(X_{1,i}, X_{2,i}|Y^n, X_1^{i-1}, X_2^{i-1})\\
&- H(X_{1,i}, X_{2,i}|f_1(X_1^n), f_2(X_2^n), X_{1,1}^{i-1}, X_{2,1}^{i-1}, Y^n) && \text{(A14d)}\\
&= \sum_{i=1}^{n} H(X_{1,i}, X_{2,i}|Y_i)\\
&- H(X_{1,i}, X_{2,i}|f_1(X_1^n), f_2(X_2^n), X_{1,1}^{i-1}, X_{2,1}^{i-1}, Y^n) && \text{(A14e)}\\
&= \sum_{i=1}^{n} H(X_{1,i}, X_{2,i}|Y_i) - H(X_{1,i}, X_{2,i}|W_{1,i}, W_{2,i}, Y_i) && \text{(A14f)}\\
&= \sum_{i=1}^{n} I(X_{1,i}, X_{2,i}; W_{1,i}, W_{2,i}|Y_i),
\end{aligned}
$$

where (A14a) follows from the fact that conditioning reduces entropy, (A14b) and (A14d) are obtained by the definition of conditional mutual information, (A14c) is the chain rule of mutual information and (A14e) follows from the fact that $X_{1,i}, X_{2,i}$ is conditionally independent of the past and feature of X_1, X_2, Y given Y_i. In (A14f), the definition of $W_{1,i}, W_{2,i}$ is used again.

References

1. Han, T.; Yang, Q.; Shi, Z.; He, S.; Zhang, Z. Semantic-preserved communication system for highly efficient speech transmission. *IEEE J. Sel. Areas Commun.* **2022**, *41*, 245–259. [CrossRef]
2. Adikari, T.; Draper, S. Two-terminal source coding with common sum reconstruction. In Proceedings of the 2022 IEEE International Symposium on Information Theory (ISIT), Espoo, Finland, 26 June–1 July 2022; IEEE: Piscataway, NJ, USA, 2022; pp. 1420–1424.

3. Korner, J.; Marton, K. How to encode the modulo-two sum of binary sources (corresp.). *IEEE Trans. Inf. Theory* **1979**, *25*, 219–221. [CrossRef]
4. Pastore, A.; Lim, S.H.; Feng, C.; Nazer, B.; Gastpar, M. Distributed Lossy Computation with Structured Codes: From Discrete to Continuous Sources. In Proceedings of the 2023 IEEE International Symposium on Information Theory (ISIT), Taipei, Taiwan, 25–30 June 2023; IEEE: Piscataway, NJ, USA, 2023; pp. 1681–1686.
5. Amiri, M.M.; Gunduz, D.; Kulkarni, S.R.; Poor, H.V. Federated Learning with Quantized Global Model Updates. *arXiv* **2020**, arXiv:2006.10672. [CrossRef]
6. Gruntkowska, K.; Tyurin, A.; Richtárik, P. Improving the Worst-Case Bidirectional Communication Complexity for Nonconvex Distributed Optimization under Function Similarity. *arXiv* **2024**, arXiv:2402.06412. [CrossRef]
7. Amiri, M.M.; Gündüz, D.; Kulkarni, S.R.; Poor, H.V. Convergence of Federated Learning Over a Noisy Downlink. *IEEE Trans. Wirel. Commun.* **2022**, *21*, 1422–1437. [CrossRef]
8. Stavrou, P.A.; Kountouris, M. The Role of Fidelity in Goal-Oriented Semantic Communication: A Rate Distortion Approach. *IEEE Trans. Commun.* **2023**, *71*, 3918–3931. [CrossRef]
9. Liu, J.; Zhang, W.; Poor, H.V. A rate-distortion framework for characterizing semantic information. In Proceedings of the 2021 IEEE International Symposium on Information Theory (ISIT), Virtual, 12–20 July 2021; IEEE: Piscataway, NJ, USA, 2021; pp. 2894–2899.
10. Dobrushin, R.; Tsybakov, B. Information transmission with additional noise. *IRE Trans. Inf. Theory* **1962**, *8*, 293–304. [CrossRef]
11. Wolf, J.; Ziv, J. Transmission of noisy information to a noisy receiver with minimum distortion. *IEEE Trans. Inf. Theory* **1970**, *16*, 406–411. [CrossRef]
12. Guo, T.; Wang, Y.; Han, J.; Wu, H.; Bai, B.; Han, W. Semantic compression with side information: A rate-distortion perspective. *arXiv* **2022**, arXiv:2208.06094. [CrossRef]
13. Wyner, A.; Ziv, J. The rate-distortion function for source coding with side information at the decoder. *IEEE Trans. Inf. Theory* **1976**, *22*, 1–10. [CrossRef]
14. Slepian, D.; Wolf, J. Noiseless coding of correlated information sources. *IEEE Trans. Inf. Theory* **1973**, *19*, 471–480. [CrossRef]
15. Wagner, A.B.; Anantharam, V. An improved outer bound for multiterminal source coding. *IEEE Trans. Inf. Theory* **2008**, *54*, 1919–1937. [CrossRef]
16. Lim, S.H.; Feng, C.; Pastore, A.; Nazer, B.; Gastpar, M. Towards an algebraic network information theory: Distributed lossy computation of linear functions. In Proceedings of the 2019 IEEE International Symposium on Information Theory (ISIT), Paris, France, 7–12 July 2019; IEEE: Piscataway, NJ, USA, 2019; pp. 1827–1831.
17. Cheng, S.; Stankovic, V.; Xiong, Z. Computing the channel capacity and rate-distortion function with two-sided state information. *IEEE Trans. Inf. Theory* **2005**, *51*, 4418–4425. [CrossRef]
18. Gastpar, M. The Wyner-Ziv problem with multiple sources. *IEEE Trans. Inf. Theory* **2004**, *50*, 2762–2768. [CrossRef]
19. Cover, T.M.; Thomas, J.A. *Elements of Information Theory*; Wiley: New York, NY, USA, 2006.
20. Ku, G.; Ren, J.; Walsh, J.M. Computing the rate distortion region for the CEO problem with independent sources. *IEEE Trans. Signal Process.* **2014**, *63*, 567–575. [CrossRef]

MDPI AG
Grosspeteranlage 5
4052 Basel
Switzerland
Tel.: +41 61 683 77 34

Entropy Editorial Office
E-mail: entropy@mdpi.com
www.mdpi.com/journal/entropy

www.ingramcontent.com/pod-product-compliance
Lightning Source LLC
Chambersburg PA
CBHW061757210926
51850CB00006B/581
9783725858071